To my dear Graham & Casey,
from Edward 22.09.25

DENMARK'S CATALYST

"Awake, and let your amen thunder"
Grundtvig
from the hymn, The sun now shines in all its splendour

DENMARK'S CATALYST

*The Life and Letters
of N.F.S. Grundtvig*

Edward Broadbridge
and Hans Raun Iversen

∼

"*My life is to fight*"
"*Fight! was my song*"

Aarhus University Press

DENMARK'S CATALYST. The Life and Letters of N.F.S. Grundtvig.
© Edward Broadbridge, Hans Raun Iversen, and Aarhus University Press
Illustrations selected and annotated by Edward Broadbridge
Language Consultant: Hanna Broadbridge

Typeset by Narayana Press
Cover design by Jørgen Sparre
Printed in Denmark by Narayana Press 2023

A recording of all the texts is available free at www.unipress.dk

This book is number six in the series 'N.F.S. Grundtvig: Works in English'
Series editors:
Niels Henrik Gregersen, Ove Korsgaard
ISBN 978-87-7219-826-2
ISBN 978-87-7219-827-9 (epdf)
ISBN 978-87-7219-828-9 (epub)
ISSN 2246-7025

Published:
vol. 1. *The School For Life. N.F.S. Grundtvig on Education for the People* (2011)
vol. 2. *Living Wellsprings. The Hymns, Songs, and Poems of N.F.S. Grundtvig* (2015)
vol. 3. *Human Comes First. The Christian Theology of N.F.S. Grundtvig* (2018)
vol. 4. *The Common Good. N.F.S. Grundtvig as Politician and Contemporary Historian* (2019)
vol. 5. *The Core of Learning. The Philosophical Writings of N.F.S. Grundtvig* (2021)
vol. 6. *Denmark's Catalyst. The Life and Letters of N.F.S. Grundtvig* (2023)

Published with the financial support of Danish foundations. For a full list see p. 11

Aarhus University Press
www.unipress.dk

INTERNATIONAL DISTRIBUTORS

Oxbow Books Ltd.	ISD
The Old Music Hall	70 Enterprise Drive, Suite 2
106-108 Cowley Road	Bristol, CT 06010
Oxford, OX4 1JE	USA
United Kingdom	www.isdistribution.com
www.oxbowbooks.com	

The carbon emission of this printed matter is evaluated to 1,73 kg CO2e according to ClimateCalc.
www.climate calc.eu. Cert. No. CC-00159/DK

Contents

Illustrations · 7

Foreword · 9

Notes on Contributors · 12

Abbreviations · 13

I   THE LIFE

1. The Making of Modern Denmark · 17
2. The path enlightened by our fathers' worth · 33
3. Little God's child, what troubles you? (1783-98) · 45
4. I must write or I must die! (1798-1803) · 57
5. Staring at her beauty (1803-08) · 73
6. Are you yourself a Christian? (1808-11) · 91
7. Fight! was my song (1811-15) · 111
8. Time will tell the Truth (1816-21) · 127
9. I am only cut out for preaching! (1821-26) · 141
10. Freedom our watchword must be in the North! (1827-32) · 155
11. A lean agreement is better than a fat conflict (1833-38) · 177
12. I have never spoken to so many ears (1839-44) · 197
13. I always know better than most people (1845-51) · 217
14. She is not dead, she sleeps awhile (1851-54) · 241
15. Youth and Old Age play Hide-and-seek (1855-63) · 259
16. Old enough have I become now (1864-72) · 283
17. Grundtvig the Man · 303
18. Grundtvig's Legacy in Denmark · 321
19. Grundtvig's International Reception · 339
20. Sources · 361

Appendix 1 Memorials to Grundtvig · 379

Appendix 2 Grundtvig's Addresses · 382

Appendix 3 Grundtvig's Marriages and Descendants · 383

Appendix 4 Grundtvig's Political Career · 384

Appendix 5 Monarchs and Bishops in Grundtvig's Time · 385

Bibliography · 387

II THE LETTERS

Writers, Sources, and Dates · 399

Foreword to the Letters and Dates · 401

Letters 1-70 · 402

Grundtvig's Works · 498

Indexes · 501

N.F.S. Grundtvig. Works in English · 510

Afterword · 513

Illustrations

1. Map of the Kingdom of Denmark-Norway at Grundtvig's birth · 16
2. Population percentage and distribution by trade in 1787 and 1870 · 19
3. The Four Estates of the Realm · 22
4. Roskilde Provincial Assembly in 1835-36 · 24
5. Social changes in Grundtvig's lifetime · 26
6. Landscape with view to Udby · 32
7. Residents of Udby vicarage 1787 · 40
8. Memorials to Grundtvig's parents · 42
9. The fertile fields of Zealand / The Jutland heath · 44
10. Registry of Grundtvig's birth · 45
11. Udby Vicarage · 48
12. The Jelling stones · 52
13. Thyregod Church in Mid-Jutland · 54
14. Aarhus seen from the north · 56
15. Aarhus Cathedral School in Grundtvig's time · 58
16. Jens Stougaard, Grundtvig's teacher · 59
17. Grundtvig's Copenhagen · 62
18. University of Copenhagen, c. 1800 · 64
19. Henrik Steffens teaching in Breslau 1813 · 67
20. Facsimile of Grundtvig's handwriting 1802 · 69
21. Grundtvig's Denmark · 72
22. Egeløkke Manor · 74
23. Lady Constance Steensen de Leth · 75
24. The British bombardment of Copenhagen 1807 · 86
25. *The Masked Ball in Denmark. A Vision* 1808 · 90
26. Valkendorf's Hall of Residence · 94
27. Poul Dons · 95
28. Christian Molbech · 97
29. The megalith in Gunderslev Wood · 98
30. Frederik Sibbern · 100
31. Svend Hersleb · 102
32. Grundtvig's timetables at the Schouboe Institute, 1808-10 · 104

33. Grundtvig's and his father's pulpit in Udby Church · 110
34. A godly assembly in a farmhouse room · 114
35. Roskilde Cathedral · 119
36. Grundtvig's Bible · 126
37. *Danne-Virke* 1816-19 · 135
38. Grundtvig 1820 · 140
39. Lise Blicher · 143
40. The Church of our Saviour, Christianshavn · 145
41. Professor of Theology, Henrik Clausen · 151
42. Grundtvig 1831 · 154
43. Strandgade 4B · 156
44. Trinity College, Cambridge · 164
45. *Nordic Mythology 1832* · 170
46. The pulpit and altar in Christian's Church · 173
47. Sorø Academy · 176
48. Grundtvig welcomes Thorvaldsen home from Italy · 182
49. The Freedom Pillar · 187
50. Grundtvig's educational thinking · 190
51. Vartov Hospital Church in Grundtvig's time · 195
52. Grundtvig wearing his knighthood order 1843 · 196
53. Grundtvig praying 1843 · 198
54. Princess Caroline Amalie 1830 · 200
55. Christian Flor, founder of Rødding People's High School 1844 · 205
56. Grundtvig delivers his 'Bragi Talks' 1843-44 · 207
57. Elizabeth Fry reading to prisoners in Newgate Prison 1823 · 210
58. Skamling Hill 18th May 1843 · 211
59. Grundtvig 1847 · 216
60. Grundtvig's Circles of Life · 218
61. Grundtvig intoxicated with Odin · 223
62. Kierkegaard taming a woman · 224
63. People's march to the King · 225
64. Johan, Svend, and Meta · 227
65. The Constituent Assembly 23rd October 1848 · 231
66. Marie Toft 1844 · 234

ILLUSTRATIONS

67. Lise Grundtvig in mid-life · 235
68. Marie Grundtvig c. 1852 · 240
69. Rønnebæksholm today, rebuilt after Grundtvig's death · 245
70. Grundtvig's pavilion at Rønnebæksholm · 254
71. Grundtvig (74) and his 3-year-old son Frederik 1857 · 258
72. Asta Grundtvig, c. 1861 · 261
73. Grundtvig's and Asta's 'Happy Home', Gammel Kongevej 148 · 263
74. Grundtvig 1862 · 270
75. Grundtvig's doctrinal structure in diagram form · 276
76. Grundtvig baptising a baby in Vartov Church · 277
77. Grundtvig pronouncing the Benediction in Vartov Church · 280
78. Asta and Grundtvig 1865 · 282
79. Christen Kold in mid-life · 287
80. Grundtvig 12th April 1867 · 288
81. Grundtvig's baptismal bowl · 292
82. Grundtvig's study and library of over 8,000 books at Great Tuborg · 294
83. Grundtvig 1869 · 297
84. The ending of Grundtvig's last sermon · 299
85. Locket with Grundtvig's hair · 300
86. Grundtvig's grave · 301
87. Grundtvig in Udby Church c. 1810 · 302
88. The four needs counterbalanced by the four fears · 311
89. Rødding People's High School today · 320
90. 28th April 1948, the first Danish Lutheran women pastors · 325
91. Grundtvig and the women's movement · 327
92. Grundtvig, the children's friend · 335
93. Six English biographies · 338
94. Clinton, Iowa, c. 1890 · 340
95. Grundtvig International Secondary School, Nigeria · 354
96. The London Grundtvig Conference 2018 · 358
97. The first biography of Grundtvig 1882 · 360
98. The Grundtvig Memorial Rooms at Udby · 378
99. Grundtvig's Church · 381
100 Celebrating midsummer at Vartov · 386

Foreword

Through the power of his work and personality and as "an agent that provokes or speeds significant change or action" Nicolai Frederik Severin Grundtvig (1783-1872) can rightfully be called the catalyst of modern Denmark. For he contributed decisively to gathering the Danish people into a nation with a common identity – and a search for the common good. His weapon was the pen – "the pen's a spear" – with which he carved his way into Danish hearts and minds, particularly through his hymns, his songs, and his ideas on education. However secular Denmark may seem today, the Danes still live with the resonance of Grundtvig's thoughts in their foundational beliefs – in freedom, in happiness, in dialogue, and in moderation.

Grundtvig's motto, "My life is to fight", is a fair judgement on himself, for he never ceased to be, in Sid Bradley's encapsulating words, a "warrior-scholar"[1] for God and Denmark. 'God' and 'Denmark' do not sit easily with one another nowadays, but to understand Grundtvig they must be taken in tandem. Behind all his thought lay the servant's wish to work for the glory of God, as God was working for the glory of Denmark. So, however pugnacious and self-willed Grundtvig was throughout most of his life, so humble was he before God – as his hymns and sermons attest. He knew himself to be a proud man, and he was in an ongoing battle with his own character. Only God could humble him, and this too was a constant theme in his work. All theologians have emphasised God's grace in the *salvation* of humankind, but drawing on Irenaeus Grundtvig stressed the very same grace at work in the *creation* of humankind. Grundtvig is the great hymnwriter to the Creation, to Nature. This essential grounding explains the sense of joy that he brought to Danish Christianity. No wonder that those of his countrymen who emigrated to America in the 19th and 20th century with Grundtvig in their luggage were known as "the happy Danes".

Crucial to the book's treatment of Grundtvig is the demonstration of how *active* he was, not just as a great thinker but as a great doer. The Danish word *ildsjæl*, 'fiery soul', describes him in a nutshell. Grundtvig's Christian-Danish passion was the greatest source of attraction for his followers. Naturally, it also created antagonists, including

---

[1]. GS 1989-90, 235.

Søren Kierkegaard, for Grundtvig was a divisive figure. But all would agree that he was *in touch with his times*, as a historian of the Danish past and prophet of the Danish future. He equated history with experience, and his prophetic choices for Denmark have proved wise: an interactive education, dialogue and innovation, and the pursuit of happiness for the common good. Many fiery souls after him have been equally active.

This biography underpins the series, 'N.F.S. Grundtvig. Works in English', by portraying the man both behind, and in, the work, and by showing how his ideas developed over time. He was a poet before he was a pastor, and an educator before he was a politician.

The dates at the start of each chapter signify important moments in his life, while the chapter quotations, mostly from Grundtvig himself, attempt to capture the essence of their content.

We owe a debt of gratitude to all previous biographers. We do not claim to present much new material, only a new, coherent interpretation which confirms Grundtvig as the single most influential person in the making of modern Denmark. Fortunately, he left behind an extraordinary number of books, articles, diaries, and letters, all of which have been supplemented by memoirs of those who knew him, and by numberless articles. We have consulted four kinds of sources:

1. Primary sources: books, articles, letters, diaries, and Grundtvig's own memoirs.
2. Grundtvig's Works/*Grundtvigs Værker*, the new digitalised variorum edition, available online in Danish, c. 1000 works/36,000 published pages.
3. Secondary sources: contemporary memoirs, biographies, illustrations (cartoons/photographs), and articles, especially from the annual publication, *Grundtvig Studies*.
4. Critical works on Grundtvig on a specific theme or subject.

This biography is being published simultaneously in both English and Danish, and to this end the flow of chapters is identical. Footnotes in the English version are largely limited to sources available in English, but we owe it to the many Danish authors quoted to append references also to them, so those in parentheses denote Danish-language only. The English biography, written in the past tense, takes into consideration the international readership by people largely unfamiliar with 19th century Denmark in general and Grundtvig in particular. The Danish biography, written in the present tense, quotes and discusses more Danish sources and takes for granted a working knowledge of the country and its history. The fact that Edward Broadbridge has had prime responsibility for the English version and Hans Raun Iversen for the Danish one is also reflected in their writing styles.

The last section of the book brings an English translation of 70 selected letters from and to Grundtvig. They supplement the biography and authenticate important events and attitudes in his life; in a sense they may be read as a small biography in its own right.

Edward Broadbridge and Hans Raun Iversen

FOREWORD

We are deeply grateful to the following for reading the manuscript and contributing to this book:

Ingrid Ank, Peter Balslev-Clausen, Hanna Broadbridge, Jørgen Carlsen, Niels Henrik Gregersen, Neil Keeble, Ida Kongsbak, Ove Korsgaard, John Nicholson, Harald Nielsen.

Our thanks also go to the following for the information they provided:

Ahmed Akkari, Gudrun Jessen, Ray Carlton Jones, Liselotte Larsen, Lone Kølle Martinsen, Jes Fabricius Møller, Dorrit Røtting.

Finally, we wish to record our appreciation for the outstanding support from our publishing team at Aarhus University Press over the years: Sanne Lind Hansen, Rikke Kensinger, Jørgen Sparre, and Ulrik Hvilshøj.

We thank the following foundations for their generous contributions to this volume:

Dronning Margrethe og Prins Henriks Fond
Augustinus Fonden
Den Hielmstierne-Rosencroneske Stiftelse
Carlsen-Langes Legatstiftelse
Konsul George Jorck og Hustru Emma Jorcks Fond
Aage og Johanne Louis-Hansens Fond
Jens Nørregaard & Hal Kochs Mindefond
Pastor Niels Møgelvangs Litteraturfond
Svend Grundtvig og Axel Olriks Legat
VELUX Fonden

Notes on Contributors

Authors

Edward Broadbridge (b.1944) BA London, MA Aarhus, taught English and Religious Studies at senior high schools in Denmark 1967-2008. Among his many theological translations are books on Ruth, Luke, Paul, and Titus of Bostra, as well as translations of 50 Danish hymns in *Hymns in English* (2009). He is also a librettist for Danish composers, and a writer/director of children's musicals. His translations of Grundtvig began with *A Grundtvig Anthology* (1984) and include the first major appraisal of Grundtvig in English, *Tradition and Renewal* (1983), as well as *Grundtvig as a Political Thinker* by Ove Korsgaard (2014), and most of the essays in *Building the Nation. N.F.S. Grundtvig and Danish National Identity* (2015). He is the translator of Anders Holm's *The Essential N.F.S. Grundtvig* (2019), and editor of the quarterly *Grundtvig Newsletter*. He is the translator and editor of the 6-volume series 'N.F.S. Grundtvig: Works in English' (2008-23).

Hans Raun Iversen (b.1948) MTh Aarhus (1976), Doctor of Divinity Uppsala (2012), was Researcher in Missiology at Aarhus University 1974-82 and Associate Professor in Practical Theology at Copenhagen University 1982-2018. He has conducted over 20 courses for English-speaking students on Grundtvig's theology and specialises in church research – emphasising relationships between church and people in Denmark and the influence and perspectives of Grundtvig. He has published extensively in Danish. Among his books in English are *Church, Society and Mission. Twelve Danish Contributions to International Discussions* (Copenhagen, 2010) and *Spirit and Life-Form. The Home, the People and the Church in Grundtvig's Time and Today* (Montreal, 2013).

Language Consultant

Hanna Broadbridge (1945-2022) MA Aarhus, English & Japanese, married Edward in 1967 and was a teacher of English at senior high schools in Denmark 1971-2009 and lecturer in English at the Royal Academy of Education 1978-2003. She was also an external examiner in English at all the Danish universities 1998-2015, and an official interpreter for the Danish legal system. She sat on the board of representatives for DanChurchAid, was chair of the Diocesan Council of Aarhus Diocese, chair of the Lutheran Committee of the Council of International Relations in Denmark, chair of the North Randers area deanery, and chair of St. Clement's Church Council, Randers for 25 years.

Abbreviations

We have retained the same Danish abbreviations in the English book

N.F.S. Grundtvig. Works in English, published by Aarhus University Press

TSFL	1. *The School For Life. N.F.S. Grundtvig on Education for the People* (2011)
LW	2. *Living Wellsprings. The Hymns, Songs, and Poems of N.F.S. Grundtvig* (2015)
HCF	3. *Human Comes First. The Christian Theology of N.F.S. Grundtvig* (2018)
TCG	4. *The Common Good. N.F.S. Grundtvig as Politician and Contemporary Historian* (2019)
TCOL	5. *The Core of Learning. The Philosophical Writings of N.F.S. Grundtvig* (2021)
DC	6. *Denmark's Catalyst. The Life and Letters of N.F.S. Grundtvig* (2023)

Grundtvig's Works in Danish/Biography

BFOTG	LETTERS FROM AND TO GRUNDTVIG/*Breve fra og til Grundtvig* I & II, ed. Georg Christensen & Stener Grundtvig. Copenhagen: Gyldendal 1924-26
DDS	THE DANISH HYMNBOOK/*Den Danske Salmebog*. Copenhagen: Det Kgl. Vajsenshus Forlag, 2003
DUB	DIARIES AND NOTEBOOKS/*Dags- og Udtogsbøgerne*, ed. Gustav Albeck. Copenhagen: C.A. Reitzel 1979
GEEG	GRUNDTVIG'S MEMOIRS AND MEMOIRS OF GRUNDTVIG/*Grundtvigs Erindringer og Erindringer om Grundtvig*. Copenhagen: Gyldendal 1948
GP	GRUNDTVIG'S SERMONS 1-12/*Grundtvigs Prædikener* 1-12. Copenhagen: Gad 1983
GS	GRUNDTVIG STUDIES/*Grundtvig Studier*. Copenhagen: Grundtvig-selskabet, 1948-
GV	GRUNDTVIG'S WORKS ONLINE/*Grundtvigs Værker Online*, 2009-
HS	THE PEOPLE'S HIGH SCHOOL SONGBOOK/*Højskolesangbogen, 19. udgave*. Copenhagen: Forlaget Højskolerne, 2020
MM	WITHIN LIVING MEMORY/*Mands Minde*. Copenhagen: Schønberg 1877
PS	POETICAL WORKS I-IX/*Poetiske Skrifter I-IX*. Copenhagen: Schønberg 1880-1930
US	SELECTED WRITINGS I-X/*Udvalgte Skrifter* I-X. Copenhagen: Gyldendal 1904-09
VU	SELECTED WORKS I-X/*Værker i Udvalg* I-X. Copenhagen: Gyldendal 1940-49

Grundtvig's Works in Danish/Letters

BFOTG   LETTERS FROM AND TO GRUNDTVIG I-II/*Breve fra og til Grundtvig* I-II, ed. Georg Christensen & Stener Grundtvig. Copenhagen: Gyldendal 1924-26

BUSCK   GUNNI BUSCK. LIFE IN A COUNTRY VICARAGE/*Et Levnetsløb i en Landsbypræstegaard*. Edited by Henrik Beck. Copenhagen: Schønberg, 1869, 2nd enlarged edition 1888

CA   SIX LETTERS TO CAROLINE AMALIE, 1843, from *The Dane/Danskeren*, ed. Nygård, F., Schrøder, L. og Grundtvig F.L., vol. 5: Oct. 1890-April 1891, pp. 195-220. Kolding 1891

GBHH   GRUNDTVIG'S LETTERS TO HIS WIFE DURING HIS ENGLAND TRIPS 1829-31/ /*Grundtvigs Breve til hans Hustru under Englandsrejserne 1829-31*, published by his grandchildren. Copenhagen: Aage Marcus 1920

GS   GRUNDTVIG STUDIES/*Grundtvig Studier*, published annually by the Grundtvig-Selskabet af 8 September 1947

INGEMANN   GRUNDTVIG AND INGEMANN, A CORRESPONDENCE 1821-59/ *Grundtvig og Ingemann – Brevvexling 1821-1859*, published, and with a foreword, by Svend Grundtvig. Copenhagen: Society for the Promotion of Danish Literature, 1882

MOLBECH   CHRISTIAN MOLBECH AND NIKOLAI FREDERIK SEVERIN GRUNDTVIG. A CORRESPONDENCE/*Christian Molbech og Nikolai Frederik Severin Grundtvig – En Brevveksling*, collected by Christian K.F. Molbech. Copenhagen: Gyldendal 1888

RØRDAM   PETER RØRDAM. LEAVES FROM HIS LIFE AND CORRESPONDENCE /*Leaves from his Life and Correspondence*, ed. Holger Rørdam. Vols I-III. Copenhagen: Schønberg 1891, 1892 & 1895

SIMESEN   N.F.S. GRUNDTVIG AND HIS CLOSE FAMILY DURING THE FIRST SCHLESWIG WAR, ed. Inge Simesen. Copenhagen: Gad 1933

I

THE LIFE

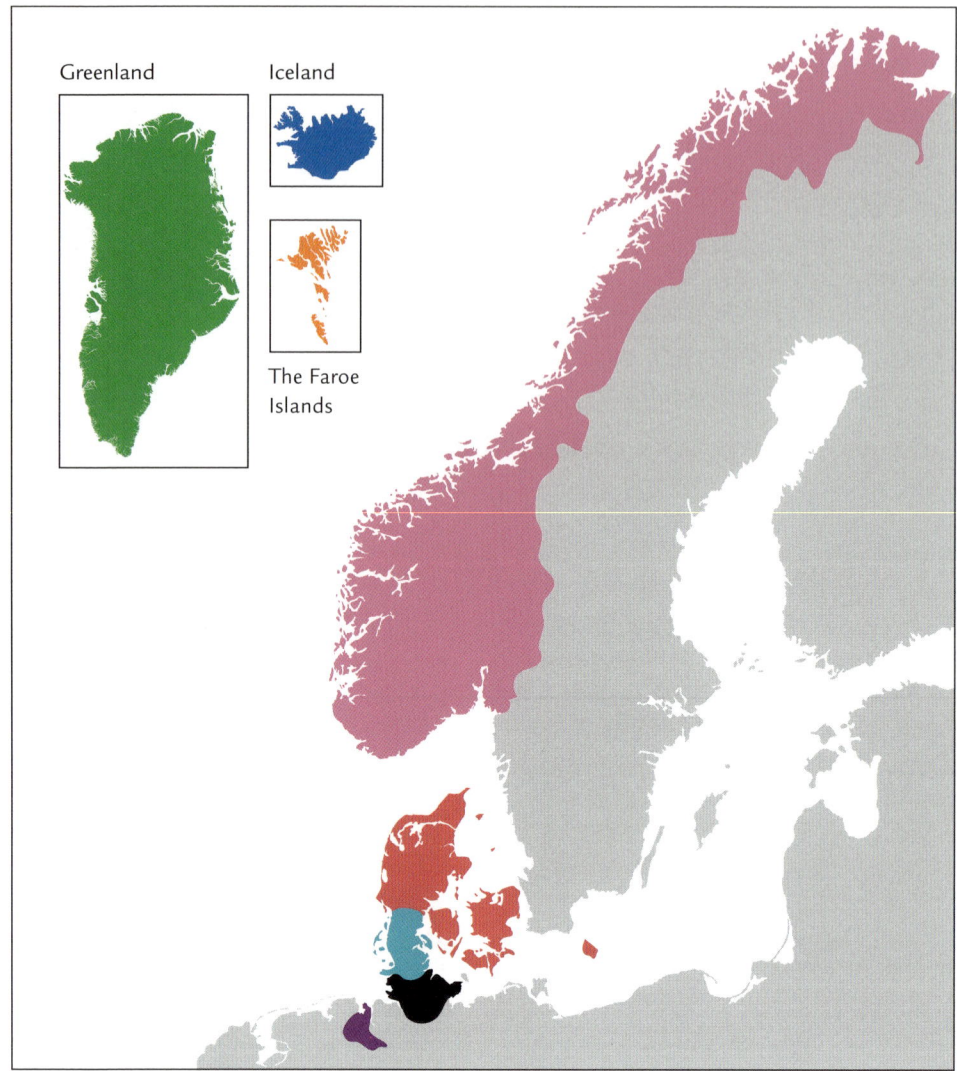

1. Map of The Kingdom of Denmark-Norway at Grundtvig's birth

1. Oldenburg, lost in 1774
2. Norway, lost in 1814
3. Schleswig-Holstein, lost in 1864 – North Schleswig returned in 1920 as South Jutland
4. Iceland, lost in 1944
5. The Faroe Islands – part of the Kingdom of Denmark, but self-governing since 1948
6. Greenland – part of the Kingdom of Denmark but self-governing since 1979

1. The Making of Modern Denmark

Nicolai Frederik Severin Grundtvig (1783-1872) lived in a unique period in Danish history. During his lifetime the Kingdom of Denmark lost four-fifths of its territory, including Norway. Would it even *survive* as an independent country? Strong forces wanted it to become either part of a Scandinavian union or a vassal state of Prussia – and not even the King of Denmark was averse to the idea! Ultimately, Grundtvig was instrumental in the revival of his people and the reinterpretation of their history in a new national self-understanding. This catalyst role makes him a figure of interest for readers worldwide, especially those facing similar challenges today to the ones that Denmark faced in the 19th century. He is an essential figure in any discussion about freedom and democracy, history and nation-building, heathen mythology and Christian faith, and, most of all, lifelong learning. Not for nothing is he known as "the father of adult education".

"My life is to fight!" said Grundtvig, "The tongue's a sword, the pen's a spear!" These words appeared in *Nordic Mythology 1832* and sum up the stance that he took throughout his life. He saw himself as a Viking 'shield-warrior', defending the Christian faith and the Danish nation, attacking all challengers, and seeing his whole life as a battle, first with himself, then with the Church, and finally with society in general. In a letter to his friend and fellow hymnwriter Bernhard Ingemann dated 27th November 1824, he admitted that he was better at expressing disagreement than solidarity with someone:

> I am the armour-bearer of the spirit, much better at making myself understood to enemies than to friends. I can express my particular view and my strong and deliberate antipathy to whatever is base, self-opinionated, and toothless in our times, but only very obscurely can I express my fellowship with those who have a feeling for the Spirit.[2]

Grundtvig died just six days short of his 89th birthday, having lived twice as long as the average Dane of his time. Had he died at the age of 42, like his contemporary Søren Kierkegaard (1813-55), he would not have had much to show for his warrior-stance beyond his new translations of ancient texts, some philosophical thoughts on human life, and a handful of original hymns. Aged 42, in 1825, Grundtvig's greatest works still lay ahead of him: *Nordic Mythology*, the pioneering volume on education for the people; *Song-Work for the Danish Church*, the huge collection of original and translated hymns; the mature thoughts of his *Basic Christian Teachings*; and his frequent parliamentary contributions to the establishment of 'government by the people'. He preferred the Danish word *folkestyre* (lit. people rule) to 'democracy', a foreign import. Above all, Grundtvig gathered the forces of the past, Nordic and Christian, and acted on them as a catalyst. He helped to build them into the foundation of the country's future, even as Denmark was undergoing the severest test in its history. His legacy is to be widely regarded as the major founding figure of modern Denmark.

---

2. (INGEMANN, 37).

Grundtvig had prodigious talents and boundless energy, both of which he put to good use for his country. He read voraciously; an inventory of his library at his death counted 8,963 volumes.[3] He published c. 1,000 works in 36,000 pages, and wrote some 1,500 hymns and songs. In his time he was Parliament's most voluble speaker. He transformed himself from a conservative monarchist into a freedom-loving democrat without losing his roots among the common people or his respect for the King. He realised the importance of literacy and education for all Danes and developed his own original ideas about a 'school for life'. He strongly believed that the roots of history and religion – in Denmark's case Nordic mythology and Christianity – were fundamental to the development of his country, so his 'fight' was to raise his people's awareness of their unique history and to ground them in its cultural, social, and national ideas. These are what Denmark is best known for today: political accountability, a strong, effective state, and the rule of law. In *The Origins of Political Order* (2011, 14) Francis Fukuyama presents Denmark as a good example of these three fundamental democratic ideas, noting: "For people in developing countries 'Denmark' is a mythical place that is known to have good political and economic institutions: it is stable, democratic, peaceful, prosperous, inclusive, and has extremely low levels of political corruption. Everyone would like to figure out how to transform Somalia, Haiti, Nigeria, Iraq or Afghanistan into 'Denmark'."

Much of what happened in Denmark was inspired by, and even compelled by, what happened in other parts of Europe. Denmark's transformation from a multinational to a national state may therefore be seen as an overture to the transformational processes in Europe, especially in Germany, England, and France. These did not find a preliminary conclusion until after the First World War, when the Austria-Hungarian and the Ottoman empires were dissolved into smaller national states.

Conditions of life 1783-1872

Although Grundtvig's Denmark was smaller than it had ever been, its population in the 19th century was on the increase:

1801	1,000,000 (excluding Norway)
1834	1,231,000
1850	1,415,000
1880	2,000,000
1901	2,500,000.[4]

From 1660 to 1814 the Kingdom of Denmark-Norway was a single absolute monarchy. In 1733 the Danish government had passed an 'adscription' law, which forced all 14 to 36-year-olds to remain in the area of their birth, under the watchful eye of the lord of the manor, who owned all the land on which they worked. In 1764 this restriction had been

---

3. (Toldberg, 35).
4. Today the population is approaching 6 million.

tightened to include all 4 to 40-year-olds. Personal freedom did not exist. The government – i.e. the King in Council – gradually realised the economic potential for the country in promoting agriculture, which in turn required improvements in education and greater legal security for the peasant farmers. From 1788 all Danish agriculture was therefore reformed, allowing for much greater freedom and increasing progress in cultivation and trade. The reforms were widely welcomed, and by 1815 two-thirds of the peasants actually *owned* their farms. Higher earnings meant more livestock and thus more manure, better crops, an improved diet, and therefore a lower death rate for children. The population increased markedly, with villages growing faster than towns, and agriculture becoming the dominant source of income.

2. **Population percentage and distribution by trade in 1787 and 1870**

	1787	1870
Population	0.8 million	1.8 million
Agriculture	43	44
Labourers	25	16
Crafts and industry	14	21
Fishing and shipping	3	3
Trade and business	3	5
Professionals	7	6
Rich and poor without an occupation	5	5

Source: Erling Olsen, *Danmarks økonomiske historie siden 1750*. G.E.C. Gads Forlag, 1967, 20.

It is much harder to calculate the economic growth of the country, which depended on many and various factors including: an unwise financial policy leading to the state's bankruptcy in 1813; siding with Napoleon against Britain and the subsequent loss of Norway to Sweden in 1814; and a European agricultural crisis between 1818-28. However, *after* 1828 prosperity began to return to all sections of Danish society and real economic growth more or less doubled in the course of Grundtvig's lifetime, at least for the peasant farmers.

At Grundtvig's birth in 1783 the population of Denmark numbered just under 1 million, rising to just under 2 million by his death in 1872. Throughout his life, 75% of the people lived in the country, where most farmers paid each other in kind and only a few took their wares to market. The emphasis on agriculture set the pattern for the next 150 years; by the mid-20th century Denmark was still living mainly off its agriculture. Not until the 1870s did the industrialisation of Denmark really gather speed, motivating country people to move to the cities for work opportunities and a better standard of living. Life in the country could be terribly hard, and for the same reason Danes also began to seek farming opportunities *outside* the country, emigrating in particular to North America and Argentina. Between 1820 and 1930, no fewer than 336,000 Danes left for the USA. Industry did not finally overtake agriculture as the largest export provider until 1963.

The growing freedom of mind and body

All over Europe people were classified into 'estates' with widely differing life-conditions. From the Middle Ages onwards Denmark was divided into four 'estates of the realm': the nobility, the clergy, the citizenry, and the peasantry. In the so-called 'Danish Law' of 1683, the 'peasantry' included peasant farmers, villagers, smallholders, and cottagers, i.e. the bottom layer of society, which constituted 70% of the population. The social structure in Grundtvig's day favoured the first estate of the realm, the nobility, meaning the lords of the 800 or so manors dotted round the country. Their tasks were to administer the king's justice, to distribute the produce of the manor to the cities and trades, and to provide soldiers, should the king choose to go to war. Administering justice allowed the lord the right to punish corporally all household members on the manor estate; adult males could do the same to their servants and their children – though by the Danish Law of 1683 not to their wives. Corporal punishment of servants was abolished in 1921, of school pupils in 1967, and eventually of *all* children in 1997.

Human rights were not a determinant in Grundtvig's early life, but came to the fore in the first democratic Danish constitution from 1849, which allowed for freedom of speech, religion, and political organisation. The even more basic right to have control over one's own body and the fruits of one's labour was hard to handle by legislation. Until the abolition of adscription in 1788 most people's 'bodies' belonged to the lord of the manor. Not until an agreement between workers and employers in 1899 did the former gain the legal right to strike to improve their life-conditions. Grundtvig returned time and again to the British Habeas Corpus Act of 1679, whereby no one can be denied physical freedom without a legal judgement to that effect; this he called "the firm foundation of their freedom".

The most conspicuous examples of people who lived without control over their own bodies during Grundtvig's lifetime were, apart from Danish women in general, the Danish West Indian slaves. From 1839 to 1848 Grundtvig was a member of a small committee working for the abolition of slavery in the Danish West Indian colonies of St. Thomas, St. John and St. Croix (now the US Virgin Islands). For some years he had argued that full freedom for all his compatriots in Denmark should take priority over the case of the African slaves in faraway West Indies. In the late 18th century criticism of slavery was coming to a head in England. Denmark took the lead in 1793 by forbidding the transport of slaves from the Danish colony in present-day Ghana to its colonies in the West Indies. Britain followed in 1807-08. In 1833, Britain abolished slavery in all its colonies except for India and Ceylon, bringing Denmark under considerable pressure to follow suit. In the event the Danish slaves in the Caribbean managed to free themselves by rebellion in 1848 before the new constitution in Denmark in 1849 made all forms of slavery illegal.

Women were largely subservient to men in Grundtvig's Denmark. Enfranchising women in the constitution of 1849 was never up for debate. The family, and in particular the head of the household, decided who could marry whom and with what dowry, and only the pastor could ratify the marriage before God and society. The husband was required by law to treat his wife respectfully, but it was not until 1880 that she could dispose over her own assets legally; married women achieved legal authority in 1899 and the right to vote in 1915 for *all* women. Equal parental custody was allowed in 1922. In Grundtvig's day divorce was frowned upon by both the Church and the State; in 1800 there were still only 100 divorces a year in the whole of Denmark. By 1925 divorce was a free right – though on specific legal grounds.

As regards their cultural and social position, until the 1870s Danish women were in general referred to by the German term *fruentimmer*, literally a 'female staying (and working) in a room or chamber'. Grundtvig preferred to talk about women using the word *kvinder* (present-day 'women'), in accordance with his respect for all the significant women in his life – from his mother and his nurse to his three wives and the many other women in his social circle. This was also in accordance with old Nordic mythology, where women were not just the object of man's love but also and often active shield-warriors in their own right. Grundtvig regularly referred to them as the ideal Danish women, *Dannekvinder*. or Dane-women.

The four estates converge into one people

Grundtvig was born into the second estate, the *clergy*, but his father's relatively high social status was not matched by his income in a rural parish. Although Grundtvig lived close to 70 years of his life in Copenhagen, he always maintained that his roots were in the country – in the gently rolling hills around Udby where he spent his first 9 years, and on the Danish heath around Thyregod where he spent the next 6. He belonged to the *land*, and strongly believed that social change should come from the grass roots where the great majority of the people lived.

Grundtvig was acutely aware of the peasant wisdom that lay behind the many country proverbs and sayings. He collected and published 3,012 of them in 1845 under the title *Danish Proverbs and Sayings*. If and when the people were to be given their say in the running of the social and political life of the nation, the new nation-state should bear in mind this great store of folk wisdom. With the coming of democracy in 1849, the four estates gradually faded into the background. The legal privileges of the nobility were abolished – although today there are still some 200 so-called 'noble' families in the country, by and large a titular privilege. Little by little the three other estates became social classes, so that pastors and farmers, bankers and butchers all share one status nowadays. Similarly, although the very *first* franchise of 1849 was limited to 15% of all Danes, this nevertheless meant that 73% of all men over 30 had the vote. In 1915 the franchise was extended to all men *and* women over 25; it currently stands at 18 years old.

Grundtvig was born 7 years after the American revolution in 1776 and 6 years before the French in 1789. Who knew *what* would happen from then on? Was this the wind of freedom or of chaos? Grundtvig was conservative by nature, believing that Denmark was unique in having an *enlightened* absolute monarch who really *did* listen to his people – and who then did the right thing *for* them. The King's Law of 1665 had actually legitimised this relationship, with 'representatives of the people' establishing the king's absolute rule and the order of succession to his first son. Not only was Denmark unique, Grundtvig argued, it was also a country divinely blessed! Mob rule in 1789 and Napoleon's imperial ambition

3. The Four Estates of the Realm.
In the illustration from Bishop Frans of Viborg's album (c.1600) a sword is granted to the nobility, a sceptre to the king, a book to the clergy, and a flail to the peasantry.

in the 1810s had destroyed the French nation; the same must not be allowed to happen in Denmark. Philosophically, Grundtvig was already conjecturing that the future might lie with 'people rule', i.e. democracy. Already in 1819 he wrote in *On Church, State, and School*:

> ... We can also quite reasonably get it into our heads that the agreement between every man's demand and the interests of all can only be brought about by each man giving his vote and everything being decided by the most votes.

King Frederik VI (ruled 1808-39) admired Grundtvig for his translations into Danish of the Icelandic and Norse[5] sagas, as well as of the great Anglo-Saxon epic poem, *Beowulf*, dating from the 8th century. He gave him an annual grant, and paid for his 3 trips to England in 1829, 1830, and 1831. Grundtvig was both flattered and honoured, and came home full of ideas of freedom based on education for *life* rather than for an occupation. When His Majesty dragged his feet at the very thought of 'government by the people', Grundtvig went

---

5. 'Norse' relates to the Viking Age of the 9th and 10th centuries, when the Norsemen reached as far as Canada, North Africa, and Central Asia, and wrote their Norse Sagas. Otherwise the preferred term throughout is 'Nordic'.

along with him, until both bowed to the people's pressure, and the King established four provincial advisory assemblies from 1835. Although these included citizens and farmers, the keyword for the King was 'advisory'; they were not to enjoy any *real* power.

Nonetheless, the stone was now rolling. It gained momentum with the demands for greater freedom that the four assemblies recommended. When Christian VIII succeeded Frederik VI in 1839, he was expected to *meet* these demands, and when he failed to do so, disappointment turned into active popular dissatisfaction. The National Liberal Party increased its pressure on the King, and when revolutions again broke out all over Europe in 1848, there was no way back for Denmark. To avoid any whiff of a popular uprising, Frederik VII signed the new democratic constitution into law on 5th June 1849. Grundtvig's ambiguity about the move is apparent in a witty speech he had given, with women present, as late as 26th April 1848:

> ... not only am I royally minded, but more recently I have noticed that I am more royally minded than I ever realised myself! Now it is no longer enough for me just to *have* a king; now I would like to be a little king myself and see nothing but other little kings around me, just as long as we have learned the noblest art of all: the royal art of controlling oneself. Naturally I want to see nothing but small queens of Denmark around me too, not just where I am going to speak but *everywhere*, provided they have a little self-control (even if they are wearing crowns), and no claim on the government, but in all modesty settle for perhaps not a *powerless*, but nevertheless only an *advisory*, voice.[6]

Grundtvig nevertheless became a member of the Constituent Assembly that drew up the new constitution which legally moved the people from four estates into one nation. He promoted all forms of 'Danishness' to weld the country together, one of his favoured combinations being 'Fatherland and Mother-tongue' – linking history, territory, and governance to language and culture. Above all, in order to understand themselves Danes must learn about their past, and then learn *from* it. Their forefathers' experience was paramount in this process.

The new Danish reality

Denmark's geographical position may be a good way north of Europe's centre, but it was never independent of the rest of Europe. More often than not, what happened south of Denmark was a determining factor in its history, its development – and even its destiny. The country comprises the Jutland peninsula north of the German border plus 406 islands. The chief of these are Zealand (with the capital Copenhagen) and Funen. In area, Denmark is slightly bigger than the Netherlands, slightly smaller than Estonia, and about the size of the US state of Virginia. To move around the country, island ferries were essential – and also efficient. Whole trains transferred onto ferries to sail across the Little Belt and the Great Belt until two bridges, built in 1938 and 1998, linked the west to the

---

6. *TCG*, 252.

4. Roskilde Provincial Assembly in 1835-36.
On the plinth in the centre is a bust of King Frederik VI. To the left sits the Royal Commissioner, Anders (A.S.) Ørsted, later prime minister (1853-54). To the right, with his face turned towards the standing speaker, is the assembly president, Joachim (J.F.) Schouw. Heliograph by Vilhelm Pacht after a drawing by an unknown artist. Royal Danish Library.

east by road and rail. Denmark is simultaneously *protected* by water and easily *accessible* by water. Indeed it has lived off its water for much of its existence, both as a naval and as a fishing nation. The former helped Denmark to build a small empire, trading with its colonies abroad in India, West Africa, and the West Indies. But in the early 1800s the navy was lost, Norway was lost, and later the twin dukedoms of Schleswig-Holstein were lost. Multi-cultural, multi-lingual Denmark became a small heterogenic nation-state – all in Grundtvig's lifetime.

Two potentially dangerous political factors had emerged in Europe around 1800: a growing nationalism, and competition for supremacy in Northern Europe. The French revolution shocked citizens across Europe. When the French king and queen were executed in 1793, and Napoleon Bonaparte seized power in 1799, monarchies such as the Danish feared for their lives. Caught between the major powers the Danish king took Napoleon's side *against* Britain and set up a peace alliance with Russia, Sweden and Prussia – a fateful move. Copenhagen was shattered first by the British attack in 1801 and then by the British destruction of half the city in 1807. Denmark had chosen the losing side, with the loss of Norway at the Kiel peace negotiations in 1814 as a result. 'Denmark' in this case meant the absolute monarch himself, who since 1665 had enjoyed complete control over all three branches of power: the legislative, the executive, and the judicial.

In the meantime Prussia, which had been defeated by France in 1806, was back on the move. The old Holy Roman Empire had gone, but a new Federated States of Germany was formed in 1815, and looked to add the Danish duchies of Schleswig and Holstein to their number. This failed in the First Schleswig War (1848-51) but succeeded in the Second Schleswig War (1864). In 1870 the Federated States of Germany went on to defeat France, and from the mid-19th to the mid-20th century the now unified Germany was the strongest power in Europe. Denmark had to be very careful of its huge southern neighbour, but could not prevent Nazi Germany from occupying Denmark between 1940-45. Since the 1950s, however, and Denmark's entry into the European Union in 1972, there has been a new attitude of mutual respect on both sides.

In the midst of the political and military turmoil in Northern Europe, a strong existential, cultural and philosophical questioning was taking place: Who are we as a nation? Do we have a common way of thinking and acting that *unites* us? In Denmark, the academic and cultural elite had put down its roots in classical Latin and Greek culture. From the 1750s onwards the existential inspiration and cultural standards of Denmark followed Germany in the philosophies of rationalism and romanticism. Grundtvig was at first fascinated by German literature and philosophy, especially Goethe, Schiller, Fichte and Schelling, but he was critical of German rationalism and turned to his indigenous Danish cultural heritage of Nordic mythology and the oldest sources of Denmark's history. Among these he included the epic Old English poem, *Beowulf*, set in Denmark and Swedish Götland. He coupled these with his awareness of Scottish liberal ideas, and his practical experience of an industrialising England, where on his visits he was particularly struck by the repeated question: "Yes, but what do *you* do, Mr. Grundtvig?"[7]

As he made his way from country boy to city pastor, Grundtvig became increasingly aware of the injustices inherent in pre-democratic Denmark. His conscience was slowly awakened to the need for *reform*, but never for revolution. He was still both a royalist and a champion of "the educated world" at this point. He was 47 years old before he published his first genuinely political work, the 72-page *Political Observations with Regard to Denmark and Holstein* (1831).[8] Prophetically, Grundtvig pointed out that the revolutions around Europe were creating a "new world of peoples", based on the irrefutable fact of language preference and mind-frame. He predicted that German-speaking Holstein could therefore no longer be part of Denmark and that sooner or later Schleswig would divide into a Danish-speaking and a German-speaking area; and indeed the former happened in 1864, the latter in 1920. In the same work Grundtvig also proposed "a high school for the pursuit of learning by the people and for civic training, which on the one hand would give students who wish to be part of the educated world the education that is actually required of them, and on the other hand would give the state a yardstick with which to draw its border-line." Grundtvig argued for freedom of expression, but only for those who had some learning, i.e. mature students and academics. Only later, as his ideas on freedom progressed, did he support an almost unrestricted press freedom. It is

---

7. (Schrøder 1901, 105).
8. TCG, Text 15.

significant that Grundtvig wrote most of his works on education between 1831 and 1847, i.e. in the period between the announcement of the four Provincial Advisory Assemblies in 1831 and the change in the political system in 1848-49. Despite his reservations about democracy, Grundtvig was carried along by the tide, and his conversion to 'government by the people' was relatively swift.

The following diagram illustrates the many major changes during Grundtvig's lifetime:

5. Social changes in Grundtvig's lifetime

1783	1872
King's sovereignty	People's sovereignty
United monarchy	Nation-state
Royal law	Democratic constitution
Religious duty	Religious freedom
Mono-religious society	Multi-religious society
Multi-lingual	Mono-lingual
Time of the Estates	Time of the People

Source; Ove Korsgaard, *The Common Good* (2019) 25.

The last transition in the diagram is the one that concerned Grundtvig most – the Time of the Estates becoming the Time of the People. His earliest political concern for the Danish people was to improve the lot of the peasantry – not to introduce a democratic constitution. He realized that there can be no democratic nation – big or small – without a common identity for the people who belong to it. Since there can be no national identity without national educators, and since there is nothing for the national educators to teach without a foundation in history, Grundtvig cultivated what Anthony Smith calls a "cult of the ancestors".[9] This was the purpose of his plans for a people's high school. Five teachers were indispensable, he asserted: for Danish language and literature, Danish history, Danish geography, Danish songs, and Danish law.

Changes in local life

In most respects the lords of the manor were the king's representatives in local society. For instance, when Grundtvig sought to improve the miserable schooling conditions in Udby in 1811, it was to the local landowner, the king's local administrator of education, that he had to write – and without much success, it must be added. Nevertheless, as the local landowners gradually lost power after the agricultural reforms, it was the pastors who took over as local leaders, including local schooling. The Education Act of 1814 was one of the most progressive in Europe, stipulating that all children should receive educa-

---

9. Hall et al, 51-78.

tion regularly between the ages of 7 and confirmation (between 14 and 19).[10] This meant that in Denmark primary education *preceded* industrialisation. Following this reform, local community/parish councils came into being in 1841, with the pastor as a sitting member and most often the council chair, plus 4 to 9 other males elected by and among the peasant farmers. This was extended in 1867 into a 'municipality', charged with the administration of local affairs outside the boroughs, i.e. the major towns and cities. Following this, pastors were gradually phased out of local executive administration, though they retained their powers within the Church until the 20th century.

The new liberal politics introduced a general taxation and conscription. Tithing was replaced by an annual church tax at the beginning of the 20th century, and all farmers were gradually made freeholders. Grundtvig's demand for "freedom for Loki as well as for Thor" (two opposing gods in Nordic Mythology) was being implemented slowly but surely. The speed was often determined by economic factors and technical development.

Grundtvig and his fiancé Lise had to wait 7 years before he had enough income to marry her; by then he was 34 and she was 31. The marriage age of the day was thus surprisingly high, 30 for men, and 28 for women. In Grundtvig's time a household was a self-sustaining entity. Just as the country was governed by the king, and the manor by the lord, so was the household governed by the husband. All production and early education took place in the household, where leisure-time was at a minimum. Among the landed gentry and the clergy it was common to send children away to be educated by other families, when such an arrangement was convenient to both. Grundtvig's 6 years away from home, from the age of 9 to 15, is an example of this. By today's standards of freedom and security Grundtvig and his family lived a rather poor and economically insecure life.

Until around 1850 all hot meals in peasant homes were prepared over an open fire. Meat was boiled, fried, or roasted on a spit, but in the main, like fish, it was preserved either salted or smoked. Only during slaughtering, was the meat fresh; any mincing, which was rare, was done with a knife. Eaten with the meat were bread, cabbage, or preserved vegetables, such as dried peas, bottled beetroot, or apples, while fresh fruit and vegetables were only eaten in season. Around 1850 three major arrivals changed the home: the iron stove with an oven, the mince grinder, and the potato, a late arrival on the dinner table, and served with the meat or the fish. In the late 1800s the cooperative movement, often initiated by local students from the Grundtvigian people's high schools, improved all areas of agriculture, enabling fresh meat and dairy products to be transported, while by the end of the century Copenhagen was sampling both *smørrebrød* (open sandwiches) and fancy cakes. In this development, energetic people managed to create freer conditions for their own lives, opening many new branches of business and production, free of previous restrictions.

---

10. To this day there is no compulsory school attendance in Denmark, only a compulsory teaching duty.

From State Church to People's Church/*folkekirken*

At the Reformation in 1536 the Danish king, Christian III, followed its leading protagonist Martin Luther (1483-1546) and its doctrinal Augsburg Confession of faith in 1530. Grundtvig was proud to have been born precisely 300 years after Luther. The 28 articles of the Augsburg Confession were the bedrock of Grundtvig's faith and remain legally valid to this day. The first ten articles can be summarised as follows:

1. God is Triune: Father, Son, and Holy Spirit
2. The natural sin of human beings is redeemed through Holy Baptism and the Holy Spirit
3. God's son, Jesus Christ, is the incarnation of God. Jesus has atoned for human sin and reconciled humankind to God
4. Human beings are saved (justified) only through faith in Jesus Christ
5. To ensure that the gospel of Jesus Christ is preached throughout the world Jesus has established the Church and the holy ministry
6. Good deeds are the fruit of faith and salvation
7. There is only one holy Christian Church, and it is found wherever the gospel is preached in its truth and purity and the sacraments of Holy Baptism and Holy Communion are administered according to the gospel
8. The twin sacraments are always valid because they are instituted by Christ
9. Baptism at any age is necessary, and signifies the grace of God
10. Christ's body and blood are truly present in, with, and under the bread and wine of the Sacrament. (The Lutheran doctrine of the real presence is more accurately and formally known as "the Sacramental Union", differing from 'transubstantiation')

Christianity was the king's religion. It was superior to all other religions, adhered to by all citizens, and disseminated to the Danish colonies. This included the people of Greenland following the arrival of the Danish missionary Hans Egede in 1721. Under the absolute monarch, a law was passed in 1735 making church-going compulsory in Denmark. It proved impossible to enforce and was widely ignored, and contemporary records show that by 1783, the year of Grundtvig's birth, only 10% of Danes went to Sunday service. However, the apathy towards church-going must not be interpreted to mean that the Danes were either irreligious or ignorant about Christianity. They simply could not see how worship could be relevant to their situation as peasant farmers. German pietism had made an impact in the 18th century but was now marginal. The only innovation was a Christian revival among lay people in the form of so-called 'godly assemblies' outside the Church. Grundtvig was favourably disposed towards *anyone* who wished to worship, and in his early years he considered himself a revivalist preacher, but he stayed *within* the Danish national church throughout his life, also when the State Church became the People's Church in 1849. All who were baptised were members, meaning 99.6% of the population in 1849. They attended the rituals of baptism, confirmation, wedding, and funeral, but the majority found the worship and the pastor's long dogmatic sermons tedious. Today secularisation and immigration have brought the number of members of the People's Church down to 73.2% (2022), with another 10% belonging to other recognised religious bodies. As in Grundtvig's day membership comes automatically with baptism. All members of the People's Church still pay the annual church tax of 0.87% on average (2022), and 75% of the population attend a church gathering at least once a year. In this respect the Danish churches differ from most others in their widespread support among the people.

Trained as a theologian and seeing himself as a Christian prophet in the Old Testament style Grundtvig was at the heart of the transformation of the Danish Church. He opposed the bishops who wanted the new People's Church to be the same as the old State Church, but he drew the line at a democratically-elected synod to govern the Church. His ideal was the free congregation under the state umbrella, but with no state interference in the faith or the life of the congregation – a system that has aptly been termed, "well-organised anarchy".

Education for life

When Grundtvig was born, young children had two duties: to help in the household as soon as they could, and to learn Luther's *Small Catechism* by heart in order to be confirmed in their faith in their early teens. Without confirmation they could not be considered adults. The Roman Catholic sacrament of Confirmation had been abolished by Luther and the Danish king, but it was reintroduced in 1736 by Christian VI, not as a *sacrament* but as a means to educate loyal, Christian citizens. Like other Pietists of the time, the King thought his people had become ignorant of their Christian faith. In consequence of this restrictive measure, without baptism and confirmation one could not marry, become a soldier, run a business, be a godparent, witness in court, or take Holy Communion. The parish clerk helped with the teaching of confirmands alongside a number of other duties, being the middleman between the pastor and the peasantry. Slow learners of the catechism were browbeaten, and the totally recalcitrant were detained until the pastor was satisfied. Confirmed youngsters were issued with a character reference book, which also listed bad or criminal conduct. Grundtvig protested long and hard but in vain at this intertwining of Church and State politics and demanded that there be no *civil* consequences of people's faith or of their standing in the church. He argued that the teaching of confessional Christianity should be removed from all public schools, as this was an issue for the Church only. This finally happened in 1975.

From 1736 the State had had to ensure that all youngsters had access to teaching *before* their compulsory confirmation. The Education Act of 1739 had introduced a teaching duty available for all children, which involved the inculcation of selected religious texts, but also included the training of reading and writing abilities. In 1791, Denmark opened its first teacher-training college in Copenhagen,[11] and, as we have already seen, Denmark's Education Act of 1814 instituted 7 years of education free of charge for all children, as well as the opportunity to lead the singing in churches on Sundays! In the country children attended every other day, in the cities every day. Not every child went to school of course, for parents needed them on the farms so much so that they ignored the threat of fines for absence – and for the most part got away with it. This resulted in the opening of many new schools run by gradually more qualified teachers and the opportunity for children to be active in church. From 1814 onwards city children went to school 6 half-days a week, and country children 3 half-days a week. The basic subjects were Reading, Writing, and Arithmetic. In 1820 a Teachers' Association was founded by teachers in private schools. By 1880 some 200,000 children were attending country schools, only 40,000 town and city schools.

Songs and ballads were not uncommon in Grundtvig's youth, but they took a huge step forward with his own contribution from the 1830s onwards. Referring to the 1840s, the folklorist Karen Toxværd wrote in 1914: "In those days the peasants bought neither books nor ballad collections, but they sang a lot, and when they learned a ballad, they wrote it down on any piece of paper they could get hold of, and sewed the pieces together in a book."[12]

The people's high school movement and its counterpart, 'Danish Society', a popular society for the promotion of Danish, consciously employed community singing to further Grundtvig's ideas and to consolidate 'the Fatherland and the Mother-tongue'. After Grundtvig's 34th lecture in the Within Living Memory series in 1838 the audience spontaneously broke out into song – Grundtvig's *own* song about the Danish naval hero, Peter Willemoes, who had fought against Lord Nelson in 1801. By tradition, this was where the widespread Danish custom of community singing was born. At the famous meeting on 4th July 1844 at Skamling Hill there was both community singing and choral singing, including the song that was to become Denmark's national song, 'There is a lovely land.' National songs soon became an integral part of Denmark, witness this excerpt from the 21-year-old Peter Boisen, the teacher of 37 students at Uldum People's High School in 1859:

> I sing for all I am worth, and they roar along with me like thunder! I urge them to sing from the heart, even though they sound no better than the owls of the night. The schoolroom ceiling is far too low, so the tobacco smoke and the fumes of the many people present gather under the beams and drip down, worst of all on the teacher's platform, so I have to put on my raincoat! But it makes no difference; there is such *spirit* here and always good humour; that is the main thing![13]

Grundtvig was always interested in what young people were learning. In the 1840s he even edited school textbooks with patriotic songs and Norse and Greek myths.

---

11. Preceded by cf. Reims, France 1685, and followed by Concord, USA 1823, Genadendal, South Africa 1838, and Chester, UK 1839.
12. (*Dansk folkemindesamling: dafos.dk.*).
13. (Skovmand, 158).

So, how well equipped were the children to be the good citizens needed for the coming Time of the People? On 25th July 1851 some 10,000 people gathered at Lejre, the legendary home of Denmark's prehistoric kings. They were celebrating Constitution Day and a famous victory over Prussia at Idstedt. Grundtvig was proud to be invited as the main speaker, and as he left the meeting to take the train back to Copenhagen, he passed a group of happy country girls and asked two of them how they liked the two songs they had sung: 'Denmark, loveliest field and meadow' (by himself) and the new victory song, 'Danes have won the vict'ry'. The girls said they liked the tunes, but did not know the words. Grundtvig encouraged them to learn both by heart, for they were the rhythmic pulse of the new Denmark.

6. Landscape with view to Udby.
Painting 1853, Vilhelm Kyhn. Frederiksborg Museum of National History. Photo: Hans Petersen.

2. The path enlightened by our fathers' worth

"He is above all a rooted man."[14] With this bold statement, Grundtvig's English biographer, Donald Allchin, asserts that we cannot understand Grundtvig without digging deep into the four roots of his heritage and his own self-understanding. He is primarily rooted in the history of Denmark and the history of Christianity, and these two histories merge into his understanding of God's purpose in the incarnation of Jesus Christ. This third root is *world* history, as Grundtvig makes clear in his three works on the subject in 1812, 1814, and 1817, and in the three later volumes, *Handbook of World History* 1833-43. However, there is a fourth and in many ways an even richer root nourishing Grundtvig: his own family history. To illustrate or justify his choices and battles he repeatedly turns in prose and poetry to his ancestors, and not least to the four generations of pastors on his father's side. Thus the word 'forefathers' appears no fewer than 162 times in the five previus volumes in this series.

Grundtvig himself believed that it was the family that decided who you were and who you might become. This is apparent not only from his many references to his forefathers in his own life, but also from his only personal attempt to write a brief biography. When his patron, Count Christian Danneskiold-Samsøe died in 1823, Grundtvig and his brother-in-law, Pastor Poul Glahn from the Count's parish, decided to publish a book about the Count's life and achievements – though in the event the book was never published.

In the high-flown and often freely imaginative style of the times Grundtvig wrote a detailed draft of his contribution in which he expressly rejected the idea that we are born with a *tabula rasa*, an empty tablet upon which our family and environment can freely etch their influence. Instead he paid tribute to "the ancient tenet that everyone takes after what they have come from". Grundtvig had no modern theories about the relation between heredity and environment, yet his entire organic thinking affirms that we must never neglect, let alone reject, the context into which we are born. As with the multitude of peoples throughout world history, as with the many and various historical churches, as with the generations that make up the history of Denmark, and as with every single individual, we all stand on the shoulders of our predecessors. Every new-born child is unique, and will lead a unique life, however long or short; but in Grundtvig's time it was the family that set the basic framework around that life.

In depicting the most important features in Grundtvig's ancestral history we follow his first great biographer, Frederik Rønning, and his third son, Frederik Lange Grundtvig: on the basis of comprehensive source studies, both men published their works in 1904. For the family history we follow primarily his son Frederik's notes, collected in *The Origins of the Grundtvig Family*. From the list below, going back to 1618, we can see that on his father's side between 1706 and 1811 Grundtvig had no fewer than 11 'forefathers' who were pastors, all of them on Zealand – an ancestry that was a major influence on his own self-understanding. He was proud of this patrilinear descent:

---

14. Allchin, 1997, 16.

Morten Tuesen (died 1618), Mayor of Nykøbing
father of 8, including

Jørgen Mortensen (1609-57), also Mayor of Nykøbing
father of

Morten Jørgensen Grundtvig (1642-77), alderman
& Hans Jørgensen Grundtvig (1644-1700), alderman, recorder (1682) in Nykøbing
father of 5, including

Morten Grundtvig (?- 1736), recorder in Nykøbing
& Niels Hansen Grundtvig (1670-1737), parish pastor in Svallerup (1706)
& Jørgen Hansen Grundtvig (1671-1712), parish pastor in Kregme-Vinderød (1697)
father of 6, including

Isak Jørgen Grundtvig (1697-1767), parish pastor in Strø (1722) & Hillerød (1725-34)
& Otto Jørgensen Grundtvig (1704-72), parish pastor on Sejerø (1732)
& Vallekilde-Hørve (1760)
father of 9, including

Jørgen Grundtvig (1733-87), parish pastor on Sejerø (1760) and in Ledøje-Smørum (1772)
& Christian Grundtvig (1737-97), parish pastor in Gladsaxe-Herlev (1780)
& Enoch Grundtvig (1744-85), parish pastor in Ude & Oppe Sundby (1778)
& Johan Ottosen Grundtvig (1734-1813), parish pastor in Odden (1766) & Udby-Ørslev (1776)
father of N.F.S. Grundtvig and 4 siblings, including

1. Otto Grundtvig (1772-1843), parish pastor in Torkilstrup, Falster (1800), rural dean (1805), parish pastor in Gladsaxe & Herlev (1823)
2. Jacob Grundtvig (1775-1800), pastor in Guinea (1799)
3. Niels Grundtvig (1777-1803), pastor in Guinea (1802)
4. Ulrikke Grundtvig (1782-1805)
5. **Nikolaj Frederik Severin Grundtvig** (1783-1872), called Frederik
father with Elisabeth (Lise) Blicher (1787-1851) of

1. Johan Nikolai Blicher Grundtvig (1822-1907), historian & archivist
2. Svend Hersleb Grundtvig (1824-83), literary historian and folklorist
3. Meta Cathrine Marie Bang Grundtvig (1827-87), in 1847 m. Peter Boisen, who became Grundtvig's curate 1854-62

and father with Ane Marie Elise Toft, née Carlsen (1813-54) of
Frederik Lange Grundtvig (1854-1903), folklorist and pastor in Clinton, Iowa, USA (1883-1900)

and father with Asta Tugendreich Adelheid Reedtz, née Krag-Juel-Vind-Frijs (1826-90) of
Asta Marie Elisabeth Frijs Grundtvig (1860-1939)

Patrilinear descent

As we can see from the above list, the name 'Grundtvig' was first used by Morten Jørgensen Grundtvig around 1670. Researching the name, Grundtvig's son Frederik noted:

> As far as we know, this is the first time the name 'Grundtvig' appears in written records; it is also spelt as Grundtwig, Grundtwiig, Gruntwij, Gruntvig, Grundwiig and Gruntwiig. Its origin is unknown, but it is undoubtedly a place-name. N.F.S. Grundtvig writes that it 'very likely' comes from Rørvig. But this seems less than probable. Possibly on Ise Fjord there was a place called 'Grundtvig'.[15]

On his father's side Grundtvig came from a family of active villagers in the fishing-port of Nykøbing in North-west Zealand (pop. 1740=350; 1787=532). They assumed local responsibility on the village council, and included two local mayors and a number of village 'recorders', or record-keepers. Although in 1700 the pastor and the recorder had fallen out with each other, the latter, Hans Jørgensen Grundtvig (1644-1700), nevertheless encouraged two of his own sons to study for the priesthood. This was a sure way to climb the social ladder, despite the surplus of theology students queuing up to become parish pastors. Eventually, the two sons did become pastors, while a third became the recorder in Nykøbing, Zealand.

Most of the sons and male cousins read theology at Copenhagen University with a view to a permanent pastoral benefice afterwards. The majority of Grundtvig's patrilinear uncles and distant cousins also became pastors, as did his three elder brothers, Jacob, Niels, and Otto. There were not so many other studies available at Copenhagen University, where Theology functioned as a 'mother-subject' for many others. The supreme professional title was 'Professor of Theology', towards which many other professors aspired – at least until 1830:

> Around 1830 at least half of the university's roughly 1,000 students from the Faculty of Theology occupied prominent positions in society. However, in the course of the century the situation changed, and by 1900 the faculties of Medicine, Law, and Theology were more or less the same size, with 500 students in each, whereas the Humanities and Natural Sciences were somewhat smaller.[16]

Grundtvig's family of pastors had its background in semi-prospering citizens, most of them devout and orthodox pastors, but also powerful figures, who often had to work under difficult conditions. He himself was most impressed by his grandfather Otto's ability to assert himself physically in the face of refractory parishioners and a confrontational, drunken parish clerk on the island of Sejerø. Grundtvig's son Frederik recounts the episode:

---

15. (Grundtvig F.L., 17).
16. (Grane, col. 325).

Close to the church there was an inn, where up to Sunday service a number of farmhands would always sit drinking. He wished to put an end to this unacceptable practice, but all his admonitions were in vain. One Sunday morning before church Otto turned up at the inn. There sat his parishioners drinking around a long oak table. He spoke harsh words to them about their ungodliness; but one man, Mads Jutland, sitting at the end of the table became so furious that he leaped up, drew a knife from his belt and said, "What has it got to do with him? If he does not control himself, there will be an accident!" At this the pastor tore open his cassock, bared his breast, went up to him, and shouted in his face, "Stab me, if you dare!" And when Mads Jutland let the knife fall, Otto said, "You coward! You dare to *threaten* me, but not to *stab* me!" And straightaway he gave him such a box on the ear that the man fainted. "I am going to church now," he said, as he left the inn. "Whoever wants to can follow me!" And they all got up and followed him.[17]

There were also debilities in the family. Aged only 37, Otto's brother Isak was pensioned off as chapel pastor at Fredensborg Palace for his mental fragility, while one of father Johan's brothers lost his mind and died, aged 38. Quite often sons who rejected the priesthood fell on hard times. Another of Johan's brothers emigrated first to England, then to Germany, then to Russia, where he disappeared without trace.

When Grundtvig was a child in Udby he read about the achievements of Martin Luther and felt a 'Little Luther rising up in me".[18] He later identified closely with Luther, on whose insights he built and then transcended. Within his own family he was encouraged to identify with the brave Pastor Otto who bared his breast to the knife, ready for a fight:

> You bravely bared your breast
> against the reckless knife
> that threatened you with steel.[19]

Yet Grundtvig realised that his grandfather's courage was ultimately in a good cause:

> For that holy sound you prayed,
> when your organ-pipes were played;
> there was nought but parish wonder
> when you spoke with voice like thunder
> roaring at the people's sin,
> when you preached the end is nigh,
> sought the Word to clarify.

The impact of 'the forefathers' was reinforced even after Grundtvig's death, when his son Frederik, unable to shake off his father's influence, emigrated to the USA. Long after his

---

17. (Grundtvig, F.L., 47-48).
18. (*New Year's Morning*, 1824, st. 68).
19. (*Roskilde Rhymes*, 1812).

father's death Frederik had a dream which he described to his brother Svend in a letter dated 27th September 1881:

> Last night I dreamed that I was out on a big river. Three boats came up. In the one sat my father, in the second my grandfather, and in the third my great-grandfather. All three of them looked sad, but my father and grandfather embraced me and kissed me on the brow without saying anything, and their boat went away. So only my great-grandfather remained (i.e. Otto, ed.). He looked very much like my father. But his face was smaller, his eyes somewhat bigger, and his hair and beard dark grey. He spoke in a gruff tone, asking me why I would not stay in the Fatherland, and threatening to have my name deleted from the family tree. He refused to hear what I had to say, but turned round and rowed away. But some time later he came back, and now I could barely recognise him. The tears were running down his cheeks, and he embraced me and kissed me softly on the brow.[20]

Matrilinear descent

In 1731 Grundtvig's grandfather Otto married Marie Lauenstein (1706-55). She bore 11 children in 14 years, including Grundtvig's father, Johan, in 1734. The legacy from his father's family that weighed on Grundtvig's one shoulder weighed no less heavily than the legacy from his mother's on the other. For his mother's family were just as insistent that the boy should make something of himself in order to honour *her* family. Was he not *proud* to inherit the name of 'Bang', famous throughout generations of Danes? When Grundtvig's mother, Cathrine Marie Bang, aged 20, married Johan, aged 33, in 1768, he had just been called to his first pastorate at Odden, Zealand. She in contrast had grown up on the manor estate of Egebjerggaard, North Zealand, as the daughter of Niels Bang, a King's Councillor of the 2nd Rank and Steward of the Royal Manor in Odsherred. She was proud to trace her descent back to the famous Hvide family, whose oldest-known forefather was Skjalm Hvide (died c. 1113). Cathrine had 8 siblings and 8 step-siblings. Among the former was Frederik Bang (1747-1820), a highly-respected doctor at Frederiks Hospital, Copenhagen, and stepfather of Jakob (J.P.) Mynster, Bishop of Zealand (1834-54), who turned out to be Grundtvig's theological adversary. Another of Cathrine's siblings, Susanne, was the mother of the philosopher, Henrik Steffens, a cousin who was to play a major role in Grundtvig's understanding of Romanticism. In 'To Cathrine Marie Bang, My Beloved Mother' (1815) Grundtvig acknowledged his debt to his mother:

> Once you bore beneath your heart
> all my sight and song submerged,
> brought them to this world in pain,
> from your womb this bard emerged.
> In the ancient hero-days
> he has roots through you inspired,

---

20. (Høirup 1955, 84).

and a sense of song and self,
with your noble blood acquired.[21]

In his close study of Grundtvig's relationship to his ancestry on both sides, Steen Johansen states that in appearance Grundtvig resembled his mother, while in later life he looked just like his cousin Oluf, again on his mother's side; this was true both of his facial features and especially his mild but somewhat inscrutable eyes.[22] Like Grundtvig, cousin Olaf had 'an enormous desire to write and rhyme', as well as a vitality that was characteristic of his mother's family rather than his somewhat sterner father's side. It was not only Luther who taught Grundtvig to "go forward through life cheerfully", as he himself put it;[23] he had also inherited this trait from his mother's family. It was the mental instability on his *father's* side that occasionally surfaced in the son. Grundtvig accepted this: "People's spiritual abilities, like their physical features, depend largely on their origins."[24] Other features that Steen Johansen notes are Grundtvig's height, c. 172-73 cm (quite tall for the time), his build, described as 'sturdy' and 'straight-backed', and his long-lived family.

Cathrine was a strong-willed woman, whose motto was: Rather dead than irresolute! She had been advised to smoke tobacco for her health and this she did from a long pipe. Grundtvig's tribute poem to his mother acknowledged that it was she who taught him to read and write, and then kept him at his studies until he left home, aged 9.

Mother, I will not spell out
how I caused you since to moan;
no one in this vale of dust
knows except for God alone.
But my thanks I bring you here,
bless you with good Jesus' grace;
let my harp sing out for you
sinking in your warm embrace.[25]

Grundtvig sent the finished poem to his mother and in a letter dated 5th July 1815 she thanked him with the words: "I have read your verses to me and was much moved by them" (Letter 11).

Both his mother Cathrine, and his paternal grandmother Marie, had kept four of their sons at their books in order for them to follow their forefathers into the Church, despite the small clerical income. Each pastorate functioned as a farm, but in contrast to the manor farms where inheritance could pass from father to son, there were no inheritance

---

21. No. 129 in *LW*.
22. (Eller, 18).
23. (BFOTG I, 43).
24. (*A Brief View of World History in Context*, 1812).
25. No. 129 in *LW*.

rights for children of *retired* pastors. Once the pastor left the living, that was that – as Grundtvig was to discover in 1813 when he applied for his late father's living and was rejected. His talents were indeed many, but despite being already 30 years old his pastoral experience was by then limited to the last two years in Udby. It is fair to conjecture that the same sense of legacy and duty that in 1810 brought him home from Copenhagen also kept him in his parents' affection on his path to serving the Church. After 1810 there was one task more important than all others, and that was to witness to God and to His purpose with human life.

A distinctive though not unequivocal testimony to Grundtvig's relationship with his parents and their respective family traditions can be found in Letters 2 and 3. When father Johan's health was definitively failing in 1810 and they called their son home to help out in the parish, Grundtvig showed his filial duty to his father but made it clear that he had another calling than the Church in mind, one that he would rather not abandon (Letter 2). In a missing letter, his mother took him severely to task for his hesitant response, to which he replied with unusual intensity in a self-justifying defence of his literary calling (Letter 3). He acknowledged their albeit limited financial support throughout his life so far, but he was unwilling to help them out in their old age – at least for the time being (Letter 4). In the end, however, he bent his will to his mother's wish and returned home – at the price of a mental breakdown and a religious crisis.

If the boys in many an educated family were to become pastors, what about the girls? Most of them married and settled into their husband's position, though for some this came later rather than sooner; they were called upon to give priority to their aging parents, especially if it was the father who outlived his wife – as in grandfather Otto's case. In addition, married brothers and sisters often 'inherited' an unmarried sister, who lent a hand in the household or in some cases even managed it. Grundtvig himself knew the magnitude of the task: what was a poor son to do if there was no sister to look after his parents when they grew old? On 7th March 1805 Grundtvig was back in Udby, where not only the maid and his mother were ill, but also his sister Ulrikke, who was suffering from an abdominal inflammation. She had been his "best friend" in childhood, but now Grundtvig tersely wrote in his diary:

> I would be so sad if my sister died, though not so much for her sake. With her lack of money, beauty, unusual talents, and the cheerfulness of a warm soul, she will hardly be happy. I would be sad more for my own and my aging parents' sake, for who would then look after their house? Who would take care of my ailing mother? It would be sad, and if I lost a sister, I would probably also lose my mother.

Ulrikke died shortly after, aged 23. Among her belongings was a love-letter from the young student who had taught her to play the piano!

7. Residents of Udby vicarage 1787.

1. Johan Grundtvig, husband 53, married, parish pastor
2. Cathrine Maria Bang, 40, married, wife
3. Jacob Ulric Hansen Grundtvig, 12, unmarried, child
4. Niels Christian Bang Grundtvig, 10, unmarried, child
5. Ulrica Eleonora Grundtvig, 6, unmarried, child
6. Nic. Frideric Severin Grundtvig, 4, unmarried, child
7. Apollone Hald, 19, unmarried, sister's daughter, housemaid
8. Lauritz Feld, 38, unmarried, tutor, MA
9. Rasmus Madsen, 24, unmarried, servant, head farmhand
10. Ole Jacobsen, 20, unmarried, servant, second farmhand
11. Bodil Peders Datter, 31, unmarried, servant, cook
12. Sidse Christofers Datter, 30, unmarried, servant, scullery maid
13. Malene Jens Datter, 55, unmarried, living on alms
14. Maria Jörgens Datter, 11, unmarried, poor fatherless child

National Archives, Copenhagen.

The struggle against early death and poverty

Emphasising Grundtvig's family roots – including those he himself engendered – is not solely in order for us to begin at the beginning; it is also in order to argue for a *continuity* that ran throughout his life. This is before the individualism that characterises our age today, where 'family' has become an ever-more-diffuse concept. In Grundtvig's day 'family' meant primarily the *household*, i.e. the family itself and all other residents. In the 1787 census there were 14 people living in the vicarage at Udby. Everyone contributed to the farm maintenance and the household welfare, but Pastor Johan's stipend was the sole income from outside the home.

The extended family here comprises the Grundtvig core family, house tutors, house labourers, and various other accumulated members. With these roots in the South Zealand countryside in the late 18th century Grundtvig was born into a family of which he was always proud. The legacy of the forefathers can be seen in the Christian names of the sons: thus father Johan's middle name was 'Ottosen' (son of Otto). Grundtvig's first brother was named after his grandfather, his second brother after his mother's stepfather, his third brother after his mother's father, and his sister after her maternal grandmother. Grundtvig himself was baptised 'Nicolai' after the husband of his late paternal aunt, followed by 'Frederik Severin' after the same aunt, Frederikke Severine.

Although life expectancy at the time was no more than 40, we can see from Grundtvig's family tree that many of his ancestors and siblings died much older: his grandfather Otto at 68, his father Johan at 79, and his brother Otto who reached the ripe old age of 60. Against these figures Grundtvig's own 88 years and 11 months are nevertheless incredible, especially since he never took exercise, smoked a strong pipe tobacco, and slept many a night in an armchair. At 50 he called himself an old man, while at 55 his lecture series 'Within Living Memory' was couched as memories and conclusions from a long life coming to an end. And yet he remarried and fathered a child, and then remarried and fathered yet another child at the age of 76! Quite extraordinarily, all five of his children actually *survived* him – their deaths coming respectively in 1883 (Svend, aged 59), 1887 (Meta, aged 60), 1903 (Frederik, aged 49), 1907 (Johan, aged 85) and 1939 (Asta, aged 79), 67 years after her father's death. Grundtvig was deeply grateful for their lives and their good health, as he wrote to Lise from England: "Thank you, dear Lise, for eleven years of loving companionship and for our lovely children" (Letter 20, 1829). And again, writing of their three children, Johan, Svend, and Meta, he speaks of "the threefold love-tie that our children represent" (Letter 32, 1831).

Throughout the generations listed above outright poverty never touched the Grundtvigs, but occasionally they lived close to the poverty line – until, that is, N.F.S. Grundtvig himself married his second and third wives, both wealthy widows. By comparison, once the death duties had been paid, grandfather Otto could leave nothing to his children. Father Johan for his part had lived a decidedly spartan life for 6 years as curate to older pastors. He had to take out a loan to buy the vicarage in Odden, when he finally became parish pastor in 1766 at the age of 32. When he moved to Udby in 1776, the old vicarage there had to be totally renovated, while from his meagre salary he had to pay the house tutors

8. Memorials to Grundtvig's parents.

A memorial to Johan at Udby Church, and a memorial to Cathrine at Egebjerggaarden (south of Nykøbing, Zealand) where she was born in 1748; on the granite stone erected in 1915 she is teaching her son to read. Photo: Edward Broadbridge.

and then the sons' schooling and university expenses. Actual earnings from the vicarage farm were paltry, and the size of the tithes that the parishioners owed him fluctuated considerably. Illustration 7 shows a household of 14 people with only one earner – Johan.

The uncertain outlook for his sons, Jacob and Niels, led them to offer their pastoral services abroad. Initially, Jacob was intended for the Danish colony of Greenland, but in the end, and at a 3-year interval, they both went to the tiny Danish colony on the Gold Coast – in present-day Accra, Ghana. From 1659-1850 Denmark had a small but profitable colony here. Its trade was not only in gold and ivory, which were sent back to Denmark, but also in thousands of slaves, who were sent to the Danish West Indies. After 4 years pastoral service, Grundtvig's elder brothers could expect to find a living back in Denmark – but they died of malaria and neither of them made it home. Jacob had been a resounding success, Niels a resounding failure. But rooted in the Church they had both been: Grundtvig's parents, Johan and Cathrine, had four sons, who all became pastors.

The reason that the Grundtvigs did not go bankrupt in Udby was that mother Cathrine had a brother, Major Carl Bang (1754-1806), who had married the rich widow of a brewer in 1798. When the major died in 1806, followed by his wife in 1807, the assets were divided between the two families, and Cathrine inherited the substantial sum of 3014 rigsdaler.[26] This explains how Johan could provide his son with the 200 rigsdaler needed for his pastoral vestments when he was appointed curate in Udby in 1811; at last his parents could see him in the pulpit of his childhood church. The path had been "enlightened by his fathers' worth".[27]

---

26. A rigsdaler was the Danish name for the silver coin first minted in 1518 after the discovery of vast silver reserves in Bohemia. It was in use in Denmark long before the word *daler* was officially minted on the coin in the late 18th century, until it gave way to the present-day *krone* in 1873. At that date the conversion rate was 1 *rigsdaler* = 2 *kroner* = c. 100 *kroner* in 2022.
27. No. 86 in *LW*.

9.
Above. **The fertile fields of Zealand.** *Marklandskab med en bro*, Vilhelm Kyhn, 1858. SMK, National Gallery of Denmark.
Below. **The Jutland heath.** *En jysk fårebonde på heden*, Frederik Vermehren, 1855. SMK, National Gallery of Denmark.

3. Little God's child, what troubles you?
(1783-98)

Grundtvig's father recorded his son's birth and baptism in 1783 thus:

10. Registry of Grundtvig's birth.
On 8th Sept., which was a Monday after the 12th Sunday after Trinity, at 3 o'clock in the afternoon my dear wife Catharine Maria Bang was safely delivered of a son, who on the 10th inst. was baptised by me at home and named Nicolaj Frideric Severin Grundtvig. The midwife, Mrs Carstensen, carried him.

The baby boy who was to become the great catalyst of modern Denmark came into the world on a Monday afternoon in early autumn. The birth took place in the vicarage at Udby on the island of Zealand in east Denmark. In attendance was a midwife, 'Madame Carstensen', who two days later had the honour of holding baby Frederik when his father, Pastor Johan, baptised him in their home.

This was common for a pastor, and not uncommon for those who could afford to pay a pastor for a home baptism. The important next step was to present the new-born child in church at the first opportunity. Grundtvig baptised all five of his children at home:

Johan	– 14th April 1822 at Torvestræde 7, Præstø
Svend	– 9th Sept. 1824 at Prinsessegade 52, Copenhagen
Meta	– 27th May 1827 at Prinsessegade 52, Copenhagen
Frederik	– 15th May 1854 at Frederiksholms Kanal 16, Copenhagen
Asta	– 10th Feb. 1860 at Gammel Kongevej 148, Copenhagen

Contemporary written records from Grundtvig's birth to his 17th year are hard to come by. The most important source for his childhood is Grundtvig himself. By and large we can rely on him to tell the truth about himself, though naturally his perspective changes as he moves through life. Among his surviving papers are bundles in small octavo of the diaries that he kept between 1802-06. These cover his last weeks at Copenhagen University, his return to his home surroundings in Udby, and his first months as house tutor at Egeløkke Manor. Only fragmentary pages remain of his original diary for 1802-04, but in the course of four days in 1806 (27th-30th May), he rewrote this account of the first 19 years of his life. To achieve a distancing effect he wrote about himself in the third person:

He had no siblings at home except a slightly older sister, with whom he could never agree, and since she was the weaker, he usually got his way. He regards this as one of the most important reasons as to why he turned to reading, since he has never been any use with his hands, apart from turning pages.

The second autobiographical source consists of two poems 'Our Garden at Udby' (1811)[28] and the lengthy *New Year's Morning* (1824), published when Grundtvig's memories are respectively 20 and 30 years older than the actual events. In both cases the adult Grundtvig 'stages' himself as the *child* Grundtvig experiencing the events and moods of his early years.

A country bookworm

'Frederik', as Grundtvig was called, enjoyed a privileged childhood in relation to most other Danes of the time. His three elder brothers had all left home by the time he was 3, so he was left to share it with his 1-year-older sister, Ulrikke. She was both his play-mate and his quarrel-mate. His mother Cathrine battled to teach young Frederik the alphabet, (especially the letter O, he recalled) but once it was mastered, he became on his own admission "a lifelong bookworm". In this respect he took after his father Johan, who in 1762 had bought the collection of historical and theological books that stood on the shelves in the Udby vicarage. Indeed Johan had published 3 books himself: *The Bliss of a God-fearing Land* (1774), *An Exposition of the Catechism according to the Doctrine of Salvation* (1779), and a Danish translation of *Phaedrus's Fables* (1785). They were poorly received, and a fourth book remained in manuscript without a publisher, but the young Grundtvig would doubtless have found inspiration in seeing his father's name on the title-page of no fewer than 3 books.

Best of all, Grundtvig remembers the garden at Udby, at first a place of comfort and confinement for the toddler, but later a

> Garden, spreading broad and wide
> round the ancient rectory,
> to those happy childhood years
> homeward you are leading me!
> ...
> Lying in the garden green
> watching heaven, wondering
> how was even God allowed to
> walk upon such flimsy clouds?
>
> Often I would lie here too,
> when I was an older boy;
> this time with a book to read;
> Chronicles were all my joy

---

28. No. 105 in *LW*.

as I made a merry march
to the end of world and time.²⁹

In 1788 the 57-year-old Bertel Faurskov arrived in Udby as the new schoolmaster. He was a country boy from Funen who had read Theology but had never qualified as a pastor. In his diary Grundtvig recalls (in the third person) his experience of learning Latin with Faurskov in 1789:

> He (i.e. Grundtvig) learned part of the little dictionary and Baden's *Grammar Book* by heart, but he did not understand a word of it, for his learned teacher explained hardly anything, and even when he did, he never lowered himself to Frederik's level of understanding. The only thing he acquired from all this learning-by-rote nonsense was that his memory was sharpened at the cost of his judgement.³⁰

This was Grundtvig's first meeting with 'school' – and without doubt it was a 'school for death', as he later called such institutions. Rote-learning implanted factual knowledge but killed the child's spirit.

However, in 1776, the same year in which the Grundtvigs arrived in Udby, another pastor's son, 30-year-old Christian Feld, had taken the job of parish schoolmaster – prior to Bertel Faurskov. When Christian Feld left in 1784 to finish his Theology degree, his younger brother, Laurids, deputised for him, and thus came to teach Grundtvig's elder brothers, Jacob and Niels. Feld appears in the list of residents in Illustration 7, as house tutor to Jacob and Niels. Between 1788-90 Feld held a pastorate on the islands of Hirsholm off the north-east coast of Jutland, and Jacob and Niels moved in with him. In 1790 he was called to the living at Thyregod in mid-Jutland, and again Jacob and Niels moved house, until they were admitted to Viborg Cathedral High School. Jacob graduated in 1795 and Niels in 1796, after which they studied Theology in Copenhagen. They both died early as young pastors in the Danish colony on Africa's Gold Coast, before their little brother, Frederik, knew them. Laurids Feld kept in touch with the Grundtvig family through his annual visit to Udby, where the young Grundtvig enjoyed his company and his challenges. When he was 8 years old, Feld promised him a silver watch, if he proved that he had read Kall's *World History*.³¹ When Feld returned the following year, Grundtvig demonstrated his knowledge and got the silver watch.

Grundtvig's move to Thyregod aged 9 must have been something of a wrench. Yet such a move was not uncommon at the time for the children of clergy, and may very well have suited the boy. Feld had been part of the household at Udby, and Grundtvig placed great trust in the man whose teaching skills and conservative theological solidity none doubted. Grundtvig was not only leaving home, he was also exchanging the rolling farmland around Udby for the "dark-brown heath" of Jutland. It may sound

---

29. No. 105 in *LW*.
30. (DUB 1979, 45).
31. Abraham Kall (1743-1821) wrote *General History of the World for Use in Schools* in 1776.

11. **Udby Vicarage.**
Grundtvig was born in a room adjoining the wing on the right. The vicarage was Grundtvig's home from 8th September 1783 until 15th September 1792. Udby was his home in what he called his "happy childhood years". During his curate days (1811-13) he lived in the wing on the left. The wing now houses the Grundtvig Memorial Rooms. Lithograph by Lars Kornerup, c. 1883.

strange to us that the boys whom the unmarried Feld taught soon adapted to their new surroundings; Feld's sister, Tryfona, ran the household, and there were the other men and women around – housemaids and farmhands. All in all the safest haven for Grundtvig was Pastor Feld.

> Thyregod and Laurids Feld!
> Thanks, my teacher, loud and clear
> for the many days now past!
> Like a son I hold you dear;
> if of aught I should complain,
> it would be my willing mind,
> coupled with your father's care,
> far too often made me blind:
> so much so that you forgot
> how my pride in this pursuit
> fed a bad and bitter root.[32]

---

32. No. 105 in *LW*.

Like the budding family pastors before him, Grundtvig soon came to terms with his new situation. He was not particularly sociable in his early adolescence, but he would doubtless have been shaken by the illness and death of one of his new fellow-students. He later called his 6 years at Thyregod his "silver age", following his "golden age" in Udby. He learned Greek, Latin, and the history of Christianity; he read widely from Feld's library and welcomed the parcels of books that regularly arrived at the vicarage from a local circulating library. In his final year at Thyregod he was reading the latest books and journals on rationalist Christianity, such as *Jesus and Reason*, a weekly journal published between 1797-1801 by Otto Horrebow. But he was also reading their more orthodox counterparts, such as the periodical, *The Bible Defends Itself*, published between 1797-99 by Grundtvig's uncle, Bishop of Zealand Nicolai Balle. Grundtvig sided with Balle, who defended orthodox Lutheran Christianity and the truth and integrity of the Bible against the upstart rationalists.

The caring household

Probably as early as 1808 and as a result of Count Danneskiold-Samsøe of Gisselfeld's interest in Grundtvig's *Nordic Mythology* that year, the wealthy count began to take a patron's interest in the young writer; in 1818 he even financed Grundtvig's wedding reception with Lise. In Grundtvig's contribution to the unpublished biography of the Count, he wrote in 1823 that the Count's good heart and upright being was rooted in the caring household of the family home at Gisselfeld. This love was a prerequisite for the nobility to be able to attend to affairs of state:

> ... for where the heart does not even link the nearest and dearest to each other, even less can it link the *totality*. We are in a labyrinth where no exit seems possible. If the self-important nobleman is a *stranger* to tender feeling and happiness, and is full of overweening, ruthless ambition, his household becomes selfish and ungovernable, and the cramped and confined peasant farmers become sluggish and mean-spirited.[28]

Grundtvig goes on to underline the importance of household life in the vicarage, where in order to serve the people, the Church, and the state, the family must ensure that its sons gain a solid training in the priesthood. Based on his own experiences from Udby and Thyregod he adds:

> The vicarage was not a private property but a borrowed tent; and yet it was a holy sanctuary. As the highest instance, God's honour linked the pastor to the entire human society, but the calling itself linked him to the household circle and his children to the state as their only earthly haven.[33]

---

33. (Jens A. Nielsen, 'Grundtvig og Gissenfeld', *GS* 1962, 29).

The 'household circle' is central to Grundtvig's thought, for it is here that faith, hope, and love can grow, where mistakes can be made and forgiven, where tears and smiles can go hand in hand. In the poem 'My Mother' (1822) Grundtvig pays tribute to his mother's 'tearful smile', a sentiment that contains pain borne with love. He is reminded of this when he sees her looking at his own first-born son, Johan:

> Your tearful smile shall not expire,
> your offspring shall inherit!
> for to my new-born son you showed
> your rainbow-coloured spirit:
> each child is blessed and passes on
> till spirit melts in radiant sun.[34]

In the Thyregod vicarage this mother-love was replaced by woman-love in the warm kitchen and man-love in the farmhands' tender care for the birds in winter. The poem 'In Praise of Jutland' (1815) speaks of the wheat and rye, hard-won from the heath, "with promise of daily bread,/and stores against the cold ahead." Grundtvig deeply admires the farmhand who takes the time to feed the birds in winter:

> That sound I never heard before
> which mem'ry now is keeping:
> a little finch close by the door
> outside the barn was cheeping,
> as once a Jutland farmhand strewed
> a little corn for small birds' food
> one frosty day in winter.[35]

Grundtvig draws on this motif in many a hymn, such as 'Little God's child, what troubles you?' from 1855 where, referring to Mt 6:27, he writes:

> Ploughing nor sowing is their task,
> nor do they sow in case of need,
> yet when the peasant of hunger dies,
> each little bird can find a seed.
> All praise to God![36]

The birds of heaven and the songs they sing are part of God's caring household. So too are the bees on the Jutland heath. The young Grundtvig was fascinated by beekeeping

---

34. (PS V, 99).
35. No. 117 in *LW*.
36. No. 4 in *LW*.

at the vicarage, as he recalls in his talk on England and the industrial revolution on 14th November 1838 in the series Within Living Memory. He can

> compare England's daily industry in the natural world with *bees*, those congenial flies which since my childhood I have loved as much as I have hated all others. In fact, gentlemen, you have probably not been so familiar with bees from childhood as I have, when my greatest amusement on the brown heath was to see them collect nectar and swarm.[37]

Language-learning

Although both his parents, and especially his mother, spoke 'the King's Danish' during his first 9 years in Udby, Grundtvig had learned the dialect of east Denmark from the other household members and all the Zealanders around him. In his next 8 years in Jutland, the west Danish dialect took hold. Occasionally he accompanied Pastor Feld on house visits around Thyregod, and once he travelled with him to Feld's native soil in Salling, gaining a first-hand impression of Jutland peasant life. Every summer Feld accompanied the young Grundtvig on his month-long visit home to Udby, a 200-kilometre journey that took several days and passed through a number of dialects on the way. Already at this early age Grundtvig would have been registering the variants in his mother-tongue, sensing that they carried an identity and a culture. His interest in languages was being nourished in the process. He was beginning to learn the local proverbs by heart – and thus the local wisdom: "An old friend and an old path do not let you down", or, more politically, the rhyme 'Were the peasant not bound, he'd be worse than the hound". He was later to collect and publish such gems.

On these trips home Grundtvig would also be passing the various monuments to the past – including the famous royal grave mounds and runic stones near Thyregod.

Grundtvig was himself conscious of his upbringing: "Though a Zealander in speech,/ to Jutland's roots my sources reach"[38] ... "Since my origins and upbringing divided me between Zealand and Jutland, many turns of phrase of the ordinary man have lodged in my head, which has been quick to learn them; they above all have taught me what Danish I know."[39] The Reformation in Denmark began in Jutland, where there was a land-link to Germany. Grundtvig drew on this fact to develop a theory that there was once a unique tribe in North Jutland and Halogaland in North Norway who alone possessed the qualities needed to save the twin kingdom. The corruption of Christianity and Denmark was centred on Copenhagen, whereas it was from the countryside that salvation would come, particularly from those who were armed with both history and the deeds of their forefathers. Several times he sought benefices in North Jutland or a teaching appointment at the new university in Oslo.[40] He was conscious of his double Danish legacy – from both

---

37. TCG, 137.
38. (*Latest Picture of Copenhagen*, 1815).
39. (*Dane-Work* III 1817, 81).
40. Christiania officially became Oslo in 1925.

12. The Jelling stones.
The little stone reads: "King Gorm raised these stones after Thyra his wife, Denmark's pride". The big stone reads: "Harald won for himself all Denmark and Norway and made the Danes Christian". The country was already semi-Christian, but in 969 Gorm and Thyra's son Harald erected this stone to signify that he had unified the twin kingdom in the Christian faith. The Viking gods gradually succumbed to the overwhelming influence of Christianity, which was also politically expedient from the need to trade with Christian Germany. The first missionary to the Danes, Willibrord, from Northumberland, England (c. 710), was unsuccessful, but Ansgar of (801-65), later Archbishop of Hamburg-Bremen, enjoyed widespread success and to this day is known as 'the apostle of the North'. Between 950 and 1060 eight dioceses were created, while three-quarters of Denmark's 2000 or so stone churches were built *before* the Reformation. The image on the larger stone is known as 'Denmark's baptism certificate' and is reproduced on the inside cover of the Danish passport. The Christ-figure is challenging rather than suffering – a truly Viking Christ. Photo: Alamy.

Zealand and Jutland. His father's family were from Zealand, but he traced his mother's family lineage back to Jutland roots: to be a real Dane one must be born in Denmark, he believed. To be acquainted with both Zealand and Jutland was a double blessing.

When Grundtvig finally returned to Zealand after 8 years in Jutland, he found it somewhat difficult to discard his Jutland accent – as well as his attire, which marked him out as a country boy among city dwellers. He himself noted this in his diary for 28th November 1802 when he was looking back on his last two years in Copenhagen. Nevertheless, the Zealand dialect gradually reasserted itself, thanks not least to the memory of his childhood nurse in Udby, Malene Jens Datter (1733-1810). The crippled Malene had been a resident at the vicarage since 1769 – long before the Grundtvigs arrived; she lived there for over 40 years in all.

Malene was a gift of a nurse for Grundtvig. She read to him, talked to him, told him stories, answered his questions, and most memorably *sang* to him – the hymns and songs and the rhymes and rhythms of Grundtvig's childhood. Indeed, she had once sung a hymn to him that brought tears to her own eyes – to the young Grundtvig's dismay and amazement:

> It is the literal truth that I am in debt to Malene for many idioms in my translations of Saxo og Snorri … When I am in doubt about how to phrase something or other, I often think, What would Malene say?[41]

In the poem 'New Year's Morning' (1824) Grundtvig praises her as his 'language-mistress'. As an adult he wished to give back this gift to the Danish people: hymns that were enchanting and memorable.

Later in life a number of Grundtvig's linguistic choices in his hymns proved unacceptable to the hymnbook compilers. In his book on *Grundtvig and South Zealand*, Morten Bredsdorff takes as an example a verse from the hymn, 'There sat a fisherman deep in thought'. Although written in the King's Danish, it is best read and understood through the South Zealand dialect that Grundtvig grew up with:

> He did his job and he drew his net,
> it weighed far beyond his wishes;
> his boat was listing, his net was split,
> so full was it now of fishes.
> Then Simon called to his friends for aid,
> between the fishers the catch was made,
> though they were all close to sinking.[42]

This is hardly 'poetic' but it is riveting: it is Grundtvig as narrator of stories in the vernacular. This is how the people spoke. There is doubtless more of the Zealander than the Jutlander in Grundtvig, but his respect for the latter is beyond question: 'Jutlander' is a badge of honour in his *World History* (1812). Either way, Grundtvig's loyalty to the Danish soil and the peasant farmer was formed at an early age; it was from the bottom-up that Denmark was to be revived and enlightened.

Even more important than nature is history. To understand a people one must understand both their natural surroundings, their historical experiences – and their language! Grundtvig had a strong sensory response to places, as Thyra Holt's book *Memorable Places in Grundtvig's Life* testifies; it contains photos of no fewer than 80 sites to which Grundtvig refers in his hymns and poems, reflecting this sensory response. Through the nature, history, and language of east and west Denmark, Grundtvig could pride himself on being Danish through and through.

---

41. (Bredsdorff, 1983, 20).
42. No. 14 in *LW*.

13. Thyregod Church in mid-Jutland.
Laurits Feld was pastor here from 1790-1805. The plaque on the outside church wall at Thyregod reads: "In this church the hymnwriter N.F.S. Grundtvig confirmed his baptismal vows on 15th April 1798." Photo: National Museum of Denmark.

After 6 years in Thyregod Grundtvig was ready for the next stage in his education. From his childhood homes in Udby and Thyregod he could take with him a sense of history and literature, a practical Lutheran faith from two vicarage homes, and a knowledge of Latin, Greek, and Danish that would stand him in good stead. Not least was he aware of the trials and tribulations of *translation*, as he moved backwards and forwards between the three languages. Turning Latin into Danish was hard enough, but turning Danish into Latin was fiendishly difficult.

Finally, having demonstrated before the congregation in Thyregod that he knew by heart Luther's *Small Catechism* and a number of hymn verses, Grundtvig was confirmed at the age of 14½ by Pastor Feld on 15th April 1798, the 1st Sunday after Easter. Due to the distance from Udby to Thyregod his parents were absent from the ceremony. Confirmation conferred a form of adulthood on the youngsters. Boys wore their first suits and girls their first dresses. They could now legally marry, become godparents and soldiers, testify in court, and take up a craft or business – and, if admitted, they could go to high school. A few months later Pastor Feld accompanied Grundtvig to Aarhus Cathedral High School, which he was to attend for the next two years of his life.

The last word on Grundtvig in his early teens goes to the parish clerk's wife, Mrs Bering, whom Christian Thyregod has recorded as follows:

> The parish clerk's home was close to the churchyard. The boy often came into them for a chat and a bite of something from the generous lady of the house. But just as often he would turn round, lost in his thoughts and, as she said, "... a bit strange, so it was hard to make head or tail of him." Then one day Mrs Bering exclaimed, "Heavens above, either he's mad or he's cleverer than other people!"[43]

---

43. (Thyregod, 56).

14. Aarhus seen from the north.
Not much more than a small town with the cathedral dominant. Painting c. 1850 by Peter Holm. ARoS.

4. I must write or I must die!
(1798-1803)

Aarhus Cathedral High School

Within the space of 5 years, between September 1798 and October 1803, Grundtvig began and completed his formal education – at high school *and* university. The plan all along was for him to take holy orders, and the path to this goal took him through Aarhus Cathedral High School and the Faculty of Theology at the University of Copenhagen. The origins of training for the priesthood went back to medieval times, when candidates studied the ancient languages and catholic philosophy at monasteries attached to the cathedrals. At the Reformation the monasteries were replaced by Cathedral *schools*, where boys also served as choristers, and could earn a little pocket-money at weddings and funerals. Aarhus Cathedral was founded around 1195, but the school itself was founded in 1540. The main subjects were Latin, Greek, Bible Studies, and Luther's Christian Doctrines. In 1739 Mathematics and Philosophy were introduced, and from 1775 'Danish' at last received a place in the syllabus.

Grundtvig had just turned 15 when Pastor Feld accompanied his talented but self-willed pupil on the 85-kilometre journey to Aarhus. The school was not a boarding-school, so Grundtvig lodged with a shoemaker and his family in nearby Skolegade 42. He says very little about this experience, except that he would occasionally read aloud to the family, a pastime he enjoyed and one at which he excelled.

The 15-year-old boy passed the school entrance exam with excellent marks, and the school's principal, Thure Krarup, had no hesitation in placing him in the top class; Grundtvig could expect to graduate after two years. He thereby avoided falling victim to the ritual humiliations that the top class often inflicted on the four bottom classes. He was also spared the poor teaching of the 'hearers', unqualified teachers whose task was to hear the boys recite their lessons. The mechanical grind of this 'rote-learning' remained in place even after the reforms of 1739, when the total number of such schools was reduced from 58 to 20 and their annual intake increased. Since the school was a preparatory school for the civil service, the education was free. Indeed, as a pupil in the top class Grundtvig earned 30 rigsdaler a year from singing in the cathedral: at Sunday worship, at weekly prayers, weddings and funerals; and at special services. Given his lack of musicality he was doubtless a 'shadow-singer'.

Grundtvig's two teachers were Principal Thure Krarup and Vice-principal Jens Stougaard. At first they differed in their opinion of the boy: Krarup was impressed, but Stougaard let Grundtvig know that he was immature and should really be in the bottom class. Grundtvig determined to prove him wrong – and he was so successful that Stougaard gradually took the place of Pastor Feld as the boy's mentor. Stougaard taught him Latin and Greek, in which Grundtvig was already well-versed. The new subject was

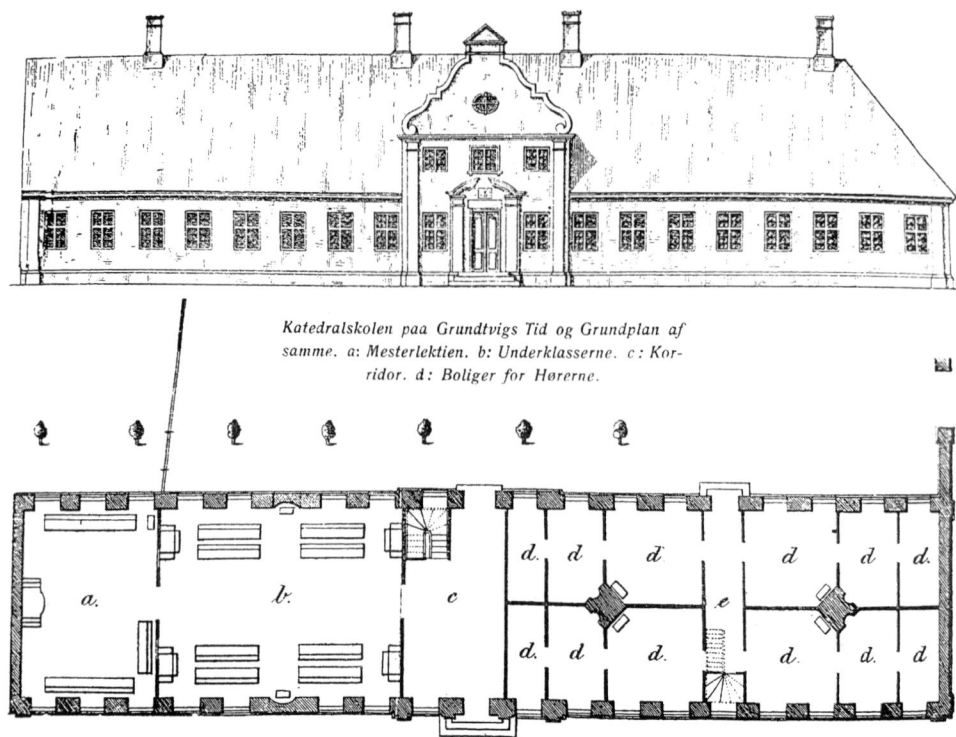

Katedralskolen paa Grundtvigs Tid og Grundplan af samme. a: Mesterlektien. b: Underklasserne. c: Korridor. d: Boliger for Hørerne.

15.
Above. **The facade of Aarhus Cathedral High School in Grundtvig's time**
Below. **The four divisions of the school**: a) The top class, *Mesterlektie*, b) the bottom classes, *Underklasserne*, c) Corridor, d) living-quarters for 'hearers'.

Hebrew, taught by Principal Krarup, to prepare the class for reading the Old Testament in the original language. At Hebrew, on his own admission, Grundtvig did *not* excel. Also new to him was oral Latin, in preparation for the Latin lectures and debates at university. Two other new subjects were Religious Studies and Astronomy, taught by Krarup, and History and Geography, taught by Stougaard. Especially in History Grundtvig impressed his teacher, but he was largely bored by Religious Studies, which also included devotions, prayers, and hymns, all in Latin. As in the Thyregod vicarage he availed himself of the school library and read books on the classics, Christianity, and not least Nordic mythology.

Grundtvig describes his two years in Aarhus in widely differing terms. In his diary from 1804 they were "simply awful" – but he also turns the criticism on himself. On the one hand he ironically presents himself in pigeon French in the 3rd person as 'Missure Frederik'; on the other he confesses to his most embarrassing experience so far. In the Cathedral at Easter 1799 he had put paper strips in the collection box instead of money – and got away with it! When he repeated the prank at the Pentecost service he was discovered – and publicly rebuked by Krarup. In private, Stougaard asked him whether he had been led along by others or was indeed penniless. Grundtvig was tongue-tied, but would

16. Jens Stougaard, Grundtvig's teacher.
Lithograph by Anton Winther, post-1937. SMK, National Gallery of Denmark.

not lie and answered no in both cases. Most likely he had spent the collection money on his two new interests, card-playing and pipe-tobacco. On Grundtvig's last day at school Principal Krarup praised him to the skies, but the young man was clearly more affected by Stougaard's tears as they bid goodbye to each other.

In 1811, looking back on his schooldays, Grundtvig acknowledged the "lazy pride within my soul" in his Aarhus years, which is a telling, honest touch. He also paid tribute to his teacher:

> Doughty Stougaard! Often you
> looked at me with noble pain,
> bade as father, begged as friend;
> but self-willed my heart was then
> and straightway closed up again.
> Yet however I played up,
> never did you give up hope!
> Both your wishes and the tear
> that you shed on this young fool
> in your fatherly farewell
> touched me deeply, these I kept.
> And whatever else has gone.
> those remain forever dear;
> in my eye I see that tear.
> Thanks, our Father God on high!
> Stougaard! Worthy teacher! Thanks![44]

---

44. No. 105 in *LW*.

His retrospective view of Aarhus took a further turn when he realised the educational poverty of those two years. By 1838 he is comparing his plans for a 'school for life' with the 'school for death' he attended in Aarhus. He proudly recalled the very first time he became aware of the outside world, when his first teacher in Udby, Bertel Faurskov, announced that the Russians had defeated the Ottomans in December 1788. Now, aged 55, he remembered nothing from Aarhus because the world outside had not yet encroached upon him. His verdict was irredeemably damning!

> In a little nook on the Jutland heath I had kept alive my sense of the great outside as well as of homely pleasures and natural vitality; in less than two years at the Latin School I turned into such a cold, self-opinionated, stunted individual that I cared not a jot for the great struggle in the outside world that I had followed with spirited interest until the day I set foot in that bewitched Latin school ... At our most transient and vulnerable age, the fearsome blindness of our ingenuous forefathers confined us in a circle so inimical to natural vitality in the highest sense, and so empty of that which ennobles, so full of what can demean, deaden, and damage us as people.[45]

Grundtvig's final judgement on his Aarhus years is passed, at the age of 80, in 1863. It is hard to determine from the following whether it was the fault of the school or himself. Either way, his schooldays were a total waste of time:

> Even though it lasted only two years, I forgot everything: not only about Napoleon and what was in the news, but also about church history, church attendance, and my childhood teachings. The cause was boredom, pipe-smoking, card-playing, and a life of idleness with my books under my arm. When I graduated to Copenhagen in 1800, there was no thought of going to church, except when, because the bishop was my father's brother-in-law, I attended the funeral cortège of Bishop Balle's wife in the Church of Our Lady.[46]

Grundtvig's four separate judgements on himself do not tally, but in general he describes his adolescent self in Aarhus as immature and uncommitted. As in Thyregod there is no mention of any *friends* – these came later, in Copenhagen. There was little to do outside school and church, no distant horizons or spiritual hills to climb. But we must give him credit that he came to realise this, and was mature enough to put part of the blame on himself. As we have noted, when the idea of a 'school for life' took hold, it was tempting to contrast it with the 'school for death' that he and his contemporaries attended. Yet it was in these two years in Aarhus that he laid the groundwork for his prodigious academic energy – for the time when he could set the challenges himself. The poet, the historian, the translator – they all have their base in his Aarhus days. Above all, the power of language and history was taking hold – the power that later led him to teach himself Old English, Old Norse, and Old Icelandic. In *Grundtvig as a Philologist* the philologist Helge

---

45. (*Within Living Memory*, 270).
46. (Schrøder 1883, 68).

Toldberg points to Grundtvig's outstanding command of languages and his extraordinary gifts as a translator.[47] Toldberg's contemporary, Gustav Albeck – himself a student at the Cathedral School and later Professor of Nordic Literature at Aarhus University – wrote a brief but penetrating account of Grundtvig's schooldays, *Grundtvig's Dreadful Schooldays*, in which he concluded:

> Grundtvig's rich talents – however liable they were to be diverted – only did justice to themselves as a result of his academic upbringing. We dare not think of the loss that our culture could have sustained, if Grundtvig had truly decided to drop his schooling – and made good on that decision.[48]

After eight years in Jutland, from September 1792 to October 1800, Grundtvig returned to Zealand, to study with the best and brightest at the ancient University of Copenhagen, over 300 years old. Theology was his subject – for everyone expected him to become a priest.

University of Copenhagen

In Grundtvig's time, high school graduates entered university through an exam in their first term. Grundtvig passed this exam and was formally enrolled on 7th November 1800, just six weeks after leaving school.

The University of Copenhagen was founded in 1479 on the authorisation of Pope Julius. After the Reformation, the Faculty of Theology became the most prestigious school at the university, graduating students who had previously read philosophy and languages (and even law and medicine); from 1629 all prospective pastors were required to pass this Theology exam.

With so few grants available, Grundtvig's short tertiary education was not uncommon in those days. His step-cousin, Jakob Mynster, gained an M. Theol. at the age of 19! Analytical thinking and interaction between professor and student were not expected, so for 3 more years Grundtvig was a bright but, on his own confession, a somewhat lazy student, bored with rote-learning, with no particular view about God or his own calling – a typical self-conscious, angry young man. His interests lay elsewhere. He wrote poetry and history; he joined an amateur theatre called 'Thalia', and began writing drama; he copied out excerpts from the many books he was reading – but all apparently to no avail. Halfway through his university studies, aged 19½ he wrote in his diary under the headline 'Confession': "It has been my lot never to complete anything… I am well aware that it is of no use, yet I cannot see when this rage will end."

Grundtvig had to find his purpose in life *outside* the university, which offered him only constitutional lethargy and a mechanical grind of reading the Bible and Classics. At an existential level Grundtvig continued where he left off in Aarhus. His theological studies

---

47. (Toldberg 1946, 92 ff).
48. (Albeck 1945, 23).

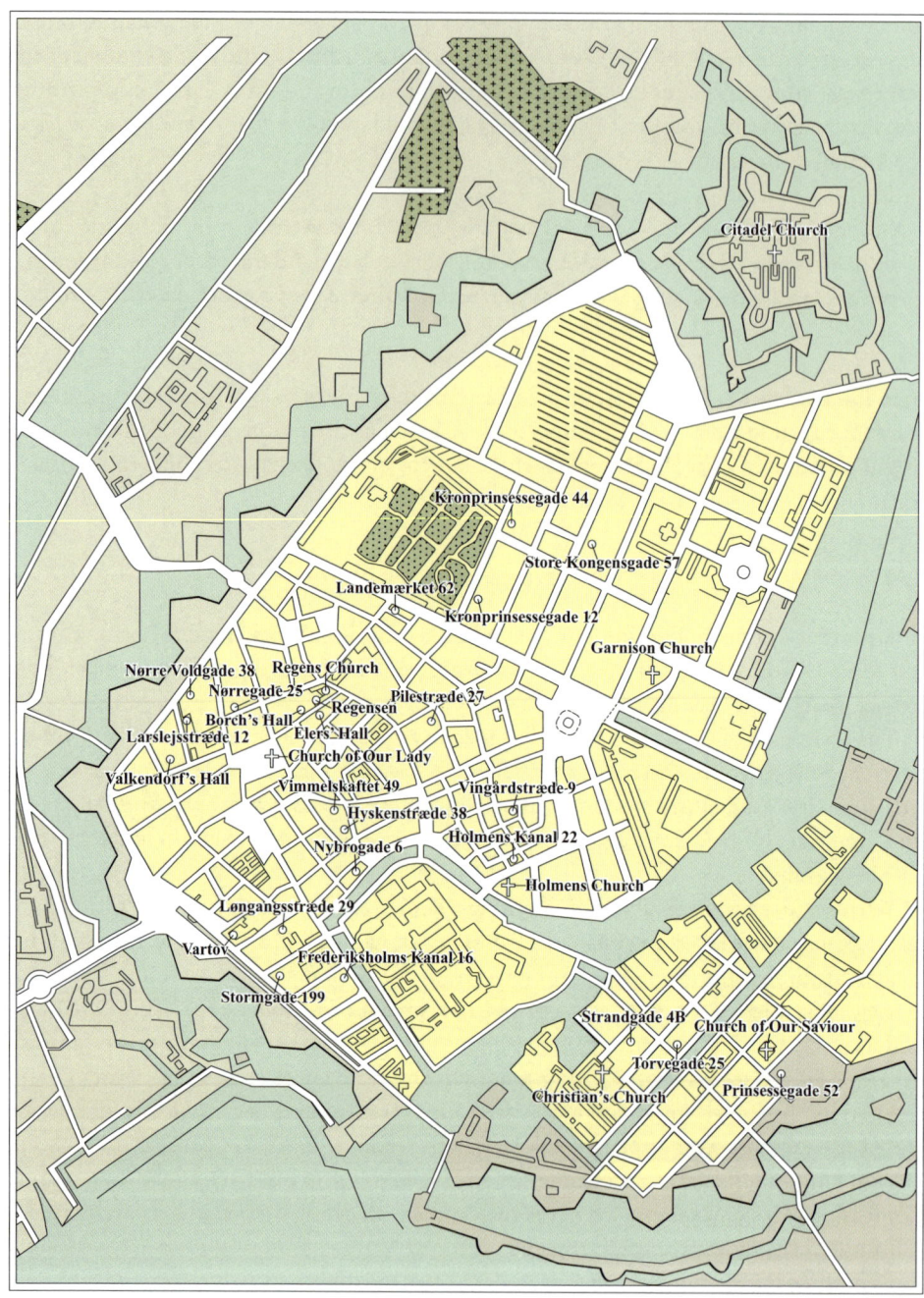

17. **Grundtvig's Copenhagen.**
With a population of around 100,000 in 1800 Copenhagen had roughly the same number of inhabitants as all the other market towns put together. The old city is in the centre, the military citadel in the top right-hand corner, and Christianshavn in the bottom right.

were more about getting through the syllabus than about the passion and revelation of coming to grips with living Christianity. For better for worse, there was no compulsory attendance at university, so Grundtvig skipped lecture after lecture without a qualm. It was the professors' fault for being so boring.

Compared to Aarhus, Copenhagen was fortunately full of attractions beyond the auditorium – and not just passing amusements. Where he really did thrive was in the best libraries and bookshops in the country, and in the intellectual conversations that could be held over the card-table with his fellow-students. As before, he read his way to knowledge, and learned especially from the historical experience of others. In volume 5 of this series, Experience with a capital E is central to Grundtvig's philosophical ideas and to his attack on all speculative and rationalist philosophy. Human experience is found in the reading of human history, and for Grundtvig the experience of his forefathers – going back to Christ – was becoming central to his thought in these university days. When he had to return home to see his parents in Udby, it was not just the cultural or even the intellectual life of Copenhagen that he missed. It was being away from the world of books coupled with the lack of "witty conversation and amusing pastimes" at home that was debilitating. On one occasion he came across a book in his father's library on the history of Iceland, and he devoured it. Throughout his life he proudly called himself a 'bookworm', and when he was not pursuing some external activity, he invariably turned to reading history in its very broadest sense.

Grundtvig is his own unforgiving assessor in describing his transition from school to university, how he went from being a little 'genius' to becoming a 'midget'. He attributed part of this to his external appearance on arrival in the big city. Wearing the attire of a poor farmhand from the provinces he cut a drab figure in the capital; nor did he do much to improve his looks – at least not until he was mobilised as a soldier in 1801 and could briefly wear a soldier's uniform! He was fluent in the South Zealand dialect of his childhood and the Jutland dialect of his adolescence, but in the eyes and ears of the Copenhageners he lacked style. He was not destitute, but his proclivity towards both the card-table and his long-stemmed pipe were a drain on his income. To sustain him, he received a total of 8 rigsdaler a month from four people: his father Johan, his elder brother Otto, his rich Uncle Joachim, and his old teacher Pastor Feld. His mother sent him packages of dry food, and he received an evening meal from Uncle Frederik, served with lengthy devotions and moral lectures.

Grundtvig makes no direct mention of his lodgings. We owe our knowledge of these to Royal Librarian Steen Johansen, a giant among the giants who founded the Grundtvig Society in 1947. Johansen searched the archives so diligently that he has provided us with the full list of addresses where Grundtvig lived in his 89 years (see Appendix 2). During most of his university years he seems to have lodged with master tailor Jacob Møller in Lille Brøndstræde 162 – in the poorer end of town. Before this he may have stayed briefly with rich Uncle Joachim at Store Kongensgade 51 (now 57-59), where his elder brothers, Otto and Jakob, had stayed while they were studying: if so, it was most likely only to sleep or read.

Grundtvig's study of Theology came in the midst of the rationalist period of Chris-

18. **University of Copenhagen, c. 1800.**
The building burned down in the English bombardment of 1807 and its replacement opened in 1836. Royal Danish Library.

tianity, from 1788-1830. Christian Rationalism argues that Truth is determined through reason and factual evidence rather than revelation and doctrinal tradition. Gone too was the belief that the university should deliver fealty to the absolute monarch and train its pastors to keep order in the kingdom; there was room now for reforming ideals and cosmopolitan thought, especially from Germany, while the classic bible and doctrinal studies were now supplemented by Philosophy and Church History as well as textual criticism and biblical criticism.

As for his own faith, Grundtvig was relieved that church attendance was no longer obligatory – so he stayed away for all three years of his university life. He did not *abandon* his faith – only his churchgoing. When he calls himself and his like-minded students 'heathen', he means they are neither orthodox Lutherans, like his father, nor 'revivalist' Christians. The revivalist movement arose in the first half of the 19th century, largely as a lay people's Christianity; it was practised outside the church walls in the so-called 'godly assemblies', and was characterised by personal conversion and observable conviction. With an anachronistic expression we could call Grundtvig and his fellow-students 'cultural Christians' at this point – a present-day designation for the vast majority of those who are not 'church Christians'. They were, and are, rationalist in thought, more or less irreligious, yet 'Christian' by virtue of their culture, their view of history, and their social values. In Grundtvig's case, however, he never denied God's existence nor disbelieved the Bible.

Having passed his university entrance exam in October 1800 Grundtvig immediately had to prepare for exams in Philosophy (theory and practice), Physics, Mathematics, and Astronomy; trainees for the priesthood should be able to construct their Theology on this basis. On 10th April 1801 he again passed with a good mark (*laudabilis,* praiseworthy), but a further exam awaited him that autumn in Latin, Greek, Hebrew, plus Philosophy/ Philology with textual exegesis in History, all depending on what the professor had taught. Since the professor would also be the examiner, the obvious way to pass the exam was to attend his lectures; but many students thought otherwise. Attendance was only moderate, and the majority turned to private coaches who could predict what the exam would most likely contain. One of Grundtvig's history teachers was Professor Abraham Kall, whose *General History of the World* he had read as a boy, but as a teacher Kall was less than adequate. Grundtvig passed this exam with only a moderate mark (*haud illaudabilis*, not unpraiseworthy).

Grundtvig could now begin on the Theology courses, taught by five professors, but none left a mark on him. Among them was his father's brother-in-law, Nicolai Balle, who was not only a rationalist but a super-rationalist (one who admits truths beyond reason); he was also the best theologian in Denmark at the turn of the century. He had abolished the exorcism prayer at Baptism in 1783 – and thus relieved Grundtvig's father of praying it at baby Frederik's baptism that year. Balle was best known for his *Textbook for the Evangelical-Christian Religion for use in schools*, 1791.

Grundtvig took his final exams in October 1803 and passed with a *laudabilis*, which was enough to get him a job. Looking back on what he had learned, he called it "schoolboy knowledge". There was no sense of enlightenment and no staff-student interaction – two areas where his own educational philosophy was later to make its mark.

If Grundtvig was not attending lectures and studying, what *was* he doing? He was certainly spending his money. Before leaving the capital on 29th November 1803, he listed his debts: "46 rigsdaler to Master Tailor Møller, 20 rigsdaler to Grocer Zimmer, and 4 rigsdaler to my private coach, Svendsen". Although he spent money on his pipe tobacco, there is no evidence of any debauchery – or of much study for that matter. Much later, in a letter to his step-cousin Jakob Mynster dated 22nd December 1812, Grundtvig wrote of his younger self that his "inherited seriousness of purpose, his poverty, his pride, and his ambition kept him apart from the pleasures of the world. I was a Pharisee of the strictest sect. I was known in the world as 'a moral person' and of that I was proud."[49] He was so poor that at one point he had no money for his private coach or for his woodfire, so in the winter of 1803 he went home to Udby for 3 months. In short, neither the teachers, nor the syllabus, nor his fellow-theologians actually influenced him. It was three experiences outside his Theology studies that left the biggest mark: the first had nothing to do with the university, the other two did.

On 18th March 1801, aged 17, Grundtvig registered as a soldier. On 28th March, as part of the student militia, he was issued with a uniform and a gun. All diplomatic communications had broken down and the British fleet under Vice-admiral Nelson was bearing down on Copenhagen to deter Denmark from becoming a French ally. Napoleon had

---

49. (BFOTG I, 109).

already conquered much European *land*; he was not to be allowed to conquer the seas. The First Battle of Copenhagen on 2nd April 1801 was a short-lived affair. On the quayside of 'Langelinie' Grundtvig heard the roar of the guns and saw the smoke from a distance, but although he was trained as a firefighter, he was inactive, as the two navies fought it out at sea. On hearing that the Russian tsar had died, the Danes realised they could cut ties with the French without fear of Russian retaliation, so they accepted the peace terms offered by the British, and all parties returned to base.

Skougaard and Steffens

The two major experiences of Grundtvig's university life were his meeting with Peder Skougaard (1783-1838), "the only friend of my youth" – and a series of lectures ushering in the Romantic era by Grundtvig's cousin, Henrik Steffens.

In his introduction to *Nordic Mythology 1808* Grundtvig acknowledged his debt to Skougaard for putting him on the track of the great Icelandic 'Edda' sagas (Snorri) and the history of the Danes (Saxo): "You it was... who led me to the wise ancients, Snorri and Saxo, in whose tracks I wandered towards the Edda's mystical forest". Grundtvig and Skougaard met and became friends in 1801. Skougaard was from the island of Bornholm in the Baltic Sea, 180 kms east of Copenhagen. He was studying Mathematics, but he had a rare knowledge of the early sources of Danish history, a subject that had always fascinated Grundtvig but which had not yet inspired him to any worthwhile poetry. Unusually for Grundtvig their friendship held steady throughout their lives, not least because Skougaard was so generous in his help. With a young man's eagerness Skougaard published his critical *Description of Bornholm* in 1804, which under the prevailing censorship laws against defamation cost him 14 days on bread and water, a substantial fine, and lifetime censorship. He was marked for life by this rejection and died in poverty in 1838. But it was Skougaard who pushed Grundtvig towards writing the history of ancient Denmark, and towards translating original sources into modern Danish. This was to be Grundtvig's future mission – with branches into theology, the Church, education, and politics, and an enrichment of the Danish language in his many hymns and songs.

His second major experience touched on his poetic view of life. On 11th November 1801 at Elers' Hall of Residence, Grundtvig's 10-year-older cousin on his mother's side, Henrik Steffens, began a lecture series. These 'Lectures on Philosophy' introduced the new movement, Romanticism, to Denmark. Steffens had studied in Germany and had actually met the German philosopher Schelling, and the poets Goethe, and Schiller, so his lecture series broke new ground for the rationalist students. One of these was the poet Adam Oehlenschläger (1779-1850), whose response was immediate and overwhelming – in stark contrast to Grundtvig's. In mid-1802 Oehlenschläger and Steffens had a 16-hour meeting of minds; their long walk and restaurant dinner concluded at 3 o'clock in the morning. The next day Oehlenschläger wrote the most famous Romantic poem in the country's history. Entitled 'The Gold Horns' it commemorated the two 5th century gold horns found in South Jutland in 1639 and 1734. Unfortunately, on the night between 4th-5th May 1802 they had been stolen from the Royal Art Chamber by the goldsmith, Niels Heidenreich,

19. Henrik Steffens teaching in Breslau 1813.
After painting by Arthur Kampf, 1891.

and immediately melted down into jewellery and coins. The culprit was arrested and given a life sentence in 1803. Oehlenschläger's poem, and indeed the whole book, *Poems 1803*, celebrates the central ideas of universal romanticism, and is subtitled 'A glimpse of the ancient past'. In these words Grundtvig was to find much of his subject-matter. Oehlenschläger himself went on to become the national poet and author of Denmark's national anthem, 'There is a lovely land'.

Grundtvig recorded his immediate response to Steffens in his diary:

> tonight I did not understand more of what the lecturer said than that he intended to tear down Kant and Fichte, and himself rise above their ruins.

36 years later he reflected on his experience of Steffens:

> I had completely forgotten he existed, except that I remember from my childhood how he had shown me pictures in the first peepshow. He was now 28 ... and there was a stumbling-block in his *style*: it was rather *German* in a number of respects and full of all kinds of

made-up words that I had neither seen nor heard. But the tone in which he spoke, the fire with which he breathed, struck me at once![50]

In the winter of 1803-04 Henrik Steffens gave a further lecture series, this time on Goethe and romantic poetry. By now Grundtvig was a regular listener, and increasingly aware of the influence of these lectures. Oehlenschläger immediately, and Grundtvig gradually, acquired a new self-understanding from this experience, for Steffens was such a powerful, innovative speaker:

> All history begins with the gods. Behind all history lies mythology ... The source of all existence is religiosity ... I call 'prose' the degrader of even that which bears the manifest stamp of the Eternal to a mere Finite. I call 'poetry' that which even in the Eternal finds the stamp of the Finite.[51]

As Uffe Jonas writes in his introduction to *Living Wellsprings*, quoting Grundtvig's letter to Bernhard Ingemann of 26th November 1824:

> Even though he made sure to keep a certain critical distance to his cousin, Grundtvig always acknowledged "a sense of spiritual kinship so strong that my own historical-poetical efforts are basically just a continuation of his in 1803."[52]

In his own sense of self, Grundtvig was already a 'writer' – with the right to tell his diary that Oehlenschläger's linguistic forms in *Poems 1803* "lack correctness". He himself was experimenting with both prose and poetry, and in 1802 had even produced a short 3-act comedy, *The Schoolmasters*, which he sent off to the Royal Theatre. It received a rapid rejection. Grundtvig was unsuccessful with his writing until he was ready to adopt and later to rework the *Romantic* view of life. What he did realise, as he wrote in his diary, was: "It is the same with me as with Horace,[53] I must write or I must die."

What were the fruits of Grundtvig's education in Theology? In the introduction to *Human Comes First* (2018), the Danish theologian, Niels Henrik Gregersen, characterises Grundtvig as "a theologian of classic calibre and scope". He continues:

> Apart from the breadth of Grundtvig's view of the Christian faith, the most original contribution of his theology is his cultural agenda, developed in the context of his creation theology after 1832. Indeed, a school of theological thinking has developed around Grundtvig's cultural agenda known as *Scandinavian Creation Theology*.[54]

---

50. (MM, 273).
51. (Quoted from Rønning 1907, 61 and 63).
52. LW, 32-33. (INGEMANN, 36).
53. Horace (Quintus Horatius Flaccus) 65-8 BCE, Roman poet, satirist, and critic.
54. HCF, 52.

20. **Facsimile of Grundtvig's handwriting 1802.**
The poem is no. 104 in *LW*.

In the light of Grundtvig's later reputation as a theologian of the highest calibre, we may justly ask how much his university studies contributed to his later reputation. Very little, must be our conclusion. We know that throughout his life his own theology of creation and salvation differed from the critical textual analysis of the Bible and history that the university theologians taught. Grundtvig and the Faculty of Theology shared a mutual dislike of each other, and Grundtvig never taught at the university. But seen from his own perspective, knowing which way *not* to go was no bad thing, especially if, as he believed, he was intellectually their equal – and spiritually their master.

Meeting Lise

At university Grundtvig gave little time to personal relations and was happy in his own company. But in 1800 his elder brother Otto had become Pastor of Torkilstrup on the island of Falster, and Grundtvig preferred his brother's company to his parents'. There was more *life* here, more rewarding *conversations*; and it was only 3 kms to Gundslev, where the rural dean, Diderik Blicher, lived with his wife and their four attractive daughters, Marie (20), Pouline (18), Lise (16), and Jane (14). Around 1st January 1802, the 19-year-old Grundtvig fell head over heels for Marie, but by the time he had graduated from university she was already engaged to Poul Glahn, five years her senior and training for the priesthood. Although Marie and Poul did not marry until 1808, Marie was firmly out of Grundtvig's reach. The somewhat dazed young man, now in love with his own unfulfilled passion, was looking for a girl who was looking for him, as Abrahamowitz so pointedly puts it.[55] At Sunday service on 4th March 1804 Grundtvig preached in his brother Otto's church, and sat next to Lise Blicher at lunch that day. His diary confirms his change of heart: "She means to me now almost what her eldest sister meant to me then. I know of no girl I like more than her."

Being Grundtvig, he questioned himself. Was this his vanity speaking? Or perhaps his sexual desire? Was he indeed in love? Was this what love is? Or was he in love with being in love? Had he fallen in love on the rebound from Marie? Nine months later he confided to his diary: "... in my calmest moments it seems stark staring mad for me to become engaged to a poor girl of my own age with *my* prospects. I am in my 22nd year and would be fortunate to get a calling before my 26th year." Even then he and any would-be wife would have to tighten their belts. The choice was between heart and head, between the "bridal couch" and "such a debt that anxiety would be my only lot for the rest of my life." In this dilemma Grundtvig's head won the day; he stayed single.

---

55. (Abrahamowitz 2010, 33).

21. Grundtvig's Denmark, showing places mentioned in the text.

5. Staring at her beauty
(1803-08)

Between passing his Theology degree in October 1803 and starting his first job as house tutor on Langeland in March 1805 Grundtvig spent a frustrating time trying to make both ends meet. For the first seven months he was forced to return home to Udby, thence to his brother Otto in Torkilstrup. Although by virtue of his degree he was qualified to teach, he could not face the drudgery of high school Latin and Greek; he was going to be a *writer*. Having discovered the extraordinary mythology of the Icelandic Sagas, he decided to teach himself Old Icelandic: "The desire to learn Icelandic filled my soul!" The two languages were distantly related, and Grundtvig pored over an Icelandic grammar book in order to decode the language; at the same time he was beginning to think about translating it into modern Danish, and for this purpose he was missing the academic libraries of Copenhagen. Scraping together enough money for the ride back to the capital that summer, he stayed for 6 weeks first with his friend Peter Skougaard at Pilestræde 110, and then with his cousin Jakob Trojel at Hyskenstræde 38-39. There was no supply teaching available, nor did his plan to publish reworkings of historical episodes meet with any interest. He next decided to write a dissertation on King Knud the Great – the same king who is known in English-speaking countries as King Canute (c. 995-1035) and who also gave his name to the English county of Kent. Grundtvig's aim was to prove that he was anything *but* great, but this too turned out to be beyond both his knowledge and his means. He told his diary that he was totally out of sorts: "I sit alone ... Death stands in my mind's eye ... a gentle liberator from the bonds of vanity."

A teaching post nevertheless did appear when a distant relative, Pastor J.H. Edsberg, wrote to cousin Jakob that Captain Carl and Lady Constance Steensen de Leth were looking for a house tutor for their young son, Carl junior, at Egeløkke Manor. Here was an appointment that was easy to manage and would provide him with some financial resources. It would also allow him time to *write*, and would situate him close to the four Blicher sisters and his own brother, Otto. The first shock came when he realised that the job was on Langeland, not Falster, much further away from Copenhagen – and the attractive sisters. The second shock came at the interview with the Captain's brother-in-law, who began by asking the applicant if he spoke French! For once Grundtvig's vitriolic temperament came to his aid; he was visibly angry at this new requirement and demanded that he be told on the spot whether he had the job or not! At the end of the interview he was appointed! He agreed to an annual remuneration of 150 rigsdaler, plus board and lodging; he was expected to speak German and a smattering of French, i.e. the languages of the nobility.[56]

In those days the journey to Langeland went via Falster and Lolland, so Grundtvig

---

56. (GEEG, 37-39).

22. Egeløkke Manor.
Drawing from a painting from c. 1840 by F.M.E. Fabritius de Tengnagel (1791-1849). The manor is first mentioned in 1426. The above building is the one Grundtvig knew. It was rebuilt in 1846.

planned to stop off at Gundlev vicarage and pay his respects to Lise Blicher. He reached the port of Nakskov only to find the ferry was cancelled because of sea ice. Back he went to Udby, still unsure about Lise. Not until March 1805 did he finally arrive at Egeløkke Manor, where he was to spend the next 3 years of his life. Grundtvig was now 21, Captain Carl 29, Lady Constance 27, and Carl junior 6.

Tutor at Egeløkke Manor

Grundtvig's relatively humdrum life was turned upside-down by what happened next. He fell in love with the lady of the manor, Lady Constance Leth. As Illustration 22 shows, at Egeløkke Manor he had stepped up a class – from poor student to landed nobility – and away from the Church calling that had been his parents' hope and expectation. His employer was rich: Captain Carl owned both Egeløkke Manor and Steensgaard Manor a little further to the north. The captain's wife, Constance, whom he had married in 1796, came from the nobility, being the daughter of State Councillor Michael Fabritius de Tengnagel and his wife Adophine Leth from Vejlegaard Manor on mid-Funen. Michael de Tengnagel and his daughter Constance de Leth both had the French 'de' between their names to denote that a forefather had been knighted. The 6-year-old Carl also had a nurse, Bine Lassen, who had advanced from the position of housemaid to that of Constance's trusted friend. Both she and Grundtvig were now members of a caring household and both sat at the dinner table with the rest of the family and the guests who regularly visited. For the three years that Grundtvig was at Egeløkke (1805-08), the house language was Danish, but when German guests arrived, for instance from nearby Tranekær Manor, it was German, the preferred language of the court, the aristocracy, the civil service, and

23. Lady Constance Steensen de Leth.
Portrait by Jens Juel, pre-1803.

the landed gentry. At the time, the southern Danish border was just north of present-day Hamburg. Grundtvig had not learned German in school, and managed as best he could, for "no one forced me to use it".

Initially, Grundtvig was out of his depth. Being something of a loner, an outsider, a country boy, he was not expecting the nobility to be so accommodating, so friendly. But must he really speak *German*? Was he not in his heart of hearts more at home among the peasant farmers of Jutland? Apparently not. He swiftly adapted to his new circumstances and soon he even began to enjoy them. Not only could he be himself, he could even begin to feel at home among the nobility. He derived some pleasure from his teaching, he was reading German, French, and English,[57] he found time to write – and he also had this beautiful woman to admire.

The admiration soon turned to infatuation, then to adoration. Everything that happened in his 3 years at Egeløkke is coloured by this experience. 18 months into his stay he confided to his diary:

> I came here open to amusement, and with a desire for the second sex. Had I not fallen in love, my pupil would never have got on so well! And I would already have held a rather high position in the School for Lust.[58]

Grundtvig distinguishes between *vellyst* (lust) and *lyst* (pleasure). He was later to name his own high school 'Marie's pleasure', for the people's high school was to be pleasurable. The appellation no doubt had something to do with living so close to a woman – in the same house, occasionally in the same room – alone. The closest he had come to this physical feminine presence had been with Lise Blicher, but he respected her partly as the dean's daughter and partly as his junior. Nothing could ever possibly have got out of hand with

---

57. DUB 229.
58. (Ibid., 232).

her, even if kisses may have been exchanged in a game of blind man's buff. Constance was totally different. She was married, she was six years his senior, she was his employer, she was well-educated, she spoke German and French, she was a conversationalist – and she even sang! Moreover, she treated Grundtvig as an equal, which Lise could never have done. Conversation at the dinner table – often with guests – could range from literature, where Grundtvig was sometimes her equal, to music, where he was not. And then there was her body language. Constance was not only physically attractive, she was also naturally charming to everyone. Her genuine *joie de vivre*, her smiling eyes, her laughter, the offer of her hand to the gauche Grundtvig ... No wonder he was captivated by "the blissful exchange of loving glances and the intoxicating handshakes"; for she did not discourage him.

In December 1805 he wrote in his diary:

> I came here. I read in the fair lady's eyes, and what were all the books in the world compared with that? What could I learn from them that was so dear as her resting her gaze on me with such tenderness? What was all reading and talk compared to silently staring at her beauty? Like the feeble lamp is to the radiant sun.[59]

By September 1806 his diary was positively sensual:

> With its dark blanket the night covered my world, only for me in dreams to conjure another world, more beautiful, more blossoming. In dreams the hand that I kissed warm by day clasped my bowed neck, drew my beating breast to the heaving bosom that by day merely enchanted my gaze and pressed my mouth firmly to the blushing lips that dispensed kisses ten times sweeter than the harmonious sounds that by day intoxicated my ear.[60]

Grundtvig clearly knew that his passion for a married woman was illicit, impossible, yet apparently unstoppable. In 1808 he wrote to his new friend, Christian Molbech, about the experience (Letter 1):

> O how I fought against the rising passion! With what strength have I forced my soul into the most exhausting pursuits to calm the storm that raged in my innermost being! But all in vain. It was like trying to stem the rushing mountain stream with a bucket.

Constance was musically gifted, and instrumental in the lasting transformation in Grundtvig in the world of music and song. So far he had considered music as comprising not much more than church hymns and popular songs. But when Constance actually *sang* to him, his heart melted. In one of his 'Bragi Talks' in 1843 he was to admit that "Unfortunately I myself am very unmusical ... I do not understand music at all." But in

---

59. (Ibid., 282).
60. (Ibid., 373-74).

the presence of Constance he made a real effort to appreciate its communicative power. In his diary for 23rd June 1805 he described the turning-point:

> I thought I lacked a taste for music ... but you, Palmine (a cover-name for Constance, ed.), awakened me from my cheerless dream with your pure, artless voice. Every note of yours pierced my innermost being. Far from weakening my feeling for the graces of Nature it was a ... point of brilliance in its crown, engendering unity and harmony in all my feelings ... I learned more powerfully than a thousand other proofs that music ennobles life, diminishes sorrow, and makes happiness itself more happy.

Classical music of the day was largely confined to the Royal Court, the Royal Theatre, and the *soirée* in Copenhagen. Grundtvig had never experienced the fascination of watching musicians and singers practise their art, and he had no defence against Constance's drawing-room performance as she sang to him. He returned the romantic experience by reading aloud to her from among others *1001 Nights*. Reason yielded to feeling at Egeløkke.

Despite his pain, both the short and long-term consequences of Grundtvig's love for Constance were largely positive – as he himself gradually came to realise. Initially he felt the pangs of forbidden love, and questioned whether it was being requited from Constance's side. He suffered the guilt and shame of his erotic dreams and the useless admonitions of reason. In the first passionate love of his life he was caught in a cultural clash and a personal impasse that he could not resolve. He came close to wounding Constance as deeply as she was wounding him, and he feared that she was playing with him, even though from her side there was not much more than a warm, unmistakable, kindness.

The last evidence of his passion are the 92 pages torn out of his diary for 1805, presumably because he feared that their content would somehow become known. Nevertheless, it says much for the besotted young man that he actually *wrote* them. This is a huge step forward in his understanding of his poetic, romantic self. In the end no lasting harm was done – neither to Constance nor to Grundtvig.

A tutor's work

Initially, Grundtvig admitted in his diary that he was ill-equipped to teach Carl: "I often did not know what to do with him." But little by little he began to build a relationship with the boy and to learn the rudiments. He believed that his passion for Constance spilled over into his teaching – and all the better for that! But employer and employee did not quite agree on how to educate the boy. Constance was much taken by the free educational upbringing advocated by Jean-Jacques Rousseau in *Emile, or On Education* (1762). Children who were allowed to develop naturally without social constraints will develop their fullest potential, both educationally and morally. Constance also wanted her boy to learn French so that he could be a man of the world. Grundtvig could not oblige on either count; he spoke very little French and knew nothing about education other than what he had been through himself – hardly a recipe for success.

Grundtvig demanded calm and consistency to carry out his teaching-plan for Carl, but far too often Constance made playtime dates for her son and his friends, or there were outings or visitors, or such-like. When Grundtvig complained, she took to meeting Carl's requests for a diversion with, "Alright with me, what does Mr Grundtvig say?" Mr Grundtvig was not amused. He considered himself responsible not just for teaching the boy but also for raising him to be an upright, cultured citizen. Compared with the outward appearance of propriety "the harmonious development of his spiritual powers ... is far more important", he wrote, and Constance's attitude to her son's education was somewhat irresponsible.

The subjects that Grundtvig and Carl were to share were Writing, Reading, Grammar, Arithmetic, Geography, and especially History and Danish. From 1st March to 19th November 1806, Sundays included, Grundtvig kept a teaching record which runs to 90 pages with the title: *Lesson and Mark Book for Carl Steensen Leth*. Again Grundtvig is his own historian. He had been teaching Carl for the best part of a year, and had reached some important conclusions about education. He rejected the quantifying marking system of the schools and acknowledged that perhaps "when I am least satisfied with his progress, that is when he deserves the greatest praise – and *vice versa*." This is the earliest example of Grundtvig's educational insight – on such ideas he would later base his "school for life". But his own teaching abilities were limited.

In his best moments Grundtvig was fully aware of his own human failings and pedagogical shortcomings, so the diary also served to remind him that learning was more important than teaching. This was the beginning of his child-centred approach to education, and corresponds with *Emile*. The child's needs come before the teacher's demands – and here Grundtvig's Christian beliefs played their role. He was raising Carl not just to be a good citizen and inherit his father's wealth, not just to be a cultivated citizen and socially-conscious lord of the manor; he was raising him to inherit eternal life! Grundtvig outlined his educational philosophy in the lengthy introduction to the diary, before closing with a prayer:

> Almighty God! I can only plant and water, You alone can make things grow. Do so, O Lord. Fill me with ten times the warmth when I plead Your case, and the case of virtue for this young boy! Make his heart gentle, so that it may melt at the description of the wretchedness of this world that I seek to help him rectify! In particular, when with tears in my eyes I depict the temptations that will surround him in his youth and adulthood, let Your Spirit make my tongue eloquent, and let my words stamp themselves indelibly on his innermost being, so that they become an insurmountable wall between him and all vice. Amen, let it be, dear Lord!!![61]

From his own experience Grundtvig knew the need for both a moral upbringing and for a genuine warmheartedness in the boy, and now and then he had moments of great joy when he noted his pupil's progress, not least when Carl confided in him. Often indeed

---

61. (DUB, 23x).

Grundtvig chided *himself* for breaking his principles, for scolding the boy vehemently, and for frightening him. Below are four typical entries in the lesson-plan:

> 8th April 1806
> The natural history of the pig was repeated and remembered poorly. Norway, Italy, Hungary, Helvetia, Sweden were repeated and remembered well ... In general I was satisfied with both him and myself.

> 9th April 1806
> The natural history of the deer was repeated and remembered ... The French and German words – 33 – were repeated and remembered rather well, if I except occasional mistakes with the definite articles.

> 14th April 1806
> We began with addition and subtraction of numbers, but then Carl asked me to write a little verse for his mother in honour of her recent birthday (on 11th April, ed.), and himself supplied me with the content. I neither could nor would reject the boy's good idea, and thus in a sense the afternoon was lost. But we both won: I won his love to a greater degree, and he won my increased interest in both his heart and his intelligence.

> 6th May 1806
> The natural history of the reindeer was repeated ... The Persian monarchy was analysed ... but I lost my temper with his repeated inattention over some of the numerals.

On the other hand Grundtvig could admit that his teaching was not only gratifying; it also kept his mind off Constance:

> These teaching lessons were so enjoyable for me, and well calculated to take my attention away from unpleasant objects; they gave me peace of mind. On such occasions I recognise twice as much how beneficial this profitable occupation is for me.[62]

Young Carl did not much care for his teacher, if we are to believe his own, much later, account in 1890 in *From the Chronicles of the Day*, a monthly journal for literature, art and politics:

> Grundtvig was a queer fish, when he was young. Repulsive, overbearing, dictatorial, and hard-hearted: I doubt that he had any friends in his early youth ... Grundtvig was my teacher, I never had cause to find fault with him, he taught me untiringly. However, he was also a hot-tempered man and he treated me rather strictly – but I will not complain, it might have been deserved.

---

62. (Bugge 1965 op. 96).

Grundtvig was not the first teacher to discover that theory and practice can be at odds! He had no teaching experience, but he was full of good intentions; he had only one pupil in his class and only a mother to deal with. But sympathy for Carl must not undermine the teaching experience that Grundtvig was gaining: his challenges at Egeløkke would stand him in good stead later in life. After 6 confused months in the job, he decided to leave. To his surprise, he was asked to reconsider his decision by the boy's father, who was well aware of Grundtvig's infatuation with his wife. When Grundtvig learned that his possible replacement was a drunkard, a womaniser, and a charlatan who might seduce Constance and destroy Carl junior, he made a life-changing resolution. In order to protect Constance and Carl he would remain at his post and use his *reason* to come to terms with his infatuation.

Partly to demonstrate his capabilities and partly to keep himself entertained out in the country, Grundtvig took charge of the reading circle at Egeløkke – primarily for the pastors on the island. But he did so in a somewhat overweening style that initially bore little fruit. The pastors resented Grundtvig's manner – until Constance persuaded them to join nevertheless, and once the pastors allowed Grundtvig to have his way, the project was reasonably successful. For his part Grundtvig got to read the books he ordered for the book club, including major works by Friedrich Schiller (1767-1805), Johann Fichte (1762-1814) and Friedrich Schelling (1775-1854). This provided him with the impulse to produce his own work, though it is often hard to trace his thought back to any specific predecessor.

His soul's captor, or his faithful friend?

A number of biographers have pointed out that Grundtvig arrived at Egeløkke a rationalist and departed a romantic. In fact it was ultimately his own reason and morality, coupled with Constance's propriety, that saved him. He took a deep breath and turned his unhappiness to his own advantage, as he wrote in his diary for 10th September 1806:

> I must call it good fortune that my love was unfulfilled, since it made me active and contributed to an increase in my knowledge.

What Steffens had talked about 4 years earlier in his lectures on the romantic soul was now lived experience for Grundtvig. To combat his unrequited passion he turned to reading – and especially to writing. Whatever happened earlier that year to cause this change of attitude towards Constance remains unknown. Scholars have speculated on the mysterious reference in his diary for 6th May 1806, painstakingly reconstructed by Gustav Albeck:

> ... with her. My undemanding [worship?] may at times have raised her to an elevated position, but that can never be enough for her, since she has become used to a quite different kind, one whose instincts are animal or highly refined sensual pleasure, which has its eye solely on its own gratification without casting a glance at the eternal law of morality or the higher dignity of humankind. So it is to my good that she finds herself in that situation,

for her lower level puts me on a higher level, one that I might never have climbed to, if I had possessed her [love?].

It would seem that Grundtvig was blaming Constance for 'seducing' him and was drawing the conclusion that she was morally inferior to him. By withstanding her temptation, he had proved himself the stronger. A fragment from his diary for 17th July 1806 seems to point in this direction:

> But now she boldly stood before me, declared with the holiest assurances that my suspicions were unfounded, and shook me with the pronouncement, as painful as it was justified, that she was now fully aware that my love for her was a sham, for I could not possibly love a woman whom I believed to be sunk in the deepest swamp of animality. With bitterness and disgust she painted a picture of what she must be, if I was right. I must, she said, not just be lustful, but my whole life must also be a detestable mask. "I treat my husband with love and tenderness! What must I be if at the same time I fluttered from one embrace to another – what you think, and I will say, 'A public whore!'"

We are seeing here a clash not only of genders, but also of cultures. There was clearly pain on both sides, but Grundtvig had not read the codes of the nobility and could not gauge how Constance felt about *him*. An additional reason may be that it was difficult for Grundtvig to grasp in general how others felt about him. How *he* felt about *them* took priority due to his preoccupation with his own higher calling. At Egeløkke, blaming the innocent Constance helped him to withdraw from her – and then to concentrate on himself and his writing again. His honour was intact – or so he convinced himself.

From many other sources in Constance's archives it is clear that in spite of her often romantic bearing, she always adhered to certain formalities when dealing with her staff, including the tutors that came after Grundtvig. Perhaps the closest we can come to the truth about their relationship lies in the letter she sent to her best friend and confidant, the local pastor, Christen Graae. It was New Year's Eve 1820, and she had just dismissed a tutor of whom her husband was obviously jealous:

> I am often misunderstood. Which of us is guiltless? ... But I stand free and calm in the face of the storms that seek to crush me. My innocence has so often been violated; I cannot defend it, but may God grant to all the peace that is in my soul. I did not go out into the world cold and indifferent; my feelings were too tender and my blood too warm for that. I know that I have left my love in people with whom the world attributed to me the grossest offences.[63]

How then did Grundtvig and Constance retain their care and cooperation for Carl over the next two years – and how did they establish a loyal, confidential friendship that lasted until Constance's death in 1827 at the age of 49? Why did Grundtvig not just walk away from Egeløkke, lick his wounds, and count his blessings? The evidence that he wanted

---

63. (Rønning I, 2, note 5, 185-86).

to remain in touch with Constance lies in the seven poems that he wrote for her on her birthday each year between 1805 and 1811. Written on Maundy Thursday the 1811 poem is formed almost as a meditation "on the faith, hope, and love of Jesus", against which Grundtvig sets his relationship to Constance in the new light of friendship: "Be till death my true and loyal friend,/ as such a friend in me you now possess." On this plane of Christian friendship with Constance he could now move on in his life. Proof that Constance was relieved at this outcome and genuinely wished Grundtvig well in his engagement to Lise Blicher can be seen in Letter 8:

> ... my heart braves all life's changes and remains as loyal and constant as ever to my friends. And you, Grundtvig, are my friend! I shall never forget you and I wish that you lived closer. Please send me a few lines now and then, and let us be tried and trusted friends whom nothing can separate, with Lise one day becoming a link in that chain. Greet her from me, though I do not yet know her. I hope you bring her here some time and that she will like me – of that I am sure ....

While the practical relationship to Constance gradually found a tolerable balance on both sides, Grundtvig found it far more difficult to explain what insights his unhappy infatuation had given him, as well as the personal price he had had to pay. The feeling of pain and loss stayed with him, and found expression in the pathos of his wedding poem to Lise's sister, Marie Blicher, on 15th May 1808, as she married Poul Glahn:

> My heart was also granted
> Love's ever-gushing spring,
> but not the life attendant
> that Love's success can bring;
> my harpstrings can no sweet song play
> except upon your wedding day.
>
> When pleasant days are passing
> and you walk side by side,
> when in his arms you linger
> so proud to be his bride,
> withdraw a simple kiss and send
> it to your own, and sorrow's, friend.[64]

Channelling the romantic drive

The transition from rationalist theologian to romantic poet went via Grundtvig's awareness of his moral culpability, as the following episode shows. As a Master of Theology Grundtvig was licenced to preach sermons, but not to administer the sacraments. When

---

64. (PS I, 27f).

Constance's good friend, the above-mentioned Pastor Christian Graae, invited Grundtvig to preach in Bøstrup church at Sunday service on 10th August 1805, his sermon drew on a recent experience he had had with two officers of the dragoons, staying at Egeløkke, whose language he deemed improper. Grundtvig began his sermon with a prayer, directed not least to himself:

> Almighty God, worthy of adoration, You who implanted reason in us to govern our desires, You who through Your beloved Jesus, taught us to know and use our abilities to suppress our passions; grant us the will and the strength so to employ Your wise provisions that we promote our true earthly and eternal well-being.[65]

The New Testament text was 1 Corinthians 10:6-13, where Paul advises the church that "we should not commit sexual immorality" (v. 8). Grundtvig gave an account of the temptations where men should control themselves, such as when they cannot afford to marry before they are quite old, or when young people are brought up in a shady environment where their parents are poor role models. Morality is anchored in religion, and religion is being scorned by those of high rank; their right to sensual pleasure is confused with the freedom which is thought to "animate the finer breed". Grundtvig named no names, so people could think what they liked, but having pointed to the social and human consequences of immorality, he added:

> ... to the few of you who have still not forgotten what you owe God and His commandment... pray with me and for me that when I meet you beyond the grave I shall not have cause to blush and be ashamed of myself.

Whether or not Grundtvig's prayer was answered, we can read in his birthday entry for 8th September 1805 that he was beginning to see a light:

> ... of course one can be tempted to prefer eternal death to eternal life, whose bliss we can only glimpse and whose misery one only felt. But in my innermost being I feel as strongly as possible a desire for life – even stronger than love. Only now do I hear the heavenly Spirit speaking clearly through Paul: when all has perished, what remain are faith, hope, and love.

The very next day Grundtvig began a brief study entitled, *What Constitutes Poetry?* Here he comes with the following definition, "Poetry is everything that bears the hallmark of Eternity... whose first determining element lies within the limits of experience: otherwise its purpose is defeated." In other words, the link between heaven and earth must be anchored on earth. In his own case he could not deny his love for Constance, for he must be true to his experience; instead he had to live with it, and try to make poetry of it. A bridge must be built between the Eternal and the Finite, as he wrote in his diary on 10th September 1805:

---

65. (Rønning I, 2, 12-13).

> ... Poetry must conjure forth a fairer existence than our day-to-day reality, but equally it must be seen from a final point as an ascending chain whose first determining link lies within the limits of our experience; otherwise it fails in its aim. The ordinary person cannot penetrate the higher form of poetry; for him it is a waste.

This notion of two worlds was now Grundtvig's focus, but not in the platonic sense. His love for Constance was real – and grounded. So must his poetry be.

On the way out of his romantic passion for Constance Grundtvig turned first to the main source of knowledge about the Nordic gods and giants of old, the *Poetic Edda*, and not least to the forbidden love of the young god Frey for the giant woman Gerda; for gods and giants must not mix.

Snorri Sturluson (1179-1241) was an Icelandic historian, poet, and politician, who wrote the *Prose Edda* or *Younger Edda*, a narrative of Nordic mythology. Grundtvig's Danish translation was published in 3 volumes in 1818-22. His other comfort was Saxo (c. 1160-post 1208), who had worked as a scribe in Copenhagen for the great Archbishop Absalon (1128-1201). Saxo's *Deeds of the Danes (Gesta Danorum)* was handwritten in elegant Latin in 16 volumes. The early volumes contain mainly legendary material, but references to documented events become more and more common in later volumes. *Gesta Danorum* was first published in 1514; by the 1770s Bertel Sandvig (1752-86) had published translations of old Danish and Norwegian poetry, inspirational sources which Grundtvig himself owned, according to his library stocktaking of 1805. Grundtvig's very first *published* article, written in July 1806, appeared in the literary journal *Ny Minerva* that October and was his response to a rationalist interpretation of the *Poetic Edda* by Professor of Theology Jens Møller. In Grundtvig's romantic rejoinder he drew on the fruits of his Icelandic studies to pursue his idea that poetry must bridge the two worlds of the Finite and the Eternal. For both Grundtvig and Oehlenschläger, Iceland was a holy isle, the spiritual home of the Nordic gods. Grundtvig later wrote to his friend Poul Dons that the Nordic myths could not *end* his suffering, but they could channel it.

He followed this article with his first published scholarly study, *On Religion and Liturgy* (1807), as his contribution to the topical debate on the revision of the Church liturgy. This time he asked, "What is Religion?" and found his philosophical answer in whatever bridges the gap between the finite valley of humankind and the eternal land beyond the sea. We send out Poetry *over* the sea, but it loses itself in the clouds; we build a boat out of Philosophy to sail *across* the sea, but the towering waves force it back to shore.

Most notable in the work is the emphasis Grundtvig places on music as part of the bridge:

> We come now to singing, the central point in liturgical poetry, in which all that we can produce of the sublime and the beautiful is united. Poetry must be clothed in harmonious verse and rest on melodic rhyme, and to this is added the intensifying music. We must be raised far above this earth, and a glimpse of eternal life must float over our heavenward gaze.[66]

---

66. *TCOL*, 165.

This was written four years before Grundtvig composed his own first hymn, but it is a pointer to the direction in which he was now travelling. He was in no doubt about the truth of the Trinity, or the atoning death and resurrection of Jesus Christ. What he doubted was himself – and his *own* faith.

A third article from his busy life at Egeløkke – in between teaching Carl junior! – was *On the Advancement of Learning, with Particular Regard to the Fatherland* (1807), which like *On Religion and Liturgy* anticipates his later work. Niels W. Bruun writes in his introduction to the study:

> We should also note the first usage in this essay of other principles and practices that form Grundtvig's idea of "the school for life", which crystallises in 'the people's high school'. These include: Danish as the mother-tongue; Danish literature, especially poetry, as its expression; the importance of history as lived human experience; a religious mind that acknowledges a supreme Maker: and the idea that the school should be a *nursery* for the branches of Learning rather than a factory.[67]

65 years later, Grundtvig was still championing these ideas. He deliberately employed the term 'learning' (*videnskabelighed*), which was normally reserved for higher education and beyond. In Grundtvig's definition it includes the cultural education that he had been exposed to at Egeløkke, from where he carried with him into the future a copy of the Bible that Constance had given him.

Egeløkke in perspective

With new knowledge from his experiences of the opposite sex and of teaching Grundtvig left Egeløkke having learned the hard way that feeling and reason must live side by side. A useful by-product came with the insight that one's own emotions are often the result of a close bond with another person. He arrived back in Copenhagen in April 1808, where he was able to establish contact with four young men like himself whose friendship would accompany him through the coming years. Moreover, he was now reflecting on Steffens' lectures 8 years previously and concluding that the sense perceptions which can only be expressed in poetry are anchored in God's love and eternal life, a crucial perception on which he would build in the future.

Alongside these insights had been the practical experience of mixing with the nobility – a steady job, board and lodging, a domestic set-up based on the family, and literary discussions with Constance and the reading circle – not to mention a visit in 1807 from his friend, Peter Skougaard, who encouraged him to pursue his Icelandic interests. One other visit was also a transformative experience for him. In August that year the English were threatening to bombard Copenhagen in order to dissuade the Danes from siding with Napoleon; there was high drama on Langeland when the Danish army marched across the island on their way from South Jutland to Copenhagen. First Lieutenant Peter

---

67. Ch. 6 in *TCOL*.

24. The British bombardment of Copenhagen 1807.
Painting by Christoffer (C.W.) Eckersberg (1783-1853), SMK, National Gallery of Denmark. Fearing that the Danes would side with Napoleon, the British rejected the Danish claim to neutrality. In the indiscriminate rocket attack on the city, the first ever on a European capital, hundreds were killed and more than a thousand buildings destroyed, including Copenhagen Cathedral. Crown Prince Frederik of Denmark accepted an armistice after the Danes had lost 15 warships and the British none. The British then sailed 15 Danish battleships, 15 frigates and 30 brigs and gunboats off to England. Despite his fondness for England, Grundtvig stood by his country, saying it was an action in which "Denmark gained more honour than England, indeed gained all the honour, while England has gained all the shame."

Willemoes was quartered at nearby Tranekær Manor, the home of the commanding officer on Langeland, Count Frederik Ahlefeldt-Laurvig. Constance, Carl junior, and Grundtvig, now an army chaplain, had all moved to the greater safety offered by the castle, and as the army passed through, they made the acquaintance of its First Lieutenant, who was briefly quartered at the castle. This was the same Peter Willemoes who had fought Lord Nelson 6 years previously with great credit to his reputation. Constance was starstruck, as indeed was Grundtvig: the charming Willemoes was the first commoner hero in Denmark, a man who left an indelible impression upon all who met him. Nevertheless, the Danes could not prevent the horrific British rocket bombardment of Copenhagen in early September which destroyed the cathedral tower and half of the city. Of particular sadness to Grundtvig was the loss of the cathedral's carillon, or 'Song-Work' as it was known, which used to play out across the city. He lamented the destruction and wrote the poem 'Looking Back at Copenhagen' beginning with, "Pitiful, there you must stand,/... sick and dismembered."[68]

The later untimely death of Willemoes in action, killed by an English cannon-shot in 1808 moved Grundtvig to write a poem for his gravestone and two memorable songs. 'The ships engaged on the sea at dusk' commemorates the heroes of the battle, while 'Gather round, you maidens spry' celebrates Willemoes himself.[69] The latter was published in 1810, set to music by Christoph Weyse in 1837, and is still a popular song in the *People's High School Songbook*.

Intoxication with the gods

Grundtvig was not alone among European academics in seeking to rehabilitate the ancient gods, a movement that culminated artistically in Wagner's Ring Cycle. But as Flemming Lundgreen-Nielsen points out, Grundtvig was alone in trying to link the *pre*-Christian to the Christian.

Grundtvig's biographers agree that the period beginning here is aptly called his "intoxication with the gods" (*asarus*, lit. 'god-drunkenness'). The paradox of new horizons opening on the background of unrequited love is captured in 'To my friend, Poul Dons', 1808:

> Opened to me is the great Nordic past,
> joyful between gods and giants I flow;
> yet is my overbrimmed heart still aghast,
> those who have loved, ah, they alone know:
> Love's searing pain can be muffled, not muted,
> deadened the heartache, but never uprooted.

In his own mind Grundtvig had turned his unrequited love to his advantage. It inspired him to produce half a dozen works laying down tracks that he would later pursue, including his first version of *Nordic Mythology 1808*, later superseded by his masterpiece *Nordic Mythology 1832*.

Grundtvig's most resounding romantic expression of his Egeløkke experience is the poem, 'Hill by the Beach at Egeløkke',[70] which he started in 1807 but did not finish in its final form until 1811, by which time he had reverted to his childhood Lutheran faith. It begins as a poem about Nature, but soon turns to gratitude to God for the pain from which the poet has learned, a just chastisement:

> You, though, who build up on high,
> over the stars in Your art,

---

68. No. 118 in *LW*.
69. Nos. 98 and 99 in *LW*.
70. No. 150 in *LW*.

> honour and praise be all Yours!
> Thank You for wounding my heart,
> Thank You for sending me pain,
> Thank You for making me wise!

Now that his gaze has been opened by the Spirit, he can turn to poetry, to philosophy, to mythology and history, for the search has ended most surely in the Bible. He:

> looked for a Saviour and found
> falling to prayer,
> God everywhere:
> Found him in the poet's song
> found him in the wise man's rhyme,
> found him mid the Nordic throng
> of myths that span the tracks of time.
> Clearest, surest, though, of all,
> found him in the Book of Books.

His Danish biographer Hal Koch distils the essence of Grundtvig's great drama at Egeløkke as

> ... the love that said yes to life in all its dominion and all its horror, even when tossed about on stormy seas amid roaring waves with no sight of land. On such terms do we dare to, are we willing to, say yes to life, to *accept* it? ... The drama lay in the fact that his meeting with Lady Constance had awakened the very *life-force* in him, a power stronger than the glow of falling in love. He sensed that within him were forces he had not felt before, splitting his conventional existence asunder. Love is a spark of the very flame of existence, lying in wait and pointing towards eternity.[71]

---

71. (Koch 1944, 39-40, EB's translation).

Maskeradeballet i Dannemark

1808.

Et Syn

af

Nik. Fred. Sev. Grundtvig,
Kandidat i Teologien.

Kjøbenhavn, 1808.
Sælges hos Hofboghandler J. H. Schubothe.
Trykt hos Andreas Seidelin.

25. *The Masked Ball in Denmark. A Vision* 1808.
The title-page of Grundtvig's first publication, with his three Christian names abbreviated, followed by his title, MA Theology/*Kandidat i Teologien*.

6. Are you yourself a Christian?
(1808-11)

Around 15th April 1808 Grundtvig left Egeløkke and Constance behind him and moved back to Copenhagen. Six weeks later, with the help of Professor Nyerup, who had assisted him with material from the university library and had the right of nomination to the residence, Grundtvig was boarded, free of charge, at Valkendorf's Hall of Residence – at last among his own kind! Here there were young university-trained men with cultural ambitions and contacts to professors, writers, opinion-makers, and in some cases, their wives. In the course of the next three years Grundtvig put his painful romantic experience at Egeløkke to good literary use, but he was increasingly dogged by the question, Are you yourself a Christian? In 1810 he answered it positively and suffered a mental breakdown in the process.

With the publication of *Nordic Mythology* in 1808 Grundtvig began to be taken seriously as a writer, especially as a poet rather than as a literary critic. He was gradually accepted as an unmistakable, and indeed unavoidable voice, but he was argumentative in the extreme. He was admitted into literary circles but not for long, let alone lecture halls, or university auditoria. Second, he became a high school teacher at the Schouboe Institute – standing in front of a class of intelligent 16 to 17-year-old boys for the first time at the age of 25. And, as with little Carl Steensen-Leth, he took the job very seriously. Third, his newly-discovered emotional awareness found a response in the acquisition of new friends, the like of which he had never experienced before. Their influence on him will be described in greater detail below. Suffice to say here that he was *conscious* of their friendship and support, and he began to exchange both his ideas and personal experiences with them, to which the letters below bear witness. Grundtvig nevertheless found it difficult to sustain any friendship without testing it, mainly through argument – and he regularly took his friends to task for misunderstanding or misinterpreting him. Last but not least, his forefathers now 'caught up' with him, in the sense that he realised with a shock that he was not being as loyal to the pastoral calling he was destined to follow as he was to his poetry and his friends.

Our best sources for Grundtvig's life in the period 1808-11 are his published works from the time, and the public controversies in which he was involved. He no longer wrote a diary, and since he was living among new-found friends he wrote fewer letters. Those to and from his parents are of great importance (Letters 2, 3 and 4), while from his 'Within Living Memory' talks in 1838 we have his evaluation of his time at Valkendorf's Hall of Residence.

Early publications

While on Langeland Grundtvig did a stocktaking of his library, listing 106 books.[72] He added to this number with his own very first independent publication on 15th March 1808. *The Masked Ball in Denmark. A Vision* is a minor work, no more than a 21-page pamphlet in prose and poetry, attacking his countrymen's lack of concern over the British navy's fire-bombing of the capital city six months earlier and the subsequent confiscation of the entire Danish navy. While Rome burned, its citizens were dancing the night away, he wrote. More specifically, the popular masked ball at Christmas 1807 in Tranekær Manor on Langeland had raised Grundtvig's ire at the country's broken spirit and inclination to frivolity. Early in the book "the floor shook under the dancers", but at the end when Old Denmark dies, "the dancers fall lifeless to the floor." The dramatic tableau ends with Old Denmark's funeral pyre in the nation's hall under the signs of Christ's cross and Thor's hammer. The choir sing:

> High Odin, White Christ!
> Settled is your former clash,
> both are sons of the All-Father!
> With our cross and sword afire,
> here we consecrate your pyre:
> Both of you have loved our Father.[73]

Grundtvig's vision of Denmark's spiritual downfall was fulfilled physically with the state bankruptcy of 1813 and the loss the following year of the twin kingdom of Norway after 278 years under one Danish-Norwegian king. It was on these ruins that he determined to build a new and better Denmark – this time on a Christian foundation. He nevertheless came to realise that the comparison between Odin and Christ was inappropriate. In the light of his decision in 1811 that he *was* a Christian, he admitted in his revised version of *The Masked Ball* in *Little Poems* (1815) that he should never have juxtaposed the two or sought "wisdom outside Christ".

However, this later retraction did not affect his wholehearted acceptance of the Viking/Nordic mythology as a predecessor of the Christian faith, for it contained both sublime poetry and deep human truths, and thus the purest understanding of the eternal life that lay, in his phrase, "beyond the sea". This is already apparent in his Egeløkke diaries and in the letter to his friend Christian Molbech in 1808 (Letter 1). Even before Egeløkke, Grundtvig had taught himself rudimentary Old Icelandic, enough to read the body of Icelandic literature dated to 800-1000 CE. Following his *Brief Thoughts on the Edda* (1806) and *On Nordic Mythology* (1807) in December 1808 he published his first major work, *Nordic Mythology 1808*.

The core argument in the book is that Nordic mythology *surpasses* Greek mythology,

---

72. (Toldberg, 28)
73. No. III in *LW*.

not least in the inner coherence of its narrative, albeit with many digressions and complications. In brief, the All-Father (Energy) does battle with the self-created powers (Mass), led by the giants *(jætter)*. They are attempting to lure the All-Father's special creatures, the gods *(æsir)*, led by the cunning Loki, into a conspiracy to seize power. Only with the help of divine female wisdom *(the Norns)* are the gods freed. Though Loki falls, the gods fight on against both the All-Father and the giants in a battle so intense that at its culmination *(Ragnarok)* all perish. In the final stanzas "the earth rises up from the sea and is green and beautiful" – a new world is born.

The moral of the story is that any and every self-assumed life must disappear, before all things can be filled with eternal life – granted by the All-Father. Grundtvig saw this as representing the purest concept of the battle between good and evil, and of a perfect harmony – even before the coming of Christ. He eschewed any Greek idea that the gods 'rule over' certain areas of human life, nor was he interested in reworking the individual source-materials; his goal was a symbolic unity that he himself constructed.

During the period 1806-10 Grundtvig could not see that just as there was no practical solution to his passion for Constance, nor was there any ultimate salvation in living in the world of Nordic mythology. His "intoxication with the gods" would not result in any immediate practical solution – only in more books. His one consolation was his discovery in the *Edda* that the All-Father had made woman *superior* to man in her power and purity. In his diary for 12th June 1807 he wrote, "Everything is the work of the Norns," and later that year, "I am peculiar in believing that man belongs with the moon and woman with the sun", as though he wished to say that it was the woman who, as the higher being, shone her rays on the man and made him radiant. Wisdom lay with the Norns!

Nordic Mythology 1808 had a mixed reception. Grundtvig was commended for his poetic talent and his appreciation of the pre-Christian wisdom embedded in the myths; but he was criticised for the vagueness of his theology, his odd interpretation of the source material, and the inconsistency of his blank verse. Undaunted, he ploughed on, publishing *Scenes from the Death of the Giants' Life in the North* in 1809, in which he depicted the legendary heathen hero Palnatoke's conflict with the first Christian king of Denmark, Harald Bluetooth (d. 986). Grundtvig's heart is with Palnatoke, but his head is with the Christian priest, Odinkar, who enjoys the ultimate victory.

Grundtvig's homespun word 'Scenes' *(optrin)* constitutes a problem in his presentation of the Nordic myths. There is neither dramatic tension nor character insight in any of his figures; they merely speak Grundtvig's thoughts on life and death, truth, and falsehood, light and dark etc. in static tableaux with no sense of action or plot. Both these first books proved to be artistic and publishing failures, but as a spiritual Nordic bedrock Grundtvig was forming the adage that he later came to be known by: "Human comes first and Christian next".

Four new friends

When Grundtvig left Langeland for Valkendorf's Hall of Residence in Copenhagen in 1808 he was for the first time open to other adult friendships. Over the next few years

26. Valkendorf's Hall of Residence.
Originally a monastery, the hall was founded in 1589 by Christoffer Valkendorf (1525-1601), a Danish statesman and landowner.
Source: *Et Mindeskrift i anledning af Hundredeaarsdagen*, 1883

he was fortunate enough to meet four other young men with whom he could interact in both oral and written conversation: Poul Dons, Christian Molbech, Frederik Sibbern, and Svend Hersleb. All four were born within three years of Grundtvig, and all had been influenced by the new romantic wave from Germany, introduced by Henrik Steffens in his famous lecture series in 1802-03.

Poul Dons, 1783-1843

Grundtvig's son-in law and curate, Peter Boisen, died in 1861. He had been married to Grundtvig's daughter Meta since 1847 and had become Grundtvig's curate at Vartov in 1854. His successor was the 25-year-old Kristian Köster (1836-71), a deep admirer and faithful servant until his premature death – the year before Grundtvig's. He it was who collected material on Grundtvig and Dons for a portrait that was published in 1875.

Poul Dons was born in the Danish West Indies, where his father was stationed. He arrived in Copenhagen in 1799, but, unlike Grundtvig, he was immediately overwhelmed by Henrik Steffens' lectures on Romantic philosophy. So far, Grundtvig's publications had been received in silence, but Dons sent him his first response, a poem lamenting such a negative view of Denmark. Grundtvig later wrote in gratitude that his debut would indeed

27. Poul Dons.
Artist unknown. Royal Danish Library.

have been a miserable failure, "... were it not that a young man of Christian faith – with a heartfelt love of all goodness and ancient Denmark but with less acquaintance with the wretchedness and deep corruption of the times – had found my view too bleak and wrote this in verse to me."

In their younger years Dons and the next friend listed, Christian Molbech, were good friends, but they fell out over Steffens' lectures. Where Dons was passionately influenced by Steffens, Molbech turned instead to Rousseau, so their ways gradually parted. It was in Dons' home that Grundtvig first met the poet and hymnwriter Bernhard Ingemann, a man of equal poetic sensitivity to Dons. When Ingemann experienced religious misgivings in 1811-13 it was Dons who helped him through the crisis. Dons was already a supporter of, and a support for, Grundtvig. When Grundtvig was out of town, Dons kept him informed about life in Copenhagen; he procured books for him, and dealt with his publishers. On one occasion, in 1813, he even ventured to criticise Grundtvig's spidery script: "... your poor handwriting deserves such reproach that I shall overlook it here so as not to hurt you overly; but please make it *better* in future!" Dons was a sensitive man who tried in vain to soften Grundtvig's attitude to the poet Adam Oehlenschläger, to his friend, Christian Molbech, and to the later Bishop of Zealand, Jakob Mynster.

With his nerves and concentration affected, Dons had to give up his job with the Widows Pension Fund in 1821 and retire to West Zealand, where he died, a weakened man, in 1843, still loyal to Grundtvig, as two late letters testify. Dons' family traced his weak nerves to Grundtvig's crisis in 1810, when Dons witnessed Grundtvig's own mental breakdown. Nor is there any evidence in Grundtvig's two existent letters to Dons of his reciprocal care for his friend; in both of them Grundtvig writes mainly about himself (Letter 8). Grundtvig reserved his care for Dons to his *writings*. He wrote several birthday poems to him, and dedicated a poem to him in 1811 with thanks for his help during his breakdown. In 1813, in his pastoral role, Grundtvig even presided when Dons married his wife, Henriette. The two centrally-placed stanzas in Grundtvig's memorial poem, 'Poul Dons' (1843) come as close as possible to the truth about his friendship:

> All was seeing, all was hearing
> all that life he echoed best,
> all to which he looked and listened,
> all of that rang in his breast.
> He stood by us in our starkness,
> in his sunshine and my darkness –
> close to Ingemann and me!
>
> Then convulsed and blown to pieces,
> seared by fire and overstrung,
> burning as though self-ignited,
> tottering as though half-drunk.
> Tired his eyes from endless twinkling,
> none could help, and without winking
> eyes were glazed, his fire was quenched.[74]

Christian Molbech, 1783-1857

Grundtvig's relation to Christian Molbech through their letters and poems is the subject of another book, collected by Molbech's son and published by Grundtvig's biographer, Ludvig Schrøder, in 1888. Molbech was born exactly a month after Grundtvig. He graduated from Sorø Academy in 1802, and two years later joined the staff of the Royal Danish Library, where he rose to the position of Chief Librarian in 1823. With no formal training

---

74. No. 144 in *LW*.

28. Christian Molbech.
Drawing by A. Jensen, 1920.

he became a historian, reaching a career peak in 1839 by helping to found the Danish Historical Society and the *Danish History Journal* (*Historisk Tidsskrift*). Already in 1829 he had become Professor of Literature at the University of Copenhagen, while in 1830 he was also made Director of the Royal Danish Theatre (1830-42). His prodigious talent and work ethic resulted in *The Danish Dictionary* (*Dansk Ordbog* 1828-33) and the *Danish Dialect Dictionary* (*Dansk Dialektleksikon* 1833-41). He wrote a pioneer work, *Historical Annals for Enlightenment and Education in the History of the North, specifically the History of Denmark* (3 volumes, 1845-51), which established the chronology of Danish history. As a literary critic he is remembered for his savage reviews of the works of Hans Christian Andersen and of Grundtvig's friend, Bernhard Ingemann. As a teacher of literature he counted Søren Kierkegaard among his students in 1836.

When they met in 1808, Molbech and Grundtvig were both fully-fledged Romantics and had shared the experience of unrequited love. Grundtvig immediately confided his passion for Constance to his new friend (Letter 1). The two also shared a love of vernacular Danish, which Grundtvig demonstrated in his designation of his country nurse as his "language mistress", and which was fully evident in Molbech's *Danish Dialect Dictionary* (1841). They were also in total agreement about the state of the nation. As Molbech put it, "Denmark still stands... and the old, proud power of the Northerners is not completely

29. The megalith in Gunderslev Wood.
A.P. Madsen, 1862.

dead; it is only slumbering. It may slumber a little longer, but as long as it is not dead, it can still be awakened!"[75]

Their most memorable experience together was the walking-trip to Gunderslev Wood on 26th August 1808. Grundtvig was on tenterhooks as he approached the megalith – the 'altar-stone' where he assumed the Vikings had worshipped. Molbech took a more sober approach: "It was such a lovely summer morning on 26 August when my friend Grundtvig and I left Sorø Academy to look for the place where the tradition had created desire and expectation in equal measure." After the trip Grundtvig wrote his lengthy passionate poem, 'Gunderslev Wood',[76] whereas Molbech wrote about the beauty of nature in the wood.

When Grundtvig suffered his mental breakdown in 1810, Molbech supported him, without quite understanding its religious origins: "I wish with all of my heart that you soon recover your full powers, with peace in your soul, and that a joyful hope will soon be active in your life."[77] But when Grundtvig resolved his crisis by turning back to his childhood Lutheran faith, he himself knew that a break with Molbech was sooner or later inevitable: "I shall probably never agree with anyone on the nature of my sufferings, and

---

75. (MOLBECH, 10).
76. No. 112 in *LW*.
77. (MOLBECH, 56).

least of all with you, who do not believe that any Devil exists."[78] Both agreed that their friendship was more one of the spirit than of the heart.

Their differences came to a head when Grundtvig published his *World History 1812*, a theodicy with a foreword claiming "the cohesion of all times with Christ at their centre". The German philosophers and other rationalists were misguided, wrote Grundtvig. Molbech and other enlightened Christians of the time could accept that the Bible contained the highest ideals, but they took exception to the miracles and supernatural events, preferring to get to the core of Jesus' teaching. They found Grundtvig overbearing in his endless condemnation of others.

Although their relationship cooled, it was not put on ice. They exchanged letters sporadically, and Molbech even invited Grundtvig to tea in the 1830s. But a single episode illustrates the breach, and it concerns Constance. When Grundtvig was at his lowest ebb, Molbech wrote to Constance with the suggestion that it would be good for Grundtvig if the two friends visited her. Constance, knowing of Grundtvig's illness, rejected the idea. Then in July 1813 Molbech arrived unannounced at Egeløkke, allegedly on a visit elsewhere on Langeland. Constance gave him the cold shoulder. She still thought kindly of Grundtvig and was shaken by the arrogance of his former friend.

Nevertheless, Grundtvig and Molbech were still writing letters to each other in the 1830s, including this from 1837:

> If you could be prevailed upon to make the long trip from Christianshavn to come to tea with my wife tomorrow (Sunday) evening at 7.30 and spend two or three hours with us, it would greatly please
> Your old friend
> C. Molbech

∽

Frederik Sibbern, 1785-1872

From his arrival in May 1808 to his departure in December 1810 Grundtvig shared the same room with Frederik Sibbern at Valkendorf's Hall of Residence. Sibbern lived there from 1806-11. He was a brilliant scholar, winning 3 gold medals for the annual prize at Copenhagen University. He read Philosophy and Poetry but finally graduated in Law in 1810. Following a study-trip to Germany in 1811, he became Professor of Philosophy in 1813, retaining the title for the next 57 years. Sibbern introduced Grundtvig both to the academic elite of Copenhagen – including the talented Ørsted brothers, the scientist Hans (H.C.) Ørsted (1777-1851) and the lawyer and politician Anders Ørsted (1778-1860) – and to the literary stronghold where Professor Knud Rahbek and his equally powerful wife Kamma Rahbek held court for the writers, opinion-makers, and scientists of the time.

Like Molbech, Sibbern had put behind him an unfulfilled passion for a married woman, none other than Anders Ørsted's wife, Sophie, who also happened to be the sister of

---

78. (Ibid., 64-65).

30. Frederik Sibbern.
Portrait by Christen Købke, 1833.
SMK, National Gallery of Denmark.

the famous Romantic poet, Adam Oehlenschläger. Sibbern was a decided Christian, enamoured like Grundtvig with literary Romanticism and German philosophy. But both turned away from the German idealists and worked in a specifically Danish tradition of phenomenological life-philosophy, Sibbern with a psychological, and Grundtvig with a historical-poetic, orientation. The two friends planned to publish a journal together on philosophy, poetry, and history, with Sibbern in charge of the first subject and Grundtvig of the other two. The projected title, *Odin and Saga*,[79] was Grundtvig's idea. In February 1810 they sent out a prospectus, but were sorely disappointed when only 39 people responded positively and they had to shelve the plan.

It was Sibbern who accompanied Grundtvig home on the fateful trip in December 1810 during his mental breakdown. Sibbern not only shared a room with Grundtvig, he also shared the frightening experience that followed. Recovering in his childhood home in Udby, Grundtvig thanked him profusely for his kindness (Letter 5), but their ways were soon to part. Before Sibbern left for Germany in 1811, Grundtvig wrote him a farewell poem, including the lines:

---

79. In Grundtvig's usage of Nordic mythology Saga is the goddess of history.

We pondered both the cause of life's confusion,
but never reached a mutual conclusion:
we two had such a different path in mind.
So when we left the capital behind,
you longed to see a distant foreign throng,
while I turned homeward, where I now belong.[80]

Sibbern for his part moved on to a most successful 'philosophy-trip' in Germany, meeting Fichte, Schleiermacher, Hegel, and Schelling as well as Germany's greatest poet, Goethe himself.

Although the friendship ebbed away, they followed each other's career from a distance. Like Molbech, Sibbern had Kierkegaard as his pupil in philosophy. He also enjoyed considerable success as a writer, including a tribute in 1826 to Sophie Ørsted, the lady for whom he had once conceived an unrequited passion. He followed this with *From Gabriel's Letters to and from Home*, which is considered a major work of Danish Romanticism. He even wrote a utopian novel, *Statements concerning the Contents of a Writing from 2135*, in which the right to private property no longer exists and religion has become no more than theoretical moral teaching.

∼

Svend Hersleb, 1784-1836

Among the friends that Grundtvig made at Valkendorf, he received the greatest practical help and solidarity from Svend Hersleb, who was 'inspector' at the hall during most of Grundtvig's residence. Hersleb lived there from 1805-10. Like Poul Dons and two of Grundtvig's heroes – the playwright Ludvig Holberg and the naval hero Peter Tordenskjold – Hersleb was from Norway.

Hersleb graduated in Theology at Copenhagen University in 1807, after which he taught at the Schouboe Institute in the capital. He was then appointed to the newly-established Oslo University in 1811, where together with Stener Stenersen he founded the Faculty of Theology. He was Professor of Theology in Oslo from 1814 until his death in 1836. In 1816 he helped to found the Norwegian Bible Society, and he was also elected to the Norwegian Parliament in 1827, serving a single term. In 1812 he made every effort to get Grundtvig to come and teach in Oslo (Letter 9).

Hersleb was by nature quiet and reticent, but he burned every bit as much as Grundtvig for Christianity and history, and it was on these two subjects that the two had their warmest conversations. When Grundtvig was out of town, it was Hersleb, like Dons, who kept him up to date; he also helped with the proof-reading of Grundtvig's publications, though he did not always agree with their content. He was critical of Grundtvig's *World History 1812*, for example. Nonetheless, when Hersleb left for Norway, he wrote to Grundtvig: "Thank you, my noble Danish, Christian friend, for every sign of friendship

---

80. (PS I, 324).

31. **Svend Hersleb.**
Lithograph by E. Bærentzen & Co., nd.

while we were together. Only God knows when we shall see each other again, but we shall always meet as friends."[81]

Through Hersleb Grundtvig also came into contact with two slightly older Norwegians who were teaching at Copenhagen University: Professor of Philosophy, Niels Treschow (1751-1833) and Professor of Greek, Georg Sverdrup (1770-1850). All three supported Grundtvig for a teaching appointment in History at Oslo University, newly-established in 1813, but much as he loved Norway and wanted the job Grundtvig had other commitments in Denmark. Moreover, his qualifications as a university History teacher were limited and his personality controversial.

Grundtvig's farewell to Hersleb took a major turn, when in 1814, as part of the Kiel Congress peace plan, Denmark was forced to cede Norway to Sweden and then had to stand by as the Norwegians declared independence and adopted their own constitution. Hersleb, a Norwegian, supported the move; Grundtvig, a Dane, was against it (Letter 12). Despite their differences, Hersleb later admitted how much he missed Grundtvig – and he even offered him financial support.[82] His letters from 1815-16 reveal how indebted he was

---

81. (BFOTG I, 177).
82. (Ibid., 379).

to Grundtvig for the theological views he was teaching at the new faculty in Oslo. Long before the Danish pastors, Norwegian pastors were familiar with Grundtvig's theology. The correspondence declined gradually and ended in 1825, when Hersleb took exception to Grundtvig's new view of the Bible as subservient to the preceding oral Christian tradition. Nonetheless, in honour of his friend, Grundtvig baptised his second son "Svend Hersleb Grundtvig". and had long ago written a loving poetic eulogy, 'To Hersleb' (1810), recalling his friend and hoping to meet him again on the other side:

> Perhaps alone from a beloved woman
> can bliss untainted fall within our fate,
> perhaps on earth we never find the one
> who matches our desire for *the* soul mate,
> but what I know and what I celebrate:
> I never found so many winning traits
> in any man, beloved friend, as you![83]

The value to Grundtvig of these and other friends lay both in their physical presence at Valkendorf's Hall of Residence and in their intellectual responses to his views. Grundtvig had retained no friends from his childhood or his schooldays – and only Peter Skougaard from his time at university. His emotional collision with Constance and her rejection of his covert advances had shaken him. He was now alone in Copenhagen, surrounded by male equals who took him for who he was – a somewhat cantankerous but always enlivening presence. He remembered the years 1808-10 as "two of the happiest and proudest, most active and instructive years of my life".[84]

The real world came even closer when he became a classroom teacher.

The Schouboe Institute

Just over 6 months after returning to Copenhagen, Grundtvig was appointed teacher of History and Geography at the Schouboe Institute, a prestigious high school for boys in the heart of Copenhagen.[85] His new friend at Valkendorf's Hall of Residence, Svend Hersleb, already taught Greek at the school. Grundtvig was attracted by the salary, and, despite his own high school experience, by the opportunity to put his knowledge of history into practice. From around 1st November 1808 until March 1811 Grundtvig was a practising teacher – his second experience as such.

The Schouboe Institute had been opened in 1794 by Frederik Schouboe (1766-1829). It rapidly gained a good reputation, but it nevertheless had to close in 1814 as a result of falling numbers. In the years that Grundtvig taught at the school, educational reform of the entire Danish school system was in the air, culminating in the Education Act of 1814.

---

83. (PS I, 176).
84. (MM, 327).
85. Present-day Niels Hemmingsens Gade 24.

Skoleåret 1808–09

	Mandag	Tirsdag	Onsdag	Torsdag	Fredag	Lørdag
kl. 11–12		Hist. 3. kl.		Hist. 3. kl.	Hist. 3. kl.	
kl. 12–13		Hist. 4. kl.		Hist. 4. kl.		Hist. 4. kl.
kl. 15–16			Geogr. 4. kl.		Geogr. 4. kl.	
kl. 16–17	Hist. 5. kl.	Geogr. 5. kl.	Hist. 5. kl.	Geogr. 5. kl.	Hist. 5. kl.	

13 ugentlige timer.

Skoleåret 1809–10

	Mandag	Tirsdag	Onsdag	Torsdag	Fredag	Lørdag
kl. 11–12						
kl. 12–13						
kl. 15–16	Hist. 4. kl.	Geogr. 4. kl.	Hist. 4. kl.	Geogr. 4. kl.	Hist. 4. kl.	
kl. 16–17	Hist. 5. kl.	Geogr. 5. kl.	Hist. 5. kl.	Geogr. 5. kl.	Hist. 5. kl.	

10 ugentlige timer.

32. **Grundtvig's timetables at the Schouboe Institute, 1808-10.**
Grundtvig's timetable for his final school year 1810-11 is unknown, but there is a clear improvement in the placing of his teaching hours from the first to his second year. He taught far more History than Geography. One of his classes consisted of 13 boys aged 16-18. In Denmark, school on Saturday did not end until 1970.

As before, Grundtvig took his teaching responsibilities very seriously. He chose as his watchword for his pupils: "Pursue God and Learning alone", and even before he began, he had written a programme of his aims in history. These he read out to his very first class:

> We shall keep an eye on the examinations, but our true goal is somewhat higher. We shall attempt through history to make a closer acquaintance with the family whose members we are, and with the whole human family. We shall learn to kneel in the dust for the wisdom of the Eternal God, who has led our people through prosperity and adversity, through light and darkness, to a knowledge of Him and of true happiness.[86]

He followed this with a warning:

> It grieves me that I cannot end here. It grieves me very much that I might have to consider the possibility that some of you will work against me rather than for me, and that some of you, through laziness, inattention, or childish irresponsibility may attempt to disturb or interrupt the steady flow of my teaching – or may embitter me in the lessons I devote to you, and waste the happiness that I consider to be the highest reward for my endeavour.

---

86. (Rønning II, 96).

We note here that as a teacher Grundtvig wished not only to give the class a love of history, but also to save their souls. To this end he also wrote poems about his teaching life, and gave hand-written copies to individual pupils: "To Sporon, as a testimony of my satisfaction and the grand hopes I place in him. May he never disappoint them." Or to Peder Møller: "To Møller, the school's best student, as a sign of my total satisfaction. G". In the spring of 1811, as he was about to leave the school, Grundtvig wrote 'Farewell to my Pupils' – and gave a copy to young Poul Sporon:

> Dear young friends, now listen to my words!
> on your hearts this farewell speech emboss:
> Turn away from this world's vale of tears
> to the Holy One upon the cross!
> There alone the soul's true health is found.[87]

Before they met him, his students had thought that they could play around with him, but Grundtvig mastered the class with his penetrating look alone. One of them, Christian Bødtker (1794-1874), recalled in 1858 with what vitality Grundtvig had related the story of Leonidas's bravery at the Battle of Thermopylae. Despite its widespread use, no corporal punishment was needed in Grundtvig's classes. Bødtker also remembered how Grundtvig would pace up and down the classroom, and once when he heard beatings and screams from the class next door, he could not contain the outburst, "Those tyrants!"

Grundtvig's teaching experiences have been underemphasised in many previous books. His 3 years with young Carl on Langeland, and his 2½ years with teenage high school boys were a major influence on his later life and educational ideas. In both cases, despite his penchant for solitary reading and writing, he was forced to turn outwards, to think of others, and to see the exciting effects of his teaching, as he watched the boys grow in stature and knowledge. He was now in the real hustle and bustle of preparing and teaching lessons, yet still planning to make his name as a writer. Much later, Grundtvig's teaching experience of history when he was aged 25-27 stood him in good stead when he came to address larger audiences, aged 55-56, in his famous lecture series, *Within Living Memory* in 1838.[88]

Personal ambition or filial duty

In response to a letter from Christian Molbech Grundtvig wrote on 13th June 1809:

> You are right to be surprised to have had nothing from one who otherwise loves to write letters; but it was not until Sunday that I more or less regained my senses after losing them for 10 days.[89]

---

87. No. 134 in *LW*.
88. *TCG*, 49-171.
89. (MOLBECH, 40).

Knud Eyvin Bugge notes that these are "the first symptoms of the breakdown that was to follow roughly a year and a half later".

The immediate cause of Grundtvig's nervous tension was his aging father's intimation in the spring of 1810 that he wanted his son back in Udby as his curate. Initially, with a writing plan and an unfulfilled literary ambition ahead of him, Grundtvig kept the thought at a distance (see Letter 2), but he nevertheless qualified himself on 17th March by preaching a 'dimissory' sermon before the university authority, Professor Peter Müller and a few others in an otherwise empty Regens Church. In answer to the sermon's title, 'Why has the Word of the Lord Disappeared from His Church?' Grundtvig let fly at the poor quality of Danish pastors: "The servants of the Lord ... think they can build a different and better foundation than the one that Jesus is Christ, so it is no longer Him whom they preach". This is Grundtvig in prophetic mode – yet it is also a theology student unsure of his *own* Christianity. He was rewarded with an honours mark from the professor.

All might have been well, had it ended there. But against convention Grundtvig *published* the sermon – on 14th May. It sold like hot cakes and was the talk of the town, but it caused much discomfort among a number of Copenhagen pastors, chief of whom was Archdeacon Frederik Plum. By 29th May he had collected enough signatures to send a formal complaint to the royal government over this young upstart and his "insulting accusations not against an individual but against the entire clergy". The sermon's very title was considered offensive.

In a letter to Professor Müller and the Faculty of Theology Grundtvig protested his innocence. His sermon was merely a call to arms. But when the government asked the university for a response, the faculty found itself in an awkward position; had not its examiner awarded *honours* to the brilliant student? It agreed to no more than a reprimand. The Bishop of Zealand thought otherwise: "The Danish clergy has the right to feel offended, indeed grossly insulted." To avoid a church scandal he nevertheless agreed to a "serious reprimand". The university's Academic Council summoned Grundtvig to an internal disciplinary case on 5th November, but Grundtvig was having none of it. He wrote an appeal to King Frederik VI himself, asking for a proper court case in which he could defend himself against these unjustified charges. On his government's advice the King rejected the complaint and ordered Grundtvig to appear before the Academic Council on 12th January 1811. A crestfallen Grundtvig feared that he might never be allowed to preach again. In a state of mental and spiritual turmoil – as a result not least of this whole sorry saga – he bowed his head, obeyed the King, and received a warning and reprimand from the university rector: "the publication of the sermon, the proclaiming of its contents in public, and the demand that the case be tried in court seem to reveal a conceited yearning to create a stir."[90]

In the midst of this minor crisis a major one blew up. Grundtvig's forefathers finally caught up with him. On 9th October 1810 he was sitting alone in his room reading *History of the Prussian Empire* by August Kotzebue (1761-1819). He had got no further than the 13th century, when he lost his temper at the description of how Prussia was christianised under "the withered cross":

---

90. (Nielsen 1889, 111).

I had shivers down my spine and not only did I throw the book down, I leapt up as though I had been seized by a mighty Spirit, calling me to be a Reformer... [There followed] a couple of months of proud but quiet passion during which I read the Bible in earnest for the first time since childhood – especially the prophets – as well as the hymns of Luther and Kingo.[91] I prayed and pondered over how a reformation, especially with pen and ink could be accomplished in our day and age.[92]

He added that he was "at once crushed by the questions: Are you yourself a Christian? Do you have forgiveness of sins?" He was debating within himself whether a people's relation to Christianity was a matter of life and death for its survival; was the real question *not* the relation between heathen mythology and Christianity but between *history in general* and Christianity. This thought was to occupy him for the rest of his life.

At this turning-point in his life he was writing both his last 'mythological' poem, *Idun, A New Year Present for 1811*, and his first Christian hymn. The former began with 'To My Dear Father, Johan Grundtvig', who celebrated his 50th anniversary as a pastor on 5th December 1810.[93] The second, his haunting Christmas hymn, 'Lovely is the midnight sky', closes with the following words appended: "The Lord's name be praised and His incomprehensible love be glorified." Taken together the two works represent Grundtvig's farewell to the past and his embrace of the present.

Mental breakdown

Grundtvig's relationship to his parents had become increasingly difficult – so much so that by 1810 he preferred not to spend much time at all with them and their old-fashioned orthodox Lutheran views. Much to their dismay, he had not yet *resolved* to become a Lutheran pastor – and Pastor Johan was now 75 years old. When the call came from his parents to return home and help his father, Grundtvig not only prevaricated, he even sought a pastorate in Præstø rather than Udby – a post he had no chance of getting. Or perhaps he could go to England?

Eventually, already in a state of nervous tension, Grundtvig decided to take the carriage home to Udby. Being his friends and seeing his condition Molbech, Dons, and Sibbern were worried. Sibbern described the beginnings of Grundtvig's mental breakdown thus:

> He stayed in bed in the morning in such a state that we sent for his uncle, Dr Bang. He declared that Grundtvig was not suffering from a physical illness, but was in an inner conflict for the salvation of his soul. I then undertook to drive down to his aging father, who was the pastor in Udby... In the evening when we came to Vindbyholt Inn, we decided to stay there until dawn the next day. We went to bed, but Grundtvig sat up and worked on his farewell poem to his students at the Schouboe Institute, while I fell asleep. But deep into

---

91. Thomas Kingo (1634-1703), Danish hymnwriter.
92. (*Church Mirror* 1871, 370 ff).
93. No. 128 in *LW*.

the night I woke up. Grundtvig was on his knees in a corner of the room praying with such a loud voice that it was like to waken the whole household. I tried to calm him down, but it took a long time. Finally, when it was light, we got a carriage and drove on to Udby. On the way Grundtvig told me that he had felt the Devil like a snake physically winding itself around his body. In Udby it rather surprised me that when I told his father about his son's condition, he was quick to compose himself. "My son has religious scruples (*anfægtelser*)." He knew what lay ahead.

It is a quite extraordinary gift that enabled Grundtvig all his life to turn his pain and pleasure into poetry charged with emotional energy:

> O Jesus, let a stream of tears
> from in my heart come teeming!
> O make me warm, O make me soft
> so out of me comes streaming
> the evil that still tortures me
> as I my distance keep from You
> and makes me Satan's servant.[94]

Grundtvig's mind was in turmoil, but he nevertheless could see through himself. On 17th February 1811, two months later he wrote to his friend Christian Molbech:

> The life I am leading is not exactly pleasant. God's chastisement has not yet ended, though I have some hope in my Saviour that God will soon forgive and grant me the strength to resist the Devil. What has further troubled me of late are the impure and blasphemous thoughts that continually pursue me and rise up inside me without my having the strength to push them away. I know you do not believe in the Devil's temptations, and I earnestly hope that you never have to be persuaded of them, for they are frightening![95]

While Grundtvig was recovering at home, his father had already sought and been granted his retirement – from 1st January 1811. He had been unable to retire before then because the pension he could receive would not pay off his considerable debts to left and right.

Grundtvig went back to Copenhagen to receive his reprimand, and returned again on 28th March to pass the required catechism exam. On the advice of the retired Bishop Balle, the new Bishop of Zealand, Frederik Münter, appointed Grundtvig on 3rd May to be curate at Udby. Together with another ordinand he sat and passed the bishop's written and oral exam on 24th May and was ordained in Trinity Church on 29th May 1811. As he wrote in the poem 'Farewell to my friend, F.C. Sibbern' in June 1811, attending pastors laid their right hands on his head and prayed for him, a moment and an act that changed him for ever:

---

94. (VU I, 303).
95. (MOLBECH, 58).

> Th' apostles at the Pentecostal Feast
> invested were with pow'r to testify,
> and in that week I too was thus ordained
> called as priest to serve the Lord on high.
> The gifts of grace are multitudinous,
> but all are by the self-same Spirit giv'n;
> when brothers touched my head with outstretched hands
> requesting that the Lord breathe life from heav'n –
> the Spirit's breath of love and pow'r and truth,
> in loving grace might thus on me descend –
> my prison-bonds were ruptured – and my fears;
> the wellsprings of my heart burst into tears.[96]

Just as the impetuous Grundtvig was saved from himself at Egeløkke through Constance's handling of his infatuation, so was he helped out of his nervous exhaustion by his friends' care and his parents' patience and understanding. It was as if he was coming home not just physically but also spiritually. He felt that this was truly his Christian awakening. As Anders Pontoppidan Thyssen writes:

> Grundtvig's new standpoint was his childhood Christianity, founded on the stories, pictures and 'myths' of the Bible, understood as literal truth. In full consciousness he broke with the intellectual and cultural orientation of his time, both the rational and the romantic. He gave up his own great plans and became his father's curate.[97]

This great turning-point in Grundtvig's life – the acceptance of God's grace and its revelation in His Son – changed his entire orientation. In the words of Hal Koch:

> Christ is now the centre of everything, of Christian life, of history, of poetry, of learning... [Grundtvig has] reached the edge of human existence, and with a prophet's authority he speaks of what he has seen and heard, for his visions are a dynamic and living reality.[98]

Grundtvig not only accepted his destiny, he embraced it – as a revivalist preacher and a priest who was learning by doing. In the two years that followed – until his father's death in 1813 – he took upon himself both his forefathers' legacy and the role and accompanying tasks of a country curate. With a genuine pride that he was a fifth generation priest, he now stood alongside his elder brother as Pastor Nikolai Frederik Severin Grundtvig.

---

96. (PS I, 326).
97. (Thyssen 1991, 20).
98. (Koch 1940, 199-201)

33. Grundtvig's and his father's pulpit in Udby Church.
The Latin inscription, NEC MINUERE NEC ADDERE translates as 'Deduct nothing, Add nothing'. Photo: Edward Broadbridge.

7. Fight! was my song
(1811-15)

Grundtvig's fight to achieve personal clarity was followed by a fight to be sure that he had received the faith and was indeed a Christian, and an active one at that. He was inducted into the parish of Udby and Ørslev by his elder brother, Pastor Otto Grundtvig, on 16th June 1811. Looking back on the event in his sermon for the 5th Sunday in Trinity 1833 he was overjoyed to have left "the nauseating capital" where he had been "chained to books" and to have arrived in Udby "under God's open heaven."

As assistant pastor, Grundtvig's curacy forced him to think of the many others in the parish beside himself. He could not write letters to them or books about them, he must preach and be among them. However proud and humbled he was to be a priest at long last, he was now a *servant* of the Lord, no longer free to come and go as he pleased. He had been set among 'the common people', whom he professed to have understood from his country childhood in both Zealand and Jutland. Up to this point his occasional preaching – in Udby and on Falster and Langeland – had been as much the work of an orator as of a caring pastor. Now he had to give his parishioners *sustenance*, not just from the pulpit but also beside the sick-bed in the cottage. He took Sunday services in the two churches, baptised, married and buried his parishioners; he taught and confirmed the youngsters of the parish; he went on house-visits when called upon; and he had the overall responsibility for both the local schooling and the relief of the poor in the parish.

This was all a result of a 'revival' of his childhood and family faith. He wrote in a letter to his friend Pastor Wilhelm Østrup, who had been a curate on Langeland when Grundtvig was at Egeløkke (Letter 6):

> I have more or less learned to humble myself under God's mighty hand, and when with the help of the Holy Spirit I have learned it fully, then I know He will raise me in His own good time.

As he came to terms with this reorientation of his life, Grundtvig kept close to his Bible, where he believed the Word of God was directly communicated to him. From his reading he obtained comfort and strength to face the task ahead – and at least occasionally when he opened his own copy, he must have thought of Constance, who had given it to him with her blessing (illus. p. 126). His primary aim now was no longer a revival of Nordic mythology but a revival of Nordic *Christianity*. For this the Bible was the lynchpin around which his world-view revolved. He saw himself as both the Old Testament prophet who initially rejected his God-given role, and the direct successor of the Christian reformer Martin Luther, with whom he closely identified.

With Grundtvig's first pastoral appointment came two benefits. One was being closer to his parents, from whom he had once distanced himself. Grundtvig now lived in a separate wing of the old home in Udby, from where his respect for his father grew with the new job. He was following not only in his father's but also in his *fore*fathers' footsteps – and indeed in his three elder brothers' footsteps. The second benefit was a regular income. This was enough for him to pluck up courage to send a marriage proposal to Lise Blicher – via her sister, Marie, that is. Satisfied with Marie's return letter announcing Lise's acceptance – and not a little satisfied with himself – Grundtvig talked to his parents and then wrote to brother Otto on 21st September 1811 (Letter 7):

> Our parents are pleased with my engagement, and God has so ordained it that it was very much in my thoughts eight years ago. It has been completely out of them many times since, but it kept coming back, and in the end it seemed that nothing was to come of it. I could tell you so much about how wonderful I think my choice is, but I am beyond the age when one thinks everyone else is overjoyed to hear the paeans of praise one sings to one's beloved. It is enough to know that you agree with me that she is a gentle girl.

He also received congratulations from Constance (Letter 8):

> I have received the news of your engagement with joy and sincere understanding; if you have indeed changed, as you write, then it will be a happy marriage.

Pastoral duties

By and large Grundtvig was welcomed into the parish, thanks to his father's reputation and his obvious need for an assistant. The young Grundtvig's revivalist sermons were accompanied by a number of Thomas Kingo's popular hymns from the old hymnbook of 1699, in which he featured with 85 out of 300 hymns. 'Kingo's Hymnbook' was much to the older parishioners' satisfaction, for he took the need for faith seriously. Sin and mercy, perdition and salvation, Jesus and the Devil, this was the stuff of Grundtvig's sermons. Faith *obliged* one to action, especially on behalf of the poor, and here too Grundtvig was trustworthy. One spring a farmhand had to ask Grundtvig senior for seed corn, because Grundtvig junior had given it all away to the poor during the winter. The son is reported to have said, "But father, what is it we *preach?*"[99]

Grundtvig's occasional house visits in particular left a deep impression on him. He described one such to Poul Dons in a letter dated 28th April 1812 (Letter 9):

> I have told you before that in my position I have many a hallowed joy. Yesterday I again experienced the most wonderful moment beside an old woman's deathbed. Oh how gratifying, how comforting it is for our eyes to see how powerful is the Word of God in driving away the bitterness of death! You should have seen how her tired eyes were transfigured when I pronounced the blessing over her that is beyond all comprehension; how weak, how almost speechless, she was to respond – but with a sign to let me understand how the

---

99. (Rønning II, 2, 9).

words poured into her heart and lit up her innermost eye with a glimpse of the glory of Eternity! Oh my friend! What are all the joys of the world compared to this! How dull is the image that even the spiritually animated poet calls forth of the excellence of faith and the radiance of Eternity compared to the moment that not only meets our gaze but also refreshes and radiates our heart.

As with Constance, real life was proving more powerful than the imagined reality of poetry, even though writing about an emotion afterwards could help to confirm and settle it in the memory. Grundtvig enjoyed a similar experience with his young confirmands, whom he endeavoured to root in the same form of orthodox Lutheran piety that he himself had finally embraced. For him, it was not enough to manage with Bishop Balle's book on the Catechism from 1791, or the *Evangelical-Christian Hymnbook* from 1798. His pupils had to borrow copies from the old people in the parish of Pontoppidan's *Exposition of Luther's Catechism* from 1737. Erik Pontoppidan (1698-1764) had chosen as the original title *Truth that Leads to Godliness*, taken from Titus 1:1. His 'exposition' consisted of some 750 numbered questions followed by correct answers, which were used to prepare candidates for Confirmation. In their lessons, from 9 am to 3 pm, candidates had to learn to sing by heart the core hymns from 'Kingo's Hymnbook'. After the hymn-singing came Grundtvig's prayers, followed by Grundtvig's story-telling, and then his examination of the pupils' knowledge of both the Bible and Luther's *Small Catechism*, followed by another hymn and a prayer. Grundtvig was a hard but deeply caring taskmaster; he was in the business of saving their souls, so nothing was too much trouble. He was later known to have fallen on his knees and prayed for his confirmands one after the other by name – with tears in his eyes.[100]

Among the other tasks that he took on as assistant pastor were the schooling conditions in the parish. Grundtvig's very first letter to a newspaper had been a complaint about the lack of schooling on Falster, where his brother was pastor.[101] Now he pleaded for funding for a teacher in Udby to replace the inadequate parish clerk, and for a new school in Ørslev. Church and school should work together, he argued, and on 3rd November 1811 he wrote to the county dean that as a "director of souls" Grundtvig too would one day have to render his account for the souls that had been entrusted to him:

> Immeasurable is the damage done, if for several years, or even just one year, children should forfeit the education for their salvation which is their due; this is a direct consequense of the lack of the necessary books and the teacher's wretched life. We can force them to go to school, but we cannot *make* them cast their sorrows aside and work with aspiration and a light mind.

Only 4 days later he received a positive response from the school's directors; apparently the poor farmers were willing to pay more, but the well-to-do were not. How the matter was resolved we do not know, but Grundtvig was on the children's side – for the sake of their salvation and the future of Denmark.

---

100. (Høyer-Christensen, 1935, 55).
101. (*Politivennen*, January 1804).

34. **A godly assembly in a farmhouse room.**
Drawing by Christen Dalsgaard, 1869.
Lars Pedersen at Sværup Mill. Especially on Langeland Lars Pedersen drew large crowds of up to 400-500 people in the open air. A contemporary witness wrote: "Lars Pedersen came forward and in plain man's language spoke of the sufferings and death of the Saviour. Such well-known things ... and yet it was quite different from in church!"

The 'godly assemblies' and the revivalist preacher

The 'godly assemblies' comprised gatherings of revivalist Christians, especially among the common people, from c. 1790-1840. They were highly critical of the established Lutheran church and held their own religious meetings, often with itinerant preachers.[102] In his theology and his focus on a 'revival' of faith in Jesus Christ as personal saviour, Grundtvig could be counted among the revivalist preachers at this point in his life. But although he spoke up for the movement's freedom to exist, he never wished to be counted its promoter. He had his own godly assembly in the church of his forefathers and was now enjoying the respect and positive expectation and response of his parishioners. He preferred to be among sinners like himself rather than in an assembly of devout pietists, and he believed that theologically-trained and apostolically-ordained pastors were better mediators of the Word of God than untrained lay preachers, however inspiring they might be.

Seven of Grundtvig's sermons have been preserved from his years in Udby, including his induction sermon on 16th June 1811. His text was Ephesians 4:10-16 on the Church as members of the body of Christ and himself as a shepherd to his flock. His appeal was highly emotional:

---

102. Text 2 in *HCF*.

> There are those present who have seen me baptised in this house of the Lord, and many who have seen me grow up in my father's home. Indeed you have called my father *your* father for so many years that you might regard me as your brother.
>
> Finally, if you see me being thoughtless as a result of my shortcomings, I beg that you neither imitate nor despise me, but recall what our merciful God also reminds us of, that we are mortal clay, and that I do not cease to be a weak and sinful person just because I am your companion.[103]

As was the case in Grundtvig's day, the pastor, and in particular the country pastor, was a learned person whose role carried great authority – however well or badly it was discharged.

Two guiding principles characterise Grundtvig's revivalist Christianity: trust in God's biblical Word and openness to the animating Holy Spirit. In the course of his first year at Udby he read the New Testament several times from start to finish, often a regular 3-4 chapters a day. He also worked hard on his Greek and his weaker Hebrew, for trained pastors should know the entire Bible in its original languages. Indeed, so rich did he make himself in knowledge of the Bible that he could summon up chapter and verse, whatever the subject. In an article on 'Idol Worship' from 1813 he wrote of his "blind faith in the Holy Scriptures according to their literal, word-for-word meaning". He judged everything by the Bible – and he loved to judge! However, he was also willing to be judged *by* the Bible, if others could prove him wrong. Time and again he emphasised that the Bible only activates people through their living appropriation of it – as he said on the 2nd Sunday in Advent 1813:

> We are born *by the side of* the Bible. It spoke to us when we were infants, before we could hold its words apart. It pronounced God's peace and blessing on us in Holy Baptism. It beckons and calls us every day, and if we open our ears and eyes and hearts to its glory and divine speech, then it is ours – ours with all its comfort, ours with the comfort that is overflowing to the hosts of people and tongues that none can count!

Newly converted and anxious for all the lost souls in his parish, indeed in the whole Church, Grundtvig could not free himself from the warning tone in these early sermons. Judgement will come, and woe betide those who have not lived up to their Christian duty – in particular the pastors of the realm! He called upon them all to take up the sword as "warriors of Jesus Christ". Just such a dramatic sermon roused his parishioners on All Souls Sunday 1812, and was later published under the title 'Why are we called Lutherans?' It began with a broadside verse against the head of the Roman Catholic Church:

> Listen now, Pope, while I here abide,
> I long but to be a thorn in your side;
> when I am dead, then are you no more!
> Thus declares Luther! Take heed therefore!

---

103. (Høyer-Christensen 1935, 47-48).

Luther is then praised for having translated the Bible from Hebrew and Greek to German, followed by dire warnings about God's anger which has found expression not just in the biblical Flood but also in the earthquake in Lisbon in 1755. The lengthy sermon comes to its crux in the following exhortation:

> Let us advance in the spirit of Luther, for that is *God's* spirit: let us strive manfully to pull down the fortresses that are raised up against the Word of God. With the sword of the Spirit – whose wondrous power to wound and heal we are sensible of – let us go in open warfare against all evil, against hypocrisy and sloth of the soul, against manifest infidelity! Let no human fear or earthly concern bind our tongues! Let no one dupe us into believing that our corruption is so little that we do not need to trumpet it forth! Do we not see how vice walks without shame? How lust swaggers round? How luxury saps our strength? Do we not hear how loudly piety and virtue are scorned? Do we not see the churches empty, the people cold, and the Bible in the dust?

This was typical of Grundtvig's Udby sermons – and of the revivalist preaching of the times. In her online introduction to the work Vanja Thaulow has noted almost 200 biblical references and allusions, and adds: "Here and there are long passages in his argument that are not much more than an accumulation of biblical quotations".[104]

Like many pastors before and since, Grundtvig believed that his sermons deserved a much wider audience than the Sunday morning congregation could give them, so already in November 1812 he published a prospectus for people to sign up for a collection of his sermons from an entire church year!

Publications and the literary scene

Despite being seriously busy with his pastoral work in Udby, Grundtvig had every intention of continuing to get his works into print. There were no takers for this latest prospectus and again the project was abandoned, but he nonetheless ploughed on publishing regardless: 11 works in 1811, 10 in 1812, 8 in 1813. Nor did he feel that he was serving two masters; in his own eyes he was priest *and* poet. The nation, its culture, its Christianity were all one – or at least *should* be. He also gladly sat in judgement on other writers and was irked when they did not appreciate his efforts to correct them. One such was the great poet, Adam Oehlenschläger, whose rebuff occasioned the following response from Grundtvig, dated 23rd June 1812:

> Believe you me, it has cost me many a hard struggle to expose myself to the anger of the very men whose friendship I wish to enjoy, but what use is that? I have my commission, and to that I must attend. Even if Heaven and Earth conjoined against me, and all others abandoned me, I would not be alone, since God is with me – provided I speak and practise His Word.

---

104. (GV).

7. FIGHT! WAS MY SONG (1811-15)

Perhaps even more disastrous was his attempt to befriend his step-cousin, Jakob Mynster, eight years his senior. Like Grundtvig he had recently had a 'breakthrough' experience, as he called it, but he had no wish to discuss this with his over-zealous cousin. He not only rejected Grundtvig's repeated requests, he indiscreetly let the correspondence circulate – and into the hands of the above-mentioned Kamma Rahbek, lady of letters and salonist. About Grundtvig she wrote the following to Molbech:

> I have stood by him and defended him for as long as I could live with myself, because I have sincerely had a good opinion of him and believed that he was hard done by. But from his letters to Mynster, which were not only insolent but also seemed to me rather stupid – and later from his *World History*, I have simply given up on him.[105]

Grundtvig had once been taken seriously on the literary scene, but his publications following his Christian revival – one might almost say 'conversion' – were not well received. He had come to the conclusion that history was the spiritual bearer of God's Truth, and that the Christian consciousness of all Danes therefore needed to be raised to understand this. All people had been made in His image, and despite the Fall, they had all retained a streak of that image. They needed to *know* that!

On 12th August 1811 he had begun work on a book provisionally titled, *A View of God's Housekeeping over Time, mostly with the Jewish People from the Bible and Other Books for the Use and Benefit of the Man in the Street in excerpts by Grundtvig*. The long-winded title did indeed include the Danish word *husholdning* (lit. 'householding'), which is an extraordinary image of God at work in His household. Needing to shorten the title he turned it into *A Brief View of World History in Context*. When the book was published, on 30th December 1812, its format alone was challenging: a poem of dedication to his patron, was followed by a lengthy foreword, and then the text itself. A quarter of this covered from the Creation to Luther, and a whole half covered from Luther to 1811. Most of the Danish monarchs were also covered, from Harald Bluetooth onwards. Last of all came page after page of corrections, to which Grundtvig added new annotations adding up to 13,500 words! This testifies to Grundtvig's eagerness to print, to his inability to cohere his thoughts, and to poor proof-reading. Grundtvig began his self-defence and his blame-sharing with the words:

> Despite the untiring diligence that my friends, Dons and Hersleb, have applied in searching through my crows' feet, a number of printing errors have crept in. This should neither surprise nor offend anyone.

The print-run of 450 copies was swiftly sold out, but such was the negative reaction, not least to the many errors, that the book remained out of print for almost a century. Grundtvig's message was otherwise simple: the whole of history is centred around the coming of Jesus Christ:

---

105. (Nielsen 1889, 166).

Human beings may act, but there is also an intervening God. This is my philosophy of history, and I wish it to be so for others. I stand by the great revolution of, and for, our species that was set in motion by the rise of Christianity. I see it involving itself in everything, shining forth in everything, like a mainspring that always works for the best, and for victory over all opposition from free people.

World history is a collaboration between God and humankind, a historical theodicy proving that "God works for the common good of those that love him".[106] Grundtvig's many critics considered the idea of God's deliberate intervention in history as backward-looking, and were especially offended by the book's concluding pages, which lambasted some of Grundtvig's contemporaries. To take one example, in 1783 Professor of English Thomas Bruun had published *My Leisure-hours or Tales from Boccaccio and Lafontaine*, a versified reproduction of some of the more lubricious tales of the two writers. Grundtvig pulled no punches:

Thomas Bruun ... has defiled many a paper with ungodly and lewd jests and has shamefully abused wit and harmonious verse to poison the holy wellspring of faith and virtue.[107]

Others who fared no better were the poet Jens Baggesen, and Grundtvig's own uncle, Bishop of Zealand, Nicolai Balle, whose Christian textbooks were counted inaccessible to "the common people". Even Voltaire was not spared, "the most spiteful, incomparable enemy of Christian and all things holy".[108] It was not just the fact that Grundtvig needlessly criticised some of his contemporaries, it was the fact that he did so in a book of world history! Nor was the criticism all negative. Despite the personal snub, Grundtvig wrote of Oehlenschläger: "His poetical works are ... a bouquet of flowers whose peer cannot be found in Denmark – and barely in Germany!"[109] Natural scientists in general were criticised for failing to accept the centrality of God's Revelation to humankind, so when news of Grundtvig's book reached Hans Christian Ørsted in Paris, he responded thus:

This person's foolishness and tastelessness knows no limits. Without any knowledge on the subject he dares to mock the greatest and noblest products of human reason. Anything that is not genuinely 'Lutheran' is an abomination to him. He shuns the inner light and the searching reason in equal measure.[110]

Grundtvig's third book, *Roskilde Rhymes* (1814), a history of Denmark in verse running to 7,103 lines, received its first public presentation in the form of a recitation on 4th October 1812. The occasion was a clerical conference in the cathedral city of Roskilde, 35 km west of Copenhagen. Grundtvig drew on Stephanus Stephanius's translation of Saxo's

---

106. Rom. 8:28.
107. (US II, 374).
108. (Ibid., 290).
109. (Ibid., 235).
110. (Nielsen 1889, 169f).

35. Roskilde Cathedral.
With the adjoining halls where the clerical conference took place. Photo: Nils Jepsen.

Deeds of the Danes from 1645 to assert that the name 'Roskilde' derived from 'Rosen-kilde' meaning a wellspring that waters a field of roses, which he linked to Isaiah 35:1-2. There is no mention of roses in the original Hebrew, only of the crocus or meadow saffron, but both the King James version and Grundtvig's bible have upgraded the crocus to a rose, so he was in good company.

Grundtvig located the figurative wellspring at Roskilde Cathedral from where its waters have spread across the land and refreshed the people:

> Our Rosen-kilde water
> has from springs divine been streamed;
> the city is baptised and
> by the cross of Christ redeemed!
> You are now a Christian flower,
> wellspring for a rosy bower.

In the poem's fictive plot, 'Copenhagen', the daughter of Roskilde, has raided the bishop's palace and the royal castle, but the cathedral with its royal graves remains the collective centre of Danish, and thus Christian, history and identity. The poem 'follows' Grundtvig as he walks around the cathedral recalling those who lie buried here, great Danes all. He runs through 800 years of Danish history, grieving over the current status of Christianity in the North and urging his clerical colleagues to action before it is too late:

> In the North one sickly bud
> lingers from that glorious rose;
> can it flower here so late,
> where the Rosenkilde flows?
> This the danger that I fear:
> with so little time to run,
> if it bloom not in the North,
> then its time on earth is done.

Not until 9 pm on that evening in Roskilde, after a day's business and a goodly dinner, did Grundtvig stand before his colleagues in the Cathedral Library and deliver an excerpt from his major new poem. He himself thought he left a good impression, but there is evidence to prove otherwise. To many it sounded like Grundtvig's dimissory sermon all over again: everyone else needed shaking up, and only Grundtvig had seen the light. As he recounted the feats of the sixteen bishops of Zealand, some of the elderly deans nodded off, while the current bishop, Frederik Münter, kept himself awake by studying the contents of the bookcases. When in the course of his reading Grundtvig actually mentioned the bishop *by name*, Münter dropped the book he was reading on the floor by accident. The loud bang woke the whole room up – to hear Grundtvig ending at full blast:

> Onward, pastors, on to battle,
> lest your tears be amply poured!
> All who hold their Saviour dearest
> did so with the Spirit's sword!
> ...
> Pastors, poets, heed your calling,
> act thereon, that it be shown!
> Speak but what to God is pleasing,
> loud in voice and cadent tone!

Grundtvig's general call to arms becomes more specific in the poem 'Peace' from 1813, where the whole nation is encouraged into a Christian revival:

> Always I sang what I had on my mind;
> inside I fought, so Fight! was my song!
> Brief is our time and our task is to fight,
> life here on earth is a battle!
> ...
> Long must we fight both in voice and in word

ere we can rightfully sing peace is won;
never on earth did a heart melt in love
ere it was swollen by blood rushing on.
Who can know peace if they never have fought?
Where is the saved man who never has suffered?

...

I do not mourn because you have to fight!
All I would mourn is that you in your life
never perceived what was needed for peace,
nor in your time chose to fight.[111]

When *Roskilde Rhymes* was finally published on 1st February 1814, it received little attention. In the paper *Dagen (Today*, 5th February 1814*)* the editor, Knud Rahbek praised especially the songs on King Christian IV, but when Grundtvig's erstwhile friend, Christian Molbech picked up his pen, he wrote that Grundtvig "has truly drowned much of his poetry in endless verse".[112]

Death and division

Between the oral recitation of 1812 and the publication of *Roskilde Rhymes* in 1814, Grundtvig had to come to terms with the death of his father. In the middle of Advent 1812 Grundtvig had sat beside the frail old man and read him a passage from *Roskilde Rhymes*, full of memories of his father and including praise for "how with zest you clarified the Gospel for the people". Old Johan leant over to his son and there and then blessed him – not with a wish but with a statement of his faith: "The Lord will comfort you in your last hour as you have comforted me; for you have sung the psalms of Israel's God." On Christmas Eve 1812 Grundtvig wrote to his friend, Poul Dons (Letter 10):

> My ancient father is still alive, but living a miserable life. His body is so wasted that he cannot stand on his feet; his thoughts are so distracted that only in a rare moment can he speak or understand an intelligent word, even though he recognises us and to some degree knows what he is saying.

Johan Grundtvig died on 5th January 1813, aged 78. His wife, Cathrine, survived him by 9 years.

Johan's death meant that his benefice and vicarage were technically vacant. Both father and son had hoped that the young could succeed the old, and Grundtvig wrote directly to the King with this in mind (Letter 11):

---

111. (PS III, 126f).
112. (MOLBECH, 75).

> My aged father has now died in the Lord, and I am a shepherd without a herd. By the Grace of God and Your Majesty I therefore request most humbly that I be allowed to tend one such. Since an application requires some substance, I venture to name the congregations for whom my father was shepherd for 36 years and where my conscience testifies that I have not laboured for two years as a mere hireling.

But the King, via his bishop, had others in mind, and Grundtvig's application was turned down – as was his appeal for help with a teaching appointment in History at Oslo University. He was allowed to remain in Udby for six months, but then both he and his mother would have to leave. In November 1813 Grundtvig and Lise therefore moved back to his mother-in-law's large apartment at Holmens Kanal 22 in Copenhagen. Cathrine went to live in Præstø, where she had friends. In his almanac for 1813, Grundtvig wrote: "On 27th October my mother and I left the vicarage in Udby, and now I have nowhere on earth that I can call my home." No flock to tend, and no church in which to preach.

Before he left Udby, Grundtvig stood before his congregation on 15th August 1813 and held his farewell sermon, beginning with his beloved word, "Beloved!". The text was the Parable of the Unjust Steward (Lk 16:1-13), but he turned it to speak of the housekeeper who was losing his housekeeping job. He acknowledged that he may have failed, but then so had others in their hardheartedness to his preaching. As a dismissed householder, he feared that another would come and destroy what he had built up. Time and again he appealed to his congregation, "You, my beloved!". In exalted state, he ended up repeatedly using Christ's own words from John's gospel:

> I will not leave you as orphans.[113] For your father and my father in Christ Jesus lives in heaven, and He will give you a Comforter who will remain with you, namely the Spirit which the world cannot receive, because it sees Him not and knows Him not; and then I shall know that the Spirit which is within you is stronger than the one that is in the world. See, I am going away[114] and I do not know what will befall me … Because I have said these things to you, you are filled with grief,[115] but your hearts are not fearful.[116] Though we be parted a little while, we shall meet again, and our hearts will be happy and none shall take our happiness from us. Amen![117]

No pulpit left

On the very same day that old Johan died, Denmark was technically bankrupt. The absolute monarch, Frederik VI, to whom Grundtvig was appealing for a new job, had chosen the losing side in the Napoleonic Wars. The loss of the Danish navy to the British, the

---

113. Jn 14:18.
114. Jn 8: 21; 16:5,7.
115. Jn 16:6, 33.
116. Mt 14:27.
117. (*Biblical Sermons*, 2nd ed., 85f).

destruction of areas of Copenhagen, widespread unemployment, and the devaluation of the currency had negative effects throughout the country. The government printed more money, but in vain. In 1807 a bushel of corn cost 7 rigsdaler, by 1813 it cost 130. On the exchange the Danish currency fell from 83 in 1808 to 1 in 1813.

In *To the Fatherland concerning its State of Affairs and its Dangers*, published on 23rd July 1813, Grundtvig bemoaned the dreadful state of affairs. In a 10,000-word defence of Christianity and an attack on the "futile strife and bloody game" of the great powers,[118] he castigated those who sought a new world order like the Romans, and those who blamed the Jews for the mess the world was in. Denmark should turn its gaze inward: "It is we ourselves, it is our lack of faith that we must fear, that is what is destroying us!" This latest harangue was anonymously attacked in *Danish Literary Times*: "The ugliest feature in Grundtvig's character is undoubtedly his lack of love." The reviewer proved to be none other than Hans (H.C.) Ørsted, the famous physicist and discoverer of electro-magnetism. The touchpaper was lit for a lengthy feud between the two.

Grundtvig could not contain his righteous anger against the country's loss of faith and its consequent downfall. A year later, on 6th October 1814 he again spoke at the clerical conference in Roskilde, reading aloud from his latest discourse, *On Polemics and Tolerance or On Dispute and Resignation*. Again he was confrontational: "... if Christianity is true, any tolerance of opinions, speech, and action that conflict with it, is a shameful betrayal of God, Truth, and humankind". In other words, the Danish clergy were still asleep!

On request Bishop Münter acquired a copy of the manuscript and lamented that Grundtvig had learned nothing from his dimissory sermon experience and the subsequent reprimand four years earlier. This time he took sterner disciplinary measures: Grundtvig was to stop urging his fellow-pastors to mend their ways, otherwise he was finished as a priest.

Grundtvig continued preaching wherever he could get a hearing, but within a short while only the pastor at Frederiksberg Church was willing to let him into his pulpit. Without his own church, and with such limited access to other pulpits, after a final sermon on Boxing Day 1815 Grundtvig solemnly laid down his preaching ministry. He immediately dramatized the situation thus:

> It was assuredly a heavy task for me to make this sacrifice, but a far heavier one to end here what I had only half started. After a lengthy struggle it is now possible for me, with tears in my eyes, calmly and in all sincerity to extend this declaration to the whole of the Kingdom of Denmark and hereby relinquish the right to be a public teacher in the Church, a right granted me by my pastoral ordination and guaranteed to me by law.[119]

Much later, in 1839, he wrote to his English friend, Rev. Nugent Wade – who served as chaplain to the English delegation in Elsinore from 1833-39 – an *Open Letter from a Friend to an English Priest*, in which he looked back on his situation between 1813-15:

---

118. (US II, 729).
119. (*Biblical Sermons,* 2nd ed, 493-94.)

> I felt both the call and the power to take up the cudgels for the Lutheran Church in the land of my fathers, and I rightly regarded the capital city as the arena where the battle should be joined and the victory won ... But I soon found the pulpits of the capital closed to me. I did not lack an audience in Frederiksberg Church, but even the pastor there, who wished to keep his good neighbours, was soon in doubt and no longer wished to swim against the tide.[120]

As the Copenhagen churches closed ranks against this turbulent priest, Grundtvig was already opening up another front on which to pursue his rescue mission of the North. Already in September 1815 he had published some 'test translations' into Danish of Saxo's *Deeds of the Danes* (from Latin) and Snorri's *History of the Nordic Kings* (from Icelandic). This would be one of the paths he trod as he went his own solitary way.

---

120. (US VIII, 195).

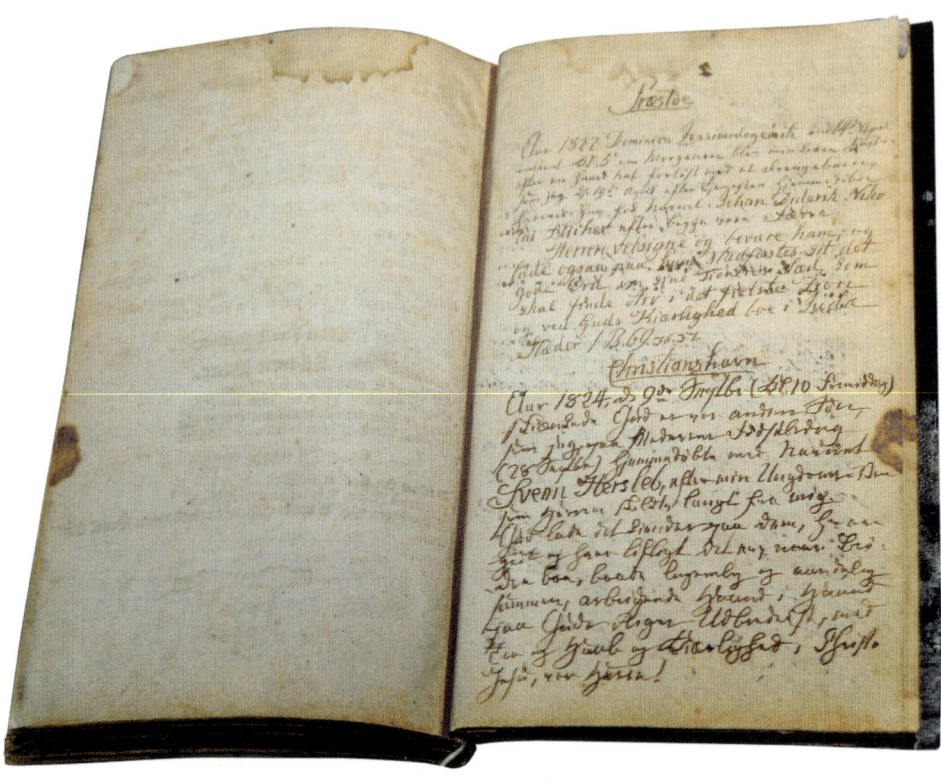

36. Grundtvig's bible.

In his preserved bible in the Grundtvig Memorial Rooms at Udby Grundtvig has written that it was a present from Constance Leth, dated 17th April 1807. At the time (1805-08) Grundtvig was staying in the manor home of Carl and Constance Leth, tutoring their son and infatuated with Constance. The translation is known as *Christian VII's Bible* from 1787. On the inner end-paper Grundtvig has noted certain important events in his life: births, confirmations, and deaths. He notes under 'Præstoe', the town where he was pastor at the time: "In the year 1822 ... on 14th April around 5 am, my dear wife was delivered of a boy child ..." Under 'Christianshavn' he writes: "In the year 1824 on 9th Sept. (10 am) God granted us a second son." And then: "1851 Jan. 14 my beloved wife *Elisabeth Christine Margrethe Blicher* passed away, my faithful spouse for a whole lifetime ..."

8. Time will tell the Truth
(1816-21)

Grundtvig's workload in this period was stupendous. In March 1814 his brother Otto wrote to him: "Congratulations on your busy work with your new history book! But in the meantime do not forget to think about Lise and the future."[121] Grundtvig had been attracted to Lise since 1804, and had become engaged to her in 1811, yet still there was no chance of her marrying the poor, churchless pastor. "No prophet is accepted in his home town," said Jesus,[122] a saying with which Grundtvig could wholly identify, his home town from now on being Copenhagen. He had therefore decided to withdraw into a 'tumulus', as he called it, a warrior grave mound, where he could write and write and write: three major translations, published between 1818-20. The first of these was Saxo's Latin history of the *Deeds of the Danes*, the second, Snorri's Icelandic *History of the Nordic Kings*, and the third, the epic Old English poem *Beowulf*.

Grundtvig deliberately translated the first two into his own characteristic Danish, "so that for the lay reader who cannot penetrate the substantially different linguistic tone in the originals the entire work of translation can manifest itself as an organic unity."[123] In the preface to the first of two volumes of Saxo, Grundtvig himself wrote:

> Such old books are like vessels of gold and silver. If they are to be improved they must be melted down and like the phoenix rise from the ashes. Only then can their proper likeness be achieved, and only then can the books become what they should be as expressions of various eras: separated by their letters but united in spirit!

According to Grundtvig a translation should be idiomatic rather than literal. It should pass from heart to heart and thus serve to awaken a people from their slumber. In principle it should be written for the average citizen – in contrast to the previous translation from 1644 by Stephanus Stephanius. In practice Grundtvig was well-equipped for the task from his experiences in the countryside of Udby and Thyregod, and in the cities of Aarhus and Copenhagen. Grundtvig's versions of Saxo and Snorri gained him a few more readers, one of them being Professor of Theology and History, Jens Møller, who wrote to him on 7th February 1819:

> ... no other living Dane or Norwegian could transform the ancient chronicles into popular books (*Folkebøger*) to the needs and tastes of our common people. It is true that you could

---

121. (Rønning II, 2, 190).
122. Lk 4:16-30.
123. (Toldberg 1946, 113).

have achieved your goal with a little less 'poetic freedom', but I for one am extremely satisfied to have the body of Saxo and Snorri hereby wrapped in Grundtvig's garments.[124]

Of course there were critical voices, not least among those who preferred a more elevated style, but Grundtvig would have none of it. In *The Danish Literary Times* he defended his choice with the following metaphor:

> The good woman, Denmark, must gather the words of her Norwegian bridegroom in her heart and then seek to represent his opinion so honestly and faithfully – and without rejecting her own language – that he would *gainsay* her, he would take her hand, lay it on his heart, and movingly say: 'That is what I meant! Please be my tongue and translator!

The four volumes in all, two of Saxo and two of Snorri, cemented Grundtvig's reputation not only as an able, independent, and idiosyncratic translator but also as a national historian with roots in the soil of the Nordic forefathers. The books also attracted the attention of the language expert, Rasmus Rask, who suggested the two of them together should turn their attention to the Old English epic poem *Beowulf*, but then Rask left town on one of his many 'language trips' and Grundtvig carried on alone. Under the title, *Song of Praise to Beowulf. A Gothic Hero-poem from the last Millennium*, his translation was published on 7th August 1820. According to Sune Auken, the result was Grundtvig's "only unequivocal academic success,"[125] but there were, unfortunately, few readers. Looking back on his hermit-life in the 'tumulus' Grundtvig commented:

> I had set aside my weapons and staff, so to speak, and buried myself in a mound of Saxo, Snorri, and the ancient Anglo-Saxons, who sang about Beowulf the Geat and Hrothgar the Danish lord. This was in order if possible to lure or drag them up to the light of day and give them a little company that in my view was better than their customary readership. There I remained for 7 years, more or less ignorant of what was happening in our little world ... When I surfaced again in 1823 and began to look around, I cannot tell you how dismayed and depressed I was, almost to the point of desperation .... I felt like one who believes he had only slept a single night but had in fact been dead for hundreds of years ... The epic poem of *Beowulf*, which I had imagined would entertain people, found no readership; the *Deeds of the Danes*, from which I had expected heroic deeds, did not budge an inch.[126]

In 1817 Grundtvig reworked and republished his *World History* from 1812 and 1814. His purpose, in a nutshell, was to let history take the place of philosophy:

> All true Learning must in every way be *historical*, since Reason finds nothing in itself except as a measure of temporal Truth and must search outside itself to find the core of Learning. It is

---

124. (BFOTG I, 506).
125. (Auken, 230).
126. *TCG*, 160.

historical because human beings develop over *Time* and can only be understood *within* Time, and because it can only be understood in part, and can only be ended with the end of Time.[127]

'Universal history', a phrase much-used by Grundtvig, is a common resource for the whole of humankind. By now he was moving away from the imposition of biblically-based judgements on all and sundry, and moving towards history as an independent area in its own right. History and Truth are the work of God, as demonstrated by Christ. In Grundtvig's desire to unfold this truth about human life, he was taking a new step towards his later phrase, 'Human comes first and Christian next'. In its simpler explanation it means that 'We are all human before we become Christian'; but the phrase can also be interpreted historically to mean, 'As they were a people, so did they become Christian'.[128] Here again, Grundtvig was moving towards a creation theology which asserted that all things are made by God and *nothing* should therefore be despised or rejected. Despite the Fall, human beings retain within them a residue of the image of God. His prophecy, unassailable in all its simplicity, was that "Time will tell the Truth", a proverb that he applied both to himself and to history. Yet at the same time we know that no simple objective truth exists independent of a life or an age. Grundtvig formulates it thus in *On Human Beings in the World* (1817):

> only perfected human beings can completely and clearly understand themselves, and … only through *history* can we get to know the human mystery in all its depth and breadth, and grasp as much of it as Time has revealed and clarified in its passage.[129]

Confronting Enlightenment and Romantic philosophy

The perception of history and Christianity outlined here is closely linked to, and later merges with, the Mosaic-Christian view that is displayed throughout Grundtvig's work. Many of the features of his view of life and his own contribution as historian and poet were taken up in the 20th century by historiographers, epistemologists, hermeneutists, linguists, inter-textualists etc, even though no modern philosopher thinks so essentially *historically* as Grundtvig. The link between Grundtvig and 20th century philosophy is that both kinds of thinking built on the work of German philosophy in the 18th century, even though Grundtvig surprisingly seldom makes specific reference in chapter and verse. In his first year at university in 1800 he assimilated the philosophy of the Enlightenment, not least the principle of contradiction from Christian Wolff (1679-1754): light cannot be dark, truth cannot be falsehood, life cannot be death etc. The principle stood him in good stead as he defended the truth of Christianity and insisted that the Christian Creed should retain the rejection of the Devil before it accepted the Trinitarian God. Already in 1806 he mentioned in his journal the idea of 'universal history' as proposed by Friedrich Schiller (1759-1805), who in a lecture in 1789 considered the extent to which previous ages have con-

---

127. (*On Danish, Language, and History*, 1816).
128. TCOL, 275.
129. Ibid., 69.

tributed to the development of humanity. Another influential German philosopher was Johann Herder (1744-1803), who emphasised that the Romantic writing of history was being written for the dead as much as for the living, for we are for ever in *dialogue* with the past. But by 1816 Grundtvig was taking strong exception to a number of German philosophers:

> Did Wolff not pretend that history did not exist? Did Kant not claim it was invalid? Did not Fichte try to prove the same thing? Did not Schelling endeavour to turn it into a mere reproduction of the development of Natural Man and a prototype of his self-enlightenment?[130]

From inside his 'tumulus' Grundtvig battled on doggedly. In 1816 he decided that his multiplicity of ideas were best presented in *journal* form. Who better to write every one of the 16 editions single-handedly than the bard himself? For he now considered himself not just a poet, but also a bard, a *skald* in Danish. Skalds were composers and reciters of epic poems which honoured heroes and their deeds and encouraged their emulation. Grundtvig was honouring his forefathers.

Reflections and resonances

Nowadays we tend to think of history, and not least national history, as part of our cultural inheritance, passed down from one generation to another, and available to our scrutiny. Versions of our history emerge with the years; they can be haggled over, but we should show our history loving care, for it is ours and no one else's; its resonance can be heard. Similarly, we should honour and respect the histories of *other* peoples. For all history has an *impact* on its peoples – for better, for worse. In the 16 editions of *Danne-Virke* that Grundtvig wrote, proof-read, and published, he developed his particular theory of reflections and resonances on the relation between the past and the present. Since the imprint of the divine life is reflected and resonant in our earthly life throughout history, it is incumbent upon us to *learn* from it. For certain patterns are repeated: the present can *learn* from the past. Whether or not it chooses to is a different matter.

Grundtvig went further than this, however. The past and present are inseparably *intertwined*, in the sense that the present also sheds light on the past. This view gave Grundtvig a new impetus towards a revised understanding of his ancient forefathers, the creators of Nordic mythology long before the coming of Christianity to the North in the 10th century. Its dynamic content reflected a dynamic people – and the impact of Christianity on the North was equally dynamic. Mythology is not just a precarious precursor of Christianity, whose divine purpose will be fulfilled in the course of time. As Anders Holm writes: "In the final instance, being aware of this resonance is being conscious of the transfiguration *and* the resurrection. The idea is that the heathen myth is *transfigured* in the Christian reality and is thus meaningful – a radical *resurrection* in history."[131] Before 1810 Grundtvig had been thinking in terms of mythology, between 1811 and 1815 he had been thinking in

---

130. *TCOL*, 277.
131. (Holm, 2001, 71).

terms of revivalist theology, but now, from 1815 onwards, he was thinking first and last historically. He now saw his own role as *skald* as being focussed on the reflections and resonances that had coloured especially Danish history in the course of time.

Grundtvig brought this new direction to bear on his poetic works. He began to rewrite old song lyrics in present-day Danish. A good example is the ballad of Thyra Dannebod entitled 'Denmark, loveliest field and meadow', composed around 1685 by Laurids Kock. It became very popular with Danish soldiers in the Schleswig conflicts of the 19th century, and has remained so to this day. Thyra Dannebod was Queen of Denmark from 935-50 and is still credited with raising a huge defensive rampart along the southern Jutland border against the Germanic tribes on the other side. Archaeologists have since dated the original 'Dane-work' rampart back to c. 500 CE. For Grundtvig in *his* time this border wall was as much to ward off German cultural influences as to defend the kingdom from the Prussians beyond it. The battles of Bjarke and Hjalte for Denmark are another example. Grundtvig drew on the resonance or 'echo' of their stories to write 'See the sunrise', with its typical call to arms:

> Waken, Danish heroes, waken,
> tighten belts, be not mistaken,
> day and deed are fighting rhymes![132]

Like so much else in Grundtvig's works, this line of thought has its roots in Christianity. We cannot understand the risen Christ (the second Adam) without knowing about the first Adam and his fall from grace. A further instance had its genesis in Grundtvig's Bible-reading in 1810. In the Book of Revelation he came to the seven churches of the apocalypse. Rather than ground them in the actual text, where they refer to 7 churches in present-day Türkiye, he imagined them as the seven churches of the western world: Jewish, Greek, Roman, Anglo-Saxon, German, and, in Grundtvig's time, the Nordic church. The seventh and last church would be at some point in the future – and in India, the land of ancient Hindu wisdom. On the one hand therefore, the past must be reinterpreted in the light of the present – and especially in the light of Christianity. On the other hand, Christianity itself is subject to history. Like true poetry, true history is a kind of poetic creation. True poetry is found only in God, and must be experienced by us as a revelation – the proclamation of a "mystery hidden".[133] Such revelations of varying power that can leave traces in us are to be found, according to Grundtvig, in mythology, history, the life of a people, and especially in the Bible.

From here on Grundtvig finds his opposites in the systematic philosophers who prefer to understand life and history through reason alone, without realising that human beings see only *in part*. One day all will be revealed and we shall see "face to face", as Paul says.[134] The full Truth *will be revealed*! Theologians must also learn that human experience has affected our view of Christianity for over 2000 years, for the 'revelation' is continuous:

---

132. No. 97 in *LW*.
133. Rom 16:25. (*Dane-Work* 3: 236).
134. 1 Cor 13:12.

Human beings are at the head of it all and their lives are set on a historical course, at the end of which, like Professors of History, they are created Doctors of Theology. It follows from this that in God's eyes no other study is needed for Philosophy than History.[135]

Two core quotations on philosophy have been singled out for the title-page of Grundtvig's philosophical writings, *The Core of Learning* (2021):

- Philosophy is an expression of the human endeavour for wisdom (1816)
- Philosophising without Faith is the same as looking without eyes (1817)

The very *titles* of Grundtvig's studies in *Danne-Virke* present his thinking on a whole range of subjects:

On Historical Learning, or the Concept of History (1816)
On Human Beings in the World (1817)
On Truth, Greatness, and Beauty (1817)
On Revelation, Art, and Learning (1817)
On Proverbs (1817)
On the Relation between Learning, Experience, and Sound Common Sense (1817)
On the Church, the State, and the School (1819)
On the Word/Language and the Mother-Tongue (1819)

In their introduction to *The Core of Learning* (2021) Kim Arne Pedersen and Anders Holm summarise Grundtvig's contribution to Philosophy thus:

These philosophical-religious studies are key to understanding thought-structures which recur in the educational, poetic, theological, and political writings that constitute the first four volumes of this series. The visionary historical-poetic thought, often seasoned with ideas from the Bible and history, is a distinctive form of *knowledge* for Grundtvig, a form of orientation, as he seeks to understand human beings in Time and Space. When compared with the stringent academic thinkers of his time such as Kant and Fichte, it is here that Grundtvig reveals his originality as a philosopher.

Skald, poet, and hymnwriter

An increasing number of people who were kindly disposed towards Grundtvig often worried about his combative temperament and polemical writing-style – characteristics which as a rule he himself believed to be part of his prophetic call as a national *skald*. One of his most loyal and long-time supporters was Pastor Christen Olsen who wrote to him in a letter dated 5th November 1816. Olsen's brother-in-law – an honest man but not

---

135. *TCOL*, 199. (*Dane-Work* 3, 260).

especially knowledgeable about history – had much enjoyed the latest number of *Danne-Virke*. Olsen goes on to say:

> I myself have enjoyed *all* of them, but I must tell you straight out that I think it is a waste of time for you to *scold* your opponents. Just pretend they do not exist and carry on regardless! There are more people than you think who *welcome* your work and they are somewhat put off by these remarks.[136]

Grundtvig's image of himself as a *skald* was closely linked to that of the revivalist preacher and the national prophet. In *Roskilde Rhymes* he even talked to himself as such:

> Let your quaking heart be glad:
> *skald* you are by fate and call!
> How you see the source of life
> is your task to teach to all.
> You in whom the flower grows,
> spread abroad the perfumed rose!
> You are crowned life's scout and guide
> standing by the Master's side.

The Easter Lily (i.e. the common daffodil), first published in *Danne-Virke* on 27th May 1817, is a good example of Grundtvig the bard becoming Grundtvig the hymnwriter. The original poem of 2,500 lines was couched as a spoken, unacted drama. In the prologue the bard asks the daffodil a number of questions. The scene then moves to the Cross, around which stand four Roman soldiers and a Pharisee exchanging views on the death of Jesus, culminating in the resurrection and songs of praise. The drama returns to the present with songs of praise welcoming the truth of the resurrection:

> Saga, yes, I saw it clear!
> From the dead he rose in glory,
> gave our hope a pledge so dear
> in the Easter morning story.
> What are seal or shield or sword
> 'gainst our valiant risen Lord?
> These are chaff His breath sends flying,
> who redeemed us by His dying.

Grundtvig was low in spirits when he wrote the drama, likening himself to the 'peasant flower' of no worth. But his understanding of the resonance of the past paved the way for him to experience Christ's real presence in Holy Communion, where God is plainly active. Of the original drama six verses have found their way into the current Danish

---

136. (BFOTG I, 435).

hymnbook and are accounted among the best lines that Grundtvig ever wrote.[137] In the penetrating 5th verse of the hymn sung today, Grundtvig's metaphor of the daffodil for the chalice is quite extraordinary:

> Easter flow'r, should one strong drop
> from your golden cup refresh me,
> there the wonder will not stop,
> you will raise me, new enflesh me.
> Morning song and cockcrow clear
> in your golden cup I hear,
> waking with the dead at the dawning
> of a rose-red Easter morning.

Grundtvig likens the 'peasant flower' to his own situation, then to the whole of Denmark's situation, and finally to that of Christ, an outcast who became a saviour. Grundtvig's fellow-poet, Jens Baggesen, was willing to exchange his entire poetry corpus for the honour of having written this poem.[138]

Two more major hymns from Grundtvig's flowing pen also saw the light of day in 1817 – proof that even without a church or a pulpit he was still a man of deep faith. Although he later became known as the 'poet of Pentecost', in these early days he concentrated his hymn-writing more on Easter and Christmas. 'O ring in now a Christmas blessed' was published on 23rd December 1817, and three years later, to the very day, came 'A child is born in Bethlehem' – a perennial favourite, especially with children.[139]

The unemployed curate

Since 1813 Grundtvig had been calling himself an "unemployed curate". He had lost both his job in Udby and the opportunity to preach in the pulpits of Copenhagen, but he still longed for a church of his own, seeing himself as a pastor-in-waiting. The problem was his own self-image as a reformer of the Danish Church, of Danish Christianity, indeed of the Danish *people*. His ambition, as he wrote in *New Year's Morning* (1824), was to be a "little Luther"! Blowing his trumpet loudly, he closed his *World History 1817* with the following words:

> History can testify on Luther's grave that nowhere was he so assiduously followed as in Denmark. And although history must remember the visionaries who, wearing their own suits of feathers, have sought to surpass both the Bible and Luther, History must also admit that Denmark has raised no visionaries whatsoever unless it be the author of this book. He has sat on Luther's grave with his Bible open, he has crossed his shepherd's staff with his history staff and tears in his eyes. If I be a dreamer, then I dream alongside God's prophets,

---

137. No. 26 in *LW*.
138. (Holm 2001, 129).
139. Nos. 7 and 10 in *LW*.

37. **Danne-Virke 1816-19.**
Photo: Edward Broadbridge.

Martin Luther and history itself. My dream is not only that the heavens and the earth shall pass away, but that every word of Jesus will endure, so the gates of Hell will never gain power over His Church Saga. The Word will perform wonders and we shall celebrate Martin Luther until the coming of the heavenly, eternal Truth!!![140]

To whom could he turn for a church of his own? There were three options: 1) the Bishop of Zealand, who had twice reprimanded Grundtvig. 2) The Royal Chancellery, i.e. the King's government. And 3) the absolute monarch himself, King Frederik VI. Grundtvig preferred the third option and appealed to the King, newly returned from the Vienna Congress at which Denmark lost Norway to Sweden in the Napoleonic Wars settlement. After eight months abroad, Grundtvig welcomed the King home in May 1815 with 'The Year of our Fathers. A Danish Poem to His Majesty Frederik VI'. Its gist is that Denmark had failed to honour its forefathers and was paying the price. Unless the forefathers' solidly-based Lutheran Christianity were allowed to return and flourish, the country was done for – and what is more, the heirless King's family would die out! Renewed hope was needed; hope would benefit not only the Fatherland but the King's family, for God would grant him a son to ensure that the North survived! In the final stanza Grundtvig linked the future of both King and country to his own future:

---

140. (US III, 729).

> I call and I call
> on the fairest of kings;
> I hope and I hope
> for the mercy God brings.
> O let not my song fall
> on deaf ears, in vain!
> Your soul shall one morning
> enjoy its refrain,
> when all clouds are parted
> and over your kingdom
> you witness the sun rise again.

Of course Frederik VI was aware of Grundtvig's position – and of his linguistic and translation gifts. After the publication of the 'test translations' in 1815 the King promised Grundtvig financial help, once his versions of Saxo and Snorri began to be published. In 1816 Grundtvig asked the King to appoint him pastor of St. Knud's Church in Odense – again in vain. He then turned to option 2. In 1817 he wrote a letter to the government pleading his case for the Citadel Church in Copenhagen (Letter 14):

> For these reasons I am taking the liberty of asking the illustrious institution to recommend me for this living, one that is neither lucrative nor distinguished, but which allows me the opportunity, at a time when it undoubtedly needs it, to keep repeating the ancient commandment to fear God and honour the King, and to continue my literary pursuits, the obvious purpose of which is to awaken a genuine love of our country and a desire for literary art.

Again he was passed over. He opted to stay in Copenhagen and he even applied for the curacy at the Church of our Saviour *free of charge,* for "every day my longing grows to preach God's Word, so if I cannot get a benefice in the capital, I shall have to begin seriously applying elsewhere."[141] He then applied for curacies in Aalborg, Vartov "my fervent and well-founded wish",[142] and Slagelse; again and again he was passed over. But the tide was beginning to turn.

First, the King acknowledged the publication of the first volume of Saxo's *Deeds of the Danes*. He awarded Grundtvig a grant from 1818-24 of 600 rigsdaler annually from the state treasury, the equivalent of half a professor's full salary. At last, after seven long years of engagement, Frederik could afford to marry Lise. Partly in renewed promise, and partly in defence of himself, he had written to her in 1815:

> Girl, I never dared to promise
> that your steps were lightly shod;
> steep the ladder up to heaven

---

141. (Abrahamowitz, 142).
142. (BFOTG I, 509)

narrow is the path to God.
To a skald you gave your faith
heard his harp and words a-flowing
so, where you see sharp thorns now
know that there his crown is growing.[143]

The wedding – at last

At last, in 1818, he could support a wife! On 12th August Nikolai Frederik Severin Grundtvig married Elisabeth (Lise) Christina Margretha Blicher in Ulse Church, with his brother-in-law Pastor Poul Glahn presiding. Glahn had married Lise's sister Marie. The wedding and reception, held in Ulse vicarage, were paid for by Grundtvig's patrons, Count and Countess Danneskiold-Samsøe.

The couple moved into their first home, Løngangstræde 29, in the heart of Copenhagen, and Grundtvig wrote to his mother-in-law to tell her how happy he was (Letter 15). In the December edition of *Pictures of Copenhagen* that year Grundtvig acknowledged that however little he had contributed to it, he now felt "ever deeper that peace serves Denmark best". He was now willing to admit certain mistakes – even though his opponents bore a greater share of the blame.

Among his many songs, 'Far higher are mountains elsewhere on the earth' from 1820 is a perennial favourite. It was written in honour of his poet-friend Christian Pram, who had been appointed to a post in the Danish colonies in the West Indies. Its original title was 'Denmark's solace', an allusion to the loss of territories to stronger powers, but its 'solace' lies in praising Denmark. This is not to the detriment of other countries – which may be far fairer, far richer, far wiser – it is just that they are not *Denmark*, which has its own matchless virtues. This form of quasi-humble self-assertion was a tonic to the Danes as they emerged from the difficult first two decades of the century into what came to be known as its cultural Golden Age. The song, which was widely adopted from the 1840s onwards, ends with two of Grundtvig's most famous lines, often quoted as the basis of the social mindset in Denmark:

In this lies our wealth, on this tenet we draw:
that few are too rich, and still fewer too poor.[144]

The newly-married couple were safely and happily ensconced in Copenhagen when, out of the blue, Grundtvig was told on 2nd February 1821 that he had been appointed pastor of the parish of Præstø and Skibbinge, the very same parish where his mother was living. The surprise was all the greater in that Grundtvig had actually preached in Præstø in the summer of 1820 and had considered applying for the pastorate but had decided against it! He was now ensconced in the beloved capital city and Præstø was 90 km and a day's journey away. One conjecture is that the King had taken Grundtvig's work to heart and

---

143. (*Little Poems* 1815).
144. No. 91 in *LW*.

wished to reward him; another is that Grundtvig was no longer the flea in everyone's ear. Whatever the explanation, word soon got round that the unruly priest was leaving town for his own church in Præstø. As he prepared to depart, the sympathetic pastor at Holmen's Church, Frederik Gutfeld, offered Grundtvig his pulpit; and even Queen Marie Sophie invited him to preach for the Danish Cabinet. In a letter to Christen Olsen dated 9th February 1821 Grundtvig reasoned thus:

> I was at last called in Jesus' name to preach the Word of the Lord, and in my frailty I have stammered out what God has taught me to sing: a hallelujah therefore, since I know that the way of the Lord is always right... yet it is true that since I preached here last summer it has been against my wish, or rather my expectation, to come to Præstø.[145]

He added that he would rather have had a calling in Copenhagen where he could preach to the students, "if they will listen, and if they refuse, what hope is there for the country?"

Grundtvig was installed in the pastorate on Palm Sunday, 15th April 1821. Three months later he received a letter from his friend, Bernhard Ingemann, which likened Præstø Fjord to the Bay of Naples! Ingemann began the letter with the Danish phrase *'Tak for sidst'* (Thanks for our last time together), which is unknown in English, but is used throughout Denmark.

> First, a heartfelt 'thanks-for-last' to you and your wife, and warm greetings to you both from the two of us (my beloved and I) – and from many others, to whom I shall return. I know more or less now how you and your wife are living from day to day, with the Bay of Naples before your eyes, Danicised and embellished by the beech-tree hills of Zealand and free of volcanoes and volcanic people! From now on I shall be sitting beside you among the bookcases in your quiet study listening to the pigeon cooing below until there is a knock on the floor and we go down to the (admittedly) little family which, God willing, can grow with the years. Peace and God's blessings on the new house, joy and contentment with your church, and every happiness in your good deeds! ...[146]

---

145. (BFOTG II, 3).
146. (INGEMANN, 1).

38. Grundtvig 1820.
Painting by Christian (C.F.) Christensen, Frederiksborg Museum of National History. Grundtvig owned this first portrait of himself and hung it in his sitting-room. Christensen was better-known for his theatre backdrops, especially for Bournonville's ballets.

9. I am only cut out for preaching!
(1821-26)

The parish of Præstø was Grundtvig's first permanent pastoral calling, and with it came a wide range of new responsibilities. As curate to his father from 1811-13 he had carried out the pastoral duties attached to baptism, confirmation, weddings, and funerals, as well as house-visits when called upon. It was now eight years since he had served a parish, so all these duties he resumed in Præstø, along with a wide range of administrative tasks. These included supervision of both the local schools and the local social agencies – as well as the maintenence of the parish registries. In 1646 Christian IV had imposed this latter duty on all parish pastors, meaning that for government use they had to register births and deaths and all other church functions linked to their parishioners.

This important socio-cultural responsibility – keeping the church registry, which is also the civil registry, up to date – still lies with the senior pastor in a parish, who is therefore known literally as the 'church-registry-keeping pastor'. When the diocesan bishop used to come to the church on an official 'visitation', the books had to be in order, or it would be noted in his report. When asked about the registry in 1821 Grundtvig's verdict on his own prowess was as follows:

> Since one is a poor witness in one's own case, the above testimony is best left to the bishop or the rural dean, who check through the church registry on their pastoral visitations, but if I am to say what *I* think, then naturally I think rather well of myself![147]

After his breakdown in 1810 and his decision to join the priesthood, Grundtvig was never in any doubt about his ability as a preacher, or the rectitude of his cause, but he had mixed feelings about moving back to the country. He had wanted a parish in Copenhagen (population 100,000), but the King had sent him to Præstø (population 900). On a normal Sunday, churches at the time were attended by roughly 10 % of the population, and Grundtvig was luke-warm about serving *all* his parishioners whatever their faith or lack thereof. On the other hand, his own mother lived in Præstø, and it was a great relief for her and the family that he now had a parish, a living wage, a home of his own, and a newly-married wife to live with (Letter 13). Grundtvig actually arrived in Præstø *before* Lise, and the letters which they sent to each other between 13th April and 4th May 1821 testify to a mutual love and an excited hope; they were both determined to make the best of it. When Lise finally moved in, it was together with a maid and her unmarried sister Jane, who kept her good company. This allowed Grundtvig to get on with his churchwork and his writing. A pattern was forming.

---

147. (Eriksen & Broch, 14).

Pastor in his own church

The driving-wheel in Grundtvig's developing theology was the Sunday sermon. As with most pastors it forced him down into a gospel text and up into an expectant audience, however small it might be. He could count on his mother's presence most Sundays as well as a number of orthodox Lutherans who saw the liturgy as comforting and his sermons as inspirational. Grundtvig had always placed oral speech before the written word, so in his Sunday sermons he now had the opportunity to take up what he called 'the living Word' of the Gospel to enlighten and enliven his congregation. We are fortunate to have all of his Præstø sermons and can see the great pains he took with them. The Lutheran sermon of the time had certain characteristics; it had to be biblical, exegetical, and evangelical, and it was often didactic, dogmatic, and polemical; it always was and still is a challenge to the pastor. Just before he arrived in Præstø he wrote to his friend, Christen Olsen, about the sermon he was preparing "I have been working on it since Monday morning and it is not until now, Friday evening, that I am thinking of *writing* what I am going to say."[148]

Grundtvig's first sermon in Præstø was not markedly different from his first sermon in Udby ten years previously. In both cases we must remember that he had been reluctant to *accept* the calling. He had been sent by the King – and thus by God – to preach "the faith that has strengthened my departed forefathers":

> Praise be to God that with this conviction I can commence this calling to you as your pastoral carer. I come not in my own name, nor in the name of any human wisdom or any human superior, but in the blessed name of our Lord and Saviour, Jesus Christ!

Grundtvig also took his confirmands very seriously, for their souls were at stake. Confirmation lessons in Præstø lasted from 9 am to 3 pm three days a week in the winter half. Some 50 years later the Præstø pastor, Nicolai Bondesen, published a number of statements both from Grundtvig's registry records and from the confirmands' recollections. Grundtvig noted the "warmth" and "increasing sensitivity" of some of the girls, whereas one girl was deemed "rather silly". The boys' reports varied from "good" and "sound" and "with a soft heart", to "very good" and "a bright lad" but "appears cold". The children for their part were impressed by the order he kept in the classroom and the pride of place he gave to them when he asked the local VIPS not to sit in the chancel, as was their custom, since he wanted this to be free for the confirmands to come closer to the altar. During this only confirmation service he held in Præstø, on 14th April 1822, and recorded in the town archives, both he and his confirmands became so emotionally overwhelmed that he had to hold a lengthy break in order to calm down the children – and himself too no doubt. Bondesen also notes that Grundtvig's sermons were extensive, enthralling, and emotive: "He himself was often so gripped that the tears flowed."

---

148. (BFOTG II, 4-5).

39. Lise Blicher.
Date and artist unknown.

As the parish pastor Grundtvig also had to submit reports on everything that the central administration wished to direct on the King's behalf. He derived some pleasure from the decision by the school commission on 31st October 1821 to acquire Saxo's *History of Denmark* and Snorri's *History of Norway* in the new popular translations he himself had published. The local archives document his attempts to improve teaching qualifications and his unremitting work as chair of the parish public assistance committee. Here, as in Udby, he set a good example with generous gifts to the poor, when they came to his door.

While Grundtvig was hard at work, Lise gave birth to their first son on 14th April 1822. Grundtvig baptised him at home, naming him 'Johan' after his own father. The new-born baby's grandmother, Cathrine, lived long enough to see her grandchild, and Grundtvig was deeply touched by her "tearful smile". She passed away five months later on 17th September 1822. Grundtvig held the funeral service and buried his mother in Præstø churchyard. In the church registry he wrote: "Blessed are they who die in the Lord" (Rev 14:13).

Partly because of its relative isolation and its heavy workload, Grundtvig never really settled in Præstø, witness the letter that he wrote to the King on 22nd August 1822, i.e. *before* his mother's death, asking to be transferred back to Copenhagen as soon as possible (Letter 16):

> Two perpetual curacies in the capital are currently vacant: the one at Trinity Church, the other at the Church of Our Saviour in Christianshavn, and I am gratefully content with whichever of these Your Majesty sees fit most graciously to grant me.

To Grundtvig's surprise and joy, and against the advice of Bishop Münter, the King was listening. On 6th November 1822 he was appointed 'perpetual curate' at the Church of Our Saviour in Copenhagen, and was inducted on the First Sunday in Advent. At last he had arrived in a city church of his own – and with a capacity of 1,200. That December the Grundtvig family moved into Torvegade 25 in Christianshavn, an island integrated with Copenhagen.

Curate in the Church of Our Saviour

Grundtvig's reputation went before him, and not everyone welcomed him back to Copenhagen. Already on 5th January 1823 Jakob Mynster, the curate at the Church of Our Lady (since 1922 the Cathedral) and an old rival, attended Grundtvig's Sunday service and wrote of the sermon:

> Today I heard Grundtvig preach to large numbers in the beautiful church. An animated speech, better constructed than is usual for him but without sufficient depth – a sermon should also be edifying. But in general he preaches the gospel as the servant of the law ... aimed more towards hatred for the unbelievers rather than love of the faith.[149]

Without mentioning Grundtvig by name Mynster later added: "With some people it is like with elephants and lions; I am glad to have seen them, but I do not want any further contact with them."[150]

Whatever the opposition, Grundtvig now embarked upon three of the most spiritually exciting and productive years of his life. He had his first permanent job in one of the foremost churches in the capital city, he was happily married, and he was the father of a new Grundtvig generation. His sermons now revolved around What is True Christianity and Is Christianity True? – which were also the titles of his two major published works of the time. In April 1823 the Grundtvigs moved house yet again – this time to Prinsessegade 52, close to his new church. Here they were to remain for 4½ years – and to live through another major upheaval.

Among the subjects Grundtvig raised in his sermons was the law's demand that all church members should take Holy Communion at least once a year. His response on Maundy Thursday 1823 is among the first examples of his refusal to *force* Christianity upon anyone; freedom of conscience was essential here: "Unless Holy Communion is taken out of love and an inner need, it is an abuse and a profanation."[151] Behind these words lay the coming clash between the State Church, which dictated church rules for the people, and the People's Church that would allow freedom of worship from 1849 onwards.

The tone of Grundtvig's preaching was gradually changing. His emotional pitch was often high, and he was beginning to turn more towards praise and hope and less towards

---

149. (Rønning III, 1, 15).
150. (Ibid., 9).
151. (GP I, 187).

40. The Church of Our Saviour, Christianhavn.
Photo: Edward Broadbridge.

warning and condemnation. He could not help being occasionally dogmatic, but there were now signs of humility coming from his pulpit. If Mynster had attended divine service just four days before he actually did, he would have heard Grundtvig's New Year sermon 1823 extol how God was working His purpose out *through* the Church and confess the limitations of all preachers:

> Clearly God Himself is working towards this end; for although we must admit that none of us preach His Word with such vitality and passion, such pith and zeal as we should – and which He would grant us the power to, if we fervently and persistently beseeched Him, it is nonetheless preached among us these days by many with more life and power than in more recent times.[152]

In his sermons, his hymns, and his poetry, Grundtvig now sought to work out for himself the relation between the Bible, the faith, and the essence and expression of Christianity. In his sermon for the First Sunday in Advent 1823 he preached on the text: "the hour has already come for you to wake up from your slumber, because our salvation is nearer now

---

152. (Ibid., 102).

than when we first believed. The night is nearly over; the day is almost here."[153] Afterwards he could not get the words out of his head; they captured all that he was thinking about faith and salvation. A new day was dawning; *this* was the quintessence of his faith. The word 'new' was taking on a different and wider meaning for him. As a result he was inspired to write two of his most extraordinary works: his spiritual autobiography, *New Year's Morning*, and an early version of his greatest hymn, 'The Land of the Living'. The longing for eternity informs both.

Writing his way to clarity

Published on 12th August 1824 and running to 312 11-line stanzas *New Year's Morning* was Grundtvig's longest poem to date. On publication it sold less than 20 copies.[154] Critics have called it a "hinge", a "pivot", and "Grundtvig's greatest individual literary work",[155] but it is a difficult poem to penetrate and interpret, as his friend Bernhard Ingemann experienced it:

> Your song can never be dark speech to either me or your closest friends; but when you become so deeply absorbed in the ancient North and ride Sleipner with old greybeard over the deep, then you must not insist that many should follow you. So you are not to denounce any of your countrymen or your friends.[156]

'Old greybeard' is a reference to Odin, and 'Sleipner' to his 8-legged horse. The opening line of the third stanza is simple enough: "God's peace and good morning in fields and on hills!", but the poem soon turns to a penetration into ancient history in order to prophesy the future. Like King Hadding from Nordic mythology, and like Christ in *The Harrowing of Hell*, the poet visits the land of the dead, Hel, in order to recall the past. A woman shows him the wall dividing the living from the dead. She wrings the neck of a cockerel and throws the dead bird over the wall, whereupon it crows on the other side. The image is vivid and unmistakable: resurrection cannot come about before death *and* the descent into the realm of the dead. Grundtvig is now integrating the *pre*-Christian stories into his understanding of the lessons of history and Christianity. As Sune Auken puts it: "They help Grundtvig in his effort to make people in the North realise the great continuity they are part of."[157]

The Church and music historian, Jørgen I. Jensen, pays particular attention to the "symphonic" nature of the poem: "the stanza-rhythm, the huge, violent, occasionally apocalyptic scenes, and the overall colossal form":

---

153. Rom 13:11-12.
154. (Jensen, 2017, 64).
155. (Introduction in GV)
156. (Rønning III, I, 58).
157. (Auken, 459).

Grundtvig has sought to *bore his experiences into the future*, not because, everyone should take note of him, but ... because he had discovered that his own story, far from being smooth and lineal, was in itself a symbol of the great forces, the great dangers, and the great opportunities for his fatherland ... [The poem] employs a ferocious rhythm which gives the impression that it is boring not only into the future but also deep into the mountain of memory. This can lead us to think of the equally awe-inspiring yet simultaneously fascinating tunnel-diggers that are linking areas in Copenhagen that have never been linked before."[158]

New Year's Morning is a self-biographical prophetic poem in which an immense amount of material, memories, narratives, and visions merge. They may be theologically somewhat opaque, for here in the summer of 1824 the eschatological hope for the future is supreme. As Jørgen I. Jensen notes, "Grundtvig the poet knew something that Grundtvig the theologian did not."[159]

The contrast between *this* life and *another* life beyond, is the theme of 'The Land of the Living', a poem that has been divided into two hymns in the current *Danish Hymnbook*: 'O life lived in Christ' and 'I know of a land'.[160] Here we find Grundtvig's deepest understanding of the link between the two:

> O wonder-full faith:
> our bridge swaying over the ocean's dark face
> from bleak realms of death to the warm shores of life,
> defying the coastline where ice-floes are rife;
> live lowly among us, it pleases You best,
> our Lord and our Guest!

Grundtvig locates the love of God which makes our earthly life a gift in its *real presence* in faith, hope, and love, both here and beyond. Christ, the incarnated heavenly guest on earth, has recreated the link to love that was damaged at the Fall:

> O life lived in Christ!
> You grant to our hearts what the world never prized:
> what faintly we glimpse ev'ry day, ev'ry hour,
> yet lives deep within us, we feel it empow'r;
> my land, says the Lord, is both heaven and earth,
> where love has its birth.

Both poems had their seeds sown by Grundtvig's cousin, Henrik Steffens, in his lecture series in 1802-03 introducing the new Romantic movement to Denmark. In 1823 Steffens had published *On False Theology and the True Faith*, and in autumn 1824 Grundtvig was eager

---

158. (Jensen 2017, 36 & 74). The reference is to the new Metro system, opened in 2002.
159. (Ibid., 149).
160. Nos. 41 and 65 in *LW*.

to meet him in Copenhagen for a theological discussion. Expecting Steffens to understand him – as he believed he had understood Steffens – Grundtvig was deeply disappointed to find his cousin so unsympathetic to his work (Letter 17):

> It was to be expected that my interpretation of the spiritual conditions of the North, and especially of Denmark and its deep historical importance, would offend you, but not that you would denounce my entire view and all my Song-Work!

In his own view Grundtvig was moving towards his vision of Denmark as "history's Palestine, the land where Christianity will reach its highest earthly transfiguration" – a goal which Steffens found far-fetched; he advised Grundtvig to stick to preaching!

We may well ask at this point to what extent Grundtvig was still a 'romantic' in 1824 – and for that matter, for the rest of his life? There is no contradiction between romanticism and Christianity, indeed the former was partly inspired by Christian impulses such as medieval mysticism, radical reformation, pietism and so on. Grundtvig's high estimation and unflinching embrace of poetry would hardly be likely without his moorings in the romantic view of art and life. Indeed he is at his best as a lyricist when he cuts loose as a romantic poet. There are similar romantic forces at play in his view of history, mythology, the people's spirit, the nation, and of the spiritual importance of Nature. But he was neither a loner nor a dreamer building castles in the air. He sought to discover what it *is* that the Church, the people, and he himself are actually *nourished* by.

In *New Year's Morning* Grundtvig dramatised his struggle to reach a coherence between faith and action, but admitted he had failed:

> I learned then, poor sinner,
> in midwinter's cell
> that light without heat is
> a torment of Hell,
> no tears were forthcoming
> for God or for friend,
> dread only, then brooding,
> then dread yet again.
> I fought like a Viking
> to love's living wellspring,
> determined to transform myself!
>
> You earth-clod, you sinner!
> What can you expect?
> What flesh calls 'transform'
> must the Spirit reject.
> To be like the Master,
> yet do without God?
> No! Honour Him, follow

> the path that He trod,
> From dying to living
> to Him alone given
> to lift Himself up and take wing![161]

In his struggle to be like Christ, "love's living wellspring", Grundtvig realised he came up short, for the light of his faith was not matched by the heat of his action. Yet again we see Grundtvig analysing himself and discovering a cold heart in a "torment from Hell". He must break his stubborn will and *surrender* himself to God's saving grace.

On the home front Grundtvig and Lise were blessed on 9th September 1824 with a second son, named and baptised 'Svend Hersleb Grundtvig' after his friend Svend Hersleb, now Professor of Theology at Oslo University. Despite this welcome addition to his family Grundtvig was in low spirits; the curacy was demanding too much of him, both in terms of his working hours and his pastoral duties for people without faith. He wanted to *write* rather than fulfil his many church duties; and despite the pressure, he remained poetically fertile. At the Christmas morning service 1824, he read aloud to his congregation a poem that proved (in its subsequent hymn-form) to be one of his most popular: 'We greet you again, God's angels bright'.[162] An eye-witness testified that Grundtvig could barely hold back the tears as he did so.[163] In this jubilant hymn uniting earth and heaven the link between human beings is mediated by "God's angels ... treading up and down the scale of their hymn-singing," a quite extraordinary image. The meaning of the enigmatic 'Christmas grief' in the last verse is discussed to this day:

> O may we but see that joyful day
> before our life is ended;[164]
> for then like a mother giving birth
> our pain will soon be mended!
> Our Father in heav'n, let this be so
> and Christmas grief transcended!

The last line encapsulates not only Grundtvig's hope that the birth of Jesus will raise his spirits, but that in the Christian faith a birth lies next to a death – and thence to a resurrection.

The 'matchless discovery'

In April 1825 Grundtvig joined forces with two members of his congregation, Doctor of Philosophy Andreas (A.C.) Rudelbach and the theologian Jacob Lindberg, to publish the

---

161. (*New Year's Morning*, 21).
162. No. 8 in *LW*.
163. (Borup, 81-82).
164. Lk 2:25-35.

anti-rationalist journal, *Theological Monthly*, which ran to 39 editions until September 1828. In the very first lines of the very first number Grundtvig wrote:

> Shall I speak or keep my silence,
> quell my pent-up words by choice,
> or throughout the North take licence,
> lend the Church my bardic voice?

The question was of course rhetorical. For four years he now had the opportunity to argue in print his case against rationalist Christianity. He was gradually working his way towards a new understanding of his *own* Christian faith. In the process he was inspired by the Church father, Irenaeus (c. 125-c. 202), who had known Polycarp of Smyrna (c. 69-155), who had known Ignatius of Antioch (30-107), both of whom had known John, the only apostle to write a gospel. What a lineage! Grundtvig was circling around the concept of 'the Rule of Faith', which Irenaeus had used in his book, *Against Heresies*, hinting at the oral tradition in the oldest congregations. Reading Irenaeus in the original Greek (and even translating him into Danish), Grundtvig came to the conclusion that "the Rule of Faith" was the Apostolic Creed! Before any of the books in the New Testament were written, the faith was being formed orally, especially in connection with baptism, and circulated in and around Palestine. In his evening sermon for the 31st July 1825, Grundtvig proclaimed: "Whatever the Bible says, it is absolutely certain that the Creed which Christians at all times and in all churches have confessed is, and can only be, the *Christian* Creed."

After a long search Grundtvig had at last discovered his true rock. On this rock he would stand for the rest of his life, whatever winds might swirl around him. What brought him this far? He had resolved the dilemma between oral and written history in favour of the former. True Christianity, both historically and existentially, began with the first Christians formulating their faith and acting on it. This was the Church's one foundation, led and driven by the Holy Spirit. It is this living Church that strengthens Christians in their faith, especially through the twin sacraments of Baptism and Communion.

Grundtvig was no longer alone in this decisive battle against the rationalists. A number of younger theologians both in Denmark and in Germany were criticising the university teachers and the pastors who were disregarding their obligations to the five symbols of the Danish Church as set out in the King's Law of 1660: the three creeds from the Church fathers (the Apostolic, the Nicaean, and the Athanasian), the *Confessio Augustana*, and Luther's *Small Catechism*.

In his first *programmatic* Church hymn, 'Dare a single soul remember?', published late in 1825, Grundtvig wrote the following remarkable verse, in which God and humankind are both *builders*, with the joint aim of gathering around "the heavenly Eucharist":

> Only by His hand creating
> are the Father's halls composed;
> only by His Son descending

41. Professor of Theology, Henrik Clausen.

is our human clay transposed.
We below must build in beechwood
– with the song-thrush in our midst –
no more than a humble guest-room
to the heavenly Eucharist.[165]

In passing we should note that although the phrase 'matchless discovery' is now in general usage, it was not Grundtvig's invention, but was first used sarcastically by Søren Kierkegaard.[166]

---

165. From 'Dare we yet recall the tender'/*Tør end nogen ihukomme* (DDS 348).
166. See p. 273.

The Church's Retort

A major problem for Grundtvig was that it was the rationalist theologians at university who were training students for the Christian ministry. Were they actually *teaching* the faith, or were they only interested in biblical criticism? On 20th August 1825 the young Professor of Theology at Copenhagen University, Henrik (H.N.) Clausen published *Catholicism and Protestantism: Their Constitution, Doctrine and Ritual*. The gist of this voluminous work was that Catholicism built on the Church, whereas Protestantism built on Scripture. Given that Grundtvig had just made his discovery that it was *Protestantism* that built on the Church, i.e. the oral tradition in the congregations, it is hardly surprising that he was out with his pen as soon as he received his subscriber's copy. By 5th September he had published *The Church's Retort*, refuting Clausen's argument and demanding that as a false teacher he should resign his post. The book was reprinted twice within weeks and became the talk of the town. Grundtvig had plunged his hand into a hornet's nest that included 88 of Clausen's student supporters, whose support for their professor he addressed in no uncertain terms (Letter 18). To Grundtvig's astonishment Clausen sued him for libel and a year later won the case. Grundtvig's accusatory words were deemed 'null and void', he was fined 100 silver Rigsdaler, and placed under lifelong censorship, meaning that anything he wished to publish must first pass the police censor.[167]

While he was still awaiting the verdict in the libel case, Grundtvig published on 28th April 1826 a collection of hymns for the 1000th anniversary of the arrival of Christianity in Denmark with the missionary Ansgar in 826. Professor Clausen's father, Henrik (H.G.) Clausen, happened to be the county dean, and as such was Grundtvig's superior. For the millennial celebrations he turned down all Grundtvig's contributions on the grounds that they were not in the authorised hymnbook. Grundtvig was furious; no one was listening to him. He sought an audience with Frederik VI and on 8th May he asked permission to resign his office as a pastor in the State Church. The request was granted – without a pension. Once again he was a pastor without a church. A number of sources testify to Lise's loyalty also over this decision. She is said to have gone into his study, put her arm around his neck and said, "I see what is troubling you; you fear for your wife and children. Forget us, and trust in what the Lord is asking of you. He knows how to put bread on our table."[168]

Perhaps there was more than anger and disappointment behind Grundtvig's resignation. Steen Johansen suggests that "Even if there had been no Clausen and no libel trial, Grundtvig would doubtless have found an excuse to free himself of his curacy in order to pursue his studies; there is no doubt about that."[169] Grundtvig himself provided some evidence of his obvious frustration in a letter dated 28th August 1826 to his old Norwegian friend, Pastor Wilhelm Wexels: "… I am only cut out for preaching, not for the day-to-day pastoral life" and added that as an enlightened Christian one cannot be a pastor in the

---

167. See *HCF* chs 1 and 4.
168. (Nielsen, 1889, 278).
169. (GS 1949, 90-91).

State Church "with a good conscience without knowing deep down that one would rather not, and that one is only doing it for the sake of the Word."

Grundtvig was now free to pursue his writing full-time, on the limited budget that his various grants allowed him, but the problem remained: How can a prophetic priest best reach his audience?

42. Grundtvig 1831.
Painting by Christian (C.A.) Jensen, 1831. Ny Carlsberg Glyptotek. He also painted the 1843 portrait on p. 196.

10. Freedom our watchword must be in the North!
(1827-32)

The censor's hammer finally fell on Grundtvig's work, *On Religious Freedom*. Despite its controversial content Parts 1 and 2 were allowed to be published in the January and February 1827 editions of *Theological Monthly*. Grundtvig was arguing for three freedoms for the individual: 1) to be allowed to worship *outside* one's parish under a pastor *of one's own choosing*, thus breaking the 'parish-tie' that limited people to the confines of their own parish, 2) to be allowed to be confirmed by the *State* and not the Church, thus breaking the compulsion of the Church-State tie, and 3) to be allowed to be married without confessing the Creed, again releasing people from the compulsion to confess their faith before they could be married. Grundtvig defended these three demands as "human rights". However, when Part 3 was laid before the censor, the content was considered too subversive to be published. Grundtvig was now demanding that in the name of freedom of worship (already enshrined in the American Bill of Rights) people should be allowed to *leave* the State Church and set up their own independent churches! In April the censor, representing both the State and the King, confiscated Part 3.

Down-hearted but undeterred, Grundtvig had already decided to write his literary will. When *N.F.S. Grundtvig's Literary Testament* was published on 23rd February 1827 it proved to be more of a prophecy than a last will and testament. In a somewhat melodramatic stocktaking of his situation he also seriously addressed the unity between the divine and the human spirit. Linking the Nordic myths to the Christian faith he enigmatically called his understanding of this coherence between God and His Creation "the key to my hideaway and the clue to my labyrinth"

> ... because the battle between the Aesir and the Jætter [the Gods and the Giants, ed.], with Valhalla and Gimle [Heaven and its palace, ed.] was the equivalent of the battle that the poet found first and foremost in his innermost being and saw illuminated in the Bible. That is why there is no fundamental contradiction between the poet's vision and his writing; he did not turn away from the Bible Spirit when he pursued the Nordic Spirit, nor did the Giant Spirit ever leave him when he sought to be enlivened and guided solely by the Great Spirit which created all things new on earth. Spirits that can unite do not exclude each other, and in the Spirit's kingdom the ruler is not just above all others but all others are *in* Him and He is All in All. What is the spirit of history, of human history, if not God's own steering Spirit of the true Christian faith in the Bible as it symbolically depicts our human path? It is the fighting Spirit of humankind, the same as the Nordic Giant Spirit, when it has truly understood the human riddle in all its deep mystery, the human struggle in its every sense, and the human goal, however high it may soar to correspond to the depth of its wishes![170]

---

170. (US V, 176).

43. Strandgade 4B.
Above the lower door bottom left is a commemorative plaque recording that "Here lived the pastor and hymnwriter N.F.S. Grundtvig 1829-40".

This was a radical expression of Grundtvig's understanding of his freedom as a Christian theologian, perhaps spurred on by his own experience of losing his freedom of speech.

He was already at work on his collected sermons, when Lise gave birth on 23rd May to their third child and first daughter. Eleven days later in their home at Prinsessegade 52 Grundtvig baptised her Meta Cathrine Marie Bang Grundtvig, 'Cathrine Marie Bang' being the maiden name of Grundtvig's mother.

Grundtvig as husband and father

Having occupied four different homes in the past 5 years, father, mother, and three children moved yet again – this time in April 1828 to Strandgade 4B, Christianshavn – with Frederik's German Church as their neighbour (now Christian's Church and referred to as such from now on). Here they were to live for the next 12 years, the longest stay in the whole of Grundtvig's life. The roomy apartment was organised to give the family breadwinner the maximum opportunity to write. His study and library occupied four windows – until a backroom later became available. The rest of the family, Lise, her sister, Jane, the three children, and a housemaid, had to make do with two smaller rooms, which also served as a bedroom and a dining-room. The apartment was later reorganised to make less room for Grundtvig and more room for the family. This information comes from Marie Blom, the daughter of a colonel whom Grundtvig had known in earlier days and a regular visitor to the Grundtvigs since their respective children had become playmates. She noted that apart from the mealtimes Grundtvig

... spent the whole day and night in the room I have described, where the dust from the books and his incomparably strong Dutch tobacco created a dense fog... He was a very serious man. In his house, seeing and obeying him were one and the same thing... Once he was at his writing-table, he was not easy to approach, but he was a kind, hospitable host, and if there were no distinguished guests present, he amused himself with his children, both his own and us... In inviting so many people to share his daily life, he made great demands on his wife; they were not especially heavy demands, but they were absolutely indispensable; Grundtvig was a most hospitable and charitable man...[171]

Marie Blom characterised Lise Grundtvig as the exact opposite of her husband:

... As well as being orderly and extremely thrifty, she had the beautiful gift from nature of being able to serve even the simplest of meals... All this came from her loving, and in the best sense humble, heart, coupled with a grace that she and her sisters must have been given in the cradle. We could gather from the children's random remarks the difficulties that she had taking care of the essential cleaning of her husband's room – where he lived day and night for lengthy periods – not to mention getting him to undertake a full change of clothing at least once a week... Mrs Grundtvig managed it all without appearing to be busy and without the air of martyrdom whereby every domesticity forfeits a payment.

We cannot be certain about the family's income in the years 1827-29 apart from the gifts from faithful friends and the King's annual grant of 600 rigsdaler between 1818-27. Royalties from Grundtvig's works would have been limited.

Three months after moving home, on 14th July 1828, he published *A Brief Chronicle of the Bible for Children and the Common Man*, lovingly dedicated "to Christian parents and children in the name of the Lord". This was a textbook of Bible stories and Church history, and a revised and enlarged version of his previous edition from 1814. The book proved popular with parents, schoolteachers, and pastors and was used in homes, schools and churches (for confirmation lessons). By the end of 1828 he had also finished a new history book, for boys aged 10-16 in the grammar school. *Rhymed Chronicle for Children* followed not only the model of the first book ever printed in Denmark, the original *Danish Rhymed Chronicle* (1495), but also the latest pedagogical precepts for the teaching of history, with an introductory overview followed by digestible events, and with a link to geography. Grundtvig had his own personal teaching experience from Egeløkke and the Schouboe Institute to draw on, and had also begun to teach history in the home-schooling of his two young sons. His innovation now was to present history in *rhyme*, in the knowledge that children learn poetry more easily than prose, and enjoy reciting it. Svend in particular was fascinated – at the age of four. The uncontroversial book was passed by the censor on 24th February 1829 and published 10 days later. In 52 chapters of roughly 3 pages each Grundtvig presents people and characters from the history of Europe with a moral lesson to follow. Thus, he takes the story of King Canute, who in Grundtvig's version once

---

171. (Barfod 1898, 21f).

put his foot in the River Thames and commanded the tide to stop. When the water had reached his knee, he withdrew his leg and pointed out to his court that only those who recognise the validity of their king will obey him!

Alongside *Rhymed Chronicle for Children* Grundtvig published *The Flow of Time*, a chronological map depicting the flow of European history, with an accompanying commentary. The book was based on the German original by Friedrich Strass published in 1803, which Grundtvig had bought in 1808 and used in his history lessons to the young Carl Steensen-Leth at Egeløkke. Its originality lies in its visual impact, which replaced all the tables that stretched over many pages in previous history primers. History was like rivers, flowing in and out of one another and being joined by tributaries; the Egyptians and the Hebrews flow with other peoples into the great kingdom of Alexander the Great, and so on. The *Rhymed Chronicle for Children* ran to seven editions and *The Flow of Time* to five, making them the most popular of Grundtvig's works on history.

The Education Act of 1814 had given children the right to 7 years teaching rather than a *school attendance* law, which thus allowed for home teaching. Grundtvig himself had been home-taught and judged it best for his own children. But at Strandgade 4B it was left to Lise to teach the boys literacy and numeracy. Grundtvig adopted his own liberal pedagogical views and demanded diligence from the boys. The lessons were Geography and History in addition to Nordic Languages and Literature. They were also taught Religious Studies and Greek, but not Latin, and thus they could not pass the matriculation exam to university – a circumstance which his son Svend later deplored. At this early stage in their lives Grundtvig was not concerned about university entrance, and he associated Latin with his own rote-learning at the 'School for Death" in Aarhus. He even wrote a poem in 1839, 'An Open Letter to My Children', maintaining how wicked and wasteful it was "to sacrifice our lads with cheeks a-glowing/to Latin Grammar and a certain death."[172] Grundtvig's concern was to hear an improvement in their oral reading and comprehension skills. The boys progressed to reading his own translations of Saxo and Snorri as well as starting on classical Greek. After a morning devotion, Johan and Svend were left to themselves with a reading assignment. The boys were to be educated for *life*, and at a later stage they therefore had to learn a trade: Johan learned bookbinding and Svend carpentry. According to his wife, Laura, Svend took all this in his stride, but it was not so with Johan, who was a much slower learner.

Christmas with the Grundtvigs 1832

Since this biography is also concerned with the everyday life of the subject, we venture to bring an account of Christmas with the Grundtvigs as recalled by Marie Blom (1824-1901), then aged 7½. The year was 1832 when, as is the custom in Denmark, the Grundtvigs celebrated Christmas Eve, together with the Schmidt and the Glahn families.[173] In Marie Blom's memoirs she recalls that there were three large oil paintings on the living-room

---

172. No. II in *TSFL*.
173. (GEEG, 135-36).

wall: of Grundtvig, his mother, and Lise, in that order. The Christmas tree was in the bedroom, visible from the living-room. Everyone had tea and Christmas cake, then the candles were lit on the Christmas tree, and the presents were opened. Writing much later, Marie could not remember her own presents, only that the children, Johan aged 10, Svend aged 8, and her younger brother Vilhelm, aged 6, all received a felt-covered folding-chair according to their size, "one that was an unfailing aid to sitting upright! Svend already seemed to be an extraordinarily lively boy, who was here, there, and everywhere he was not meant to be!" Johan on the other hand had good manners and was well-behaved. Later in the backroom the children and the young people gathered to play Christmas games. It seemed to me that no one was particularly amused by them ... We all ate in the bedroom and had porridge. Apart from grace being said there was no religious ceremony."

The Three Trips to England: 1829, 1830, 1831

1829

Grundtvig had long imagined seeing the original manuscript of the anonymous epic poem *Beowulf* in the British Museum in London. Angles from Schleswig and Saxons from northern Germany had settled in east England around 450 CE, replacing the Romans in the process. In the 9th century Vikings from the North arrived in England and north-west France, where they were known as Normans (i.e. north men). For Grundtvig the English were therefore fundamentally a Nordic people. It had also made a deep impression upon him that the most important sources for the legendary Danish king, Skjold, Odin's son and progenitor of the royal house of Denmark, came from Saxo's *Deeds of the Danes* and *Beowulf*, which runs to 3182 lines. The text that Grundtvig had used for his own translation in 1820 differed slightly from the original manuscript in the British Museum. In a conversation with Frederik VI in 1828, the King had asked him what he was working on, to which he responded "Nothing, Your Majesty, unless it should be that Your Majesty would send me to England to study the Old English manuscripts, which may prove to be of significance to Denmark." The application (Letter 19) was finally accepted late that year. Grundtvig was granted 2000 rigsdaler for the purpose, and began to take English lessons in Copenhagen from Carl Mariboe, a 28-year-old businessman newly returned from 5 years in London and now offering his services as an English teacher. Grundtvig had originally proposed to be away for a whole year, but had since cut the time to 3 or 4 months. His friend, Peter Fenger, offered to house and teach 6-year-old Johan while Grundtvig was in England, but in a letter dated 21st March 1829 Grundtvig wrote:

> ... If [the Lord] calls me away during the boys' childhood, I know of no friend whom I would rather take my place as father to Johan than you; but in such a brief absence as the trip to England appears to involve, I prefer not to separate the boys or ask of my wife another absence besides my own. At the moment there is no hurry for J's progress in knowledge, and, God preserve us, Møller [the house tutor] will keep what he *has* learned in good order,

while I would rather have a less involved hand teach him to write and reckon, which as yet he cannot manage at all.

England awaited him, and he left Denmark in good spirits and with great expectations. He had reworked into modern Danish excerpts from the above-mentioned *Rhymed Chronicle*, and for once he was well reviewed. Another of his books for children, *Chronicle of the Bible*, had even pleased a 'Naturalist', who had no need of any transcendent God. Moreover the Bishop of Zealand, Friederich Münter, was supplying him with a letter of recommendation for the Archbishop of Canterbury, William Howley.[174] He informed Rasmus Fenger of all this and more (Letter 20).

> ... my *Rhymed Chronicle* seems to please all sides. The other day I spoke with a man who openly admitted that he was a Naturalist, but who nevertheless thanked me for my *Chronicle of the Bible*, which he let his children use and found it admirable. The Bishop is recommending me to the Archbishop of Canterbury, and I hear that the distinguished literary world is very pleased about my trip.

The journey, his first out of Denmark, was truly arduous. He departed Copenhagen on Sunday 3rd May in a sailing-ship going north round Elsinore. Battered by a westerly wind and then becalmed it was only on the following Saturday that the ship sailed out on the North Sea. Not before Wednesday 13th May did he sight the Suffolk coast, and finally on Friday 15th he disembarked at Limehouse, east London, after a voyage of 12 days. Approaching London he had noted in his diary the number of new-fangled *steam*ships sailing in the opposite direction!

Grundtvig spent most of the summer of 1829 with a transcriber in the basement of the British Museum, studying the Anglo-Saxon manuscripts, in particular the only surviving manuscript of *Beowulf*. Although he had letters of introduction, this was his first trip away from his wife and children for 3 months, stuck in the museum, and trudging home to a landlady who offered him a simple fare of meat and potatoes. He went to church on Sundays and met a few English theologians, but for the most part he was lonely and lost, at home in neither the language nor the city. He wrote home to Lise on 4th June that he had now learned the meaning of loneliness and that he would return "a more loving friend, husband, and father". By 30th June 1829 he was truly downhearted: "I cannot get used to the life here – or rather the death. Every time I try to make somebody's acquaintance I lose even more hope of success."

Lise too was lonely, missing her husband's colossal presence in her life. Already on 30th May she wrote:

> For almost all of the first three weeks you were gone I lay alone in the bedroom with our three dear children. Once they were asleep, I was surrounded by an emptiness, for I could not peep in to you once in a while. I have felt this more and more, even when there are people

---

174. William Howley (1766-1848), a High Anglican, was Archbishop of Canterbury from 1828-48.

around me. I have told you how in my childhood I wished I had wings; this will happen even more often now. If only I could at least I could *give* this letter wings ...[175]

Although he gradually adapted to his new way of life – feeling more alone rather than lonely – Grundtvig never really enjoyed 'Babylon', as he called London. It was simply too *busy*, and he missed his home comforts, but he learned to adapt and by August he was really managing quite well (Letter 21).

Another powerful London experience was his visit to a school to see the new teaching methods for himself. Grundtvig's interest in education was now becoming more practical. He himself was aware of the great Swiss educationist, Johann Pestalozzi (1746-1827) and his philosophy of "Learning by head, hand, and heart". He knew of the English educationists, Andrew Bell (1753-1832) and Joseph Lancaster (1778-1838), who had introduced the concepts of mutual instruction and the monitorial system whereby the teacher personally observed the pupils' learning. He had encountered Rousseau's free upbringing in Constance's wish for her son to be taught "like Emile". From the German Johann Basedow (1724-90) he had learned that good teaching should strengthen a child's faith, independence, and self-confidence. Basedow had published his educational treatises, *Elementarwerk*, in 1768, and from 1753-61 he had been Professor of Moral Philosophy at Sorø Academy in Denmark.

The school that Grundtvig visited at Borough Road, Southwark had been founded in 1798, and was run by the British and Foreign School Society on the new teaching principles of Lancaster, a pioneer of universal free school education. Its main aim was to enable poor children to read the Bible, the innovation being older pupils teaching individual groups of younger pupils. Despite Grundtvig's initial scepticism he witnessed the system at work and praised it afterwards for its "liberal spirit". But even after a number of such positive experiences his verdict on his 4½ months away was damning: "What I have put myself through in this cold, dead, monstrous world-city cannot be described in words!"

Grundtvig had forgotten his wedding anniversary on 12th August until he was writing the date on a letter to Lise. Life in London was looking up, and his book purchases were clearly a source of great satisfaction (Letter 22). Safely returned to Copenhagen he nevertheless reflected on the lessons he had learned in London, the greatest of which he described thus: "The English stick to their guns, so the more I attacked the English way of doing things, the more they said, 'Well what do *you* do then?' And I was struck to the soul, for I had to admit that they were right. The most important thing about a man is that he *does* something!"[176] He remained in touch with John Bowring, among others, and sent him a copy of his poems with an accompanying letter, which testifies to his acquisition of the English language (Letter 23).

Something was already happening in Grundtvig's inner being. He came home from England a changed man – both as husband and father. He made contact with the poet Oehlenschläger; he revived his friendship with Molbech; he even heard Bishop Mynster

---

175. (GBHH, 8).
176. (Schrøder 1901, 105).

preach a "beautiful Christian sermon". He refused to be drawn into a polemical battle over the Church, leaving this to his younger supporters. This was most unlike the Grundtvig of old.

1830

Between Grundtvig's first and second visit to England, the British Parliament, led by the Duke of Wellington and Sir Robert Peel, had passed the Catholic Emancipation Act, allowing Roman Catholics roughly the same rights as Protestants. This extraordinary measure represented a huge step in the battle for religious freedom; a bilateral Parliament had in practice ended the divine right of Protestant kings, even though the British monarch to this day must belong to the Church of England. Again Grundtvig was impressed by the powers and workings of Parliament.

On 11th May 1830 Grundtvig returned to England for another 4 months to study the Anglo-Saxon manuscripts, first in London, then in Exeter to see the 10th-century *Exeter Book* of poems. His letter of introduction from the Archbishop of Canterbury, William Howley, praised him as "an eminent Nordic Scholar ... employed by the King of Denmark ... If you can show him any civility, you will find him a well informed and agreeable acquaintance, and well worth cultivating."

The second trip was much more exciting and successful than the first, as Letters 24 to 29 testify. Among his experiences was a visit to St. Paul's Cathedral on 3rd June, where he saw 10,000 children from London's charity schools (Letter 24). Grundtvig was fond of children and later helped Queen Caroline Amalie found a charity school in Copenhagen. Life in Exeter was very different from London. People were more welcoming, Grundtvig spoke better English, and he was allowed to sit alone with the manuscripts in the Chapter House. He also made trips to Bristol, Oxford, and back to London, where his acquaintances, Mr and Mrs Heaton, invited him to a dinner party on 24th June. Seated next to him at the table was the vivacious 26-year-old Clara Bolton, who revealed a deep knowledge of Greek mythology. Grundtvig was entranced until past midnight – when she invited him to her country home at a later date. He immediately wrote to Lise that he had met "the most interesting lady" and that he did not know whether she was unmarried or a widow... "Do not be jealous of your grey-haired toothless husband!" he wrote (Letter 25).

Unbelievably, and to his great embarrassment, Grundtvig then learned not only that Clara was *married* but that her husband had been present at the dinner-party! In some bewilderment he declined the invitation, only to be scolded by Lise in her next letter: "I am rather put out by your refusal to visit Mrs Bolton ... You do not know *how* she might have helped you, precisely because she *was* married. I am not jealous, I am angry!" (Letter 27). Grundtvig never forgot Clara and wrote a poem about her, 'Clara' (1844) 14 years after the event:

> Clara's breath my mouth unlocked,
> the rock was split, the water streamed;
> Like a morning dream she knocked,

then disappeared – or so it seemed:
For ev'ry time a harp-string sighs,
Clara floats before my eyes!

Inspired as he was by the oral tradition that lay behind both the New Testament and the Old English poems, Grundtvig was planning to put his considerable knowledge of Anglo-Saxon literature to good use *in England* (Letter 26). On the advice of the publishing house, Black, Young, and Young, he drew up a subscription plan to finance the publication of the ancient manuscripts in new editions, including *Beowulf*, the *Exeter Book*, and Layamon's *Chronicle of English History*, written in 12th-century Middle English poetry. He wrote to Bernhard Ingemann on the subject (Letter 30): "I have had the opportunity in the said prospectus to tell the English what I think of their unnatural indifference to what they ought to venerate, even if it were not their own!"

Although initially disinterested, the prestigious Society of Antiquaries now agreed that such an edition was desirable, but not with a foreigner as its editor. In spring 1831 they sent out a rival subscription plan and, to Grundtvig's dismay, a number of subscribers who had been on his *own* list now appeared to be jumping ship.

During this second England trip Grundtvig saw the consequences of industrialisation for himself. The new machinery "not only makes such a noise that no one can hear a word, it also blackens and roasts everything that comes within its range. Moreover, it turns people by the thousands, large or small, into no more than minor players, mere appendices to the machinery ... they are gradually replacing all the old artisans and making them mere tools in the engineer's hands, thoughtless slaves in the factory-owner's yard."[177] This time his letters home to Lise were more full of news and less of his loneliness (Letters 28 and 29). In his biography of Grundtvig from 1944 Hal Koch writes that Grundtvig moved from wonder to admiration when he compared England with the backwater of Denmark, and realised that the pre-condition for all this 'activity' is freedom – personal and public freedom. He left England at the end of his second trip determined to waken Denmark from its slumber.

1831

For Grundtvig's third trip he was recommended with the words, "He is a most zealous and able student of Anglo-Saxon literature and visits Oxford to look at what you have in that Department. He has published a translation of the Saxon poem *Beowulf* into Danish and other works on Nordic mythology." However, the main goal of his 2½-month trip was Trinity College, Cambridge, from where he wrote home to Lise on 14th June: "I have never had such good days in England as here, where I have joined a circle of knowledgeable, friendly, Christian clergy and professors whom I visit when I am not poring over manuscripts." Among these was Professor William Whewell (pronounced 'you'll'), whom Donald Allchin calls, "the most wide-ranging [man] in the spread of his intellectual interests, scientific, philosophical, and literary. Here at last Grundtvig was

---

177. TCG 140.

44. Trinity College, Cambridge.
Photo: Alan Copson Pictures / Alamy Stock Photo.

meeting a man of something like his own calibre".[178] William Whewell (1794-1866) was a polymath, with knowledge of the sciences (mechanics, physics, geology, astronomy) as well as economics, history, philosophy, theology, and law, the latter giving rise to the Whewell Professorship of International Law. He wrote poetry and sermons, and translated Goethe. In 1831 Whewell was Master of Trinity College, Cambridge. Grundtvig was both enthralled and flattered by the attention and kindness he received. He was invited to dine together with the students and the dons, and in letters from Cambridge (19th June and 13th July) he wrote home to his wife, Lise, full of enthusiasm (Letters 32-33).[179] He also took time to correspond with Bernhard Ingemann on the state of the Danish Church (Letter 31).

Grundtvig was deeply impressed by the university's tutorial system and the closeness between teacher and student – not least by the fact that they dined together in the college dining hall with the staff at the top table and the students on crosswise parallel benches all down the hall. The staff and the young men seemed to be sharing a common goal, the pursuit of learning, in a common dwelling, the university college. Both staff and students were to be found in the chapel, the library, the lecture-hall, the tutorial room, and the dining-hall. Grundtvig was pondering the basic elements of his educational

---

178. GS 1993, 243.
179. For Grundtvig's English poem to Whewell see no. 140 in *LW*.

philosophy for a People's High School. Back in London he wrote to Lise: "If I had you and the children here and you were as accustomed to the country and the language as I am, I should not mind living here for a few years in the hope of better times to come for my work in Denmark."

Yet all was not well with his marriage. On August 11th, the day before his wedding day that year and the third in a row when he had been in England, he wrote (Letter 34):

> Dear Lise, it is in the nature of things that married couples at our age no longer show such tenderness for one another as when they were younger. But I would be dishonest if I did not take this opportunity to say that it has truly worried me that last winter there seemed to be not just a constant cloud on your brow, but something strange placing itself between us. I do not know what it is. You will recall that I have said it before, but the only reply was a stronger impression of the hidden anguish that troubles you. Only He who has our hearts in His hand can heal your wounds, and far be it from me to say that I am innocent, as my grumpiness and my oddities must of necessity become more disagreeable as the years go by, especially in our straitened circumstances.

His Anglo-Saxon book project was also faltering. Admittedly by the autumn of 1831 Black, Young, and Young had 70 of the 80 subscribers needed to go ahead and print, and Grundtvig was offered the opportunity to collaborate with his English rivals, but he hesitated – for too long it would appear – and the chance never came again. On the positive side, as Sid Bradley writes: "Grundtvig's English prospectus certainly galvanised the English scholarly establishment ...; by virtue of substantial textual and interpretative work on *Beowulf*, Grundtvig established a place among pioneers of modern Anglo-Saxon scholarship."[180]

In Denmark Grundtvig always thought he knew best and was often self-contained. In contrast, on the England trips he sought out as many people as possible in Church circles, often Unitarians, and in cultural circles, provided he had a letter of introduction, an invitation, or a reference that would open closed doors. These conversations added new perspectives to the impressions he had gained from reading the *Edinburgh Review* and the *Westminster Review*, to which he subscribed for 8 and 4 years respectively. The former was a periodical from 1802 to 1929, which both argued the left-of-centre political cause and paved the way for modern literary criticism. The latter was from 1824 to 1914 the official organ of the philosophical Radicals, who promoted the utilitarian philosophy of Jeremy Bentham (1748-1832), maintaining that we should measure our moral standards against the maximisation of happiness.

Especially on his third trip, centred on Cambridge, Grundtvig landed in the midst of an intense cultural debate that corresponded in many ways to what was going on in Denmark. Should politicians follow the liberal market economy as promoted by Adam Smith (1723-96) and Jeremy Bentham (1748-1832), or should they follow the poet and social philosopher Samuel Taylor Coleridge (1772-1834), who argued against the unregulated free

---

180. Bradley, 350.

market, warned of the dangers of rampant industrialisation, and called for reforms to help the poor contribute better to society. Grundtvig's host in Cambridge, Professor Whewell, was a Coleridge man, as was his friend, Frederick (F.D.) Maurice, who later became one of the founders of Christian socialism. Grundtvig was deeply inspired by the level of debate, the freedom of speech, and, not least, the beauty of the college and the closeness of its community. Denmark, he thought, should aspire to something similar in Sorø on Zealand, a cultural centre for Denmark's history and education since the monastery was established in 1142. After reading in the *Edinburgh Review* of the plans for a University of London,[181] he had already written an article in 1827 in which he envisaged a People's High School for young men in Sorø.

In 1838 he proclaimed his love of England in his lecture series 'Within Living Memory':

> Gentlemen, in general I am an admirer of England, and if I were not a Dane, I would prefer most to be an Englishman.[182]

Shakespeare and Grundtvig

One of the most powerful poetic attractions in England was Shakespeare. As a young man Grundtvig had tried his hand at writing drama, and even acting, and he had acknowledged its difficulty. In his estimation, as a dramatic poet of history and the human mind Shakespeare had no equal; his genius should be linked to Denmark and the North:

> how better can [this preliminary reflection] be concluded than with the best omen for ... the resurrection of the North – namely, with the great prophet of universal-historical learning? For that is what William Shakespeare is, and that is why, like all prophets, he is honoured most after his death and outside his homeland. Indeed, those of us here who possess the ancient mythical prophecy must look with the greatest wonder at how the life of humankind in all its wonderful historical development presented itself to the bard, and how it was struck by the lightning of his prophetic insight. There will be hardly a single chapter in the great universal history we are awaiting for which the most suitable heading could not be found in "Shakespeare's Histories", as they are so appropriately called.

In 1969 Morten Bredsdorff wrote an English summary of his essay on Grundtvig and Shakespeare, in which he noted that Grundtvig's

> ... own knowledge of Shakespeare's text was not very extensive as he did not have any command of English and had to be content with reading A.W. Schlegel's German translation of the great Elizabethan.
>
> In England Grundtvig immersed himself with growing enthusiasm in Shakespeare's plays in the poet's own language. With delight he discovers that in his famous poem on the

---

181. See ch. 1 in *TSFL*.
182. *TCG*, 85.

"Sweet Swan of Avon" Ben Jonson has emphasized Shakespeare's lack of erudition. Grundtvig here finds proof that as a son of the common people the poet has escaped the shackles of the despised Latin schooling and has given unbounded expression to the genuine spirit of the Anglo-Saxon people in his historical plays. Shakespeare now becomes an ally in the exposition of Grundtvig's cultural policy and philosophy, according to which the peoples of northern Europe have been suppressed by classical humanism, and thus prevented from unfolding their original genius.[183]

In *N.F.S. Grundtvig's Literary Testament* (1827) he had called Shakespeare "the master-poet in the new Europe, whom not only poets but also book-lovers must learn to respect, if they are to enjoy any kind of esteem in the North." Great was his joy on 20th June 1829 when, as he noted in his diary: "I bought Shakespeare's works in 6 volumes for £1".

Luther and Grundtvig

In between his trips to England Grundtvig was pondering his relationship to Luther. He followed Luther's teaching that the Word of God was not the actual word on the page in the Bible but the activated word when heard and *believed*. It did not come alive until it was preached in the sermon, recited at Holy Baptism and Holy Communion, and employed in pastoral care and pastoral teaching. "The living Word" was thus becoming one of Grundtvig's characteristic concepts. He had already examined its content and meaning in *On True Christianity* (1826) and *The Truth of Christianity* (1826-27), and had concluded that through the power of the Spirit the Word creates *faith*. His reforming zeal now sailed close in the wake of Luther, and resulted in a direct question: *Should the Lutheran Reformation Really Continue* (1830-31).[184] Two Grundtvig scholars, Holger Begtrup and Hal Koch, consider this a "major work" in the corpus, despite it only being 80 pages long. Grundtvig answered his own question in the title with a resounding ...

> 'Yes, of course'. For life in the Lord's Congregation must not merely be sustained, but must grow in purity and power until it becomes like His own life on earth. The light must not merely be lit but must be transformed from glory to glory,[185] and shine over the whole earth.

Just as Luther purged the Roman Catholic Church, so did Grundtvig feel the need to purge the Danish Lutheran Church in order to penetrate to its core faith. As Steen Kullberg writes of Grundtvig in his introduction to the text:

> ... he criticises pontificating theologians and self-satisfied 'modern' pastors who threaten the 'old-fashioned' Christians – amongst whom he wished to be counted ... he and his kind

---

183. (GS 1969).
184. Ch. 3 (3 extracts) in *HCF*.
185. 2 Cor 3:18.

can no longer share the Church with those who refuse to acknowledge the confession of the Creed as the condition for acceptance into the Universal Church.[186]

Of equal interest are some of the central tenets of Luther's theology which Grundtvig considers *deficient*, including: his neglect of the oral tradition behind the Creed and its long history in the living Church; his misplaced trust in the Bible as the sole norm for the Christian faith; his underestimation of the importance of Church history as the learned experience of our forefathers' faith; and his acceptance that the *Confessio Augustana* of 1530 can be regarded as an 'article of faith' on a par with the Apostolic Creed. Grundtvig wrote, "A border sharper than before should now be drawn between what all Christians must believe and confess and what must be left to the free working of the Spirit and the individual Christian." Again he was distinguishing between the role of *faith* as opposed to the free workings of the Church, the School, and the State. The belief that faith was confirmed in the Creed at Holy Baptism was a view that Grundtvig was to hold for the rest of his life:

> At Holy Baptism pastors are like the guardians of Zion in the power of the Spirit. When the Bishop stands at the altar, truly mirroring the good shepherd who lays down his life for his flock, when the congregation joyfully lets the light shine on good deeds, and when the scholars keep vigil over the Book with their night-lamp lit by the light from the altar, making sure that the church door is open for exit as well as entry – then all is in its Christian order and the Lutheran reformation is complete.

Grundtvig's admiration for Martin Luther found poetic expression in a sentence from his *World History*: "His greatness is like that of the mountains, it becomes clearer the higher the sun rises."[187]

Grundtvig's first political work

Political Observations with Regard to Denmark and Holstein was published on 7th January 1831, between Grundtvig's second and third trip to England.[188] The three motivating factors behind this first political work were: the revolution in France in 1830 and the fear of a similar movement in Denmark; Grundtvig's positive experience of democratic politics and freedom of speech in England; and the mounting pressure from the southern dukedoms of Schleswig, where Danish and German were spoken in equal measure, and Holstein, where German was the sole language. Norway had been lost in 1814; were the dukedoms also to disappear? Grundtvig's conclusions were also threefold: the Danish absolute monarch was the best suited to solve the problem; freedom of speech was essential to a solution (also for the censored Grundtvig); and in this burgeoning 'age of the

---

186. *HCF*, 91.
187. (quoted in Borup, 71).
188. Ch. 15 in *TCG*.

peoples' it was the *people* of the dukedoms who should decide their future. For a society to cohere around 'freedom', the people, and especially their representatives, must cherish higher ideals than feathering their own nests. *On the Church, the State, and the School* (1819) contains the remarkable phrase 'republican virtues' in the following sentence about 'the people': "They must be full of republican virtues, and must possess integrity, patriotism, and altruism to the highest degree!"[189] In the dukedoms themselves Grundtvig's work was considered important enough to be translated into German in order for it to contribute to the political debate in Schleswig-Holstein.

Nordic Mythology 1832

On his return to Denmark from his three invigorating trips abroad, Grundtvig was more than ever determined to reawaken the Viking spirit that in his poetic imagination had overwintered in England. He immediately set about putting his new life philosophy into print in a new and totally revised version of his *Nordic Mythology* from 1808. Combining his knowledge of the Nordic myths and Anglo-Saxon poetry with world and Church history he produced a work which has been considered by all Grundtvig scholars to be a highpoint in his writing career. In particular the first 100 pages reflect his understanding of the spiritual power of Shakespeare's "universal historical learning". History, says Grundtvig, has produced four major peoples: the Jews, the Greeks, the Romans, and the Nordics:

> I maintain that when we regard the world of the spirit with Nordic eyes in the light of Christianity, we get the idea of a universal historical development of art and learning that embraces the whole life of man, with all its energies, conditions, and achievements. This idea liberates, strengthens, and delights all that is in harmony with the temporal welfare of the individual, the nations, and the whole race of man. It cannot help but lead to the most perfect enlightenment of life that is possible in the school for life.[190]

It was the sons and daughters of the Nordic spirit whom Grundtvig was addressing, and this included the British – that much he had learned from his visits to England. It was the latent Nordic spirit – still visible in the immense enterprising activity of the British on the cusp of the industrial revolution – which Grundtvig wished to harness as a chariot horse to his Nordic ambition. Paramount for him now was the liberty of the *people*, as heralded in the American Declaration of Independence and the slogan of the French revolution. 'The people's spirit' was to be a key concept in his understanding of the nations and their drive towards self-government. In the introductory poem, *Rhymed Letter to our Nordic next-of-kin*, Grundtvig writes with such power that the words still burst off the page:

---

189. *TCG*, 176.
190. *TSFL*, 57-58.

45. Nordic Mythology 1832.
In lines 4, 5, and 7 the first word *Frihed* (Freedom) is underlined.

> Freedom our watchword must be in the North!
> Freedom for Loki as well as for Thor...
> Freedom for all that from spirit is sprung,
> that never is changed but is outraged by chains;

Freedom must reign everywhere, also between enemies such as the trickster-god Loki and the sky-god Thor; each must be heard so that they can do battle with what is Truth, and thus unfold the power of the Spirit. Freedom must be secured with the aid of "the Mosaic-Christian view" – defined by Grundtvig scholar Ole Vind as "the view of the history of the human race as a world drama of ongoing optimistic development".[191] However, Christianity as a *faith* must otherwise be kept out of the equation. This allowed Grundtvig to keep house with the "naturalists of spirit", the deists and humanists whom he had met in large numbers in London. They too would be part of the gathered community that would become a nation-state. In this joint "school for life" myths were useful as symbols for the illumination of human life: Grundtvig's Danish word here was *sindbilleder*, literally 'mind-pictures'. Standing on the shoulders of our forefathers we will make increasing progress, for

---

191. (Vind, 432).

... man is not a monkey, destined first to ape the other animals and then himself until the world's end. Rather is he a glorious, incomparable creature, in whom divine powers through thousands of generations proclaim, develop, and enlighten themselves as a divine experiment, in order to show how spirit and dust can permeate one another and be transfigured into a common divine consciousness.[192]

In this condensed view of humankind and history, Grundtvig compares the monkey, which can only do what it is trained to do, to the human being, borne by spirit and capable of changing the future. The central word is 'experiment'. Human life and the whole of history are an open process, with an unknown result. Only time will tell the truth, but the foundation is that human beings are made in God's image.

Like most other philosophers and historians of the 19th century Grundtvig believed in evolution, though as a Christian romantic, not as a Darwinist scientist. Just as historically both the North and he himself had come through an Age of the Gods (childhood/imagination), followed by an Age of the Heroes (youth/feeling), now he was deep into the Age of Activity/ Working (adulthood) with its emphasis on reflection and afterthought and its understanding of the link between 'spirit' and 'dust'. This alone would bring about "a cohesion between idea and reality, between the world of the spirit and the world of the hand, between our view of humankind and its tangible great achievements."[193] Ideas were not much help if they could not be realised for the benefit of the common good; so industrialisation was a twin-edged sword. Grundtvig's amazement at the *activity* of the English was tempered by his fear of what the cotton mills and coal mines would do to the spirit of the people. Since industrialisation would doubtless be the future for Denmark, how could the country develop as a *single*-edged sword? If capitalist profit-making could be curbed, Denmark had a golden chance to control its development and create a society that also felt like a *community*. Even before its publication Grundtvig was excited about *Nordic Mythology*. He was aware that he was not only breaking new ground but was building on ideas that he had first visited twenty years earlier. On 7th January 1832 he wrote to Bernhard Ingemann about the Aesir, the gods associated with war and conquest, and the Vanir, the gods associated with fertility, wisdom, wealth and the future (Letter 35):

It was quite strange after twenty years to come back to the heights on which all youthful dreams are dreamed and all visions have their source – to see how everything in the dimmer light appears clearer and takes up a closer acquaintance with the Aesir and the Vanir. We must admit that it was the product of the decent, genuine natures, and that all the enthusiasm that we felt for them was more than worthy.

Grundtvig wrote endless drafts for his introduction to this *magnum opus* and was well satisfied – and relieved – with the result. The book marked a new start in his efforts to

---

192. *TSFL*, 57-58.
193. (Grell 1992, 124).

reform Denmark. During the 6 years that this chapter covers, these writing efforts had, despite his censorship, amounted to over 1,500 published pages. The idea of a school for life was taking shape.

Back to the pulpit

Grundtvig had reached another watershed in his life. Over the past six years he had made great strides in his understanding of the roles of the Church, the State, and the School (i.e. education). England had been the stimulus he had needed. From now on his main contribution to the Church would no longer be polemical but practical – as a pastor, as a hymnwriter, as a teacher. And it would be on behalf of the people, whatever their faith or lack of it. Right now, however, he was more concerned with the dissemination of freedom – in both the State and the School, as *Political Observations* (1831) and *Nordic Mythology* (1832) testify.

To help him test this decision in practice the circle around him approached the King and then the Chancellery for permission to form a free Danish/German congregation with two pastors: Grundtvig and the German-speaking Dane, Lorentz Siemonsen. Grundtvig decided to bypass the law. He 'borrowed' a friend's large home on Lime Kilns Road (*Kalkbrænderivej*) and preached to a full 'Lime Kiln congregation' two Sundays in a row. So great was the interest to hear him that he was about to move to a larger venue near the shipyard, when the police got wind of his activity and put a stop to it. Grundtvig himself then approached the new Bishop of Zealand, Peter (P.E.) Müller, who was much friendlier than his predecessor. The request was granted. From 4th March 1832 Grundtvig was allowed to preach in Christian's Church – though not to administer the sacraments.

At the entrance to the church is a plaque which reads: "This stone shall speak to future generations that N.F.S. Grundtvig worked in this church from 1832 to 1839 without being allowed to administer the Lord's Baptism and Communion but as a free preacher of God's living Word. Here, under difficult conditions he prepared the awakening of the life of the Danish Church and church singing which through him later issued from Vartov to the glory of God. Where the Name and Word of Jesus Christ is confessed and preached, there is truly the Kingdom of God, however frail its beginning."

With his return to the pulpit came Grundtvig's choice to remain *inside* the Danish State Church for the time being and to fight his cause from within, for that is where the people were already. His zig-zag path to this decision is worth retracing briefly: he had moved from demanding order in the State Church (1825) to demanding its partial dissolution so that the individual could break the parish-tie (1827), to seeking permission to leave and establish a free congregation (1831) to finally agreeing to become pastor of an authorised semi-free congregation within the State Church (1832). As late as 1866 he was still threatening to leave it.

His preaching was also changing course. He now sought to preach and pray "on behalf of life" in order to water the shoot that had been planted in baptism. The very text of his prayers and sermons took on a higher tone, as if the Holy Spirit were present not only in the sacraments but also in the sermon. They became quieter, more reflective and

46. The pulpit and altar in Christian's Church.
Photo: Edward Broadbridge.

personal, with more entreaty and encouragement. As Christian Thodberg has shown in his exemplary editions of Grundtvig's sermons, the style became almost liturgical – as in his introductory prayer to his sermon on the First Sunday in Lent 1832 together with a full congregation:

> O God! Father of our Lord Jesus Christ!
> Our forefathers' God and Our Gud!
> You who alone do wondrous things!
> Praise be to You and Your name for ever!
> Let our hearts burn within us,
> as you speak to us.
> Reveal the Scriptures to us,
> create a pure heart within us,
> and renew a constant Spirit in our innermost being.
> Do not leave us as we grow old (lit. 'under the grey hairs'),
> but let us make known Your care
> and Your power for all those who are to come.
> Be our children's God,
> as You were our forefathers God,
> that they may remain in Christ,
> as in Baptism they were grafted into Him!

Grundtvig's elevated spirit was moving towards the poetry of hymn-writing, and not least to the sense of joy and liberation that he associated with the resurrection. Over the next five years this was to be a central impulse. We can gain a feeling for this elation in the second verse of the Easter hymn, 'Take the black cross from the gravestone', which he recited to his congregation on Easter Day 1832:

> Heaven darkened, as He faded,
> shedding blood for all our woes;
> darkness waned, the grave was lighted
> as transfigured He arose.
> Let our praises Him adorn
> sweetly in this Easter dawn:
> Jesus Christ broke wide the prison!
> See the God-man is arisen!

Above all, Grundtvig's decision to stay within the established Church necessitated a redefinition of the Church in Denmark as the people's church *(folkekirke)*. The concept of the people's church *(Volkskirche)* is first attested in the writings of Friedrich Schleiermacher in 1822-23 where it denotes a church created by the people and not by the state. It is in this sense (and without further significance) that Grundtvig first uses the word in a sermon for Pentecost (Whit) Monday 1832:

> I know that in the 17th century it was not far from a pastor's thought that he should be a 'pope' – on a large or small scale; perhaps in a church created by the people *(folkekirke)* or a private chapel, or even at home with his children.[194]

Once the *folkekirke* was established by law in the 1849 constitution as "the Danish people's church", Grundtvig used the word extensively; for instance, it appears no fewer than 29 times in a single text, 'The People, the People's Church, and Popular Belief in Denmark (1851).[195]

A further event in 1832 is worth noting, Grundtvig's first published collection of hymns, entitled *Historical Hymns and Rhymes for Christian Teaching*. In her online introduction to the work in GV Else Riisager recounts the working process that Grundtvig could occasionally adopt when requested to change a line or two. The collection contained 68 hymns and songs, and included 29 hymns by Kingo, 9 by Brorson, and 22 by Grundtvig, who worked in close collaboration with his publisher, L.C. Hagen. Grundtvig's supporters, Lorentz Siemonsen and Sigfred Ley, followed the process, the latter noting in his diary for 9th September 1832:

> Hagen enjoys visiting Grundtvig these days. He tells him which hymns he wants altered and Grundtvig sits down in the corner of the sofa and writes them! ... The other day Siemonsen suspected him of changing the *old* hymns. Grundtvig defended himself somewhat but finally said, "You see, Siemonsen, it makes no difference, for when someone comes and asks me to do my best, I dare not say no![196]

---

194. (Thodberg, 5, 230).
195. Text 10 in *HCF* (2018).
196. (GEEG 153).

47. **Sorø Academy.**
Drawing by Just Michael Hansen, mid-19th century.

11. A lean agreement is better than a fat conflict (1833-38)

It was a risky business living as an unpaid preacher in an open congregation with no organisation. Grundtvig counted on God's blessing and his own good fortune, as well as on his good friends and benefactors. Occasionally his congregation supported him, as with the silver-plated cup and Danish ducats that they gave him for his 50th birthday in 1833, or the new cassock presented to him at Easter 1838, but by and large he depended on the financial support of his faithful friends, especially Gunni Busck and Peter Fenger.

He remained hyper-active in two increasingly separate areas which had once been united in his head and heart. Where the aim of the younger Grundtvig had been to bring people to Christ through fiery tracts and sermons and polemical attacks on his 'enemies', the older Grundtvig was now distinguishing far more clearly between the Church and the School, and generally between what should be handled in Church and society respectively. For the Church he wrote a vast number of hymns; for the School (i.e. education) he wrote numerous articles advocating the education of the peasant farmers who made up 70% of the population. This more mature Grundtvig was better able to integrate the two entities through his burgeoning interest in Danish politics and his ongoing revision of Danish history. It was in the 1830s that Grundtvig at last received genuine appreciation as a public figure. This was due not least to his realisation that a milder tone encouraged a greater dialogue, both with his erstwhile opponents and with his newfound admirers. As a 'freelance' pastor in Christian's Church, he attracted a large number of congregants, even though he was still not allowed to administer the sacraments. His sermons were becoming softer in tone, and by 1838 he could announce: "I have abandoned my previous claim that the more 'fight' there is, the more 'life' there is ... so in every sense now, a lean agreement is better than a fat conflict."

Throughout his life Grundtvig wore a coat of many colours: the theologian, the hymn-writer, the historian, the poet, educator, patriot, and politician. Each of these appellations accurately describes him during this period; his ideas were changing with the times, his compass was set in different directions, and all the while his productivity was astounding.

The theologian

As a theologian, Grundtvig was becoming less intense about the need to save souls and more trusting in God's ability to ensure the survival of the Christian faith – just so long as the Church preached the Word and administered the sacraments. In an exchange with Frederik Barfod, the latter relates: "He once told me, 'You are not a Christian, Barfod, and you may not become one until late in the day, but I am not worried about you, for you are a truth-lover, so you will also *find* the truth, either here or hereafter'. It was the warm and gentle words, 'here or hereafter', that left such an indelible impression upon me."

The creation theology that Grundtvig was developing here is based on God's love, first as Maker, then as Redeemer – as Creator and Re-creator. The human life granted at the Creation must serve as a resource, a force, and the basis for our understanding of the *second* creation in Jesus Christ. Grundtvig had reached a new understanding of the relation between the human and the Christian. All humans can view life as their common property and experience, but the Christian faith is a new creation of a new life *within* the old life; moreover, it is a gift, not a coercion. As he wrote in 1837:

> Human comes first and Christian next,
> this is a major precept;
> our Christianity comes free,
> a gladness pure and perfect,
> but gladness only in the end
> for those who truly are God's friend
> and Truth's right noble kindred!
>
> They who would *truly* human be
> while on this earth still living,
> lending an ear to Truth's own word,
> to God the glory giving,
> if Christian faith is *the* true way,
> though 'Christian' they be not today
> they will be so tomorrow![197]

Thus the foundation of Grundtvig's theology and world-view in the 1830s was the relation between what is human and what is Christian – as he wrote in a poem 'To My Sons' (1839):

> Honest heathens, Turks, and Jews,
> God loves each and ev'ry one,
> hates the honeyed devotee
> who *pretends* to be His son

Grundtvig could thus formulate the purpose of life for all human beings – Christians and heathens alike – as follows:

> Though of clay, yet *human* being,
> strong in Spirit, strong in heart
> God in humankind to honour,
> our Creator's work of art![198].

---

197. No. 123 in *LW*.
198. (HS 197, 2).

With reference to the bloody revolutions of 1789 and 1830 Grundtvig went so far as to claim "there were traces of our fundamental human spirit even in the middle of Paris."[199] The true essence of humanity is as central to *human* life as Jesus Christ is to *Christian* life, and the life that God granted humankind at the first Creation forms part of our human experience when Jesus comes to earth at the second Creation, the Redemption. The two express God's creative power in relation to his Creation:

> First time as the good Creator
> God took clay as Maker mild.
> Second time, as sin-forgiver,
> gracious God redeemed His child![200]

Though rare for a Lutheran, Grundtvig set the theology of creation on the same level as the theology of salvation and redemption, thus requalifying the traditional Lutheran teaching of the dominance of sin in all human life. The second Creation/Redemption – through the working of the Holy Spirit in Baptism and Faith – manifests the Christian faith as a new creation of a new life *within the old life*. The old, created life that Christians share with non-Christians is still there.

In the Grundtvig archives there is a draft for *The Danish Four-Leaf Clover*[201] which best illustrates this reflection on human life alongside the Christian life:

> Both these lives still exist and are easy to reconcile; I know because I *live* them! It may be on a small scale, but it is nevertheless so real an experience that I can feel them trying to reproduce themselves in me – not in a confusion as they once were but separately, under their own names. I no more want the life of the Danish people to be Christian than I want it to be French or German! A *real* life is neither more nor less than it *is*, and it only works and *manifests* itself as it truly is.

From his article, *Is Faith Truly a School Matter* (1836), we can see how much Grundtvig had changed his mind – as he happily admitted! Here he now argued that all religious instruction should be *removed* from the school curriculum, for faith is a "matter of the heart". It cannot be received from God through 'the School' but only through 'the Church', where it can be strengthened by other Christian believers.

Freedom of belief within the State Church

In a letter to Bernhard Ingemann in 1836 Grundtvig had argued that "the spoken word is the only living, effective expression of the Spirit" (Letter 37). He was now sure of his view of history and mythology, but he still grappled with the question of whether the

---

199. (VU IV, 284).
200. (GSV IV, no. 212).
201. See ch. 5 in *TSFL*.

Church should actually *allow* religious freedom and make greater room for this "effective expression". As we have seen, he had chosen to remain within the State Church, but questioned whether the freedom to leave it and establish an independent church should be granted to others. He wrote a substantial contribution to the question in *An Impartial View of the Danish State Church* (1834),[202] prefacing the work with a biblical quote: "Where the Spirit of the Lord is, there is freedom."[203] He was now arguing that all forms of compulsion should be abolished and people should at least be able to "break the parish-tie" that had bound them to their local church and pastor from time immemorial. They should be allowed to remain *within* the State Church since "the faith of our fathers would indeed always present the state with its most diligent, faithful, and obedient citizens."[204] It was therefore in the State's and the King's interest to reorganise the Church so that there was room for Grundtvig and other like-minded Christians. His dilemma was that although he did not want the Church to split into free churches and sects – for what would that mean for the unity of the people? – he wished to preserve its historical core in old-fashioned Lutheranism, even when he was at odds with its view of the Bible.

By 1834 Grundtvig was arguing for "a free state Church, with a free congregation,"[205] which would allow: 1) a breaking of the parish-tie, 2) civic confirmation and wedding rituals, and 3) withdrawal from the State Church. Pastors should be permitted the greatest degree of freedom as regards doctrine and ritual, while churchgoers could change congregation if they so wished, or create their own – either inside or outside the State Church. Against this, Bishop Mynster wished to retain the State Church in its present form with a few minor changes, while Grundtvig's old adversary, Professor H.N. Clausen, was arguing for a Church *Synod* as a solution to the increasing problem of allowing more freedom while retaining the State Church.

The State Church was by definition in the hands of the State or the King. With inspiration from England Grundtvig therefore called it an 'Establishment Church',[206] with which the government could do as it liked. On this point he was right, but not on two others, where his views were unrealistic. He argued first that the State could seek an alliance with, and help to organise, any free congregations that had no defined doctrine and ritual, and second, that their pastors should enjoy total freedom. Both ideas were non-starters, and could end up sending churchgoers round in circles as they looked for a congregation where pastors did not use their freedom to change both doctrine and ritual.

---

202. Ch. 5 in *HCF*.
203. 2 Cor 3:17.
204. *HCF*, 126.
205. Ibid. 135.
206. (VU III, 316).

The hymnwriter

In the years 1835-37 Grundtvig was also hard at work writing hymns, up to a hymn a day at the height of his powers. He had written a number of fine hymns before, but a reform of the liturgy was in the air, church attendance was declining further, and the turgid tempo of contemporary hymn-singing was sucking the life out of the hymns. Grundtvig had already mentioned in a number of sermons that hymns should be sung at 'walking-speed'. His friends, not least Gunni Busck, who had been a warm supporter since 1821, encouraged and even financed him to concentrate on a new collection of his *own* hymns (Letter 36) – and Grundtvig set to work. In the summer of 1835 he rented a summer residence for the family 13 km north of Copenhagen and walked, often with his two sons, back and forth to Christianshavn, composing as he went. He usually had a particular tune in mind to which he could fit a stanza or a verse. In a letter to Busck dated 28th July 1835 he wrote: "Out there I hum the old hymns and my ear thrills to the sound, with the blue sea and the blue sky before me."

The hymns were published successively in pamphlets and collected into a first volume of 401 hymns on 13th September 1837 under the title, *Song-Work to the Danish Church*. The 'Song-Work' referred to the bells in the spire of the Church of Our Lady, which had been destroyed by the British bombardment in 1807. Dedicated to "The Danish congregation and my pastoral friends, Gunni Busck and Peter Fenger", Grundtvig's *Song-Work* not only rebuilt the carillon figuratively but added new bells in different tones – with hymns for the entire church year. The throats of the singing congregation were now the new tower for the *Song-Work*. In contrast to the solemnity that surrounds the sacraments of Baptism and Communion, hymn-singing allows the congregation to sing to the Lord both loud and long; in its hymn-singing the sense of community in the faith is at its highest. In a letter to Gunni Busck he was clearly delighted with the result – "to the Lord's praise" (Letter 38) and to both Busck and Ingemann he spoke of a "new song" in the Danish Church (Letter 39).

Grundtvig's strengths as a hymnwriter are multiple. He wrote freely *from the Bible*, his hymns being an integral part of his theology. Indeed, in his hymns he is at his best as both poet *and* theologian. Take, for instance, his extraordinary image of heaven as a meeting-place for friends and our true 'Fatherland' at the end of the hymn, 'We welcome with joy this blessed day':

> And so may we reach our Fatherland
> where days are forever vernal;
> there stands a castle so fair and grand
> with halls full of joy supernal.
> Then cheerfully may we there converse
> with friends in Your light eternal.[207]

---

207. No. 53 in *LW*.

48. Grundtvig welcomes Thorvaldsen home from Italy.
Grundtvig's fame was now such that he was among the leading Danish figures who welcomed the world-famous Danish sculptor Bertel Thorvaldsen home from Italy in 1838. In this panel of a frieze by Jørgen Sonne, painted in 1847, which surrounds the exterior of the Thorvaldsen Museum in Copenhagen, Grundtvig is sitting with his hat doffed. Photo: Ole Haupt. Thorvaldsen's Museum.

Grundtvig is moving into a poetic, Christian world of his own. The originality of those last two lines is a lyrical and theological masterpiece. Our resurrected souls will not just rest in peace in the next world, they will actually *converse* with one another in halls full of joy. Second, he wrote *for the divine service* with all its rituals, so his hymns were for the most part a rewriting and a reinforcement of the liturgy. Third, with his prodigious knowledge of other churches in other times and in other languages he was able to rework hymns into Danish from Hebrew, Greek, Latin, Old English, German, and Nordic sources to serve his purpose. Even well-worn Danish hymns came under his reforming pen, such as 'We welcome with joy this blessed day'. This in itself was a confirmation of the power of the original source to inspire not only the living spoken word but also the living *singing* word. For Grundtvig, divine service was the essential form of Christian fellowship, merging the heavenly with the earthly and the dead with the living:

> Saints on earth and saints in heaven
> share the same Church, this we know,
> He on high of this assures us,
> He who knows all depths below.[208]

Of the 1,500 hymns and 20,000 verses that Grundtvig wrote, many are long and/or long forgotten, but among them are so many 'bells of bronze', all cast in one piece, that they resonate throughout the central tenets and fields of Christianity, praising the persons of the Trinity, the Church Year, Christian life and human life. The *Song-Work* is an amazing *work of song*. On its appearance composers of hymn-tunes set to work under Grundtvig's inspiration to produce an extraordinary number of tunes worthy of his original hymn-texts.

The historian

Grundtvig waited in vain for reviews of *Nordic Mythology* from the previous year. The book was neither widely read nor even reviewed on publication. Only few understood the significance of its content, but it was to prove central to the movement that was beginning to use the name 'Grundtvigian', as some of his followers called themselves. Meanwhile he pressed on with a new version of his *World History*: the first volume, from Genesis to the Destruction of Jerusalem in 70 CE (1833); the second, from 70 CE to the Fall of the Byzantine Empire in 1453 (1836), and the third from 1453 to 1715 (1843). Even after 1,800 printed pages Grundtvig could get no further; 18th century rationalism proved beyond his reach. Each volume was prefaced by the same quotation from the Swiss historian Johannes von Müller (1752-1809): "Where there is most life, there is the victory".

All his history writing is marked by an honest attempt to draw on the original sources, which is why he added the sub-title to all 3 volumes of the *Handbook*: "*According to the Best Sources*". Grundtvig respected the credibility of in particular the Mosaic-Christian sources

---

208. No. 66 in *LW*.

that represented the foundation of history as God's plan for humankind with Jesus as its midpoint. To these sources the Bible belonged.

In 1837 Grundtvig was persuaded by his younger friends to hold a series of lectures on the history of the last 50 years. What motivated him to set out on such a journey? Grundtvig was gratified by the young men's enthusiasm, he was always keen to stand before an audience, and he was not at all dismayed by his own ignorance on the subject, as he wrote to Bernhard Ingemann (Letter 41):

> This is an area of history that I have completely neglected and in general held in contempt, so to turn it to good use I had to go back to the roots in particular of the French Revolution and deal with this singularly most unpleasant and generally poorly treated moment in history. I am in the middle of it right now, and although I could do with a little encouragement, I nonetheless need all the time available to be ahead of events by the end of the holiday. Between the two of us, I was getting desperate, partly because there was so much to read up, and partly because my memory will not be as reliable as it was in my youth. In the case of a history lecture, which must not be read from a manuscript, but must be true story-telling, that is an embarrassment.

This self-belief was yet again the driving-force. Grundtvig, now in the eleventh year of his censorship constraint, needed the King's permission. His application met with a ready response and between Christmas and New Year's Eve 1837 he was informed that the censorship ban was to be lifted on 4th January 1838. Around this time he wrote one of his most famous songs, celebrating what Flemming Lundgreen-Nielsen has called "the power and intimacy of the mother-tongue, as spoken and sung by mothers and young girls"[209]:

> Mother's name is a heav'nly sound,
> as broad as blue oceans swaying;
> Mother's voice is the baby's joy,
> and gladdens when hair is greying.
> Joy or need, so sweet its breath,
> sweet in life and sweet in death,
> sweet in time hereafter.[210]

When Bishop Mynster allowed the lecture series to take place, Grundtvig set to work – and was never more than a couple of lectures ahead of himself! Between 20th June and 26th November 1838 he gave 51 lectures at Borch's Hall of Residence to an expanding, and increasingly enthusiastic, audience. Grundtvig's belief in the power of history as the greatest tool of learning culminated in this lecture series, later entitled *Within Living Memory*.

---

209. (GS 2007, 57).
210. No. 87 in *LW*.

The lecture hall seated 250, but 600 were present at the final lecture. What his male-only audience clearly warmed to was Grundtvig's belief that the key to understanding a people's spirit and its characteristics is found in its history – and not just the history of Denmark and the Danish forefathers. The range of lectures included the recent history of several European countries – Greece, Spain, Italy, France, Germany, as well as the USA. Nor was it all names and dates. Grundtvig discussed the concept of 'public spirit' in England, and his fear of 'the mob' in revolutionary France. He praised the Greeks' fight for freedom, and deplored 'the shadow of Rome', meaning the Roman Catholic Church.

Grundtvig's belief that *no* history can be viewed 'objectively' since the viewer is always *subjective* is well argued in the second of his lectures, on 22nd June. He simply consulted his sources and presented his views, which were quite common for the time. Of the USA he said: "may I ask you to note that the country was in general populated by *Europeans*". Democracy as a system of government was flawed; Grundtvig preferred the 'enlightened monarch' who 'listened to his people'.

The lecture-series caused quite a stir in the capital city! The day after the lecture on 17th October, Frederik Barfod wrote: "When Grundtvig descended from the lectern, the assembled audience sang his song about Willemoes for him; they gave him back his own song by way of thanks... and this was without prior agreement."[211] The impact was such that it established the model for the popular talk and communal singing which is so prevalent in societies and associations in Denmark today. Grundtvig was now genuinely *popular* in both senses of the word, being considered 'of the people' as well as admired 'by the people'. His own 'living word' had proved a great success, and this encouraged him in his educational philosophy.

He kept returning to the question: What makes a people *distinctive* in history? His answer was: Begin with their mythology and examine the thoughts and deeds of their heroes and villains. What are the hazards they must overcome? And above all, how do they move towards freedom and peace? In that same second lecture he praised the freedom granted to the Danish peasant farmers in 1788 when adscription (a form of serfdom) was abolished. Later, in 1797, a 20 m-high Freedom Pillar was erected in the heart of Copenhagen. Grundtvig regarded the abolition of adscription as an important step on the path to a society based on increasing equality, but he was still not ready for any form of *democracy*.

Grundtvig's basic view in the lecture series was that we must concern ourselves with history in order to learn about ourselves and others. We cannot understand what we need as an organic people until we have studied our history, both in its general movement and in its particulars. If a mythology contains a high god, then our present king must be strong; if we want to know what 'the people' are thinking, we must know their history. If Odin holds a consultation with all the gods, then our king also needs an advisory council. Above all, the peoples of the world must not *copy* one another. To ensure that this does not happen Denmark needs a people's high school that can teach the people about themselves and their history, their geography, their language, their songs, and their laws.

---

211. No. 99 in *LW*.

Occasionally Grundtvig drew on his own experience to tell this essential history. When he first heard Steffens lecturing on the new romanticism, he did not understand him, for he was mired in the mud of the Aarhus Cathedral School that he had attended. Where he had once claimed that 'salvation' came from the country and decay began in the city, he now stood on a university rostrum to praise Copenhagen as "a beautiful city" and claim of the Freedom Pillar that:

> Here in Denmark at least, that represents the freedom of the spirit, of the mother-tongue, and of all beneficent powers, so just as the morning lark sang on the Freedom Pillar in *The Harvest Festival*, so am I sure that the evening larks will gather in flocks to fly up from it and sing heaven a good deal closer to them![212]

The optimism that Grundtvig expressed in poetic language is characteristic of his – and the 19th century's – evolutionary view of history. In his New Year's Day sermon 1838 he proclaimed that Denmark was on the way to a "Danish and Nordic golden year that will radiate through history as one of the most prosperous and envious periods of the human race on earth".[213] Such optimism has been hard to sustain in the 20th century and beyond. To this day his view of history as a *spiritual* rather than a temporal development is both condemned as naïve yet also praised as prophetic. Balancing the one against the other Ole Vind argues that Grundtvig is on firmer ground in his anthropology of spiritual history when he says that through the Word, the life-force in humankind can "propagate, proceed and develop the life of our forefathers and thereby create history, as opposed to the human species remaining a kind of monkey, identical in a thousand generations and without heroic deeds and a history. His view of history as God-driven is the most fundamental feature of his view of life, and the nucleus of Grundtvig's works. From this it follows that his view of *Church* history is an integrated part of his comprehensive philosophy of history, so he feels no need to write about it as a separate subject. Summarising his view of Grundtvig on this point Vind concludes:

> The core of Grundtvig's anthropology of *spiritual* history is his view of humankind as being defined by *spirit* and belonging to the supra-individual world of *spirit* which is also the world of *history*. This contains a truth that reaches beyond Grundtvig's time-bound biblical and Christian imagery".[214]

The educator, the patriot, and the people's high school

Education and patriotism were inseparably linked in Grundtvig's mind, like two prongs on the same fork. In the course of the 1830s he was working his way towards an understanding of the concept of 'Danishness': how to define it, how to practise it, and how to

---

212. TCG, 58. *The Harvest Festival* (1790) was a musical play by Thomas Thaarup.
213. HCF, 394.
214. (Vind, 559).

49. The Freedom Pillar.
Erected in 1797 in commemoration of the abolition of adscription in 1788. The four statues around the obelisk symbolise Fidelity, Justice, Civic Virtue, and Agricultural Industry. SMK, National Gallery of Denmark.

promote it as part of every child's education. In 1836 he published *The Danish Four-Leaf Clover*, arguing that the four leaves of the clover were the King and the People (the ideal form of government), and the Fatherland and the Mother-tongue (Grundtvig's indelible marks of kinship). Four more tracts followed, one for each of the subsequent years:

1837: *To the Norwegians concerning a Norwegian High School*
1838: *The School for Life and the Academy at Sorø*
1839: *On the Union of Learning in the North*
1840: *Appeal for, and Concept of, a Danish High School in Sorø*[215]

It is worth recalling that while he was publishing these works he was busy collecting hymns for *Song-Work to the Danish Church*, preparing lectures for *Within Living Memory*, writing songs such as 'Mother's voice' and 'Enlightenment', and preaching every Sunday at Christian's Church.

Initially, Grundtvig was concerned with Higher Education – not for the academics but for the new and eager civil servants who were to help the Danish monarchy and government in the education and formation of its citizens to greater participation in the affairs of state. His inspiration came not least from his trips to England, and in particular to Trinity College Cambridge, where all manner of subjects were being taught and studied and there was above all *interaction* between staff and students. This was to become a keyword in Grundtvig's educational philosophy and a central part of his legacy to the world. He also came to realise that the same interactive philosophy could be used right down to the youngest children – and to the lesser-educated peasant youth out in the country. The academic youngsters were still fast asleep in the city when the country youngsters were up and about using their practical skills on the farms. The two were well contrasted in Grundtvig's poem, 'Enlightenment', from 1839:

Is spelling right or wrong a light
alone to scholars given?
O no, God grants this good to most,
His light a gift of heaven.
The sunrise on the peasant shines,
but on the scholar never,
enlightening the agile man
in all his bright endeavour.[216]

In the 'school for life', as he called it, education was not to be a dusty degree in Theology and a knowledge of Latin; it was to be a contemporary understanding of *Denmark* and *Danishness*. Children young and old should *enjoy* school, and teachers should inspire their

---

215. Chs 7, 8, 9, and 12 in *TSFL*.
216. No. 10 in *TSFL*.

pupils by being enthusiastic about the subject in question. In a letter to Gunni Busck on 28th July 1835 he wrote:

> All our efforts to make young people and country people think and know anything that is strictly *coherent* is foolishness; we should simply try to tell them what we are excited about at the moment and leave it to time and their digestion to make sense of it spiritually, just as they do with bodily food.

Even before he arrived in England in 1831 for his third trip Grundtvig was employing the phrase 'people's high school'. Already in 1827 he had written *The University in London and the Academy at Sorø* as a contribution to the lively debate about the use of the buildings that until the Reformation had formed the monastery of Sorø 80 km west of Copenhagen. Indeed, this was where Saxo had written his famous *Deeds of the Danes*. Since 1623 the buildings had housed – under the name Sorø Academy – various clerical, military, and academic institutions for the youth of the nobility. Thus Grundtvig refers to the academy as the 'Knights College'. Despite large donations from Danish cultural life – such as the fortune that the Danish-Norwegian professor and playwright Ludvig Holberg had donated on his death in 1754 – the Academy had been forced to close in 1798. But in conjunction with the cultural growth of the Danish Golden Age (1800-50) Sorø Academy had re-opened in May 1827 in the newly-constructed main building, a landmark for Sorø's exceptional status. The concept of a 'people's high school' first appeared in 1831 in *Political Observations on Denmark and Holstein*, where Grundtvig wrote: "in few places, if anywhere, is there a High School for popular learning and civic education that gives 'the non-academic' the opportunity for both education and skills training."[217] Sorø was to be the prototype, and Grundtvig captured its revolutionary nature in a brief fable which he called 'The Academy in Sorø – a Sweet Dream'.[218]

> A man comes into the academy but finds it empty – there are no students. He meets someone and asks, "Where are all the students?"
> "They are on holiday!"
> "Then where are all the teachers?"
> "They are at the exams!"
> "But how can they be there if the students are not present?"
> "It is the *teachers* who are being examined! The examiners are the oldest farmers in the area, those who have lived longest and most intensely."

Grundtvig was not a systematic thinker, but that does not stop us from trying to gain a systematic overview of his thought. Ove Korsgaard has made a brave attempt.[219]

---

217. Ch. 15 (extracts) in *TCG*.
218. (Most likely from 1837. Christensen 1983).
219. (Korsgaard 2018, 116).

50. Grundtvig's educational thinking

Life sphere	Civic sphere	Learning sphere	Religious sphere
School	Civic school	Grammar school	The Lord's school
Educational form	Public (grade) school	University	Church school
Type of school	School for Life	School for Pleasure	School for Song
Primary room	Lecture room	'Workshop'	Church
Genre	Speech-conversation	Experiment	Sermon
Goal	Capability	Learning	Virtues
Pattern	The people	The universal	God (*imago dei*)

As Korsgaard's diagram shows, the central element in the people's high school was to be the lecture hall, though elsewhere students could also formulate their thoughts in conversation and reciprocal teaching. Learning together interactively, students would be better equipped for life in general – and predominantly in its civic and vocational sides. The 'narrative' element, *story-telling*, was to be a central methodology from first to last in all education. In his introduction to *The School for Life* (2011) Korsgaard writes:

> Life as it is lived and history as it has been experienced, constitute the narrative element in Grundtvig's educational thinking. More than any of his contemporaries he is aware that personal identity and collective communities have a narrative as their prerequisite. Without narratives there is no individual and popular identity. Human life and social life are structured by the narratives that are passed on to the next generation. According to Grundtvig, 'the School for Life' must build on the narrative and the dialogue as its most important educational methods.

As a pedagogical concept the School for Pleasure in the diagram above is somewhat diffuse, but as we have seen, Grundtvig wanted students to enjoy their schooling whatever their age. We need to enjoy a subject before we can first gain and then increase a knowledge of it. This is what he meant by his famous lines in the song 'Here is a revelation':

> It has been well contended:
> We never comprehended
> what first we did not love![220]

At university level Grundtvig proposed a joint Nordic University in Gothenburg for Denmark, Norway, and Sweden, with two faculties, one for History (i.e. the humanities) and one for Natural Science. The inclusion of the latter, in stark contrast to his previous antipathy towards the sciences, doubtless reflected his experience in 1831 at Cambridge Uni-

---

220. No. 79 in *LW*.

versity, where he was befriended by Professor William Whewell, who was both a priest and philosopher *and* a mathematician and minerologist! During his trip Grundtvig not only met 'the father of the computer', Charles Babbage, but also himself visited the university's astronomical observatory (Letter 32). Using this experience Grundtvig proposed that the university in Gothenburg should be a living workshop for experiments that could bring about new insights into the general conditions of humankind and develop a tradition for free research in all areas: ... "a Nordic University must arise to eclipse not only those in Berlin, Göttingen, and Wittenberg but even the colossi in Paris, Oxford, and Cambridge".[221]

In a later and more developed proposal from 1847, Grundtvig wanted the people's high school to have an agricultural purpose:

> Running a successful home farm alongside the High School would be both pleasurable and beneficial, and if the school were surrounded by workshops where all the crafts were well run, the pleasure and the benefit would be excellent. It is a joy for every living soul to see the brisk movement of human life in many useful directions that in a single word could be called 'enterprising'.[222]

Under 'Educational form' in the diagram we also find Grundtvig's concept of a Church School, though this was never really defined. In his sermons from 1837 Grundtvig referred increasingly to "the Lord's School", which would seem to extol the virtues from 1 Cor. 13: to "bear, believe, hope, and endure all things" while putting "the ways of childhood" behind us. Throughout our lives we are apprentices to the Master:

> Far from being able to master His ordinances or, from our impoverished understanding, to discuss and correct His mysterious words regarding Baptism or Communion, we should emulate Maria and sit humbly at the feet of the Master, watching His lips and storing up His words in our hearts.[223] The student is not above the teacher, but everyone who is fully trained will be like their teacher.[224]

Our human circumstances are also our Christian circumstances as we grow and develop. Like children learning to walk, we are held by the Spirit's reins as we follow Christ's example:

> As we live life
> we are by God instructed,
> in joy, in strife,
> are carried and conducted:
> we walk in reins,

---

221. *TSFL*, 236.
222. Ibid., 334.
223. Lk 10: 38-42.
224. Mt 10:24; Lk 6: 40.

the Spirit trains,
led by our Father's host of angels.[225]

The question for Grundtvig, which he never answered unequivocally, was how Christians can be "carried and conducted" when they are in "reins". He was doubtless thinking first and foremost of the divine service, of Christ's own words 'carry and conduct' in the sacraments and the hymn-singing, all of which lift us beyond ourselves. By "the Church school" he probably meant the congregation's *schooling* – as a parallel to the civic school. The sermon is part of this schooling, being for Grundtvig often both catechetic and exhortatory, but there should also be a Christian education *outside* the pulpit – and even outside the educational system in general. Faith should not be taught or encouraged in a *civic* context, it belonged in a *church* context. *Is Faith Truly a School Matter?* he wrote in 1836; and his answer, contrary to the practice of the time, was a resounding no! Like his Nordic University, Grundtvig's 'Church School' never materialised as an institution, but how to *progress* in the faith remained a church matter, for the Holy Spirit was holding the reins of God's children. The actual contents of Grundtvig's Church School – lectures and discussions on the Christian faith and Church matters – were nevertheless taken up and continue to be fostered in other fora today.

Just as there are three spheres in life, so should there be three forms of school. Public/Grade School must aim at the people and their life, the University must study the universal conditions of life, while the Church School/the Lord's School must direct itself towards God and the understanding of humankind as created in His image. For Grundtvig there is a *Christian* way of life, just as there are Christian virtues. There are overlaps between the three schools, which in the last resort are dealing with the same human life that we share. He can therefore envisage, for instance, that aging clergy could take up residence in the University in order to receive and contribute to new theological insights.

The 'Danish Society'

More or less in direct continuation of the history talks in 1838 Grundtvig involved himself in two enterprises that were to influence his future activity. In February 1839, at the request of several of his audience, he established the Danish Society, a debating society in Copenhagen with himself as autocratic chairman and his friend Frederik Barfod as secretary. To begin with, the few participants sat at a round table, an absolute innovation and conducive to conversation but later up to 100 participants were present, depending on who was invited to lead the debate; for popular speakers like Grundtvig the audience was already in place half an hour before the start. The society met every Tuesday evening at 7 p.m. As often as not – over 100 times – it was Grundtvig himself who opened the evenings with a song from a custom-made book of 102 songs, later primarily national songs. Grundtvig's first three 'test lectures' were concerned with the aims and keywords of the society: the mother-

---

225. (DDS 379, 8).

tongue, the memory/history, and hope. Grundtvig only relinquished his position in 1845.

Flemming Lundgreen-Nielsen has made an exhaustive study of 'Danish Society' and concludes that despite its small significance it was "one of many signs of the increasing democratisation under Christian VIII's shrinking autocracy."[226] It was in Danish Society that Grundtvig acquired the practical experience necessary for all subsequent chairpersons of associations and principals of high schools – from actually *running* a dynamic organisation. Lundgreen-Nielsen credits him for the hard work and the considerable success he achieved: "Grundtvig's evening-school for the living word in the capital was a trial run for the people's high school, Denmark's greatest educational success."[227] The same writer has studied the archive material for the lectures, including the reports of the ever-present police spies, and concludes that for Grundtvig Danishness meant "love, peace, lack of a desire to conquer, faith in a God-given fortune, modesty, which are replaced by courage and toughness, when external provocations come too close."

The society acquired six branches throughout the country as the interest in a 'living conversation' about the country grew, and new tracks were laid for the activities of societies and associations in general. In Grundtvig's case, it was difficult to get a word in edgeways, such was his dominance. Princess Caroline Amalie wrote of one such 'talk' by Grundtvig for the ladies of the court: "Dear Grundtvig prefers to hear himself speak, and we prefer that to be the case!"[228]

Grundtvig's closer contact to the court via the princess, who was to become queen in 1839, showed itself in the second half of the 1830s in his gratitude to Frederik VI for his relatively stable autocratic government over 40 years. To celebrate the occasion in 1839 Grundtvig wrote a 75-verse poem, 'The Golden Year' in which he lauded the absolute monarch who listened to his people:

> The King's hand, the people's voice,
> both are strong and both are free!
> Both have had their home in Denmark
> long before we came to be ...[229]

How does Grundtvig know the last line to be *true*? Because it was the same system under Odin and the gods back in mythological times!

> Odin, King of all Valhalla
> though not giv'n to games with odds,
> at the ash-tree Yggdragsil con-
> vened his court with *all* the gods.[230]

---

226. (Feldbæk 1992, 77).
227. (Ibid., 78).
228. (VU IV, XXVII).
229. No. 136 in *LW*.
230. (PS VI, 233).

For the new *Queen* Caroline Amalie's birthday in 1841 Grundtvig made a speech in which he asserted that Denmark's guardian spirit was "of a woman's nature, a kind of queen in the invisible world with whom the 'Dane-woman' has much in common ... here in Denmark the higher life force known as 'spirit' lies more in the heart than the head."[231] 'Dane-woman'/ *Dannekvinde* is Grundtvig's own innovation, an abstraction which included all Danish women as being both singular and special. Already in *The Danish Four-leaf Clover or A Partiality for Danishness* (1836) Grundtvig had attempted to define her as "sweet as both a mother and a spouse, and the mother-tongue on her lips is of course as sweet as can be."[232]

Full-time Pastor again

Without a stipend Grundtvig was fortunate to be able to rely on friends such as Peter Fenger, whom he thanked for yet another donation (Letter 42). As a *full-time pastor* Grundtvig had spent remarkably little time in the Danish Church. Leaving aside his separate preaching engagements, so far his pastoral career had been as follows:

1811-13 Curate at Udby Church
1821-22 Pastor at Præstø Church
1822-26 Curate at the Church of Our Saviour

Thus by 1838, aged 55 years, he had been a full-time pastor for only seven years. Now, however, he had a strong motivation to return to the pastoral role. His sons, Johan, 16, and Svend, 14, had not yet been confirmed, and Grundtvig saw it as his paternal duty to perform this ritual for his sons. The King was obliging and Bishop Mynster gave way: better now to have the unpredictable man inside the Church rather than outside. Grundtvig's application in March 1839 to become Pastor of Vartov Church was granted and on 9th June 1839 he was inducted into the living where he would remain until his death, 33 years later. His stipend was relatively comfortable, 800 rigsdaler per annum.[233] After flitting backwards and forwards for half a century, he now settled into his new uncomplicated role, which consisted mainly of leading worship in the church at Vartov on Sundays and Wednesdays. There was no other parish work as such. Vartov, at Løngangsstræde 24, was built in 1722-55 as a hospital and care home for elderly people and the chronically ill. Strictly speaking, the church was part of a secular institution, so Grundtvig's official English title would have been 'chaplain'.

Grundtvig felt close to his two sons at this point. In 1839 Johan had registered Grundtvig's entire book collection to 4,030 volumes, which was to double by his death.[234] Grundtvig had also given Svend a copy of a handwritten ballad from 1656 which his son

---

231. (Feldbæk 1992, 58-59).
232. *TSFL*, 156-57.
233. (GEEG, 227).
234. (Toldberg, 1946, 30).

51. **Vartov Hospital Church in Grundtvig's time.**
Grundtvig was pastor here from 1839-72 and preached his last sermon here two days before his death.
Royal Danish Library.

was encouraged to compare with the existing version. When Svend discovered that the latter was seriously deficient compared to the former, the seeds were sown for Svend's later career as a folklorist, particularly as a collector and publisher of folk tales and songs. On 6th October Grundtvig duly confirmed his two sons, and wrote for the occasion one of his greatest poems, 'Open Letter to My Children'[235] with the oft-quoted words that are the quintessence of Grundtvig's philosophy of life:

> A plain and cheerful, active life on earth
> as this, I would not for a king's life barter,
> the path enlightened by our fathers' worth,
> where high and low-born share an equal charter;
> our eye, as it was made, to heaven turned
> alert to beauty, and by greatness greeted,
> yet knowing where the deepest longings burned
> alone by God's great light shall be completed.

From now on for Pastor Grundtvig there were to be no more fat conflicts and far more lean agreements. It was, however, not that easy...

---

235. No. 131 in *LW*.

52. **Grundtvig wearing his knighthood order 1843.**
Painting by C.A. Jensen. The Hirschsprung Collection.

12. I have never spoken to so many ears
(1839-44)

As pastor of Vartov Grundtvig was back in the pulpit for the Sunday morning service, Sunday Evensong, and the Wednesday evening Communion service. On this foundation alone he built up a congregation of dedicated worshippers, among whom was the Queen of Denmark, Caroline Amalie. He left pastoral care to others and concentrated his spiritual energies on his hymns and sermons. All his sermons from 1839-45 have been published and reveal primarily his developing theology of 'The Word', which for him is *physical* as well as spiritual. Christ is therefore 'fully' present in the Words of Institution at the twin sacraments of Holy Baptism and Holy Communion, inasmuch as we use the words *from His own mouth*: "This is my body …, this is my blood". Grundtvig idiosyncratically added the words of the Creed to the two sacraments to represent the earliest form of faith as instituted by Christ to His apostles. In the last verse of the hymn 'Jesus, where is it I find You?'[236] (1843), Grundtvig answers the question thus:

> Jesus! I have truly won You:
> I am Yours and You are mine!
> Now your dwelling-place is sited
> in our midst, both fair and fine:
> At Your Word we all must take You –
> as it lives, despite our death –
> spoken to us with Your breath.

Grundtvig was barely installed as pastor of Vartov before he sought and received from King Frederik VI a 3-year grant extension for his scholarly work. All that remained was for the King to support his idea for a people's high school at Sorø Academy. But on 3rd December 1839 the King died.

As Prince Regent of Denmark-Norway from 1784-1808 Frederik VI had initiated the agricultural reform of 1788 that set the peasants free to seek work outside their native manor and thus reorganise the land around the villages. Under his absolute monarchy, from 1808, the Education Act of 1814 had imposed the teaching duty of all children between the ages of 7 and 14, and in the same year he had granted full civil rights to Jews living in Denmark. Against these achievements weighed the loss of Norway, also in 1814, and the tightening of the law on censorship in 1835 with the majestical argument, "None but we alone are capable of deciding what is best for the state and the people." On his death Frederik VI had effectively reigned for 55 years, 24 as Prince Regent and 31 as King. He was succeeded by his nephew, Christian VIII (b. 1786) and Queen Caroline Amalie (b. 1796).

---

236. (*Song-Work* III, no. 253).

53. Grundtvig praying 1843.
Pen and ink drawing by Johan Lundbye, a noted artist in the Danish Golden Age who was killed by accident in the First Schleswig War in 1848. Royal Danish Library.

Even before the new king and queen were crowned, Grundtvig received his first major honour. The new royal couple had celebrated their silver wedding on 22nd May, on which date Grundtvig was awarded the Order of the Dannebrog for his contribution to Danish life and letters. He repaid the mutual admiration with a poem, 'Song for their Majesties' Silver Wedding on 22nd May 1840' in praise of *all* Danish monarchs: "The name may change with pain/but not the King's heart." In another poem to be read at the late king's funeral, Grundtvig wrote that "he did not even harm a fly," a line which Caroline Amalie asked him to change to "the birds all sang when he passed by". Grundtvig obliged for the funeral but held fast to his original one in the published edition.

On 28th June 1840, King Christian VIII and Queen Caroline Amalie were both crowned and *anointed* – as a symbol, reaching back to King David in the Old Testament, that they were chosen by God; the practice was discontinued after the 1849 Constitution was enacted. Caroline Amalie was Christian's second wife. His first wife (also his cousin), Charlotte Frederikke, had given birth to a son (later Frederik VII), but also had a child out of wedlock; she was summarily divorced and exiled to Horsens in Jutland. King Christian on the other hand fathered a number of other children outside his marriage to Caroline Amalie.

Grundtvig the royalist

At this point in his life Grundtvig's royalist acclaim knew no bounds. He wrote page after page of speeches and poetry in honour of the late king, and published a collection of 'royal poems' that sold 20,000 copies and helped to popularise Grundtvig's name. He clearly appreciated the patronage he had received from the monarchy, while for his part Frederik VI had enjoyed the role that Grundtvig and others had cast him in as 'father of the nation'. Did His Majesty not act according to the law of the land and out of love for his people? Was it not thanks to the King that there was no Parisian mob stirring up trouble on the streets of the Danish capital?

In the wake of the lecture-series *Within Living Memory* Queen Caroline Amalie invited Grundtvig to court to give a similar series on the history of the North for herself and the ladies of her chamber. Grundtvig willingly obliged, and the Queen and the pastor struck up a friendship that was to last for the rest of Grundtvig's life. She was 13 years his junior, and as 'Princess Caroline Amalie' she had financed and opened a pioneering charity school in 1829 for poor children between the ages of 2-7; they were cared for from 9 am to 7 pm, while their parents eked out a living in the city. Grundtvig was enthusiastic about the initiative and in 1841 the Queen asked him to be the director and accountant of the management board for another new school which she opened that year for 7 to 14-year-olds 'on Grundtvigian principles'. She herself determined that "the children shall learn Bible stories and religion, but also reading, writing, and arithmetic ... to give them a good understanding of life, so they become skilled artisans and housemaids."[237]

The day-to-day teaching was undertaken by Peter Boisen and a Miss Jacobsen, and the small school became noted for its progressive ideas, such as an end to corporal punish-

---

237. (Barfod 1900, 105).

54. Princess Caroline Amalie 1830. By Louis Aumont, a noted portrait painter. Royal Collection, Rosenborg.

ment and an end to Latin! Yet, contrary to Grundtvig's ideas noted elsewhere, the teaching of the Christian faith was central! When Christian VIII issued a decree exempting the school from state control, it became the first Grundtvigian Free School in Denmark. For its inauguration Grundtvig wrote the *Free School Song*, 'Where Spirit has a mouth and voice'.[238] Here was a school where learning was to be enjoyed.

---

238. No. 81 in *LW*.

Unlock each ear to happiness,
God's Word to you is winging!
Spread wide the people's mouth that they
through you may do the singing!

Speak loud the truth of great and small
of heav'nly things sincerely,
For all that God has done is good,
and child-eyes see quite clearly!

When the owner of Strandgade 4B terminated the apartment contract with Grundtvig, he and the family were forced to move again – to his 11th new address in Copenhagen since 1813 and his 9th with Lise. Once more Lise scouted around and found a 2nd-floor apartment in the city centre. Johan was 18, Svend 16, and Meta 13, and Auntie Jane 48 when in April 1840 they moved into Vimmelskaftet 49, where they remained for the next 10 years. The 1845 census lists the 5 Grundtvigs and two housemaids at this address. Quite remarkably, for the next 3 years Grundtvig appears to be *settled*. He was working as hard as ever – on two more volumes of his *Song-Work* and a Danish translation of the Anglo-Saxon poem *The Phoenix*. The bird that rises from its own ashes was a motif that he returned to throughout his life. It was in his introduction to *The Phoenix* that he wrote of his love of England:

> I count the summer months that I spent in London and Cambridge as being among the most pleasant and most instructive in my life.

It is not an exaggeration to say that by 1842 Grundtvig was becoming a court favourite. The Queen invited him to give another series of lectures on history, and from 9th November 1842 to 26th May 1843 he again obliged.

While he was busy writing, lecturing, and preaching, he was shaken by the death of his elder brother Otto and his friend Poul Dons. Otto died in January 1843, aged 60. Born nine years before Grundtvig, Otto had trodden a quieter path than his brother. He married Maria Amalie Balle in 1798 and had a daughter, Bolette, in 1808. In 1823 he became Pastor of Gladsaxe outside Copenhagen, where he remained after Maria died in 1833, aged 55. Grundtvig officiated at Otto's funeral and held a speech in which he praised his brother's loyalty:

> ... His brotherly friendship endured every trial, and that is saying a lot! For it is spoken by a brother whose path through life was not only beset with thorns, but was so uncommon that he retained only true friends to the end, friends like my Otto, who, despite whatever can weaken or break a friendship in this world, did not allow himself to be removed from one whose heart met his early on.[239]

---

239. (Brun I, 176).

Grundtvig also commemorated his brother in the poem, 'At the Funeral of My Brother Otto':

> My eldest brother and my first good friend,
> a gentleman has passed away,
> and brother-chats of old ways in our home
> no more shall see the light of day.
> Like sunny weather, dew and rain, our talks
> as matters of a kind heart stay;
> as round our rectory forget-me-nots
> are fading in my autumn day.[240]

Three months later his old friend, Poul Dons, died. Grundtvig's poem mourning his loss – and the loss of loved ones in general – is his most moving meditation on death. Faced with our fear of the grave, how should we leave this world? In 'To bid this world farewell aright' Grundtvig recalls that Christ Himself died, but that He will come again, and, in Grundtvig's astonishing vision, as a *friend*:

> Come in the hour the last watch lies
> in clothing I can recognise,
> and sit with me in gladness,
> and talk to me, as friend to friend,
> of how we soon shall meet again
> and soon forget all sadness!
>
> Come as You wish! I know Your call!
> You said that here and thence we all
> shall recognise Your greeting;[241]
> In spite of this world's weary noise,
> our heart can burn to hear that voice
> and comfort find in meeting.

A month later Grundtvig was grateful for Queen Caroline Amalie's offer to finance a 3-month trip to England for himself and his son Svend, for the father to pursue his theological interests, and for the son to dig deeper into the folk-songs of Britain. In a letter to Bernhard Ingemann dated 1st May 1841, Grundtvig admitted that his home-schooling of his children had caused them problems, for without Latin they could not sit the university entrance exam. This was made clear to him by his younger son, Svend, now aged 14:

---

240. No. 132 in *LW*.
241. Jn 10:4.

My younger son came over to me the other evening and asked if I had anything against him becoming an engineer officer, since he could not take the university entrance exam like the others. This was a hard nut to crack. It is true that at that point I had not reckoned on my sons going to university because I was waiting for the new times to come ... but right now he is sitting deep in the Iliad, the Danish and English heroic ballads, and the genealogy of the nobility.[242]

4th England Trip, 1843

Father and son left Copenhagen on 8th June 1843, travelling overland to Hamburg and thence by ferry to London. Grundtvig's main purpose (he even called it a 'mission') was to cast a critical eye on the Church of England and persuade its leaders to move with the times – i.e. to think like himself! Oxford was the centre of a movement among High Church Anglicans in the 1830s-40s to reinstate some older traditions of faith, including more ceremony and ritual, an increasing use of vestments, and with Holy Communion as the absolute focus of the worship.

In a letter to Queen Caroline Amalie dated 2nd July 1843 (Letter 46) Grundtvig outlined his view that the Anglican Church was still at the stage of *sola scriptura* (scripture alone) as the sole criterion for the Christian faith. Grundtvig believed that he himself had moved on:

> If these main figures *are* papists at heart, the whole edifice is in danger either of becoming one with the Catholics or of going into liquidation. But since they are serious, reverend, and, as far as can be judged, upright and sincere men, they may be able to put *themselves* back on the right track when they see that Christianity *in origin* in both faith and creed is *independent* of Scripture.

The doors of access to several of the leading Anglicans had been opened by Grundtvig's English friend, Rev. Nugent Wade, who had been the English chaplain at Elsinore from 1833-39. Wade also generously opened his home to the two Grundtvigs and arranged contacts for his friend in both Oxford and Edinburgh. Through his reading of *The British Critic, Quarterly Theological Review*, the mouthpiece of the High Church movement from 1837-43, Grundtvig was well-informed about the "new Anglicans" and their leader, John Henry Newman. He admired Newman's attacks on rationalism and his historical approach to Church doctrine, but he crossed swords with him on the apostolic succession. This is the teaching that bishops represent a direct, uninterrupted line of continuity from the Apostles of Jesus Christ through the laying on of hands. In *Should the Lutheran Reformation Really be Continued?* (1830) Grundtvig had pinpointed "what we in Denmark have lost since the Reformation but always missed, a real Episcopal Consecration. This the good Lord will restore to us in his own time."

His meetings with the High Anglicans bore no fruit for the Anglicans and only little fruit for Grundtvig, in that he now rejected even more firmly a State Church, a Synodal Church, and an Episcopal Church – in favour of a free congregational Church. He was happy to call himself 'catholic' in the sense that "we belong to the everlasting historical Church which has come down to us through Rome ... we are Catholics, with and not

---

242. (INGEMANN, 246).

against Luther".[243] In *Church Teachings* (1842) we find Grundtvig's core understanding of true Christian and Church practice:

> If we therefore live truly in the Lord, when we enter the Apostolic Church, we must leave behind our scriptural knowledge, the Bible, and *all our books*. We must sit at the feet of the Apostles and listen to what they have to tell us all in the name of the Lord. Only thus will we gain a truly *living* understanding of the universal Church as an apostolic community of baptised believers who have kept, and *will* keep, the Lord's commandments.[244]

Since Svend wished to gather folklore material from Scotland, they travelled to Edinburgh, where 600 pastors had threatened to leave the State Church in protest against the sole right of secular patrons to appoint pastors (Letter 44). Grundtvig sought out their leader, Professor Thomas Chalmers, but failed to persuade him of his trichotomic faith in Holy Baptism, Holy Communion, and the Holy Creed, all instituted by Christ. During the trip he kept his patron Queen Caroline Amalie, well-informed about his comings and going (Letter 47). He returned home strengthened only in his belief in his own faith. In England Grundtvig was much taken by the role of the bishop as Apostolic successor, but by 1845, when the High Anglican John Henry Newman converted to Roman Catholicism, he had changed this view quite radically.

The People's High School Project at Sorø

When the principal of Sorø Academy died in December 1842, Grundtvig hoped that with its falling attendance the future of the Academy would be discussed at the highest level and a progressive principal appointed. He was granted an audience with Christian VIII and presented the King with a copy of the newly-printed *New Year's Wishes in Danish Society*. Grundtvig seized the opportunity to advance his ideas for the reformation of the Academy once more, and the King allowed him to deposit a new application, in the form of a letter dated 9th February 1843. Here Grundtvig reasserted his desire for a patriotic education and the awakening of a new national awareness to release the cultural bonds and tensions of an older social awareness linked to differences of rank. Grundtvig's nationalism was clearly not of an aggressive, imperialist kind, though he would always take up arms in Denmark's defence. As Uffe Jonas points out in his introduction to *On the Establishment of Sorø Academy as a People's High School (1843)* Grundtvig's nationalism was directed solely inwards towards nation-building and civil society. The focus was to be on "the voice of the people" – their language, history, narrative tales, and current needs – in order to promote a civil society of self-motivated, self-organised, and self-learning citizens. The school should promote "the People's character, the Fatherland, and the Mother-tongue", or in Danish: *Folkelighed, Fædreneland* and *Modersmaal*. There was to be no Latin teaching and no examinations. The aims of the People's High School were threefold: 1) to develop a narrative culture of history

---

243. (US VIII, 387).
244. (Ibid., 454f.).

55. Christian Flor, founder of Rødding People's High School 1844.
Photograph from c. 1860. Flor (1792-1875) was a pastor on Zealand before he taught Danish at Kiel University. Inspired partly by Grundtvig's *Nordic Mythology 1832* he founded Rødding and defended the Danish cause in Schleswig, not least through writing manuals of the Danish language for Germans.

and poetry, 2) to encourage practical self-education, and 3) to advance the communication of learning through interaction and the living word. To achieve these goals Grundtvig proposed the appointment of a number of new teachers in various subjects with specific qualifications:

1. A teacher of Danish, a story-teller who can bring alive the mother-tongue not just in books "but primarily as it comes alive in the mouth of the people, with all its richness of pithy adverbs and strange idiosyncrasies".
2. A teacher of History who knows and loves the "history of the Fatherland and can relate it with spirit", i.e. a story-telling historian.
3. A teacher of Poetry and Song who can sing and play and knows the tradition of the "folk-songs, in both their older and newer form" and who can "make the stones dance in time; ... the people's folk-songs, when used naturally, have been the most fruitful means of education from time immemorial".
4. A teacher "who has looked around the Fatherland and knows not only where the towns are situated and the beautiful local views but also the people's pursuits and occupations and their predominant frame of mind".
5. A teacher of Danish Law who can "give young people a true and living idea of the state constitution and the legislation of the Fatherland, then and now".

Grundtvig was for the first time willing to touch on the difficult question as to who was qualified to be a teacher at this innovative school. In his view, only his friend Bernhard Ingemann, already a teacher at the Academy, passed muster, for "he has something of a warm heart for the people's cause". However, he would need "three or four capable colleagues" while the rest would have to be dismissed. Only time would tell "which popular forces the Academy already has in its lap and how large the number of applicants will be".

In the event, the first people's high school was founded by Christian Flor on 7th November 1844 at Rødding in Schleswig, not waiting, as Grundtvig did, for the King and the authorities to take the lead. In Schleswig the need to promote the Danish language and Danish history was even more urgent than in the rest of the country. Flor had even written a book to help German speakers learn Danish, *Lehrbuch der Dänischen Sprache*.

Just this once we shall pursue the theme of the people's high school beyond the dates designating the extent of this chapter. Not least thanks to Caroline Amalie Grundtvig enjoyed more political influence in the final decade of the reign than as a member of the Constituent Assembly and the new Parliament from 1849. After many attempts Grundtvig persuaded the King to issue a resolution of 27th March 1847 regarding Sorø Lower Secondary School/*Real-Højskole*", but with entrance qualifications, a final examination, and an emphasis on 'a rational agricultural economy'. Despite these restrictions, Grundtvig decided to interpret the resolution as a victory for his attempt to reorganise Sorø Academy as a people's high school. The King, who was now solidly behind the Sorø project, offered him the pastorate of Sorø, but Grundtvig turned it down, preferring to strike his blows in Copenhagen. In a letter to Bernhard Ingemann dated 26th July 1847 he considered the

56. Grundtvig delivers his 'Bragi Talks' 1843-44.
This time women were allowed to be present, which Grundtvig found inspirational. The five men at the back are probably representatives of the church, the university, and the police. Drawing by Johan Lundbye, 1841. Frederiksborg Museum of National History.

possibility of moving to Sorø, and whether he could leave all his children and half his library behind. Although Ingemann was subdued in his response, Grundtvig's optimism led him to write the winter solstice hymn 'White clouds are greying' with its repeated line, 'Yet we bear our torches with gladness', for 'Christmas will bless the New Year'.[245] But the King's death early in 1848 put an end to his hopes.

Bragi Talks

On Grundtvig's return from England Queen Caroline Amalie asked him yet again to give a series of talks, this time 25 public addresses at Borch's Hall of Residence on Mondays, Wednesdays, and Fridays between 20th November 1843 and 31st January 1844. He called them 'Bragi Talks' after Bragi, the god of skaldic poetry in Nordic Mythology, the fully published title being *Bragi Talks on Greek and Nordic Myths and Ancient Legends for Ladies and*

---

245. No. 74 in *LW*.

Gentlemen (1844). For the first time, ladies were present at these well-attended lectures, and biographers have noted how Grundtvig repeatedly addressed them in an unconsciously paternalistic, flattering, manner. His old friend Frederik Sibbern was present with his young daughter and found the talks inspirational but wrote, perhaps on her behalf, that they lacked a direct introduction to the two mythologies.[246]

Modern critics have been more positive, arguing that Grundtvig was deliberately *not* examining mythology and its sources, but expounding them into the present-day. He was using the texts as he would use a biblical text for a sermon. Sune Auken argues that the talks lie in a direct line back to *Nordic Mythology 1832*; Katrine Frøkjær Baunvig characterises the talks incisively as "civil-religious sermons",[247] while Sophie Bønding, in her GV introduction to the work writes:

> The style throughout is associative and digressive; the tone is light, jovial, and occasionally flirtatious towards the ladies. Grundtvig often comments on their presence and takes their side against the men, as he puts comments and attitudes into the latters' mouths. It is clear that in the published book he has sought to retain the oral form of expression ... In the talks Grundtvig manages to embrace ordinary day-to-day situations as well as the evolving lines of world history, and to make both relevant to the development of his understanding of myths.[248]

Grundtvig was among the first to attempt this kind of 'talk' in which he updated the past to the present, and of course he was unsure of himself at times. What he *was* sure of was the eagerness of his audience, the success of this form of 'the living word', and especially of the attentiveness of the younger women, who despite their obvious interest at this level were not allowed to study at university until 1875. Such regular, informative talks by outsiders have since become an integral part of all societies and associations in Denmark.

The dedication in the book, translated in the first stanza below, was to "Denmark's Queen Caroline Amalie the First", and was clearly an invitation to spiritual interaction between the sexes. The second stanza, from the afterword to the book, presents Grundtvig's view of the "Danish woman":

> Queen of all the Danish regions,
> lands of love o'er hill and dale,
> in your breast of ages legion
> burns a heart that cannot fail;
> Of Greek goddesses a sister
> in your lap I with your permission
> pouring out my Bragi talks! ... [249]

---

246. (SU XIII, 492).
247. (Auken, 530-36; Baunvig, 86).
248. (GV).
249. (US VIII, 494).

Mother shared, at whose full breast
Danish man is nourished
Mother sweet, at whose behest
Danish man has flourished!
Since I saw the light of day
always and in every way
You and your trustees
I have sought to please.[250]

Finally, we cannot be absolutely sure of what Grundtvig actually *said* at these talks, since, as with his printed sermons and previous lectures, the manuscript he sent to print was revised. Sophie Bønding draws a parallel with Grundtvig's Foreword to his printed speech, *On the Historical Conditions of the North*, held originally on 20th October 1843 in the Scandinavian Society, where he said:

> ... it is only the written draft of the speech that is printed here and not the speech as it was given, which could only be expressed orally and in any case was not a pre-written text to be read aloud. It had a characteristic spirit of the moment, and I have just as little spoken every word that is printed here as I have written down every word that I spoke. Were I to do so, then goodnight to the speaker and the writer, who were best served by shutting their mouths and laying down their pens![251]

Grundtvig and freedom

Grundtvig's view of human freedom extended further and further as the years passed. A good example is his encounter with Elizabeth Fry in 1841. On a lengthy trip with her husband around Europe Queen Caroline Amalie had met the Quaker anti-slavery advocate and prison reformer Elizabeth Fry, and had invited her and her brother, Joseph Gurney, to Denmark. Being fluent in English and a friend of the Queen, Grundtvig was asked to accompany Mrs Fry as interpreter, and his social conscience was shaken by the experience. They visited the Copenhagen prisons on 24-25th August 1841, and in the course of a few hours in her company his previous ignorance and condemnation of Quakerism were put to shame. Elizabeth Fry was shocked to find prisoners of conscience in the cells and prisoners for life still in chains. In a letter home dated 30th August 1841, she wrote: "We found Baptist ministers, excellent men, in one of the prisons, and many others of this sect suffered much in this country, for there is hardly any religious tolerance."[252] Grundtvig had also spoken words of comfort to the prisoners, as Joseph Gurney noted in his journal: "They were also addressed by the celebrated pastor, Grundtwig (*sic*), a truly spiritual man, who seems to depend on a divine influence in his preaching."

---

250. (SU XIII, 785).
251. (US VIII, 478).
252. *Elizabeth Fry, A Quaker Life*, ed. G. Skidmore (AltaMira Press 2005) 223.

57. Elizabeth Fry reading to prisoners in Newgate prison 1823.
A great reformer, Fry (1780-1845) championed the Gaols Act of 1823 which segregated prisons by gender. Women's prisons also had female warders. Photo: Photo 12 / Alamy Stock Photo.

As evidence of Grundtvig's ability to renew his thinking and change his standpoint, only a day after the English Quakers' departure he gave a talk to the organisation 'Danish Society' in which he spoke of:

> the famous English woman, Mrs. Fry, whose art consists ... of touching the hearts in the prisons and awakening sympathy for their unfortunate inhabitants. ... What it was in Mrs. Fry that made a deep and spiritually wholesome impression on me was not her distinctive opinions and views on the nature of salvation but the gentle seriousness, sincerity, and veracity of her speech. It was not her predilection for prisons and their inmates, but the general human love that shone from her countenance and embraced all those whom she met – in short, her noble human nature, completely unaffected throughout a whole human age. She burns for her extended, charitable activity, yet she is cultivated to a rare degree of consciousness, thoughtfulness, and self-assurance.[253]

The incarceration of Baptist ministers was a result of their defiance of the law forbidding re-baptism of confessing adults who had already been baptised once as children. Grundtvig went on to write an attack on this law, *On Religious Persecution* (1842), in which he argued that all forms of religious persecution should cease forthwith.

---

253. TCG, 208-09.

58. **Skamling Hill 18th May 1843.**
Lithograph by unknown artist. In the early 1840s Skamling Hill became the rallying-point for South Jutlanders to assert their right to speak Danish in the dukedom of Schleswig. In 1844 Grundtvig gave a rousing speech here to the crowd of 10,000. Royal Danish Library.

Like a number of other powerful women, Elizabeth Fry exerted a deep influence on Grundtvig and moved him further towards a social commitment to action rather than just words. His re-evaluation of the *practical* activities of the Quakers is reflected in his new edition of *World History* (1845), where, remarkably, he places George Fox (1624-91), the founder of the Quaker movement, alongside Luther and Calvin for his "great and beneficial influence on civil society" and his "new view of the relation of the revelation and Christianity to human nature".[254]

Similarly, when the United Kingdom forbade the slave trade, the British and Foreign Anti-Slavery Society sent a representative to Copenhagen to persuade Denmark to free its slaves in the Danish West Indies. Grundtvig was drawn into the movement, which at a meeting of the Provincial Assembly in Roskilde in 1844 recommended the release of all slaves, but the Assembly nevertheless stalled with the tenuous argument that the economic consequences for the slave-owning Danes were unclear.[255]

Grundtvig struck a further blow for freedom in July that year with his most famous speech of all. On 29th March Christian VIII had unwisely issued a decree stating who could and who could not speak Danish in the Schleswig Provincial Advisory Assembly.

---

254. See chs 18-19 in *TCG*.
255. Ibid. chs 20-21.

The Schleswig Association protested loudly – speaking Danish was the right of every Dane. The King responded by banning and dissolving the association, and followed this with an official summons for police interrogation of its leaders on charges of high treason and *lèse-majesté*. A day later, on 4th July – a date deliberately chosen in honour of the USA – the provocation served to gather an estimated 10,000 people at Skamling Hill in Jutland, where the hills are an echo chamber for the speaker. Grundtvig spoke for an hour and a quarter on what he called "the birthday of Danishness" and of the necessity for North Schleswig to cultivate its Danish roots.

Afterwards he wrote proudly to Queen Caroline Amalie (Letter 49):

> ... I [have] never spoken to so many ears at one and the same time, nor with Dannebrog [the Danish flag, ed.] waving, the beechwoods singing, and the Baltic Sea surging before my very eyes. I have never before spoken for so long yet so fluently, so cheerfully yet so forcefully, and never in front of such an enthusiastic audience.

Siding with her husband, the Queen was not amused, and for a while she gave Grundtvig the cold shoulder – until she came to see matters from the pro-Danish side and resumed their friendship.

The Second Mental Breakdown

It is hard to grasp that from March until September of 1844, Grundtvig was suffering from an attack of depression. In February he had begun another series of historical talks at court, but by March he had to cancel them. He contracted a mild case of mumps, and being now 60 he began to reflect on his imminent death – and possible perdition. In May 1844 he visited four pastor-friends, all of whom were dismayed at the state he was in. The fourth, Gunni Busck, prayed the Lord's prayer with him, and Grundtvig then asked him to copy down the hymn that was forming in his mind.[256] The hymn, 'Dear child, sleep sweetly'[257] was a lullaby to himself; it remains one of his most popular hymns, especially for baptism:

> God's fingers have signed you,
> His cross has defined you
> on brow and on breast
> a child by Him blessed.
> No devil shall harm His creation!
> In baptism's bowl
> your heart and your soul
> may rest in the hope of salvation.

---

256. (Borup, 156).
257. No. 68 in *LW*.

God's active intervention with Christ's own words becomes a personal reality for Grundtvig, who finds strength in identifying himself with the child who trusts in God's real presence. During this second breakdown, he received much care from his beloved daughter, Meta, who turned 17 on 24th May, a care that he later acknowledged in 'To My Own Meta' (1845), when she became engaged to Peter Boisen:

> My dearest, young daughter! My brain was once ill,
> my head was bemused, yet my heart soft and still;
> when madness once threatened
> and friends feared the worst,
> you fondly stood by with a smile through your sigh,
> my dear, only daughter,
> as I stand and see you this fine summer's eve
> and whisper, Goodbye![258]

Still out of balance, Grundtvig, now 60, met a 33-year-old married woman, Louise Hemmings, with whom he was briefly infatuated. She reciprocated his admiration; they walked around in public view, hand in hand, with Grundtvig occasionally kissing her hand and her cheek. It would appear that it is this new intoxication that inspired him to turn his experiences of Constance Leth at Egeløkke, Clara Bolton in London, and now Louise Hemmings in Copenhagen into the poem from 1848 commemorating all three of them as 'Dearest ladies'.[259]

We have no way of knowing what his wife Lise felt about this public admission of his affections outside the marriage. Meanwhile, her jack-in-the-box of a husband was writing to Peter Rørdam on 6th August (Letter 50), "I have regained all my spiritual strength, God be praised; indeed I have even had it increased."

From his letters from England in 1843 we know that Grundtvig was at odds with his 20-year-old son, Johan, whom he took to task (Letter 45):

> ... I cannot take all the blame but must give you the lion's share, since it is certain that I have given you more and greater proof of my love than you have given me of yours, so I have first claim on your trust.

Referring to Johan he wrote to Lise on 9th August 1843 that he hoped Johan "was thinking of doing something decent that was both useful and enjoyable, since until that happens I am very concerned about his future." On their Silver Wedding Day, 12th August, they were again separated by the North Sea; Grundtvig sent his gratitude and greetings three days later (Letter 48):

> Thank you, dear wife for all your love for me through 25 years and for the children you have conceived and borne! By the goodness of God we still have them and have lost none. He

---

258. Ibid. no. 133.
259. Ibid. no. 154.

gave us and them health into adulthood before our eyes! If the children also thank God, as we hope, for giving them loving, Christian parents, then our joy is singular and our silver wedding day a special occasion for us all, even though we are unable to be physically together. Kiss the children for me and greet our friends wherever you are and wherever you come.

When Grundtvig returned from England, the couple celebrated their 25 years together and Bernhard Ingemann wrote a song for the "greying songbird' and his "pious, faithful dove".[260] For his 26th anniversary a year later Grundtvig wrote a poem for Lise in which he remembered the cold welcome he gave her letter in England and ruminated on the ups and downs of married life. Their silver wedding had come and gone, their golden wedding lay ahead:

> Your letter flew light o'er the sea;
> it did not make me reminisce.
> No kiss did I thus bestow on it
> to pay for your heart-warming kiss;
> empty of flame and of yearning and loss,
> your letter and greeting found me somewhat cold,
> where once we enjoyed the love-making of old.
>
> Strange is the skaldic life's lot!
> I see where our marriage is heading:
> a born-again summer of love,
> the daybreak of our *golden* wedding.
> Longings, sweet yearnings, they come and they go;
> the old man embraces the bride of his youth,
> calls with his kisses her 'lovely in truth!'[261]

---

260. (Brun I, 186).
261. (PS VI, 509-10).

59. Grundtvig 1847.
Painting by Constantin Hansen, a wedding present for Grundtvig's daughter Meta and her husband Peter Boisen. Royal Danish Library.

13. I always know better than most people
(1845-51)

At the heart of Luther's teaching on the structure of society lies the home, the fundamental unit of production – and reproduction. The home is run by the householder/breadwinner together with his domestic/child-nurturing wife. Beyond home life lies the next social structure: public life, the village, the town, the city – ideally an extension of the life of the home. In Luther's day this 'life of the people' was controlled by the landowner, the prince, or the king – each of them with the same paternalistic function as the householder. Beyond the home and the village lay the third circle, church life, the *Christian* life. In an article on life in Denmark in 1851 Grundtvig turned the concentric circles into a triangle, and summarised the relation thus:

> What we call home life, public life, and church life are not three separate lives of the individual, any more than they are of the people! They are three sides of the *same* life in the triangle of the heart. If we are tempted to take only one side of the triangle as *real* life, it is only because life for a people or an individual has a favoured side that seeks to capture the whole attention.[262]

All three sides are essential to a full human life, says Grundtvig. Home life is the 'favoured' side, being the nucleus of faith, hope, and love: "If human kindness is missing in the home, there is no point in looking for it in other areas of life".[263] The simple diagram below shows how the one circle encompasses the other.

In all three circles faith, hope, and love are both the goal and the driving-force toward that goal. Their sustenance comes from God – to the home, to the community, to the Church. This has been so throughout Christian (and even pre-Christian) history. Love itself starts in the home and in the parents' love for their children.

Given what he described as his 'golden years' in Udby and his 'silver years' in Thyregod, Grundtvig's later domestic life was much like his childhood pattern. He was head of the household, he had a loving, loyal wife, and was father to three healthy, intelligent children. Sickness was rare, and never disastrous; and, as we have noted, all his children would survive him.

Church Life

Working from the outer circle to the inner circle is a journey towards increasing pressure in Grundtvig's life. In this outer circle, we see the battle for freedom intensifying both

---

262. (*The Dane* IV, 604).
263. (Ibid., 605).

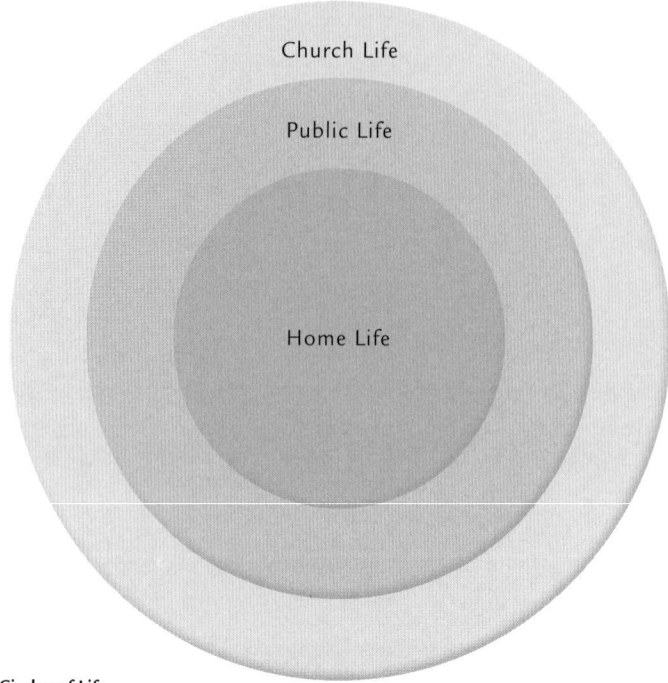

60. Grundtvig's Circles of Life.

inside and outside the Church. Grundtvig had long ago distanced himself from his early judgemental stance as regards people's faith. Under the sting of his own censorship he had been moving towards his mature, liberal, view of the Church's role in the community. Freedom of faith and worship was his goal. He had been helped in this process by his first three visits to England, where he began to realise the paradox that freedom is best developed in a healthy competition. As the English poet, William Blake (1757-1827) wrote: "Without contraries is no progression. Attraction and repulsion, reason and energy, love and hate, are necessary to human existence."[264] This was also Grundtvig's experience with Elizabeth Fry in 1841, for instance. His original prejudiced view of the Quakers conflicted with his actual experience of her in practice – and on that occasion, as we have seen, she won him over. Grundtvig held strong views on many subjects, but few so strong that he could not change them sooner or later, especially under the influence of an intelligent woman. In Elizabeth Fry he saw the *effects* of faith, which he rightly believed must always be *alive*. The decisive point about faith is, as Kaj Baagø writes, "that it is living, which it can only be where it is in conflict. And in order that the conflict of life may unfold itself in every sphere, freedom is essential. The demand for freedom for competitive conflict is entirely in accordance with the view of English liberalism."[265]

264. *The Marriage of Heaven and Hell* (1790).
265. (GS 1955, 103).

Grundtvig applied this freedom of faith to both his people and his church. When he was accused of confusing Danishness with Christianity, he responded with an article in *Danish Church Times* entitled *A People's Identity in Relation to Christianity*.[266] Just as "human comes first and Christian next", so does a person's, or a people's, identity come before their *Christian* identity, though the one follows closely on the other because they are linked by God:

> At least where Denmark is concerned, I am sure that by advancing religious freedom and the life, culture, and identity of any people by all means possible Christianity will win more respect and influence than it has ever enjoyed before. This ... will happen because religious freedom and a people's identity are what Christianity, in order to work in the spirit, must either find, or must create, if it is missing![267]

Ole Vind formulates it thus in his introduction to Grundtvig's essay on identity in *Human Comes First* (2019):

> For Grundtvig, all the peoples of the earth had their place in a divinely-created world order. The burgeoning awareness of 'Danishness' to which he contributed to such a high degree called for a *sense of community* with both predecessors and successors as a prerequisite for all spiritual life, including the Christian. If true Christianity was to survive, it was crucial that it did not make itself master over the newly-awakened life of the people but simply offered them the Gospel as a spiritual gift to believe and follow.[268]

In Grundtvig's historical view, God had a special role for the North – and an even more special role for Denmark *within* the North. In his sermon for the 4th Sunday in Epiphany 1849 he employed a powerful metaphor to illustrate this relation, one that he knew would create opposition:

> When I speak thus about the Kingdom of Our Lord Jesus Christ as being so closely linked to our little earthly people and our kingdom that they *accompany* each other, are surrounded by *the same* dangers, and will be saved *together* – either as I understood it on this day of the Lord last year as two boats that sail side by side on the sea, or, as I see it today, as a little boat built in Denmark, with Jesus and his disciples onboard – I know that some will think this objectionable ...

Sailing side by side the Kingdom of God and the Kingdom of Denmark cannot but interact: a growing awareness of Danish identity will accompany a confirmation of its Christian life, and vice versa. For example, when Luther translated the Bible into German (from which it was translated into Danish in 1550), the language of the people was hugely

---

266. Ch. 9 in *HCF*.
267. *HCF*, 193.
268. Ibid., 189.

enriched by new metaphors, new similes, new proverbs, and so on, while all the time still *bearing the Word of God*. On the other hand, if the Christian life was vapid, the people's life would tend to be so too. Grundtvig could just as little live without Danishness and his Christian faith as he could live without a roof over his head and a family to care for. This extraordinary identification reaches its apex in the last two stanzas of the poem 'Self-examination', dated Pentecost Eve 1848:

> Even if God did not want all hearts offered
> though we be father and mother and wife;
> should I not give up my Danish uniqueness
> safely to consummate this Christian life?
> Would I be willing for my Saviour's sake
> to live without Danish while I am awake?
>
> No, I would not, I must readily venture,
> though all else will my Lord ever transcend;
> nowhere on earth could I otherwise prosper,
> were all my Danishness days at an end!
> Even in heav'n, at the very last day,
> there I would find it transfigured, I pray.[269]

According to Grundtvig, we are created *in the image of God*. In His eyes we have an inborn dignity and value much greater than any we can attain on earth by our own striving or the ascription of others.

The Evangelical-Lutheran Church in Denmark

Grundtvig's emphasis on a people's identity (*folkeligheden*) allowed him, albeit reluctantly, to accept the new Constitution's definition of the Church in 1849. It is still in force today, word for word: "The Evangelical-Lutheran Church is the Danish people's church and as such is supported by the state". Already in 1834 Grundtvig had made it clear that the State should have no influence whatsoever over the individual's faith, nor over what the Church confessed; so when the above definition partially perpetuated the idea of defining all Danes as 'evangelical-Lutheran', he voted against the proposal in the Constituent Assembly! He nevertheless still thought it embarrassing that a pastor should *by law* have to baptise, confirm, and marry people whom he knew to be non-believers – let alone administer Holy Communion to them!

In his article, *The People, the People's Church, and Popular Belief in Denmark* (1851)[270] Grundtvig formulated three practical instructions for a 'people's church' which respected the life and cultural identity of a people *as created by God*:

---

269. (PS VII, 50).
270. Ch. 10 in *HCF*.

1. The Church is there for the people and not the people for the Church.
2. The title 'People's Church' is the emptiest of all if it fails to address and satisfy the people's heart.
3. The Church must seek to know its people, to speak their language, and to inform them about themselves.[271]

He practised these principles himself only to a limited degree, but he was pleased to tell Bernhard Ingemann in a letter dated 13th January 1848 that Peter Rørdam was proving how a Christian life could develop with such energy and enjoyment that it was a true testimony to others:

> When in the pulpit it occurs to him, and he says, "I think it would be nice to sing 'A child is born in Bethlehem' (or whatever), I sing the first verse and you join in!" – the whole church sings along! Even when they were gathered to elect the parish council, he persuaded the farmers to sing a song or two about Frederik VI, to everyone's enjoyment ... I often wish that I could lead the singing with my confirmands, so I could create a bit more life than all my talk can achieve.

We have noted how unmusical Grundtvig knew himself to be, how he shunned composers and concerts, and cared little for the fine arts in general – but when it came to writing hymns and songs, he had no rival. His metrical and rhyming sense, his down-to-earth imagery, his sheer joy in being a redeemed child of God are both incomparable and *memorable*. He wrote hymns in abundance, and hoped that his work would be well received for publication by the hymnbook compilers. Not for the first time he was disappointed. When Bishop Mynster published a supplement to the *Evangelical Christian Hymnbook* in 1843, he included only one of Grundtvig's hymns, a deliberate snub. Several of his hymns appeared in *Church Hymns* (1845), but this too was rejected by the Pastors' Assembly because too many of them were written 'by Grundtvig'! The only way out was small-scale publishing of his own – in the form of pamphlets that were tried out with his congregation of enthusiastic singers in Vartov Church. On Christmas Day 1845, with Queen Caroline Amalie among the congregation, two of his hymns were sung, 'A child is born in Bethlehem' and 'Jesus Christ, how we praise Your name'.[272] Grundtvig ended his Christmas Day sermon by reflecting on the vision he had experienced before writing the hymn, 'We greet you again, God's angels bright'[273] back in 1824. Like the angels on Christmas night, uniting heaven and earth in the birth of the baby, the hymn descends and ascends in metaphors:

> God's angels go treading up and down
> the scale of their hymn-singing!

---
271. (VU V, 379, 389 and 392).
272. Nos. 10 and 80 in *LW*.
273. Ibid., no. 8.

For all who have yearned He sends His Son,
to earth His peace is winging!
The portal of heaven opens wide,
His kingdom God is bringing.

Beginning in 1845, Grundtvig's pamphlets, *Festival Hymns*, eventually went through ten reprints, with new hymns being added on the way. In 1845-46 his friends, Johannes and Rasmus Fenger, published *Hymns and Songs for Christmas* (28 by Grundtvig), *Hymns and Songs for Holy Week and Easter* (45 by Grundtvig), and *Hymns and Songs for Ascension and Pentecost* (35 by Grundtvig). This was a church within the Church that Bishop Mynster could do nothing about, not least because the Queen was a regular worshipper at Vartov.

Just as Grundtvig's 'Within Living Memory' lectures in 1838 came to be the model for "a talk with some songs" in modern-day Denmark, so did the hymn-singing in Vartov Church form the basis for modern-day hymn-singing in the Danish Lutheran Church. Grundtvig's congregation sang 'unauthorised' hymns, with tunes that might even be from well-known folk-songs. Moreover, they were singing them faster than usual – although only occasionally and never in the tempo of today. They were derided by some as "Vartov gallops"! However, by virtue of Grundtvig's charismatic presence and his animated singing-growl Vartov hymn-singing became an added attraction. Queen Caroline Amalie and the rest of the congregation united around these hymns and felt a warmth and a sense of friendship in singing them heartily together. Here was a vitality in the singing, an intensity in the prayer, a depth of thought in the sermon, and a solemnity in Holy Baptism and Holy Communion; here the Gospel was proclaimed, confessed, and testified to in rousing hymn-singing. This was what Grundtvig had been fighting for since 1825: Christ's presence in the congregation being praised by his people.

Grundtvig and Kierkegaard[274]

In a capital city where the great satirical dramatist Ludvig Holberg (1684-1754) had amused theatre audiences in the 18th century the heavyweight presence of Grundtvig was an obvious target for satire. In 1840 Meir Goldschmidt (1819-87), whose ancestor had founded the Mosaic community in Copenhagen in 1684, established *The Corsair* as a satirical weekly. It went after Grundtvig with such phrases as "the old eagle Grundtvig" or fictive titles like "Scenes from Grundtvig's Giant Life" and "An Open Letter to German Heretics Found in an Attic in Vartov". Indeed, the journal was considered so scurrilous that at one point Goldschmidt was fined, briefly imprisoned, and sentenced to life-long censorship. In its heyday *The Corsair* reached an audience of 3,000. But the attacks on Grundtvig were nothing like as vicious as those on Kierkegaard, attacks which seriously dented both his reputation and a self-image much frailer than Grundtvig's.

Søren Kierkegaard (1813-1855) was 30 years younger than Grundtvig and treated him with respect, but regarded his theology as no more than a poor version of the established

---

274. The subject is treated at length by Anders Holm in his Afterword in *TCOL*.

61. Grundtvig intoxicated with Odin.
Grundtvig's "intoxication with the gods" is caricatured by Constantin Hansen in 1846. Grundtvig, arms casually folded, is riding Odin's 8-legged horse, Sleipner.

State Church views. In his diary for 1839 Kierkegaard noted how for the first time he attended a Sunday service with Pastor Grundtvig. The sermon was not a sermon, he wrote, but a history lecture with edifying tones, "a walking-tour of the imagination in which one's legs could not keep up."

In *Concluding Unscientific Postscript* (1846), Kierkegaard made his first sally against Grundtvig: "Can we build eternal salvation on historical knowledge?" He found Grundtvig's preaching historically untrustworthy as well as insensitive to the individual and the truth that can lie in subjectivity. Where Grundtvig's focus was on the living congregation and the Christian insight and experience that he himself had acquired, his youthful counterpart believed that faith was released and born only in the individual. Kierkegaard first shunned, then vitriolically attacked, the 'easy Christianity' of his day – without challenge, without risk, without cost, and without pain. Both being self-assertive, they were unlikely ever to find much common ground. Suffice it to say that Grundtvig is remembered as the promoter of the collective and Kierkegaard as the guardian of the individual. In Denmark Grundtvig is celebrated for his hymns and his high schools, Kierkegaard for being the

62. Kierkegaard taming a woman.
Peter Klæstrup's caricature in *The Corsaire*, no. 278, 16th January 1846. In *The Seducer's Diary* (1843), Johannes the Seducer's project is to educate and inform the young girl, Cordelia. Johannes has been wrongly regarded as Kierkegaard's alter ego, whereas he is in fact protesting at the male treatment of women of the time.

'father of existentialism'. At this point Grundtvig took little notice of Kierkegaard's attack, but this was to change later on.

Public life

The second circle, Grundtvig's and Denmark's public life, covers six of the most important years in their intertwined history. Denmark was moving away from an outdated absolute monarchy towards a modern democracy, at the same time as the southern border was being contested with Germany, more specifically Prussia. Throughout this chapter and beyond, 'Germany' is used to designate the people south of the Danish border. At the time, however, Germany as a nation did not exist. The modern state consisted of a 'German confederation' of states, Prussia being the largest and the northernmost. The Danish dukedoms of Schleswig-Holstein were only twin in name, for North Schleswig was predominantly Danish in language, culture, and spirit, while South Schleswig was predominantly German, as was the whole of Holstein. Democracy and war were just around the corner. The four Provincial Advisory Assemblies were all leaning towards a more representative form of governance, and Grundtvig actively encouraged them.

Ove Korsgaard introduces volume 4 of this series, *The Common Good*, with a snapshot of the crucial revolutionary year in modern European history, 1848 – and never more so than in Denmark. Five dates are noted:

Folketoget til Kristiansborg den 21de Marts 1848. Grundtvigs Bolig var paa 2den Sal af den forreste Bygning til højre.

63. People's march to the King.

On 21 March 1848 12-15,000 men, mostly Copenhageners, gathered in a procession to the King to demand a democratic constitution. Grundtvig watched the procession pass Vimmelskaftet on Strøget from his 2nd floor window.

1. 20th January – Christian VIII died, aged 61, and was succeeded by Frederik VII.
2. 21st March – a crowd of 12,000-15,000 people marched through Copenhagen to the Royal Palace to demand a democratic constitution in which Denmark retained Schleswig but surrendered Holstein
3. 29th March – Civil war was a reality between Denmark and Schleswig-Holstein, as the German-minded majority seized power in the duchies and demanded independence from Denmark.
4. 22nd September – Denmark set all its slaves free in the Danish West Indies
5. 5th October – the Constituent Assembly was elected to draw up the new constitution

20th January 1848 – 21st March 1848

In December 1847 Christian VIII inspected the corvette Valkyrie, newly returned from its maiden voyage to the East Indies. He caught a cold that turned into a fever that was treated with blood-letting that caused an infection that led to his death on 20th January

1848. The King had held out for as long as he could against a new constitution, but on his deathbed he told his son and heir Frederik "to give the Danish people and the duchies (i.e. Schleswig-Holstein) a joint constitution". Two months later the march on the Royal Palace culminated in the handing over of a petition, drawn up by the National-Liberal leader, Orla Lehmann, for a new constitution for a democratic Denmark, including Schleswig but excluding Holstein. Lehmann challenged the King with the famous words, "We implore Your Majesty not to drive the nation to the desperation of self-help!" The King gave way, and Denmark received the royal assent to its new constitution on 5th June 1849. The day has been a national holiday ever since.

In a letter to Queen Caroline Amalie (Letter 51), Grundtvig admitted that 'people power' was inevitable. As we can see in Illustration 63, Grundtvig had watched the march to the Palace from his second-floor window. Was this the dreaded mob who might even assassinate the King, as in France, or were these intelligent citizens, determined to introduce greater freedoms for their people? Hans Christian Andersen wrote that there was "something rather menacing about meeting these almost foreign hordes, these faces unknown to me," whereas the young writer, Mathilde Fibiger, rejoiced that "on 21st March a new life began for me ... my heart was beating with a proud self-awareness." As for Grundtvig, his friend Pastor Vilhelm Birkedal recorded, "... he was not happy ... In those days he was like a lion fuming in a cage."[275]

Grundtvig was champing at the bit, eager to tell "the reading world" that they should reject all that is not Danish. The very day *after* the march, he published the following:

> The words 'German' and 'Swede' are often used by our writers, but we never see the word 'Dane'. Indeed, some might think that I made up the word *myself*, if it were not for the fact that, as chance would have it, two hundred years ago it was written down by Shakespeare in *Hamlet, Prince of Denmark*!

This was Grundtvig's opening salvo in his new publishing venture, *The Dane*, a self-penned, 8 to 10-page weekly journal which was to run for four years. In September 1848 as many as 300 subscribers were recorded. It closed on 27th December 1851 with these pregnant lines from Grundtvig, a man changed by his new circumstances:

> Long live Denmark's Danish 'woman',
> she who gave all Danes their start;
> Blessed be all man's friend in spirit,
> she who reads the human heart!

29th March 1848
The First Schleswig-Holstein War, from 1848-51, is known in Denmark as the Three Years' War. It had its origins way back in 1460 (Schleswig) and 1814 (Holstein). In the former case Christian I (1426-1481) had acquired the twin duchies "forever together undivided"/

---

275. TCG, 19-20.

64. Johan, Svend, and Meta.
Drawings by P.C. Skovgaard, 1846-48. Museum Sønderjylland and SMK, National Gallery of Denmark.

ewig tosamende ungedelt. In practice Schleswig had been Danish until the more German-oriented Holstein joined the German federation after the Congress of Vienna (1814). The Congress had redivided Europe after the Napoleonic wars. The prospect of being ruled by a democratic Danish Parliament rather than by a German-friendly Danish king was not to the Holsteiners' liking, so on 23rd March 1848 they formed their own government. Tensions increased, and in May 1848 the German army occupied North Schleswig. Denmark had a volunteer army, so Grundtvig's two sons immediately enlisted and were sent to the southern front. Their proud father wrote to them occasionally, but left most of the letter-writing to Lise (Letters 52-58). Battles, an armistice, and then more battles ended with a decisive Danish victory at the Battle of Idstedt on 25th July 1850. Danish casualties were 2,128 dead and 5,797 wounded. German casualties were 1,284 dead and 4,675 wounded. Johan and Svend lost 4 friends from their youth.

The lasting solution to the siting of the Danish-German border was not reached until 1920, but when it did come, through a referendum of both Danes and Germans, the idea that Grundtvig had proposed in 1848 won the day. North Schleswig became Danish, and was known from then on as South Jutland/*Sønderjylland*. South Schleswig and Holstein became German. Grundtvig's thinking was ahead of its time: cultural and religious freedom should be a human right for both sides. Danes should not govern Germans, and vice versa. The dividing-line was the mother-tongue.

Throughout the war Grundtvig insisted that it was the duty of all Danes to fight the threat from Germany, for every people had the right to the identity that God had given them. He asserted this in a letter to his son Svend, assuring him that he was doing his duty in fighting for his homeland (Letter 52) and repeated it two years later (Letter 57). Yet in the equally solemn name of 'freedom', Grundtvig also opposed any form of national conscription, for no one should be *compelled* to fight. Similarly, he agitated *for* army chaplains but *against* compulsory worship for the soldiers. He shared with all Danes the belief that God was on their side and that their cause was just. On 24th May in *The Dane* he published a patriotic song that is sung to this day: 'Land of my fathers':

> Though things now look dark,
> the Almighty knows
> your foes here below
> are also His foes;
> they are foes of the Truth from above,
> they are foes of the lineage of love;
> their destiny never to thrive,
> for the Ancient of Days is alive![276]

Grundtvig and his countrymen were patriotic Danes, but they were no longer imperialists. A thousand years earlier the Vikings had sailed to Iceland, Greenland, and Newfoundland; they had conquered half of England, founded Dublin in Ireland and had traded with Russia, Türkiye, and North Africa. The Danes were determined to keep what little they could. They were still 'a people'. Grundtvig's 'people's identity' stemmed from the Old Testament concept of "the twelve tribes of Israel", corresponding to the 12 sons of Jacob (aka 'Israel') in Deuteronomy 27: 12-13. The Israelites were the first recorded people to have worshipped a single God, Yahweh. They regarded themselves as God's chosen people; if they obeyed His commandments, He blessed them, if they disobeyed, He punished them. Grundtvig's view was inclusive, in the sense that *all* peoples (even the Germans!) had

---

276. Dan. 7:13. (HS 382, 2).

the right to self-determination – but only within their own cultural territory. Grundtvig always preferred the Danish word *folkelighed* to *nationalitet*, which he called either "dog Latin" or "gobbledygook".

Who then, could count themselves *Danish*? In 1848 Grundtvig wrote an extraordinary poem entitled 'Of the people is our watchword' in which he asked the question and provided the answer:

> People! What defines a 'people'?
> What does 'of the people' mean?
> Does the nose or mouth distinguish
> how a 'people' can be seen? ...
> There were 'peoples' long before us,
> great or small with that word blessed,
> whether there is still a 'people'
> we must now put to the test: ...
>
> Of a 'people' all are members
> who regard themselves as such,
> find their mother-tongue sounds sweetest
> and their Fatherland love much; ...
>
> If we get true Danish statutes,
> Danish schools in which to learn,
> Danish concepts, Danish farming,
> then our old fame will return:
> 'Gifted Danes live by the ocean
> peace and joy their heart's devotion';
> then in deed and poetry
> 'of the people' all will be.[277]

This may seem reasonable. Any people can simply substitute their name for 'Danish' and the poem's sentiments are theirs. Nevertheless, Grundtvig was seriously challenged on the subject, when the 'people' involved were the Jews; for they had their identity from God, so how could they be *Danish*? Were they not doomed to wander forever? The number of Jews in Denmark in 1800 was around 3,000, the vast majority of them living in Copenhagen. Grundtvig took their side in a dispute with Bishop Mynster as to whether Jews could sit in the new government, but he questioned whether the above-mentioned satirist, Meir Goldschmidt, could be a *true* Dane. What Grundtvig always claimed of Christianity, that it was universal and all-embracing, he could not say of 'Danishness', for a guest "may put his fingers in the holy water, but he does not thereby become consecrated."[278]

---

277. No. 82 in LW.
278. (*The Dane* II, 691).

22nd September 1848

In Grundtvig's long campaign for freedom of speech, freedom of the press, and freedom of worship, his attention was drawn in the late 1830s to the plight of the 30,000 or so slaves working for Danish slaveowners on the sugar plantations in the Danish West Indies. The islands of St. Thomas (acquired 1672), St. John (1718) and St. Croix (1733), were sold to the USA in 1917 for $25 million and renamed the Virgin Islands. Denmark had forbidden the slave trade in 1792, but not slavery as such. Grundtvig joined an anti-slavery committee and drafted an unpublished letter in 1839 in which he argued that "many of our fellow-citizens undoubtedly want slavery to cease on our Danish islands as soon as possible and in a good way. We are therefore inviting like-minded people to a meeting to discuss to what degree this wish can be reasonably realised through the establishment of a similar anti-slavery society".[279] When the natural scientist and politician, Joachim Schouw, took the initiative to reorganise the Danish anti-slavery committee in 1843, Grundtvig declared that he would continue as a member "with pleasure". He was even more pleased after he had given a lecture to the Scandinavian Society on 17th January 1845, when his old opponent, Professor H.N. Clausen, proposed a toast to him and was loudly applauded by those present.

The decisive year for the release of all slaves was 1848. Off his own bat the General Governor of the Danish West Indies, Peter von Scholten, proclaimed their freedom to a large gathering of rebellious slaves in Fredrikssted on the island of St. Croix on 3rd July that year: "Now you are free. You are hereby emancipated". Fortunately for him, Frederik VII endorsed the decision later that year. The next question was compensation for the slave-owners, who had held the right of property over the slaves. Grundtvig strongly rejected this claim in an interjection on 14th December 1848 at the Constituent Assembly. No one had any "right of property" over any other human being. His words were even reported in one of the island's newspapers, *St. Thomas Times*, on 27th January 1849. Knud Eyvin Bugge's definitive book on the subject concludes that in his anti-slavery work, Grundtvig underwent his first experience of working together politically with influential men who could show him the way in politics. It was in the spring of 1848 that Grundtvig finally realised that the future lay with some form of democracy rather than a royal autocracy.

5th October 1848

It is typical of Grundtvig that although he was reluctant to become involved in preparations for the new Parliament, he simply could not help himself joining in, for "I always know better than most people".[280] Elections for the Constituent Assembly that was to draw up the new constitution began on 5th October 1848, with both local elections (114) and royal designations (28). In the former, Grundtvig lost the Nyboder seat by 313 votes to 369 to Captain Nicolai Tuxen. He lodged an official complaint about voting irregularities and received 2,000 signatures to support a *royal* designation. He was allowed to

---

279. Text 22a in TCG.
280. (3ÅRSKRIG, Letter to Johan, 01.09.1848).

65. The Constituent Assembly 23rd October 1848.
The two main architects of the new constitution are on the right: Ditlev Monrad (holding his top hat) and Orla Lehmann. Grundtvig is almost invisible, seated behind Lehmann's left shoulder. Painting by Constantin Hansen, 1860-64. SMK, National Gallery of Denmark.

stand for election again, this time on 6th November in Præstø, against Hans Hansen, a weaver. Under pressure to give way to the popular Grundtvig, a former *pastor* of Præstø, Hansen agreed. Grundtvig stood instead against his former confirmand, Jens Jensen, who encouraged everyone to vote for Grundtvig! With his election speech written by his good friend, Pastor Peter Rørdam, Grundtvig won by 573 votes to 11 and duly took his seat on 8th November. He wrote to his sons of how his despondency had turned to delight (Letter 53). Of his subsequent work in the Assembly he wrote to Johan (Letter 54):

> In the circumstances it is a necessary drama in which I have volunteered to take part on condition that I do not have to play anyone but myself! ... I believe that even when we seem to be no more than actors, it nevertheless feels that for men like us – who wish for the best, know what we want, and dare what we must – this feeling is not futile since, like all who give birth, it carries its foetus for a long time *unseen*!

In his Assembly work he managed to insert into the constitution a clause that ensured 'public access to the courts and oral proceedings therein', but he was dissatisfied with the thinness of the constitutional document and when the final agreement was voted on, Grundtvig abstained. Did this really represent 'the will of the people', was it not rather the will of the few? The franchise extended only to 15% of the Danes, namely "all men of good character over 30 who owned their own homes". Where were the peasant farmers in all this? argued Grundtvig. The answer was that although in 1846 they had formed the Friends of the Farmers Association in an alliance with the National Liberals, as yet they had no political clout at the highest level. As Letters 55-58 show, he voiced his concern to his sons and told them how proud he was that they were fighting for Denmark. His argument for standing for the new Parliament was that "I owe something to the voters who elected me last year and partly that as a Member of Parliament I am more assured of the freedom of my voice and my pen".

Grundtvig was now a powerful figure with considerable support. Already in 1817 his friend Svend Hersleb had written from Norway that "there are quite a few who call me a 'Grundtvigian'; indeed I have even been called such in print!"[281] The epithet suggests that 'Grundtvigian' referred to some kind of political grouping. From 1825, however, it was also used to describe Grundtvig's Church view. Independently-minded as he was, he disliked the term. He wrote in 1847 that "what the so-called Grundtvigians may have done has nothing to do with me; I am totally unaware of them. I have never been one to form a party!"[282]

Educational work

While waiting for his new People's High School to find a form, a venue, financial support, and the royal assent, Grundtvig published three books for youngsters in school: *Danish Proverbs and Sayings* (1845), *Greek and Nordic Mythology for Young People* (1846) and *Danish Heroic Ballads for School Use* (1847) as well as *Folksongs and Other Songs for 'Danish Society'* (1840-47). Sales of the first three were poor, whereas sales of the folksongs went much better. The royal assent for the new school finally arrived in March 1847 with Christian VIII's decree for the reorganisation of Sorø Academy into what might look like a people's high school. Grundtvig was encouraged to write his last major work on the subject, *A Congratulation to Denmark on the Danish Dimwit and the Danish High School* (1847). In the words of Uffe Jonas, Grundtvig was "discreetly mocking its official style and Latin and German influence, while humorously promoting the everyday language of the people in an attempt to further his case. The work is thus a tour de force of ancient Danish proverbs and sayings, most of which have since gone out of use... the Danish word *dummerhoved* (translated in the title as 'dimwit') is a word-play on *Dumkopf*, the German nickname for the provincial and uneducated Danes; they did not realise that they were actually *Germans*! In a rhetorical move, Grundtvig turned the word to his own advantage to satirise German rationalism. Thus the plain and silly Danes are exalted against the more lawful and rational Germans."[283]

---

281. (BFOTG I, 467).
282. (*Danish Church Times*, 1847, col. 34).
283. TSFL, 300.

In December 1847, to Grundtvig's dismay, the King issued a further decree announcing that the school would remain under the Danish state. Worse still, three weeks later the King was dead, and with him, Grundtvig's hopes of a people's high school.

However, at some point in 1850 Grundtvig received a visitor by the name of Christen Kold, who wanted to open a small school for farm children on Grundtvigian principles in order to "animate them", as he said. Together with a friend, Kold found Grundtvig smoking his pipe and told him he wanted children aged 14 to 16. Grundtvig said that was too young; 18 and over was better! When Kold asked for help regarding financial support, Grundtvig advised him to draw up a petition to that effect, and that Grundtvig's signature would be the first. Kold himself had saved 500 rigsdaler, to which the petition successfully added 600, plus 50 of Grundtvig's own money – and Marie Toft another 100![284]

Home life

One woman in Grundtvig's life was moving away from him, and another was moving closer. In July 1845 his only daughter, Meta, became engaged to the young theologian, Peter Boisen, a great admirer of Grundtvig and a teacher at Queen Caroline Amalie's Charity School. It was also Boisen who led the singing at the meetings of Danish Society. Grundtvig took the news hard; he was both close to Meta and protective of her and was reluctant to 'give her away'. She had looked after him in his recent depression and his home would be all the emptier without her. Boisen was a much softer man than Grundtvig, whose petulant outburst at the news of the engagement cut her to the quick: "I thought you wanted a man!"[285] Grundtvig wrote a poem to his 'dearest young daughter', 'To My Own Meta' (1845), recalling her happy childhood, praising her virtues, and offering her his hope: "May your heart be with my spirit laden".[286] He was losing her, but nevertheless presided over the wedding on 29th October 1847, after which Meta left home for good.

In the autumn of 1845 a woman, her mother, and her two sisters arrived unannounced at Grundtvig's second-floor apartment in Vimmelskaftet to seek his advice. Lady Marie Toft was a passionate Christian and held revivalist meetings in her country manor of Rønnebæksholm, 100 km or so south-west of Copenhagen. She left it to the local pastors and laymen to do the preaching, but when they were not present, she herself led the prayers and hymns. During the winter she and her family lived in the city, in Nørregade 25 (now no. 5), close to the cathedral. Marie was grappling with many questions of a religious nature, and since she could get no satisfactory answers from her pastor friends, she had decided first to attend services at Vartov in 1844, and then to approach the source of their inspiration, Pastor Grundtvig himself.[287] She had called once before that spring, but Grundtvig was not at home.

---

284. (GEEG, 223).
285. (https://tidsskrift.dk/fundogforskning/article/view/40995/46586) retrieved 23.05.23.
286. No. 133 in *LW*.
287. (GS 2016, 14).

66. Marie Toft 1844.
Portrait by an unknown artist.

67. Lise Grundtvig in mid-life.
Drawing by unknown artist at unknown date.

Marie was 30 years younger than Grundtvig and a widow. She had lost her father when she was five, but was otherwise living the privileged life of a manor house owner. In June 1840 she had married Harald Toft, Master of the Royal Hunt, but 16 months into the marriage he died of tuberculosis. Marie inherited his manor and three months later gave birth to their daughter, Haralda. Her mother and two sisters moved in to help out, but Marie ran the manor on her own with a staff to whom she was closely attached; they in turn had great respect for 'Lady Marie'. Grundtvig, though not totally inimical to the revivalists, had dutifully received her, was impressed by her firm views, but was nonetheless unmoved by them:

I saw her visit as something of a provocation, and it was not long before I asked her mischievously what kind of a South Zealand manor-house was it that Bishop Mynster said boasted a revivalist meeting of 500 souls! 'To be sure', she answered, 'though the boast and the figure are mere gossip, there can be no other manor on Zealand in mind than Rønnebæksholm.' Lady Toft's short, sharp response pleased me greatly.[288]

It is noteworthy that Grundtvig cited even his enemy of the time, Bishop Mynster, in order to tease Marie. In fact there was room for no more than 50 people at her revivalist meetings. The conversation became vociferous, Grundtvig dismissed the revivalists as being of no account, and the two parted company on polite, but irreconcilable, terms. Grundtvig did not expect to see her again.

But he did. Marie Toft began to attend Grundtvig's services in Vartov Church: "I simply had to hear Grundtvig give the blessing from the altar; I had looked forward to it for so long!"[289] When Grundtvig was invited to speak at a meeting of Danish Society in Næstved, he accepted her offer to overnight with several other guests at Rønnebæksholm nearby and to preach in the local church. His refusal to attend her revivalist meeting met with an equally strong refusal from Marie to attend his talk. One of the guests was a mutual friend, Eline Boisen. In the course of the few days spent together, she recorded how the relationship became "very warm between Grundtvig and Lady Marie".[290] For her part Marie wrote to her friend, Pastor Mads Melbye, that as a preacher Grundtvig had "a wondrously powerful giant spirit with a childlike devout, loving heart."

This was not the first time that Grundtvig was so attracted: Marie Blicher, Constance Leth, Clara Bolton, Louise Hemmings, he was charmed by beautiful, intelligent women – but never ever could he pursue them further. This time a beautiful, intelligent woman was approaching him, a married man, and he was both flattered, frightened, and determined to maintain his intellectual superiority. Marie for her part was also deeply attracted. During the winter she became a regular churchgoer at Vartov and sat in the front pew. The following year she again invited Grundtvig to Rønnebæksholm for his talk to Danish Society, only this time she attended it.

Warmed by his new flame Grundtvig again began to write poems about love and 'the Dane-woman'. Eline Boisen was pained to see how Lise was becoming depressed and wasting away into a sickly old woman, while Grundtvig did nothing to discourage Marie:

Last winter Lady Toft of Rønnebæksholm came to town and Grundtvig was the perfect gentleman, day in day out. When she visited the Grundtvigs, he kissed her hand, and neither he nor Lady Toft took the slightest notice of the lady of the house... At home Grundtvig was bad-tempered and hard-hearted, but with Lady Toft he was the fine cavalier. She was aware that it was hurting Mrs Grundtvig so much that she would rather not see her... The

---

288. (Bojsen-Møller, 13-14).
289. (Ibid., 15).
290. (Ibid., 37).

whole relationship was as public as possible and offended everyone who was not inclined to idolise Grundtvig.[291]

Eline's husband talked to Marie's sister, Jutta, who remonstrated with Marie – on her knees, but to no avail. Lise realised what was happening, but was helpless – and in declining health. She became ever more isolated from her husband, but nevertheless still thought caringly about him. She wrote to her sons, "He lives so alone and he feels so lonely; that is what often pierces my heart, without my being able to do anything about it." Their sons had got wind of the situation with Marie, and while Svend was home on leave in February 1850 he wrote to Johan that their father was dividing his time "between Parliament and the Tofts". Johan wrote back ... "What else is it but the desire always to be idolised and played up to?"

In a number of letters Lise expressed her concern for the pressure of Grundtvig's political work. He often got steamed up and became fretful, and at 63 he was too old for such a burden.[292] Grundtvig himself told Johan that he could no longer write from the heart to his friends; either he would be misunderstood, or he had to 'play a part' with them.[293] No one in his circle understood that he was unhappy with his loyal, indefatigable wife, a woman whom everyone else liked and admired. Perhaps he must even sacrifice his sons in the war against Germany. In the poem 'Solitary state' from November 1849, he lamented his situation thus:

... sitting day and night,
a bird alone upon the shed,
the world an empty desert waste,
as in the grave among the dead.

The long-suffering Lise was now called upon to find a new apartment for the family, somewhere near Vartov, as Vimmelskaftet was no longer available for rent. Apparently, it was Marie who found them a smallish apartment home in Løngangsstræde, and after 10 years in Vimmelskaftet they moved home. Lise was not satisfied and went in search of something larger. She found what she was looking for on the second floor of Stormgade 199, and once again they moved – on 10th October – but immediately afterwards Lise began to feel poorly with a slowly progressive dropsy (now known as 'edema'). She managed to see her new grandchild, Meta's daughter Elisabeth (born 21st April 1850), and in mid-November to write long letters to her sons at the front, but by 22nd December Meta was writing to Svend that after 6 week's illness she "feared that our beloved mother will not recover".[294]

On 22nd November in Vartov Church Grundtvig presided over the wedding of his

---

291. (Ibid., 40).
292. Letter of 27th October 1848.
293. Letter of 10th July 1850.
294. (3ÅRSKRIG, Letter 334).

friend Peter Rørdam to Marie's sister, Jutta. At the small reception he recited a newly written-poem extolling the virtues of true love and home life, pleasures which he now felt were being denied him. He doubtless never imagined that he should provide pleasures for *Lise*. As her life moved to a close Lise was nursed by her niece, Louise Schmidt. Her son-in-law, Peter Boisen,[295] informed Johan and Svend of what happened on 14th January 1851:

> Sunday morning she was clearly turning for the worse. When I wiped the sweat off her brow, it was cold. It froze me to the bone with the sense that this was the chill of death. She was in great pain, as her stomach was so tense that she could find no rest and wanted to be moved all the time. "Dear Meta, help me!" still rings in my ears. Meta was a faithful daughter to the very end. She and Louise Schmidt were almost constantly by her side. They kept watch that night. The old man went in and out and truly wished to comfort her, but he could hardly hear her and she could barely speak. He did have one good exchange with her, when she asked him, "They will hear my *voice* from the grave. Will my *soul* stay in the grave?" On Monday I spoke a bit longer to her, and it was obvious that she was expecting to die, "My faith has not been so strong, but our Lord will not leave me at the end." I thought I heard her say, "They have all been so good to me ... our Lord has preserved both my sons!" But she could not manage to say any more about you. She then wanted to see Elisabeth. She kissed her and said, "We shall meet in heaven." At 2 in the morning she woke up from a brief sleep and said. "A miracle has happened. I felt the dropsy leave me!" She wanted to get up, and we all went into her, including your father, but she had a natural bowel movement, which was why she wanted to get up. She had never had this before throughout her sickness. It caused her a lot of pain to be lifted up and laid down again. This continued until Tuesday at noon, when, with much difficulty, she got up for the last time. From then on she lay quite still – without pain and half asleep. Fenger arrived and thought it would last until the evening. Meta had kept watch two nights in a row, and I managed to get her to rest for a moment on the bed, as the others had done on the sofas, while I sat and watched over her and Aunt Pauline came in and out. She seemed to be asleep with her eyes half-open, breathing without apparent discomfort. When I looked at her at 2 p.m., she lifted her left shoulder, almost imperceptibly, and then she almost stopped breathing. I immediately called in Meta and the others, and she arrived just as she took her last breath. She got what she deeply wanted, peace and quiet in her last hour. Just a shrug of the shoulder, and she passed on into the long sleep, from which, she once said, "The Lord will wake me up!" Your father, who had gone out for a while, came home at the same time. I told him first what had happened, "Go in Jesus' name!" he said and broke into tears.

Lise Grundtvig died on Tuesday 14th January 1851, aged 63. Grundtvig immediately wrote to his sons to inform them of her death (Letter 59). A month later he told his friend Bernhard Ingemann of their joint suffering before the end came (Letter 60):

---

295. (3ÅRSKRIG, Letter 249).

I could no longer comfort or gladden the noble soul with the melancholic mind, nor could she comfort or gladden me. I also need far more of both than the world realises, or with God's help, will ever know.

The last word goes to Queen Caroline Amalie, who later mentioned three women she had "always looked up to": her predecessor, Queen Marie, Countess Reventlow, and, most of all, Lise Grundtvig.[296]

---

296. (Barfod 1900, 31).

68. Marie Grundtvig c. 1852.
Portrait by N.P. Holbech. Photo: The Picture Art collection / Alamy Stock Photo.

14. She is not dead, she sleeps awhile
(1851-54)

Lise lay in an open coffin at home for a week and was then carried over Langebro to the Church of Our Saviour, where she was buried on 21st January 1851. The grave has since been removed, but there is a memorial plaque to her on the church wall. Grundtvig's eulogy to his wife soon turned into a eulogy for the Christian faith:

> Not earth only heaven, not time only eternity, can heal the wounds that death inflicts. I stand here today, an old man, taking a perceptible step towards his own grave, burying his children's mother, the bride of his youth, who for forty years, including seven years before her promise at the altar, lovingly shared prosperity and adversity, but mostly the latter. I myself am at a loss, and have nothing to say to those who have lost a tender mother, a dear sister, a precious female friend. I have nothing except what the Creator has given us all with our human hearts: tears to shed for ourselves and our loved ones, for our human life in death's dark vale, which like the flower of the field is resplendent and fragrant today but withers and dies tomorrow, so no one knows its whereabouts ...[297]

Bernhard Ingemann, who was a childhood friend of Lise and one of her many admirers, chided Grundtvig for the paucity of his eulogy and the lack of a memorial poem from his otherwise bountiful hand. The best the widower could manage was a rather ambiguous poem for his granddaughter Elisabeth's (Lise's) first birthday, in which he wished:

> ... that you may answer to your name,[298]
> and be 'Dane-woman' unexcelled:
> much greater will your loss be mourned,
> your memory more sweetly held
> than she whose weary foot here trod
> who rests till we meet face to face,
> who left to you both Christian name
> and then her smile, a gift of grace.[299]

The year of mourning that traditionally followed a partner's death began, understandably, with Grundtvig wanting his family around him – and a new address. His two sons, back from the war, moved with him into the new, much larger, apartment at Nybrogade 6. The year of mourning also saw two significant events in his life.

---

297. For the full eulogy see ch. 48 in *HCF*.
298. Elisabeth means 'fear of God'.
299. (PS VII, 368).

The first was his reading of a new novel, *Clara Raphael. Twelve Letters*, already a scandalous success. 'Clara Raphael' was both its title and its protagonist, a young woman who writes twelve letters to her friend, Mathilde, about the frustrations of being a woman in a man's world. Its foremost authority, Lise Busk-Jensen, has called it "the first manifesto of the women's movement".

The author of the book was the 20-year-old Mathilde Fibiger, who had approached the leading literary critic Johan Heiberg, with a view to the anonymous publication of her brief but powerful novel. Heiberg was swept off his feet by it, and not only published the book in December 1850, but also wrote a lengthy sympathetic introduction. Like Mathilde Fibiger herself, Clara is a 'governess', a woman employed as a private tutor to a child, in Clara's case on the island of Lolland. Fibiger's radical ideas of an independent life received short shrift from the critics, but when Grundtvig read the book in May 1851, he was overwhelmed. For here was a woman who wanted the privileges of a man, and Grundtvig found her arguments irrefutable. In his one-man journal *The Dane*, he reviewed the book with admiration – and yet with a little reservation.[300] On the one hand, he immediately acknowledged the power of the main character in his poem: "Clara lit the beacon-fire/in the fight for women's rights".[301] Here indeed was a 'Danewoman' *and* a 'shield-maid'! On the other hand, Grundtvig rejected Clara's solution to her problems: to live in a platonic relationship with a good husband with no children and no Christian faith. This was not 'home life' as Grundtvig understood it. At a more principal level Grundtvig concluded:

> ... since one must always be a living human before one can become a living Christian, Clara is clearly closer to the Kingdom of God than the pastor who goes to confession and the girl who wants to convert her, without yet having her living feeling of what human beings – made in God's image yet in their deepest fall – are and must be, in their own and in God's eyes ...[302]

For Grundtvig, a platonic marriage is no more than a friendship. There is nothing wrong with friendship of course, even if the friends have a 30-year age difference – as he wrote to Marie in 1848:

> Hearts of equal disposition
> breathe together love's sweet breath,
> disregard all reputation,
> never change in spite of death.
> Friendship shuns what came before it,
> cares alone for what comes after,
> born to last eternally.

---

300. Ch. 33b in *TCG*.
301. No. 155 in *LW* & ch. 33a in *TCG*.
302. (*The Dane* IV, 327).

Good the man and good the woman
who can see how theirs has been;
caring only for that friendship,
counting not the years between.
Thinking even at the grave-edge
of God's heaven and each other:
friends for ever and a day.[303]

The second event was Grundtvig's only other trip outside Denmark apart from the four trips to England. This was the culmination of his speaking engagements at a number of meetings promoting the concept of 'Scandinavia' as a regional federation with a shared monarchy, army and navy, and customs and postal services: the three languages, Danish, Norwegian, and Swedish, were mutually understandable. The linguistic and cultural 'Scandinavist' movement of the mid-19th century proclaimed the common heritage and cultural unity of the Scandinavian countries. It was popularised by among others Hans Christian Andersen in his 1839 poem 'I am a Scandinavian'. After a visit to Sweden he wrote to a friend, "All at once I understood how related the Swedes, the Danes and the Norwegians are, and with this feeling I wrote the poem immediately after my return: 'We are one people, we are called Scandinavians!'" The Norwegian Students Society had invited Grundtvig and his two sons to Oslo for a week in June 1851, and the visit was a triumphal progress. The Danish prophet was in town! He enjoyed the adoration of the Norwegian students, preached to the Norwegian Parliament in the Church of Our Saviour, and enjoyed the hospitality of the widow of his old contact, Stener Stenersen, who back in 1814 had tried, and failed, to get Grundtvig to come to Norway. After the visit Grundtvig wrote a letter of deep thanks to Stenersen's daughter, Vilhelmine (Letter 61). A bonus for the family came when Grundtvig's elder son Johan announced that he had fallen in love with Vilhelmine! They married in Oslo in 1855 but moved to Denmark and provided Grundtvig with 5 grandchildren.

Marie Toft

Grundtvig put the following words about Lady Marie into the mouth of a farmer working at Rønnebæksholm:

> She looked so kindly on the children and all of us, and she told us what to do, because she knew about everything! She could speak to our Lord – let alone to the farmers – much better than our pastor could! ... She was every bit the queen of the kingdom, and it was fascinating to see how the counts and the barons bowed and scraped for her; it made no difference whatsoever, for she always spoke as kindly and just as often to *us* as she did to them.[304]

---

303. (PS VII, 116).
304. (US X, 29).

From all else that we know of Lady Marie Toft, this captures her spirit best. She was knowledgeable, open-minded, industrious, and unpretentious; and had run the manor single-handedly for 10 years, since her husband's death. Frederik Barfod called her "strong, warm-blooded, and high-born".[305] She not only fulfilled all Grundtvig's hopes and expectations of a woman, she also enjoyed his absolute admiration. For Marie's part, we have no independent record of her feelings for Grundtvig, so we must trust him when he writes in *Lady Marie's Monument* (1855):

> ... she often leaned over to me and said, "I want to be with you."[306]

Lady Marie invited Grundtvig to her 38th birthday on 4th August 1851, where he was presented to her family as her new fiancé. He brought with him four new love-poems, one signed by Frederik the Pastor, the other by Frederik the Bard, and the third, his most famous love-song of all. In the first, 'All the Father does is great', he writes that love and eternity are one and the same thing:

> Love and everlasting life
> are a single choice:
> life becoming like to God,
> lived through our heart's voice.
> With a root divine such love
> as life's wellspring from above
> flows eternally![307]

The third poem questions in the title what it is that makes them so attracted to each other – 'What is it, my Marie?', and the following stanzas provide the answer:

> It is because we wish for
> each other as we are,
> because we two can carry
> each other as we are,
> because awake or dozing,
> our mouths will soon be closing
> together in a kiss! ...
>
> We join ourselves together
> in faithfulness and love
> with Death's eternal conqueror
> who came down from above,

---

305. (GEEG, 171).
306. (Ibid. 37).
307. No. 157 in *LW*.

69. Rønnebæksholm today, rebuilt after Grundtvig's death.
Photo: Edward Broadbridge.

>   in honour of the Father;
>   He now our dust will gather
>   into the Spirit's arms.[308]

Grundtvig's experience of love as being God-given meant that he believed himself to have been miraculously opened up to the very source of life, and, indeed, to a glimpse of Paradise. On 7th September he published a hymn to this effect in *Danish Church Times*. The first two stanzas of 'Uneasy heart' reflect his troubled soul, despite God's providence and the blessings of baptism from Christ's own mouth, but in stanzas 3-5, God's love is triumphant – as it was in Grundtvig's personal life:

>   She waits at the threshold, the loveliest bride!
>   Will *you* not go with her and walk by her side,
>   embrace her and welcome God's gift of a guide?
>   ...
>   Wherever she dwells is the angels' abode,
>   wherever she sojourns will lighten your load;
>   there rise all our hopes, on us faith is bestowed.

---

308. No. 95 in *LW*.

> God's peace is a queen, He Himself for her sighs!
> Whoever will marry her truly is wise;
> where she has a home, there is God's Paradise.[309]

Modern commentators understand the 'bride' in the hymn to be a symbol of God's feminine love, even of the Holy Spirit. For Grundtvig, however, the bride at the threshold is also Lady Marie herself, with her coach and coachman, just as she was when she once arrived at his home in Nybrogade 12. As Magnus Stevns has pointed out, in Grundtvig's hymns, especially those based on Greek and Latin texts, "the heart is feminine, faith is feminine, grace is feminine – and all are of royal blood. The Church is both bride and mother, the entire Christian people is a feminine people, which is why the Church speaks with a woman's voice".[310] Grundtvig's eschatological view of history coloured this new experience of love, linking 'the moment' to 'the end of time' through 'Christian marriage'. A few days after Lise's death he was preaching on the Wedding in Cana, and later in the year he wrote an entire article, 'Christian Marriage',[311] and a poem to Lady Marie in which he believed that a Christian marriage is concluded when a woman and a man go to the Lord's table together:

> When we knelt before the altar,
> you, Marie, with your friend,
> how we shared our thoughts and feelings!
> Into one our souls would blend!
> here our hearts were burning,
> into one were turning
> in the name of our dear Lord[312]

News of the engagement, a mere 200 days after Lise's death, came as a shock to many. Grundtvig's friends, Bernhard Ingemann and Gunni Busck, were distressed at the haste and the disregard for conventional mourning-rites. On the other hand, he was congratulated by Queen Caroline Amalie, who wrote: "I imagine that the intrepid Lady Toft is a woman after your own head, just as you are a man after her own heart; two matching souls of the same nature" (Letter 62).

But how would Grundtvig's children react to the news? Grundtvig tried to share his happiness with them while understanding their sadness in a poem on the anniversary of Lise's birthday, 28th September, 'To my dear children'. Speaking of himself, he wrote:

> You cannot conceive his contentment,
> though none can a *mother* replace;

---

309. (*Song-Work* IV, 2, 288).
310. (Stevns 1950, 85).
311. No. 25 in *HCF*.
312. (PS VIII, 127).

a 'stepmother's' name smacks of winter,
and yet when the grave we must face
a stick for support is most precious,
and golden a loving embrace.

He was asking his children to honour their mother's memory – but she was dead! Could they not move on with him to the living?

Despite their initial concern, both Ingemann and Busck did just that, and the latter agreed to marry them in his church at Brøndbyvester, 10 km west of Copenhagen. When 9th October arrived, Grundtvig was agitated as to whether his two sons would join his daughter Meta and son-in-law Peter Boisen in attending the wedding, but as he waited inside the church, he heard the sound of swords being delivered in the church porch, and the two men arrived in full military uniform. Their father's frown broke into a smile, and the couple were married – also to Ingemann's satisfaction. In a letter dated 5th November he wrote:

> ... What has transpired with most of your friends has also happened with me: we could not get into our heads what was in your heart. It did not match with our ideas of time (i.e. a *year* of mourning, ed.). But since matters really had to follow your ideas rather than ours, your good friends chose rather to keep silent than to join the 'conversation'. The best solution to undoing the knots of Time is Time itself. When you are at home in your new situation and I am only half a stranger in your house I shall no longer postpone visiting you with the kindest wish for you and yours.

They spent the summers at Rønnebæksholm Manor and the winters in Copenhagen. In April 1852 they moved from Grundtvig's apartment at Nybrogade 12 to Marie's palatial apartment at Frederiksholms Kanal 16, which housed 16 residents, including members of Marie's family and seven servants.

Early on in their relationship Grundtvig described how their 'elemental agreement' (*grundenighed*) on Christianity was equally fundamental on humanity in general, on a people's identity, and on Danishness: "I never met a man or woman with whom it was such a pleasure and comfort to exchange one's views as this wonderful woman," he wrote.[313] Grundtvig's admiration for Marie also included her socially-minded care for her tenant farmers, an attitude which also coloured some of his parliamentary speeches. For at Rønnebæksholm Marie had abolished all forms of forced work, had shared out the licence to hunt on the estate, and had encouraged her farmers to *buy*, and thus own, their hitherto rented properties – at half price! She even ensured that they did not get into a debt that they could not repay. In her lifetime she sold nearly half the property out of her hands. As Grundtvig wrote of her motivation::

---

313. (US X, 36).

There must be in all Danish hearts a desire to do what one can to reach agreement and a firm pact between all those who have more and all those who have less of God's green earth, and have the pleasure of owning it, watching it flower and bear fruit. Like true Danes they make common cause against all pen-pushing, puerility, and meanness, which would otherwise destroy all human freedom and independence, all noble pride, honour, and dignity.[314]

The most comprehensive assessment of Grundtvig's pre-nuptial poems to Marie on this 'elemental agreement' and his hymns about love being God's gift to humankind has been undertaken by Peter Balslev-Clausen. He demonstrates how Grundtvig's love for Marie actually strengthened his Christian faith, as "faithful hearts in winter/flower in joyous spring". In a Christian context these 'faithful hearts' are identical with 'like-minded souls'. Grundtvig's love is eros, philia, and agape, all in one: namely, the kiss and embrace, the friendship and admiration between equals, and the unconditional love for others – for example a spouse or in a family. All three of these Grundtvig defined as feminine, as being *of a woman*. In a profound insight Balslev-Clausen writes that for Grundtvig "Woman is not only the male equal, but more than that; she is also the *prerequisite* for the man to find the coherence between his human and his Christian being... so that his deeds and his dreams can be realised through the peace that she mediates."[315]

By coincidence or God's purpose, Marie can also trace her ancestry back to the same Danish 11th century earl of Zealand, Skjalm Hvide, as Grundtvig's own mother, Catherine. This is one of the resonances of history that brings the two fortunes together. The insightful Queen Caroline Amalie was again ready with a precise formulation of the relationship in the draft of an unsent letter. Of Grundtvig and Marie she wrote: "... it is my firm conviction that this connection will give his whole being the consummation that he still needs ... I can rejoice in the hope that it will bring an equilibrium to Grundtvig's entire conduct of his life."[316]

In the summer of 1852, Grundtvig and Marie invited Mathilde Fibiger to Rønnebæksholm, partly to give her a respite from the negative criticism her book had evoked, and partly to give her time and space to write a sequel to *Clara Raphael*. Mathilde later counted these two or three months the happiest of her entire life. During her stay, Grundtvig arranged for her to give a public speech about her work. There was no precedent for such an event with a *woman's* address, and Grundtvig knew that he was challenging the norm. Word of the plan got round to Mathilde's brother, who wrote two letters in July 1852 urging Grundtvig not to pursue this path. Marie answered back that they did not *own* Mathilde. Grundtvig ignored the polite warning, and was unprepared for what transpired on the day. The politician Fredrik Bajer wrote in his memoirs how he had been told that after Grundtvig himself had spoken, Mathilde was finally on the rostrum and about to deliver her speech, when a sturdy squire lifted her up and set her down on the

---

314. (Ibid., 32).
315. (Balslev-Clausen 1991, 219).
316. (Ibid., 239).

ground again. The story may be apocryphal, but it says much for Grundtvig's new-found dynamic on behalf of women.³¹⁷

A foundation, a depression, a celebration, a death

Grundtvig first suggested founding a 'Danish association' for the promotion of the national spirit back in the 1830s, but it was not until 7th March 1853, and with Marie's encouragement, that 50 or so men sent out an invitation to both men *and* women to join the new organisation to discuss "the common good". Most pressing was the fear of South Jutland being drawn away from Denmark into Germany after the inconclusive end to the First Schleswig War in 1851. Meetings should also include "refreshments and songs", and should work towards the establishment of its own people's high school for the young men of the countryside. At the first meeting on 3rd May Grundtvig was elected chairman, and in his speech of acceptance he referred to the "March days in 1848" when it came to him "in a flash of lightning that a Danish association of men and women in their thousands was indispensable." A further aim was to close the distance between the capital and the provinces – an ongoing concern in most countries to this day. The first number of the society's weekly journal, *Dannebrog* (the name of the Danish flag), was published already on 21st May and on Constitution Day, 5th June, people gathered in large numbers to celebrate the event. Some 15,000 people marched to the Royal Palace at Christiansborg. Although the King decided not to show himself, he was given three cheers, after which Grundtvig shouted, "Long live the Constitution. May it overcome all its enemies!" (Letter 63).³¹⁸

Despite his harmonious marriage, Grundtvig again sank into a depression. In 1810, 1844, and now 1853 he could not fight off the gremlins. Was this an old family shortcoming – bearing in mind that several of his family had suffered similarly? Was it a fear of death from the outbreak of cholera in Copenhagen from June to October that year? In a city of 130,000 people 7,519 were infected and two-thirds of them died. Perhaps it was a hidden guilt over his treatment of Lise, as compared with his current sense of being blessed beyond belief with Marie. Or perhaps the independently-minded Marie had upset him somehow. Whatever the cause, this depression was worse than the last one – and the very worst was yet to come. On this occasion he did acknowledge the attack, and even apologised to Caroline Amalie in a letter dated 12th September for his lack of communication. He had suffered

> ... a deadly sickness... like that of 1844, but more inwardly than outwardly. For that very reason it almost blew out the wish to live and seemed to eat away at my life-force. In such miserable circumstances I prefer to go quiet, and to retire from the world, since I can neither lie to it nor show it any honest participation.³¹⁹

---

317. (Korsgaard 2018, 175).
318. (Brun II, 13f).
319. (BFOTG II, 530).

One remedy for Grundtvig was to translate into Danish extracts from the Greek New Testament. The idea was not new. In the years when he was translating works in Latin, Icelandic, and Anglo-Saxon into Danish, (1810-20) he had also considered translating the Bible, first and foremost the New Testament. The translation never materialised, but in between times, and particularly during his depression in 1844 and now in 1853 he turned to the New Testament. Grundtvig knew the Bible more or less by heart, and found comfort and inspiration in translating especially extracts from the New Testament Letters. In 1853 alone he produced handwritten translations of the Letter to the Ephesians, the First Letter to the Corinthians, Peter 1 and 2, and John 1, 2, and 3. These have been published in full in 2018 by Jette Holm, Helge Kjær Nielsen, and Ruth Østerby. Among the authors' remarks are that here and there Grundtvig translates the same Greek word differently, and that his sentences are far longer than in other translations, with a plentiful use of the conjunction 'and', only sporadic punctuation, and a penchant for exclamation marks. The authors conclude that the translations are marked by Grundtvig's theology and are thus somewhat freer than all previous attempts in Danish; this goes for his theology of the Image of God, of the Holy Spirit, of the Redemption, and of growth.

Marie was a good therapist. Three times a day she walked him round Rønnebæksholm; she read to him – not least from his own sermons – and she encouraged him to write them out in fair copy for publication. Grundtvig still had enough strength to be driven into Vartov and take the Sunday service, despite the outbreak of cholera. Marie, ever faithful, kept him company. What is more, by mid-August she was pregnant with their first child. She was 38, he was 70.

In the circumstances Grundtvig would most likely have preferred to celebrate his 70th birthday on 8th September that year in solitude. But Marie was having none of it. She arranged a surprise party for him at her own birthplace, Gammel Køgegaard, 50 km away, with family and friends and a birthday present of 7,000 rigsdaler, collected by Danish and Norwegian friends. The gift would help to establish a people's high school bearing his name. Grundtvig was overwhelmed – and deeply grateful, as his letter to Bernhard Ingemann demonstrated (Letter 64). By Christmas that year Marie could tell him that she was expecting their child. What more could he ask for? His joy was complete – and so was hers, according to Nanna Boisen, Eline Boisen's eldest daughter, who was 19 at the time:

> Lady Grundtvig was exceptionally good to the 'old man'. She was always caring for him, reading to him, singing hymns to him until he fell asleep in the evening; and she was not far short of her confinement at the time.[320]

On 15th May 1854 in their Copenhagen home Marie gave birth to a healthy son. Grundtvig's joy rings through his letter to Gunni Busck, written the day after the birth (Letter 65). The boy was baptised 'Frederik Lange Grundtvig' by his father in their home ten

---

320. (Stoklund Larsen, 54).

days later, on Ascension Day. He was named 'Lange' after Rasmus Carlsen-Lange, who owned Gammel Køgegaard Manor, where Marie was born. Frederik Lange was Marie's second child after Haralda, and Grundtvig's fourth. But on the same day as the baptism, Marie realised that she was unable to suckle the child; she contracted an infection that resulted in an inflammation of the breast. By 7th June this had become an abscess, and Marie was unable to attend the ceremony in Vartov Church on 18th June, where little Frederik's baptism was confirmed in church. Marie's life ebbed away; on her deathbed she whispered to Grundtvig that she found peace not in the words "In Jesus' name" but in the words, "In *our Lord* Jesus' name".

Marie Grundtvig died on 9th July 1854, aged 40. Grundtvig's shock is captured in his poem:

> 'She is not dead, she sleeps awhile,
> upon her mouth is still a smile,
> her cheeks are warm I find.'
> That was my whisper late that day,
> as though in sleep she passed away,
> the fairest of her kind.[321]

As Marie's coffin was about to be carried out of their apartment in Frederiksholms Kanal, Grundtvig was "deeply moved, speaking through tears, kneeling in prayer beside the coffin and then sobbing his heart out as he followed it down the stairs with his brother-in-law Hans Carlsen under the one arm and his son-in-law Boisen under the other."[322] Grundtvig himself conducted the burial service at Vartov Church on 17th July, beside the oak coffin of his wife. This time his eulogy was in contrast to the one he held for Lise 3½ years before:

> My friends, there was such a rare similarity between our hearts and souls, our thoughts and feelings, our view of human life in this world, its purpose, its struggle, its victories. So from the very first moment to the last we could speak of these out of each other's hearts like two childhood friends, created to live and die with each other. That is why we rarely knew which of us would put into words what we both were thinking and that is why we could walk so happily together... And the little blessed child... is a living image of the great and imperishable hope that grows to comfort us over all temporal loss and is illuminated to prophesy the glory of eternity. He, together with his child-angel, who always sees the Father's face in heaven, is to me a little angel from God who will always let me see his mother's face, as in Paradise, and he will accompany me to the gates of Heaven.[323]

---

321. No. 159 in *LW*.
322. (Begtrup 1925, 53).
323. No. 49 in *HCF*.

Marie's coffin was transported to Køge, 40 km south of Copenhagen, and was laid to rest in St. Nicholas Church, from where it was later moved to a vault in the grounds of her birthplace at Gammel Køgegaard. Grundtvig returned to Rønnebæksholm and went into mourning. Four days after the funeral he wrote to Bernhard Ingemann (Letter 66), paraphrasing Job's words:[324]

> ... in every sense she belonged to God. He gave and He took and, despite all the objections of the world and our self-love, the believing soul cannot but add, "God be praised!" He gave so richly as to exceed the boldest expectations, and He took so like a father as to exceed even there all expectation once He had given us, in the blessing of a little boy, a living memorial and a living hope. With His blessing, our loving Christian life together will not only be reflected in him but will be reborn with His glorious increase.

Grundtvig wrote of his loss to his three grown-up children (Letters 67-69). Meta took him to task:

> So often in your life you have told me that no earthly love can compare with the love between parents and children, yet now, when our Lord has not only let you keep all your children but has even granted you a little son in your old age, it makes me very sad to see you write that life has no joy in it for you. I understand it when you say you can only live in the past and the future, but your past also belongs to your children, and truly they belong together with those who love you deeply. Indeed, father, if I did not think it was proof that you place greater trust in me than in your sons, it would sadden me all the more than it already has. You have not mentioned in a single letter to me that my love for you was a joy – it seems to me as though it was more of a burden, but you had not the heart to tell me straight out. Yes, father, you do not understand the power you have over me, for a loving word from you is one of my greatest joys, just as an unloving or an unfriendly look is a great sadness to me. That is how it has been all my life and that is how it still is at the moment.

There was one other practical matter that Grundtvig had to take care of in connection with Marie's death – her inheritance. At their wedding in 1851 they had signed a marriage contract, or so Grundtvig thought. On Marie's death the manor was to be passed down to her 13-year-old daughter, Haralda, whose uncle, Marie's brother, Hans Carlsen, was her guardian. It now transpired that the document was invalid, since it had not been ratified. Hans Carlsen, who himself owned Gammel Kongegaard, Marie's birthplace, suggested to Grundtvig that they should send the marriage contract to the King for ratification. This would make the teenage Haralda and Grundtvig's baby Frederik the sole heirs of Marie's estate. Grundtvig rejected the proposal; this was not the King's business. He therefore asked for all Marie's goods and chattels to be treated as being under joint ownership, but Marie had already signed away Rønnebæksholm as a deed of gift to Haralda before the

---

324. Job 1:21.

wedding. The "law's delay" saw the court appoint a guardian, known only as 'Olsen the Transcriber' for the now 2-year-old Frederik. He took the case to the supreme court and lost it in 1856. Frederik received 17,379 rigsdaler, Haralda inherited the manor and 8,689 rigsdaler, and Grundtvig inherited nothing from Marie.

Such was their admiration for Lady Marie that on 4th August 1855 the peasant farmers and smallholders at the manor raised a memorial stone to her in a wood on her property. Grundtvig himself led the procession. The inscription reads:

> Love and great respect have caused this pillar to be raised for Anna Marie Elise Grundtvig, née Carlsen. From 1839 to 1854 she was the owner of Rønnebæksholm: she abolished forced work, granted hunting licences, and transferred her right of ownership not to her own but to the benefit of her subordinates. Thus her memory will last for ever. Her soul is with God's angels, she was loved by Our Saviour. She was loved by us.
> *Rønnebæksholm's peasant farmers raised this monument on 4th August 1855*

In the same year, 1855, Grundtvig published his memoir of Marie: *Lady Marie's Monument*. Here he spoke of the kindness of the farmers in raising the monument as well as the closeness of his relationship to Marie, but he also made a reference to the people's high school that he and Marie had hoped to open at Rønnebæksholm:

> Since like me she saw the true enlightenment of the Danish people as the only thing that with God's help could save them and direct them, my idea of a proper Danish people's high school, especially for farmhands, never found more fertile earth than in her. If I ever get to actually build such a high school then it can only be called 'Marie's Pleasure'/*Marielyst* as being both what she really wanted and what she urged as best she could... She also had the great plan, which was strangled at birth, that all manor-house owners on Zealand and the small isles should make a 'contribution' to its establishment, and the only obligation she laid upon those peasant farmers who were themselves educated was that they should shun their own advantage, think the matter through, and contribute 100 rigsdaler to such a Danish educational establishment.[325]

After Marie's death Grundtvig was in mourning, but he was not a broken man – far from it. He wrote 20 new love-poems to Marie, in which he seems almost as happy as when she was alive. She was dead and buried, but her body, soul, and spirit were with God, and that was a state which Grundtvig himself yearned for. He lived in the belief that God's love embraced all, saints and sinners alike, and every Sunday he read and heard the words of Jesus telling him so – the Words of Institution for the two sacraments, the Lord's Prayer, the Creed, and the Blessing. In between were prayers, songs of praise, and a sermon to the glory of God. Life in the shadow of Paradise was an all-powerful experience for Grundtvig, with Marie now one of the "saints in heaven" while Grundtvig remained with the "saints on earth" – or so he hoped. His experience of love in the years with Marie

---

325. (US X, 33).

70. Grundtvig's pavilion at Rønnebæksholm.
Ever mindful of Grundtvig's wish to write in peace and quiet Marie had this pavilion built for him in the spring of 1854. Grundtvig called it 'Kindness'/*Venligheden*, but Marie died before he could start using it. Photo: Edward Broadbridge.

and her sudden death tested his faith, a faith he best described in the hymn 'O life lived in Christ' as "our bridge swaying over the ocean's dark face/from bleak realms of death to the warm shores of life".[326]

In her book, *The Shadow of Paradise: Grundtvig in Love and Crisis*, Birgitte Stoklund Larsen delves deeper into the paradox that Grundtvig's faith was *strengthened* by Marie's death. One of her conclusions is that Grundtvig's tears were not only a healthy consolation but also an emotional confirmation of his faith and a driving force for the poems to Marie that now flowed from his pen. She points in particular to the poem 'My Friend-wife', written a month after Marie's death:

> I once had such a flower, I once had such a bird,
> my friend-wife was beauty on sight;
> Not even the most beautiful garden could enjoy
> an equal to my eyes' delight!
> A rose three times over it was![327]

Grundtvig's poem presents, says Stoklund Larsen:

---

326. No. 41 in *LW*.
327. No. 158 in *LW*.

his report from the inner dialogue between himself and Our Lord ... No one less than God himself had said 'Congratulations!' on the birth of the little son. God too had caught the eye of Marie, a flower and a bird, a friend-wife so beautiful ... Marie was quite simply so lovely that God wanted her back.[328]

Grundtvig's philosophy of womanhood

There are just as many layers to Grundtvig's philosophy of womanhood/*kvindelighed* as there are to his philosophy of a people's identity/*folkelighed*. We have already seen how, in addition to women's many other virtues, both Nordic mythology and Denmark's history presented women as ready for fight. On 5th July 1848, long after he became attracted to Marie, he had written a long poem, 'In Praise of Dane-woman'; Dane-woman was particularly admirable, being born to both action and love. Such a prototype woman was Margrete I of Denmark (1353-1412), who gathered Denmark, Norway, and Sweden into the Calmar Union which she ruled from 1389-1412. The union lived on long after her – until 1523.

The poem begins with admiration for Marie Toft and her daughter Haralda – 'Mother sweet and daughter fine' – but goes on to speak of Dane-woman as a 'shield-maid', daughter-in-arms with Freya, goddess of love, beauty, fertility, war, and clairvoyance. Even more important than these mythological references was Grundtvig's changing view of the role of women in Christianity, Since faith was 'a matter of the heart', the image of God was best revealed *in* the heart, as we read in Paul's letter to the Romans: "For it is with your heart that you believe ... "[329] In his definitive study of the significance of the heart in Grundtvig's works Erik Krebs Jensen writes in 'The heart as the image of God' (1977):

> The open heart is sensitive and impressionable and thus a prerequisite for the interactive conversation between God and the heart to come about through Jesus' mediation ... For Grundtvig love on earth is an image of love in heaven. God is love, and where love is alive among human beings, it is an image of God's love that we have inherited from the Creation.[330]

Human love is not just a reflection and resonance of divine love, it is actually *part* of it, by virtue not of human endeavour, but of God's goodness. Though the heart is neither male nor female, it is the essence of womanhood. As Krebs Jensen writes:

> The heart is the hidden feminine in everyone. With its mother characteristics it receives God's masculine creative force, the spirit, and can in due course give birth to a song of praise to its Creator, the song by which God will also be known on the final day.[331]

---

328. (Stoklund Larsen, 98)
329. Rom. 10:10.
330. (Krebs Jensen, 84 & 88).
331. (Ibid. 91).

In the 1,626 hymns in Grundtvig's *Song-Work to the Danish Church*, the word 'heart' appears 1,723 times. Thus, the role of the female heart in the sequence from creation to salvation is of the essence in the mediation of the Christian faith. Grundtvig was forever grateful for this from his childhood onwards, thanks to his mother, Catherine, and his 'language mistress' and songstress, Malene Jens Datter. It is on this basis that the Church *itself* must be understood as the 'bride of Christ', and the love of woman. Grundtvig ended his hymn, 'How the Church is like God's kingdom!' (1851) with the affirmation that the heavenly fullness of Christ's love should be understood through our experience of married love here on earth:

> All the earth cannot compare with
> what we trust and know and share:
> here on earth we have His heaven
> in Our Saviour's loving care![332]

There can be no misunderstanding here. If 'the woman' has a key position in Christian life, she must also have it in human life. In Synnøve Heggem's doctorate from 2004, the woman "... is the basic human, the prototype of what it means to be a person".[333] The expression 'basic human', (*Grund-Mennesket*), comes from a verse in Grundtvig's *Danish Raven-gall* (1860), where, though aware that Adam was the first to be created, he adds:

> Nor must it be forgotten
> that ever since our Adam's death
> the basic human being,
> life-mother, is the fount of life
> and source of our life's calling.[334]

Grundtvig's understanding of womanhood even stretched to speaking of women as 'female bishops', as in 'We can feel we must learn daily' from 1855:

> He sent Mary of Magdála
> with the Word of Life that day.
> Who would dare forbid a woman
> thus to follow in her way?
> Christian maidens, Christian mothers,
> you shall not be chained by others!
> Who would dare restrain your mouths!
>
> Only when such pious women,
> like the great age of the Word,

---

332. (*Song-Work* IV, 227, 8).
333. (Heggem 2004, 75).
334. (US X, 481).

> serve the Lord as 'female bishops',
> use their tongues so they are heard,
> will the heart by speech exciting
> make all childlike souls delight in
> Heaven's Kingdom here on earth![335]

In an even later poem, 'Earth and heaven, be united' from 1868, Grundtvig further pursued this line of thought in the extraordinary image of love as 'God's own begotten daughter':

> Love, God's own begotten daughter,
> beautiful and fair beside,
> everlasting smile and laughter,
> is the Son's own rightful bride:
> heav'nly groom and earthly bride,
> at God's table they reside.[336]

If we today are to hold firm to the concept of a genderless image of God, we risk doing a disservice not only to the Incarnation but also to the history of Christianity. Grundtvig therefore had his work cut out to introduce his view of womanhood in a Church dominated by men. Synnøve Heggem, describes it thus:

> In his attempt to rehabilitate women in the rhetoric of his hymns, he turned for inspiration to mythology, catholicism (both the Eastern and the Western Church), to protestant theology and his own theology as well as his own experience, and not least, to what had not yet been fulfilled: women's own account of themselves as religious subjects, not least as possible stewards of a religious office speaking from their own women's hearts as equals in regard to the divine.[337]

The crucial point is that love, as humanly experienced, is to be understood in the light of Christian love, and vice versa. They are not identical, but they *are* of the same nature, even though God's love, which is eternal, far surpasses woman's love.[338] There is nothing important that men are, or can do, which women are not capable of being and doing. In contrast, there is much that women are, and can do, by virtue of their heart's warmth and their ability to give life. Men can only attempt to imitate this, they cannot unfold it as strongly as women. They can only try to cling to the power over existence with which women's basic humanity is endowed. This was Grundtvig's *experience*, as he sensed it, and felt the call to prophesy about the power of 'womanhood'.

---

335. No. 78 in *LW*.
336. No. 127 in *LW*.
337. (Heggem 2004, 493).
338. (Ibid., 283).

71. **Grundtvig (74) and his 3-year-old son Frederik 1857.**
Frederik is wearing a dress, as was the custom at the time for boys not fully toilet-trained.

15. Youth and Old Age play Hide-and-seek (1855-63)

As we have seen in chapter 13, Church life, Public life, and Home life are three concentric circles in Grundtvig's world which also overlap each other. Whereas we worked from the outside inwards in chapter 13, we reverse this process here, to emphasise how Grundtvig's new view of womanhood and his need for companionship were so important to him in this period.

Home life

In 1848 21-year-old Countess Asta Tugendreich Adelheid Krag Juel Vind Frijs (b. 1826) married Count Holger Christian Reedtz (b. 1800), the owner of Palsgaard Manor in Jutland, and a Privy Councillor to the King. A week after the birth of her fourth child, her husband died – in February 1857. Lady Asta had already lost her parents when she was only one year old, as well as her cousin Clara Carlsen in 1852. Clara was buried in the graveyard named after her on Køge Ridge. It is reasonable to conjecture that Asta wanted the stability and companionship that a new father-figure would give both herself and her family. The wealthy countess and her four children moved to Copenhagen. Among her long-standing friends from earlier days was Lady Marie Toft, so Lady Asta had been well-informed about Marie's relationship to Grundtvig. For much the same reason she too was attracted, despite him being 43½ years her senior. Indeed, she was young enough to be his *grand*daughter, let alone his daughter. As with Marie, it was another pastor who advised her to contact Grundtvig with her questions about the Christian faith.

Grundtvig for his part was also on the move. On 1st April 1855 he and his little son Frederik rented a smaller apartment at Nørregade 5 with the child's nanny, Maren Pedersen from Rønnebæksholm, and the housekeeper Sille. He moved yet again in October 1857, this time to Nørre Voldgade 38 – his twentieth address in Copenhagen. At some point in the mid-1850s he also decided to let his beard grow.

At face value the new relationship looked like a repeat of Grundtvig's previous one to a wealthy widow. Grundtvig was conceivably looking for a new mother for Frederik, as well as for the companionship of a woman who would care for him, now that he was 74 years old. This indeed was Asta's next step in the relationship, to be Grundtvig's live-in carer. According to a letter of 30th November 1857 from Peter Rørdam to his sister Bolette, it was Asta who took the initiative:

> Last time I wrote, I told you not to draw any conclusions from what you heard concerning Grundtvig and Lady R; but now I am saying that it has been seen before that a mighty

fortress has been taken by constant storm!!! You may think what you like, but you must not open your mouth! Do you understand!³³⁹

A charming episode is related concerning Asta, her loyal housemaid Else Marie Rasmusdatter, and Asta's 4-year-old son, Niels Juel, who, in the presence of his mother, turned to Else Marie one day and said, "I dink Mummy should barry Dundtvig, 'cause when Mummy dits on de dofa, Dundtvig dits on de dofa, and when Mummy dands on de foor, Dundtvig dands on de foor."³⁴⁰

Grundtvig wanted more than a nurse. Early in December he proposed marriage to her, and Asta accepted. On 12th February 1858 they attended Holy Communion together in Vartov Church, with Gunni Busck presiding. This was tantamount to a formal engagement in Grundtvig's view, and two months later, on 16th April, they were married in Asta's apartment on Vesterbrogade in Copenhagen with Peter Fenger presiding. Grundtvig was genuinely amazed at his good fortune:

> All agree with 'third time lucky'!
> Rarely though in any land
> are so many goodly weddings
> granted any married man!...³⁴¹

When he heard a passer-by in the street say to her neighbour, "Look, there goes old Grundtvig with his new springtime piece!" he was not annoyed, but flattered.

Asta renounced her ownership of Palsgaard Manor, but retained an annuity of 1,000 rigsdaler as well as 2,000 rigsdaler for her four children: Sophie (b. 1849), Niels, (b. 1853), Louise (b. 1855), and Holger (b. 1857). A few months into the marriage she purchased a large villa at Gammel Kongevej 148, Frederiksberg, which Grundtvig renamed Happy Home (*Gladhjem*), after Odin's residence in Valhalla in Nordic mythology. They moved in with their five children under ten years old, and resided there with seven servants for the next eight years. In the marriage contract Grundtvig agreed to share the household effects with Asta – except for his 6,000 books.³⁴²

Grundtvig was, as ever, concerned for his children. As we have seen, Johan had married the daughter of one of Grundtvig's friends in 1855, but against Grundtvig's wishes he became a member of the Danish Parliament for the National Liberals from 1858-61, and again from 1864-66. Johan later became Keeper of the Royal Archives. Meanwhile, eight months after Grundtvig's third wedding, his son Svend married Laura Bloch in Vartov Church with Grundtvig presiding and urging the couple to receive God's blessing like the good wine served at the Wedding in Cana.³⁴³ Svend went on to become Professor of

---

339. (Rørdam II, 59-60)
340. (Søndergaard, 128).
341. No. 161 in *LW*.
342. (Søndergaard, 130).
343. Jn 2: 1-12.

72. Asta Grundtvig c. 1861.

Nordic Philology, a Danish literary historian, and an eminent ethnographer. He was a systematic collector and publisher of Danish traditional music and folk tales, and it was he who, after his father's death, took care of his literary legacy. But he too was a National Liberal! As for Meta, we must assume that the father-daughter relationship improved after Grundtvig accepted her criticism of him following the death of Marie; she herself lost her husband, Peter Boisen, in 1862. He had been a teacher in Caroline Amalie's Charity School before becoming Grundtvig's curate at Vartov in 1854.

Now into his third marriage, Grundtvig summarised his wives in three verses in the poem, 'To My Asta' (1858):

> Sisterly was my first dear wife,
> smelling of violets sweet;
> seldom indeed more idyllic a life
> under the sun could one meet,

wealth was but small, yet fair was fate,
ours from Christmas to autumn late!

Motherly was my second wife,
sparkling as bright as a gem,
ours was a bold, romantic life
Artemis spun on the loom,
then in her womb another child
I hymned, and bewailed aloud to the skies!

Daughterly is my third sweet wife,
fairy-like floating she goes;
This is a rich, enchanted life,
roses grow out of the snows!
Youth and Old Age play Hide-and-seek,
games and kisses in Christmas week![344]

The 'games and kisses' extended beyond Christmas week. In the late spring of 1859 Asta became pregnant, and on 10th February 1860 she gave birth to a little girl – her fifth child. Grundtvig wished to commemorate his three wives and celebrate his new-found good fortune, so he named the baby Asta Marie Elisabeth Friis, a prestigious surname from his wife's side, and baptised his new daughter at home on 18th March. When the baby was 'presented' in Vartov Church on 8th April, Grundtvig's sons, Johan and Svend, were among her seven godparents.[345]

Grundtvig had already fathered one child beyond his 70th birthday; here was another. At the grand old age of 76, Grundtvig was deeply moved by this addition to his family. The following year he wrote 'To My Wife Asta':

So I look with double pleasure
on my pretty child today,
who with other tender flowers
peeps out now above the clay,
may her gladness never cease
at my latest 'springtime piece'.[346]

As the above three stanzas testify, in Grundtvig's eyes all three marriages were successful: the first was an idyll, the second a romance, the third a fairy-tale.[347]

Physically, Grundtvig was gradually slowing down. He suffered from swollen legs,

---

344. No. 160 in *LW*.
345. (Søndergaard, 137).
346. No. 161 in *LW*.
347. No. 160 in *LW*.

73. Grundtvig and Asta's 'Happy Home', Gammel Kongevej 148.

ankle sores, and 'red skin', while his eyesight was also fading and his use of a magnifying glass increasing. With Asta's help he rose later, and conducted morning prayers for the whole household. Maren Pedersen's beautiful voice led the singing until she married in 1860 and left the household. Grundtvig was beside himself with the loss, and at Maren's final morning prayers, he openly wept as he paced the floor. She had meant so much to him and Frederik over the past six years that he himself sponsored her wedding.

Happy Home was also a busy home. Grundtvig carried on working in his study, while the six children played and learned elsewhere. He was especially attentive to Frederik, who, his two elder brothers noted when Frederik was 5 or 6, was being given much more freedom than they themselves had enjoyed. Their father answered that one is better at bringing up children when one is old![348]

Grundtvig received many a visitor eager to tap him for a wise word, often on theology. He was generous with his time in this respect, as Ernst Trier, one of the great inheritors of the Grundtvig legacy, found out in his youth. In 1859 Asta invited the 18-year-old theology student to Happy Home to meet for the first time his future mentor. He records that Grundtvig's words "... issue so perfectly plainly from his mouth, and he would listen with such noticeable patience to one's questions and show one the way ahead." But Trier re-

---

348. (Brun II, 239).

ceived short shrift when he told Grundtvig that he did not always understand his sermons; the old man bridled at any criticism and responded that they demand a pre-existent faith in "the Lord as He *is*, present among us and as close to us as the Word in our mouths and hearts." Add to this, it does not appear to have crossed Grundtvig's mind that his sermons were occasionally impenetrable, due partly to the intricacy of his thought and partly to his complex syntax. Generally, he preached to "the insiders" as he remarked critically on himself in 1861, meaning those who would understand him.

Another visitor was sent away empty-handed, as Grundtvig himself relates. On 9th July 1855 a "simple Jew of the artisan class ... a good-natured and honest creature" who had married a "common Christian woman", had wished to be baptised, but Bishop Martensen had refused to allow the man's parish pastor, his teacher in the faith, to perform the sacrament. Grundtvig had no wish to get involved and thought the man's knowledge was below par and his motivation lacklustre. The man then argued that not only did Jews welcome converted Christians but that there was many a Christian who knew *less* than him. Grundtvig felt that the man was undermining the holy sacrament, and he could be of no help, for he did not believe that the man was serious. From the pulpit the following Sunday Grundtvig argued that Baptism and the gospel were wasted on "such indifferent people" who "were not seeking the Kingdom of Heaven". It was God who was the active element in Baptism in *creating* faith; He was so, however, "only when we wish for it".

A further approach to Grundtvig came from the young baroness Elise Stampe (b. 1824), who wrote asking for guidance on the efficacy of Holy Baptism and Holy Communion, the two sacraments in the Danish Lutheran Church. Although nowadays Holy Communion forms part of the Sunday service liturgy, in Grundtvig's day it was a service for which one had to register beforehand. In their lengthy correspondence in the summer of 1856 Grundtvig was remarkably patient, being straightforward as regards Baptism, but reticent about Elise's wish to partake of the holy meal *every* Sunday. Her twin argument was that this is what the early Christians did, and that it is in Holy Communion that absolution is pronounced. He was aware of the need, perhaps even greater among women, but noted that catholic nuns did not seem to profit from their frequent access to the sacrament. In Grundtvig's final letter in the correspondence, dated 13th September, he wrote:

> I can only loosely touch on your comment on the feeling of the Lord's 'living presence', since on the one hand this is both glorious and important, yet on the other hand both an obscure and difficult matter, which especially convent life has taught us to think cautiously about. However, when the Word of Jesus Christ as both the Grace and the Truth has become a living reality within us, then that Word will always be a holy lamp in the night that burns until the dawn.[349]

Grundtvig's friend and fellow-politician, Sophus Høgsbro, who had known Grundtvig through all three marriages, noted the welcoming atmosphere at Happy Home, which had a more homely feeling than his previous residences:

---

349. (BFOTG 2, 573).

During the time of the Constituent Assembly, I never saw any farmers in his house, such as his close friends Jens Jørgensen and Cornelius Petersen; nor did I in the days of his second marriage. But now, in his third marriage, farmers who were also MPs, such as Peder Larsen Skrappenborg, and far less-known people were regular and very welcome guests there.[350]

Further testimony to the happy household came from the Norwegian poet, Bjørnstjerne Bjørnson, who visited Happy Home on 8th July 1860, where there were children everywhere. Afterwards he wrote:

> I was invited to dinner by old Grundtvig yesterday, whose latest wife ... recently bore him a daughter .... All these young children play and make noise around him, and the old children's friend is perfectly happy with this ... He lives in a country house out of town with a large garden and a big play-area for the children with a swing, a doll's house, a playroom, and a very small Icelandic pony called Sleipner. A farmhand holds the rein while they ride madly round in the garden! ... On the other side of the garden door sits his little, devoted wife, the former countess, who has offered him her fortune and her hand to sweeten his last days. She looks after his every need.[351]

Grundtvig's home life, public life, and church life merged into a single circle when on 29th May 1861 he celebrated his 50th anniversary in the priesthood. The day began with a children's choir singing outside his home one of his best-known hymns, 'We welcome with joy this blessed day'.[352] They then hoisted the Dannebrog flag that they had sewn and shouted hurrah in his honour. At 10 am Grundtvig presided at a service of celebration in a chock-full Vartov Church, with 50 pastors present. The dowager Queen Caroline Amalie presented him with a 7-armed candelabrum, a gift from his friends in Norway and Denmark, with the words, "May this gold candelabrum remind you of the light that now shines in the Danish Church." The King granted Grundtvig the rank of Bishop on the occasion, but the Minister of Culture, Ditlev Monrad, went one step further and at the celebration he promoted Grundtvig to the actual *title* of Bishop; he was hereafter often addressed as 'Bishop Grundtvig' both at home and abroad.[353] The King was not amused and Bishop Martensen was furious with Monrad, calling his action "a prostitution of his title of Minister of Church Affairs."[354]

Late in the afternoon a number of his friends gathered for dinner in a large well-decorated tent in Grundtvig's garden. A group of young people arrived and sang, and the sum of 3000 rigsdaler was handed over for the publication of Grundtvig's hymns and spiritual songs. The gift was put into a fund administered by his friend, Pastor Gunni Busck and three other friends, who published three large volumes of Grundtvig's hymns

---

350. (Søndergaard, 131).
351. (Ibid., 138).
352. No. 53 in *LW*.
353. E.g. *Bishop Grundtvig, Prophet of the North*, E.L. Allen (James Clarke 1947).
354. (BTOFG II, 38).

in 1873, 1875, and 1881. Busck also presented him with a gold coin minted in his honour from donations from the Vartov congregation. Grundtvig made a speech of thanks, which was followed by more singing and speeches, including greetings from the Jutland farmers and the Norwegian students. Between 10 and 11 pm torches were lit all round the garden, after which a farewell song was sung and the celebration ended.

Grundtvig's son Johan and his daughter Meta were present, but not Svend. Johan even proposed a toast to Asta, his second stepmother, but 4 years his junior! This toast pleased Grundtvig immensely and helped to compensate for Svend's absence due to military duties, though Svend did send a telegram that also delighted his father. Five days later he wrote about the occasion to Svend and Laura (Letter 70):

> It was as delightful as such a day can possibly be, and I had therefore wished so deeply that I could share it with you who are so close to my heart! Your sentiment on the day itself was a doubly joyful surprise, when I was forced to believe my own eyes and see what I had never imagined – that the telegraph really can and does convey poetry! ... Thanks too for your letter to my wife! She will write back, I am sure. Johan also drank to her health on the great day!

Public life

For Grundtvig Public life was conducted in all of society (*det borgerlige selskab*), which is as important for God's creation as Church life is for the Christian community. State and Church must grow *alongside* each other. However, in seeking to strengthen the individual into a competent contributor to the people – across rank, class, gender, faith, domicile, and wealth – the State is secondary. A people's education that focuses solely on the individual does not deserve the name of 'education': the individual and the group must understand themselves as part of the community and the Fatherland. Grundtvig's use of 'Fatherland' refers solely to 'the nation of one's fathers', which he often used alongside 'Mother-tongue', the language of one's mothers. Together they are the pathway to 'the common good' – the title of volume four in this series, where the phrase appears 40 times! In an article from 2022 Ove Korsgaard went so far as to suggest that with this phrase in mind Grundtvig ended up a 'republican' in the pre-politicised use of the phrase, for the Latin words *res publica*, from which the English word derives, mean no more than 'public matters'. A 'republican' believes that supreme power is held by the people and their elected representatives, who in turn consider the country a 'public matter'. The State, the Government, Parliament, and the Courts must govern in the people's interest – and with the people's knowledge, understanding, and acceptance. The three instances must be kept on a rein so that they do not abrogate power to themselves; if they do, in an elective democracy they can regularly be replaced. The Danish constitution of 1849 built on this principle, copying it from the Belgian and the Norwegian constitutions, and, like them, following Montesquieu's original idea in *The Spirit of Law*, 11, 4. (1748) of the separation of government powers into the executive, the legislative, and the judicial.

For most of his life Grundtvig believed that the best form for governing public matters was through the enlightened monarch listening to the people's will. Only very slowly did he come to accept a more limited role for the monarch and a greater influence of the elected representatives in Parliament, for the king was a symbol of stability, and the power that chose governments, whereas 'governments' could come and go. As Denmark took its first small steps between the introduction of democracy in 1849 and Grundtvig's death in 1872, the country experienced no fewer than twelve governments – all for 'the common good'!

In the same period, Bismarck was using his Prussian military power to subjugate and unite 39 individual German-speaking states into a single centralised nation, culminating in 1871. From early in the century, Grundtvig had fought to consolidate and inspire the Danish people to become aware of their history and their identity – for their very survival was at stake. In his capacity of parliamentary politician from 1850-58 he involved himself in all manner of affairs, when he thought that the relationship between the individual, the people, and the state was becoming lop-sided. He was against the idea that it was the *state* that should look after its citizens, for that was the individual's duty. He therefore opposed a number of measures that we would now take for granted: the civil servants' demand for pension rights; the right of dependents to state maintenance; compulsory school attendance, and compulsory general military conscription. These would require not only much higher taxes, but would work against the independence and voluntary spirit that was the core of a healthy life for the people. At the same time, the state must be limited in its scope through the individual's right both to freedom of speech, and to be brought before a judge within 24 hours of arrest. We have already noted that Grundtvig's successful contribution to the new Constitution was 'public access to the courts and oral proceedings therein'. To this day, unless a judge rules otherwise, public access is a constitutional right.

Grundtvig's belief that all life was dependent on the invisible, God-given, inter-human 'spirit' also affected his political views. Spirit is *power*, expressed through language, and demanding freedom in the life-forms in which it works. The Danish-American, Ernest D. Nielsen, emphasises that Grundtvig is always "on the trail of the Spirit".[355] A sense of what constitutes 'true life' is a sense of the "Spirit's life on earth",[356] which is in constant movement and works best when contraries are in play. *Combat* is therefore essential to life, between light and dark, good and evil, even between tradition and renewal. Grundtvig's lines from *Nordic Mythology* resonate here:

> Freedom our watchword must be in the North!
> Freedom for Loki as well as for Thor.
> Free is the Word in the Spirit's new world,
> which the Word has created on this earthly shore,
> ... and only in battle does life make a stand,

---

355. Nielsen 1955, 13.
356. No. 131 in *LW*, st. 12.

> Where, even when power is hidden in steam,
> loudly it shouts: My life is to fight!...
> Freedom for all that from Spirit is sprung...

For Grundtvig the cause of freedom also stretched to the physical battle against the invading Germans, so he rejected the armistice agreed with them in 1848. Denmark should fight on! Freedom could not be rolled back into subjection; once tasted it was the elixir of the Spirit. Again he was experiencing how 'combat' was absolutely essential between Members of Parliament, as it was for the electoral system that pitted one candidate against another. Logically, therefore, when the Constitution was revised in 1866, and new voting restrictions imposed, Grundtvig was furious; for a second time he had to run for Parliament and vote against the bill on the Constitution! Democracy was now part of his vocabulary: a right, once given can not be taken back.

Another basic tenet of his political views lay in the bedrock of his Christian conscience. We have seen how his visit to the Copenhagen prison with Elizabeth Fry in 1841 had affected him, as did the demand of the slaveowners in 1848 that they should be compensated by the Danish state for their loss of income. The free action of the Spirit in work and trade, along with a socially balanced land reform and a voluntary charity initiative, was the combination that for Grundtvig best ensured the people's sustenance and social order. The nobility could retain their titles, but all their accompanying rights should be abolished, and their land sold off to the peasant farmers at modest prices, just as Marie Toft had done at Rønnebæksholm. From the Christian sense of justice, it is the *people* who own the Fatherland soil, which was given to them by God to share out and cultivate as best they could. Grundtvig further supported not only the equality of opportunity for public office but also the Trade Act of 1857, which largely followed his views on freedom of trade. For him, the freedom of independence took priority over equality of opportunity, since only in freedom can the common good be pursued; a state-dictated equality of opportunity was a slap in the face for freedom.

In 1848 he had amplified his position in an article entitled 'The Danish, the German, and the French Cause', in which he saw his position as both a bridge and the golden middle way:

> Such a bridge over what experience teaches us can neither be waded through nor vaulted over, and that is what I propose and advocate as the golden middle way. I remain quite calm when some call me 'conservative' because I *defend* the bridge, and others call me 'revolutionary', because my goal is to *cross* the bridge and reach a brand-new state of civil society. In this new society, our unassailable human rights are truly asserted, the people are truly considered the owners of our land and our kingdom, and we aspire to all the liberty, equality, and brotherhood that we may reasonably suppose awaits us – given the nature of the times and our people, with their increasing enlightenment and better education.

The following year he went one step further, proposing that the young veterans of the First Schleswig War should be rewarded with a livelihood:

In fighting and winning for old Denmark, these brave and healthy lads are *conscious* of their love of the Fatherland, and they will also learn from their wars how wrong things can go when everyone commands, and no one obeys, and that there is only a joint loss when everyone seeks to save his own skin and not to help towards the common good. If we could provide a self-owning farm on good terms for all these young lads who have fought with honour for the fatherland, who have gone through hell and high water, and who wish to become regular farmers, then we would be killing two birds with one stone. For we would be showing them a just appreciation for their risking life and limb for us all, and we would be securing for the fatherland a race of farmers who with God's help, from generation to generation, would protect our realm and our peace and have an eye as to what best serves the security and peace of Denmark![357]

It was at the beginning of this period that Grundtvig experienced one major parliamentary success, on 4th April 1855, with the passing of the bill to 'break the parish-tie'. This may seem a small victory to modern readers, but it was a victory for freedom of worship in Grundtvig's day, repealing a law from 1683 that had allowed parishioners to worship outside their parish but not to be 'administered' there, e.g. receive the twin sacraments.[358]

Grundtvig's understanding and genuine admiration for the female nature also led him to speak up for women in various fora, including Parliament in 1857:

I therefore deeply welcome the present bill as part of a larger bill to give these rights to women concerning inheritance and access to conducting lawful business, be it craft or trade. I welcome it not least because I deeply desire with this undoubted relaxation of the law that far from wishing to be men, our women should endeavour to be truly *women*! For I am certain that as women they have a call and a purpose and an ability that can and must be demonstrated in order to show that they are a revelation of human nature which in no sense whatsoever is either inferior, or less important, or less reliable than it is in the best of men.[359]

However, when the above-mentioned Trade Act was passed in 1857, he lost his claim that women had an "inalienable human right" to full authority in legal and financial matters. Parliament was not yet ready for this move, which only became law in 1908.

The most powerful driving-force behind Grundtvig's political work was his Christian faith, as Per Øhrgaard writes:

Christianity comes first and last for Grundtvig, but for it to become manifest there must be *people,* indeed there must be *a* people among whom it can grow. And there is only a people

---

357. Ch. 32 in *TCG*.
358. *HCF* 127-35.
359. No. 33d in *TCG*.

74. Grundtvig 1862.
Portraits by Constantin Hansen,
Frederiksborg Museet, and
Wilhelm Marstrand, Copenhagen City Hall.

where there is a history, hence Grundtvig's intense occupation with both world history... and with Nordic Mythology.[360]

As we have seen, Grundtvig linked *England* to the Nordic countries. In England practice often came before theory; one acted first, then discovered whether the action/experiment was successful or not, and only then did one form a theory. For an unsystematic thinker like Grundtvig, this was a satisfying procedure. Moreover, England was needed as an ally against Germany. As he wrote in 1853, for Denmark, "the only possible way out is a permanent union between the three Nordic kingdoms and the more than half-Nordic England."

When he rose to speak in Parliament, his audience rarely knew what to expect. Grundtvig's speeches could switch from the philosophical to the humorous to the ironic to the deadly serious without him always being aware of where he was going. Occasionally the old warhorse would give such vent to his anger that he broke parliamentary protocol, but for the most part he was witty, if long-winded. The opening of his speech on a revision of the Constitution in 1855 is an example of these two traits; he clearly loved to hold the floor:

> I cannot ask the honoured house for permission to *bore* it, for I never allow anyone to bore me and cannot ask it of others! Instead I shall endeavour to be as *un*boring and as brief as possible, though I dare not promise to be *very* brief today. I must further apologise if, like other honourable members, I begin a little *outside* the main subject, as I cannot come at it in any other way...

In the summer of 1862, Grundtvig sat for his portrait by two of the greatest painters of his time, neither of whom was pleased to know what the other one was doing. Even the set-up was the same, the same chair and table, and the same red glass with a long spoon in it for the sugar-water it contained. The family in Copenhagen preferred Hansen's portrait, whereas the painter Joakim Skovgaard preferred Marstrand's.[361]

Constantin Hansen's picture was bought for little Asta by her godmother, Charlotte Neergaard, and hung first in Johan Grundtvig's home. Asta bought Marstrand's portrait for 300 rigsdaler and gave it to her step-son Frederik in her will. It is now in private hands.

Church life

Conflicts with Bishop Martensen and Søren Kierkegaard

Behind *Basic Christian Teachings* lie not only Grundtvig's deepest thoughts on the subject but also half a century of theological struggle to "hammer his thoughts into unity", in Yeats's phrase. But this does not mean that he remains unshaken when the two leading theologians of the time, Bishop of Zealand, Hans Martensen (1808-84) and Søren

---

360. Hall et al. (ed.) 2015, 226.
361. (Saxtorph, 47-50).

Kierkegaard (1813-55) contested the validity of his theology and thus his church work and his existential foundation.

When Bishop Mynster of Zealand died in 1854, the succession lay between another old Grundtvig adversary, Henrik (H.N.) Clausen, and Hans Martensen, a Grundtvig admirer in his younger days, who became the new bishop. Martensen was a first-class systematic theologian, whose works have been translated into a number of languages and are read to this day. Like Mynster, he feared the dissolution of the Danish Church, if it started splintering into 'free' congregations such as Grundtvig was advocating. Martensen's further reservation about Grundtvig concerned the latter's young supporter, Christian Kragballe, who edited the periodical, *Church Collector*, where Grundtvig often published his work between 1855-62. Kragballe believed that the 'effects' of Baptism depended on the sensitivity and strength of faith of the baptising pastor, and when he approached Bishop Martensen in 1856 with a request for ordination with a view to becoming curate to Pastor Peter Rørdam, his baptismal views were a hindrance. Grundtvig persuaded Kragballe to modify them, but to no avail. Martensen held firm to the view of the Early Church which at the beginning of the 4th century had condemned Bishop Donatus for claiming that the sacraments were deprived of their validity if they had been administered by a priest who had sold out to the Romans during the persecutions of Emperor Diocletian from 285-305. Kragballe continued as a teacher until he was finally ordained by the Bishop in 1872.

Grundtvig understood Martensen's position. The 'effect' of Baptism does not depend on the pastor at all, only on God's act of love, for which the pastor is merely a medium, though of course he should be trust*worthy*. This was indeed the core of Grundtvig's theology, that it is *God* who is active in history. We mortals are dependent on our subjective feelings, imagination, and experiences, but there is a further, objective, reality beyond us to which we only have access through our senses. The sacrament must be believed and felt to work by the recipient, what Grundtvig calls 'the sense of Truth', which is available to all congregants and beyond all worldly authorities. This necessity of subjectivity here is summed up in the famous words: it "lives deep within us, we feel it empow'r".[362] This view might well have appealed to Kierkegaard, but he went after the man rather than the ball and singled Grundtvig out as the worst of them all, since his only interest was to create a safe little haven for himself. Grundtvig for his part was peeved by the criticism and returned it in kind.

There may have been a cold wind blowing between Grundtvig and Martensen over the rejection of Kragballe, but it did not destroy their relationship. According to Grundtvig's first biographer, Hans Brun, Queen Caroline Amalie invited them both to Sorgenfri Palace, and when Grundtvig stretched out a hand to Martensen, the latter took it with tears in his eyes.[363]

In Martensen's first sermon as bishop he had called his predecessor, Bishop Mynster, "a witness to the Truth", which was too much for Kierkegaard, who prepared the wither-

---

362. No. 41 in *LW*.
363. (Brun II, 139).

ing attack on the Danish Church that filled the last year of his life. Martensen, his former university teacher yet only five years his senior, was one of many who "play at Christianity, and make a fool of God."[364] Both Martensen and Grundtvig were shocked at Kierkegaard's tone, and the feud rumbled on. Martensen refused to be drawn any further publicly, and concentrated on his episcopal duties and his sermons, a genre to which he gave premier status, and where, as a systematic theologian he was of the highest calibre. Like Mynster he felt that Grundtvig's insistence on the freedom to establish congregations outside the State Church was a slippery slope.

Kierkegaard wrote the following scathing evaluation of Grundtvig:

> As a thinker, Grundtvig is a genius; but so instantly a genius that the ingenious impulse or the Ingenious One's experiencing during the idea has, in respect of the mental constitution, something in common with what an apopletic seizure is for the corporeal. An idea seizes him, he is astonished, is affected, he wants to render the whole of humanity happy with his matchless discovery (...) The moment he has an opinion, no matter what, it is the absolute, the matchless [den mageløse], the sole source of blessedness (...) whether it be his depiction of the foul ignorance of the age or his radiant prospects into a matchless future, or ingenuous wonderment over his own self, that once again he has made a matchless discovery.[365]

Seen with the benefit of nearly 200 years hindsight Grundtvig and Kierkegaard had more in common than they could realise at the time: 1) they are both against German idealism in their theory of cognition as a philosophy of life; 2) they are both to a large degree conservative royalists; 3) they are rounded by the same Lutheran inheritance and critical of the doctrine of original sin; 4) they are both marked by revivalist Christianity with a pietistic strain, though neither of them is a pietist; 5) they both have a high degree of veneration for their fathers, even though they feel they have outgrown them; 6) they are both extremely critical of state-administered, conventional Christianity without a personal commitment; and 7) they share a fundamentally existential approach to human life and the Christian faith, an attitude that reveals itself in at least three areas: a) both follow the fundamental approach that "human comes first, and Christian next"; b) both are artistically existential in their central forms of expression, Grundtvig as a poetic skald and Kierkegaard as a poetic prose-writer; and c) they both emphasise 'simultaneity with Christ' as crucial to true Christianity.

There are of course significant differences between the two. While Grundtvig makes a *distinction* between culture and Christianity, Kierkegaard has an *absolute* separation. While for Grundtvig the Church with its living congregation is the place of mediation for the forgiveness of sins, the Church for Kierkegaard, and in particular its major emanations such as the state church in Denmark, are *damaging* to true Christianity. The Church has become a mass theatre. Instead of burgeoning and 'emerging', it is stagnating, and all

---

364. (*The Instant* no. 4, July 1855).
365. Bradley, 274. Bradley's translation.

church leaders should kiss the dust and apologise – best of all they should be pensioned off. Grundtvig on the other hand argued that the sacraments should create a "clean conscience and hope of God's glory which is the evangelical submission of Christianity and which will, after the new Covenant, be the fruits of Baptism for all believers."[366]

Grundtvig could only shake his head at Kierkegaard's view of the Church, yet he was sympathetic to the younger man's wish to throw out all the dead wood that had accumulated over the years. Grundtvig argued that freedom of worship should be available to all – without the state's interference. If this were so, wrote Grundtvig, there would even be room for a *pastor* Søren Kierkegaard, who could then see if his form of New Testament Christianity was practicable! Freedom of conscience should also be granted to the individual pastor, said Grundtvig, but this proved not only impossible in a state church, but also controversial, with several of Grundtvig's faithful supporters arguing against him.

Central to Grundtvig's Church life were both the oral and the written word. He always preferred the oral; it was not just the marks on the page that distinguished humans from animals, it was the verbal communication through which we interact in meaningful sounds and share our deepest thoughts and feelings. Thus the Bible, or any other book for that matter, only comes alive when it is read by an inspired person. Oral presentations always contain a 'dramatic' element only potentially present in the written word: we do not get spirit from reading a book, we read the book with the spirit we have. When we read the script of *Hamlet, Prince of Denmark*, we are a huge step away from actually watching the drama unfold before us onstage. From contemporary reports of Grundtvig's oral presentations, we can see that they had a dramatic quality. Grundtvig enjoyed communicating his ideas, and was aware of the power of his speech and his personality, no more so than when he was preaching the Word of the Lord before a willing audience. Only in his later years could he preach a sermon without moving his body at all. By all accounts Grundtvig's voice from the altar and the pulpit was deep, gruff, articulate, and penetrating. Despite his inability to sing in tune it was nevertheless he who was the channel for the spirit behind the hymn. Of course in many cases it was actually he who had written it!

During the eight years that this chapter covers Grundtvig was continuously productive, as poet, theologian, and historian. Two works stand out: his theological *magnum opus*, *Basic Christian Teachings* (1855), and his poem *The Seven Stars of Christendom* (1860).

Basic Christian Teachings

Between 1855 and 1861 Grundtvig published a series of articles in *Danish Church Times* on the basic tenets of his theology. Grundtvig believed that his version was an improvement on Luther's *Small Catechism*, to which he was nevertheless indebted. Indeed in *New Year's Morning* (1824) he had actually called himself "the little Luther".[367] The 21 articles were first published in a collected book in 1868. 15 of these have been translated into English

---

366. *HCF*, 289.
367. (US IV, 269).

in *Human Comes First* (2018) with a lengthy introduction by Hans Raun Iversen, to which interested readers are referred. In its original form *Basic Christian Teachings* still serves as a useful work for theology students in the Department of Dogmatics seeking an overall view of Grundtvig's Christianity. A few chapter titles give a flavour of its content: The Christian Baptismal Covenant; On our Third Article of Faith; The Lord's Prayer; The Christian Signs of Life; Faith, Hope, and Love; The Divine Trinity. In contrast to Luther, Grundtvig omits any article on the Ten Commandments of the Old Covenant in his determination to concentrate on the New Covenant and how God is addressing us today. The two sacraments of Holy Baptism and Holy Communion are central, encapsulating Grundtvig's belief that:

> Only at the font and table
> do we hear God's Word to us.[368]

By contrast, the sermon is not *God's* words. God only speaks to us *directly* in the Words of Institution at the Lord's Supper, in the Apostles' Creed, and in the Lord's Prayer in addition to the Aronitic Blessing and Peace Blessing. All else – the hymns, the prayers, the other blessings, even the readings – have been instituted by human hand. After 1825, almost every time Grundtvig spoke of 'the Word', he was referring to these three incidences, in which Christ himself is present: "Only in the Spirit is God with us and only through the Spirit does God work in us, from the Day of Ascension to the Day of Judgement."[369] In this context, the Danish word *Ordet* is a constant challenge for the translator, for it denotes three separate yet interlinked concepts: 1) the Word of God, Jesus Christ, the *logos*, as in Jn 1: 2); the Word as transmitted directly by Christ in the above three incidences; and 3) language *as such,* i.e. *words.* We are in communication with the divine through all three, but where Danish often uses the single word, *Ordet,* English has the choice of three: the Word, words, language – and the translator must compromise. What is not in doubt for Grundtvig is that Christ's living words (the Word) have been passed down to us, from generation to generation:

> The audible testimony of the Church of Christ at Baptism ... has been transmitted from mouth to mouth and from generation to generation as the Word from His *own* mouth which must never leave the mouth of His Church and from which His Spirit shall never depart but always accompany and seal that testimony. This then, in its truest, strictest, and most blessed sense is the 'basic Christian teaching ... '[370]

God's call demands a response, as Grundtvig wrote in a poem entitled 'The Eternal Word of Life' from 1855-56:

---

368. (*Song-Work* V, 385).
369. HCF 279.
370. HCF 242.

> If you trust what you have heard,
> add your Yes, and Amen too,
> then with water and the Word
> my right hand baptises you;
> you are thereby born anew,
> so will matchless joy ensue.

In the chapter on 'The Divine Trinity' towards the end of *Basic Christian Teachings* Grundtvig touches on the subject of a 'Christian doctrinal structure':

> Thus, although with the Christian enlightenment that we have gained we must have been cured of the delusion that we can clarify and describe what we have neither experienced nor can experience in this life, we can nevertheless *glimpse* what a Christian doctrinal structure would look like as a design for the new Jerusalem.[371]

In the authors' reading this doctrinal structure could be schematised thus:

75. Grundtvig's doctrinal structure in diagram form

Oral Word of Life	The Apostolic Creed	The Lord's Prayer	The Words of Institution
Life Expressions	Faith	Hope	Love
Life Signs/Church Characteristics	Confession of Faith	Preaching the Word	Song of Praise
The Trinity	The Holy Spirit	The Son	The Father
The Kingdom of God	Justice	Peace	Joy
Eschatology	The Forgiveness of Sin	The Resurrection of the Body	Everlasting Life
Humankind	Spirit	Soul	Body
Outward Humankind	Hand	Mouth	Heart
Inward Humankind	Life-force	Truth	Love

Reading across: the Oral Words of Life from the Lord's own mouth in row one create the corresponding Life Expressions in row two, which immediately reproduce themselves in row three as Church Characteristics. The diagram further corresponds to the three persons of the Trinity, the Third Article of the Apostolic Creed, and Grundtvig' anthropology.

Grundtvig's earlier idea that Jesus himself dictated the Creed to the Apostles in the 40 days between the Resurrection and the Ascension is historically incorrect. Experience,

---

371. HCF, 370.

15. YOUTH AND OLD AGE PLAY HIDE-AND-SEEK (1855-63)

76. Grundtvig baptising a baby in Vartov Church.
Drawing by Wilhelm Marstrand, c. 1860.

however, shows us something else. Grundtvig is therefore experiencing a poetic *truth*, for without doubt the Christian faith grew out of *something* as it can be felt in Baptism and the Lord's Supper. In a revision of an earlier hymn he asserted in 1864:

> We are, with thanksgiving,
> both touched and are living
> in Christ, in the Word that God gives.
> When that Word is spoken
> and love is its token,
> then truly that name in You lives.[372]

The Seven Stars of Christendom

The alternative translation of the Danish original is *The Pleiades of Christendom*, since the reference is to the cluster of seven stars known in English as 'the Pleaides' or 'the Seven Sisters'. The *Christian* reference is to the cluster of seven churches in present-day Türkiye (then Asia Minor) referred to in Rev 1-3, where the Holy Spirit instructs John of Patmos: "Write on a scroll what you see and send it to the seven churches: to Ephesus, and to Smyrna, and to Pergamum, and to Thyatira, and to Sardis, and to Philadelphia, and to Laodicea." Each letter declares the successes and failures of the seven churches and encourages them to be strong in the faith. Grundtvig took up the concept of seven churches to delineate the *chronological* history of Christianity and the characteristics of each church, from the original Hebrew church, through the Greek church, the Latin church, the English church, the German church, and the Nordic church. Grundtvig's seventh and final church lay in India, somewhere in the future. He had been working with the idea since 1810, and it now took the lengthy form of some 450 stanzas. Grundtvig's common themes, such as Baptism being the decisive moment of acceptance, are at the heart of the narrative, which leads to a new life in the Spirit interacting with the people's history, culture, and language.

The work by the South African missiologist, David Bosch (1929-92), *Transforming Mission. Paradigm Shifts in Theology of Mission* (1992), explores what happens to a people when they are gradually permeated by the Christian faith – the process sometimes referred to as 'inculturation', meaning the new shape that Christianity takes in a local culture, and the way a local culture is transformed by Christianity. In his book *Translating the Gospel. The Missionary Impact on Culture* (1989) Lamin Sanneh (1942-2019) from The Gambia, a Muslim convert to Christianity who taught at the Yale Divinity School for 30 years, spells out how Christianity works as a movement of new translations of the message of Christ in the cultures of the world. In his own way Grundtvig did very much the same as these modern missiologists.

Which linguistic and cultural forms of expression can Christianity take over from the local culture – as Paul does with the statue to the unknown god in Athens (Acts 17:23)? Grundtvig was at his most inspired when he came to the Nordic Church, where

---

372. (No. 397 in *DDS*, 'Trods længselens smerte').

he presents Christianity as a modest *guest* on its arrival in Denmark. This appearance of a foreign religion is dated to the year 826, when Ansgar, later known as the 'Apostle to the North', was allowed to build the first church on Danish soil in Hedeby, 50 km south of the present-day Danish-German border. Grundtvig describes Christianity as a foreign guest in an already religious society, the 'host' being Nordic mythology:

> When we saw this stranger first,
> though an angel of the Lord,
> he appeared a foreign guest,
> needing only room and board,
> lodged with humble folk at heart,
> never sought a clash to start,
> or to disrespect his host.[373]

Other works

In the winters of 1860-62 Grundtvig gave a series of talks on the same subject to a circle of friends at Happy Home; these were published in 1871 under the title *Church Mirror, or a Study of the History of the Christian Church*. A poem of over 4,500 lines followed in 1860 with the title, *Danish Raven-gall*, a reference to Odin's two ravens, Munin and Hugin. Where Odin is the symbol of the Nordic spirit, Munin represents 'memory' and Hugin 'thought'. In the poem Grundtvig calls himself Knytling, which is best translated as 'little attachment', derived from the same word for 'knitting'. He seeks to be the 'little attachment' to the ravens as he surveys Nordic history poetically. He then turns into the biblical dove (Christianity), and finally into the phoenix, the bird which in ancient Greek and Egyptian mythology is associated with the sun god. Rising from its own ashes, it symbolises resurrection and immortality. In its flight in the poem the bird announces what it sees – also one and a half generations into the future, taking the narrative to 1910. Difficult as it may be, the poem carries the powerful message that Nordic mythology and Christianity *need* each other, at least in Denmark.

Grundtvig continued to revise and publish works on language and history. His revised edition of Saxo's *Deeds of the Danes* appeared in 1854-55, and the third and final volume of *Handbook in World History* came out in 1856. A new edition of his *Beowulf* translation, based on his own transcript from the British Museum in 1830, was published in 1861. Grundtvig's prodigious output of hymns and poems continued. In 1855 alone he wrote over 70 hymns to the single tune of 'God's Church still stands, an ancient house'.[374] The same year also saw the publication of one of his most popular hymns, written for the silver wedding of his friends Peter and Louise Fenger. To this day 'How sweet to travel the road ahead'[375] is sung at many church weddings in Denmark, as well as outside the bedroom window

---

373. (Grundtvig 1860, 188f.).
374. No. 42 in *LW*.
375. No. 71 in *HCF*.

77. Grundtvig pronouncing the Benediction in Vartov Church.
Painting by Andreas Bennike from the early 1860s. Bennike and his family were worshippers at Vartov. The symbolism of the so-called 'altar pulpit' from 1755 was intended to convey not that the pulpit was superior to the altar but that it rested *on* it in a vertical axis. The experiment has not since been repeated, and all modern churches emphasise the horizontal axis.

of the celebrating couple early in the morning of the silver anniversary – and even at the golden anniversary.

> How sweet to travel the road ahead
> for two desiring to be together,
> for joy is double when we are wed,
> and sorrow's storm-winds much lighter to weather.
> How sweetly valid
> to travel married,
> when we are carried
> on wings of love.

78. Asta and Grundtvig 1865.
Photograph by Bertel Budtz Müller.

16. Old enough have I become now
(1864-72)

Having begun chapter 13 with 'Church Life' and chapter 15 with 'Home Life' we begin this final chapter in Grundtvig's life with 'Public Life', for in 1864 Denmark suffered another humiliation – the loss of its three dukedoms, Schleswig, Holstein, and Lauenborg in a disastrous war with Germany. The defeat affected the last eight years of Grundtvig's life, with repercussions running right up to 1920, when the border agreement along the principles (language and mind-set) promoted by Grundtvig in his lifetime was ratified by a referendum throughout the area. North Schleswig became Danish and South Schleswig and Holstein became German. Denmark was neutral during the First World War, but under Nazi Germany war broke out again in 1939. Denmark was again invaded by the Germans in 1940 and occupied until 1945, when the country was liberated by the British. With the entry of Denmark into the EU in 1972, the free flow of people and goods brought the border people closer and closer together, and Denmark and Germany are now the best of neighbours. Some 50,000 Danish speakers live in South Schleswig with 50 Danish schools and churches, as well as Danish libraries, youth centres, and associations. A German minority of 15,000 lives in South Jutland in Denmark.

Public life

By the beginning of 1864 Denmark was enjoying a number of new freedoms. Democracy was slowly beginning to function, Copenhagen had torn down its outer walls and was expanding rapidly; gas lighting had been introduced; a farmers' savings bank had opened; and the first agricultural people's high school, at Frederiksberg, was flourishing. But the dukedoms of Schleswig and Holstein were a perennial problem.

Among the many causes of the Second Schleswig War two were decisive: the rise of Bismarck, who became chancellor of Prussia in 1862 and claimed Schleswig and Holstein for the German Confederation; and the unexpected death of the Danish King Frederik VII in November 1863. He had no direct heir, so the crown passed to his second cousin, the Schleswig-born Prince Christian of Glücksburg, who took the throne as Christian IX. Under pressure from the National-Liberals and in breach of the London Protocol of 1852, the new king reluctantly ordered that the 1849 constitution should be further applied to Schleswig, though not to the more German-minded Holstein. The whole of Denmark feared the northbound march of the Prussian-Austrian army, which had entered Holstein on Christmas Eve 1863 and was pushing on towards the Danish border with Schleswig. Whose side was God on? In January 1864 Grundtvig had a dream, which he turned into a poem called 'Childhood':

> A little girl lay sleeping
> protected by God's hand;
> she dreamed of heaven's kingdom
> and of her Fatherland.
> ...
> As Germans threatened Denmark,
> she dreamed a vision clear,
> that gave her lasting comfort
> and calmed her ev'ry fear.
>
> She recognised quite clearly
> Our Lord upon a horse;
> with sword aloft and ready,
> intent upon His course.

Grundtvig's dream confirmed what he would believe to the end: that God would realise His great sixth congregation in Denmark in His plan towards the coming of His kingdom on earth. However, politically, Denmark had no allies, and could muster no serious defence when the heavily-armed German troops crossed into Schleswig on 1st February 1864. The Danish army retreated to Dybbøl, where it was finally overwhelmed on 18th April with the loss of around 1,700 Danes.[376]

The defeat was unbearable. Not only a quarter of Denmark's land but also around 200,000 Danish-minded Schleswigians were brought under Prussian control – and forbidden to speak Danish. For Grundtvig the coming of the Kingdom of Heaven on earth had been linked to the fate of the kingdom of Denmark. How could he salvage *anything* from this wreckage? To his credit he did not fight shy of the subject. In a series of poems he recalled the courage of the Danes of old, castigated the Germans, rallied the country, and looked to better days ahead. In 'Consolation Letter to Denmark', published on 8th June 1864, he compared the loss of the duchies to that of the Widow of Nain, whose son Jesus brought back from the dead (Lk 7:11-17). Just as the widow had lost a son, so had Denmark's sons sacrificed themselves to save Mother Denmark; and just as Jesus had raised the widow's son to life, so, with God's help, the young Danes would rise again:

> So all skalds throughout our country
> shall predict your vict'ry fame,
> and your son, once more grown youthful,
> shall to glory raise your name,
> teaching Germans still offended:
> Here the Roman Empire ended!

---

376. See map on p. 72.

The last line is a quotation from the so-called 'Eider Stone', which until 1806 was placed above the south gate of Rendsborg on the River Eider in present-day North Germany. It bears the Latin inscription: EIDORA. ROMANI TERMINUS IMPERII, (Eider, the limit of the (Holy) Roman Empire).

Politically, Denmark was at sixes and sevens. Sweden and Norway had refused to come to Denmark's rescue, so the 'Scandinavist' political movement ended up with no more than a common advisory council. The National-Liberal government had promoted a disastrous war, and the powerful manor-owners insisted that a revised constitution should give them a chamber *of their own*, an Upper House, the *Landsting*. When the bill passed into law, Grundtvig's protest against this further limitation of the people's franchise led to him offering his candidacy for Parliament yet again – at the age of 82! Once elected, he took his fellow-members to task for their lack of democratic understanding. In 1866 his final speech to the Upper House of Parliament summarised the positive position to which he had come after his luke-warm acceptance of democracy back in the 1840s:

> I hope already today to prove that a new element will be added to the parliamentary debate when I as a member take the stand on behalf of the unchanged constitution of 1849. I do so as a senior parliamentarian who, although not among the idolizers of the old constitution, has nevertheless participated actively in its genesis. The talk here is not of *introducing* the general franchise but of *abolishing* it. We are being urged to change the basic premise, and on top of that to move backwards with a brand-new Upper House ... We have neither a united Parliament nor any other legal means by which, even though the King and the people were in complete agreement about this, to compel a privileged and stiff-necked Upper House![377]

Asta was present in the gallery at this final speech and praised her husband's oratory, while castigating his critics. She wrote to her friend Caroline, her children's tutor:

> Grundtvig's farewell speech yesterday was a masterpiece, as if one of our ancient poets had come back to defend the cause of the people and of Denmark. He spoke such strong, powerful, and true words, and yet with such mildness that our hearts were inwardly moved. But I cannot tell you how disgusting it is to *enter* the chamber, like entering a castle of trolls! I guarantee you I am not exaggerating. They mock and crow, whenever Grundtvig and the Farmers' Party (*Venstre*) say anything, and they deliberately close their ears and shut up their hearts. Carl Ploug[378] sent us *such* a look with the most abominable expression on his face. Dear oh dear, God help Denmark with such a parliament![379]

Again Grundtvig's protest was in vain, but again events subsequently proved him right.

Recovery from the defeat to the Germans in 1864 was remarkably swift and unexpected. Reduced to a modest, mono-lingual nation, the country rallied to Grundtvig's undying

---

377. For the full speech see no. 37 in *TCG*.
378. Carl Ploug (1813-94) was a Danish poet, editor, and National Liberal MP who sided with the manor-owners.
379. (Søndergaard, 171).

optimism and to the famous words of the poet, Hans Peter Holst, from 1872, "What is outwardly lost must be inwardly gained!" The long-lasting result of this thinking was the cultivation of large tracts of heathland and the formation of co-operative movements by the farmers that increased production, exports, and profits. The principles were: One man, one vote in a democratic system; joint use of machinery; and shared profits. The first such co-operative in Denmark was formed in Thisted, West Jutland in 1866 by Hans Christian Sonne, who adapted the principles of the pioneers from Rochdale, England, where, in 1844 28 poor textile workers had founded the world's first co-operative society. Following Sonne's initiative within a decade 160 new co-operatives had been established. Absolutely in the spirit of Grundtvig, Sonne also ensured that 2½% of the joint profit should go towards a Meeting House with a Library, a cultural feature of the Danish co-operative movement ever since. The first dairy co-operative was set up in Hjedding also in West Jutland in 1882.

The People's High School

In a draft for an article on 'A People's Identity' Grundtvig grappled with the problem of the *distance* between the multitude of peasant farmers, whom he considered 'truly Danish', and those, like himself, whose "literary language, written laws and organisation of affairs, our taste and our cultural education, in fact our 'privileged positions' in general, are far from being 'truly Danish'." If renewal was to come 'from the country', it was not going to be he and his pastor-friends who would apply his ideas in practice. The acknowledgement of this distance is a credit to Grundtvig, as is his attempt to bridge the gap with the concept of a '*people*'s high school', but how and what should the high schools *teach* to bring the two together? It was fortunate for Grundtvig that already in 1850 and again in 1852 Christen Kold had visited him to ask for financial assistance with his schools, for Kold proved to be the most successful developer of Grundtvig's ideas in practice.

Kold had started out aged 15 as a house tutor in his home area of north-west Jutland, before qualifying as a teacher and being influenced by revivalist Christianity at Snedsted College of Education. Such teacher training centres had begun when the first Danish College of Education (*seminarium*) opened at Blågård, Copenhagen in 1791. Several more followed, but the uptake was small. By 1821 over 800 teachers had been trained but the methodology was old-fashioned. Not until the late 19th century was teacher training modernised in Denmark. Otherwise a university degree, mostly in Theology, qualified teachers to teach in the grammar schools. Kold's career took a major turn when he and an enterprising friend, Pastor Ludvig Hass, became missionaries in Smyrna (today Izmir) in Türkiye for 5 years, before he returned home in 1848 and enlisted in the war over Schleswig. In 1850 he wrote down his progressive ideas in *On the Primary School*, which opens with a child-centred chapter entitled 'Teaching according to the children's abilities and needs'. Aimed at the teaching of 7 to 14-year-olds the book unfortunately remained unpublished until 1877. Temperamentally as stubborn and dynamic as Grundtvig, Kold left a good impression on 'the old man' and especially on Marie, who had wanted him to be the director of Grundtvig's projected people's high school. Instead, Kold opened his own people's high school at Ryslinge in 1851. Kold's idea of a people's high school

79. Christen Kold in mid-life.
Lithograph 1912, unknown origin.

differed considerably from Grundtvig's in that he wanted its main dynamic to be revivalist Christianity. He built one school up and then left it to build another, preferably in the shape of a cross. Even when he finally married four years before his death, he would often sleep in the loft with the farmhands in winter. Teacher and student should be as close to each other as possible, for high school life was and is *family* life. Kold and his students lived a simple life, and often found their 'interaction with the living word' around a practical task. The man was a great story-teller, and ensured that his students sang the hymns and songs of the fatherland. He was also the first to open a school for girls – in the summer of 1863.

In his memoirs (1921-25) one of Kold's students, the 18-year-old Klaus Berntsen, a later Prime Minister, recounted how in the early 1860s Kold had turned up at Grundtvig's home in Copenhagen with eight youngsters from Funen. They had never before been to Copenhagen and wanted to hear and see Grundtvig. Berntsen noted that not only was Grundtvig most hospitable in his welcome but that Kold was somewhat in awe of the great man:

80. Grundtvig 12th April 1867.
Photograph by Georg Rosenkilde. Grundtvig wrote a verse below the picture, saying: "There is no danger he will burst/from all the praise that he received:/'As learned skald he quite outmatched/what other writers had achieved'." It is signed "Nik. Fred. Sev. Grundtvig 1867". Royal Danish Library.

I was astonished to see Kold sitting like a schoolboy by Grundtvig's side. Kold, who at home always spoke so powerfully and strongly, sat here humbly asking questions and quietly listening to every word of Grundtvig's. The conversation was about prayer ... When we came out into the street, Kold said, "Well, you see, when I get together with Grundtvig, I do not feel any desire to talk, only to listen. In the course of the year I gather together a lot of questions which I cannot clarify myself; then I come here to see Grundtvig with them all, and miraculously he helps me get them all sorted out![380]

---

380. Davies 1931, 171.

In Grundtvig's lifetime over 80 people's high schools opened, and though many of them soon closed, the movement continued, with the following 9 still at work to this day:

1844	Rødding Højskole
1848	Uldum Højskole
1851	Ryslinge Højskole
1856	Marielyst Højskole
1865	Askov Højskole
1865	Vallekilde Højskole
1866	Rødkilde Højskole
1866	Thestrup Højskole
1867	Bornholms Højskole

As late as the 1920s only 7% of the students came from the towns. Grundtvig was far from alone in motivating the successful integration of the Danish peasants into the new democracy, but his insistence on the necessity of education was its prime mover. Kold for his part was the great executor of Grundtvig's ideas. It was Kold who made practical work the half of a school day, Kold whose brilliant story-telling, especially of the Bible, left a deep mark on all his students, Kold who insisted on living and dining with his students, and Kold whose charismatic presence watered the seeds that Grundtvig had sown. In a very practical sense he was more Grundtvigian than Grundtvig.

Church life

In the course of the 1840s and 1850s a number of Grundtvig's friends moved closer to him in Copenhagen: Gunni Busck, Johannes and Peter Fenger, and Peter Rørdam. There were many others of Grundtvig's persuasion who also attended the celebrations of his anniversaries, and the annual church meetings and friends' meetings at which he was the central figure. Among his friends he now counted royalty and nobility, politicians and farmers, pastors young and old, not to mention his weekly congregation at Vartov Church. Grundtvig had not only risen in the ranks, he had gathered his own around him.

However, though probably flattered, he was not keen on the concept of 'Grundtvigians', as if he were some kind of cult. Even Bishop Martensen used the term in his 112-page book, *A Defence Against the So-called Grundtvigianism* from 1862. Also Grundtvig's detractors happily used the term 'Grundtvigianism' negatively. In the winter of 1862-63, Grundtvig relented somewhat in his criticism of that word, and was willing to use it to his advantage ironically. He wrote in his memoirs in *Church Mirror*:

> If God allows me to live to next Pentecost, then I shall have completed 25 years at Vartov Church; and if I were to count the number of people I have confirmed, the effect on the direction of living Christianity would be *insignificant*. But considering the effect that the Vartov congregation and their hymn-singing – under the designation 'Grundtvigianism' – has had on the world, not just in the capital city but in the whole of Denmark, it cannot

be doubted that in recent years a core has gathered to form a 'Christian, Danish, free congregation'.[381]

Grundtvig did indeed live to celebrate his 25 years as the pastor of Vartov Church. His duties were few, and his Sunday congregation was large, faithful, receptive, and above all, *living*. The great Norwegian writer, Bjørnstjerne Bjørnson, said of the hymn-singing at Vartov that it was "more powerful than any mission."[382]

Of the many hymns that Grundtvig continued to write in these years, the one that has lasted best is 'Bless'd were you, the eyes that saw him' (1864).[383] This praises not only those who saw Jesus walking in Palestine, but also those who see him today as he speaks to us during Baptism and Holy Communion. The contrast comes in the first and last verses:

> Bless'd were you, the eyes that saw Him,
> God's own Son – and were so stirred!
> Bless'd were you the ears that heard Him
> and grew wiser at His word,
> He whose speech in God's love grafted
> truth and grace together crafted ...

> Bless'd are you, the eyes that see Him,
> God's own Son – and are so stirred!
> Bless'd were you the ears that heard Him
> and grew wiser at His Word!
> Hearts who once that Word accepted
> by Life's Tree became protected.

Whether it was caused by his failing health, his fear of death, or the defeat to Germany, Grundtvig suffered a fourth mental breakdown in 1867 – this time suddenly, in public, and in the pulpit of Vartov Church before a congregation of 500 worshippers. The immediate trigger may well have been his preparation for Annunciation Sunday that year, when he identified himself with the Angel Gabriel bringing the good news to Mary. He imagined that his own words, his touch, and even his kiss could help the women in his congregation to conceive and bear God's children, including the dowager Queen Caroline Amalie! Grundtvig's attempt to implement this fantasy took place the following Sunday, Palm Sunday, 14th April, when he urged each and every one of his congregation, including the unconfirmed, to take Holy Communion there and then. If they refused, they should leave. Since the law allowed only those who had given formal notification of their intent to take Communion and also forbade the unconfirmed from doing so, Grundtvig was

---

381. (*Church Mirror*, 395-96).
382. (GEEG 227).
383. No. 19 in *LW*.

not only breaking the law, but also breaking new ground. Was this his idea of a 'free church' and a 'free pastor'?

There were many who testified to what happened next, and all agree that it was strange. The strangeness lay first in the fact that the bent-backed old man was standing upright, moving with apparent ease without his stick, and looking 30 years younger. He took off his glasses and told the congregation that he could read without them! At the Absolution that began the service his curate, Pastor Køster, noted how Grundtvig turned to the dowager Queen Caroline Amalie and said, "Peace is granted to Denmark, let the King of Prussia come!" According to Pastor Fredrick Hammerich, at whose marriage Grundtvig had presided in 1836 (in Grundtvig's own sitting-room!), an exalted Grundtvig high up in the pulpit pressed his arms to his heart and said:

> I am so happy! For 84 years I have been working to move out of myself and let our Lord move in, and today for the first time He has done so. Now I can sing: Death, where is thy sting? Grave, where is thy victory? That is what God has taught me to sing today, and what you should all learn to sing with me! ...

Hammerich next describes the baptism that followed:

> There was a little child striking out with its arms like a little bird with its wings. I was standing close by and saw and heard everything. As the baptism was about to begin, the child stretched out both its hands towards Grundtvig and smiled at him. Grundtvig exclaimed, "Little one, be happy indeed for what is about to happen to you! I will tell you something that will make you so happy, that it is just such little children as you that belong in the Kingdom of God".

Finally came Holy Communion. Together with Pastor Hammerich, Pastor Helweg, and Grundtvig's curate, Pastor Køster, Grundtvig distributed the bread and wine to among others his unconfirmed son, Frederik. So many partook that the service was reported to have lasted almost 5 hours.

One of those who refused to take Holy Communion that day was Skat Rørdam, later Bishop of Zealand, who called Grundtvig's behaviour scandalous: "It was neither more nor less than a satyriasis!" a hypersexuality. Svend Grundtvig said his father should be committed to a mental hospital for treatment, but Asta would have none of it.

Grundtvig realised he had embarrassed himself and his congregation. The following day he drafted a letter of resignation, explaining that on the one hand he was indeed "out of balance, but on the other hand it was the Holy Spirit itself that had overwhelmed him." Some believed that the water in his legs had transferred to, and was affecting, his brain.

After several days Asta gave way and Grundtvig was taken to a retreat in Frederiksdal, North Zealand, where he remained until mid-September. A young doctor was in constant attendance, and Asta and Frederik were with him in the house – to help ensure that his manic state was not replaced by a deep depression. The children's tutor, Caroline, took them to Jutland until further notice. Grundtvig's old friend, Peter Kierkegaard, now Min-

81. Grundtvig's baptismal bowl.
In this bowl Grundtvig baptised his first two children. In 1865 he donated it to Ryslinge Independent Church. Photo: Rie Thygesen.

ister of Cultural and Church Affairs, delayed his acceptance of Grundtvig's resignation in the hope that he might recover, and indeed that is what happened.

The border between prophecy and mania is fluid in Grundtvig's illness in 1867. For instance his prophecy that God's daughter would be born in Denmark forms part of his theological view towards the end of his life, and after his recovery he was not afraid to repeat this claim. The following year at the Friends' Meeting, he said: "... here in the North God created another little Holy Land where He revealed His glory ... here in a sense he would spiritually bring up the heavenly Father's daughter, just as He brought up His son in the regions of Galilee."[384]

In an article in GS 2007, Synnøve Heggem, summarised Grundtvig's view of 'the feminine as a bride':

> We meet the bride-figure with many varying faces: the Nordic goddess Freja in the role of bride of Christ; the young singing bride; the old bride; the bride as a microcosm relative to others and the world; as man and as priest in a concrete church-political sermon; as mother, daughter and sister; and not least as the Daughter of God.

---

384. (US X, 561).

Thus, in 1867 Grundtvig was breaking with the triune tradition when he spoke in the same breath both of Mary as 'Our Mother' as well as of 'God's daughter'.

One of Grundtvig's lasting *personal* dilemmas was whether to remain in the established church or attempt to set up an independent congregation. We saw earlier how in principle he supported the revivalists and their law-breaking open-air worship, but refused to join them in practice. The Evangelical-Lutheran Church in Denmark, to give it its official, and to this day constitutional, title, was the church of his forefathers, and of his great predecessor, Martin Luther. At the same time Grundtvig feared that splitting the church would weaken the Danish nation, even break it apart. Nor could he be sure that his friends and supporters would follow him into the unknown. Moreover, he already enjoyed a relatively independent existence as Pastor of Vartov Church, which contained an increasing number of worshippers who wished to be numbered with his flock. Grundtvig's ideal of a 'free church' was already half realised; why risk more? He felt forced to take sides in the case of his friend Vilhelm Birkedal, who had had Peter Fenger among his teachers at Borgerdyd High School and later came under the influence of Grundtvig's preaching both at the Church of Our Saviour (1822-26) and at Christian's Church (1832-39). From 1840-49 Birkedal had been pastor in the parish of Sønder Omme and Hoven in West Jutland, where in 1843 he wrote and published a book that Grundtvig was so grateful for: *The Church Year. A Picture of the Christian Life-Journey* (Letter 43). From 1849-65 Birkedal was pastor of Ryslinge, south of Odense on Funen, where Christen Kold was the house tutor. In 1865 Pastor Birkedal, now an opposition member of Parliament, was dismissed from his pastorate for inflammatory speech. In the crisis year of 1864 he had prayed publicly: "God grant the King a Danish heart, if that is possible!"

Grundtvig supported Birkedal's right as an MP to say what he liked, and be allowed to continue as a pastor. Birkedal refused to leave his pulpit and with the support of his congregation he set up an alternative church, first in a barn and then in a custom-built church financed by friends – the first in the country in 1865. Grundtvig welcomed the Ryslinge innovation and rejoiced that for the first time since Constantine the Great made Christianity the state religion, a congregation had not been dictated into being from above, but had grown up from below by popular demand. The Ryslinge Independent Church remained within the fold of the Danish People's Church, and Grundtvig donated to the church the baptismal basin in which he had baptised his first two children.

The Danish words *valg* and *menighed* mean election (choice) and church congregation respectively. The Danish-English dictionary has no corresponding English word, only the explanation that a *valgmenighed* is a "congregation formed by the voluntary union of a certain number of members of the Established Church." The implementation of the new constitutional right to freedom of worship placed the established Danish Lutheran Church in a dilemma after 1849. Could people come together from various parishes and set up their own churches as independent congregations *within* the established church?

Under the Independent Congregations Act of 15 May 1868 Parliament recognised the Ryslinge church as an independent congregation under the People's Church (and the Bishop's supervision). Following this, a number of such congregations appeared across the land; at the time of the present publication there are 29 of these inspired by

82. **Grundtvig's study and library of over 8,000 books at Great Tuborg.**
Royal Danish Library.

Grundtvig. They are not to be confused with the Free Churches, which are outside the People's Church altogether.

Another Grundtvig supporter and MP, Sophus Høgsbro, brought a bill before Parliament to endorse the concept of independent congregations, and after a lengthy battle it passed into law in 1868. Independent congregations of at least 50 members could choose their own pastor and pay for him and the upkeep of their church. They were released from the need to pay tithes to the established church, but nevertheless remained its members, being answerable to the bishop for their choices. Another freedom had been won, even though by 1897 there were only 15 such congregations in the country.

Even in his final days Grundtvig was an impressive figure, as the English literary critic Sir Edmund Gosse (1849-1928) attested in *Two Visits to Denmark 1872-74* after attending worship in Vartov Church:

> After sitting more than half an hour, surrounded by strange, fanatic faces, and women who swung themselves backward and forward in silent prayer, the word was passed round that the Bishop would probably be unable to come. The congregation began to sing hymns of his composition in a loud, quick, staccato manner invented by the poet, which was very little like the slow singing in the State churches. Suddenly, and when we had given up all hope, there entered from the vestry and walked rapidly to the altar a personage who seemed to me the oldest human being I had ever seen. Instantly an absolute silence prevailed throughout the church, and then there rose a sound as though some one were talking in the cellar below our feet. It was the Bishop praying aloud at the altar, and then he turned and addressed the communicants in the same dull, veiled voice. He wandered down among the ecstatic worshippers, and stood close at my side for a moment, while he laid his hands on a girl's head, so that I saw his face to perfection. For a man of ninety, he could not be called infirm; his gestures were rapid and his step steady. But the attention was riveted on his appearance of excessive age. He looked like a troll from some cave in Norway; he might have been centuries old.

Home life

On 8th September 1863 Grundtvig celebrated his 80th birthday at Happy Home. Asta had plans for her husband, knowing that he thrived on company. In 1857, 1859, and 1861 three Nordic church meetings had been held in Copenhagen (Denmark), Lund (Sweden) and Oslo (Norway). The plan was to meet again in 1863, but it never came to fruition; instead eleven pastors and eleven laymen invited all Grundtvig's supporters to a so-called 'Friends' Meeting' in Copenhagen on 9-10th September, after they had greeted Grundtvig on his 80th birthday the day before with songs and speeches.[385] Asta and friends of Grundtvig saw to it that similar gatherings – of up to 1,000 'friends'! – were held at Happy Home around Grundtvig's birthday in 1865 and 1866. At the latter Christen Kold was invited, and Grundtvig was rewarded by a speech in which Kold expressed his gratitude: he had been inspired to become a teacher through understanding Grundtvig's *World History* (1817) as God's plan for humankind, and then wanting to open a school so that others could read the great work.

At the end of September 1867 Grundtvig moved house for the last time, to a large villa at Strandvej 123 in Hellerup, called Store (Great) Tuborg. Originally 'Tuesborg', it

---

385. Grundtvig's speech at this meeting in 1863 is no. 50 in *HCF*.

has since lent its name to a famous Danish beer. The move was Asta's idea and financial undertaking, occasioned by Grundtvig's mental breakdown in 1867. With over an acre of land Great Tuborg faced east across the Øresund Strait to Sweden, so Grundtvig could watch the sun rise and enjoy the capacious room that he used as a study and library.

As Asta had hoped, Grundtvig recovered slowly but surely from his illness in his new home. In November 1867 he was well enough to give the welcoming address to the new students at his high school, and on 22nd December he held his first service in Vartov Church. By then he was already preparing his 16-year-old son, Frederik, and Asta's son, Niels Juel Reedtz, for their confirmation in Vartov Church, at which he presided on 19th April the following year.

In 1921 Asta, Grundtvig's youngest daughter, recalled her happy childhood to the newspaper, *Berling's Times*:

> There was lots of room at Great Tuborg, both in the house and the lovely garden, but it was also needed. As well as mum and dad we were six children, the tutor, the housekeeper, the maids, and the coachman, Peter. Then there were the guests, nearly always guests, especially on Sundays, family and friends from town and country, from Norway and Sweden. It all reached a climax in the big garden parties on 8th September, when several hundred people gathered.
>
> However, Christmas Eve was relatively quiet. My dad ... had to take the long journey into Vartov the following day, whatever the weather. It was mum who made Christmas for us children ... The Christmas tree was in the sitting-room, decorated with lilies, roses, flags, and cones ... Even though we lived modestly and simply, Mum's Christmas presents were beautiful and expensive, and we children, me especially, also got the loveliest of presents from the dowager Queen Caroline Amalie.[386]

The housemaid who was present takes up the story:

> When we were all together, old and young, the double-doors were opened and your dad came in with your mum on his arm, and I can see his face, mild and happy and with clear blue eyes, looking at the tree from top to bottom. He sat down for a while as we sang 'Christmas with gladness sounds' and then he went into his room, where there was always someone to read to him ...

Asta ended her Christmas memory with the words:

> Once dad had gone, we got our presents and danced round the tree, which was then 'plundered' and immediately carried out. By 10 o'clock everything had to be quiet in the big house.[387]

---

386. (Søndergaard, 190-91).
387. (Ibid.).

16. OLD ENOUGH HAVE I BECOME NOW (1864-72)

83. Grundtvig 1869.
Photograph by Budtz Müller. Royal Danish Library.

The Friends' Meetings continued in 1868, 1869, and 1871, now at Great Tuborg, where a large tent was set up in the garden. At dusk, coloured lamps were lit around the garden and the speeches and songs continued. One of the meetings even concluded with a small fireworks show. Grundtvig revelled in the company, and in the opportunity to speak to all these friends, old and new, particularly on the subjects of freedom in the Church and the Church's relation to the people. At the 1871 meeting, the 88-year-old 'old man', as he was often affectionately known, began his speech with the words of the patriarch Jacob/Israel: "I am about to die, but God will be with you".[388] At 88 this is hardly a prophecy, more of a reassurance that his God-granted spirit will live on in his friends.

Among the guests in 1871 was Pastor Ludvig Hertel, who later wrote of these Friends' Meetings:

> The party of friends was like a Christmas Festival, the feast of the home, when the whole family gathered in Copenhagen around the old chief, who stood among us like a father. We owe the Friends' Meetings some of the best memories of our lives, and we can rightly say that nothing in the history of the Danish Church can compare to these meetings and the group of men who spoke at them.[389]

August 1872 was to be the last month of Grundtvig's life. He changed the ending of one earlier poem and wrote a new poem about himself and his faith, a powerful conclusion to a long life. *Open Letter to My Children* was written for the confirmation of Grundtvig's sons, Johan (b.1822) and Svend (b.1824) in October 1839. It was published in 1841, but it was not until August 1872 that Grundtvig, encouraged by his friend Ernst Trier, rephrased some of the central lines into three verses beginning with the line, "A plain and cheerful, active life on earth". These words ring through the history of popular education in Denmark. They rank with the most famous in Danish literature and are as good a characterisation of the Danes as any other. Grundtvig added his conclusion in a new final quatrain for the song – with a veiled reference to himself and those coming after him:

> The track is ready, short or long the race,
> it is for people's good, it is for growing;
> if 'Well begun is half done' are the days,
> then just as lovely is the sunset glowing."

Grundtvig's final poem, 'Old enough have I become now', was untitled. His son, Svend, gave it the title 'Farewell', when he published it in 1880. It concludes with a quite extraordinary image of the soul sailing into harbour, with God's Spirit as the rudder, God's Word as its compass, and God's table as the gathering-place.

> Where God's Spirit is the rudder
> and His Word the compass true,
> as in fairy-tales the hour-glass
> of eternity runs true;
> straightway without trial or wait,
> opens the eternal gate.

---

388. (VU VI, 429). Gen 48:21.
389. (Søndergaard, 187).

84. **The ending of Grundtvig's last sermon.**
Source: *Et Mindeskrift i anledning af Hundredeaarsdagen*, 1883

Jesus Christ! The very title
shall for evermore be praised!
By His love embraced and nourished
are our hearts to heaven raised;
no more to this earth enthralled
to God's table we are called.

Last sermon
On the very last Sunday of his life, 1st September 1872, Grundtvig preached a very brief sermon on the ten lepers healed of leprosy and the one who turned back to say thank you – the grateful Samaritan who worshipped Jesus and who was rewarded with the words,

85. Locket with Grundtvig's hair.
The practice of cutting a lock of hair from the recently deceased was common in the 19th century. The locket is in private ownership.

"Your faith has saved you" (Lk 17:15-17).[390] Grundtvig pointed out that the Samaritan had neither rights nor duties according to the Law of Moses, but followed the only right path and turned back to give God the glory:

> Only this faith in God's fatherly loving-kindness can give birth to the heartfelt gratitude from which the true word of thanks issues to express our reciprocated love for our fatherly God. He opens our hearts to offer the reciprocated love of His children which makes it possible that our divine Father's love can save us wretched sinners from the power of all falsehood, darkness, and death and transfer us from Satan's power to the kingdom of God's beloved Son, where home-coming sons and daughters for ever compete to give thanks in the name of our Lord Jesus Christ. Amen!

---

390. *HCF.* 440-41.

86. Grundtvig's grave.
Grundtvig is buried beside his second wife, Marie, in Clara's Cemetery on Køge Ridge. Contemporary drawing. Royal Danish Library.

Grundtvig's death and burial [391]

On Monday 2nd September 1872, a day after preaching his final sermon and six days before his 89th birthday, Grundtvig died peacefully. Asta and the children had gone to the zoo in Copenhagen, and Grundtvig was sitting in his armchair listening to his son, Frederik, reading to him. Grundtvig wished to take a nap, so Frederik left him. When Asta arrived home, she realised her husband was very poorly. She called the doctor, who administered a stimulant, but to no effect. Grundtvig died a few minutes later. He was carried into the bedroom and laid on his bed, where he remained until the evening of the 5th, when several hundred men and women gathered round the coffin for speeches and hymns. Asta's daughter, Asta, together with a personal friend of the family, Louise Skrike, cut a lock of his hair and placed it in a locket.

The coffin was then carried to the Church of Our Saviour, where the funeral was held on 11th September with some 2,000 people present including 300 pastors. The coffin was then taken to Copenhagen railway station, where it was transported to its final resting-place on Køge Ridge – next to Marie.

---

391. For details see *HCF*, 450-51.

87. **Grundtvig in Udby Church, c. 1810.**
Painting by Professor Carl Thomsen 1901. Royal Danish Library.

17. Grundtvig the Man

We began this biography with Donald Allchin's statement that Grundtvig was a "rooted man", and that he came from a long line of Lutheran pastors whose roots he himself watered. Grundtvig grew up in a male-dominated society, with strong father-figures as his childhood experience – and his adult goal. From God via the king in his palace to the lord in his manor to the pastor in his vicarage, all the way down to the peasant farmer in his cottage, it was men who were head of the household. Grundtvig also acknowledged a huge debt to his forefathers – and took pride in his 'foremothers' in the Hvide family.[392] Sons are more important than daughters and should follow their father's lead. However, in the case of Grundtvig's children there were flies in the ointment: despite their father's wishes neither Johan nor Svend became pastors, and he himself was partly to blame since he refused to teach them Latin at home, a necessary qualification for the priesthood. His beloved Meta took him to task for his self-pity, while son Frederik had to emigrate to escape his father's reputation. Little Asta was too young to do other than love and respect her aging father.

Into this traditional masculine self-image that Grundtvig inherited and cultivated came a series of women who shook it, turned it inside-out, and eventually coerced and humbled him into a genuine recognition of *their* value – both to him and to the future of the world. On this count, Grundtvig died a very much wiser man about the twin nature of humankind, aware of God's love in a wholly different dimension than in 1804 when he first set eyes on Lise. Grundtvig's published works are full of references to the twin life (*tvillingliv*) of God and humankind and of man and woman. Outside his marriages two women in particular affected his view of 'the feminine': Constance Steensen-Leth and Clara Bolton. We are fortunate to have access not only to Grundtvig's thoughts and feelings in his diaries, letters, and poems; we can also be astonished at the honesty with which he wrote them down – and in the case of his poetry, *published* them.

Half in jest, half in earnest Grundtvig imagined in 1848 a time when every man could be a little king, with himself as first monarch and with a flock of queens around him, provided that he and they could exercise "self-control".[393] This was Grundtvig's way of coming to terms with people power. He was still an out-and-out royalist, but this position would gradually change within the next couple of years. Ahead of him lay the new *democratic* constitution and the gradual transfer of the king's power to the people. A further change was looming in his attitude to women, for the patriarchal views which he had held for the first 65 years of his life were turned topsy-turvy by his new-found passion for Marie, who challenged his manhood without undermining it. With Marie he came to see 'the feminine' in a different light, and his praise for her and other like-minded women, such as Mathilde Fibiger, was absolutely genuine. This is another trait

---

392. See p. 37.
393. *TCG*, 252.

in Grundtvig that makes him *our* contemporary too: a self-confident, self-centred man, trying to come to grips with "the other half".

The man and his faith

During Grundtvig's long life Denmark underwent a major transformation – from autocracy to democracy, from three countries and three languages to one nation and one language, from enforced religious conformity to religious freedom. These all left their mark on him, but he certainly left his mark on them, for he moved with the times, and in several cases, notably education, he was ahead of them. Throughout his life he considered himself someone special, with a God-given calling. The paternalistic trait in Grundtvig was part and parcel of his Lutheran inheritance, which he defended with tooth and claw as a pastor and self-styled prophet. In casting himself in the prophet mould especially from 1810-25 he could verbally chastise the Church and its prelates, and chide both the slow-thinking country peasants and the shallow city know-alls who had removed God from their daily lives. From his probationary sermon in 1810 to his polemic against Professor Clausen he was the warrior-scholar. With the help of both Lise's understanding and the punishment of censorship, Grundtvig became somewhat less strident after 1825, and even more so after his three trips to England. He now thought less about what had gone wrong and more about how to put it right.

Grundtvig's view of the Bible changed in 1825 from Lutheran orthodoxy, in which scripture alone (*sola scriptura*) was the primary source of the Word of God. He called the Bible dead letters unless it was brought to life by God's enlivening spirit in the reader. However, to a group of guests after the Friends' Meeting of 1863 Grundtvig said, with his hand on the Bible, "I venture to believe everything written in this book".[394] Furthermore, in spite of the advances of science, he never surrendered the Bible's Ptolemaic universe in which the sun revolves around the 6,000-year-old earth. Does not the sun come *up* and go *down*, not just for the poet but for all people? Science was one thing, lived experience another.

The Bible, said Grundtvig, is the book of Christian enlightenment, and no one was more enlightened with biblical *knowledge* than Grundtvig when it came to transforming it into Danish poetry. He used the Bible freely and creatively, especially in his hymns and songs. Of course Eve was created from Adam's rib, but she is unique, for out of that rib come two sons, which, whatever the biblical writers thought, makes her the "basic human being... the life-mother... the fount of life and source of our life's calling" (p. 256). Another example is his treatment of the story of manna in Exodus 16, which says: "the one who gathered much did not have too much, and the one who gathered little did not have too little. Everyone had gathered just as much as they needed." In Grundtvig's hands this became one of the most famous lines when applied to Denmark, where "few are too rich, and still fewer too poor".[395]

---

394. (GEEG, 237).
395. No. 91 in *LW*.

Nowhere of course does the Bible mention Denmark, but it does mention the Seven Churches of the Apocalypse (Rev 1:11), and in Grundtvig's imagination Denmark is the sixth church in God's history in the world. In a letter dated 1st May 1841 he even goes so far as to tell Bernhard Ingemann: "[I] have not intended my sons' education to be for the present, but for the new time that I am expecting," presumably meaning 'the new Denmark' that God was ushering in. Caroline Amalie's pertinent comment in a letter to Baroness Elise Stampe dated 18th May 1844 was that he was "an age before his time".[396] If this was so, it was because Grundtvig was first and foremost a *poet*, even before he assumed all the other roles – and poets follow the strings of the heart. As he said in a talk to Danish Society on 5th November 1839:

> Once our heart has answered a question to our satisfaction, gentlemen, you are well aware that it has a corresponding influence on our life and thought, whether or not we can explain ourselves clearly and convince others that we are right. On the other hand, however clearly our *reason* can explain a question, it is quite futile if the heart is only half in it – or not at all.[397]

The poet in Grundtvig goes hand in hand with all the other roles he took upon himself as educator, politician, hymnwriter etc.: for he wrote poetry about *all* of them. Moreover, in each of these roles he is a *Christian* poet, whose Christian vision shows him the past as God's purpose, and the Kingdom of God as God's future for us. In Finn Abrahamowitz's gloss on Grundtvig, "The history of the world is testimony to the truth of faith and the certainty of its ultimate victory."[398] Although he may not differ so much from other contemporaries in the conservativism of his social and biblical views, Grundtvig is very much his own man when it comes to *vision*. For the poet-prophet sees the second coming of Christ as facilitated by the necessary transformation of the Danish Church, the sixth of the seven stars of Christendom, to welcome Him when he arrives. This was Grundtvig's vision, and this was what he worked towards – to his very last poem.

Grundtvig as seen by his contemporaries

In 1851 the *Morning Post*, the political organ of the party known as Friends of the Farmers carried an anonymous series of pen-portraits of Members of Parliament. On 28th May it was the turn of Grundtvig. He was described as a straight-backed man of a little over average height for a 67-year-old. He had a high, noble brow, "an abundance of white curls round his temples," and "clear, bright eyes":

> When Grundtvig is calm, his face has an expression of gentle thoughtfulness, but as soon as he speaks or his emotions are otherwise moved, the expression changes, often and quickly. His brow is raised, his eyes turn sharper, he begins to purse his lips, and his whole face

---

396. (GS 2005, 79).
397. (Lundgreen-Nielsen 1995, 176f).
398. (Abrahamowitz 2000, 229).

expresses power and earnestness. Then, suddenly, his features begin to move, and as he rounds his lips, the corners of his mouth lower in a pointed smile, his eyes sparkle and sink back a little, and one senses a witty remark or a stroke of irony on his lips. Yet again, this expression is also fleeting, and within a moment it can give way to one that manifests the deepest feelings or the warmest enthusiasm. In such moments his face becomes noble, even beautiful. This same alternation of expression also colours his lectures.[399]

Johan Borup began his biography of Grundtvig in 1943 with a summary of the contemporary characterisations of Grundtvig and came to much the same conclusion as the *Morning Post*. Grundtvig switched between harsh and soft, exuberant and dour, open-handed and closed-off. He could dismiss criticism with a wave of his hand, but he could also be vulnerable. Grundtvig could be impetuous, yet good-natured. He could be a modest man of the people, but then expatiate on a subject as though he were the only expert in Denmark. He could be elegant, yet opaque, conservative yet innovative, taciturn yet talkative, narrow-minded yet far-sighted.[400] Grundtvig was clearly a complex person with more facets and dimensions to his character than most, yet he was not a *split* personality. Indisputably, he was a man of great energy, perhaps bordering on the bipolar, he was a special person but in general, he was far from being neurotic.

Ebbe Kløvedal Reich's popular biography from 1972 included not only a horoscope of Grundtvig from his moment of birth – showing "a conflict between a fanatical craving to realise his high aspirations and a sentimental softheartedness"[401] – but also an analysis by a German graphologist of a handwritten page from *Rhymed Chronicle* (1828). This agreed with the previous descriptions, calling the writer "highly original ... spiritually powerful ... tight as a drawn bow ... He has a limitless ability to suffer and to live intensely" and "the clearest view in a fight".

Grundtvig saw himself as a national *skald* and Christian prophet all in one. Bishop Hans Martensen on the other hand considered Grundtvig's prophetic success to be limited to the *immediate* future:

> He has an eye for new beginnings... but less of an eye for the future beyond: it is hard to see that his prophecies have born fruit in any real sense, which goes to prove that that there must be an intervening obstacle preventing his eye from seeing clearly. What he *does* have, throughout his spiritual path, is an extraordinary eye for the immediate, for beginnings.[402]

Grundtvig would doubtless have agreed with Martensen's perceptive praise but not with his critical warning. The future that Grundtvig predicted was actually enjoying success in his lifetime. We could mention a few examples that he himself lived long enough to see:

---

399. (Dam 1983, 71).
400. (Borup 1943, 9f.).
401. (Reich, 393).
402. (Martensen 1874, 96).

- The awareness of the Danes' history, their cultural inheritance, and their language
- The prediction that the peasant farmers would benefit from the school for life
- The increase in freedom of worship through independent and free congregations
- The enlivenment of worship in Vartov Church and elsewhere, not least through his own hymns
- The early stirrings of the women's cause

Two causes that he championed but did not live to see were realised after his death:

- The extension of the franchise
- The drawing of the Danish-German border according to the will of the people

Grundtvig responded indirectly to Martensen with a lengthy poem entitled 'The connecting links', in which he invoked the Christian mystery to explain himself:

> Yet when in my cloudy speeches
> I can not make all things clear;
> neither head nor tail to follow,
> 'nonsense' as it would appear:
> even then is Christ my veil,
> He the head and I the tail,
> where His body is the Church.[403]

Reading Grundtvig's works in the original Danish we get the sense that the words tumbled out of him. He could not *stop* himself, so not every word is weighed before it is written, and not every sentence is fully formed. Most Danes can still follow and admire the beauty of his poetry, especially his hymns, but his dense, occasionally long-winded, prose presents a number of obstacles. He is simply thinking and writing too fast for his own good. Caroline Amalie could also judge Grundtvig critically, but she was far more sympathetic than Bishop Martensen. In a letter to Peter Rørdam dated 12th November 1848 she wrote:

> Perhaps you can visit Parliament in the morning and tell us how our good Grundtvig is getting on. It is always with misgiving that I think of him there. Imagine what heterogeneous people he sits amongst! I am constantly fearful that he will speak when I would prefer him to keep silent, for few really understand him.[404]

Caroline Amalie's understanding of Grundtvig was most perceptive, as she revealed in another letter to Rørdam dated 18th March 1851: "... He can have a wrong opinion about

---

403. (US X, 491).
404. (Rørdam II, 117).

many *real* things because he sees them transfigured and he wants them to appear to us as *he* sees them."[405]

This was also the experience of Grundtvig's parliamentary colleagues. When others were joining parties and pushing the party line, he sat as an independent member – his only support was for him personally. He was respected in Parliament, but he carried little weight. As a speaker he was much more at home in the pulpit, on the lecture podium, or at the Friends' Meetings. His greatest speaking success was undoubtedly at Skamling Hill in 1844 in front of 10,000 supporters. In his son Svend's introduction to *Within Living Memory*, collected and published in 1877, he wrote:

> Grundtvig's eloquence was part of his personality. He gripped you with a flow of wit and fiery passion. When he spoke, what may seem strange or strained in his writing sounded true and forthright to his thought and mood; for when he was in the Spirit, he was always stirring and lyrical.[406]

If one was tuned in to Grundtvig's speech and manner 'in the Spirit', he was most persuasive, as his friend Frederik Hammerich wrote on Grundtvig's lecture in Danish Society in 1842:

> Grundtvig was now developing the peculiarly enthralling style which he has often used since, striking ancient, long-forgotten strings that touch his audience. It is not poetry as such, yet nor is it a direct address; it plays out in all manner of colours, from whimsically jocose to the deepest seriousness, and it sweeps everyone along, if they are receptive to spiritual impression.[407]

Among his contemporaries were those who did not care much for Grundtvig, most notably the influential, cultural radical, literary historian Georg Brandes (1842-1927), who nevertheless acknowledged Grundtvig's stature. In her memoir from 1930 Brandes' lover, Gertrud Rung, records him as saying, "For my part I loathe him, but the Devil take me if he was not a great man!"[408]

Psychological theories about Grundtvig

In 1918 the first diagnosis of Grundtvig's mental state was published. *N.F.S. Grundtvig's Mental Illness* was written by a leading psychiatrist of the time, Hjalmar Helweg (1886-1960). His conclusion was that Grundtvig was a manic-depressive. Helweg wrote similar biographies with the same diagnosis of Hans Christian Andersen and Søren Kierkegaard. He is knowledgeable about most of the previous Grundtvig material and takes his cue

---

405. (Rørdam II, 187f.).
406. (Lundgreen-Nielsen 1992, 30).
407. (Ibid., 39).
408. (GS 2018, 177).

from Grundtvig's own writings before, during, and after his depressions – as well as the experiences of those who witnessed them. Helweg argues that the kind of 'minor mania' with which Grundtvig lived *all his life* is conducive to a creative productivity, provided it does not get out of hand. Helweg is open to criticism on three counts: presenting a psychiatric diagnosis of long-dead people; using secondary and non-contemporary sources for his diagnosis; and largely ignoring other significant factors that could have contributed to Grundtvig's change of mood. For instance, Helweg misses the *religious* nature of Grundtvig's crisis in 1810, misunderstands Grundtvig's understandable bewilderment of his first weeks alone in England in 1829, and fails to grasp Grundtvig's progressive understanding of 'womanhood' and subsequent flirtatious behaviour with the women at his 'Bragi Talks' in 1844. Helweg is on shaky ground when he attributes the concept of the 'happy Danes' who followed in Grundtvig's footsteps to his 'manic disposition'; there were other cultural, and not least theological, factors at work here. But Helweg's work gains from its concentration on the person Grundtvig as a man with specific psychological dispositions.

In an article from 1970 the sociologist of religion Jakob Rod argues that Grundtvig was a deprived child, who until 1810 suffered from a mild megalomania that turned to angst, which was then transformed into a "panic fear of the Devil and perdition".[409] In general, Rod believes that Grundtvig was characterised by an "inner weakness that turns to aggression"[410]– in the form of the polemical behaviour that Vanya Thaulow has analysed in her PhD, *Warrior of God. Rhetorical Criticism of N.F.S. Grundtvig's Early Polemical Writings on Theology (1810-1825)*. Thaulow also sees Grundtvig as "violating genre conventions time and again" in what nowadays would be tantamount to 'hate speech'.[411] Rod agrees that this was toned down after 1832, once Grundtvig had found his mental balance, thanks not least to his encounter with England. Against this one could argue that the Devil and perdition were part and parcel of Grundtvig's times, and that it is *our* times that have weakened these concepts. As for Grundtvig's mental *balance*, it most certainly is also out of joint three times after 1832: in 1844, 1853, and 1867.

A further diagnosis came in 1993 with Ulrich Vogel's *Knocked at the Door of Paradise. N.F.S. Grundtvig's Crises*. Vogel sets out to present an alternative psychological theory to Helweg's diagnosis of Grundtvig as a manic-depressive, namely that his removal from his home in Udby to Thyregod at the age of 9 was such a traumatic experience that he sought to rediscover his childhood security for the rest of his life – in the form of an inner fusion with God (or a woman) who could consolidate his weakened self.[412] The major problem for Vogel is that there are no sources for his conjecture, and that Grundtvig was not particularly *upset* to leave home so young. He soon learned to live with his new father-figure, and went home once a year to keep in touch with his parents. Grundtvig

---

409. (Rod 1970, 15).
410. (Ibid 17).
411. (GS 2019, 149).
412. (Vogel 1993, 73 & 84).

called his 9 years in Udby "a golden age" and his 6 years in Thyregod "a silver age". There is no evidence to prove otherwise.

In 2000 Finn Abrahamowitz published the most recent biography of Grundtvig with the provocative title: *Congratulations, Denmark*. He came to the following conclusion on Grundtvig's personality:

> Deep inside or deep down – as deep as one can come in a depression – there is the same angst that must have been there all his life, namely, the contrast between life and death. In order to come to terms with death, darkness, and falsehood, one must have faith. When that is lost, Grundtvig loses everything. In this light, his battles, his polemical writings, and his attacks on those who think differently are his inner struggle. His opponents are facets of himself and have been so since his secure childhood years in the labyrinthine paths of the vicarage garden in Udby. The longing back, and the longing for/horror of ultimate death into the Saviour's motherly bosom, lead the same way. Sometimes there is a place where the little child that is lost and cannot find the way home – when the heart trembles and the tears flow and the waves of the world are rushing in – this is when the little child begs, "Come and sit down beside me!"[413]

Thus, when characterising Grundtvig, we are faced with a set of contrasts: "Grundtvig is a fire-spouting mountain," said King Frederik VI.[414] "Grundtvig is a god-fearing Viking," said his friend Vilhelm Birkedal.[415] "Grundtvig is a depressive lover of life," said Finn Abrahamowitz.[416] Grundtvig is "counter-suggestible," said Knud Eyvin Bugge, "the more one recommended a specific view to him, the more he reacted against it. Yet Grundtvig possessed an extraordinary ability for self-revision."[417]

We have found it rewarding to analyse Grundtvig's psyche using the theory of angst outlined in the work of the German psychologist and psycho-therapist Fritz Riemann (1902-79), and his book, *Basic Forms of Anxiety* (1961/English 2009).

All humankind faces these four fundamental dilemmas on both a spiritual and a physical level. They are all four in play in Grundtvig's dilemma in 1810 over whether to pursue a writing career in Copenhagen or to return home to Udby to help his aging father. On the vertical axis (top) he has a need for independence and a fear of commitment (bottom); on the horizontal axis he has a need for development (left) and a fear of stability (right) in Udby, for stability can soon lead to apathy.

Psychologically, Grundtvig lies within a broad, known spectrum, while living out an extraordinary number of innate talents. Riemann's main point is that powerful, even dominant, features of personality can be a great strength, but they can also be a weakness.

---

413. (Abrahamowitz 2010, 290).
414. (https://grundtvig.dk/biblioteket/citater/)
415. (GEEG, 205).
416. (Abrahamowitz, 299).
417. (Bugge 2003, 51).

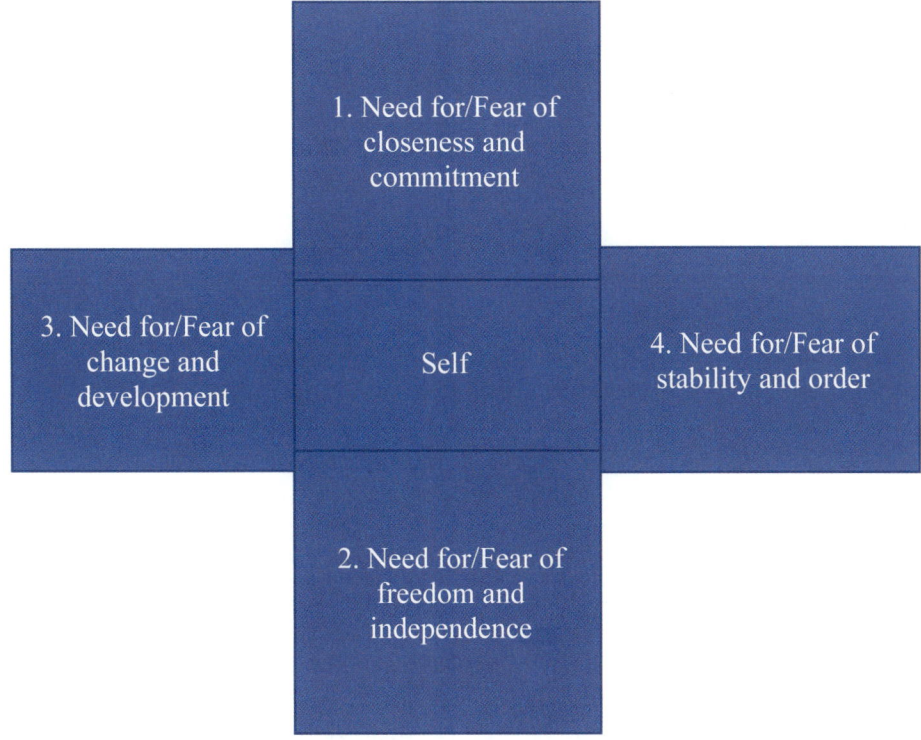

88. The four needs counterbalanced by the four fears.
In Fritz Riemann's book, *Basic Forms of Anxiety*.

1. Need for/Fear of closeness and commitment

To begin with, Grundtvig needed an audience more than he needed friends. Indeed, in his early life he appears not to have had *any* close friends – yet nor does he seem lonely. In Udby, all his brothers had left home, and he was not particularly close to his 1-year-older sister Ulrikke. The only truly powerful influences were his mother and father and his 'language mistress', Malene Jens Datter – and beyond them all his forefathers. Between the ages of 9 and 18 we have no record of a lasting friendship with any of the three other boys under Pastor Laurids Feld's tutelage or with his classmates at Aarhus Cathedral High School. Doubtless they got along well enough, as most boys do at that age. But Grundtvig was already a bookworm, as happy in Feld's library as in the fields surrounding the vicarage farm. Looking back at these years in later life he does not mention a single friend, only acquaintances with whom he could gamble his money away at cards and tobacco. At Copenhagen University Grundtvig met for the first time another young man who was on his wavelength, Peter Skougaard, who nurtured his interest in ancient history. This was the closest he came to a friendship – in a brief common literary interest rather than in a lasting common cause. At this point Grundtvig was nevertheless largely in balance with himself, his closest commitment being to his books and his early writings.

The catalyst that punctured this self-sufficient reserve and lack of commitment to anything beyond himself was his meeting with Constance Leth, when he was 22 years old. This married lady of the manor called forth in him deeply-hidden feelings, also of a sexual nature. In Riemann's terms his need for closeness to Constance dominated him, so much so that he refused to leave her employment even when the opportunity arose. On the other hand, his fear of her power *over* him, and even more so his fear of the power of his *own* feelings, were ultimately the decisive factor. She held him at arm's length and at last, albeit reluctantly, he turned away from her. His dream of Constance was most certainly unattainable, and it was therefore transformed – in the direction of Nordic mythology and poetry.

Between 1808-10 at Valkendorf's Hall of Residence Grundtvig shared common interests with four men of the same age and calibre, who became his first genuine friends, for a time at least: Christian Molbech, Svend Hersleb, Frederik Sibbern, and Poul Dons. Once he got a job in Udby, however, he moved out of their circle. Of the cultural and political acquaintances he acquired over the following years, only Bernhard Ingemann and Gunni Busck can be called genuine friends. Again, there are no signs of loneliness in Grundtvig, who was more committed to his work than his friends; if they could help him, then all well and good. He kept up a friendly correspondence with all of them. He did have two attempts at *making* friends, of winning the ear of both his cousin, Henrik Steffens, who rejected him, and his step-cousin, Jakob Mynster, who as Bishop of Zealand, passed on his distaste for Grundtvig to the Copenhagen elite. Apart from Ingemann and Busck, Grundtvig had supporter-friends in the Fenger brothers and Peter Rørdam, with whom he was truly at home; they regularly visited one another, participated in family anniversaries, and were always present at the Friends' Meetings from 1863-71.

In all these relationships, Grundtvig comes across as a self-sufficient, self-assured, ambitious *workhorse*. He admits to laziness in his school and university days, but from then on he sees himself as a gifted *skald* and prophet whose task it is to awaken Denmark to thought and action. He was ably helped by his three wives, who each in their own way nourished him, body *and* soul, bore his children, and broadened his understanding of both family and the female nature. But his work at the writing-desk was still his priority.

Grundtvig was clearly lacking in active empathy, and only rarely showed sympathy; even as a pastor he in general eschewed the role of active pastoral *carer*. Yet he never turned enquirers away from his door, including the women who later became his second and third wives. Indeed, Grundtvig *enjoyed* the role of theological consultant, especially to women who sought his company and were fascinated by his personality. As for his *own* emotions, he was better at putting them into poetry, as when Marie told him of her situation when her first husband died and she was pregnant with his child. Grundtvig responded with a deeply empathetic poetic description of what she had been through, borne by God's grace:

> Your mother-heart, forever fearful,
> gave the foetus life so far –
> through to birth, albeit painful,

under God's own gentle star:
growing now, the garden treasure,
queen of flowers to your pleasure![418]

His later poetic portraits of women such as Mary, Mother of Jesus, and Mary Magdalene testify to his growing understanding of the feminine side of human nature. For Grundtvig Mary is an image of the Christian Church, embracing love, care, and compassion. He translated a number of Mary-hymns from the Byzantine Greek and reworked them into Danish in the 1840s.

Of all the people he met throughout a long life, Grundtvig eventually became closest to his second wife, Marie, but not before they had thrashed out the premises on which they could love – and respect – each other. To her he was *devoted*, and his devotion included a large measure of gratitude. He took this with him into his third marriage with Asta, fulfilling his "twin dream" with each of them.

2. Need for/Fear of freedom and independence

Grundtvig's need for freedom and independence was strong throughout his life, never more so than in the Danish Parliament, where he shunned all party politics and stood as a lone voice. He was *fond* of that voice, and in company he preferred to talk rather than listen. At one of Queen Caroline Amalie's receptions, he fell asleep, after which she wrote to Peter Rørdam in a letter dated 4th December 1852:

> I shall have no more talks or performances ... not when Grundtvig is with me. It pains me so much to see him bored. For him to be happy he needs to talk – and we others are perfectly willing to let [him] do so. I wonder what he said about yesterday's boring evening, once he was alone with his wife! Name just *one* person who livens him up and whom *he* wants to talk to![419]

Grundtvig was not *a*social, but he did prefer to talk *at* people rather than *with* them. He was better at sharing his own opinion than sharing that of others, or at moving the conversation around. In the words of Finn Abrahamowitz, he was no good at group work![420]

In his younger days Grundtvig's temperament occasionally got the better of his judgement, partly due to his self-identification as '*skald* and prophet' – for in neither guise could he tolerate opposition. His criticism of others often took the form of sarcasm or irony. It is also a sign of his self-sufficiency, bordering on self-righteousness, that sooner or later none of his friends avoided his annoyance when they consciously or unconsciously advanced contrary opinions – a lamentable trait of which he himself was aware. In a letter to Gunni Busck dated 20th November 1828, he wrote:

---

418. (PS 8, 51).
419. (RØRDAM 2, 227-228).
420. (Abrahamowitz, 262).

> I am ... by nature an impetuous, but what is known as a 'good-natured', person. When I dare to, I can easily tweak someone's ear, but, in all seriousness, I can just as easily ask a thousand times for forgiveness. I have the kind of nature that would rather not provoke anger, and which cannot be angry for long, because it is worst for myself!

This is somewhat wide of the mark: we have plenty of examples of Grundtvig being angry, but none of him asking for forgiveness "a thousand times". On the other hand, he rarely bore a grudge for long and was willing to let bygones be bygones. For instance, he removed Frederik Barfod from the editorship of their joint periodical, yet offered him a genuine handshake when they met at Svend's wedding. The same happened with Bishop Martensen after their disagreement over Christian Kragballe's ordination, where again it was Grundtvig who reached out to Martensen.

Apart from his father, his substitute-father Laurids Feld, his Latin teacher Jens Stougaard, and the King of Denmark Grundtvig had no deep respect for other men. He did not *look up to* a single figure in the Church circles of Denmark even though as a boy he admired his uncle, Bishop Nicolai Balle; only Luther came close to winning Grundtvig's respect, and even then Grundtvig saw himself as Luther's heir and successor, called to mediate and *improve* the great man's legacy. Perhaps he came closest with Professor William Whewell at Cambridge University, one of the few men that he genuinely admired for his polymathic learning and his status as Principal of Trinity College, Cambridge.

Grundtvig's need for freedom and independence, and his unwillingness to work under any other authority than God's and his own, was a determining factor in his failure to obtain a university post, however much he would have liked the title of 'professor'. He came closest in 1813, when he considered an appointment to teach History at Oslo University, but he was not too disappointed when he was turned down. He knew that he was more fit for the pulpit and podium with an eager audience than the university platform in front of lethargic students. He never seems to have *feared* freedom and independence, provided his personal needs were attended to. This was one of the major roles of the women around him, and he took it for granted that a housekeeper, or a wife, or a daughter looked after him.

From the mid-1840s onwards, however, his respect for *women* increased incrementally, as he discovered his own feminine side and, in Jungian terms, learned to balance his archetypal *animus* with his *anima*. The seeds had been sown much earlier. At Egeløkke in 1808 and Udby in 1810 he was forced to face himself and make life-changing decisions – which he indeed did, despite the mental anguish they caused.

Later in life, he did not regard his new-found dependence on Marie as anything other than stimulating and rewarding. She was both motherly and sisterly towards him, while their invitation to Mathilde Fibiger to come and stay with them at Rønnebæksholm in the summer of 1852 was a fatherly gesture to a girl young enough to be his granddaughter. Grundtvig's personal encouragement for the young Mathilde as she faced a barrage of criticism for her novel on the emancipation of women must be seen as another sign of his own independent judgement. Grundtvig always spoke his mind – without fear or favour.

In his first breakdown in 1810 Grundtvig chided his stony heart and begged God to make his tears flow. In her book *The Shadow of Paradise*, Birgitte Stoklund Larsen makes the salient point that not only are tears the bodily expression of a change of heart, they are also a catharsis, linked to purification and new life.[421] Grundtvig not only admired the tears of others, including Mary Magdalene, Jesus, and his own mother's "tearful smile". He was emotionally capable of tears himself, as we have seen during his ordination, in the pulpit in Præstø, and at the departure of little Frederik's nanny from Happy Home, as well as his understandable weeping at the death of his first two wives. The older he grew, the milder he grew, and many a visitor noted a twinkle in the eyes of the older man. Fortunately, his family continued to increase at the same time as his need for closeness. His worst moment of loneliness came in 1867 when he was recuperating from his mental breakdown. Confined to a convalescent home, he felt himself imprisoned by his doctor, despite the close attendance of Asta and his son, Frederik.

3. Need for/Fear of change and development

Grundtvig never feared change, never protested when he was called 'revolutionary'. He defined it as being willing to move with the times. For him this meant holding on to the old bridges only in order to cross them to a new land – ultimately to the 'land of the living'. A well-known song by Hans Kaalund in the *People's High School Songbook* contains a verse that perfectly describes Grundtvig:

> Fight then we must, if life is to grow,
> not just for bread and breath,
> fight to be free in life and in faith
> till life submits to death.[422]

Folk wisdom has long held that people become more conservative with age; the opposite is true of Grundtvig. In his youth he *supported* the status quo of the absolute monarchy and the church-state connection. His argument was not with the Church of Christ but with the Danish Church *leaders*, who had fallen asleep at the wheel. In his introduction to volume 4 of this series, *The Common Good*, Ove Korsgaard notes how

> Grundtvig, with his ecclesiastical background, had an exhaustive knowledge of the old order, which in his younger days he had been unwilling to undermine. Later, however, he became a kind of spiritual leader for the many who were gradually crossing the bridge to the new order. Given the times in which he lived, one could justifiably claim that Grundtvig was a conservative who became a liberal.[423]

---

421. (Stoklund Larsen, 58).
422. (HS 88, 5).
423. *TCG*, 31.

This is a quite remarkable claim, and the progressive movement from right to left in Danish society in the 19th century only partly explains it. For against this liberalising movement there were those who fought to *retain* their privileges, including the King himself; there were those who moved with the times, including Grundtvig; and there were those who *drove* the new democracy, such as Orla Lehmann. Grundtvig moved to the left by virtue of his insight into his fellow-citizens' need for education, along with his own self-belief and unremitting tenacity. When, aged 86, he was asked if war would ever stop, he replied, "War may stop, but never the fight!"[424] Grundtvig was not a 'socialist', but his belief in *the common good* was based not least on his frightening experience of the industrial revolution in England in 1829-31. Surely the country's economy should be run for the benefit of *all*, and not just for the wealthy who claimed that they deserved their wealth because they had earned it – or inherited it. Grundtvig lived in a time of transition – from the "time of the estates" to the "time of the people" and he fought on the side of the latter. Balanced *against* this was Grundtvig's own personal comfort in coming into money when he married, one after the other, two wealthy well-born widows.

There is no sign that Grundtvig feared change and development. On the contrary, most of the changes in his life were initiated by Grundtvig himself, including his various applications, his intimidating replications, and his abrupt resignations. He was both driven and drawn by the causes for which he fought, always convinced that ultimately they were part of God's plan for him – including every setback, for "Where the Spirit of the Lord is, there is freedom" (2 Cor 3:17).

4. Need for/Fear of stability and order

Grundtvig never feared stability and order either, while his need for them was met both from above and from below. He believed that *from above* came the gift of his Christian faith, asserted first in 1810 and strengthened around 1825 in his 'matchless discovery' of Christ's presence in Baptism, Communion, and the Apostolic Creed. It was further confirmed in his belief in the unswerving onward march of *God's* history in the world. This was the rock on which he built his spiritual life. His need for stability and order here *on earth* was further met by his three wives and his five children, as he moved from the cramped apartments of his early marriage to the opulence of his later households. Grundtvig was never destitute, never wanted for food and shelter, and cut his coat according to his cloth until he moved to the happy homes of his later life.

There was a further stability and order in his stance at the writing-desk, pen in hand, and publisher in mind – even when the publisher was himself. What is most remarkable about his *local* circumstances was his willingness to move house and home. Between 1818 and 1828 he lived at 10 different addresses in Copenhagen, and between 1850 and 1859 he moved house another 5 times.[425] Each time he moved his household and his extensive library. There is no suggestion here of stability and order, nor is there in his decision to leave his wife and children for 3 months in the summer of 1829 to pursue his studies in England – and again in

---

424. (Brun 2, 673).
425. See Appendix 2.

1830, and yet again in 1831! Indeed, he was so taken with the English mentality and lifestyle that at one point he considered moving his whole family to England; in the end he took his son with him on his final trip in 1843 – leaving Lise and his silver wedding day behind him. We cannot therefore categorise Grundtvig as either a stay-at-home conservative or as a runaround adventurer. As with most aging people, Grundtvig's later life with Asta followed a fairly fixed routine, but there was nevertheless much to do: the daily writing, the visits to and from friends, the trip to Vartov every Sunday to hold divine service, and the excitement that built up and held sway around the Friends' Meetings in the 1860s. Life was never dull for Grundtvig; it was always a blessing – and there was always work to be done.

Our worst fear is to lose the source of our needs. This never happened to Grundtvig, at least until Lise passed away, by which time he was already involved mentally and spiritually with Marie. *Her* death in contrast shook him to his roots, without threatening his life-spirit. Secure in the knowledge that she was now with the Lord, he turned his face to the future, to the upbringing of her dying gift of their son Frederik, and eventually to a new wife and a new home. His mental and physical constitution continued to hold out, far beyond the norm for the time, even to a year short of his 90th birthday. He fought his way through every crisis in his life, including his breakdowns and his personal losses.

In summary

Grundtvig underwent a transformative personal development in the course of his long life, at the same time as the world in which he lived did the same. He was a man of both reflection and action, often rapidly proceeding from the one to the other. His foundations were his Christian faith and his understanding of Danish history as the key to Denmark's future – drawing on the past to envisage the future. Yet he had to *react* to the momentous events of Danish history in the 19th century, as one by one they caught him by surprise: the destruction of Copenhagen by the British in 1807, the loss of Norway to the Swedes in 1814, the enactment of people-power in the constitution of 1849, and the loss of the duchies to Germany in 1864, the advances in education and the cooperative movement in the late 1860s. Three disasters and two successes left Denmark in a completely different state in 1872 from 1783.

Through all these ups and downs it was Grundtvig who more than any pulled the Danish people together, comforting and encouraging them in their faith in God and themselves. At a personal level he took many hits, and his mental equilibrium was occasionally knocked out of balance when outside events met inner tensions. Paradoxically, the resultant shock to his system was often what moved him on – with scars to his soul but renewed faith in his mission. He was primarily a man with a *mission*. As Henning Høirup put it in 1951: "There is no point in thinking of Grundtvig's psychoses as embarrassing parentheses to be passed over lightly ... [without realising that they] are precisely one of the preconditions for his spiritual innovations .... His crises ought rather to be thought of as mental *foci*, the burning points of central significance for his development and his production."[426]

---

426. (Høirup 1951, 8).

Of all his contemporaries it was the dowager Queen Caroline Amalie who showed the deepest and most loyal understanding of Grundtvig as a person when, of his engagement to Marie in 1851, she wrote in an unsent letter, lines that are worth repeating:

> ... it is my firm conviction that this connection will give his whole being the consummation that he still needs ... I can rejoice in the hope that it will bring an equilibrium to Grundtvig's entire conduct of his life.

The queen could rest in peace after this, for, despite his mental lapses, that is exactly what happened with Grundtvig.

When applied to Grundtvig, Riemann's four categories would suggest that he lived within a broad, known spectrum where the balance may tip towards one pole, but never so far as to fall within the category of any of the four forms of anxiety in the diagram above.

Very few people survive their times as 'influencers'. Their discoveries can be momentous, but humankind moves on and builds on them with admiration and gratitude; scientists and artists alike face this destiny. We can admire the great masters and philosophers of the past, but we are inclined to believe that we know better – or at least just as well. Our forefathers are still seen to be *relevant* for our times, but not actually *topical*. Shakespeare and a few others, poets and dramatists mostly, are the exception.

A later evaluation of Grundtvig's importance came from the great Danish novelist, Martin A. Hansen, who, as Donald Allchin puts it, "saw in Grundtvig something new coming into being":[427]

> The path of personality is just as strictly defined in Grundtvig as in Kierkegaard. But in Grundtvig one has a stronger feeling that this path is quite different to that of individualism – it is in fact its opposite. In Grundtvig the personal cannot develop without immediately being transmitted and united with the personal in others. Grundtvig has the effect of an originator after the three others, Luther, Kant and Kierkegaard. The last is the Protestant consummator. Grundtvig belongs to the future, he transcends Protestantism and in him a culture seems in embryo.

In Denmark Grundtvig the historian, the politician, and the preacher are figures relegated to history. But not Grundtvig the educator, the theologian or the poet, especially Grundtvig the hymn-writer. Grundtvig's belief that learning should be a pleasure, and is for *life*, still motivates so much of our educational thought to this day. We can learn *about* him from libraries, but we learn *from* him in the words of the hymns and songs that are sung in church every Sunday or at community meetings during the week. These sustain our national narrative, our faith, and our self-belief. It is on this background that we claim Grundtvig was, and is, Denmark's greatest catalyst; his fight for freedom has left an indelible mark on Denmark, and in many ways outside Denmark, wherever freedom is under threat.

---

427. Allchin et al 1993, 5.

89. Rødding People's High School today.
Photo: Erik Smedegaard / Ritzau Scanpix.

18. Grundtvig's Legacy in Denmark

On his first visit to Denmark towards the end of the 1950s, the Grundtvig scholar Donald Allchin picked up a tourist brochure at Copenhagen Airport and read the following:

> Grundtvig, the clergyman and poet, has meant more to Danish trade than has Rockefeller to that of the United States. Rockefeller bored for oil. Grundtvig bored in the depth of the people and discovered unexpected sources of power. From the spiritual and national awakening created by him a good hundred years ago, modern Denmark arose.[428]

The brochure explained that Grundtvig had been the catalyst for the co-operative movement, which led first to general stores, and then to the dairies and slaughterhouses that put butter and bacon on the tables of the world. Grundtvig's role was to be the first to advocate the education of the farming community at adult schools. In the narrative by which modern Danes live, it is Grundtvig who gathered the people into a nation and Grundtvig who invigorated it with its forgotten history and his poetic gifts. Bishop of Portsmouth UK, Kenneth Stevenson, wrote in 1996:

> He is, above all, a man whose very national and cultural contexts make him a very Danish Dane and also a figure steeped in the Romantic Movement, with his love of the imagination, his reverence for the past, and his creative vison for turning the present into a glorious future.[429]

Grundtvig understood the relation between the present and the past as one of mirror and reverberation. The determining patterns and developments in present-day life can only be understood through the events and tracks in history in which they are mirrored or from which they resonate. Conversely, the present throws new light on, and gives new resonance to the past. First and foremost, said Grundtvig, we are reflected in the Creation, which sings to us and requires us to sing back. We then *become* the mirror and the reverberation:

> God's voice gave the dust new being
> when He made man out of clay;
> nothing can out-sing the echo
> sounding from that wondrous day;
> evermore it goes on ringing
> through our human voices singing,
> In God's likeness we were made.[430]

---

428. Allchin 2015 [1997], 13.
429. *Handing On. Borderlands of Worship and Tradition* (Darton, Longman, and Todd 1996), 98.
430. No. 49 in *LW*.

Traditional historiography would more likely speak of Grundtvig's *legacy*, but it is the *sound* of Grundtvig that is a stronger image – what modern youngsters would call his 'vibe', his resonating presence in modern Denmark. To clarify the reverberations after Grundtvig we have employed the seven categories used by Thorstein Balle in his book on Grundtvig's legacy to state education in Denmark, *Grundtvig's School Path* (2022). Balle distinguishes between:

1. Grundtvig as a *person*, i.e. the direct inspiration he provided in his lifetime to his
2. contemporary listeners and readers.
3. Grundtvig as *text*, i.e. the secondary inspiration he provided through studies of his treatment of the causes he fought for.
4. Grundtvig as *symbol*, i.e. as a point of reference to underpin an argument, though the link to Grundtvig may occasionally be tenuous.
5. Grundtvig in *reception*, i.e. as a general *ad hoc* reference to the agency of Grundtvig's 'spirit'.
6. Grundtvig as *progenitor*, i.e. as founder of a legacy to be executed by self-declared disciples or an organisation.
7. Grundtvig as *construction*, i.e. as a platform reference for particular views or a programme with a more or less marginal interpretation of Grundtvig.

In their usage over the 150 years since Grundtvig's death, these six categories have overlapped, but they all testify to the reverberations of his impact especially on education and the Danish Church right down to our time.

We have identified 8 channels along which Grundtvig's ideas have flowed – before as well as after his death:

> His personal inspiration
> His influence on education
> His contribution to collective thinking and thus to 'Association Denmark'
> His effect on the culture of hymn-singing and song
> His impact on Church teaching and congregational life
> The transition to 'organised Grundtvigianism'
> His political influence
> His overall view of the link between Christianity, humanity, and culture

The adjective coined from Grundtvig – 'Grundtvigian' – is still in use, as 'Shakespearean' is in English. But even this word is in dispute, for, as Bishop of Aarhus Henrik Wigh-Poulsen says, "Grundtvig is in many ways a help-yourself buffet; it is integral to the Grundtvigian movement that all the time there is dialogue or disagreement as to what is 'Grundtvigian'."[431]

---

431. (*Christian Daily*, 27.10.2017).

1. Grundtvig's personal inspiration

Many a fiery soul was ignited in the meeting with Grundtvig himself: his young pastor-friends, Gunni Busck, the Fenger brothers, and Peter Rørdam, and the first generation of principals at the people's high schools, Christen Kold, Ludvig Schrøder, and Ernst Trier. To follow just one of these, Ludvig Schrøder, is to see how Grundtvig's spirit lit so many fires after his death. As a young theologian Schrøder formed a theological discussion group which included Ernst Trier and two 'Grundtvigian' Norwegians, Herman Anker and Olaus Arvesen. On the way back from a Scandinavian Church Meeting in Lund in September 1859 the group met Grundtvig's son-in-law, Peter Boisen, who encouraged them to come to the inaugural Grundtvig Friends' Meeting on his birthday that year and meet the great man. Schrøder determined to follow Grundtvig's educational principles when he himself became a practising teacher of History and Nordic Mythology. He began at Rødding People's High School in the autumn of 1861 and was already appointed principal there in 1862. Men and women came for 3-month courses, the men in the winter, the women in the summer. After the defeat to Germany in 1864, the school moved to Askov with Schrøder continuing as principal – for 40 years in all. The introduction of board and lodging as well as community singing increased the school's popularity, while his wife, Charlotte, was the first of many so-called 'high school mothers'. Schrøder appointed some brilliant teachers, including Jakob Knudsen and Holger Begtrup, and remained in contact with similar schools in Norway and Sweden. Askov became the 'first among equals' of the people's high schools. Schrøder was also a prolific writer and in 1901 wrote an influential biography of Grundtvig.

But there were also lesser-known followers, not least among women. Grundtvig and his friend Peter Kierkegaard, elder brother of Søren and Bishop of Aalborg, supported women lay preachers, such as Kirstine Larsdatter from North Jutland. Her itinerant preaching gave her the nickname 'Forest Kirsten'. Like Ludvig Schrøder, in due course she became a Grundtvigian and attended the Friends' Meetings. In February 1859 the newspaper *Dagbladet* even conjectured that Grundtvig might leave the established church and start a free church with his 'lady Apostle'. This never happened, but it gives us an idea of how liberal Grundtvig was with regard to equality of opportunity. He even went so far as to present her to the dowager queen, Caroline Amalie.

Other women also made their mark among the Grundtvigians. Louise Skrike, a friend of Asta and Grundtvig, dedicated her life to his ideas, and moved away from her upper-middle-class background in Copenhagen to a village in North Jutland in 1877. She opened a winter school for young people and read Grundtvig aloud to them! She moved on to a local school and taught history from a woman's perspective. She was present at the local pastors' meetings, where one of them related that with Louise Skrike they always got "Grundtvig undiluted". She tells in her memoirs how the pietistic Inner Mission frowned on her activities as a woman, and disdained her link to Grundtvig.

There was opposition from the men, unsurprisingly. As late as 1925 Bishop Christian Ludwigs forbade missionary Anne Marie Petersen from speaking to the Independent

Congregation in Hundborg because of her association with the infidel, Mahatma Gandhi. In the spirit of Grundtvig, the congregation defied the bishop, turned itself into a Free Lutheran Church outside his jurisdiction, and invited her anyway! Nor was it a coincidence that it was a Grundtvigian Independent Congregation that pushed for the ordination of women, a move that was legalised by Parliament and resulted in Pastors Edith Brenneche, Ruth Vermehren, and Johanne Andersen being ordained in 1948 by the Bishop of Funen – since the Bishop of Lolland-Falster refused to admit them to the priesthood. Lone Kølle Martinsen's research suggests that it is not least the reverberations from Grundtvig that helped make them the first women Lutheran priests in the world.[432]

2. Grundtvig's influence on education

In Thorstein Balle's terminology, the 'Grundtvig' that we find in varying degrees behind education in Denmark is a *progenitor*. His educational precepts were implemented in four different school forms: the people's high schools/*folkehøjskoler* (for 18+), the state-run people's schools (for grades 1-9)/*folkeskoler*, the free private grade-schools (for grades 1-9)/*friskoler*: and the continuation schools (for 14 to 18 years old)/*efterskoler*.

We have already traced the influence of the first **people's high schools**, so a more recent study of them by an American anthropologist gives a better idea of how Grundtvig's reverberations are still felt today. For his book, *The Land of the Living* (1991) Steven M. Borish undertook a comprehensive study of life in the Grundtvig-Kold inspired people's high schools, in which he argued that Kold's wish to raise young people's expectations and energy for life so that they never fell back again has been fulfilled.[433] He links this to what he calls Denmark's unique non-violent path to modernisation through reform.[434] He was particularly impressed by 'the inclusion principle', the legacy of Grundtvig, which is at its purest in the life of the people's high schools:

> ... Danes are good at doing things together. For one thing, everybody knows that it is difficult to find *hygge* unless each of those present agrees to carry his or her part of the ceremonial burden. Although the task appears to be a minor one, the consequence of failure is noticeable to all. *It just will not do* for someone to sit off in corner looking lonely and dejected. Nor will it do for a person in the center of an encounter to remain sour, angry or withdrawn. Great effort is most often extended to make sure that all persons present are sitting loosely oriented to each other and included with a single interaction, governed by a relaxed and positive mood.[435]

---

432. (Martinsen, Lone Kølle (ed.), *The Great Man. New Narratives about Grundtvig*, Gad 2022).
433. Borish, 192.
434. Ibid. 241f.
435. Ibid. 285.

90. 28th April 1948, the first Danish Lutheran women pastors.
Photo: Ritzau Scanpix.

The 75 people's high schools today have diversified into 7 categories: General schools with a broad subject-range; Subject-specific schools; Sports schools; Christian or spiritual schools; Lifestyle schools; Senior schools; and Youth schools, an alternative for 16-19-year-olds to both the people's schools and the continuation schools.

Grundtvig's impact on the early people's high schools spread exponentially to Danish education in general, and by the 1920s the **state-run people's schools** were becoming known internationally for their progressive, child-centred pedagogics. The years from 1930 to 1960 can rightly be called the golden age of Grundtvig's influence on general education, when a series of laws reformed both the pupils' education and the teachers' training.

Grundtvig's ideas and Christen Kold's practice were the driving-force behind the rapid expansion of **free private schools** throughout the country after his death. The watchword was as much education as possible – for life. These first schools were run on a shoestring by individuals or married couples who lived close to, or even at, the boarding-school, sharing the students' lives. Many of them closed after only a few years, but there was no stopping the *movement*. The subjects that Grundtvig had recommended, such as History, Mythology, and Story-telling were central until the mid-20th century, when other schools such as the Workers' High School in Esbjerg (founded 1910) adapted the curriculum to suit their needs. The chief reason for the schools' success was the sharing of a small, tightly-knit community run by understanding adults with no exams and a considerable amount of freedom. Whether it was a school specialising in agriculture, in domestic science, in handicraft, or more recently, in sports and creative arts, it was the *boarding* element that was the most essential ingredient. This too was in line with Grundtvig's thinking.

Grundtvig's ideas behind Christen Kold's school in Ryslinge in 1851 were developed in 1879 through the creation of the popular **continuation schools**, boarding schools where teenagers spend a year before typically going on to high school and education in the crafts. In this way Grundtvig's idea of linking the life of the home to the life of the people is realised. These schools were originally designed to serve the rural population, but over the years they have catered for a broad range of school types. Currently over 30,000 students attend the 240 or so continuation schools, the highest number ever. Students can take their school-leaving exams here in keeping with all other schools. The schools define themselves in words that would undoubtedly have had Grundtvig's blessing, for his view of education and child development reverberates through them in a way that was far ahead of its time:

> The balance of individual responsibilities and freedoms, the primacy of learning rather than schooling, of personal development rather than training, are central... in the Free School tradition, learning is life-long, and people of all ages have the opportunity to develop their knowledge and abilities. Even more important, learning here is learning for life; its aims are not short-term or trivial but relate to the essence of the individual's being in the world. This form of education involves equal and substantial degrees of trust and of freedom.[436]

In many central areas the five Nordic countries – Denmark (including Greenland and the Faroes), Norway, Sweden, Finland and Iceland – are similar in their political and social structure, with a powerful welfare state and a high standard of living. Yet they are dissimilar in several areas, such as their education systems. We cannot speak of a 'Nordic school model' as such, far less of joint inspiration for the Nordic schools from Grundtvig. A Nordic Council was set up in 1952 as a 'parliamentary organ for official Nordic co-operation', but it is a behind-the-scenes organisation with little public or media interest. Grundtvig's hopes for a Nordic alliance and a joint university in Gothenburg were never realised. However, the fundamental tenets of the Danish people's high schools are pursued with the same vigour in the people's high schools of the other Nordic countries. The following facts are quoted from Anders Holm's *The Essential N.F.S. Grundtvig*:

> The establishment of people's (folk) high schools outside Denmark began already before Grundtvig's death in 1872. The first Norwegian school opened in Sagatun in 1864, and numbers grew from 27 schools in 1918 to 80 today. The first people's (folk) high schools in Sweden were established in Skåne in 1868. By 1918 there were 49 of them, and today there

---

436. (https://www.hojskolerne.dk)

91. Grundtvig and the women's movement.
Cartoon by Erik Pontoppidan.

are 148. In 1889 the first people's (folk) high school opened in Finland in Kangasala. In 1914 there were 27 of them, today in 2019 there are 87.

In a survey of people's high schools in 2003 Gunhild Skovmand and Knud Eyvin Bugge found some 400 schools in the Nordic countries and 300 or so outside them. Their registry included the schools, the organisations, and the teaching activities which they judged to have arisen under the inspiration of Grundtvig's ideas either directly or indirectly, e.g. via Swedish or Norwegian schools.

An interesting parallel to Grundtvig's championing of the Danish language against German was his promotion of the Faeroese language against the invasive influence of Danish, after the islands became solely Danish in 1814. Grundtvig is remembered there as having spoken up for the use of Faroese as the mother-tongue rather than Danish, the language of the Church and the law-courts. In his father's spirit, Grundtvig's son Svend was only 21 when he published a book condemning the Danish heavy-handedness and advocating the use of the Faroese mother-tongue throughout the country. Svend was also a personal friend of Pastor Venceslaus Hammershaimb, who established the Faroese orthography and the etymological basis for the Faroese language. In the current Faroese Hymnbook 71 of the 592 hymns are by Grundtvig. When Elin Jacobsen arrived from the Faroes in the 1850s to study Domestic Science in Denmark, she came under the influence of a number of Grundtvigians and the people's high schools. Back on the Faeroes she encouraged others, especially women, to do the same, and eventually the first Grundtvigian high school opened on the Faroes in 1899, the first school on the islands to teach Faeroese.[437] Nowadays it focuses on visual and performing arts, and on Faroese culture and society.

In Greenland the initiative was taken by the Danish Missionary Society, including Grundtvig's two good friends, Johannes and Peter Fenger, to open teacher training colleges in Nuuk and Ilulissat. The colleges trained teachers and catechists, but not pastors, who came and went from Denmark until 1983 when Greenland began to train its own pastors. Frederik Nielsen translated 30 of Grundtvig's hymns and songs into excellent Greenlandic, but understandably had to make compromises when it came to 'roses' and 'nightingales'. Grundtvig's influence can also be seen in the work of Jonathan Petersen, who visited Denmark in 1911-12 and later produced a Greenlandic equivalent to the *People's High School Songbook* that has enjoyed similar success in Greenland as regards church and community singing. Over 15,000 Greenlanders live in Denmark, so the cultural exchange is tangible and ongoing. A number of Grundtvigian pastors and teachers made their mark in Greenland, not least Dean Christian Schultz-Lorentzen, whose achievements included a dictionary and a grammar in Greenlandic and the establishment of the Luther Church in Greenland in 1905. Grundtvig's influence as progenitor was further served in 1985 when Nielsen published a book in Greenlandic with translations of his hymns and songs, 11 of which were recorded by the choir Appita. In the current Greenlandic Hymnbook 83 of the 644 hymns are by Grundtvig.

3. Grundtvig's contribution to collective thinking

Denmark is a land of clubs, associations, and societies. In this case we shall use the word 'association' to cover all three. The joke is that if three people get together on a project they form an association with a chair, a vice-chair, and a treasurer; then they apply for outside funding!

New arrivals in Denmark are told that if they want to meet and befriend Danes, they should join an association, such as a sports club. Grundtvig's influence here is absolutely minimal, but we can trace the origins of Denmark's success as a nation back to those early organisations in the mid-19th century that began to think *collectively*. Grundtvig refused to join a political party, but he supported a number of societies: he founded 'Danish Society' to promote all things Danish; together with 3 others he established the Danne-Virke Society to combat German influence in the duchies; he co-founded the Danish Association in 1853; he joined the Anti-slavery Society; he gave a speech and support to 'the Schleswig Aid Society'.[438] The achievements of this collective thinking in Denmark were first found in agriculture, but they have since spread to every area of Danish life, where Danes can see the fruits of their efforts. This collective movement required a local meeting-place, so in the years around 1900 no fewer than 1000 village

---

437. (GS 1989, 187-215)
438. All three are detailed in vol. 4 of the series, *The Common Good*.

halls were built – alongside the 1000 mission halls, mainly housing meetings of the Inner Mission. Nowadays there are around 100,000 associations in Denmark, the largest being typically organisations founded to combat disease, such as the Danish Heart Foundation, or to improve living conditions, such as the Association for the Homeless (SAND). Collectively these are known under the umbrella term Association Denmark/ *ForeningsDanmark*, and a third of the population is doing voluntary work in, or is associated with, them.

Professor of Political Science Carsten Jensen has written a book entitled *Equality in the Nordic World* (2021) in which he links the happiness of the Nordic world to "the four equalities that set it apart: economic, intergenerational, gender, and health. The challenge to each of these equalities is the arrival on their shores of foreigners who need time to integrate and even then may find it hard to live like the Danes, which is a litmus test in a small, homogenous country like Denmark. Non-natives are increasingly viewed as costly and undeserving of the help they receive. This contrasts with views on the elderly, whose benefits and services are all but sacrosanct."[439]

One foreign-born Dane who has taken Grundtvig to heart is Ahmed Akkari. Born in Lebanon in 1978 he came to Denmark in 1985 when his family home was bombed. His parents integrated well and sought the same for their son, but he retained his links to Islam and was a central figure in the protest against the 12 Muhammed cartoons published by the *Jutland Post* in 2005. Akkari, a trained teacher, withdrew to Greenland, where he rethought his life and was inspired by his discovery of the works of Grundtvig. He is now translating Anders Holm's introduction to Grundtvig into Arabic.

Common to most of these clubs, associations, and societies is their grass-roots origins, a phrase which harks back to Grundtvig's own formation of 'Danish Society' in 1839 and the collective thinking that flowed from the people's high schools out into the countryside and eventually into society at large. Both the origins and development of the associations follow the path denoted by 'Grundtvig in reception'.

4. Grundtvig's effect on the culture of hymn-singing and song

Nowhere else has a single person been so dominant as a hymnwriter in their country – and not far behind Grundtvig come Bernhard Ingemann, Thomas Kingo, and Hans Adolph Brorson. Grundtvig's hymns reverberate through the Danish Lutheran Church in a tradition which stretches back to the Reformation and the hymn-writing of Luther himself. Grundtvig wrote some 20,000 hymn verses, a large number of them merely humdrum and long since retired, but that still leaves 500 hymns of high quality, produced for every possible form of church service and celebration. Not all of these were popular at first, and they had to make their way slowly into the Danish hymnbook tradition. The following list shows the official name first and the vernacular name afterwards (often the name of a central figure in its composition):

---

439. (Jensen, 92)

1569	The Danish Hymnbook/Thomissøns hymnbook, the first authorised hymnbook
1699	The Prescribed New Church Hymbook/Kingo's hymnbook
1740	The New Hymnal/Pontoppidan's hymnbook
1778	The Hymnbook or a Collection of Old and New Hymns/Guldberg's hymnbook
1798	The Evangelical-Christian Hymnbook for Use in Church
1855	Hymnbook for Church and Home Prayers/Roskilde Convention hymnbook
1899	Hymnbook for Church and Home
1953	The Danish Hymnbook
2002	The Danish Hymnbook

Not until the 1953 Hymnbook did Grundtvig experience a breakthrough – with 278 out of 753 hymns being included. He is the hymnwriter who is most sung throughout Denmark – from the Free Churches across the Lutheran Church to the Roman Catholic Church of Denmark. 70-75% of all children in Denmark are confirmed at the age of 13-14; they regularly choose as their favourite hymn Grundtvig's 'Hail, our reconciling Saviour', which first appeared in *Song-Work* in 1837.

Grundtvig would have applauded the hymn-singing that fills up to half of the current liturgy, for this is the people's response to God's Word to them. On average six hymns are sung at Sunday morning service and at least one of them will be by Grundtvig. His hymns are present at Holy Baptism, Holy Communion, Confirmation, Wedding, and Funeral as well as at the major Church Festivals of the year at Christmas, Easter, and Pentecost. Modern Danish hymnwriters find inspiration in the great hymns of the past, and the last 50 years have seen a remarkable production of new hymns of high artistic quality.

In her PhD in 2013 the present director of the Grundtvig Centre Katrine Frøkjær Baunvig compared Grundtvig with the French sociologist Émile Durkheim (1858-1917) on the foundation and upholding of communities (*forsamlinger*). They are similar in their emphasis on the benefits of the physical gathering of people in communities of all kinds, but Grundtvig had the gift of actually *gathering* communities – in churches, meeting-halls, and associations – through his hymns and songs, and is consequently far better known in Denmark than Durkheim is in France. Grundtvig's words are mediated through the body and soul of living people, and he "considers congregational singing a key element in maintaining Christian (churchly) community".[440]

Grundtvig is also sung widely and on a daily basis at various gatherings *outside the Church*. The Danish singing tradition is strong and distinctive, and Grundtvig was central to its formation, for alongside his 1,500 hymns were a host of popular songs. As early as 1807, in *On Religion and Liturgy*, he had realised the importance of singing. Indeed, as we have seen, he himself is credited with being the innocent founder of the movement when his enthusiastic audience responded to one of his talks by singing his own song back to him by way of applause.[441] So popular did such songs become that by 1894 it was necessary to publish a book containing most of the songs (and hymns) that were already being

---

440. (Baunvig, 2013, 212).
441. See p. 185.

sung at the people's high schools. This book, *The People's High School Songbook* is now in its 19th edition, and each and every edition has begun with Grundtvig's hymn, 'We welcome with joy this blessed day'. Together with the *Danish Hymnbook* it is a national bestseller. The well-known TV broadcaster Paula Lorrain is a Chilean refugee who grew up in West Zealand and learned how Grundtvig still serves as a bridge from the secular to the sacred:

> Especially through Grundtvig came an understanding of Christianity's perspective. It was a language I could understand, and a sentiment I recognised in myself and my upbringing. Singing these hymns laid them down in my heart and there they stayed. Song became the link from the Larrain family in Chile to the Nielsen family in Gangergaarden [West Zealand, ed.]. So singing was my entrance to Denmark and the Church, but also the way into the spiritual world and my first clear link to God.[442]

Early on in the Covid-19 lockdown in 2020 the Director of the Danish National Girls Radio Choir, Phillip Faber, introduced a 10-minute morning-TV programme which was an unexpected hit. Under the motto "Together, each in their own way" he stood next to a piano and did warm-up exercises that became 'world-famous in Denmark' – itself a common phrase in modern Denmark. He then played and sang two songs or hymns from the entire Danish repertoire. At one point over a million of the six million locked-down Danes were watching and singing along, with Grundtvig's hymns and songs forming part of this extraordinary outpouring of national community singing. So successful was the programme that with new hosts and a 1-hour prime-time Friday-evening showing, it energised Danes to appreciate their extraordinary treasury of song.

Singing his hymns and songs brings us closer to 'Grundtvig as text', a consequence of which is that we absorb their thought and spirit and thus are affected by 'Grundtvig as reception'.

5. Grundtvig's impact on Church teaching and congregational life

In addition to hymn-singing Grundtvig's name reverberates throughout the Danish Lutheran Church in both theology and liturgy. One loud resonance in theology has been Grundtvig's insistence that God's grace extends not just to forgiveness but also to his creation, for he created us *in his image*. Not until recently has this aspect of Grundtvig's creation theology been taken up at international level – and to considerable effect. In *Reformation Theology for a Post-Secular Age* (2017) the authors see Grundtvig as a mediator between the Lutheran Reformation and modern Creation Theology, and characterise Grundtvig as "a ceaselessly active contributor to a non-Pietistic theology, which has impacted Denmark (dominantly), Norway (partly) and Sweden (sometimes!) ever since".[443] There is as much grace in God's creation as there is in his salvation.

---

442. (Larrain, 65f).
443. Gregersen et al, 31.

An example of this interaction between creation and salvation comes from Karl Otto Meyer, a Danish-minded Schleswigian who, as a hungry child at the end of the Second World War, was being sent to Denmark for a recuperating holiday. On the morning before the children left Germany they sang Grundtvig's 'We welcome with joy this blessed day'. When they reached the words 'And so may we reach our Fatherland', they were sure it referred not to heaven but to Denmark with its sunny summer and lots of food.[444] This 'interpretation' is precisely a reverberation from Grundtvig, for just as the heavenly Fatherland mirrors the earthly Fatherland, so does the earthly Fatherland receive its power and strength from, and its expectation of, the heavenly Fatherland. Singing about God's heaven brings it closer to earth – and vice versa. This was Karl Otto Meyer's rationale.

Thus the single most important thought that Grundtvig has added to the Christian faith in Denmark is that what is true in the deepest human sense is true in the deepest *divine* sense. We discover this in the course of our lives – that 'Human comes first, and Christian next'. We can always *distinguish* between the two, yet they can never be played off against each other. Pastor Christian Balslev-Olesen, former director of the aid organisation Danchurchaid, which is both a church and a people's organisation, says:

> My claim is that its success in Denmark is due to Grundtvig's legacy; it is through him that we have understood ourselves, while our partners have realised that you can be a church organisation without being a narrow, insider undertaking. Being rooted in church values we could get involved in South Africa, Palestine, illegal mining or debt default.[445]

The first Grundtvigian Independent Congregations inside the Danish People's church and the first Free Congregations outside it were pioneers with regard to congregational fellowship and community feeling. They sustained their pastors actively; they allowed a slightly freer liturgy and welcomed children to Holy Communion; they supported local outreach (*diaconi*a) and individual missionaries abroad; and they elected their own church councils from among all members over 18. They were also pioneers as regards female pastors. Over the years they have become somewhat more conservative as regards liturgy, and their sermons are no longer specifically anchored in Grundtvig's theology. Only a quarter of the 115 of these congregations could now be described as 'Grundtvigian', for the modern revival movements have left their mark in Denmark.

By contrast, Grundtvig's influence on the majority Danish People's Church has remained steady, and has even taken over some of the above elements. Worship is the primary expression of faith, said Grundtvig, and it is founded on the practice of the Early Church, not on the Bible. Svend Bjerg has called Grundtvig's understanding of divine worship "a mysterious sacramental power-centre".[446] The twin sacraments of the Lutheran Church – Holy Baptism and Holy Communion – have become an integral part of the Sunday morning service. This would have surprised Grundtvig, but perhaps not upset

---

444. (Meyer, 42).
445. (Mikkelsen and Thomsen, 131).
446. (Bjerg 2002, 7).

him. Central elements of the current liturgy which he would have appreciated are the Apostolic Creed, the Lord's Prayer, the Words of Institution, and the Benediction – and of course the Biblical readings, the hymn-singing, and the sermon.

In this field we are dealing again with 'Grundtvig in reception', and, especially after the Second World War, with new practices and forms of communication that in varying degrees can be called 'Grundtvigian'.

6. The transition to 'organised Grundtvigianism'

On the day of Grundtvig's death his friend Peter Rørdam wrote: "I think that Our Lord wished to spare him the grief of seeing discord break out among friends who have so far been in agreement but would now seem to be splitting up".[447] The first discord had to do with who should give a funeral eulogy in the church or at Grundtvig's actual burial, or not at all.[448]

The disagreement as to how Grundtvig's legacy should be administered took several different turns, as the 'fiery souls' sought to extend his ideas in practice. There was Ernst Trier, who opened a modest people's high school in 1865 at Vallekilde in West Zealand, where he drew on his family finances to build an imposing building. He extended it to include a handicraft department and a sea school, numbering 200 students of both sexes. Finally he built a gymnasium for the new enthusiasm for Swedish Gymnastics. It contained imposing paintings by Martin Nyrop and a Grundtvig motto over the entrance: "Day and deed are giant rhymes!"

One attempt to organise the many local Grundtvig-oriented groups was the foundation of Church Society/*Kirkeligt Samfund* in 1898 "to promote Grundtvig's ideas on Christianity and human life", which initiated children's work, ran church meetings, and published a magazine. It peaked in 1921 with 386 groups and fell to under 100 by the turn of the millennium. Its centre is the Vartov complex in central Copenhagen, from where it has revived its fortunes under the name Grundtvig's Forum/*Grundtvigsk Forum*, an umbrella organisation for a number of Grundtvig associations, communities, congregations and individuals, with the magazine *Grundtvig Times/Grundtvigsk Tidende* as its standard-bearer. There is a new dynamic in Grundtvig's Forum, which has also published a wealth of material on Grundtvig for use in schools for the celebration of the 150th anniversary of his death in 2022. Denmark is unique in having a close relation between the Church and School (Grundtvig's terminology), so that the Church produces ideas and course material that can be used by the School in its teaching of Christianity and other religions. The concept would be anathema in the USA, the UK and elsewhere – and it would have been anathema to Grundtvig too, for he always sought to keep Church and School apart! Nevertheless the freedom that he championed has brought this initiative about, and it has been lauded on all sides in Denmark.

---

447. (Rørdam III, 573f).
448. (Weltzer, 1954-56).

As an offshoot of the move from the headquarters in Grundtvig's House/*Grundtvigs hus* (Studiestræde 35-40, purchased 1909) to Vartov in 1947, the 'Grundtvig Society of 8th September 1947' was founded. Its aim is to broaden a knowledge of Grundtvig's work and legacy through an annual general meeting, talks and activities, and the annual publication of *Grundtvig Studies/Grundtvig Studier*. After a century of divergence these and other Grundtvig-inspired organisations live in peaceful co-existence. Together with his colleague Hans Vium Mikkelsen, former pastor of Ryslinge Free Church Niels Thomsen edited a book in 2004 entitled *What happened to the Grundtvig movement?* Its articles answer the question in various ways but they demonstrate, as Thomsen put it, that "the Grundtvigian movement did not actually become a movement until it stopped moving!" – i.e. when the various Grundtvig factions stopped fighting each other.[449]

Grundtvig is the progenitor of these heirs to his legacy. In the mission statement of Grundtvig's Forum these Grundtvigians see it as their task "to spread a knowledge of Grundtvig's ideas on Christianity and human life and to translate them into the Danish reality of today."

7. Grundtvig's political influence

Grundtvig's overall influence on Danish politics lies, in Ove Korsgaard's words, in his tireless efforts "to build a new national awareness – not least through his many songs and hymns – by placing 'the people' at the heart of the symbolic order of Danish society."[450] It is not for nothing that the fourth volume in this series, on Grundtvig's political views' is entitled *The Common Good*, for this was the ultimate goal and the reason that he voted against both the new Constitution in 1849 and its revision in 1866. They did not go far enough, they were not yet in the common good.

In his day Grundtvig remained independent of all political parties, but as a symbol he is still used by politicians from both left and right as a point of reference to underpin an argument. His name has been used in rhetorical astonishment "How could this happen in Grundtvig's fatherland?" and even to ask the anachronistic question "Would Grundtvig have wanted Denmark to join the European Union?" Politicians of all colours have found 'support' for their views in Grundtvig's works. In his PhD study Esben Lunde Larsen noted that in the period 2001-09 Grundtvig was quoted no fewer than 52 times in the Danish Parliament, almost twice as many as the next person on the list. To show how broadly Grundtvig's name is used in Danish society, when Jonas Vingegaard won the Tour de France in 2022, the editor of the national daily, *Politiken*, waxed lyrical about his *team's* victory: "This year Jonas Vingegaard and Co. represented something almost Grundtvigian in their pursuit of a solidarity that also makes room for the individual."[451]

This inclusive principle, with mutual trust in one another, is characteristic of Danish

---

449. (Thomsen's afterword in Mikkelsen and Thomsen, 200).
450. (Korsgaard and Schelde, eds. 2013, 104).
451. (*Politiken* 27th July 2022).

92. Grundtvig, the children's friend.
Cartoon by Mette Dreyer.

society in general. It has led to a high redistribution of wealth via the tax-and-benefit system, "where few are too rich, and still fewer too poor" in Grundtvig's famous words.[452] In fact Grundtvig did not expect this ideal – which he had laid down already in 1820 – to result in anything like the welfare state of today, for he opposed the idea that the state should look after its poor – that was up to philanthropists. Nonetheless, his concept of the common good has been a guideline for all Danish governments, and since the Social Democrats first came to power in 1924 there is a sense in which, whether they come from the right or from the left, all 6 million Danes are social democrats in the non-party-political sense. The majority of Danes hold firm to the social democratic principles promoting: solidarity and community; freedom and equality; rights and duties; trust and cohesion; democracy and civic education; sustainability and responsibility; and internationalism and human rights. Only the last two of these pairs did Grundtvig not live to support, even though he hinted at them. In this area of Grundtvig's political influence we meet 'Grundtvig as symbol', as a more or less conscious version of 'Grundtvig as construction'.

---

452. No. 91 in *LW*.

8. Grundtvig's overall view of the link between Christianity, humanity, and culture

Denmark is a land of cultural Christians. Whether or not the people are church-goers, immigrants with other religions, humanists or even atheists, the culture of Denmark is based on Christianity. The arrival of Muslim immigrants over the last 50 years has not changed this mental foundation. The freedoms that Danes often take for granted have been hard-won over many years; they are the essence of modern-day Denmark, and the reason its people, according to the World Happiness Report, are among the happiest in the world. Grundtvig's contribution to this sense of collective well-being is his belief that to be truly human and to be truly Christian are one and the same thing. This of course is disputable. Denmark is slowly but surely becoming increasingly secular, but its shared cultural Christianity has 1000 years of history behind it. The influence of the Danish Lutheran Church is considerably less than in Grundtvig's time, and even its parish structure is under threat, but church buildings have yet to be turned into restaurants or art centres.

"I am a cultural Christian, more or less" is a phrase most Danes would subscribe to. They add that they don't go to church except at Christmas – and occasionally for baptisms or funerals – but they are as 'Christian' as the next person. If they have any faith, it is kept under wraps – to be uncovered once a year at Christmas, when it is best seen and heard in the singing of the great hymns written by Grundtvig and others before and after him. In a podcast with Pastor Sørine Gotfredsen in 2022 the Danish Prime Minister, Mette Frederiksen said, "I've gone to church a lot, but I'm not sure that I'd define myself as a believer." Danes who do go to church recite their faith in the Creed, and sing their faith in the hymns, but outside the church they tend to shy away from talking about their faith. Still, just as all the English have heard of Shakespeare, so have all the Danes heard of Grundtvig, as a 2022 poll proved. Despite their being only seven white Christmases in Denmark in the whole of the 20th century, there is always snow at Christmas in Denmark, partly because Grundtvig says so. He went to the midnight service on 24th December 1824 and in 'We greet you again God's angels bright'[453] he wrote:

> Well met on our snowy path to church,
> as midnight cold is stinging!

The Grundtvig Centre

An increasing awareness of the decisive role that Grundtvig has played in the formation of modern Denmark led to the establishment of a Grundtvig Centre at the University of Aarhus in 2009 with the primal task of digitalizing his 1,000 or so published works for free public access. This involves the scanning of 35,000 pages, the transcribing of Gothic letters into Latin letters, the deciphering of Grundtvig's handwritten notes, the listing of published variants, and an annotated commentary on the individual works. The colossal

---

453. No. 8 in *LW*.

project is being undertaken by a team of expert philologists, historians and theologians, and when finished in 2030 the new digital edition will allow full public access to Grundtvig's works. It will further explain Grundtvig's occasionally impenetrable thinking and oblique references, and it will save untold hours of scholarly research. Grundtvig is being recognised at the highest level as a national treasure, and Parliament is investing in him.

With the digitalisation of Grundtvig's complete published works, plus the 6-volume English series, and the imminent translations of *The Essential N.F.S. Grundtvig* – into German, Japanese, Korean, Bengali, and Arabic – Denmark's catalyst is at last receiving his due. His message of learning for life and working for the common good is universal. In parliament in January 1849, in words that could equally be applied to himself, he said about other great men such as Moses and Luther:

> ... as all world history shows, a single, freeborn man who in the hour of danger rallies to the flag and leads the charge, can have a great and incalculable influence."[454]

---

454. (Lundgreen-Nielsen 1992, 177).

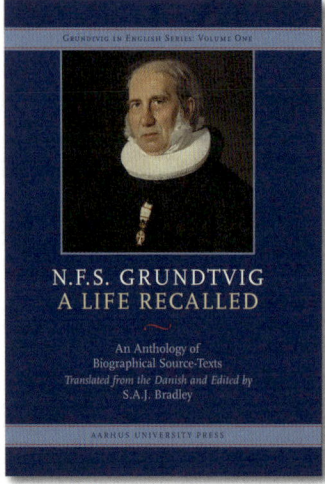

93. Six English biographies.
From top l. to r.,
1944   1955
1955   1997
2008   2019

19. Grundtvig's International Reception

The influence of Grundtvig's thought and spirit beyond the Nordic countries has been primarily in the field of education, either through Danes taking his ideas abroad or through foreigners coming to Denmark, being inspired, and trying to implement those ideas back in their own countries. A thorough treatment of both approaches already exists in *The Essential N.F.S. Grundtvig* (2019), to which readers are hereby referred. Holm looks in particular at India, Bangladesh, Japan, South Korea, and the USA. Readers are also referred to Clay Warren's afterword on the reception of Grundtvig's ideas in the USA in. *The School for Life* (2011).

Measuring Grundtvig's legacy abroad is a mixture of confirmed evidence and informed conjecture. The media that have promoted him have been *written*, such as books, translations, biographies, essays, and articles, and *oral*, such as conferences and general word of mouth. First we must look at the direct international legacy as it worked itself out in Frederik, Grundtvig's son by Marie.

We shall then illustrate Grundtvig's reception in North and South America, Europe, Asia and Africa. Within a single chapter we cannot provide more than a number of snapshots.

Frederik Lange Grundtvig

In the period 1868-1914 some 287,000 Danes – 1/10 of the total Danish population – emigrated, mostly for economic reasons. Only the eldest son could inherit the local farm, so many other farmers' sons between the ages of 15 and 29 emigrated, with 70% of them being drawn to the USA, 'the land of opportunity'. The vast majority of translations of Grundtvig's hymns and songs was undertaken by these Danish-Americans eager to share and preserve their heritage with English-only speakers. The first Danes came to Des Moines, Iowa, in 1867. Grand View College was established in 1896 as a Danish-language institution of higher learning, and achieved university status in 2008; it is the only university in the USA with Danish roots. Gradually as the Danish language gave way to English, translations of these hymns and songs became necessary. The first record we have of such a Grundtvig translation dates from 1880, when Mary Elizabeth Fellowes, an Anglican in Hartford CT, wrote 'From the grave that dark cross take' (*Tag det sorte kors fra graven*).[455]

All three of Grundtvig's sons had doubtless felt the pressure not only of the controversies that Grundtvig stirred throughout their childhood and youth, but also of the admiration that surrounded him later in life. To be the son of a living monument was no small matter, for not only was Grundtvig senior a powerful pastor, he was a force to be reckoned with in education, politics, history and even folklore. Among these

---

455. No. 27 in *LW*.

94. Clinton, Iowa, c. 1890.
Pastor Frederik Lange Grundtvig's church and congregation.

subjects, his first son Johan chose history, his second son Svend chose literature and folklore, and, at long last, his third son Frederik chose the Church, albeit 9 years after his father's death.

Frederik Lange was very fond of his aging father, who had already turned 70 when his son was born. After his father's death Frederik moved in with Svend but found it hard to concentrate on his studies. He managed to get into university and gained a degree in Political Science in 1881, the same year in which he married the Swedish Kristina Nilsson and emigrated to America "to get hold of myself... and try to become a man who knows what he wants".[456] Initially the couple settled in Wisconsin, but feeling a call at Christmas 1882, Frederik Lange mailed Svend with his deliberations about whether to become a pastor. His surprised half-brother wrote back on 29th January 1883:

> I would never dare encourage you to do so; but I shall thank God, and He will send you out into His vineyard ... This will be an unexpected fulfilment of our father's wish, as well as an unexpected continuation of the family tradition preserved through so many generations.[457]

456. (Dansk Folkesamfunds Jubilæumshæfte (1887-1912), 25).
457. (Ibid. p. 83.)

Within two years, and after a brief study of theology Frederik Lange became full-time pastor of the Danish Lutheran church in Clinton, Iowa. Of the two strands of Danish Christianity in the USA, Grundtvig's son represented the open-minded Grundtvigian strand as opposed to the stricter Inner Mission strand. His goal was the preservation of the Danish inheritance and language in the new land:

> I believe it is God's intention that by preserving their national characteristics the various peoples will come together in a collaboration the like of which the world has never seen before ... As regards the Danish people, I consider them to be betraying their God-given calling if they abandon their heritage here in America. With God's grace I believe that they can make a great contribution to the happiness of the human race.[458]

To this end he published *Songbook for the Danish People in America*[459] in 1889 containing 595 Danish items and including of course a fair number by his father. In 1887 Frederik Lange had formed the Danish Folk Society/*Dansk Folkesamfund*, a cultural rather than a religious organisation for all Danes in the USA – and one with strong links back to Denmark. But the waters turned stormy, and despite the society's initial success, the Danes gradually became culturally assimilated, much to Frederik Lange's disappointment. The newly-established Grand View College in Des Moines – "to train teachers for Danish children" – planned to use English as well as Danish as a medium. Frederik Lange called this "a disgrace, yes, treason against our people, if one is to speak the naked truth".[460] With his wife and daughter the disillusioned Frederik Lange returned to Denmark in 1900 but could not settle and died in 1903.

North and South America

The Grundtvigians v The Inner Mission in the USA

The US Census Bureau estimated that in 2019 there were approximately 1,300,000 Americans of Danish origin or descent. The early immigrants were seeking a better life – a farm of their own – and were absorbed into the mid-west as English speakers, while there are still some 30,000 Danish-Americans who continue to speak Danish on a daily basis.

The first Grundtvigians in the US actually came from Norway and preached Grundtvig's more liberal approach to faith – i.e. the Apostolic Creed – above and beyond the Bible as the sole source of God's Word. New immigrants from Norway and Denmark, clergy and laity alike, opposed Grundtvig's liberalism, and by 1871 the Danish Pastor Andreas Grove-Rasmussen could speak of a decided 'Grundtvigianism phobia'.[461] Fidelity

---

458. ('Det danske Folk i Amerika' in *Dannevirke* 13.04.1898, 3).
459. Danish title: *Sangbog for det danske Folk i Amerika*. The book ran to a sixth edition and was eventually succeeded by the English-language *A World of Song* (1941).
460. Letter to P. Kjølhede, 11th August 1898, Association of Evangelical Lutheran Churches/AELC Archives.
461. (A.L.C. Grove-Rasmussen, *Rejseberetning*, Odense, 1871, 34).

to Luther and opposition to Grundtvig became commonplace, and a lay member from Milwaukee, F.L. Mathiasen, advised Grundtvigian pastors in Denmark to remain right there. Passions were running high and culminated in the case of Pastor Adam Dan, who had been ordained by the Norwegian pastor, Johannes Müller-Eggen. Four months later Müller-Eggen declared Pastor Dan a heretic and encouraged four members of the congregation in Racine, Wisconsin to take him to court on a charge of "gross heresy and apostasy". The court found him guilty of "preaching false doctrine"; but the party adhering to him being in the majority, the court gave them the property and the original name of the congregation. By and large the Danes supported him, not least when the King of Denmark awarded him a knighthood in 1912 for his services to the country.

The pattern that emerged was that the Danish-American Lutheran Church was liberal while the American-Norwegian Church was pietistic and puritanical. Yet even *within* the Danish Church there were serious divisions between the Grundtvigians (more Creed-based) and the Inner Mission (more Bible-based) which persisted far into the 20th century. Only in the 1980s were these divisions finally resolved; the narrative that has survived to this day speaks of the Grundtvigians as "the happy Danes" and the Inner Mission pietists as "the holy Danes".

Folk High Schools in the USA

Wherever the Danish-Americans determined to keep their heritage alive they built a church and a school. The churches were for everyone, but then so were the schools, for from their very beginnings they held courses outside regular school-time. Over time the Danes integrated into American society and the people's high schools gradually lost their specifically Danish stamp. In the USA they became known as 'folk high schools', and this terminology has spread throughout the English-speaking world.

Interest from abroad encouraged the Danes into an active promotion of their own pioneering work in agriculture. The first push came with the publication in 1927 of *The Folk High Schools of Denmark and the Development of a Farming Community* by Grundtvig scholar Holger Begtrup, together with Hans Lund, Principal of Rødding People's High School, and Peter Manniche, who founded the International People's College in Elsinore in 1921.

One important visitor to a Danish people's high school was the American, Myles Horton, (1905-90). He co-founded Highlander School in Tennessee in 1932, a year after he had visited Denmark to see such schools in practice. He was inspired by the concept of the 'Living Word' and the idea of discovering one's identity through relationships with others – without the baggage of rote-learning and examinations. Songs and poetry were essential tools. Horton writes of Grundtvig:

> I saw him as a rebel with prophetic insights: a champion of the poor and voiceless... His many poems and songs carried messages of hope and joy and expressed confidence that the

Danish people, once enlivened and enlightened, would act to shape the emerging democratic society. I admired his ability to change and to learn from others.[462]

Among his students Horton numbered Martin Luther King, Rosa Parks, and Pete Seeger, all of whom received inspiration and encouragement at Highlander. It was at Highlander that the civil rights song 'We shall overcome' was born. In 2016 the US president Barack Obama acknowledged the debt that the Civil Rights Movement owed to Grundtvig in a speech to the Nordic prime ministers at a gala dinner in the White House:

> Many of our Nordic friends are familiar with the great Danish pastor and philosopher Grundtvig and the idea of the folk high school. ... Over time, the movement spread, including here to the United States, where Dr Martin Luther King, Jr was a student at Highlander Folk High School in Tennessee ... I might not be standing here were it not for the efforts of the people who participated in the Highlander Folk High School.[463]

American usage of 'folk high school' has taken the schools further and further away from Grundtvig, in that many of them are now creative arts or drama schools. For instance, Thomas Rørdam, teacher at Rødding People's High School, described his visit to a kibbutz in California in *The Folk High Schools, their Role and Activity today*. Acknowledging that because the school in question was not a people's high school in the *Danish* sense of the word, he nevertheless accepted that Grundtvig and Kold had inspired it:

> During my stay in California I visited a non-examination boarding school for young Jews. It turned out to be a rather unique experiment, built on educational inspiration from Denmark.
>
> The founder of the school and its present principal, Dr. Shlomo Bardin, had emigrated from Germany to get away from the Hitler regime. During the 30s he stayed at Danish folk high schools – Askov and Ryslinge – and what he saw and read about there, he tried to transplant to a kibbutz in California.
>
> He said to me: "It was Grundtvig and Kold and the history of the Danish folk high schools that showed me how to awaken young Jewish Americans, how to make them feel as Jews".
>
> Christen Kold had in his thatched cottage-school at Ryslinge in 1851 aimed at Christian and Danish awakening. One hundred and twenty years later Dr. Bardin aimed at Jewish and American awakening. As Christen Kold wished his pupils to become good Christians and good Danes, Dr. Bardin wished to make his students good Jews and good Americans (101-02).[464]

---

462. Horton, 52.
463. For a fuller account of Horton's debt to Grundtvig see Holm (2019) 219-24.
464. GS 2013.

Canada

In *Canada and Grundtvig* (1999) Knud Eyvin Bugge detailed the ripples of Grundtvig's educational ideas in Canada, where they were initially successful but ultimately unworkable. Bugge quotes the President of the Rural Learning Assocation of Ontario, Canada, Alex Sim, writing in 1956:

> Many of us were inspired by the Danish folk school long before we knew what it was or how it worked. We were impressed by the fact that it had aided a people to defeat limitations placed upon them by poor soil, obstinate neighbours, and a peasant population which had forgotten its art, poetry, legends, indeed the greatness of Norse culture.
>
> The Danish experiment interested us then because we were told farmers who had learned to think became, almost incidentally, efficient prosperous farmers. They became thinkers by becoming familiar with history, they became observant (a prerequisite of good farming) by learning to paint.

Several high schools were established on Grundtvigian principles, but had to close within a few years as they were not economically viable.

The Canadians' lasting contribution to Grundtvig and Denmark is the hymnal, *Grant me God, the Gift of Singing*, published by the Danish Lutheran Church of Vancouver in 2001, which has 370 hymns, including 80 translations of Grundtvig's from the Danish, singable to the original tunes.

Argentina

In 1844 Hans Fugl emigrated to Argentina and encouraged his family and then his countrymen to follow suit. The same opportunities as in the USA were available to Danes wishing to farm in Argentina, where some 15,000 took up residence between 1864 and 1914. The four Danish churches – in Buenos Aires, and further south, Necochea, Tandil, and Tres Arroyos – are all linked to the Danish People's Church, but their services are now in Spanish.

Europe

United Kingdom

Grundtvig was also becoming a recognised name in the United Kingdom, not for his Anglo-Saxon scholarship, but for 'the Grundtvigianers', who "take a brighter, happier view of life than many others ... within their community there is a warm, spontaneous fellow-feeling." Thus says Jessie Brochner in *Danish Life in Town and Country* (1903) pinpointing Grundtvig's pursuit of freedom as his most engaging quality:

> Influenced by his visits to England, freedom became the keynote of his views and writings – freedom on the old Apostolic basis, imbued with a fresh and bracing humanity, in which there was always a warm national sentiment ... The seed which Grundtvig sowed during

his long life has borne rich and manifold fruit, not only within the Church, but in many other fields. Outside the Church the rural high schools were perhaps the most important outcome of his work ... The love of freedom, which is one of the characteristics of Grundtvig's followers, has led to the formation within the Church of communities who elect and support their own clergymen.[465]

Between 1903 and 2010 Brochner's book ran into 25 editions. Today, *all* congregations within the Danish Lutheran Church elect their pastors, who are then ratified by the diocesan bishop and the monarch.

In 1910, before he became a world-famous novelist, the English writer Rider Haggard visited Denmark to look at farming conditions and the cooperative movement, for which Grundtvig's educational ideas were being given some credit. In his book, *Rural Denmark and its Lessons* (1911) he relates how he was struck by a number of things, such as that "the people have an educated look and clearly are great readers of newspapers, of which I was informed about 250 appear in Denmark". He visited Brørup Co-operative Dairy, where, one morning at 6 o'clock he watched 13,000 kilos of milk arrive from 264 co-operating members.[466]

Germany

In Germany, where Kierkegaard is the decisive Danish theologian. Grundtvig's patriotic programme for Denmark was misinterpreted by German nationalists through the early years of the 20th century to mean rampant nationalism. From here it was a short step to the Nazi philosophy of racial superiority. Quite a few Danes thought likewise and joined the Danish Nazi Party. Writing in GS 1973 Götz Harbsmeier noted:

> We sadly conclude that Grundtvig is currently known in Germany only either through a nationalistic misinterpretation or through Kierkegaard's ironic criticisms. Consequently, he is highly suspect among theologians and among educationalists he is only accepted with many qualifications, while his writings remain largely unknown. Only in most recent times – perhaps owing to tourists' experiences! – have educationalists shown a greater interest in Grundtvig.

Grundtvig, as we have seen, not only named the German Church as one of the seven stars of Christendom, he was also deeply influenced by German theologians and most of all by Martin Luther. What irked him was the German assumption of superiority, which he likened to the Roman/Latin yoke. Behind Denmark's neutrality during the First World War lay the defeat of 1864. The German Professor of Agriculture Anton Hollman had worked at the German embassy in Copenhagen and had experienced Denmark's democratisation and agricultural progress at first hand. In 1936 he published a book on the Danish People's

---

465. Brochner 1903, 27-28.
466. Haggard 1911, 7.

High School and its significance for the concept of popular culture, a book that was so popular it was translated into 8 languages.

In 1926 Grundtvig was translated into German in two volumes, especially his educational ideas. After the Second World War Grundtvig's ideas began to gain ground in Germany, so much so that by 1988 a Grundtvig conference was held in Cologne. Its organizer, Paul Röhrig, noted in the conference book, *For the Sake of Man*, an unexpectedly wide response to Grundtvig's ideas from the press, scholarly journals and the radio. In 1994 Norbert Vogel from the University of Tübingen, who had attended the conference, published a doctoral dissertation entitled *Grundtvig's Importance for German Adult Education*, in which he examined the period between 1810 and 1920. A major step forward was taken with the publication in 2010 of the first major German translation of Grundtvig's work,[467] a 1000-page book with selections from Grundtvig's historical, poetical, educational, political, and ecclesiastical writings, translated and edited by Danish and German scholars.

People's high schools in Germany, Switzerland and Austria are usually funded on a local level and provide non-credit courses mainly in the humanities. A number of them also offer preparatory classes for school exams, while the boarding schools are called *Heimvolkshochschulen* (lit. Home People's High Schools). This tallies closely with Grundtvig's wish to make school life an extension of home life.

France

In France, thanks in particular to the untiring efforts of Erica Simon (1910-93), Grundtvig became known for his educational philosophy of learning for life, learning for freedom, and learning for pleasure. In 2018 French translators produced a Grundtvig volume of educational articles entitled *L'ecole pour la vie*, which follows Grundtvig's sentence-structure more strictly than the English or German translations. Elsewhere in Western Europe interest is growing but there is not yet much literature to show for it.

Central and Eastern Europe, the Baltic Countries, and Russia

In 2002 the Czech, Jindra Kulich, published *Grundtvig's Educational Ideas in Central and Eastern Europe and the Baltic States in the Twentieth Century*. He looks specifically at Poland, Hungary, Russia and Romania, plus Estonia, Latvia, and Lithuania, noting the different receptions and attributing the legacy as much to Christen Kold as to Grundtvig. In Poland, where the first people's high school opened in 1900, the centenary celebrations for independence in 2021 included a conference on their future and a dialogue between the 20 schools and with the Polish government, which actually initiated the contact. A project has been set up entitled 'Teaching Organic Literacy in Grundtvigian Style', funded by the European Commission and the local Civil Society Development Programme in Grzybów, 85 km south of Warsaw. The Principal of the Ecological People's High School there, Ewa Smuk-Stratenwerth, writes "... we devote a lot of space to the educational thought of

---

467. (Bugge et al. 2010. 942 pp).

N.F.S. Grundtvig. We try to read the legacy of the great Dane in the face of the social, environmental, and educational challenges of the 21st century."[468]

In 1910, after a visit to the Nordic countries the Swedish Estonian Jaan Tõnisson, published a book advocating the people's high schools as a medium for preserving the language and culture of the rural farmers in the country. One such school was founded in 1920, Birkas Agricultural and Folk High School, but it had to close in 1943 when the Soviet Union annexed Estonia. After independence in 1991 the Estonians established a new school in Paskleps, and today, there are over 40 popular adult education centres and people's high schools in Estonia. As with so many Grundtvigian-inspired schools popular enlightenment takes its own course and thus the most popular topics are art, crafts, music, languages, and self-development.

Despite early efforts to transfer Grundtvig's ideas to the Hungarian system, it was not until the collapse of the Soviet Union 1991 that the new freedoms led to participation in the Grundtvig programme (see below). As János Tóth writes in GS 2018, "People's high schools helped re-establish education for the people and revival measures that resist subversion of education into mass propaganda for political indoctrination. A Hungarian Folk High School Society was established in Budapest in 2002 to contribute among other things "to the better introduction of lifelong learning activities performed in Central-Eastern Europe among EAEA and EU member-states."

The Danish-Russian Society, founded in 1924, has occasionally had Grundtvig on its agenda, predominantly his educational ideas. Initiated by Lidia Shkorkina, from 1991-97 in the city of Zhukovsky (Moscow region) a free school based on Grundtvig's principles of freedom and democracy was established. The school had 50 children and was operated by the parents, who hired the teachers and had a final say about the school programme. The tuition fees were very low and parents who could not afford to pay could contribute their work on upkeep instead, but when the municipality withdrew its support, the school had to close. In 2008 the same Lidia Shkorkina translated into Russian *A Worm – A God, On Human Beings in the World*, Ove Korsgaard's Grundtvig book. *Grundtvig and Russia*, published by the Danish-Russian Society of Zealand in 2017 and available online, is the definitive account of Grundtvig's influence in Russia. A few dedicated Russians have tried to introduce his ideas, but both before and after the collapse of the Soviet Union the necessary freedom for a people's high school has been impossible to achieve.

The Grundtvig programme 2000

By the late 20th century Grundtvig's name as an educator and founder of the people's (folk) high school had become so well-known that he was widely acknowledged as "the father of adult education", and in 2000 the European Union named their adult education plans 'The Grundtvig Programme' with the following mission statement:

---

468. Introduction to *Folk High Schools facing the challenges of the Anthropocene: What to Teach in the 21st century and How?* (Ziarno Association together with Ecological University in Grzybów, 2020).

The Grundtvig programme is a European Union (EU) education and training programme launched in 2000, aimed at helping adults to improve their knowledge and skills, further their personal development and thus boost their employment prospects. It also helps to tackle problems associated with Europe's ageing population. The programme focuses on the teaching and study needs of people enrolled in adult education and 'alternative' education courses, as well as the organisations delivering these services, the adult education sector.[469]

The statement is absolutely in the spirit of Grundtvig, including the boosting of employment prospects. His own people's high school, Marie's Pleasure/*Marielyst* (1856) offered practical courses in land surveying, agriculture, cattle rearing, chemistry, and Danish – all with the purpose of boosting employment prospects and improving the agricultural yield.

The European Association for the Education of Adults (EAEA) offers an annual Grundtvig Award:

> Every year, EAEA is searching for adult education projects from Europe and beyond demonstrating innovation and excellence in adult learning and education(ALE). EAEA Grundtvig Award calls attention to initiatives that realise new and innovative ideas, establish new partnerships, develop new methodologies and support a modern understanding of adult education. In 2022 the theme of the Award is Transformative Learning and Values.

Again, 'transformative learning and values' are central to Grundtvig's thought. His name sits alongside the other great educators with EU programmes: Comenius (grade school programme), Erasmus (education, training, youth, and sport), and Leonardo da Vinci (vocational education and training).

Asia

India

Grundtvig's idea of a national *identity* – formed through a common language, a common history, a common territory and a common culture – has taken hold in many other countries. An awareness of *belonging* is crucial to this identity, and Grundtvig was unenthusiastic about sending missionaries out to a people before they had a strong sense of belonging to a shared community. He placed education before mission, but of course he and his followers could not *control* how the locals applied his ideas. In his essay on the subject in *Heritage and Prophecy* Holger Bernt Hansen tells the story of Eduard Løventhal's mission to the Hindus in Tamil Nadu in 1872, which failed because the Hindus did not constitute a nation, not even a community. Løventhal's successor, Anne Marie Petersen, was a personal friend of Mahatma Gandhi, and in 1921 Gandhi himself laid the foundation stone for a Christian-based boarding-school for poor girls,

---

469. https://ec.europa.eu/eurostat/statistics-explained/index.php?title=Glossary:Grundtvig_programme (retrieved 23.05.23).

Porto Novo. Back in Denmark Anne Marie Petersen's Grundtvigian heritage clashed with some of the Inner Mission members of the Danish Missionary Society, who regarded Gandhi as a 'heathen'. For her part Anne Marie Petersen could see the similarity between Grundtvig's fight for Denmark and Gandhi's fight for India. The Danish Porto Novo Mission was established in Denmark to support the school, which in many ways was a shining success academically, but it gradually set Grundtvig's free school ideas aside in favour of rote learning and a plethora of examinations, while its pupils came from increasingly well-off homes that could afford to pay the school's fees. The Christian *mission* aim was also side-lined, with a mere 47 baptisms since 1920 and a Sunday service attendance of only 80 Christians among the school's 2000 pupils. In 2007 the Danish Porto Novo Mission, with its 500 members, closed down. Grundtvig had been adopted, absorbed, adapted, and transformed.

An important Indian visitor to the International People's College in Elsinore was the great Indian poet and Nobel Prizewinner Rabindranath Tagore, a visit that formed the background for the establishment of Tagore's own educational institution, Shantiniketan, north of Kolkata, now a university. Asoka Bhattacharya has written an informative book comparing the educational philosophies of Grundtvig, Tagore, Gandhi and Freire.

Another project was started by Sri Viswanathan (1928-2014) who had visited both the USA (Highlander Folk High School) and Denmark (in 1955). On returning to his birthplace in Kerala in south India he founded a non-profit project 'Mitraniketan' (Home of Friends) in 1956. 40 years later, and with the support of the Association of Danish Folk High Schools (FFD) and the Danish Aid organisation DANIDA, he founded a People's College in Mitraniketan. The non-profit organisation consists of a Kindergarten, Children's School, a Technology Centre, and a Farm Science Centre. Its current principal, says that it is a community-based college for empowering youth and women through various life-oriented and enlightenment activities – including one-year residential courses for the purpose integrating life skills and livelihood skills "as envisaged by N.F.S. Grundtvig. The education process involves opportunities for students to reflect upon their life experiences."[470] Since 2017 students have asked for certification to join mainstream employment and higher education, so the college is now forced to link with universities. This has diluted the Folk Education model to a limited extent, but the college has nonetheless sustained its holistic education system built on Grundtvig's philosophy.

The prime promoter of Grundtvig in India is Asoke Bhattacharaya in Kolkata, who came to Denmark to study Kierkegaard and returned to India with a spark from Grundtvig. His passion for lifelong learning has led to literacy and skills programmes for the rural and urban poor, for street children, and for the disabled – a contribution that in 1999 won him the UNESCO-National Literacy Mission award for his outstanding contribution to literacy. He is currently preparing a translation into Bengali of Anders Holm's *The Essential N.F.S. Grundtvig*.

---

470. Letter to the editor 2020.

Bangladesh

Supported by the Danish Ministry of Foreign Affairs 5 of the current 6 people's high schools in Bangladesh were set up in the early 1980s to combat illiteracy and poverty with a general knowledge programme and a skills-based training in handicraft, cultivation methods, and fish and poultry breeding. The Association of Danish People's High Schools liaised with the Bangladesh Association for Community Education to maintain an equal emphasis on social education and skills training, in order to equip the students with the necessary life skills for improving their situation after leaving school. A sixth school was founded in 1987 in East Bangladesh, where especially women were helped. Anders Holm visited the school in 2018 and wrote:

> Another Grundtvig-inspired initiative is Manabratan Kendra, a cultural school for children in a poor region in the Khulna district. This school was started by the author and filmmaker Tanvir Mokammel, who has written about Grundtvig and made documentaries about his influence on the people's (folk) high schools in Denmark and Bangladesh. Unlike normal schools, the children are here taught by means of song, dance, play-acting, painting, and computers.

Tanvir Mokammel attended the Grundtvig Conference in London in 2018 and said: "Like Grundtvig, we believe that people have to draw knowledge, experience, and vision from their own history and mythology."

The implementation of Grundtvig's ideas in Bangladesh was the subject of *Folk High Schools in Bangladesh* (2001) by Knud Eyvin Bugge.

China

Grundtvig's own knowledge of China was limited almost entirely to *The History of the East Indies* by the Italian Fernando Lopes di Castagneda (Venice 1578), a book which he borrowed from the Royal Library in the late 1830s and read in the original Italian, thanks to his proficiency in Latin. From this he gathered that all Chinese civil servants were classified by the number and quality of the rote-learned examinations they had passed, and since he abhorred examinations, Grundtvig railed at "the Chinese exam-system" from 1838 onwards.

Following the fall of the Qing Dynasty in 1912 Chinese educators were eager to learn from the west, and via first a Chinese translation of a Japanese book on Grundtvig and then an article in their journal *Education*, they learned that teachers

> ... for the most part use the spoken word in the classroom and do not force the pupils to learn by rote. After the teacher's talk, those who ask the most difficult questions are rewarded. This stimulates the students intellectually and activates them in their search for a happy and noble life... Being healthy in body and soul, with clear views, and full of hope, they listen to the teacher in deep concentration. They do not take many notes, but

are attentive to every word so that they can extract the mysteries behind the thoughts that are revealed to them.[471]

The anonymous writer, Jing Yu, who had almost certainly *visited* a Danish people's high school, added that five members of the current Danish government had attended such schools and that four of them were sons of peasant farmers.

According to Stig Thøgersen in his article 'Grundtvig in China' (GS 1995), Grundtvig's ideas were conveyed to the Chinese through English books, including those by Harold Foght and Holger Begtrup et al mentioned above: the latter was even translated into Chinese in 1931 and its 5,000 print-run sold out. Moreover it was Mao Zedong himself who wrote the report in 1927 recommending that the millions of Chinese peasant farmers should all be *educated*. Over the following decade Grundtvig's name became better known in China through the efforts of Liang Shuming, who saw himself as China's prophet in the style of Grundtvig and wrote of his Danish hero and the high schools:

> The idea which gave them birth was not conceived in the mind of a college professor; it was conceived in that of a prophet, a spiritual genius who understood the life and mind of the people throughout the ages, and who thereby had the vision of the special enlightenment that was needed to promote the well-being of his people.[472]

In 1934, Peter Manniche, the Principal of the International High People's College in Elsinore, visited Hong Kong, Canton, Shanghai and Beijing, promoting Grundtvig's ideas and their implementation in the people's high schools of Denmark. Then came the Japanese invasion in 1937 and the Communist Revolution in 1949, and Grundtvig was more or less forgotten, until a remarkable Chinese scholar came to Copenhagen in 2004 and began to study Grundtvig. Wen Ge's studies in Denmark culminated in 2013 with a PhD at Aarhus University entitled: *The Deep Coinherence: A Chinese Appreciation of N.F.S. Grundtvig's Public Theology*. He is currently preparing a Chinese edition of Grundtvig's writings under the title *Selected Writings of N.F.S. Grundtvig's Public Theology*, with the following sub-sections: Grundtvig's Understanding of Christian Faith; Church and State; Social Reform and Nation Building; Educational Thought Related to Society and Nation Building; Grundtvig and Kierkegaard; and five of Grundtvig's Poems.

Japan

As Japan opened up to the world around the turn of the 20th century a number of its educators looked to Denmark for educational inspiration – and that, of course, meant Grundtvig. Between 1910 and 1930 some 20 books were published on the country's agricultural development, education system, and social structure, most notably a 1911 essay by Kanzo Uchimura (1861-1930) entitled 'A Story of Denmark. A Story of how Faith and Forestry Saved a Country.'

---

471. (GS 1995, 166).
472. Ibid., 176.

Despite Uchimura's drive to adopt elements of Grundtvig's schools, no movement followed in his wake, and there was a wide variation in the 'people's schools' that *were* founded. More successful was Shigeyoshi Matsumae (1901-91), who met Uchimura in 1925 and through him discovered Grundtvig. After visiting 9 people's high schools in Denmark in 1934, Matsumae determined to implement the concept in Japan. It was a slow process in a country that was used to a certain regimentation of education – and then came the Second World War. Immediately after, in 1946, Matsumae founded Tokai University, which at last made its international mark, not least through promoting academic and cultural exchange with students in Denmark and other European countries, but as in India and Nigeria it has itself been absorbed into the accreditation system of all Japanese universities.

In 1994, Shimizu Mitsuru founded the Grundtvig Society of Japan, which now has 170 members. Meanwhile a handful of Japanese scholars have translated and published Grundtvig in Japanese, notably the social philosopher Naoto Koike. Currently, Sakaguchi Midori and Akiko Harada are preparing a Japanese translation of Anders Holm's *The Essential N.F.S. Grundtvig*.

South Korea

Several Koreans visited the Japanese people's high schools and were inspired by Uchimura Kanzo, including Lee Chan-gap, who in 1958 founded the school now known as the Poolmoo Community College for Ecological Agriculture. It offers living together and shared dormitories, morning courses in the humanities (religion, literature, history, arts, liberal arts and so on) and farming theory; and afternoon practice on the school farm: rice-paddies, field crops, horticulture, organic farming. The balance between theory and practice is maintained, except when farming demands (sowing and harvesting) are otherwise. Poolmoo encourages 'think and research projects' instead of tests and ranking. Decisions are taken after a democratic discussion. This is closer to Grundtvig's thinking than most of the other people's high schools abroad.

In 1980 Kaj Thaning's book on Grundtvig was published in a Korean edition, and interest in Grundtvig has increased markedly through the efforts of Yeonho Oh, a well-known alternative journalist, together with Seungkwan Chung (former principal of Poolmoo) and his wife Heeok Kim. Oh not only lectures on Grundtvig, he has taken a number of travel groups to Denmark, and has been rewarded with the Grundtvig Prize 2018. In gratitude Oh said, "Every time I come to Denmark I visit the Grundtvig statue at Vartov to thank him for what he has taught us. And I would also like to share the prize with my Danish friends. They have taught me who Grundtvig is, what his values are, and how he changed Danish society." Together with Haejin Chung, Yeonho Oh is currently preparing a translation into Korean of Anders Holm's *The Essential N.F.S. Grundtvig*.

The Philippines

A good example of the social and political influence of the people's high school comes from the Philippines, where in 1992 Edicio de la Torre founded the Education for Life Foundation (ELF), an organisation strongly inspired by Grundtvig's ideas, as he writes:

> ... what lay behind the birth of the folk high school movement was the early democratisation of Denmark, and in this the situation was similar in the Philippines ... Grundtvig's strongest influence on us was his philosophy of learning for life ... Education for life resonated for us because we noticed that leaders of grassroots movements, who had grown up through political movements and developmental organisations, had too narrow a training when it came to implementing projects or to political action.
>
> We regarded 'education for life' as an essential way to correct this. We interpreted it as an education for life in its totality, a holistic education that was not limited to economics and politics but included Filipino psychology, culture, family relations, neighbourliness, spirituality, and so on. Our second interpretation of education for life was all about method.

Edicio de la Torre has recorded his debt to Grundtvig in a book entitled *Grundtvig for Filipinos* (2019).

Other countries have their own experiences of adopting and adapting. In many cases the impetus from the Danish people's high schools has had to live alongside the local examination-based schools, in some cases surviving, in others being overwhelmed. Below are a number of successful adaptations of Grundtvig's ideas.

Africa

Nigeria

As in India, Grundtvig-inspired schools in Africa have come under pressure from the national and state school boards to adapt Grundtvig's ideas within the existing examination-oriented system. One such school that has blended Grundtvig into its local environment is to be found in Nigeria. Inspired by his visit to Denmark Kachi E. Ozumba (1942-2011) returned home and in 1998 established the Grundtvig International Secondary School (GISS) in Oba in south central Nigeria. Its motto is 'Education for Life', and its website quotes Grundtvig: "For all letters are dead even if written by fingers of angels and nibs of stars, and all book knowledge is dead that is not unified with a corresponding life in the reader." Writing in *Grundtvig Studies* 1993 Kachi E. Ozumba called his school "the nursery bed of Grundtvigianism in Africa." An independent boarding school with some 600 students from 12-18, it has repeatedly featured among the top ten performing schools in Nigeria based on its West African Examinations Council (WAEC) results. In 2016 the West African Quality Education awards named the school "Best in Value-based Education & Life Skill Development School of the Year", while the British Council recently awarded GISS the title: "Outstanding Cambridge Learner awards. Top in Nigeria".

GISS is proud to be "founded on our rich tradition and the Education-for-Life philosophy of Bishop N.F.S. Grundtvig of Denmark". GISS is one of three institutes that form the Grundtvig Movement of Nigeria, a non-profit-making NGO which also includes the Grundtvig Polytechnic and the Grundtvig Institute, all chaired by the founder's son, Kachi A. Ozumba. Speaking to the Grundtvig Newsletter in March 2020 he said:

95. Grundtvig International Secondary School, Nigeria.
The school announces itself as proud to be "founded on our rich tradition and the Education-for-Life philosophy of Bishop N.F.S. Grundtvig of Denmark. As an independent boarding school with some 600 students from 12-18, it has repeatedly featured among the top ten performing schools in the country. In 2020 the British Council awarded the school the title: "Outstanding Cambridge Learner awards. Top in Nigeria".

> What we find special about Grundtvig's ideas is that he focuses on educating youth, the students, for life – not just educating them to pass examinations, obtain certificates, and maybe get jobs… Education is not just to make a living but to live a *life*. It helps the full development of an individual; it enables the individual to be *aware* – cultural awareness, active citizenship, the values that make life worth living.

The school has clearly retained the link with Grundtvig but has had to adapt to the local need for qualification certificates.

Tanzania

Grundtvig's influence in Tanzania has come about largely through the Swedish people's high schools, which, following a visit to Sweden and Norway in the 1960s, inspired the first president Julius Nyerere (1922-99) to establish Folk Development Colleges (FDCs) in the country. There are now 50 or so adult colleges under the Ministry of Education; they are largely rural, situated in 24 of the 26 regions, with training in i.a. agriculture, woodwork, tailoring, motor mechanics, masonry, electrical installation, and computer skills.

We have been unable to trace any significant impact of Grundtvig in Oceania.

The Danish Church Abroad

Grundtvig's hymns have been kept alive both in Danish and in their English translations through the The Danish Church Abroad/The Danish Seamen's Church, founded in 1867. The organisation, known as DSUK, works in conjunction with the Danish People's Church in Denmark and at the time of writing numbers 48 churches, in areas where there are a relatively large number of Danes in residence or where large ships arrive in a port city. DSUK fundraises more than 65% of its funds, partly in Denmark, partly in the churches around the world. The churches are legally and financially independent and operate in accordance with local law and customs. They receive a subsidy from the Danish state for part of the pastor's salary, but must find all remaining funds themselves, from membership fees and gifts, activities, sales, and fundraising. Church services, in whatever the local language, follow for the most part the Evangelical Lutheran liturgy and practice known in Denmark.

Conferences

For the last 50 years or so there have been a number of Grundtvig conferences where his work has been discussed and new angles have been presented. The conferences have resulted in books and articles and an increasing interest in both Grundtvig in his time and his living legacy. More and more he is being seen as the nation-builder supreme of modern Denmark, one of the country's finest poets and the greatest of all its hymnwriters. Here follows a list of the major conferences and their contribution to this understanding of Grundtvig as the catalyst of modern Denmark

The 1972 International Seminar

The first serious attempt to share Grundtvig with the rest of the world in the seminar form was the international seminar on the centenary of his death, with 64 participants from Canada, Denmark, England, France, Germany, Ghana, Italy, Japan, Mexico, Norway, Rumania, Switzerland, Sweden, and the USA. The conference, held in the Danish Parliament building at Christiansborg, was led by Folmer Wisti of the Danish Cultural Institute (founded 1745) in collaboration with the Grundtvig Society.

The 1983 Copenhagen Conference

The conference at Christiansborg, Copenhagen in September 1983 celebrated the bicentenary of Grundtvig's birth in 1783. Thanks to a collaboration between the Danish Cultural Institute and the Grundtvig Society (founded 1947) the Copenhagen conference brought together over 100 scholars and educators from all over the world – with the book *N.F.S. Grundtvig Tradition and Renewal* as their foundational text. Its 3 sections – The Younger Grundtvig; Grundtvig's Basic Ideas on the Church and Education; and The Later Years and Grundtvigianism – reflected the conference title: 'Education for Life'. The conference established three areas where Grundtvig was not only ahead of his time but perpetually relevant: 1) freedom with responsibility, 2) mutual understanding, respect, and interaction, and 3) cultural identity. A 12-hymn pamphlet was also issued to all participants, who could then sing Grundtvig in English. The conference was an unqualified success, and in his summary Knud Eyvin Bugge argued that it had turned Grundtvig into "a common denominator", at least as far as Denmark was concerned.

News of the event even reached the British press, where the error-strewn *Sunday Times* article by Berry Ritchie ("Atticus") noted:

> He looked a bit like a Norse god himself, apparently, with lots of hair and beard, and he also had a lurid love-life, with three wives, four children – one when he was 77 – and a number of affairs. But he must have been hell to live with. It has been calculated that his writings would have filled between 120 and 150 volumes, including the hymns, 3,000 sermons and masses of translations. Unlike the other famous literary Danes, Andersen, Kierkegaard and Georg Brandes, Grundtvig has never been translated into English. Somehow I don't mind too much.

Ritchie's article displayed both ignorance and prejudice, but this was the last time that Grundtvig was so treated in the foreign press. He became even better known through a number of small books containing English translations of his work, as well as through foreigners who visited or settled in Denmark and discovered that "you meet him at the border", for Grundtvig has gradually permeated the whole of Danish culture.

The Cologne Conference 1988

In connection with the University of Cologne's 600th anniversary a Grundtvig conference brought together over 200 participants, mostly from Germany and other German-speaking countries, to discuss four points: Grundtvig's understanding of "Human comes first, and Christian next"; his idea of *folkelighed* (a people's spirit/nature/culture); his concept of nationalism; and the transference of his ideas into practice. The Berlin Wall fell the following year, and when the book of the conference papers was published in 1990, *Um des Menschenwillen/ For the Sake of Humankind*, its back cover underlined the importance of Grundtvig's bold ideas and radical reform proposals as a challenge to intellectual and social life in Germany. A national identity was impossible without free general education being available to all.

The Chicago Grundtvig Conference 1995

The Chicago conference in July 1995 was organised by the Evangelical Lutheran Church of America (ECLA) and the Grundtvig Study Centre, Aarhus, and brought together 45 scholars from the USA, the UK, and Denmark under the title 'Consultation'. The focus was on "Grundtvig as a potential resource for renewal in contemporary church, school and society,"[473] and it was envisaged that the consultation would be ongoing. Attention was drawn to the first major book on Grundtvig in English, Donald Allchin's *Heritage and Prophecy. Grundtvig and the English-Speaking World*, which had been published the year before. A further book consolidated the results of the conference: *Grundtvig in International Perspective, Studies in the Creativity of Interaction* (2000)

The Kolkata Grundtvig Conferences of 1999, 2003, and 2007

These three conferences were organised by Grundtvig aficionado, Asoka Bhattacharya, and supported by i.a. The Grundtvig Society for Popular Enlightenment and Human Development, Kolkata. They focused on Grundtvig in an Indian educational context, setting him alongside Tagore and Gandhi, as well as Paulo Freire. This was the first Grundtvig conference held outside the western world and was inspirational for the 150 participants, with a large contingent from West Bengal.

The Harvard Conference 2012: Grundtvig as nation-builder

In December 2012 Grundtvig was the subject of another conference, this time at Harvard University MA, organised by the Grundtvig Study Centre at Aarhus University under the leadership of Michael Schelde. Grundtvig was now a *builder*, not just of an education plan but of the very identity of Denmark. Of course he was not alone in the process, but he was both the wheel and the lynchpin that helped to roll Denmark out of its slow past and into its dynamic future. Denmark as a one-nation 'collective' was very much Grundtvig's vision. There is therefore no doubt that within educational circles Grundtvig's name has gradually been linked to progressive ideas about adult education. The keynote speaker at the Harvard conference was the US political scientist, Francis Fukuyama, who argued:

> Grundtvig and his movement are of interest because they present a case of a strong national identity being formed from the bottom up rather than by a top-down state builder using authoritarian ... Danish identity took an inclusive and tolerant form and was important in building consensus behind modern Danish democracy.[474]

In his essay on 'Grundtvig and Cultural Nationalism' Michael Böss emphasises Grundtvig's awareness that he was living in an age of rapid transition, in which he contributed to "the forging of an alliance between the mostly politically conservative but economically liberal class of middle farmers and the liberal urban middle class."[475]

---

473. GS 1996, 156, A 3-page report of the conference can be found in this issue.
474. Hall et al (2015) 44.
475. Ibid., 89.

96. The London Grundtvig Conference 2018.

Each day began with a Grundtvig hymn or song.

The London Conference 2018

In August 2018 the international conference on Grundtvig was organised in London by Anders Holm (University of Copenhagen) and Brad Busbee (University of Samford, Birmingham, AL). Its title was 'Lands of the Living', referring to Grundtvig's famous hymn, 'I know of a land',[476] and it brought together participants from Bangladesh, China, Denmark, Finland, Hungary, India, South Korea, Japan, Nigeria, Norway, Philippines, Sweden, UK, USA, all of whom had a story to tell about Grundtvig's influence on their country and themselves. The vast majority were working in education, and there was now a sense of international solidarity that had not been present at the two previous conferences. Many of the contributors were actually working with Grundtvig's educational ideas and seeking to motivate them in their respective countries.

Conclusion

All the fiery souls abroad who have felt the reverberations and ripples from Grundtvig have had to manage without a comprehensive scholarly translation of his work. With this book the 6-volume series 'N.F.S. Grundtvig. Works in English' comes to an end. There is scope now for a much wider study of Grundtvig's ideas and thus for his increasing impact beyond modern Denmark.

---

476. No. 67 in *LW*.

Biskop N. F. S. Grundtvigs

Levnetsløb,

udførligst fortalt fra 1839.

Et Bidrag

fra

H. Brun,
Cand. theol.

2det Bind.

Kristiania: Kolding: Kjøbenhavn:
Alb. Cammermeyer,   Konrad Jørgensen,   Karl Schønberg,
Hovedkommiss. for Norge.   Forlægger.   Hovedk. for Danmark.

Konrad Jørgensens Bogtrykkeri i Kolding ved J. P. Løye.

97. The first biography of Grundtvig 1882.

20. Sources

Danish books and articles about Grundtvig can be numbered in the thousands, though few of them would stand on a library shelf under 'Biography'. Many of the monographs contain important, even new, biographical information, but are classified under their themes: literature, history, theology, politics, poetry etc.

English Introductions to Grundtvig

There are two comprehensive introductions to Grundtvig in English, neither of which is a 'biography' as such:

1983. *N.F.S. Grundtvig. Tradition and Renewal*, eds. Christian Thodberg/Anders Pontoppidan Thyssen, (translated by Edward Broadbridge).
Copenhagen: The Danish Institute, 428 pp.
Published in Danish, English, German, and French in 1983, the bicentenary of Grundtvig's birth, this work has been the standard introduction to most sides of Grundtvig's life and work. Leading Grundtvig scholars of the time write succinctly about (as the sub-title states) 'Grundtvig's Vision of Man and People, Education and the Church, in Relation to World Issues Today', though these last six words are barely touched on. Among its many qualities is the chapter that compares Grundtvig with Kierkegaard, and a chapter on the Grundtvigian movement until 1900.

2019. Anders Holm: *The Essential N.F.S. Grundtvig* (translated by Edward Broadbridge).
Aarhus: Filo, 249 pp.
Anders Holm (b. 1973) is Associate Professor of Church History at Copenhagen University and a leading Grundtvig scholar. His book is an English translation of the acclaimed Danish version from 2018, presenting Grundtvig chapter by chapter as a romantic, mythologist, pastor, historian, educator, hymn-writer, politician, and Dane. It also examines Grundtvig's legacy in Denmark and worldwide. Both the English and the Danish books have the great advantage of commentated extracts from Grundtvig's works. Reviewing the book in *Theology* (Jan. 2020) Professor George Pattison wrote, "Holm's nicely laid-out and well-illustrated book does as good a job as is possible of 'introducing' a figure who cannot easily be contained within any conventional boundaries."

English Biographies of Grundtvig

1931. Noelle Davies: *Education for Life. A Danish Pioneer*.
London: Williams & Norgate, 207 pp.
Nöelle Davies (1899-1983) writes of Grundtvig that "it is as an educational pioneer that he takes international rank" as "the Father of the Danish Folk High-School" (p.69). She notes

that such a school should both foster "the personal development of the individual" and also "fit him for membership of the civic community" (pp. 69-70). In the one biographical chapter, 'The Making of the Man', she records the most important influence of his childhood being his mother, Catherine (p. 20-21). The chapter ends with Davies' assertion that Grundtvig "was ideally equipped to translate his rich experiences into action, and to take the lead in the regeneration of the Danish people" (p. 37). In 1944 Nöelle Davies also wrote a booklet entitled *Grundtvig of Denmark: a guide to small nations*. (Liverpool: The Bryerthon Press, 66 pp.).

1947. E.L. Allen: *Bishop Grundtvig: A Prophet of the North*.
London: James Clarke, 94 pp.
E.L. Allen's brief study appeared under the category of 'Modern Christian Revolutionaries' as the cover of the book announces. Of the 7 chapter titles the most interesting is 'Odin and Christ', in which Allen notes that in Grundtvig's early spiritual development Nordic mythology and Christianity were comparable, but not for long: "Odin began as a peer of Christ, but ended by laying down his sword before the Cross" (p. 39). Equally discerning is Allen's comment that the people's high school can be traced back to Grundtvig's boring days at Aarhus Cathedral High School: "Grundtvig's educational theories were the outcome of his own experience. They were a eulogy of flight by a bird escaped from its cage." Allen also emphasises the importance of "the residential college" which he hopes can be established in England.

1951. P.G. Lindhardt: *Grundtvig, an Introduction*.
London: SPCK, 141 pp.
Professor of Church History at Aarhus University, Poul Georg (P.G.) Lindhardt (1910-88) was a distinguished Danish theologian who wrote an English study in which he covers most aspects of Grundtvig briefly. He singles out Grundtvig's trips to England as turning him into a realist, and he has a final chapter on 'Grundtvigianism' with the opening comment: "At the time of Grundtvig's death the movement was strong and unanimous as never before or since" (p. 130).

1952. Hal Koch: *Grundtvig* (trans. & ed. Jones, L.).
Yellow Springs, Ohio: Antioch Press.
See Danish section, p. 369.

1955. Johannes Knudsen: *Danish Rebel. A Study of N.F.S. Grundtvig*.
Philadelphia: Muhlenberg Press, 242 pp.
The first substantial English biography of Grundtvig, was the work of Johannes Knudsen (1902-84), who became President of the 'Danish' university in Grand View College, Iowa (1942-52) and Professor of Church History at the Lutheran School of Theology, Chicago. In his introduction Knudsen emphasises the warrior aspect of Grundtvig: "Having expressed an opinion somewhat extremely in a polemical writing, he would seize it, defend it, and establish it defiantly as a dogma" – including, Knudsen, adds "the most tragic example

of the historical origin of the Apostles' Creed" (p. xi). He wisely notes that Grundtvig's educational views grew out of his religious ideas and his conception of humankind as created in God's image (p. 147). Reviewing the book in GS 1956, Regin Prenter noted that the two concluding chapters on the Church and on the nature of man "seek to show Grundtvig's significance for the modern age" and hopes not only that it will awaken interest in Grundtvig in America but that it will be "followed by translations of Grundtvig's writings".

1955. Ernest D. Nielsen: *N.F.S. Grundtvig. An American Study*.
Illinois: Augustana Press, 173 pp.
Ernest Nielsen (1902-90), President of Grand View College (1952-92), published his book in the same year as Johannes Knudsen, but limited his study to an investigation of Grundtvig's understanding of the reality of the Spirit. He emphasises Grundtvig's view of the Spirit's activity as being not only 'historical' but also the driver of progress through freedom, a key-word in Grundtvig's life and work. Nielsen adds that unfortunately "Grundtvig's writings are very difficult to read", a fact that Grundtvig himself was aware of when, quoting Horace in *World Chronicle 1812*, he wrote, "I strive to be brief but become obscure" (p.154).

1972. Kaj Thaning: *N.F.S. Grundtvig* (trans. Hohnen, D.).
Copenhagen: Danish Cultural Institute.
This monograph by Kaj Thaning (1904-94) was published in English, French, and German, but not in Danish. Thaning was a leading Grundtvig scholar of his day with his thesis, *Human Comes First – Grundtvig's Settlement with Himself*, arguing that 1832 was the turning-point in Grundtvig's life. That is when he publishes the revised *Nordic Mythology* and begins to concentrate more on being a human being and less on being a Christian. The thesis was controversial at the time, and is disputed to this day, the majority citing 1825 and the 'matchless discovery' as the more important date.

1997 (2nd ed. 2015). Donald (Arthur M.) Allchin: *N.F.S. Grundtvig, An Introduction to his Life and Work*.
Aarhus: Aarhus University Press, 338 pp.
Donald Allchin (1930-2010) was an Anglican priest, a canon of Canterbury Cathedral (1973-87), programme director of the St Theosevia Centre for Christian Spirituality in Oxford (1987-96), and honorary professor at the University of Wales, Bangor (1992-2010). From his Anglo-Catholic perspective, and after 40 years of working with Grundtvig and building on a close collaboration with the Grundtvig Study Centre in Aarhus, Allchin wrote an introduction that emphasises Grundtvig's role as mediator – between God and humankind, past and present, man and woman – and in particular between the Eastern and the Western Churches. The first five biographical chapters are entitled 'Glimpses of a Life, the second 'Five Major Themes', and the third 'The Celebration of Faith'. In his English review of the book in GS 1998 Viggo Mortensen called it "exciting and innovative", emphasising the importance of this first major study of Grundtvig in English – seen from abroad.

English Translations of Grundtvig's Works

To date no fewer than 110 hymns and 28 songs by Grundtvig have been translated into English – see the indexes in *Living Wellsprings*, 2015.

Grundtvig's hymns and songs have also appeared in English translations in *Grundtvig Studier* (GS), the annual Grundtvig journal, along with English articles, notably by Sid Bradley and Donald Allchin.[477] Each edition includes English summaries of the Danish articles.

1927. Jens Christian Aaberg: *Hymnal for Church and Home*.
Nebraska: Lutheran Publishing House, 422 pp.
This work was compiled for the Danish Evangelical Lutheran Church of America, and contains 52 of Grundtvig's hymns in English translation (out of 454 in the book), mainly by Søren Rodholm.

1953. Søren Rodholm: *A Harvest of Song*.
Des Moines, Iowa: American Evangelical Lutheran Church, 193 pp.
Søren (S.D.) Rodholm (1877-1951) emigrated from Denmark to the USA in the early 20th century, and became president of the Danish Evangelical Lutheran Church in America (1922-26), and president of Grand View College (1926-32). His book contains 22 translations of Grundtvig's hymns and songs (out of 96 hymns, songs, poems, and rhymes).

1976. Johannes Knudsen: *Selected Writings of N.F.S. Grundtvig*.
Philadelphia: Fortress Press, 184 pp.
Writing in GS 1978, Niels Lyhne Jensen, who was himself to translate Grundtvig in 1984, gave the book a very positive review: "This is the first anthology of Grundtvig's writings in English and must be regarded as an event in the field of Grundtvig literature. Translating Grundtvig is a formidable task. His choice of words, his syntax, his imagery and world of ideas present such difficulties to the translator that by comparison translating Kierkegaard or Hegel must seem like child's play. Professor Johannes Knudsen and his two collaborators, Dr. Enok Mortensen and Dr. Ernest D. Nielsen have approached the task with first-rate qualifications. There are no misunderstandings in the translations as regards language and contents, and both the anthology as a whole and the individual sections contain well-informed introductions, although they are sadly deficient in information about Grundtvig's works. But the translators' familiarity with the material has ensured a selection that in general is substantial and many-sided ... The first and largest section includes among other things selections from *The Church's Retort*, the introduction to *Nordic Mythology*, and passages from *Basic Christian Teachings* ... The poetry section consists mainly of hymns and poems on education methods, mostly from after 1832 ... The final section contains examples of Grundtvig's educational writings and his polemics. It includes amongst others *The School for Life* and the proposal for a Nordic university from

---

477. See the indexes in this book.

1837. The choice could hardly be bettered; it is substantial, varied and entertaining." Lyhne Jensen argues that Grundtvig's poems are best translated into prose, as "this is the only practicable approach; for it enables the reader to get closer to Grundtvig's special imagery".

1984. Edward Broadbridge & Niels Lyhne Jensen: *A Grundtvig Anthology*.
Aarhus, Centrum; Cambridge, James Clarke, 195 pp.
A Grundtvig Anthology is the first Anglo-Danish collaboration of Grundtvig translations. It includes extracts from Nordic Mythology, The School For Life, Within Living Memory, and Basic Christian Teachings, followed by 2 sermons and 5 hymns/poems. The volume is best seen as a forerunner of the present 6-volume series: N.F.S. Grundtvig. Works in English.

1988. Peter Balslev-Clausen, ed.: *Songs from Denmark*.
Copenhagen: The Danish Cultural Institute, 174 pp.
The book contains 22 translations of Grundtvig (out of 83 hymns and songs) by various translators already published in other books.

1991. Max Lawson: *N.F.S. Grundtvig. Selected Educational Writings*. The International People's College & The Association of Folk High Schools in Denmark, 110 pp.
The book contains works by other translators and a useful introduction on Grundtvig the educator.

1999-2001. Danish Lutheran Church of Vancouver: *Grant me, God the Gift of Singing*.
Vancouver, 420 pp.
This pioneering hymnal contains 80 translations of Grundtvig's hymns (out of 370 items). Not all of the translations match the length of the Danish originals.

2009. Edward Broadbridge: *Hymns in English*.
Copenhagen: Bibelselskabet/Det Kgl. Vajsenhus, 142 pp,
The hymnbook contains 23 translations of Grundtvig's hymns, a number which increased to 67 hymns and 27 songs in *Living Wellsprings* (2014). The Danish liturgies in translation are also included.

2009. Kristian Schultz Petersen: *New Year's Morning*.
Copenhagen: Forlaget Vartov, 191 pp.
Kristian Schultz Petersen (1921-2015) was Principal of Krabbesholm People's High School. His English translation of Grundtvig's 312-stanza masterpiece preserves the metre though not the rhyme. The book concludes with a translation of the 'The Land of the Living'.

2014. John Irons: *Easter flower! what would you here? – anthology of songs and hymns by N.F.S. Grundtvig*.
Odense: University Press of Southern Denmark, 83 pp.
The book contains 27 translations, all of which, with a couple of exceptions, are singable to the well-known Danish tunes. In his Danish review of the book in GS 2014 Peter

Balslev-Clausen wrote that the translations are neither better nor worse than previous ones, and that always "the devil is in the detail". He concludes that: "John Irons' translations will form the basis for a presentation to English-speakers of Grundtvig as a hymn and song-poet, both formally and materially."

2011-23. Edward Broadbridge (trans & ed.): *N.F.S. Grundtvig: Works in English* Aarhus: Aarhus University Press:

vol. 1. *The School For Life. N.F.S. Grundtvig on Education for the People* (2011)
vol. 2. *Living Wellsprings. The Hymns, Songs, and Poems of N.F.S. Grundtvig* (2015)
vol. 3. *Human Comes First. The Christian Theology of N.F.S. Grundtvig* (2018)
vol. 4. *The Common Good. N.F.S. Grundtvig as Politician and Contemporary Historian* (2019)
vol. 5. *The Core of Learning. N.F.S. Grundtvig's Philosophical Writings* (2021)
vol. 6. *Denmark's Catalyst. The Life and Letters of N.F.S. Grundtvig* (2023)

Co-editors in the series:
vol. 1. Uffe Jonas, Clay Warren
vol. 4. Ove Korsgaard
vol. 6. Hans Raun Iversen

Danish Biographies of Grundtvig

Apart from Donald Allchin's English work, all the important biographies of Grundtvig have been written by Danes. It is in some cases difficult to determine whether a monograph is sufficiently 'biographical' to be included in the works below or to deem it 'thematic', in which case it does not appear here. The following 18 biographies are listed in chronological order.

1882. Hans Brun: *The Life of Bishop N.F.S. Grundtvig told in detail from 1839. A Contribution*. I-II./ *Biskop N.F.S. Grundtvigs Levnetsløb udførligst fortalt fra 1839. Et Bidrag*. I-II. / Albert Kammermeyer (Kristiania, main commissioner), Konrad Jørgensen
(Copenhagen, publisher), Karl Schønberg (main commissioner, Denmark), 1,391 pp.
Hans Brun (1820-99) was a Norwegian theologian who after 1839 spent much of his time in Copenhagen, where he belonged to a group of Grundtvigians and others who regularly met in the home of the sculptor, Christopher Borch. Brun's two volumes end with 11 pages of corrections: living in Oslo he was unable to read the proofs before the books went to print. He collected numerous anecdotes about Grundtvig, and read his works as they were published. There is no evidence that the book had much influence except as a collection of material, but its strength lies in it being the very first biography as well as being the first and only source of some of the stories.

1883. Frederik Winkel Horn: *The Life and Work of N.F.S. Grundtvig. A Biographical Essay/ N.F.S. Grundtvigs Liv og Gerning. Et biografisk Forsøg.*
Copenhagen: Karl Schønberg, 485 pp.
Frederik Winkel Horn (1845-98) was a Danish literary historian, a colleague and friend of Grundtvig's second son Svend. Horn's sober biography concedes that there are many unpublished sources to which he has not had access, so he does not claim that it is comprehensive, even though it runs to nearly 500 pages. It contains little information that is not better documented elsewhere.

1901. Ludvig Schrøder: *The Life of N.F.S. Grundtvig/N.F.S. Grundtvigs Levned.*
Copenhagen: Lehmann and Stage, 233 pp.
Ludvig Schrøder (1836-1908) was Principal of Denmark's leading people's high school at Askov in southern Jutland. Having known Grundtvig personally, his biography takes the form of a popular lecture, with plenty of quotations, no references, but a comprehensive list of source material. Schrøder emphasises Grundtvig's thoughts about, and experiences with, 'the people', grounded in his country childhood in Udby. This thread is followed right to the end of Grundtvig's life, when he argued that the border between Denmark and Germany should be drawn according to the hearts and minds, language and culture, of the two peoples involved.

1907 & 1914. Frederik Rønning: *N.F.S. Grundtvig. A Contribution to the Portrayal of Danish Intellectual Life in the 19th Century I-IV/ N.F.S. Grundtvig. Et Bidrag til Skildringen af dansk Åndsliv i det 19. Århundrede I-IV.*
Copenhagen: Schønberg Press, 1,568 pp. (digitalised by the Royal Library in 2018).
Frederik Rønning (1851-1929) was a literary scholar with an extensive authorship. This massive work is the first source-based, referenced biography of Grundtvig, and ever since publication it has been regarded as the authoritative biography. It is the first source to much vital information. The title points to a contextual perspective on the intellectual and spiritual life of the whole of the 19th century. Rønning is the first to survey Grundtvig's immense and central significance for Denmark in his time, calling his story by and large "the story of the age". This view was repeated in a number of the later biographies.

1913. Hans Rosendal: *N.F.S. Grundtvig – A Life Story with Illustrations /N.F.S. Grundtvig Et Livsbillede. Med illustrationer.*
Copenhagen: Hagerup Press, 240 pp.
Hans Rosendal (1839-1921) was the influential Principal of Grundtvig's People's High School. His biography follows the tenet of "Keep quiet and let the departed speak and their spirits move," and seeks to present its subject as Grundtvig would have seen himself – often in retrospect after many years – in poetic and literary form. Stress is therefore laid on the first half of his life, for which Grundtvig had the strongest need and opportunity to revisit in the light of his memory and his contemporary situation. The illustrations consist of 7 portraits of Grundtvig and an example of his handwriting.

1918. Hjalmar Helweg: *N.F.S. Grundtvig's Mental Illness/N.F.S. Grundtvigs sindssygdom*.
Copenhagen: Henrik Koppel Press, 128 pp.
Hjalmar Helweg (1886-1960) was a leading psychiatrist of his time, and his brief book, while not a biography, presents the first attempt to deal with Grundtvig's psyche, diagnosed here as manic-depressive. His book is treated in the main text on pp. 308-09.

1925. J.P. Bang: *Grundtvig's Legacy/ Grundtvigs arv*.
Copenhagen: Church Society Press/Kirkeligt Samfunds Forlag, 2nd ed. 1930, 125 pp.
Jacob Peter Bang (1865-1936) was a moderate liberal theologian and Grundtvig supporter, also as Professor of Theology in Copenhagen from 1910-1924, when Grundtvig was out of fashion. As the title implies, his book is more about Grundtvig's legacy than about his life as such. Bang delineates 12 different areas of intellectual life to which Grundtvig has contributed: the nation, the common people, modernity, citizenship, education, the Church, foreignness, womanhood, emotions, the fight, enlightenment, and Grundtvig's view of humankind. The book ends with a discussion of Grundtvig's psyche, including the mental illness that Helweg had diagnosed as manic depression; Bang makes the point that Grundtvig *overcame* the challenges of his depression "to the benefit and growth of the people".

1929. Edvard Lehmann: *Grundtvig*.
Copenhagen: Jespersen and Pio, 249 pp.
Edvard Lehmann (1862-1930) was a liberal theologian and the first professor of the history of religion at Copenhagen University from 1900. He follows "the development of the great intellectual" and characterises Grundtvig as having "a wild, chaotic nature, for whom ... the tremors that struck ... in a lengthy fermentative process ... deepened his nature by fits and starts until it finally found its intellectual bearings." To this end he can refer to some of Grundtvig's letters, which had been published in two volumes a couple of years previously. He emphasises how Grundtvig's classical education in Aarhus and Copenhagen was the basis of both his historical writings and new versions of old poems from various languages. Lehmann is among the first to note how much Grundtvig's early thinking is influenced by Schelling and Fichte, and the idea that a life fulfilled must follow the individual conscience – as Grundtvig argued to his parents in 1810. His cultural call in Copenhagen was every bit as valid as his religious and filial call to be his father's curate in Udby. Lehmann makes an interesting point in calling Grundtvig both 'high church and 'low church' and ends his book with a chapter on Grundtvig the prophet: "Grundtvig's call was to give back to a small, weak people its belief in itself. He did so with a frantic energy – but he did it. He felt a call and followed it. And he got others to follow him".

1943. Johan Borup: *N.F.S. Grundtvig*.
Copenhagen: C.A. Reitzel's Press-Axel Sandal, 305 pp.
Johan Borup (1853-1946) was a theologian and the founder of a people's high school in his own name, which today is located by Frederiksholm's Canal in central Copenhagen. In typical high-school fashion he presents the phases of Grundtvig's life alongside the

phases that Grundtvig applies to world history – childhood, youth, adulthood, old age. He underlines how Grundtvig admired both the great, such as the most famous Danish romantic poet, Adam Oehlenschlæger, and also the small, in particular the peasant youth whom the high school movement was to lift up to a level where they could take over the leadership of Denmark. Borup is among the first biographers to accentuate Grundtvig's *political* activity as a direct consequence of his life and thought in the context of his domestic life through three marriages.

1944. Hal Koch: *Grundtvig*.
Copenhagen: Gyldendal (translated into English 1952), 205 pp.
Hal Koch (1904-1963) was Professor of Church History at Copenhagen University and for 10 years the Principal of Krogerup People's High School (1946-56). During the Second World War, when Denmark was occupied by Germany, he gave a series of well-attended and highly-praised public lectures on Grundtvig on which this book is based. Koch made a point of saying that he was not by nature a 'Grundtvigian', and for this reason his book was not coloured by any kind of canonisation. It is a reliable guide to Grundtvig, and rightly states that "both formally and professionally the hymns are the high point of Grundtvig's production" (p. 202). The Danish book's success in promoting Grundtvig's idea of a powerful spirit and tenable values for a nation meant that it merited a reprint of the Danish original in 2021.

1972. Ebbe Kløvedal Reich. *Frederik. A Popular Book on the Life and Times of N.F.S. Grundtvig/ En folkebog om N.F.S. Grundtvigs tid og liv.*
Copenhagen: Gyldendal, 402 pp.
Between 1945 and 1972 there were no new biographies of Grundtvig. Ebbe Kløvedal Reich (1940-2005) was in many ways the standard-bearer for the freedom-seeking youth of 1968. It was a time of economic growth for the welfare society and Reich's popular Grundtvig was a main contributor to the renaissance that saw a whole spate of books on Grundtvig published around the bicentenary of his birth in 1983. Kløvedal's version of Grundtvig is occasionally fanciful and not always source-based, but it makes some interesting observations. For instance, the crisis of 1810 was caused just as much by Grundtvig's inability to see a way forward with his life-form as it was by his dilemma over whether to obey his muse or his mother. Again, it was she who helped him into the pastorate in Præstø in 1821 without him even applying. The worst thing about Grundtvig's censorship was that it was now up to the state to authorise his worship of God. Finally it was the prospect of sickness and death due to the cholera outbreak in Copenhagen that led to Grundtvig's depression in 1853.

Ole Vind called the book "a combination of novel and modernist poetry ... turning Grundtvig into a freedom-fighter, an emancipated champion of the women's cause, and a psychedelic poet ... It is the most original book on Grundtvig that has ever been written and the most idiosyncratic expression of the spirit of 1968 in the Danish language."

1983. Poul Borum: *Grundtvig the Poet/Digteren Grundtvig*.
Copenhagen: Gyldendal, 281 pp.

Poul Borum (1934-96), considered by many to be the best Danish literary critic of his generation, surprised both the secular and the spiritual sector with this book. It was published in connection with the bicentenary of Grundtvig's birth in 1983 with the specific argument that Grundtvig is Denmark's best poet. When he was in the grip of his muse and his inspiration was a kind of 'fury', he exemplified the romantic poets at their best. Borum takes it for granted that Grundtvig's psyche and his poetic form were two sides of the same coin, and that his "matchless discovery of natural religion" in 1808 was part of this psychological process. This fundamental mode of religious awareness can take the form of natural mysticism and be put into practice as a kind of civil religion – a concept that Grundtvig cultivated particularly in his work with the Nordic myths. Borum also argues that, judged by literary criteria, Grundtvig's work is of the highest calibre, including his lecture series *Bragi Talks*, which many consider largely rigmarole.

1983. Ejvind Larsen, *The Living Word/Det levende ord. Om Grundtvig*.
Charlottenlund: Rosinante, 336 pp.

Ejvind Larsen (b. 1936) has been a journalist and editor of the left-wing daily *Information* and brings Grundtvig into play with Marx, Freud and Jung. In the 9 thematic essays of the book, he sees Grundtvig's life as a series of breakthroughs and discoveries from which we all can benefit: he swam against the tide and reached his goal. Larsen gives examples of how Grundtvig coped with his mental breakdown in 1810 and reacted to his popular breakthrough with *Nordic Mythology* in 1832. Like Poul Borum, Ejvind Larsen does not see a *development* from 'human comes first' to 'and Christian next', for they are an inseparable unit. Ejvind Larsen is the first to discuss contemporary problems (in this case of the 1970s) in the light of Grundtvig's thought. Reviewing the book in GS 1984 William Michelsen noted Ejvind Larsen's 'discovery' of Grundtvig's poem from 1842, 'The woman's gospel', and Grundtvig's *protestant* reverence for Mother Mary. The Grundtvig revival in the 1970s was just as much due to Ejvind Larsen as to Ebbe Kløvedal Reich, and it culminated in the bicentenary celebrations of 1983 for which Larsen published a 276-page selected texts as *Grundtvig's Birthday Present to the Danish People*, with an introduction by Kløvedal Reich.

1987. Hans Raun Iversen, *Spirit and Life-form, Home life, Public life and Church life in Grundtvig and since/Ånd og livsform. Husliv, folkeliv og kirkeliv hos Grundtvig og sidenhen*.
Aarhus: Anis Press, 263 pp.[478]

Hans Raun Iversen (b. 1948) uses as his primary sources Grundtvig's letters from England and from the First Schleswig War, as well as a number of articles in his own periodical *The Dane/Danskeren* 1848-1851. Iversen emphasises how the spirit, whose activity is free, links itself to the life-forms, where it thrives in some but is eradicated in others – as in the

---

478. The first half of the book has been translated by Edward Broadbridge as *Spirit and Life-Form. The Home, the People, and the Church in Grundtvig's Time and Today*. Montreal: IMPOR PLUS PRINTERS, 2013.

prospering people's high schools compared to the decaying grammar schools. The three 'lives' in the title co-exist in concentric circles, with home life at the centre, as Grundtvig's version of Luther's Three Estates: the Church (*ecclesia*), the household economy (*oeconomia*), and politics (*politia*). In Home life, faith, hope and love are learned and practised. In Public life these are developed through a common language, history, a Fatherland and a governing form. The outside circle includes the living and the dead, all of whom are purified through faith, hope, and love to the richness of heaven. In Grundtvig's thinking the three circles interact and overlap.

1993. Ulrich Vogel, *Knocked at the Door of Paradise. N.F.S. Grundtvigs Crises/Bankede på ved paradis. N.F.S. Grundtvigs kriseoplevelser*.
Frederiksberg: Anis Press, 144 pp.
Ulrich Vogel (b. 1961) sets out to present an alternative psychological theory to Helweg's diagnosis of Grundtvig as a manic-depressive, namely that his removal from his home in Udby to Thyregod at the age of 9 was such a traumatic experience that he sought to rediscover his childhood security for the rest of his life. The book is treated in the main text on p. 309.

2000 (repr. 2010). Finn Abrahamowitz: *Grundtvig. Congratulations, Denmark/Grundtvig. Danmark til lykke*.
Copenhagen: Information Press, 413 pp.
The most recent biography of Grundtvig has received much praise from a wide range of readers. One reviewer described how Finn Abrahamowitz (1939-2006) "sits behind the prophet and reads over his shoulder ... it is hard to imagine a better guide." The book's major drawback, however, is its lack of source references, so the author's statements about Grundtvig cannot be checked at source. Abrahamowitz was 'a people's high school man' with a wide-ranging authorship behind him before he turned to Grundtvig. With the many Grundtvig biographies to draw on he takes a balanced view rather than promote a particular theoretical interpretation. Abrahamowitz regards Grundtvig's inability to empathise with others and his own self-promotion as particular limitations, but he acknowledges that the upside of this is Grundtvig's willingness to fight throughout his life. However, on occasion the warrior-spirit was also his own worst enemy. First and foremost, however, Grundtvig was a man with a mission, one that was burned especially into his hymns and songs.

2015. Birgitte Stoklund Larsen: *The Shadow of Paradise. With Grundtvig in Love and Crisis/ Paradisskyggen. Med Grundtvig i kærlighed og krise*.
Copenhagen, Christian Daily Press, 192 pp.
Among the many thematic studies of Grundtvig in recent times, this book stands out for the quality of its biographical material. Birgitte Stoklund Larsen (b. 1960) takes the reader through the crises in Grundtvig's life with a focus on his loss of his second wife, Marie, in 1854, seen in the light of his understanding of 'love'. What carries him through the awful setback is the faith that the power of God's love can overcome his own helplessness, so he

now turns his belief in the resurrection upon himself. The book is a formidable counterbalance to the psychological interpretations of previous biographies, and demonstrates how Grundtvig *overcame* his crises through the strength of his faith.

2018. Ove Korsgaard: *Round About Grundtvig/Grundtvig rundt. En guide*.
Copenhagen: Gyldendal, 303 pp.
Ove Korsgaard (b. 1942) takes a walk round Grundtvig's conceptual world and presents him as a European thinker on a par with Rousseau, Kant, and Hegel. Grundtvig involved himself in his contemporary world, and always with a radical view of freedom, be it in education, the Church or social and political life. His purpose was to enlighten the Danish people regarding their history and language in order to gather the nation together around its true identity for 'the common good'. The book is the most up-to-date and all-round introduction to the comprehensive scholarship on Grundtvig together with Korsgaard's own contribution to it, which makes Grundtvig *topical* in the ongoing debate about identity. Reviewing the book for the daily paper *Information*, Georg Metz called it "a welcome and critical introduction and much more to the giga-phenomenon N.F.S. Grundtvig, whose importance for the history of Denmark and the national self-experience cannot be overestimated".

5. Primary sources

1877. *N.F.S. Grundtvig: Within Living Memory 1788-1838/Mands Minde 1788-1838*.
Copenhagen: Schønberg Press, 603 pp.
Collected and published by Svend Grundtvig, these talks contain the most detailed examples of Grundtvig's use of his own personal experiences. 14 of the 55 talks have been translated in vol. 4 of the series, N.F.S. Grundtvig: Works in English, 2019, pp. 41-171.

1948. *Grundtvig's Memoirs and Memoirs of Grundtvig/Grundtvigs Erindringer og Erindringer om Grundtvig*, ed. Steen Johansen & Henning Høirup.
Copenhagen: Gyldendal, 303 pp.
The Grundtvig archives are remarkably well preserved. This selection of memoirs, edited by Steen Johansen and Henning Høirup, is every bit as invaluable as the Diaries and Extracts as a work of scholarship on systematically selected and annotated texts. The editors refrain from commenting on the value of the texts as historical sources for the events they describe, an understandable decision when we know that Grundtvig's memoirs and his later reflections on them are often inseparable. Grundtvig freely drew on events from his own life to illustrate his personal views: on life in general, on the situation in Denmark, and indeed on the way of the world. As with the Diaries and Extracts, Grundtvig was always working on two or three projects at the same time, and he read widely in order to understand the subject-matter. He never found time to write his own autobiography as such, despite the extensive diaries and memories in these two books. The 112 pages of his own memoirs contain 8 chapters of memoirs up to 1824, followed by 3 memoirs of

his England trips, of his later years, and of the Church. The final 155 pages contain 69 memoirs by others of his life from 1800 until his death in 1872.

1979. *N.F.S. Grundtvig: Diaries and Extracts/Dag- og Udtogsbøger I-II*, ed. Gustav Albeck.
Copenhagen: Reitzel Press, 461 pp. + 279 pp.
In 1979 Gustav Albeck published an indispensable work in Danish to which all Grundtvig biographers are indebted. He gathered and assiduously annotated the source material that Grundtvig left behind into two volumes:

The volumes contain the day-to-day records that Grundtvig kept during his young adulthood, some of which he himself later revised with a new perspective. These are supplemented by his comments on extracts from works that he was reading as well as minutes he took of various meetings that he considered important for his work. The diaries run from 1800-07 and are followed by a few additions from 1810, 1813 and 1815 and a diary record of his first two trips to England in 1829 and 1830. From the later years there are a few entries, the last one being from 1855. Here then, we have a collection of 25 lengthy or shortish texts, the remainder of what we know to have been a larger collection.

Keeping a diary in Grundtvig's time was far from uncommon, but it was generally motivated by the wish either to commit to paper a particular experience, such as Grundtvig's secret love for Constance, or to write down thoughts to allow for later reflection, such as Grundtvig's extracts from Schiller's *The Bride of Messina*. In his early years as a writer Grundtvig sought to find his calling, and a private diary was a means of preserving thoughts and experiences that might be useful for later reflection.

2008. S.A.J. Bradley (trans. & ed.): *N.F.S. Grundtvig/A Life Recalled*: An Anthology of Biographical Source-Texts.
Aarhus: Aarhus University Press, 597 pp.
This comprehensive volume by Professor S.A.J. Bradley (b. 1936) contains translations of both the Diaries and the Memoirs. Bradley has been Professor of Anglo-Saxon Studies at the University of York and a long-time scholar of Grundtvig, with particular regard to Grundtvig's translations of Old English literature. His book draws on the three volumes mentioned above as well as on sermons, articles, and individual letters. Bradley translates a number of extracts from the first biography of Grundtvig in 1882 by Hans Brun, includes a useful timetable of Grundtvig's life, and concludes with 150 pages of lexical information on Grundtvig that is unavailable elsewhere in English – or a good deal of it in Danish for that matter.

Doctoral theses and PhD dissertations

Alongside the above biographies the series entitled *Writings Published by the Grundtvig Society/Skrifter udgivet af Grundtvig Selskabet*. currently contains 41 volumes. In addition there have been a number of doctoral theses in Danish with a thematic focus that are relevant in our context:

Doctoral theses[479]

1949 Henning Høirup on Faith and Cognition
1950 Helge Toldberg on Grundtvig's World of Symbols
1961 Sigurd Aarnes on Grundtvig's View of History
1963 Kaj Thaning on Grundtvig's View of Human Life
1969 Knud Eyvin Bugge on Grundtvig's Educational Ideas
1980 Flemming Lundgreen-Nielsen on the Active Word
1988 Helge Grell 1988 on the Creator's Spirit and the People's Spirit
1998 Bent Christensen on the Concept of Learning
1999 Ole Vind on the History and Philosophy
2004 Synnøve Heggem on the Understanding of Love
2004 Ove Korsgaard on the concept of Cultural Education
2005 Sune Auken on Mythology and Christianity
2008 Regner Birkelund on the concept of Freedom
2022 Thorstein Balle on Grundtvig's influence on the Public Schools (submitted)

Recent PhD dissertations

1989 Peter Balslev-Clausen on Grundtvig's Hymn-writing
1993 Ulrich Vogel 1993 on Grundtvig's Psyche
2009 Anders Holm on Grundtvig and Kierkegaard
2012 Espen Lunde Larsen on the concept of Freedom
2013 Katrine Frøkjær Baunvig on the concept of the Community
2013 (in English) Wen Ge on Public Theology
2013 Ole Nyborg on the Understanding of Love in Grundtvig's Sermons
2014 Therese Bering Solten on the concept of Faith in Grundtvig's Hymns
2014 Lea Wierød on Hymn-singing
2016 Jørgen Thaarup on Grundtvig and Wesley
2018 Vanja Thaulow on Grundtvig's Polemical Form.

Sources for both the Biography and the Letters

Georg Christensen and Stener Grundtvig. *Letters from and to N.F.S. Grundtvig/Breve fra og til N.F.S. Grundtvig I* (1807-1820) and *II* (1821-1872).
Edited by Georg Christensen and Stener Grundtvig.
Copenhagen: Gyldendal, 1924-26, 545 & 652 pp.
The 696 letters in these two volumes, the vast majority *from* Grundtvig, give us a glimpse into Grundtvig's personality and the most important themes and moments of his life. They are fewer and farther between in his later years, when they are more often occasioned by Grundtvig's need to justify his views. The one of the collectors and publishers of this standard collection was Grundtvig's grandson via Johan, Stener Grundtvig, a prison lawyer and later district court judge. His co-editor was Georg Christensen, a colleague

---

479. A doctoral thesis in Denmark is a higher degree than a PhD.

of Professor Hal Koch during the publication of the 10-volume *Grundtvig's Selected Works I-X/Grundtvigs Værker i udvalg I-X*, Copenhagen: Gyldendal, 1940-49.

N.F.S. Grundtvig's Letters to and from his wife during the England trips 1829-31. Published by their grandchildren/N.F.S. Grundtvigs breve til og fra hans hustru under Englandsrejserne 1829-31. Udgivne af deres Børnebørn.
Copenhagen: Aage Marcus, 1920, 203 pp.

This collection is the most important source for Grundtvig's three summer trips to England 1829-31, when he was away for four months at a time. They reveal Grundtvig's initial loneliness and disappointment at his reception – "the English are so *busy*" – and document his increasing enthusiasm for the people's dynamic and concept of freedom; but how he misses his family! Meanwhile the loyal Lise encourages and comforts her husband, ensuring him that their young children are thriving. As the letters progress, we can see how Grundtvig realises his acute dependence on his wife and children, for he has never found it easy to make friends. The book contains useful background information and a preface by Stener Grundtvig, which includes a portrait of his grandmother (d. 1851) – to whom the grandchildren are still so grateful in 1920.

N.F.S. Grundtvig and his closest family during the First Schleswig War, a correspondence /N.F.S. Grundtvig og hans nærmeste slægt under tre-årskrigen, En Brevvexling. Edited by Ingeborg Simesen.
Copenhagen: G.E.C. Gads Forlag, 1933, 525 pp.

During the First Schleswig War (1848-51) both Johan and Svend volunteered for service and were sent to the southern front with Germany, where they were both swiftly promoted and later decorated. Unlike many of their friends and comrades they survived the war. The editor Ingeborg Simesen grew up in a family that was closely linked to Laura Grundtvig, Svend's wife. As she remarks, despite all his paternal love for his sons, the fate of Denmark was uppermost in Grundtvig's mind. The majority of the parents' letters are written by Lise, who was more concerned about their sons' well-being.

Grundtvig and Ingemann. A Correspondence 1821-1859/Grundtvig og Ingemann. Brevvexling 1821-1859. Published and prefaced by Svend Grundtvig.
Copenhagen: Society for the Promotion of Danish Literature/Samfundet til Den Danske Litteraturs Fremme, 1882, 328 pp.

Svend Grundtvig inherited his father's love of history and literature and edited this complete collection of letters between Grundtvig and his most important literary friend. The two stand side by side as the greatest contributors to the Danish treasury of hymns and songs, with Ingemann being the softer of the two, as Grundtvig occasionally reminded him. In his preface Svend Grundtvig wrote that his father saw in Ingemann his spiritual partner and "felt himself fortunate to have won the friendship and sympathy of this mild poet".

Christian Molbech and N.F.S. Grundtvig. A correspondence/Christian Molbech og N.F.S. Grundtvig. En Brevvexling. Collected by K.F. Molbech and edited by Ludvig Schrøder.
Copenhagen: Gyldendal, 1888, 251 pp.
For a portrait of Christian Molbech (1783-1857) see pp. 96-99. His son collected this correspondence, which was edited by Grundtvig's biographer, Ludwig Schrøder.

Gunni Busck. Life in a country vicarage/Et Levnetsløb i en Landsbypræstegaard. Edited by Henrik Beck.
Copenhagen: Carl Schønberg's Press, 1869, 332 pp.
Gunni Busck (1798-1869) was originally a lawyer but became Pastor of Stigs Bjergby in 1824, and of Brøndbyøster in 1844. Busck was Grundtvig's loyal and eloquent supporter from his battle with the Church and the university's rationalist theology to the end of his life. Out of his inheritance he regularly donated to Grundtvig's economy and projects, not least the *Song-Work for the Danish Church*. The correspondence reveals in particular Grundtvig's thoughts on the Apostolic Creed, the recognition of opponents such as Bishop Mynster, and the need to control his own temperament.

Frederik Barfod: *Peter Andreas Fenger. A life portrait/En levnedstegning*.
Copenhagen: Carl Schønberg's Press, 1878, 208 pp.
Like his brother Johannes (1805-61), Peter Fenger (1799-1878) was a pupil of Grundtvig when he was curate to their father Pastor Rasmus Fenger at the Church of Our Saviour in Christianshavn. With their publications and organisational work both were important figures in the Church debate. Peter was Pastor of Slots Bjergby from 1827 and the Church of Our Saviour from 1855. Just as Christen Kold implemented Grundtvig's educational ideas, so did Fenger and others implement his ideas to improve the Church. Fenger was far more sympathetic towards the Revivalist gatherings and the Foreign Mission movement, but he supported Grundtvig in his overhaul of the Danish hymnbook and his battle to break the parish-tie.

Peter Rørdam. Leaves from his Life and Correspondence/Peter Rørdam. Blade af hans Levnetsbog og Brevvexling. Edited by Holger Rørdam. Vols I-III.
Copenhagen: Carl Schønberg's Press, 1891, 1892 & 1895, 284, 311, & 575 pp.
Peter Rørdam (1806-83) was in many ways the most prominent yet closest of Grundtvig's pastoral friends. He married Marie Toft's sister, Jutta Carlsen (1815-66), thereby becoming Grundtvig's brother-in-law. He was Pastor of Mern from 1841 and of Lyngby from 1856. This comprehensive set contains in particular letters to and from Grundtvig and the dowager Queen Caroline Amalie, who were both attracted by Rørdam's engaging wit and drive. The Grundtvig letters are like a correspondence between father and son, one who followed his father into the Church, unlike Grundtvig's own two sons, and became an active 'people's pastor', which Grundtvig himself never aspired to be. Rørdam was musically gifted and a useful sounding-board for Grundtvig's new hymns. Rørdam also helped Grundtvig with his political work in 1848-49 and his views on the Schleswig problem.

N.F.S. Grundtvig's Letters from England to Queen Caroline Amalie/N.F.S. Grundtvigs Breve fra England til Dronning Caroline Amalie 1843. Edited by Frederik Lange Grundtvig. Special issue of the journal *The Dane/Danskeren*.
Copenhagen: Carl Schønberg's Press, 1891.

Queen Caroline Amalie (1796-1881), who was married to Christian VIII (reigned 1839-48) was a faithful supporter of Grundtvig from their first meeting in 1838. She attended divine service in Vartov Church in the winter and in Lyngby Church in the summer, where Peter Rørdam was pastor. She sponsored Grundtvig's fourth trip to England and Scotland in 1843, from where he wrote these letters to her – collected and edited by his third son.

98. The Grundtvig Memorial Rooms at Udby.

Appendix 1

Memorials to Grundtvig

Grundtvig's Memorial Rooms

The Memorial Rooms have been furnished in Grundtvig's childhood home in Udby, in the wing where he lived when he was curate for his father, Pastor Johan Grundtvig from 1811-13. The **Information Room** contains many of his publications and the chasuble he wore as Pastor of Vartov Church in central Copenhagen from 1839-72 see p. 280. The **Small Living Room** contains the Bible that Lady Constance Leth of Egeløkke Manor gave Grundtvig in 1807 see p. 126. On the walls you can see pictures of the churches, vicarages, and manor-houses that Grundtvig frequented from 1811-21. The **Small Room** exhibits portraits of Grundtvig at various stages of his life, as well as portraits of his three wives and the many members of their families. The **Study** has illustrations of episodes and relationships in Grundtvig's many-sided public life. One grouping shows some of Grundtvig's many homes: Vimmelskaftet in central Copenhagen, 'Happy Home' on Gammel Kongevej, 'Great Tuborg' in Hellerup, and Grundtvig's own people's high school, 'Marie's Pleasure' in Nørrebro. Preserved on the writing-table are a few of Grundtvig's personal items. The plant in the window is a cutting from a cactus that Grundtvig brought home with him from one of his trips to England. The **Main Living Room** exhibits furniture from Grundtvig's study at Great Tuborg: the writing-table and chair, the writing-desk, the armchair see p. 270, a bookcase in Egyptian style, and a folding-table. The large painting was a gift to Grundtvig on his 70th birthday from Danish and Norwegian women.

Grundtvig's Church and Statues

In the Copenhagen suburb of Bispebjerg stands 'Grundtvig's Church' – built in his memory with a monumental 6 million yellow bricks! Designed by architect Peder Vilhelm Jensen Klint in the Expressionist style and constructed between 1921 and 1940, the tourist magnet merges the scale and stylings of a Gothic cathedral with the aesthetics of a Danish country church. Among its most interesting features are the three towers and the three entries on each side of the church – a symbol of the Trinity of Father, Son, and Holy Spirit. All 1,863 seats were occupied when Grundtvig's Church was consecrated by King Christian X on 8 September 1940, the 157th anniversary of Grundtvig's birthday in 1783. The church is open to visitors all year, not just at the times of services. The great Marcussen organ is regularly used for concerts. The architecture mirrors the weight and complexity of Grundtvig's spirit, which reverberates through the building.

Two statues of Grundtvig also stand in central Copenhagen, one outside the Marble Church and one in the courtyard of Vartov.

The Grundtvig Library

The Grundtvig Library is a private library, owned by Grundtvig's Forum, and open to the public. Anyone interested in N.F.S. Grundtvig is welcome to make use of the facilities. Books can be read in the library only. The library contains:

- Grundtvig's published writings
- separate editions of Grundtvig's speeches
- Grundtvig's hymns and songs
- books by Grundtvig's contemporaries
- periodicals from "the Grundtvigian era"

Anyone studying subjects related to Grundtvig is welcome to ask for a stay at Vartov in one of the guestrooms.

The Grundtvig Prize

The annual Grundtvig prize of DKK 25,000 ($3,500) was established in 2010 by Grundtvig's Forum. A list of the prizewinners can be found in Danish at https://grundtvig.dk/grundtvigsk-forum/n-f-s-grundtvigs-pris/.

The Golden Grundtvig

Since 1999 Odder People's High School has also awarded an annual Grundtvig prize of DK 10,000 ($1,500), known as the Golden Grundtvig and sponsored by architects Hune and Elkjær. https://www.odderhojskole.dk/den-gyldne-grundtvig/

99. **Grundtvig's Church** in Bispebjerg, Copenhagen. Photo: Niels Poulsen / Alamy Stock Photo.

Appendix 2

Grundtvig's Addresses[480]

Date	Address	Duration
9. 1783 – 8. 1792	Udby vicarage, Pasmergaardsvej 13, Udby	9 years
8. 1792 – 9. 1798	Thyregodlund vicarage, Vesterlundsvej 84, Thyregod	6 years
9. 1798 – 9. 1800	Skolegade 42, Aarhus, possibly elsewhere	2 years
10. 1800 – 11. 1803	Lille Brøndstræde 17 & Store Kongensgade 57, Cph.	3 years
11. 1803 – 6. 1804	Udby og Torkilstrup vicarages, Torkilstrupvej 14	8 mths
Summer 1804	Pilestræde 27, Cph.	2 mths
8. 1804 – 9. 1804	Hyskenstræde 8, Cph.	1 mth
10. 1804 – 3. 1805	Udby vicarage – and possibly Torkilstrup	5 mths
3. 1805 – 4. 1808	Egeløkke Manor, Egeløkkevej 3, Langeland	3 years
5. 1808 – 6. 1811	Valkendorfs Kollegium, St. Peders Stræde 14, Cph.	3 years
6. 1811 – 10. 1813	Udby vicarage (as curate)	2½ years
10. 1813 – 11. 1813	Store Strandstræde 20, Cph.	1 mth
11. 1813 – 5. 1814	Holmens Kanal 22 (with Lise and her mother), Cph.	6 mths
5. 1814 – 5. 1818	Kronprinsessegade 44, Cph.	4 years
5. 1818 – 8. 1818	Vingaardsstræde 9 (with Lise and her mother), Cph.	6 mths
8. 1818 – 2. 1820	Løngangsstræde 29, Cph. (with Lise)	1½ years
2. 1820 – 6. 1821	Kronprinsessegade 12, Cph.	1½ years
6. 1821 – 11. 1822	Torvestræde 7, Præstø (as pastor)	1½ years
12. 1822 – 4. 1823	Torvegade 25, Christianshavn	6 mths
4. 1823 – 10. 1827	Prinsessegade 52, Cph.	5 years
10. 1827 – 4. 1828	Prinsessegade 50, Cph.	6 mths
4. 1828 – 4. 1840	Strandgade 4B 3rd floor, Cph.	12 years
4. 1840 – 4. 1850	Vimmelskaftet 49 2nd floor, Cph.	10 years
4. 1850 – 10. 1850	Løngangsstræde 23, Cph.	6 mths
10. 1850 – 4. 1851	Stormgade 17, Cph.	6 mths
4. 1851 – 4. 1852	Nybrogade 12, Cph.	1 year
4. 1852 – 4. 1855	Frederiksholms Kanal 16, Cph.	3 years
4. 1855 – 10. 1857	Nørregade 5, Cph.	2½ years
10. 1857 – 5. 1859	Larslejsstræde 12, Cph.	1½ years
5. 1859 – 4. 1867	Gammel Kongevej 148 (Happy Home), Frederiksberg	7 years
4. 1867 – 9. 1867	Nybrovej 455, Frederiksdal (rest cure)	6 mths
9. 1867 – 9. 1872	Strandvej 123 (Great Tuborg), Hellerup	5 years

---

480. Our thanks to Lars Thorkild Bjørn for his list from 2009 and for information in Appendix 4.

Appendix 3

Grundtvig's Marriages and Descendants

Grundtvig had 3 wives, 5 children, and 9 grandchildren. Below are the descendants we have so far traced:

Grundtvig's children with Lise
1. **Johan Grundtvig** (1822-1907) married Mine Stenersen (1828-93) in 1855 and had 6 children:
   1. Johanne Elisabeth (1856-1945), unmarried.
   2. Olivia Ninni Vilhelmine (1858-73).
   3. Stener Frederik (1860-1942), married first Astrid Søndergaard Myhre (1860-98) and had 2 children: Jesper (1886-1950) and Otto (1889-1961). He then married Anna Louise Quittenbaum (1863-1951).
   4. Meta Laura (1861-84).
   5. Gustav Vilhelm (1866-1950).
   6. Johanne Vilhelmine (1869-1901).
2. **Svend Grundtvig** (1824-83) married Laura Bloch (1837-91) in 1858 and had no children.
3. **Meta Grundtvig** (1827-87) married Peter Boisen in 1847 and had 3 children:
   1. Anna Elisabeth Sysette (1850-1919) was unmarried.
   2. Nicolai Frederik (1852-1908) married Cæcilie Nielsen.
   3. Harald Immanuel (1857-1904) married Christel Bock (died); then Ingeborg Bardenfleth in 1903 and had a son, Ingolf Boisen (1904-90), Grundtvig's great-grandson. Ingold married Tove Hebo (1916-66) in 1940 and had a child: Harald. He then married Ilta Hensingius (1910-68) in 1942.

Grundtvig's child with Marie
4. **Frederik Lange Grundtvig** (1854-1905) married Kristina Birgitte Nielsson (1848-1905) in 1881 and had 1 child:
   1. Marie Margaretha Lange Grundtvig (1883 1944) married Karsten Lorange and had 3 children: Frederik (1913-99), Carsten (1915-61), and an adopted daughter, Margrethe 'Grethe' Bechshøft. Carsten married Ingalill Ceder in 1952, but had no children.

Grundtvig's child with Asta
5. **Asta Marie Elisabeth Frijs Grundtvig** (1860-1939) married Kristian Poulsen (1854-1931) in 1881 and had 2 children:
   1. Nicolai Frederik Severin (1882-1961) married Marie Andersen (1884-1935) and had 2 children: Holger Ejner Christian Frederik Grundtvig (1911-96) and Kirsten Grundtvig Poulsen (1921-2008). Holger Ejner married Else Schreiber (1911-96).
   2. Amalie Louise Benedicte (1884-85).

Appendix 4

Grundtvig's Political Career

1848: Grundtvig lost the election to the Constituent Assembly in **Nyboder** with 313 votes to the 369 of his opponent, Captain Nicolas Tuxen. Even with the signatures of some 2,000 people he was not legally appointed by the King. At a local re-election in **Præstø**, he was not elected with 573 votes to the 11 (sic) of his rival, Jens Jensen.

1849: 1st June. Grundtvig abstained in the vote to pass the Constitutional Bill. This was signed into law by King Frederik VII on 5th June, known ever since as Constitution Day. It contained a Lower House and an Upper House. 4th December: at the election to the Lower House in the new Parliament in **Præstø** Grundtvig defeated Lars Larsen by 457 votes to 374. On a bitterly cold day the turn-out was only 39.8%.

1850: The War Expenditure Act, the Local Government Act, and the Freedom of the Press Act were passed.

1851: Grundtvig spoke on Civil Marriage and International Trade.

1852: New Parliamentary Election, Grundtvig did not stand.

1853: At a local election in **Skælskør** Grundtvig narrowly defeated Søren Jensen by 571 to 563 votes. Less than 3 months later there was a general election, where in Skælskør Grundtvig lost to the same Søren Jensen with 412 votes against 582.

1854: Grundtvig won a by-election in **Præstø.**

1855: 4th April. The bill on breaking the parish-tie was passed on 4th April 1855; this was Grundtvig's greatest parliamentary success. At the general election on 14th June, the constituency of **Kerteminde** held a revote, which Grundtvig won with 499 votes to 212 for the blacksmith Niels Hansen.

1856: In Christiansborg Palace Church Grundtvig presided at the opening worship service of the 8th parliament, where he also sat.

1857: The 8th parliament passed the Trade Act granting unmarried women aged 25 and above parity with men as regards licence to trade and right to inheritance. Aged 75, Grundtvig stood down at the next general election held on 14th June 1858.

1866: On 23rd June the 83-year-old Grundtvig stood in the constituency of **Horsens** for election to the Upper House (which ran from 1849-1953) to vote against a reduction in the franchise. On 26th July Grundtvig and his fellow senior parliamentarian Anton Tscherning asked the King to stop the bill, but in vain. Grundtvig retired from politics.

Appendix 5

Monarchs and Bishops in Grundtvig's Time

The Oldenburg royal house	
Christian VII, 1749-1808, king from 1766	Caroline Mathilde of Great Britain, 1751-75
Frederik VI, 1768-1839, king from 1808	Marie Sophie Frederikke of Hessen-Kassel, 1767-1852
Christian VIII, 1786-1848, king from 1839	1. Charlotte Frederikke of Mecklenburg-Schwerin, 1784-1840 2. Caroline Amalie of Augustenborg, 1796-1881
Frederik VII, 1808-83, king from 1848	1. Vilhelmine of Danmark, 1808-91 2. Mariane of Mecklenburg-Strelitz, 1821-76 3. Louise Rasmussen (Countess Danner), 1815-74
The Glücksborg royal house	
Christian IX, 1818-1906, king from 1863	Louise of Hessen-Kassel 1817-98

Bishops of Zealand

1783-1808	Nicolai Edinger Balle, 1744-1816
1808-30	Friedrich Christian Carl Hinrich Münter, 1761-1830
1830-34	Peter Erasmus Müller, 1776-1834
1834-54	Jakob Peter Mynster, 1775-1854
1854-84	Hans Lassen Martensen, 1808-84

100. Celebrating midsummer at Vartov. The building complex known as Vartov in the heart of Copenhagen is central to Grundtvig's life and legacy. It is owned and run by Grundtvig's Forum, and includes the Grundtvig Library and the Grundtvig Academy. The latter arranges diverse lectures, study-groups, and conferences throughout the country on faith, the Church, community life, art, culture, and such-like. Also at Vartov is Grundtvig's old church, where he was pastor from 1839-72. Today it is home to the Vartov Independent Congregation. On Midsummer Day a 'Marathon Song' event is held from 7 in the morning till 10.30 at night where several hundred participants sing their way through the People's High School Songbook.

Bibliography

Titles are listed alphabetically by author

Part I: Works in English

1. Translations of Grundtvig's work

Bradley, S.A.J. (trans. & ed.). (2008). *N.F.S. Grundtvig / A Life Recalled: An anthology of biographical source-texts*. Aarhus: Aarhus University Press.

Broadbridge, E. (2009). *Hymns in English*. Copenhagen: Det Kgl. Vajsenhus' Forlag. Includes 20 hymns by Grundtvig, all reproduced in *Living Wellsprings* (2015).

Broadbridge, E. (2011-23) N.F.S. Grundtvig. Works in English, 6-volume series:
vol. 1. *The School For Life. N.F.S. Grundtvig on Education for the People* (2011)
vol. 2. *Living Wellsprings. The Hymns, Songs, and Poems of N.F.S. Grundtvig* (2015)
vol. 3. *Human Comes First. The Christian Theology of N.F.S. Grundtvig* (2018)
vol. 4. *The Common Good. N.F.S. Grundtvig as Politician and Contemporary Historian* (2019)
vol. 5. *The Core of Learning. The Philosophical Writings of N.F.S. Grundtvig* (2021)
vol. 6. *Denmark's Catalyst. The Life and Letters of N.F.S. Grundtvig* (2023)

Holm, A. (2019). *The Essential N.F.S. Grundtvig* (trans. Broadbridge, E.). Aarhus: FILO.

Irons, J. (2013). *Easter flower! What would you here?* Odense: University Press of Southern Denmark.

Jensen, N.L. (trans. & ed.) / Broadbridge, E. (trans.), Michelsen, W., Albeck, G., Toftdahl, H. and Thodberg, C.(eds.) (1984). *A Grundtvig Anthology: Selections from the Writings of N.F.S. Grundtvig (1783-1872)*. Cambridge: James Clark and Co.; Viby, Denmark: Centrum.

Knudsen, J. (trans. & ed.) (1976). *Selected Writings: N.F.S. Grundtvig*. Philadelphia: Fortress Press.

Lawson, M. (1991). *N.F.S. Grundtvig: Selected Educational Writings*. Elsinore: International. People's College/The Association of Folk High Schools.

Nielsen, E.D. (trans. & ed.) (1985) *What Constitutes Authentic Christianity?* Philadelphia: Fortress Press. A translation of *Om den sande Kristendom* (1826).

Petersen, K.S. (trans. & ed.) (2009) *New Year's Morning: 1824*. Copenhagen: Forlaget Vartov. A bi-lingual version of Grundtvig's 312-stanza poem. For translations of individual hymns and songs see Index 7 in *Living Wellsprings* (2015).

2. Biographies and introductions

Allen, E.L. (1947). *Bishop Grundtvig. A Prophet of the North*. London: James Clarke.

Allchin, A.M. (Donald). (1997, repr. 2015). *N.F.S. Grundtvig: An Introduction to His Life and Work*. Aarhus: Aarhus University Press.

Davies, N. (1931). *Education for Life: a Danish Pioneer*. London: Williams & Norgate.

Davies, N. (1944). *Grundtvig of Denmark: a guide to small nations*. Liverpool: The Bryerthon Press.

Iversen, H.R. (2013). *Spirit and Life-Form. The Home. The People and the Church in Grundtvig's Time and Today*. Montreal: Impor Plus Printers.

Knudsen, J. (1955). *Danish Rebel. A Study of N.F.S. Grundtvig*. Philadelphia: Muhlenberg Press.

Koch, H. (1952). *Grundtvig* (trans. & ed. Jones, L. from orig. Danish by Koch, H (1944)). Yellow Springs, Ohio: The Antioch Press.

Lindhardt, P.G. (1951). *Grundtvig, an Introduction*. London: SPCK.

Nielsen, E.D. (1955). *N.F.S. Grundtvig. An American Study*. Rock Island, Illinois: Augustana Press.

Thaning, K. (1972). (trans. Hohnen, D.). *N.F.S. Grundtvig*. Copenhagen: Danish Cultural Institute.

3. Other Books Contributing to Grundtvig's Biography

Allchin, A.M., Jasper, D., Schjørring, J., & Stevenson, K. (eds.) (1993). *Heritage and Prophecy: Grundtvig and the English-Speaking World*. Aarhus: Aarhus University Press.

Allchin, A., Bradley, S.A.J., Hjelm, N. & Schjørring, J. (eds.) (2000). *Grundtvig in International Perspective: Studies in the Creativity of Interaction*. Aarhus: Aarhus University Press.

Bhattacharya, A. (2010). *Education for the People: Concepts of Grundtvig, Tagore, Gandhi and Freire*. Rotterdam: Sense Publishers.

Borish, S.M. (1991). *The Land of the Living. The Danish folk high school and Denmark's non-violent path to modernization*. Nevada City: Blue Dolphin Publishing.

Bradley, S.A.J. (trans. & ed.) (2008). *N.F.S. Grundtvig / A Life Recalled: An anthology of biographical source-texts*. Aarhus: Aarhus University Press.

Brochner, J. (1903). *Danish Life in Town and Country*. London, G.P. Putnam's Sons.

Bugge, K.E. (1999). *Canada and Grundtvig*. Vejle, DK: Krogh.

Bugge, K.E. (2001). *Folk High Schools in Bangladesh*, Odense, DK: University Press of Southern Denmark.

Campbell, J.L., Hall, J.A., and Pedersen, O.K. (eds). (2005). *National Identity and the Varieties of Capitalism. The Danish Experience*. Montreal et al: McGill-Queens University Press.

Christiansen, N.F., Petersen, K., Edling, N. & Haave, P. (eds) (2006). *The Nordic Model of Welfare. A Historical*

Reappraisal. Copenhagen: Museum Tusculanum.

Desmond, S. (1918). *The Soul of Denmark.* London: Unwin.

Foght, H. (1915). *The Danish Folk High Schools.* New York: Macmillan.

Gerle, Elisabeth & Michael Schelde (red.) (2018). *American Perspectives meet Scandinavian Creation Theology.* Aarhus University: Grundtvig Study Center.

Gregersen, N-H., Kristensson, B.U., Wyller, T. (eds.). *Reformation Theology for a Post-Secular Age: Logstrup, Prenter, Wingren, and the Future of Scandinavian Creation Theology.* Göttingen: Vandenhoeck & Ruprecht.

Haggard, R. (1911). *Rural Denmark and its Lessons.* London, Longman, Green & Co.

Hall, J.A., Korsgaard, O., and Pedersen, O.K. (eds.) (2015). *Building the Nation. N.F.S. Grundtvig and National Identity.* Copenhagen: DJØF Publishing.

Hollman, A.H. (1936). *Democracy in Denmark*, part II (trans. from German by Alice G. Brandeis). Washington DC: National Home Library Foundation.

Horton, M. (1998). *The Long Haul: An Autobiography.* New York: Teachers College Press.

Institute, the Danish, (1983). *Grundtvig's Ideas in North America*, Scandinavian Seminar College.

Jensen, C. (2021). *Equality in the Nordic Countries.* Aarhus: Aarhus University Press.

Korsgaard, O. (2008). *The Struggle for the People. Five Hundred Years of Danish History in Short.* Copenhagen: Danish School of Education Press.

Korsgaard, O. (2014). *N.F.S. Grundtvig – as a Political Thinker.* Copenhagen: DJØF Publishing.

Korsgaard, O. (2019). *A Foray into Folk High School Ideology.* Copenhagen: FFD.

Korsgaard, O. (2022). *Peoplehood in the Nordic World.* Aarhus: Aarhus University Press.

Kulich, J. (2002). *Grundtvig's Educational Ideas in Central and Eastern Europe and the Baltic States in the Twentieth Century.* Copenhagen: Vartov.

Martin, G.O. (1950). *N.F.S. Grundtvig: the Man and his Theology.* New York: Columbia University.

Mortensen, E. (1977). *Schools for Life: A Danish-American Experiment in Adult Education.* Danish-American Heritage Society.

Rothery, A. (1937). *Denmark, Kingdom of Reason.* London: Faber and Faber.

Strode, H. (1951). *Denmark is a Lovely Land.* New York: Harcourt, Brace & Co.

Thodberg, C. & Thyssen, A. (eds.) (1983) *N.F.S. Grundtvig: Tradition and Renewal.* Copenhagen: Danish Cultural Institute.

Zøllner, L. (1994). *Grundtvig's Educational Ideas in Japan, the Philippines, and Israel* (translated from the Danish by Anna Marie Andersen): Vejle: Nornesalen and Kroghs Forlag.

Part II: Works in Danish

Abrahamowitz, F. ([2000] 2010). *Grundtvig. Danmark til lykke*. Copenhagen: Information.

Albeck, G. (1945). *Grundtvigs slemme Skolegang*. Aarhus: Aros.

Albeck, G. (1953). 'Grundtvigs Vej til de norrøne Skrifter', GS 1953, 103-11.

Albeck, G. (1954). 'Strandbakken ved Egeløkke og Havet'. GS 1954, 22-29.

Albeck, G. (1959). 'Huslæreren på Egeløkke'. GS 1959, 78-98.

Albeck, G. (1985). 'Den unge Grundtvig og Norge'. GS 1985, 47-66.

Albeck, G. (1968). 'Grundtvig og Jylland'. GS 1968, 9-32.

Allchin, A.M. (2002). *Grundtvigs kristendom. Menneskeliv og gudstjeneste*. Aarhus: Aarhus University Press.

Arnholtz, A. (1952). 'Grundtvigs salmer og deres melodier'. GS 1952, 7-38.

Auken, S. (2005). *Sagas Spejl. Mytologi, historie og kristendom hos N.F.S. Grundtvig*. Copenhagen: Gyldendal.

Balle, T, Haue, H. & Schelde, M. (eds.) (2013). *Nordisk pædagogisk tradition? – mellem Grundtvig og Ny Nordisk Skole*. Gymnasiepædagogik 94. Odense: Odense University Press.

Balle, T. (2022). *Grundtvigs skolevej*. Aarhus: Aarhus University Press.

Balslev-Clausen, P. (1989). *Motiv og struktur. N.F.S. Grundtvigs salmedigtning*. Copenhagen: Faculty of Theology, University of Copenhagen.

Balslev-Clausen, P. (1991). *Den vingede ord. Om N.F.S. Grundtvigs salmedigtning*. Frederiksberg: Materialecentralen.

Balslev-Clausen, P. (1991). 'Drøm og virkelighed'. Copenhagen: Hymnologiske Meddelelser.

Balslev-Clausen, P. (1991). 'Urolige Hjerte, Omkring Grundtvigs salmer fra 1851'. Copenhagen: Hymnologiske Meddelelser.

Balslev-Clausen, P. & Iversen, H.R. (eds.) (2014). *Salmesang. Grundbog i hymnologi*. Copenhagen: Det Kgl. Vajsenhus.

Balslev-Clausen, P. (2016) 'Gaade-Speil i Jærtegns Hall' (unpublished).

Bang, J.P. (1925, repr. 1930). *Grundtvigs arv*. Copenhagen: Kirkeligt Samfund.

Bang, J.P. (1932). *Grundtvig og England*. Copenhagen: Kirkeligt Samfund.

Barfod, F. (1878). *Peter Andreas Fenger. En levnedstegning*. Copenhagen: Schønberg.

Barfod, F. (1900). *Dronning Karoline Amalie*. 2nd ed. Copenhagen: Diakonissestiftelsen.

Barfod, H.P. (1898). *Minder fra gamle grundtvigske Hjem*. Copenhagen: Gad.

Baunvig, K.F. (2013) *Forsamlingen først. N.F.S. Grundtvigs og Émile Durkheims syn på fællesskab*. Aarhus University: Graduate School of Arts.

Baunvig, K.F. (2014). 'Det folkelige foredrag'. *Ved lejlighed. Grundtvig genrerne*. Ed. Auken, S. & Sunesen, C. Copenhagen: Spring.

Beck, H. (ed.) (1869) *Gunni Busck. Et Levnetsløb i en Landsbypræstegaard*, Copenhagen: Schønberg.

Begtrup, H. (1899). *N.F.S. Grundtvigs kristelige Opvækkelse i Vinteren 1810-11*. Copenhagen: Schønberg.

Begtrup, H. (1925). 'N.F.S. Grundtvig. Vartov-præster gennem 80 år – 1839-1919'. Ed. Barfod, H.P.B. Copenhagen: Gad.

Bethge L. & Hardt, N. (2020). *Danevirke. Danmarks fødselsattest og verdens kulturarv*. Danevirke Museum.

Bjerg, S. (2002). *Gud først og sidst. Grundtvigs teologi – en læsning af Den Christelige Børnelærdom*. Copenhagen: Anis.

Blom, M. (1921). 'Minder fra N.F.S. Grundtvigs og fru Lise Grundtvigs Hjem 1830-50', in *Minder fra gamle grundtvigske Hjem*, vol.1, ed. Barfod, H.P.B. Copenhagen: Gad.

Boisen, E. (1985, 9th. ed.). *Men størst er kærligheden – erindringer fra midten af forrige århundrede*. Ed. Bojsen-Møller, E., G., & J. + Haarder, B. Copenhagen: Gyldendal.

Bojsen-Møller, J. (2007). *Grundtvig og Marie – en fortælling fra Rønnebæksholm*. Næstved: Rønnebæksholm.

Bondesen, N.W.T. (1874). *Minde om Nikolai Frederik Severin Grundtvigs Præstegjerning i Aaret 1821*. Copenhagen: C.A. Reitzel.

Bonding, S. (GV). 'Indledning til *Brage-Snak om Græske og Nordiske Myter og Oldsagn for Damer og Herrer*'. http://www.xn--grundtvigsvrker-7lb.dk/

Borcak, L.W. & Marstal, H. (2022). *Fællessang – fælles sag?* Copenhagen: Forlaget Højskolerne.

Borum, P. (1983). *Digteren Grundtvig*. Copenhagen: Gyldendal.

Borup, J. (1943). *N.F.S. Grundtvig*. Copenhagen: C.A. Reitzel-A. Sandal.

Bugge. K.E. (1969). *Skolen for livet. Studier over N.F.S. Grundtvigs pædagogiske tanker*. Copenhagen: Gads Forlag.

Bugge, K.E. (2003). *Grundtvig og slavesagen*. Aarhus: Aarhus University Press.

Bredsdorff, M. (1969). 'Grundtvig og Shakespeare'. GS 1968, 33-46.

Bredsdorff, M. (1983). *Grundtvig og Sydsjælland*. Glumsø: Historisk Samfund for Præstø Amt.

Brun, H. (1882). *Biskop N.F.S. Grundtvigs Levnetsløb udførligst fortalt fra 1839. Et Bidrag*. I-II. Kristiania: Alb. Kammermeyer (Hovedkommission for Norge), Kolding: Konrad Jørgensen (Forlægger), Copenhagen: Karl Schønberg (Hovedkomission for Danmark).

Brücker, V. (1921). *Grundtvigs kirkelige Gærning*. Copenhagen: Haase.

Bukh, P. (1978). *Den grundtvigske reformation. Forkortet udgave af Anders Nørgaard: Grundtvigianismen I-III*. Aarhus: Aros.

Baagø, K. (1955). 'Grundtvig og den engelske liberalisme'. GS 1955, 7-37.

Baagø, K. (1960). *Vækkelse og Kirkeliv i København og Omegn*. Copenhagen: Gad.

Christensen, D.C. (1983). *N.F.S. Grundtvig. To Dialoger om Højskolen. Academiet i Soer – en sød drøm. Samtale mellem en Forfatter og en Bonde med Deltagelse af en magister og en Naturforsker*. Holbæk: Odin.

Christensen, G. & Grundtvig, S. (1924-26). *Breve fra og til N.F.S. Grundtvig* I (1807-20) & II (1821-72). Copenhagen: Gyldendal.

Drejer, C.M., Larsen, J.E. & Reeh, N. (2014). "Indførelsen af den indbyrdes undervisningsmetode i Danmark, dens konkrete udformning som disciplinær teknik i klasselokalet og dens internationale variationer". *Uddannelseshistorie*, 2014, 135-159.

Eller, P. (1962). *N.F.S. Grundtvig portrætter*. Frederiksborg: Det Nationalhistoriske Museum.

Eriksen, A. & Broch, B. (eds.) (1997). *N.F.S. Grundtvig. Glimt af embedsvirksomhed og privatliv. Materialesamling til undervisningsbrug*. Køge Byhistoriske Arkiv.

Fabritius, J. (1952). 'N.F.S. Grundtvigs breve til hans Hustru under Englandsrejsen 1843'. GS 1952.

Feldbæk, O. (ed.). *Dansk Identitetshistorie*, vol. 3. Folkets Danmark 1848-1940. Copenhagen: C.A. Reitzel.

Garne, K. (2016). *Romantik og kristendom belyst gennem Grundtvigs andet møde med Steffens*. Copenhagen: Det teologiske Fakultet, no. 63.

Grane, L. (ed.) (1980). *Det teologiske Fakultet*. Københavns Universitets Historie, Vol. V. Copenhagen: Gad.

Grell, H. (1988). *Skaberånd og folkeånd. En undersøgelse af Grundtvigs tanker om folk og folkelighed og deres forhold til hans kristendomssyn*. Aarhus: Anis.

Grell, H. (1992). *England og Grundtvig. Grundtvigs møde med England og dets betydning for hans forfatterskab*. Aarhus: Aarhus University Press.

Grell, H. (1995). *Grundtvig og Oxforderne*. Aarhus: Center for Grundtvig-Studier.

Grundtvig, F.L. (1904). *Den grundtvigske slægts oprindelse*. Særtryk af *Den Danske Højskole*.

Grundtvig, L. (1921). 'Fru Lise Grundtvig', in *Minder fra gamle grundtvigske Hjem*, Vol. 1, ed. Barfod, H.P.B.: Gad, 37-51.

Grundtvig, N.F.S. (1877). *Kirkelige Leilighedstaler*, ed. Brandt, C.J., Copenhagen: Schønberg.

Grundtvig, N.F.S. (1877). *Mands Minde 1788-1838 – Foredrag over det sidste halve Aarhundredes Historie, holdte 1838 af Nik. Fred. Sev. Grundtvig*. Copenhagen: Schønberg.

Grundtvig, N.F.S. (1888). *Christian Molbech og Nikolai Frederik Severin Grundtvig. En Brevvexling* (ed. Molbech, C.K.F. & Schrøder, L.). Copenhagen: Gyldendal.

Grundtvig, N.F.S. (1891). *N.F.S. Grundtvigs Breve fra England til Dronning Caroline Amalie 1843*, ed. Grundtvig, F.L. Særtryk af Tidsskriftet *Danskeren*. Copenhagen: Schønberg.

Grundtvig, N.F.S. (1920). *N.F.S. Grundtvigs breve til og fra hans hustru under Englandsrejserne 1829-31*. ed. deres Børnebørn. Copenhagen: Aage Marcus.

Grundtvig, N.F.S. (1933). *Grundtvig, N.F.S. og hans nærmeste slægt under tre-årskrigen, En Brevvexling*, ed. Simesen, I. Copenhagen: Gad.

Grundtvig, N.F.S. (1948). *Grundtvigs Erindringer og Erindringer om Grundtvig*, ed. Johansen, S. & Høirup, H. Copenhagen: Gyldendal.

Grundtvig, N.F.S. (1979). *Dag- og Udtogsbøger I-II*, ed. Albeck, G. Copenhagen: C.A. Reitzel.

Grundtvig, N.F.S. (1983-86). *Prædikener*, ed. Thodberg, C., Vols. 1-12, Copenhagen: Gad.

Grundtvig, N.F.S. (1988). *Præstø Prædikener*, ed. Thodberg, C., Vols. 1-2, Copenhagen: Gad.

Grundtvig, S. (1882). *Grundtvig og Ingemann. Brevexling 1821-1859*. Copenhagen: Samfundet til Den Danske Litteraturs Fremme.

Graae, T. (1880). *Grundtvig på Langeland (1805-1808)*. Copenhagen: J.H. Schubothe.

Hansen, P. (ed.) *Ernst Trier og Marie Abel. En Brevveksling*. Copenhagen: August Bang.

Hauch-Fausbøll, T. & Hiort-Lorenzen, H.R. (1911). 'Grundtvig'. *Patriciske Slægter. Anden samling*. Copenhagen: Dansk Genealogisk Instituts Forlag, 150-95.

Heggem, S.S. (2004) *Kjærlighetens makt, maskerade og mosaikk. En lesning av N.F.S. Grundtvigs Sang-Værk til Den Danske Kirke*. Disputats. Det Teologiske Fakultet, Universitetet i Oslo.

Hjalmar, H. (1918). *N.F.S. Grundtvigs sindssygdom*. Copenhagen: H. Koppe.

Holm, A. (2001). *Historie og efterklang. Et studie i N.F.S. Grundtvigs tidsskrift Danne-Virke*. Odense: Odense University Press.

Holm, A. (2012). 'Mellem frihed og orden. Den danske religionsmodel kirkehistorisk betragtet', ed. Christoffersen L. et al: *Fremtidens danske religionsmodel*. Copenhagen: Anis.

Holm, A. (2018). *Grundtvig, En introduktion*. Aarhus: FILO.

Holt, T. (1983) *Minderige steder i Grundtvigs liv. En fotografisk billedbog af Thyra Holt*. Copenhagen: Forlaget Rhodos.

Horn, F.W. (1883). *N.F.S. Grundtvigs Liv og Gerning. Et biografisk Forsøg*. Copenhagen: Schønberg.

Høirup, H. (1949). *Grundtvigs syn på tro og erkendelse. Modsigelsens grundsætning som teologisk aksiom hos Grundtvig*. Copenhagen: Gyldendal.

Høirup, H. (1955). *Frederik Lange Grundtvig*. Copenhagen: Gyldendal.

Høirup, H. (1961). 'Grundtvig som forkynder'. Copenhagen: *Vartovbogen 1961*.

Høyer-Christensen, P. (1935). *Kapellanen i Udby*. Copenhagen: Lohse.

Høyer-Christensen, P. (1947). *Præstefamilien i Udby*. Copenhagen: Lohse.

Iversen, H.R. (1987). *Ånd og livsform. Husliv, folkeliv og kirkeliv hos Grundtvig og sidenhen*. Aarhus: Anis.

Iversen, H.R. (2008). *Grundtvig, folkekirke og mission: Praktisk teologiske vekselvirkninger*. Copenhagen: Anis.

Jacobsen, A.C.L. (1999). *Irenæus mod kætterne. Indledning og redaktion. Oversættelse ved Kiel, U.* Copenhagen: Anis.

Jensen, E.K. (1977), 'Hjertets gudbilledlighed' in: Thodberg, Christian (ed.), *For sammenhængens skyld, ord og motiver i Grundtvigs salmer og prædikener*, 65-96. Aarhus: Institut for Praktisk Teologi ved Aarhus Universitet 1977.

Jensen, J.I. (2017). *Denne ene sommer. Grundtvigs Nytaars-Morgen som symfonisk digtning*. Copenhagen: Vartov.

Jensen, J.M. (1957). *Præsten Niels Dael, Liselund*. Aarhus: Aros.

Jensen, T. (1922). *Constance Leth. Grundtvigs ungdomskærlighed*. Copenhagen: Hagerup.

Jensen, T. (1943). *Kvinder i Grundtvigs liv*. Copenhagen: Hagerup.

Johansen, S. (1949). Anmeldelse af 'Grundtvigs Embedsnedlæggelse 1826'. GS 1949.

Johansen, S. (1957). 'N.F.S. Grundtvig og censuren'. Særtryk af *Fund og Forskning i Det Kongelige Biblioteks Samlinger* IV-1957.

Johansen, S. (1960 & 1963). 'N.F.S. Grundtvigs bopæle (adresser) i København'. GS 1960 & 1963.

Jørgensen, T. (2005). 'Dogmatikkens opgave set i religionsmødets perspektiv'. *Dansk Teologisk Tidsskrift*.

Kjær, N. (2016). *Grundtvig og kvækerne*. Books on Demand. Copenhagen: DoD.

Koch, H. (1940). 'Grundtvigs krise 1810-11'. *Smaaskrifter tilegnede Aage Friis*. Copenhagen: Schultz, 185-201.

Koch, H. (1944). *Grundtvig*. Copenhagen: Gyldendal.

Koch, H. (1945). *Hvad er demokrati?* Copenhagen: Gyldendal.

Kofoed, N. (1954). *Grundtvig som selvbiograf. Med særligt henblik på tidsrummet 1800-1810*. Copenhagen: Gyldendal.

Korsgaard, O. & Schelde, M. (eds.) (2013). *Samfundsbyggeren. Artikler om Grundtvigs samfundstænkning*. Copenhagen: Anis.

Korsgaard, O. (2018). *Grundtvig rundt. En guide*. Copenhagen: Gyldendal.

Köster, K. (1875). *Til Minde om Povel Dons. Grundtvigs og Ingemanns Ungdoms-Ven. Et efterladt Arbejde af Kristian Köster*, ed. Schrøder, L. Copenhagen: Schønberg.

Larrain, P. (2021). *Rejsen til Hjerterummet*. Copenhagen: Eksistensen.

Larsen, B.S. (2015). *Paradisskyggen. Med Grundtvig i kærlighed og krise*. Copenhagen: Kristeligt Dagblad.

Larsen, E. (1983). *Det levende ord. Om Grundtvig*. Charlottenlund: Rosinante.

Larsen, K.E. (2005). 'Missionshusene – om baggrunden for deres opførelse'. Copenhagen: *Kirkehistoriske Samlinger 2005*.

Larsen, K.E. (2007). *Fra Christensen til Krarup. Dansk kirkeliv i det 20. århundrede*. Fredericia: Kolon.

Larsen, K.E. (2022). *Kirkeretninger i Danmark. Kristendommens veje fra oplysningstid til nutid*. Copenhagen: Kristeligt Dagblad.

Lehmann, E. (1929). *Grundtvig*. Copenhagen: Jespersen & Pio.

Lundgreen-Nielsen, F. (1980). *Det handlende ord I-II*. Copenhagen. Gad.

Lundgreen-Nielsen, F. (1983). 'Grundtvig og romantikken'. (ed. Thyssen. A.P. & Thodberg, C.) in *Grundtvig og grundtvigianismen i nyt lys*. Aarhus: Forlaget Anis.

Lundgreen-Nielsen, F. (ed.) (1992). *På sporet af dansk identitet*. Copenhagen: Spektrum.

Lundgreen-Nielsen, F. (1992). 'Grundtvig og danskhed'. Ole Feldbæk (ed.). *Dansk identitetshistorie. 3 Folkets Danmark 1848-1940*. Copenhagen: C.A. Reitzel, 9-188.

Lyby, T.C. (1993). 'Grundtvigs tanker om præstefrihed – og grundtvigianernes' (ed. Nielsen, C.B. et al) *Ordet, kirken og kulturen. Afhandlinger om kristendomshistorie tilegnet Jakob Balling*. Aarhus: Aarhus University Press.

Lyby, T.C. (2005). 'Odin og Hvide Krist. Om Sune Aukens bog *Sagas Spejl. Mytologi, historie og kristendom hos N.F.S. Grundtvig*'. GS 2005.

Martensen, H. (1862, 6th ed. 1874). *Til Forsvar mod den saakaldte Grundtvigianisme*. Copenhagen: Gyldendal.

Martinsen, L.K. (2022). *Den Store Mand. Nye fortællinger om Grundtvig*. Aarhus: Aarhus University Press.

Meyer, K.O. (1983). 'Det nationale – blev det noget særligt i Danmark?' (Nissen, H.S. ed.). *Efter Grundtvig. Hans betydning i dag*. Copenhagen: Gyldendal.

Møller, E. (1950). *Grundtvig som Samtidshistoriker*. Copenhagen: Gyldendal.

Møller, J.F. (2005). *Grundtvigianisme i det 20. århundrede*. Copenhagen: Vartov.

Møller, J.F. (2019). *Grundtvigs død*. Aarhus: Aarhus University Press.

Nielsen, E.B. (1964). 'Peter Nikolaj Skougaard – hans liv og betydning for

Grundtvig'. Kristeligt Dagblads Kronik 10. februar 1964.

Nielsen, E.B. (1966). 'Peter Nikolaj Skougaard. Grundtvigs mathematiske ven'. GS 1966.

Nielsen, F. (1889). *N.F.S. Grundtvigs religiøse Udvikling. Et Mindeskrift*. Copenhagen: Schønberg.

Nielsen, H.K., Holm, J. & Østerby R. (2019). *Nypagtsbogen – Grundtvigs nytestamentlige oversættelser*. Copenhagen: Fønix.

Nielsen, J.A. (1961-62). 'Grundtvig og Gissenfeld. Hans forhold til velynderen grev C.C.S. Danneskiold-Samsøe'. GS 1961-62.

Nyborg, O. (2013). *Grundtvig og kærligheden. Kærlighedsforståelsen i Grundtvigs prædikener*. Copenhagen: Faculty of Theology, University of Copenhagen.

Nygaard, F. (1882). *N.F.S. Grundtvigs Stilling til en Udtrædelse af Statskirken og "Kalkbrænderi-Forsamlingerne*. Copenhagen: H.F. Eibe.

Pedersen, J. (1991). 'Traditionsarv og hovedanliggender i romantikken'. *Fra Augustin til Johannes V. Jensen*. Copenhagen: Museum Tusculanum.

Pedersen, K.A. (1999). 'Solen skinnede og Moder kaldte'. Grundtvigs forhold til sin mor i liv og forfatterskab. (ed. Bach-Nielsen, C. et al). *Ordet og livet. Festskrift til Christian Thodberg*. Aarhus: Aarhus University Press.

Pedersen, K.A. (2005). *Grundtvig og fundamentalismen*. GS 2005.

Pedersen, K.A. (2014). 'Det jødiske folk og folkelighedsbegrebet i 1814-krøniken'. GS 2014.

Pedersen, O.K. (2011). *Konkurrencestaten*. Copenhagen: Hans Reitzel.

Petersen, N. (1976). *Ebbe Kløvedal Reich, hans Frederik og N.F.S. Grundtvig*.

Redegørelse og debat. Kolding: Knud Jørgensens Bogtrykkeri A/S.

Possing, B. (2015). *Ind i biografien*. Copenhagen, Gyldendal.

Prenter, R. (1948). 'Grundtvigs syn på forkyndelsen'. GS 1948.

Rasmussen, J. (1998). 'N.F.S. Grundtvig og 'Rationalisterne' i årene 1825-32'. GS 1998.

Rasmussen, J. (2009). *Religionstolerance og religionsfrihed. Forudsætninger for grundloven af 1849*. Odense: Syddansk University Press.

Rasmussen, J. (2021). 'Liturgidebat: Den store ritualkamp i 1830'erne' i *Fønix 2021*, Copenhagen.

Rasmussen, M. (1983). *En konstrueret dagbog for Grundtvigs 3 Englandsrejser 1829-1831*. Copenhagen: Arken Tryk.

Reich, E.K. (1972). *Frederik. En folkebog om N.F.S. Grundtvigs tid og liv*. Copenhagen: Gyldendal.

Rosendal, H. (1913). *N.F.S. Grundtvig – Et Livsbillede. Med illustrationer*. Copenhagen: Hagerup.

Rønning, F. (1904). *Den grundtvigske slægt. Bidrag til dens historie*. Copenhagen: Schønberg.

Rønning, F. (1907 & 1908). *N.F.S. Grundtvig. Et Bidrag til Skildringen af dansk Åndsliv i det 19. Århundrede* I-II. Copenhagen: Schønberg.

Rørdam, P. (1891, 1892 & 1895). *Blade af hans Levnetsbog og Brevvexling*, ed. Rørdam, H.F. Del I-III. Copenhagen: Schønberg.

Sanders, H. & Vind, O. (eds.) (2003). *Grundtvig – nycklen till det danska?* Göteborg: Makadam.

Saxtorph, V. (1932). *Portrætter af N.F.S. Grundtvig*. Copenhagen: Gad.

Schrøder, L. (1883). *N.F.S. Grundtvigs Barndom og første Ungdom (1783-1806)*. Kolding: Konrad Jørgensen.

Schrøder, L. (1901, repr. 2020). *N.F.S. Grundtvigs Levned*. Copenhagen: Lehmann & Stage.

Skovmand, R. (ed.) (1960). *Højskolens Ungdomstid i Breve*, vol. II. Copenhagen: Munksgaard.

Stevns, M. (1950). *Fra Grundtvigs Salmeværksted*. Copenhagen: Gyldendal.

Søndergaard, K. (2013). *Asta Grundtvig, Liv og virke, slægt og venner 1826-90*: Copenhagen: Vartov.

Thaning, K. (1953). 'Grundtvigs møde med Irenæus'. GS 1953.

Thaning, K. (1981). 'Den 'mageløse opdagelse's' tilblivelse'. GS 1981.

Thodberg, C. (1989). *Syn og sang. Poesi og teologi hos Grundtvig*. Copenhagen: Gad.

Thomsen, N. & Mikkelsen, H.V. (eds.) (2004). *Hvor blev det grundtvigske af?* Copenhagen: Aros.

Thyregod, C.A. (1875). *Skildringer af det virkelige Liv*. Copenhagen: L.A. Jørgensen.

Thyssen, A.P. (1954-56). 'Det grundtvigske Møde i Middelfart 1891 og dets Forudsætninger. Bidrag til belysning af den gammelgrundtvigske Retning.' *Kirkehistoriske Samlinger. Syvende række, Andet bind*.

Thyssen, A.P. (1958). *Den nygrundtvigske bevægelse*. Copenhagen. Det danske Forlag.

Thyssen, A.P. (1967). 'Grundtvig og Spener. Især til belysning af den pietistiske Grundtvig'. GS 1967.

Thyssen, A.P. (1979). *Den danske folkekirkes struktur historisk og aktuelt belyst*. Aarhus: Aros.

Thyssen, A.P. (1988). 'De folkelige og kirkelige rødder i dansk sognehistorie'. Kristeligt Dagblad Kronik 17 & 18. juni 1988.

Thyssen, A.P. (1991). *Grundtvig og den grundtvigske arv*. Copenhagen: Anis.

Toldberg, H. (1946). *Grundtvig som filolog*. Copenhagen: Gad.

Toldberg, H. (1948). 'Nugent Wade i Helsingør. En engelsk præsts møde med Grundtvig og Mynster'. GS 1948.

Toldberg, H. (1950). *Grundtvigs symbolverden*. Copenhagen: Gyldendal.

Toldberg, H. (1955). 'Et uænset egenhændigt vidnesbyrd om Grundtvigs ungdom'. GS 1955.

Vind, O. (1999). *Grundtvigs historiefilosofi*. Copenhagen: Gyldendal.

Vogel, U. (1993). *Bankede på ved paradis. N.F.S. Grundtvigs kriseoplevelser*. Frederiksberg: Anis.

Weltzer, C. (1954-56). 'Grundtvigs sidste Fest i 1872'. *Kirkehistoriske Samlinger. Syvende række, Andet bind*.

Wåhlin, V. (1994). 'Grundtvig i politik op til 1830'. GS 1994.

Zøllner, L. (1997). *Grundtvigs skoletanker i USA, Argentina og Chile*. Vejle: Krogh.

Aarnes, S.A. (1961). *Historieskrivning og livssyn hos Grundtvig*. Oslo: University Presset.

II

THE LETTERS

Writers, Sources, and Dates

For abbreviations see p. 13-14

Number	Source	Place	Date
1. To Christian Molbech	MOLBECH, 10-16	Valkendorf's Hall of Residence	May 1808
2. To Johan Grundtvig	BFOTG I, 21-22	Valkendorf's Hall of Residence	5 March 1810
3. To Cathrine Marie Grundtvig	BFOTG I, 25-26	Valkendorf's Hall of Residence	30 April 1810
4. To Johan Grundtvig	BFOTG I, 26-27	Valkendorf's Hall of Residence	7 May 1810
5. To F.C. Sibbern	BFOTG I, 33-34	Udby	24 Dec. 1810
6. To Wilhelm Østrup	BFOTG I, 38-40	Udby near Præstø	29 June 1811
7. To Otto Grundtvig	BFOTG I, 45-46	Udby	21 Sept. 1810
8. From Constance Leth	BFOTG I, 51-52	Egeløkke	20 Dec. 1810
9. To Poul Dons	BFOTG I, 70-73	Udby	28 April 1812
10. To Poul Dons	BFOTG I, 113-14	Udby	21 Dec. 1812
11. To King Frederik VI	BFOTG I, 198		Undated (1813)
12. To Svend Hersleb	BFOTG I, 204-06	Copenhagen	8 March 1814
13. From Cathrine Marie Grundtvig	BFOTG I, 371	Præstø	5 July 1815
14. To the Royal Danish Chancellery	BFOTG I, 471-73	Copenhagen	21 July 1817
15. To Mette Blicher	BFOTG I, 489-90	Copenhagen	22 August 1818
16. To King Frederik VI	BFOTG II, 49-51	Præstø	20 August 1822
17. To Henrik Steffens	BFOTG II, 87-90	Christianshavn	6 Oct. 1824
18. To the 88 Clausen supporters	BFOTG II, 106-07		20 Sept. 1825
19. To King Frederik VI	BFOTG II, 145-46		21 May 1828
20. To Peter Fenger	BFOTG II, 158-60	Christianshavn	11 April 1829
21. To Lise	GBHH, 50-52	Mornington Place	4 August 1829
22. To Lise	GBHH, 54-58	London	12 August 1829
23. To John Bowring	BFOTG II, 179		20 Oct. 1829.
24. To Lise	GBHH, 85-88	49, Hunter St.	3 June 1830
25. To Lise	GBHH, 95-99	London	24 June 1830
26. To Lise	GBHH, 99-104	London	30 June 1830
27. From Lise	GBHH 105-06	Christianshavn	10 July 1830
28. To Lise	GBHH, 107-09	London	8 July 1830
29. To Lise	GBHH, 113-16	Exeter	25 July 1830
30. To Bernhard Ingemann	INGEMANN, 92-95	Christianshavn	2 Oct. 1830
31. To Bernhard Ingemann	INGEMANN, 124-26	Christianshavn	19 April 1831
32. To Lise	GBHH, 148-51	Trinity College, Cambridge	19 June 1831

33. To Lise	GBHH, 159-62	London	13 July 1831
34. To Lise	GBHH, 173-77	Queen Square, Bloomsbury	10 August 1831
35. To Bernhard Ingemann	INGEMANN, 130-32	Christianshavn	7 Jan. 1832
36. To Gunni Busck	BUSCK, 177-80	Christianshavn	15 Sept. 1835
37. To Bernhard Ingemann	INGEMANN, 193-96	Christianshavn	12 Jan. 1837
38. To Gunni Busck	BUSCK, 205-07		22 Sept. 1837
39. To Bernhard Ingemann	INGEMANN, 197-99		22 Sept. 1837
40. To Jacob Christian Lindberg	BFOTG II, 289-90	Christianshavn	28 Feb. 1838
41. To Bernhard Ingemann	INGEMANN, 218-20	Christianshavn	27 July 1838
42. To Peter Fenger	BFOTG II, 299-300	Christianshavn	25 August 1838
43. To Vilhelm Birkedal	BFOTG II, 373-74	Copenhagen	6 May 1843
44. To Queen Caroline Amalie	CA, 2-6	London	13 July 1848
45. To Johan Grundtvig	BFOTG II, 377-78	London	16 June 1843
46. To Queen Caroline Amalie	CA, 6-11	London	2 July 1843
47. To Queen Caroline Amalie	CA, 14-17	Edinburgh	6 August 1843
48. To Lise	GS 1952, 55-56	Edinburgh	9 August 1843
49. To Queen Caroline Amalie	BFOTG II, 402-04	Copenhagen	9 July 1844
50. To Peter Rørdam	RØRDAM II, 10-13	Copenhagen	6 August 1844
51. To Queen Caroline Amalie	BFOTG II, 461-62	Copenhagen	8 March 1848
52. To Svend Grundtvig	BFOTG II, 471-73	Copenhagen	26 August 1848
53. To his sons Johan and Svend	SIMESEN, 167-68		8 Nov. 1848
54. To Johan Grundtvig	SIMESEN, 219	Copenhagen	22 March 1849
55. To his sons Johan and Svend	SIMESEN, 267-69	Copenhagen	8 June 1849
56. To Peter Rørdam	RØRDAM II, 136-38	Copenhagen	13 August 1849
57. To Svend Grundtvig	BFOTG II, 500-01	Copenhagen	3 August 1850
58. To Johan Grundtvig	SIMESEN, 453-55	Copenhagen	8 Oct. 1850
59. To his sons Johan and Svend	SIMESEN, 499	Copenhagen	14 Jan. 1851
60. To Bernhard Ingemann	INGEMANN, 311-12	Copenhagen	18 Feb. 1851
61. To Vilhelmine Stenersen	BFOTG, 517-18	Copenhagen	17 July 1851
62. From Queen Caroline Amalie	BFOTG, 518		2 August 1851
63. To Peter Fenger	BFOTG, 525-26	Copenhagen	10 Feb. 1853
64. To Bernhard Ingemann	INGEMANN, 316-17	Copenhagen	13 Sept. 1853
65. To Gunni Busck	BFOTG, 534-35	Frederiksholms Kanal	16 May 1853
66. To Bernhard Ingemann	INGEMANN, 322-23	Rønnebæksholm	21 July 1854
67. To Svend Grundtvig	BFOTG, 538-39	Rønnebæksholm	29 July 1854
68. To Johan Grundtvig	BFOTG, 540-41	Rønnebæksholm	2 August 1864
69. From Meta Boisen	BFOTG, 541-42		12 August 1854
70. To Svend Grundtvig	BFOTG, 614-15		3 June 1861

THE LETTERS

Foreword to the Letters and Dates

Letter-writing is among the earliest literary genres, as the letters of St. Paul testify in the *New Testament*. The 19th and 20th centuries abound with hand-written letters; but the coming of the typewriter and then the digital age has left us impoverished. E-mails can seldom be literary vehicles, and biographers of our contemporaries will have few *letters* to draw on. They will find us in the clouds! Grundtvig's earliest letters were carried around Denmark in a post chaise; by 1829 they were being shipped from England to Denmark; in 1861 he received a *telegram* – but before that there are only letters!

It is typical of Grundtvig's cultural contemporaries that their letters are for the most part many, long, and substantial. A personal opening is often followed by at least five pages of views and arguments as writers share their thoughts with friends and acquaintances. There is no other form of personal communication over distance. Grundtvig in particular enjoys a good argument, especially when he is asserting his own views.

Around 500 letters handwritten by Grundtvig have survived, along with 1500 to him. The editors have selected in all 70 of these – 65 from him and 5 to him. Our aim is to illustrate the ideas and feelings of the letter-writer in relation to the biography of Grundtvig rather than to illustrate the subjects of the first five volumes in the series. Seven letters have previously been translated in *Human Comes First* (2018), and six more in *The Common Good* (2019).

Grundtvig's letters are slightly easier to read than most of what he otherwise wrote. They are directed to a specific reader, from the King of Denmark to his own two sons fighting on the German front in 1850. They could range from a few lines to several pages, the longest (not included here) running to over 10,000 words. Pride of place in this selection goes to the letters from England to his wife, Lise, in the summers of 1829-31. They offer us an insight into his observations of being 'abroad', and not least into how much he missed his family and home comforts. We can also read that he nevertheless managed to make his way in England, and surprised himself by doing so. The letter-selection begins when Grundtvig was 25 and ends when he was 73.

Of course, despite publishing almost everything he could – and often to a limited readership – Grundtvig and his acquaintances never intended their letters for publication, so it is something of a privilege to read them, and to experience him as a man like many others: self-absorbed, assertive, dedicated to his many and various projects, and proud of his family. He is easily wounded and brooks little opposition; indeed, disagreement is provocative. Grundtvig has little understanding of others, or of how they perceive him. Here, the challenging letters to and from his children are an important testimony, especially apparent in the tone of his beloved daughter Meta's letter, chiding him for his self-pity at her expense at the death of Marie in 1854.

Headnotes to letters provide contextual information about writers, recipients or occasions when these are not sufficiently evident in the letter itself. Notes are added to facilitate readability. Occasionally the writer refers to the recipient's previous letter, which is either lost or of little interest. Omissions are marked thus […].

1. To Christian Molbech

In this first letter, Grundtvig reveals to his friend, Christian Molbech his 'innermost being' as regards his first love, Constance Leth.

~

May 1808

I read your kind letter with great pleasure and am truly eager to discuss its contents with you. For progressive people there is no surer safeguard against narrow-mindedness than the exchange of ideas between those who have the same aim, whatever the path they choose and however they envisage it. Since you yourself say that in the case of such material you would prefer a *written* exchange, I do hope that this is not the last time that we converse in this way.

I think I should begin by noting that if I understood rightly the opening to your inner thoughts that you offered me, then our views are not so far apart, however divergent they may be in detail. Or perhaps there was something else ... something whose image I am searching for in the Ancient North, in the life of its gods and heroes? ... Out of anger or kindness, the Norns[481] chose a different path for me. My path is to walk between two chasms. If I seek rest in the smiling meadow, it sinks beneath me; if I pick the fragrant flower, it breathes out venom;[482] if I listen to the song of the bird, only hoarse deathscreeches reach my ears. I do not know if I ever reached too high, but I have to believe I did, for I often fell so deep that I thought I would never be able to rise again. Even now, when I think I am standing on firmer ground than when I first learned what to stand means, the earth is swaying beneath my feet; and if I fall once more, I shall never be able to rise again. You are of interest to me, but do not fear! For you must share my conviction that if my strings snap, as may happen, then one more sound from them may disturb the eternal harmony. I shall unfold my innermost being to you, and then you will understand.

To love and to live are one and the same thing. I grew up unfamiliar with nature and with no love for anything living or dead that moved outside myself. My only love was the times past, in which I lived; and when not there, my life was like that of a plant. Children's games were mostly a nuisance, and I was only really happy when I could turn to my Hvitfeld,[483] Lyksander,[484] and Holberg,[485] people of standing in the North, and gaze on the great warriors or watch the lively battles of the emperors and the popes. It was as if

---

481. In Nordic mythology, the Norns are female beings who rule the fate of humanity, much as the Fates do in Greek mythology.
482. Certain flowers exude toxic fumes. 100 such plants and flowers can be found at the Poison Garden of Alnwick in Northumberland, England.
483. Arild Hvitfeld (1546-1609) was a Danish historian and chancellor to Christian IV. He wrote the first major *History of the Kingdom of Denmark* in 1595-1604.
484. Klaus Lyksander (1558-1624?) was a Danish historian who wrote *The Greenland Chronicle* (1608).
485. Ludvig Holberg (1684-1754) was a famous Danish-Norwegian playwright.

nature, with her coldness for everything around me, sought to protect me from the fearful epoch that I had to traverse if I should dare in some way to embrace anything living. This is how I passed the age from 8 to 21. And even my unhealthy way of life – one of the few things in my existence that was not a cause of trouble – could not disturb my calm. In company I was the most stupid, the most tongue-tied, and the most boring creature. Yet at the same time my heart was laughing, for I was not what I appeared to be. I happily returned to my solitude and a well-nigh incredible cheerfulness animated me.

But then ... the time arrived when I met a lady, and I, love's coldest, bitterest derider, immediately fell in love as deeply and passionately as any mortal can. The days of old disappeared from my gaze, or rather they fused with the present that was showing itself in my beloved. I have lived in this world and embraced everything around me with love because everything seemed to be for the one cause alone: the point around which my ideas and feelings united. But brief was my bliss; for I needed only to know that I was in love before I became as unhappy as I could ever be. The civic circumstances were an insurmountable wall between us, and nature had also placed a deep gulf between our beings. O how I fought against the rising passion! With what strength have I forced my soul into the most exhausting pursuits to calm the storm that raged in my innermost being! But all in vain. It was like trying to stem the rushing mountain stream with one's hands! Years passed, and in my weakness I sank into the darkest depression. I walked some dark and trackless ways, for I had no home; the world was closed to me. My spirit lacked strength and, even worse, I lacked the desire to create a *new* one.

Now I realised the parody of the meaningful lives of the gods. Indignation stirred my slumbering powers, and Antiquity, beloved from my childhood and youth, again stood before me. This deepest of feelings sharpened my view, and where I had before seen no more than an enjoyable drama, I now saw a brilliant and consummate image of the Most High. Perhaps now you can understand what my innermost being was saying when I wrote, "I once saw an image of the Eternal. If I could have painted it as it stood before me, you would be on your knees praying! If I could express to you the pain I felt when it was no longer only for myself, your joints would tremble and your countenance turn pale! I cannot regret having seen it, and yet it is constantly swimming before my eyes, as Olympic Jupiter did before the eyes of the ancient Greeks.[486] I must find their harmonious sublimity here in the ancient North, or live in vain!"[487] Even though I am therefore moving around in Antiquity, just as even the greatest poet cannot achieve an uninterrupted life in a world of his own making, nor can I confine myself to what I have endeavoured to have reborn in myself.

My friend, when the life around me forces me to look into my deepest being and to see my place in it, it is a boon that language lacks the words to express the emptiness and suffering to which I am prey. Otherwise, if I told anyone of my state, I would make

---

486. In Greek mythology Mt. Olympus, on the border between the regions of Thessaly and Macedonia, is the home of the 12 Greek gods: Zeus, Hera, Demeter, Poseidon, Athena, Apollo, Artemis, Aphrodite, Ares, Hermes, Hephaestus; the twelfth was either Hestia or Dionysus.
487. Grundtvig quotes himself here, drawing on a passage from his study *On Nordic Mythology (Om Asalæren)*, written while he was house tutor at Egeløkke and published in *New Minerva* 1807.

them unhappy! My life is worthless, an unreality, except for what I find in her – whom I shall forever worship. How can I look at such art without despairing!![488] For as long as I can let Antiquity throw up its ramparts around me, I can live on, but if I am snatched out of its ring, there is nothing that can prevent the pursuing Fury[489] from entwining me and crushing me in her arms ...

If you feel like continuing this written conversation and if time allows, I look forward to seeing something from you. Any regularity or measuring of days and weeks is, in this context, ridiculous, so if you agree with me, then we should write when we feel like it without caring whether the previous letter has been dealt with, for we must not run away from each other!

Your friend
Grundtvig

2. To Johan Grundtvig

Although they moved apart for a while when Grundtvig was in Copenhagen, he had a loving and respectful relationship with his father, as can be seen from his poem 'To My Dear Father, Johan Grundtvig, on the occasion of his 50th anniversary as a pastor on 5th December 1810'.[490] While employed as a high school teacher of History and Geography at the Schouboe Institute in Copenhagen, Grundtvig learned of his father's increasing ill-health.

∼

Valkendorf's Hall of Residence, 5th March 1810

Dear Father,
I was deeply saddened to learn from my dear parents' letter of your infirmity and my beloved mother's distress. ... If you cannot find a living that ensures you a peaceful life, or if it costs you too much to leave the house and the congregation where you have for so long practised your holy calling, relishing life with its joys and sorrows, then you must seek to acquire an assistant in your pastoral ministry! If you think that you cannot be served by a stranger, then you know that in me you have a son who will not shirk the holy duty of coming to the aid of a venerable father in his old age and who does not disrespect the gospel of Jesus. So far I have followed the call of my heart, which in recent times has bidden me proclaim how God has never been without a witness. Nor have I imagined myself so soon taking up a post that gives the course of my life

---

488. The two exclamation marks are Grundtvig's own.
489. In Greek mythology the Furies (Gr. *Erinyes*) were three goddesses who punished men for crimes against the natural order.
490. No. 128 in *LW*.

another direction, one which is daily burdened with many chores that do not sit well with Christ's servants. But if those are the circumstances, then do not let them hold you back, for they will not hold *me* back. ...

May God Almighty strengthen you and my beloved mother as long as you may live, He who has strengthened you in so many of life's trials. This is the fervent wish of

Your devoted son
N.F.S. Grundtvig

3. To Cathrine Grundtvig

Further letters between Grundtvig and his parents did not solve the problem of his homecoming. On 16th March 1810 Grundtvig wrote a second letter home in which he offered his help but added, "I cannot unconditionally leave my position, in which I am working with keenness and success." Knowing that he might become his father's curate and needed to qualify to become a pastor, Grundtvig gave a 'dimissory sermon' in Regens Church on 17th March in the presence of his examiner, Professor P.E. Müller. Grundtvig had prepared Professor Müller with the information that this was an examination sermon and not one he would preach to an ordinary congregation. The sermon, on Mt 5:15-16, was entitled 'Why Has the Word of the Lord Disappeared from His House?' and was in essence an attack on the Danish clergy in general for being more interested in human affairs than in the Word of the Lord. Professor Müller was highly impressed and awarded Grundtvig a first-class honours degree (*laudabilis et quidem egregie*). Grundtvig was now so self-confident that he decided to publish the sermon. In the meantime his mother sent a stinging rebuke to her son. The letter is missing, but from Grundtvig's response we can gather the gist of its content.

∼

Valkendorf's Hall of Residence, 30th April 1810

Dear Mother!
I had already envisaged that my good parents would be saddened by my last letter, but I cannot help that. However, I had not imagined that your displeasure at my behaviour would go so far – as I can see from your letter with deep sadness; nor do I deserve it. Nevertheless, it ill becomes a son to rebuke his mother, so I shall only deal with what is absolutely essential.

You reproach me, dear mother with ingratitude, instability, and the cowardly frame of mind that prefers pleasure to duty. If no other duty exists but to try to fulfil all one's parents wishes, then you are right for the most part; in which case I have been in the wrong for some time now, for I have long known that it was your wish to have me as your curate. On the other hand, I believe it is our highest human duty to endeavour to consummate the work that we in our innermost being feel to be the calling of God – and that was assuredly also your intention when you let me study. I now feel that it is my call to contribute to my father's glory through the sciences, and I dare not surrender this calling in order to satisfy the wish even of my nearest and dearest. On the other hand, to break off this calling for a while under certain circumstances could be a duty, so when I heard that my father was about to give up, I felt it indeed to be my duty – if he could in no other way come to enjoy a deserved rest – to help out as his assistant. If in my first letter I had said anything other than that I offered myself unconditionally, then you would be right to call me fickle, but you yourself know that this is not the case. It is very painful for me that you and my good father have taken it otherwise than I expressly stated: that your wish does not allow you to see the matter from any other side than your own, and that you can bring yourselves to regard my scholarly activity as a brilliant trifle. For I am thereby unappreciated and you are thereby distressed. In the name of God, who sees all hearts, I cannot and must not let myself be moved thereby. I have prayed to God with all my heart and with complete submission to His will, and I venture to regard the decision I have conceived to be just that. This both comforts and calms me, even though it does not efface the painful feeling that torments me at seeing my parents suffer and believe that I am to blame. Nonetheless, the God to whose service I endeavour to devote my life, and into whose hand I confide everything as a child, will also in this matter lead everything to the best conclusion. He knows that no regard for earthly pleasure and glitter *has* determined, or *does* determine my calling.

In the light of my filial gratitude for the 20 rbd[491] you sent and all that your loving hands have given me, I cannot but be sad with what you have added. Have you ever known me to be tight-fisted or self-seeking, dear Mother? Have I ever complained about your beleaguered circumstances or the truly wretched life I must lead here? Since I received from you what I could barely live on, have I ever asked for a single shilling? I have gratefully received what you have sent me because I needed it, and I believed you could manage without it. If this is not so, may God preserve me from receiving even a single shilling before I am able to determine everything myself. No, my good mother, Favour is not my idol! My life runs along, calm and confined. I have the hope that God will grant me my daily bread, as long as I do not shun my work.

So, dearest Mother! I cannot change my decision, even if the whole world agreed to blame me, for I have not made it for vanity's sake.

With warmest greetings to my good father and little Trine,[492] I remain always, dear mother

Your deeply devoted son
N.F.S. Grundtvig

---

491. Rbd = Rigsbankdaler. In 1826 an artisan's day-wage was one-third of 1 rigsbankdaler, so 20 Rbd was roughly the equivalent of 60 days' or 10 weeks' work.

492. Before he left for the Gold Coast in 1799, Grundtvig's elder brother Jacob (1775-1800), married Anna Marie Adolph (1770-1802) and had a daughter, named Cathrine Marie (known as 'Trine') after her grandmother. When Jacob died abroad, Anna Maria and Trine moved in with her parents, but Anna Maria died in 1802 and her own mother in 1804. Being the child's guardian Grundtvig's father, Johan, took her into his keeping at Udby vicarage, until he too died in 1813. Trine and Grundtvig's mother moved to Præstø, where the latter died in 1823. Trine then married a relative of Johan's, but died childless soon after.

4. To Johan Grundtvig

Johan made a formal application to the diocesan bishop, Frederick Münter, for Grundtvig to be appointed as his curate. The bishop rejected the request on the grounds that there were already several other better-qualified curates in the diocese. Grundtvig wrote to his father on 20th April "in the firm belief that since nothing in life happens in vain, I think I should acknowledge the pointer from above that it is not yet the right time for me to become a pastor." Grundtvig's unwillingness to move back to Udby finds open expression in the letter below, softened perhaps by the gift of two copies of his dimissory sermon, 'Why has the Word of the Lord Disappeared from His House?'

∼

Valkendorf's Hall of Residence, 7th May 1810

Dear Father!
Enclosed I am sending you and my good mother two copies of my dimissory sermon. I know of no one to whom I have greater cause to dedicate them than you, good Christian father! I am sure that although the piece is short, you would prefer to see your own name on it than on any other of my works.

Dearest father, do not frown on your son, because he has had to allow one of your wishes to remain unfulfilled, but rest assured that I, who believe in the same God and Saviour as yourself, have not acted without seeking advice from them in prayer!

May God strengthen you now and for ever in soul and body, and may He preserve your paternal love for me!

With loving greetings to my good mother and little Trine I remain

Your deeply devoted Son
N.F.S. Grundtvig

5. To Frederik Sibbern

For portraits of Sibbern and Hersleb see pp. 99-103. Grundtvig was recovering from a mental breakdown when he wrote this letter of gratitude on Christmas Eve 1810.

∼

Udby, 24th December 1810

Noble friend!
You above all have first claim on my first quiet moments, for you have fought alongside

me as an honest friend! As you stood before me with hands folded in Vindbyholt,[493] so do you stand in my heart for as long as I can breathe. God be praised, I am not as unfeeling as I thought I was, even though it is true that for a long period of my life selfishness and pride have kept my better feelings in a prison where they only momentarily burst out into higher tones. I shall not go into detail here as regards the restoration of my health, since I have written about it to Hersleb and thus to you, but I wish to repeat my deepest thanks to you, good friend, for all that you have done and suffered for me. Please be assured of my friendship until I am able to repay you as fully as I should. With God's good grace I pray that day may not be too far ahead, for now I feel that I have my heart back! The postman is waiting – I must close.

Your deeply devoted friend
Grundtvig

6. To Wilhelm Østrup

Grundtvig's good friend, Wilhelm Østrup (1777-1850) was a curate on Langeland, when Grundtvig was house tutor at Egeløkke Manor. The 'visitation' that Grundtvig refers to in the first paragraph of the letter is his graphic interpretation of his nervous breakdown, including the episode at Vindbyholt Inn, where he saw and felt the Devil. Later in the letter he refers to this as a 'delusion'.

Udby near Præstø, 29th June 1811

I do not know how long it is since we saw each other or exchanged letters, but since the end of last year I have been excused. Hard times are now moving away; I am still somewhat burdened, but I have begun to raise my head, for I seem assured that my Saviour is drawing near. What am I to say about my 'visitation'?[494] Like all chastisement it seemed to lead to distress; but I thank my God and will kiss the rod, for I have more or less learned to humble myself under God's mighty hand, and when with the help of the Holy Spirit I have learned it fully, then I know He will raise me in His own good time.

You know how for far too many years I have passed for a Christian and thought myself to be such, but my Christianity was actually in poor shape, with pride and impurity building in my heart of hearts as I courted vanity's favour. I called myself 'Christian' and spoke harsh words to the un-Christian flock. Yet strictly against all Christian love I rehearsed my satirical verses and instead of working in the Lord's vineyard and assisting my aging father, I glorified in word and letter the ancient heathens and their

---

493. At Vindbyholt Inn Grundtvig hallucinated that he was being attacked by the Devil in the form of a snake.
494. i.e. at Vindbyholt Inn.

idols. No one can serve two masters,[495] nor can Christ have fellowship with Belial.[496] At harvest time last year the Lord took a wondrous hold on me, so that I felt myself snatched out of heathendom and favoured to live solely for the service of Christ. With Christian enthusiasm I seized the harp to sing of the times of Denmark and the glory of the divinity, while I searched the Scriptures. From that moment I threw off all that I considered unchristian except my pride, which had established its dwelling within me. It was now merely sloughing its skin, in that it led me to believe that I was a pious and God-pleasing man whom He had chosen to put Christianity back on its feet or at least to witness openly like the Lord's departed warriors. This pride on the one hand and a quite peculiar traffic in my nervous system brought me to such a state that I fancied I was seeing strange and wondrous visions. There is no doubt that on this path I would have become one of the proudest zealots that ever moved on earth if the good God had not taken pity on me and ripped away the veil that evil enemies had drawn over my eyes. Suddenly it was as if the scales fell from the eye of my mind; my pride and lack of love were patently obvious to me, and I was marked neither by repentance nor regret for the sins I had committed.

    I was close to despair, my brain fearing the worst, but my heart remained hard and cold. This path to the other side would have also led to ruin, if the good Lord had not inspired me with the idea of tearing myself away from Copenhagen and all worldly business to see if my aging parents could grant me room for a spiritual conversion. I went back to them, and the storm of despair abated when they partially convinced me that the strange attack on my nerves that I had attributed to the Devil, in whose clutches I thought myself to be, was only a *natural* sickness. This explanation for my 'delusion' never quite took root in me, but it was like clutching at a straw in a shipwreck – it gave me a hope of rescue. My father was relinquishing his pastoral calling, and God knows how I in my pathetic state had the audacity to offer to become his assistant. I returned to Copenhagen[497] with my hopes high, but on arrival a new sickness began which still has not left me completely. The most indecent and blasphemous thoughts pressed in on me and, as it were, played on my lips, without my being strong enough to drive them away; indeed there was even something in me that found them pleasant. The first two months of the year passed in constant struggle and dejection; I could do nothing, I could not even be properly sorrowful. Day by day I sank ever more deeply into the maelstrom of mad and blasphemous thoughts, and I was close to going under. But God's hour arrived. I was called to the capital to be catechised,[498] and here I was so fortified during my 3-month stay that I could begin to work again.

---

495. Mt 6:24.
496. Belial is an evil being (lit. worthless one) in the Hebrew Bible and is used once in the NT as a synonym for the Devil, 2 Cor 6:15.
497. Grundtvig had arrived at Udby on 21st December 1810, he left again for Copenhagen on the 29th. He was appointed curate on 3rd May 1811, was ordained in Trinitatis Church, Copenhagen on 29th May, and took up his curacy in Udby in early June.
498. Grundtvig had to answer orally a set of formal questions on Christian doctrine.

On the Wednesday before the Holy Festival of Pentecost I was ordained into the priesthood, and immediately came home here. Ever since then I have sensed God's particular strength, and with His help I hope in the name of Jesus to become master of these shameless thoughts soon. Thanks be to God, a more humble and loving heart has developed during this long struggle, and I venture to hope that it will be confirmed so strongly in the love of God the Father and Jesus Christ that I shall in all things seek God's honour. I shall renounce the world and everything in it. My induction in the very church in which I myself was baptised,[499] in the congregation which for many years had the same father as me, was very moving. My aging parents were present, and my brother inducted me. I myself preached on Ephesians 4:11-16.

Since I have to do my reading for the sermon tomorrow on God's amazing mercy over us poor sinners, I must close now. Some other time, God willing, I shall write to you about my comings and goings etc.

The peace of God be with you and with us all in the communion of the Holy Spirit!

Your friend and co-servant
Grundtvig
Write to me soon.

7. To Otto Grundtvig

Grundtvig's elder brother, Otto (1772-1843), was 11 years his senior, and pastor in the parish of Torkilstrup and Lillebrønde. It was Otto who installed Grundtvig in Udby Church in 1811. Otto's dean, Pastor Diderik Blicher, was the father of four daughters: Marie (married Poul Glahn), Pauline (married Christian Schmidt) Lise (married Grundtvig), and Jane (unmarried). Grundtvig's marriage proposal to Lise was contained in a letter to her in early September 1811. Lise's positive response was communicated to Grundtvig in a letter from her elder sister, Marie. The letter reads as if he has made a contract, first with himself, then with Lise, that he needs a wife!

∽

Udby, 21st September 1811

Dear brother!
On Monday I received your letter, for which much thanks. It was dated 7th September; perhaps you made a mistake in the date or it has taken 8 days to arrive. Anyway, that is not why I am taking up my pen; I write to inform you that in God's name I have become engaged to Lise Blicher. I shall travel to Olstrup[500] next week, God willing, and from there perhaps on through Copenhagen to Roskilde, where at the Diocesan Conference I shall be delivering my paper on the Learning of the Clergy.

---

499. For an illustration of Grundtvig's baptismal certificate, see p. 45.
500. Olstrup-Ulse is where Grundtvig will marry Lise Blicher in 1818.

Our parents are pleased with my engagement, and God has so ordained it that it was very much in my thoughts 8 years ago. It has been completely out of them many times since, but it kept coming back, and in the end it seemed that nothing was to come of it. I could tell you so much about how wonderful I think my choice is, but I am beyond the age when one thinks everyone else is overjoyed to hear the paeans of praise one sings to one's beloved. It is enough to know that you agree with me that she is a gentle, good girl. In all other things may God rule. I am not worried, least of all in this pleasant evening-hour, having written my sermon for Sunday's divine gospel.

Greet all those at home with you from

Your sincere brother,
N. Grundtvig.

8. From Constance Leth

Carl Frederik Steensen de Leth junior (31st May 1798-1889) and Vincens Steensen de Leth (2nd February 1811-93) were the two sons of Carl Frederik Steensen de Leth senior (1774-1825) and Constance Steensen de Leth, née Constance Henriette Fabritius de Tengnagel (1777-1827).

Around 16th March 1805 Grundtvig arrived at Egeløkke as the live-in house tutor to Carl junior, aged 7 years and 2 months at the time. He fell in love with the boy's mother but his passion was unrequited. After just over 3 years, around 15th April 1808 he left Egeløkke for Copenhagen. By the time of this letter, Carl junior is 13 years old and has already left home.

In time Carl became a Groom of the Royal Chamber and Vincens the Master of the Royal Hunt.

Around 26th September 1811, Grundtvig became engaged to Lise Blicher. He remained friends with Constance until her death in 1827.

∼

Egeløkke, 20th December 1811.

My dear Grundtvig,
I venture to anticipate your forgiveness for my lengthy silence, when I tell you that your last letter found me without much hope of life, following a nervous gall fever that is running around here. However long ago it happened, I still have no energy whatsoever, and it will be spring before I expect to be fully recovered. Otherwise I am extremely happy and content. Carl is a good boy, who wins everyone's favour and is very well behaved. Vincens is a lovely, healthy, thriving boy. Dear Grundtvig, please add your innermost prayers to mine in asking God to hold his hand over my children so that they may be good and useful people. Their future fate often weighs upon my anxious heart with heavy presentiments, and I am a mother for them with all the uncertainty that follows.

Since you have not yet shown any *lack* of appreciation – as you so often do – I trust that you are convinced that I have received the news of your engagement with joy and sincere understanding; if you have indeed changed, as you write, then it will be a happy marriage.

It is strange that your stay here seems to you like a sleep full of bad dreams; as far as I am concerned, everything in this world can be seen from its softer sides. I often think of how, when we were alone, you read aloud from *1001 Nights*[501] while Carl quietly dressed his dolls. You and Carl are gone and much is different now, whereas my heart braves all life's changes and remains as loyal and constant as ever to my friends. And you, Grundtvig, are my friend! I shall never forget you and I wish that you lived closer. Please send me a few lines now and then, and let us be tried and trusted friends whom nothing can separate, with Lise one day becoming a link in that chain. Greet her from me, though I do not yet know her. I hope you bring her here some time and that she will like me – of that I am sure ....

I cannot greet you from anyone, since I never go out. Saxdorf and Graae[502] are well, they come here occasionally. My devoted Bine[503] is still here and greets you together with my husband. We wish all of you everything that can make your hearts happy. May God grant you health and strength in all your undertakings, dear Grundtvig, and may you remain my sympathetic friend, as I shall ever be your unchanging and deeply affectionate friend.

Constance Leth

9. To Poul Dons

For a portrait of Poul Dons see p. 95. In Grundtvig's letter below he shares his delight over all the good things that have befallen him, including a powerful experience of pastoral care.

∼

Udby, 28th April 1812.

Dear friend,

... One piece of news that will surprise you as much as it did me is that Friedrich Schlegel in Vienna has translated part of my *Nordic Mythology* in his *Deutsches Museum*[504] to immense praise, and he is said to call me Denmark's greatest poet. I have received a very flattering letter from the man himself with an invitation to write about the North for the same museum. Such things give rise to a new struggle against pride and ambition, but we can more than overcome them through Christ, who loved us. I received both the letter and the news yesterday, and already the same day I was able to contemplate quite calmly how pleased I

---

501. The first known reference to the *1001 Nights* is a 9th-century fragment. The tales appeared in various Middle Eastern collections until they were published in a French translation in 12 volumes (1704-17). Only here does the story of Aladdin first appear (along with Ali Baba and Sinbad the Sailor). With the aid of a magic lamp and a magic ring Aladdin defeats the Sorcerer, marries the princess, and after several trials, eventually lives happily ever after.
502. Both were pastors on Langeland. The local pastor, Christen Graae was Constance's best friend and confidant.
503. Bine Lassen had advanced from the position of housemaid to that of Constance's trusted friend.
504. Friedrich Schlegel's 4-volume *Deutsches Museum* was published in Vienna in 1812-13.

was. My name will become well-known in Germany, and in a field that is fashionable among many good men they will get used to taking note of what I say. As I may have mentioned, a short while ago I learned that my dimissory sermon has been translated, doubtless on the initiative of some pietist brotherhood, and has been published in Nuremburg. Such a man is our Lord! Catholics and Pietists compete to praise me and spread my message. It is a wonder but the door seems also open to me in Germany to preach the Word of the Lord, and at the first opportunity I intend to practise writing its language. I tried to do so for the first yesterday evening that with God's help it will not prove too difficult. I am sure that you will join me in quietly exclaiming, "O, the depth of the riches of the wisdom and knowledge of God! How unsearchable His judgments, and His paths beyond tracing out!"[505]

Just between you and me, I have been proposed as Professor of History at the University of Norway. The Lord's will be done! Something in me desires it ardently. Something in me keeps me rooted here. This is perhaps best for me, but in that case may God ordain it thus that I remain here.

I have told you before that in my position I enjoy many a hallowed joy. Yesterday I again experienced the most wonderful moment beside an old woman's deathbed. Oh how gratifying, how comforting it is for our eyes to see how powerful is the Word of God in driving away the bitterness of death. You should have seen how her tired eyes were transfigured when I pronounced the blessing over her that is beyond all comprehension; how weak, how almost speechless, she was to respond with a sign to let me understand how the words poured into her heart and lit up her innermost eye with a glimpse of the glory of Eternity! Oh my friend! What are all the joys of the world compared to this! How dull is the image that even the spiritually animated poet calls forth of the excellence of faith and the radiance of Eternity compared to what at such a moment not only meets our gaze but also refreshes our heart and makes it glow.

An old Lutheran theologian has said, "It is a marvel when a priest is blessed." Those are hard but strange words; for alas, how accomplished should we not feel who have experienced such a testimony, such a prompting, such unmistakeable signs of the hidden power of the Divine. That is why it was a matter of vital concern even for Paul that he who preached to others should not himself be disowned. Praise be to the Father, who sends his Holy Spirit to help us in our frailty...

Greetings to Jette and all the friends from

Your friend
Grundtvig

10. To Poul Dons

At the time of this letter Grundtvig's father Johan had only 12 more days to live. Whenever that death might come, Grundtvig hoped to remain in Udby and assume his father's role – which was

---

505. Rom 11:33.

also Johan and Cathrine's wish. Grundtvig was clearly at home in the pastoral role in Udby, and had come to accept it as God's will for his own ministry.

⁓

Udby, 24th December 1812

Dear Dons!
Having sent off what little I managed to write today I received your kind letter, and since the postman is coming to Præstø today, I hope that you will read a few words from me at this holy time and will not be alarmed by your uncertainty about our situation.

My ancient father is still alive, but living a miserable life. His body is so wasted that he cannot stand on his own two feet; his thoughts are so distracted that only in a rare moment can he speak or understand an intelligent word, even though he recognises us and to some degree knows what he is saying. But God granted him some gloriously lucid moments last Monday towards evening. Since last Sunday's gospel reading was about John the Baptist, I could not help exclaiming to the congregation towards the end of my sermon, "Also among you there was a John!" I recalled the old man's memory of the voice of the Lord in the desert – the honest, devout servant of the Lord that he has been.

There were not many in church, but for that very reason probably only those who have come for the sake of the Word. Nearly all of them had been led by the old man along the path to salvation, so I could speak more freely, and after the sermon, and when I prayed a special prayer for the old man, there was hardly a heart that was not moved or an eye that was dry.

My father was very agitated for the rest of the day, but at bedtime, when many a child of God was assuredly saying a quiet prayer to our heavenly Father, he lay suddenly quite still and remained that way until Monday evening, when he began to speak devotional words. I doubted whether he was aware of what he was saying, but when I approached him, I sensed that we understood each other. He spoke about the peace he felt, and the pious longing to leave this world and be with the Lord. "Now," he said emphatically, "I have come so far that I would not return to this world, even if you offered me all its glory!" He attributed his victory to God's deepest mercy, and his own devout prayers.

Then it was that I told him we had prayed for him in the congregation. He was deeply moved, pressed my hand with tears in his eyes, and said, "I myself should have asked for that, but I did not have the wherewithal." During this gratifying conversation he said, "So, now I am like Jacob, when he blessed his children."[506] I asked for his blessing, especially in my calling as the servant of Christ, and he gave it to me with a heartfelt warmth that I shall not forget. He blessed my absent brother[507] and Mother, and then asked if there was anyone who otherwise wished for a blessing and a breath from him. When I named your name, as you requested, he blessed both you and your family as if he were your father. He prayed earnestly for all my friends, and when I mentioned Hersleb, he added

---

506. Gen 49.
507. Otto Grundtvig (1782-1843).

Molbech. This pleased me deeply. It seemed to be a sign that he too[508] would come to the faith which he wished for us first and foremost.

Towards the end he grew weak, and unfortunately I too grew weary with the intensity of this blessed experience. I asked him to lie down and rest, but he said he did not wish to abandon these devout thoughts. Nonetheless he was passing away. A couple of hours later, there was no pulse, and he was drawn towards death; yet after a violent battle life returned to him. Since then he has not been fully conscious. By the grace of God I am awaiting another sign of life, or at least a moment of calm, for he always prayed that he might be able to commit his soul consciously into the hands of Jesus to be preserved in eternal peace.

[signature missing]

11. *To King Frederik VI*

Grundtvig's father, Johan Grundtvig, died on 5th January 1813. Both father and son had hoped that Grundtvig could thereafter be inducted as pastor in Udby parish, which he had served for 1½ years as curate. He wrote the following plea to King Frederik VI, but his request was turned down. He remained in Udby until August, while he looked for callings in and around Copenhagen and was being considered for the vacant teaching post in History at Oslo University. He was assessed and found wanting.

Undated, spring 1813

Two years ago Your Majesty graciously granted the request of both my father and myself and appointed myself as curate to him in his advanced age.

My aged father has now died in the Lord, and I am a shepherd without a flock. By the Grace of God and Your Majesty I therefore request most humbly that I be allowed to tend one such flock.

Since an application requires some substance, I venture to name the churches for whom my father was shepherd for 36 years, and where my conscience testifies that I have not laboured for two years as a mere hireling. The calling is a good one with regard to a worldly income, and since there are many who customarily court such brides, I would not normally entertain any hope of the living. God be praised, the worldly benefit does not tempt me, for I know that He gives his allotted bread to whoever prays and works – and I seek nothing more. Indeed, in humblest sincerity I confess to Your Majesty that I do not even aspire to what I here am seeking, since it is always hardest to gain trust as teacher and adviser in a place where one has spent one's childhood.

I place all this trustfully in God's and Your Majesty's fatherly hands, and with the

---

508. i.e. Molbech.

aid of the Most High I shall be equally satisfied whether I be confirmed in my father's dwelling or bear my staff out into the wild world.

What above all I most humbly beg for is that Your Majesty will place me wherever suitable. However, if anyone should submit that the holy office in question should not be entrusted to me, I beg Your Majesty will graciously hear my plea and ask my superiors for testimony to my conduct as both a man and a pastor!

Fear God and honour the King was what my father, my grandfather, and my great-grandfather preached throughout the previous century, and thus do I preach.

"The fear of God strengthens the land and the kingdom" was the motto of King Christian IV, and his high-lauded descendants have not disavowed this. Ungodliness corrupts countries as it does individual souls: to that must all testify who love God and the King and the Fatherland, and that is my offence in the world's eyes.

May the King of Kings bless Your Majesty with all temporal and eternal blessings!

Thus prays always
Your most humble and loyal
Grundtvig.

12. To Svend Hersleb

When Oslo (then Christiania) University opened in January 1813, Hersleb was appointed to teach Theology. The following year Norway became independent of Denmark, and Hersleb accepted the break far more easily than Grundtvig, who, heartbroken at the loss of Norway, wrote the following letter to him. Despite Grundtvig's earnest appeal that Hersleb should publish his letter, Hersleb declined to do so. The correspondence nevertheless continued, and Hersleb's teaching was strongly influenced by Grundtvig until they parted company over Grundtvig's 'matchless discovery' that the Bible was not the *foundation* of Christianity. The letter shows how strongly Grundtvig could attack even his friends – and still somehow retain them.

~

Copenhagen, 8th March 1814

Dear beloved friend!
I shall begin by saying that I am your assured and faithful friend in life and death, because that is a truth. It is also a truth that I pray God will keep before your very eyes and one that you will call to mind at any time in what follows when you feel angry; for that is all that I can say about us today. To you and to Norway I must speak in the name of God. May He preserve you from being either scornful or embittered by my words. You know that I do not jest with words, and I testify that I sit here with a calm mind and with a love of you and Norway in fear of the Lord, with a humble prayer that the words may be granted to my lips to speak as I must speak, frankly and truthfully, to serve the cause of peace between us!...

You have said nothing to *me*, but I have heard your speech. Good God, how cold and alien it was! How deeply it disappointed my greatest expectations. You too, Brutus?[509] You too, my beloved friend, hit the high notes! You too shrug your shoulders as Denmark sleeps and Norway awakes. You too offer Norway a polite, somewhat haughty, farewell – with not a sigh nor a fear of the consequences, nor any sense of our straitened circumstances as a result. You too tell us that the Danish crown has cast away a jewel that is no longer worth reclaiming... No. no, dear Hersleb, with such talk your good spirit has left you! The spirit of *pride* is out to tempt you, to lead you down the slippery slope, to see if you will stand immovable beside the Lord or be blinded by the appearance and work of vanity. Have you forgotten that Norway needs a spiritual rebirth, that pride prevents love from creating and sustaining the godly person who is fitted to walk with Him in righteousness and the holiness of Truth? How can you dare to speak about a sleeping Denmark in contrast to a wide awake Norway as if Norway was more awake because it had gone berserk – as if you believed that Norway could awaken spiritually without us in Denmark? Do I really have to remind you that you yourself were still asleep when I, the sleeping son of Denmark, was wide awake? That through me the Lord told you to awaken! That through me He told Norway that the message from sleeping Denmark was also helping to awaken Norway! And that you yourself believed that Norway might have need of me, the sleeping son of Denmark, if it was to awaken!

I realise that this is tough talk and that I could easily put myself in a dim light by praising myself, but you have *forced* me to do so – and God be praised for that! At this very moment I could prostrate myself in the dust and cry from the heart, "Not us, not us, Lord! But all honour to Your name! To You belongs all honour and to us our 'shame of face'!"[510] I feel that I am nothing, and you are nothing, and your Norwegians and all of us are less than nothing unless we are in Him! But in Him are mildness, humility, and love ...

My dear friend, more than once you have given me permission to scold you, and have promised that you will correct your mistake or defend yourself! Well do so now! Test my words for yourself, and test them calmly and seriously before God in humble prayer, and then defend yourself and pour scorn on my words if you can! I know that you could, but that you will not! You must learn and feel that what I say to you here is spoken on behalf of God! I say it only because I know that both you and I, and Norway as sure as Denmark, will benefit from my words... I must test our friendship, as well as your Christian openness and love. Here are words for the Norwegians that you can have printed if you are a Christian, as you truly are...

13. From *Cathrine Bang Grundtvig*

Cathrine (née Bang) Grundtvig (1748-1822) was 14 years younger than her husband, Johan Grundtvig, when she married in 1768. Her family counted scholars and pastors and a rich history among its

---

509. "Et tu, Brute" (You too, Brutus?) were Julius Caesar's dying words in Shakespeare's *Julius Caesar* (III: i) when the emperor recognises his friend Brutus as one of his assassins.
510. II Chron. 32:21. King James Bible has 'shame of face', New International Version has 'in disgrace'.

assets. Frederik, as he was called, was her fourth son. With the motto 'Rather dead than irresolute' she taught Grundtvig to read at an early age, and he was forever grateful to her for nurturing his talents, especially his imagination. When Johan died in 1813, she moved to Præstø to live with her granddaughter Trine (1799-1823). There she had the joy of seeing Grundtvig become pastor of Præstø in 1821 and the arrival of his first son, Johan, just before she died. In his eulogy Grundtvig said: "She taught us early in our childhood to know our God and Saviour and to have Him – the living one who sees us – constantly before our eyes, to pray to Him devoutly in Jesus' name, to read, observe and prize His holy Word, and to sing His praise in the beautiful deep tones of the festival hymns of those days that have since been scorned yet never replaced. Long before this child could understand their meaning his heart was wonderfully sweetly moved and disposed towards inner piety."[511]

Written between 1808-15 and published in 1815, Grundtvig's fourth poetry collection, *Little Poems*, was dedicated to his mother with the words: "To Cathrine Marie Bang, my beloved mother". Now aged 67, she was the subject of the first poem; 11 of its 18 stanzas are translated as no. 129 in *Living Wellsprings* (2015).

Præstø, 5th July 1815

My dearly beloved son.
I received your last letter with great joy, along with the accompanying book which you have dedicated to me, for which I thank my God and you most fondly. The All-Good hears my prayers. May He bless you and your seed and ensure that you live safely in the shade of His wings. I have read your verses to me and was much moved by them. May God reward you here, and above all hereafter, where for Our Saviour's sake we shall gather for ever and be together before His throne. There we shall thank and worship Him – in a way we cannot do as we should in our mortal life. I still have my willpower and I pray each day for strength. Truly my greatest wish is that in the remaining time which the good Lord grants me I may count my days and find true wisdom in my heart and make myself worthy of His honour when His time comes – then I have comfort in this life. It was extremely kind of the King to be so gracious towards you, and I hope and know that when you begin to seek Him, God will also bend His heart to grant your requests on earth. The Almighty has the hearts of all people in His hands – as I have often experienced in this life.

May you be blessed many times and lovingly greeted by me, who shall never fail to be

Your deeply beloved mother
C.M. Grundtvig.

---

511. (Grundtvig 1877, ed. Brandt, 32).

14. To the Royal Danish Chancellery

Application for the Citadel Church curacy.

The Citadel of Frederikshavn (now known as *Kastel*) is a fortification built by Christian IV in 1644 with its own church, now Citadel Church (*Kastelskirken*). During Grundtvig's 7-year engagement to Lise Blicher (Sept. 1811-Aug. 1818) he constantly sought a curacy that would give him the necessary means to marry her. He applied for the Garrison Church (*Garnisonskirken*) and the Citadel Church in Copenhagen, as well as for curacies in Slagelse, Aalborg and at St. Knud's Church (aka Odense Cathedral). But his repeated attacks on the clergy had made him unpopular and unwelcome. He was allowed to preach at Frederiksberg Kirke, but even this opportunity did not satisfy him, and he therefore resigned in 1815. Two years later he changed his mind. Letter 14 is his application to the Chancellery, i.e. the government of the absolute monarch, Frederik VI, for a new living.

~

Copenhagen, 21st July 1817

To the Royal High Danish Chancellery
With the attached, most humble, application for the vacant living of the Citadel, Frederikshavn, I take the humble liberty of requesting the approval of the illustrious institution and of touching upon what I know has prevented your honours from recommending me to a living in the capital city. I believe I should inform you better of a matter which through a series of unusual episodes has acquired a complex appearance.

To the best of my knowledge, my disagreement with the city's pastors is the reason why the illustrious institution has hesitated to approve me. For the same reason – the fear of a scandalous dispute – I regarded my application for such a position as an offence in the circumstances, but I believe that the opposite might also be argued.

In 1810 a number of the Copenhagen clergy complained that in my newly-published dimissory sermon[512] I had insulted not any one of them in particular but the Danish clergy in general. On His Majesty's recommendation I received a reprimand, not for the content of the sermon, but because it was assumed that I had promised my examiner, Professor P.E. Müller, that I would not publish it, and that I had broken my word to him. It was my examiner's complaint, not the clergy's, that was upheld, and therefore I do not see how I could be *opposed* to the Copenhagen clergy, unless I had since complained to His Majesty or the public over my accusers, which has not been the case at all.

When I add to this the fact that the majority of the current Copenhagen clergy and none whatsoever of the Holmen Deanery have supported the complaint against me, it is quite certain that there is no fear of disagreement among the clergy, should I apply for the living at the Citadel. As far as I can see, the fear must rest on the assumption that I am a quarrelsome, cantankerous man, in which case I venture to appeal to the

---
512. See introduction to Letter 3 (p. 405).

testimony of my superiors and my public conduct, with the added claim that in all that has to do with my personal, temporal life a quiet seclusion and docility have always accompanied me.

I shall never deny that in Copenhagen and elsewhere there are pastors whose religious opinions, being distant from mine, I keenly oppose, but there is also disagreement here among the Copenhagen clergy. For as long as I use my oral and written freedom in accordance with the laws of the Fatherland, this dispute will continue whether or not I am a pastor in the capital. I venture to believe that the honourable institution subscribes to the fundamental principle that, provided they do not infringe the laws of the land, all disputes and disagreements between pastors and scholars are a matter of conscience that should not be considered here on earth.

Finally, I allow myself the humble liberty to note that it would be desirable in the circumstances that in all public discussion on religious and theological matters, it would hardly be the case that the dispute led to a victory for the only true and serviceable weapons, namely words and reason. That might be the wish of all friends of Truth, but our disagreement is too great and too widespread to be hidden from sight. Even if silence were appropriate, it is an impossible solution unless the peoples were to sink into total indifference to religion, which in turn would create such a disturbance as to inflict a mortal wound on the State. Once attacks on the faith and opinions of earlier times have become so common, they will never cease for as long as they have powerful spokesmen. And yet, if the spokesmen for times gone by truly believe in what they say, they cannot possibly keep silent, when what they regard as Truth and absolute reality is disputed and undermined. In England, France, and Germany this struggle between the old and the new is fought on a daily basis and with increasing animation. Denmark – any more than any other people who have not fallen completely asleep – cannot remain neutral. Those from whom the State at any rate has nothing to fear are indisputably those who in my opinion have the best constitution in both a political and a religious sense. In this case our Fatherland over centuries has been the calmest state in Europe.

For these reasons I am taking the liberty of asking the illustrious institution to recommend me for this living, one that is neither lucrative nor distinguished, but which allows me the opportunity, at a time when it undoubtedly needs it, to keep repeating the ancient commandment to fear God and honour the King, and to continue my literary pursuits, the obvious purpose of which is to awaken a genuine love of our country and a desire for literary art.

I apologise for the far too protracted manner that I have taken the liberty humbly to employ in this letter. The truth is that I find myself in an unusual situation, so before I perhaps am obliged to leave the city and break off my activities here, before I am performing what I truly regard to be my duty to present my case to the institution, clearly, openly, and with respect. This being so, I can at least take with me the consciousness that I have not neglected anything that I could do with a clear conscience in order to maintain an occupation and acquire a sphere of activity for which I am trained and in which I believe I can be of most benefit to my beloved Fatherland.

Humbly,
N.F.S. Grundtvig

15. To Mette Blicher

Following Grundtvig's engagement to Lise Blicher in 1811 seven years were to pass before the King awarded him an annual grant of 600 rigsdaler to undertake translations into Danish of the Nordic chronicles. Grundtvig now had the means to marry Lise and did so in Ulse Church on 18th August 1818. 20-year-old Christian Wilster attended the wedding and wrote the day after, "Grundtvig had his wedding here yesterday. I was in church and heard the ceremony. He was blissfully happy."

Grundtvig's mother-in-law was Mette Blicher (née Poulsen, 1751-1826), the daughter of a schoolteacher. She had married Dean Diderik Nikolaj Blicher (1746-1805) in 1785 and given birth to four daughters and two sons. Grundtvig had first met her in 1803 and, since the engagement, he had shared Mette's apartment in Løngangsstræde 168 with Lise (in separate bedrooms) and Lise's younger sister Jane. Grundtvig later recalled his happy days with Lise "when in my youth I found the living idyll and entered into its spirit with my youthful bride."

As was the custom of the time, he addressed his mother-in-law as 'mother' and signed himself as 'son'.

Copenhagen, 22nd August 1818

Dear Mother!
We arrived here last Tuesday evening, happy and well, God be praised, despite it being late. Lise is complaining that nothing is yet in order, but it seems to me that everything is working out fine, since we have hauled up our books and other things – and not just ours but also quite a lot of yours! Apart from the curtains it is so neat and tidy here that not even the wife of a state councillor would be ashamed.

There is a fine tea-table as smooth as a mirror that has gained Lise's attention, an unusual contribution from Schmidt.[513] So far, however, our neatness has not attracted anyone's gaze – over which I must admit Lise does not complain. No one has been here except for the Andersens and the man who had joined together to give us 6 nice large silver spoons. For these they received double thanks and three bottles of cherry preserves.

So, dear Mother, now you know our news, which I dare not conceal, since Lise claims that she has no time to write, and our Mother surely knows that my demurrals in such matters are of no use here. I intend no offence to Lise's good name and reputation by saying this! Whether or not a wife is discredited for having plenty of grit and a nose in

---

513. Christian Schmidt was Grundtvig's brother-in-law.

her slippers, I shall refrain from complaint, partly because it is not certain that this letter will escape the censor and partly because, as wives *are* in these enlightened times, I have every reason to be happy and believe that I will come out of it well!

However, it would sound much nicer if I thanked you in all seriousness for the blessed little wife you have both born and granted me, dear Mother. So I am not disinclined to say so, provided you do not pass it on to her, since I would rather not disturb her modesty!

Dear Mother, I give you heartfelt thanks for the unpretentious, devout, and charming girl you have given me to wife. May Almighty God grant that I live with her for better for worse in whatever fortune He may deal us. So may we both day by day have new cause to thank the God who joined us together, and ever to enjoy the inner happiness of each other's company! Thanks too, dear Mother, for all the goodness and comfort of the five whole years[514] that I was fortunate to experience! It is not my custom to speak often or much about such matters, but nonetheless, God be praised, to remember them and ponder them. Many times has it pained me that I could not give you the reward that you might not regard as the greatest, but nevertheless one that you could bid welcome to. I have the hope that in His own good time God will grant me the opportunity to show that whatever else I am, I am not ungrateful.

May God bless you! I must close with the warmest greetings to Pauline and Jane[515] from your

devoted son
N.F.S. Grundtvig

16. To King Frederik VI

Grundtvig was nearly 40 years old, when he wrote this application for another ministry in the church. He had been without a full-time pastoral charge, since he left his father's curacy on his death in 1813. Out of the blue, the King had offered him the living at Præstø in June 1821, but already just over a year later he is dissatisfied with the pastorate, and longs to be back in Copenhagen, not in order to minister to a congregation but in order to be a successful writer. This was not uncommon at the time. Indeed, the King, who in the event granted this request, had already supported Grundtvig's translation and publication of Saxo's *Deeds of the Danes*.

---

514. The "five whole years" refer to Grundtvig's tenancy in his future mother-in-law's property in Copenhagen before his marriage.
515. Pauline and Jane were Grundtvig's sisters-in-law.

Præstø, 20th August 1822

In Jesus' name.
Pastor of Præstø N.F.S. Grundtvig, born 1783, Master of Theology (honours) 1803, ordained 1811, hereby humbly applies for the perpetual curacy at Trinity Church, Copenhagen, or the resident curacy at the Church of Our Saviour, Christianshavn.

After completing my academic studies 16 years ago and coming before the public as a Danish writer, I had the greatest wish to obtain a living in the capital city alongside which I could successfully pursue my literary pursuits.

To this end I have sacrificed more than any scholar or poet in my Fatherland. In order to remain in the capital, where in the past I had broken new ground in my research into the Ancient History of the North, I subjected myself to the difficult task of a schoolmaster's life at what was then the Schouboe Institute. In order to bring to light the works which would survive me – such as *Danne-Virke*, *Beowulf*, and the *Chronicles of the North*[516] – I fought for seven long years (1813-21) under the most extreme circumstances, without achieving my goal: a modest living in Copenhagen. I applied for the curacy at the Garrison Church, for the pastorate at Vartov, and three times for the Citadel in Frederikshavn.

I cannot look back somewhat wistfully at the years gone by without gratefully calling to mind the grace of Your Majesty, without whose encouragement and assistance[517] it would have been humanly impossible for me endure the struggle and retain the balance of mind which is essential to the success of literary pursuits. Although I include in these proofs of Your Majesty's grace the unsolicited calling to the post that I now occupy, I cannot but deeply feel how unfavourable my position is for the pursuits for which my mind is suited – cut off from libraries, printing houses, and the company of scholars. Too often it is the formal tasks that take up my time and cast me into gloom.

May the beloved King of Denmark listen kindly to me and not be angered by the liberty of a humble subject! I am at the age when, as experience teaches, the steady purposeful activity of our powers is at its fairest flowering – but not for long! The loss now of a working-year is more than ten years ago or ten years ahead. Your Majesty has most graciously entrusted me with the delightful and honourable task of continuing with Saxo's history of Denmark, with the aim, if possible, of reviving the praiseworthy memory of our bygone kings and our forefathers' ardour for noble deeds. Wherever I stand, I shall endeavour, with God's help, to do my best, but it would be either pride or falsehood if I said that the place and the position made no difference.

Two perpetual curacies in the capital are currently vacant: the one at Trinity Church, the other at the Church of Our Saviour in Christianshavn, and I am gratefully content with whichever of these Your Majesty sees fit most graciously to grant me.

Even my opponents have attested that God has given me the gifts with which I can properly perform my ecclesiastical duties, while the fact that I, perhaps more than most,

---

516. i.e. the Icelandic Sagas and the Norwegian Sagas, published in 1817.
517. i.e. Grundtvig's annual royal grant of 600 rigsdaler.

am a pastor in the spirit of the past, of the school of Luther and Balle,[518] should never be used to exclude me from the churches of Copenhagen for as long as they have not closed Your Majesty's ears to my speech! What is also clear is that in the times that I have extolled, there was a faithfulness, an affectionate unity, a courage, and a maturity that all true friends of the people wish to be recreated as the only remedy to the national sickness that everywhere is threatening us with ruin, due to slackness, discord, and lack of faith.

In thus raising my voice louder than before to the father of our country on the throne of Denmark, it is with the consoling awareness that I am driven by the desire with God's aid to benefit this blessed land of our fathers with all my strength. I shall not surrender the hope that His Majesty will expediently hear the prayer which for a number of years has been raised by a subject who dedicated his pen to praising the God of our fathers, their highly-extolled monarchs, and their noble deeds!!

Your Majesty's most humble and loyal subject
N.F.S. Grundtvig

17. To Henrik Steffens

Henrik Steffens (1773-1845) was born in Stavanger, when Denmark and Norway were a united kingdom before Norwegian independence in 1814. Aged 14 Steffens and his parents moved to Copenhagen, where he studied Theology and the Natural Sciences: He moved to Germany and lectured at Kiel, Jena, and Freiburg before returning to Copenhagen to give nine lectures, later published as *Introduction to Philosophical Lectures*, which are credited with introducing Romanticism to Denmark in such passages as:

> Behind the visible world is an invisible one that we cannot understand. We must therefore seek this secret world, which we can only sense. Imagination and Feeling are as much a part of human life as Reason. That is why poets are chosen to proclaim the great eternal thoughts and to shine the light for thousands of souls.

As his cousin on his mother's side, Grundtvig was in awe of Steffens' intellectual prowess, foreign experience, and compelling teaching.

Grundtvig was curate at Our Saviour's Church 1822-26, when Steffens visited Copenhagen in September 1824.

---

518. Nicolai Edinger Balle (1744-1816), Grundtvig's uncle, became Professor of Theology at Copenhagen University in 1772 and then Bishop of Zealand in 1783. He published his *Textbook of the Evangelical-Christian Religion Authorised for Use in Danish Schools* in 1791, which became the authorised schoolbook on the Catechism.

6th October 1824

Esteemed cousin!
They are gone, irrevocably gone, the long-expected days when I had hoped to achieve what was so dear to my heart and what I thought would not be a matter of indifference to you. So vain are all hopes in the world of the spirit that rest only on a *reasonable* view! When I put everything together, I come close to thinking that all my efforts to reach a reconciliation with you have had the single consequence of confirming me in your failure to appreciate my literary works. It seems as if you think that I, blinded by selfishness, sought principally to attract your attention, and then lamented only that it was all to no avail. If this fear of mine is well-founded, I cannot expect these lines to effect any change in your thoughts; but, equally, I shall not spare myself these lines solely to have the comfort of that I did the little I could in the circumstances.

Unless I am much mistaken, you have more or less lost faith in the power and effect of poetry, despite the fact that, together with history, it has affirmed your entire life, and since the opposite is now the case with me, it should not come as a surprise that you regard my literary work and our agreement or disagreement about present-day circumstances and our possible effect on them as being negligible, which only selfishness can magnify through fancy. If I were not so certain of both the power of Poetry and of the unnaturalness of your denial of this, then I would keep silent. But if my work is only to be regarded as my own private business, then we have already spent too much time talking about it. But I shall not surrender the hope of reminding you of the days that you did not consider ineffective when passing on the lightning-flashes that had struck you, even though their path from heaven to earth was untraceable and their effect a mystery.

To move to the particular, do you really think that it was without beneficent consequence that you opened up to us, your audience, a view of the wondrous path of history, of Christ as its divine central point, and our epoch as the whited sepulchre – despite it not having happened in a poetic choral work or with detailed evidence? If you do, then I am sure you are mistaken! For I know that it was precisely then that the first spark in my soul of a *spiritual* view of human life was struck, a spark that not even the intervening years could turn to ash. It smouldered, then burst into flame when the hour of the Lord arrived. It was thus the beginning of all that has stirred in me since, not just as a poet and scholar, but also as a Christian and a priest. This sure and certain experience already shows me in my introspection the effects of a poetic-historical language without poetic or philosophical form, a spiritual effect which I must bless! If words from my lips have ever moved anyone to serious thought about time and eternity, then they cannot but *join* me in that blessing. And now are you to deny me the value and effect of such language, and prevent me from letting the words you spoke bear similar fruit through *me*? Honestly, you cannot be serious – any more than you can imagine that I would move a hairsbreadth from the path I am treading just because you who set me on it come with a warning! So in disapproving of my poetic-historical work, you are either offending the Nordic spirit that stimulated you into what will long be remembered and whose effect is undying, or you are assuming that my language disgraces the spirit to whose banner I swore allegiance, and you are calling it empty and impotent, or mistaken!

Here I must stop and ask, Do you *know* my work? Do you know the poetic-historical works in prose or rhyme that I have published – from *Nordic Mythology* to *Scenes from Lives of the Nordic Heroes* to *New Year's Morning*? If you indeed do, and you find them 'impotent', then I have nothing more to say, for then they are undeniably impotent in *your* view, and time will tell whose fault is that! But as far as I can gather, you are almost entirely unaware of my work, so to judge from your present view, you either find the implicit importance of the form impotent, or you regard the details of the work wildly erroneous or objectionable. That is what I think to be the case, since 'impotent' has never been an adjective that anyone applied to my work, and the general direction it takes could never displease you, since it clearly attempts to argue for a spiritual and Christian view of history. You cannot possibly disapprove of this, even if you find the way I link them together too loose, or my exposition too opaque.

It is solely on this assumption that you do not *know* my work – and that if you did, you would not find it offensive or insignificant – that I had wished to explain to you that *New Year's Morning* is to be seen only as a view of my path through life. It was to be expected that my interpretation of the spiritual conditions of the North, and especially of Denmark and its deep historical importance, would offend you, but not that you would denounce my entire view and all my Song-Work! That is unworthy of you! Even if, as you seem to believe, I were to regard Denmark through the glasses of nationalism and selfishness, many a poet and historian has nevertheless regarded his Fatherland through the same glasses without their work being scorned! I am quite sure that if you knew the history of the North and our ancient rhymes as well as I do, you would at least realise that there are deeper reasons for the poetic observer of history to have great hopes for the North in general and for Denmark in particular. It is understandable that you lack this familiar acquaintance with the ancient North and its spirit in its native form, since it was a foreign country to you in your youth. You may have sensed its great treasures and been called away from visiting it by your destiny and your studies, but for you, who are yourself animated by the giant spirit of the North, to denounce my views and hopes without *knowing* what engendered and nourished them – you cannot call that anything other than rash. To demand that I must prove the truth of my view by other means than asserting it powerfully and making its sources available is unjust of you; any other proof is impossible. You call my view of Danishness a 'judaism', and apart from it missing the mark with me, you seem to mean self-conceit of an unmerited mercy and a contempt of humankind – I must let the word stand. For I do not deny what I have expressly stated – that for me Denmark is history's Palestine, meaning the land and people,[519] where Christianity will reach its highest earthly transfiguration. What is wrong with a hope that I cannot imagine being fulfilled unless Denmark truly nurtures the best Christians in Spirit and Truth? This is my defence, for if I am conceited enough to promote myself, or if I publish the idiosyncratic ideas that arise at times from my deeply-moved, almost-singing

---

519. Grundtvig's word here is *Folkeland*.

heart as articles of *faith*, I shall not defend such behaviour. But my conscience acquits me of that charge, and I have often unambiguously declared this to be the case!

This in brief is what I had wished to enlarge on as regards my poetic-historical writings in conversation with you; this was the very least I had hoped to discuss with you. Now that the rest can no longer be made good either, I think I ought to tell you – if you will allow me an hour of quiet here at home – that it cannot be my fault that you disapprove of a good deal of my writing. I cannot separate it from my work as a pastor, but will continually strive to bring it into harmony with it.

Farewell, I know that at heart you will not be angry over an honest word and that now and then you will remember with kindness your kinsman

Grundtvig.

18. To the 88 Clausen-supporters

The Clausen libel case was a major event in Grundtvig's life, and is covered in two articles in *Human Comes First* (2018). Professor Clausen's supporters were many, including 88 students who published an 'address' directed against Grundtvig in *The Picture/Skilderiet* on 17th September 1825. Below is Grundtvig's response to their defence of their teacher. The page references are to Clausen's book, *Catholicism and Protestantism: Their Constitution, Doctrine and Ritual*.

~

20th September 1825

That you praise those you love is natural enough, nor does it surprise me that your love is blind. Remember, however, that even if you were 88 *million*, your combined voices could not overcome the unique power of Truth, and could never make 'Christian' what is *against* Christianity! Even the blind would know that this is the subject we are dealing with, the knot that we must loosen!

In your eyes, your teacher is ten times, no, a thousand times, better than me. So be it! I know how poor I am as a teacher, however great he may be! But he is not a *Christian* teacher, and I have the moral and legal right to say so out loud! What else have I done?

I am saying that when your teacher will not acknowledge the Christian Creed as the rule of faith, he is not my brother in Christ! And that is undeniably true; so why do you want him to be called what he does not wish to be? And is it good of you to show me the path to Hell for telling the truth?

If I understand your teacher and master correctly, he himself believes (pp. 231-32) that when anyone publicly presents a creed that is found to be divergent form the Church's constitutive basic principles, the Church should declare such a member to be excluded from church society until he expresses the wish to be readmitted!

Dare you *prove* that the creed which your teacher publicly presents (p. 537) and wishes to be instituted is not altogether different from all the constitutive basic principles that have obtained in the Christian Church from its foundation to the present day? Or do you claim that your teacher should be an exception to the rule?!

Have you not obviously forgotten that in insisting your teacher makes *Scripture* the rule of faith, he is arguing (p. 301) that all Paul's letters are the fruits of the oldest Christian tradition? That no word in the New Testament is expressly sealed by Jesus' highest authority (p. 308), and that (p. 308 and 343) Scripture contradicts itself in regard to both dogma and history? Or have you learned the art of deducing a non-contradictory rule of faith from a self-contradictory book?

N.F.S. Grundtvig

19. To King Frederik VI

Grundtvig learned Hebrew, Greek, Latin, and German at school. He taught himself Old Icelandic, Anglo-Saxon, and modern English. Grundtvig's German is testified to in the following:

> Grundtvig once invited the German Professor of Theology P.K. Marheineke to his house and spoke very freely with him. A witness, later bishop H.L. Martensen, wrote of Grundtvig's conversation in German: "His pronunciation was not particularly good, but I must admire how he always knew how to choose the most powerful, significant and characteristic expressions and idioms. The great language genius certainly could not deny his knowledge. Although he spoke German, one noticed immediately that it was Grundtvig who was speaking.[520]

Grundtvig's English was only moderately good before his first trip in 1829. However, after the second and third trips it had improved considerably – to the extent that he was quite proud of himself. However, being self taught at a mature age, he doubtless had a pronounced Danish accent, which announces itself especially with 'r' and 'th' sounds.

In the letter below Grundtvig asks for a grant for a whole year! In the event the King granted him 2,000 rigsdaler, roughly 10 times as much as an artisan's annual wage.

---

520. Translated from *N.F.S. Grundtvig – Schriften in Auswahl*. Knud Eyvin Bugge, Flemming Lundgreen-Nielsen, Theodor Jørgensen, Vandenhoeck & Ruprecht, (2010) p. 48. For the three years that Grundtvig was at Egeløkke (1805-08), the house language was Danish, but when distinguished visitors came, it often switched to German, the preferred language of the court, the aristocracy, the civil service, and the landed gentry. At the time, the southern Danish border was just north of Hamburg.

21st May 1828

Most gracious King
N.F.S. Grundtvig most humbly requests His Majesty's benevolent support for a year's stay in London in order to examine the manuscripts, particularly in the British Museum, which can cast light on the history of the North.[521]

Our national history in all its breadth has found a number of benefactors on the throne of Denmark which no other nation can match. Nevertheless, may posterity find Your Majesty's days appreciably distinguished for the generous support and felicitous progress which constantly crowns this illustrious project: namely, to shed light from all sides on the character of our past times and to revive the memory of our laudable and endearing forefathers!

The importance of this for the enlightenment of both the true human condition and the sure and deserving continuation of the life of our people is now becoming obvious to the great nations, such as Germany, England, and France. Despite its limitations, Denmark is so fortunate as to enjoy such goodness of its King as to be more than able to keep pace with the major countries on a path where it is both honourable and beneficial to keep up with the leaders!

Gram, Langebek, and Suhm[522] have lamented the dearth of the rich information from the history of the Middle Ages that can be found in Anglo-Saxon literature, and indeed in general from the book collections in England, where the numerous relevant manuscripts have lain almost completely idle.

In linguistic proficiency in Anglo-Saxon, Denmark has had the honour of surpassing England, and Denmark should not wait for the English scholars to take their foreign counterparts into consideration, for they have neglected to recover so very much of the history of their country. Research from Denmark into the most important manuscripts, especially in the British Museum, is now both possible and must be thought desirable.

Since my studies have rendered me reasonably serviceable for such an undertaking, I most humbly venture the following question: Would His Majesty be most graciously pleased to support a year-long stay for me in London? If so, I would most gratefully strive as far as my strength can stretch, to remedy the lack which the historians of our Fatherland have felt for so long and so painfully!

Most humbly,
Nik. Fr. Sev. Grundtvig.

---

521. The British Museum, established in 1753, was the first free public national museum in the world. Among the collections acquired from the start was the library assembled by Sir Robert Bruce Cotton (1571-1631). It contains the largest group of Anglo-Saxon manuscripts in the world, including the *Lindisfarne Gospels*, the *Beowulf* manuscript, two of the earliest copies of Bede's *History of The English Church*, and five manuscripts of the *Anglo-Saxon Chronicle*.
522. Hans Gram (1685-1748) Danish historian and philologist; Jacob Langebæk (1710-75) Danish archivist and historian, founder of the Royal Society for the History of the Fatherland; Peder Suhm (1728-98) Danish historian.

20. To Peter Fenger

Peter Fenger (1799-1878) took a degree in theology in 1820 and worked for 7 years as a high school teacher. He then became pastor of two parishes near Slagelse in south-west Zealand, an area that was known for its religious revivalists and was therefore dubbed "the Holy Land". He was on home ground here and took up the fight against the rationalist Pastor Hans Bastholm in Slagelse. In 1855 he returned to Copenhagen as pastor of the Church of Our Saviour, where Grundtvig had served between 1822-26, and where Fenger had first come under Grundtvig's influence. Thanks to Fenger, a number of Grundtvig's hymns were given new tunes by composers such as Weyse, Hartmann, Rung, and Barnekow.

N.B. Although Easter Day 1829 fell as late as 19th April, Grundtvig was still waiting for the ice to melt in Denmark before he could embark on his first England trip.

∼

Christianshavn, 11th April 1829

Dear Fenger!
May God grant you a joyful festival and a blessed Easter Day, when the Word of Faith comes alive on the tongues of children and calls down the young men whose raiment is like lightning and whose desire it is to see the wonderful deeds of the Lord among the children of humankind!

In the name of the Lord, and as far as human resolve can stretch, it has been decided that I shall travel to England. As soon as the ice melts, I intend to embark, God willing, to visit the Great Babylon with Daniel's grave![523] If the Lord into whose hands I strove unreservedly to place the matter, and whose turn of finger I therefore dare to note, is with me, then I can feel that I am not alone in that foreign country. May he also bless the trip, so that it may be fruitful in life and light, according to His Word, in whom is the source of life and in whose light we shall see light! It is also His pledge of a happy outcome to the trip at which I have flinched somewhat. I nevertheless have regarded it as both desirable, if not essential, and it now appears that the circumstances are far more favourable than anyone could imagine. The Lord has ensured that my enemies keep their peace for the time being, and my *Rhymed Chronicle*[524] seems to please all sides. The other day I spoke with a man who openly admitted that he was a Naturalist,[525] but who nevertheless thanked me for my *Chronicle of the Bible*,[526] which he let his children use and found it admirable. The

---

523. 'Babylon' (here and elsewhere) is a synonym for a large, confusing city. The OT prophet Daniel is reputed to have been buried in Babylon, Mesopotamia.
524. The *Rhymed Chronicle* (1495) is the first printed book in Danish. It consists of 115 first-person poems about Danish kings up to Christian I (d. 1481). Grundtvig translated 15 of them into modern Danish and published them in the first two editions of *Danne-Virke* (1816-19).
525. Naturalism, beginning with the Ancient Greek, Thales (c. 624-546 BCE), holds that all phenomena can be explained by scientific laws, i.e. by natural causes, without recourse to the super-natural/transcendent.
526. Full title: *A Brief Chronicle of the Bible for Children and the Common Man*, 1828.

Bishop[527] is recommending me to the Archbishop of Canterbury,[528] and I hear that the distinguished literary world is very pleased about my trip, seeing it as an advantage for Learning. I can therefore reasonably hope that the path will everywhere be paved for me to the manifold sources of knowledge that may appear to have dried up but which only need to be addressed in the name of the Lord for them to gush forth and water the soil of the Church meadow so that the harvest is crowned with a good yield!

I admit that I still cannot grasp how I shall lead a *cheerful* life abroad, far away from my wife, my children, and my friends. But I know that He lives who is better than many sons and who never tests us beyond our abilities. He offers a tolerable way out of the trial, and gives far more than we ask for or understand, so I will stammer it until I can sing it with joy!

Dear friend, ... It is as clear as sunshine to me that what we must pray to the Lord that He will set us free from what binds us, so that in whatever way it pleases Him best we may be separated from those who obviously deny and dishonour our faith; to this end quill-battles are of no use! What every Christian pastor must prepare for, if the occasion arises, is to raise his pastoral voice in the name of the Lord and without question of the consequences against the transparently un-Christian pastoral teacher and all the teachers in the Danish State Church who call into question the faith they are pledged to transmit with the urgent request to the authorities either to ensure religious freedom for Christians in the State Church or allow us to leave it! In all likelihood the opportunity to take this step will come soon! May God grant that they and every honest pastor clad in the Lord's full armour stand firm on 'the day of evil'![529] Then we shall assuredly see the salvation of the Lord, for He has not forgotten His people or relinquished His legacy. Our Redeemer is strong, and sits at God's right hand, testifying that He came to preach the Gospel to the poor, to give sight to the blind, and to set the tormented free! Amen ...

My wife sends her greetings. The Lord be with you and preserve us in the holy fellowship of His Spirit!

Your friend
N.F.S. Grundtvig

21. *To Lise*

Grundtvig's first trip to England to study the original *Beowulf* manuscript in the British Museum got off to a slow and lonely start. After a month in London he writes to Peter Fenger: "What I have experienced in myself in this cold, dead, monstrous metropolis cannot be described!" (26th June 1829). But by the time he writes to Lise in the letter below, he is much better adapted to the hurly-burly of the big city.

---

527. Bishop of Zealand, Friederich Christian Carl Hinrich Münter (1761-1830), was a German-born Dane, a rationalist theologian, church historian, philologist, archaeologist, and numismatist.
528. William Howley (1766-1848), a High Anglican, was Archbishop of Canterbury from 1828-48.
529. Eph 6:13.

34 Mornington Place, Hampstead Road, 4th August 1829

Dearly beloved wife!
Thanks for your letter of 24th July... I have moved house, in God's name, and am now living in a lovely, light room with a big green field before me, and that is as it should be, since all persons of quality move to the country in August and September! I have an appreciable walk to the Museum,[530] but once you have got used to London, you do not measure distance so much – a few miles more or less. With God's help I shall never regret the move, for Salting[531] is truly a nice young man who does not know how comfortable he has made me!

My way of life is now to some extent quite different, since Salting has shown me a dining district which, although half a Danish mile from here, is roughly only half-way to the Museum. I leave at 4 p.m., eat my two good dishes there (a rather good soup and a very good second course) and drink a cup of coffee for the same price for which I previously used to have to chew a tough piece of beef. I can also read the English and French papers there, and in the evening I have a chat in Danish or English depending on the circumstances. I came here on Saturday afternoon and on Sunday I went for a walk with Salting to the village of Hampstead, where many Londoners have country houses. The heat was really rather intense, but I very much enjoyed myself. As I think I have mentioned, I now have 4 rooms, 3 on the first floor and a bedroom on the second floor by choice. Our living-room is spacious and attractive with a small sofa and cushions on the chairs, so I can rest; and instead of it being dark by 6 p.m. in Kenton Street, I can now write at 7 p.m. in broad daylight. Best of all, if I lack anything, I only have to tell Salting, and I am truly well served.

Today, while I was out, young Wilson (son of the Consul[532] to whom Møsting[533] had recommended me) came round, and I intend to repay him the visit just to say hello and goodbye. I wish I could have said a farewell for good, but even if the Londoners bore me, God has truly looked after me and helped me gradually to improve, which is the greatest joy in life, for then we are not spoiled but are continually encouraged to appreciate God's goodness. I have now been through more or less all the Anglo-Saxon manuscripts in the Museum, so I only need to look at a few Latin ones and read a number of old English books. Now that it is too late to start on a further trip, I have a few hours to profit from meeting some good people, if only I knew where I could find them. However, what is good and useful will doubtless happen, so I shall frankly endeavour to cast all my care on the Lord who looks after us and who has Londoners in His hand no less than Copenhageners! ...

---

530. The distance is c. 2 miles (3.2 kms), a Danish mile being 7,500 m.
531. S.K. Salting (dates unknown). From 1826-33 he was secretary for the Danish General Consul in London.
532. Mewil Wilson (died 1829) was the Danish Vice-Consul in London.
533. Johan Sigismund von Møsting (1759-1843) was a Danish privy councillor.

Greetings to your friends nearby, kiss the children, and believe me when I say I long to hear Meta talking like a big, sweet girl, to see and embrace you all, and to tell my Lise how happy I am to be by her side as

Your own
Grundtvig

22. *To Lise*

Grundtvig has forgotten that 12th August marks his 11th wedding anniversary – until he takes up his pen and writes the date at the top of this letter. He has clearly had a successful stay in London and his work is done.

London, 12th August 1829

Dearly beloved wife!
Over the last few days I have waited in vain for a letter from my Lise, and I do not expect to see one this week. I was at the museum today, but I could not concentrate, so I came home with the intention of writing this letter. I did not remember that it was our wedding-day until I wrote the date at the head of the letter, but I must have had a vague feeling, since I finally took up my pen today. I also needed to explain to myself the impatient homesickness that I have been half afraid of today, and hope that it will retreat into the background behind its appropriate barriers. This is the first time we are not together on our wedding anniversary, added to which we are far apart today. But the Lord who has conjoined together what no one shall separate will just as little let space as time do that; He will knit us closer together in His love until the end of days!

I am otherwise living as well in London as it is possible away from my loved ones in a bewitched city! But that does not mean so much except that it be to the honour of God who has singularly soothed and comforted me...

The week before last I sent home a number of books that I had purchased at a bookseller to the Royal Library,[534] which I happily regarded as the first step on my homeward journey. As soon as I can obtain a shipping opportunity (with the help of an assistant at the Danish Consulate) I intend to send a number of books that I have purchase for myself to our brother-in-law Schmidt, because when I moved here the books (for the King and myself) filled my suitcase to the brim. I could see that it was to no avail, so I shall lighten my load thus.

I barely know myself why I intend to stay here to the end of the month, since my major task at the Museum – where I now work only reluctantly – seems completed, and I

---

534. i.e. in Copenhagen.

cannot pull myself together to travel anywhere else this year. Nonetheless I feel I ought to do so, if only to await the return of John Miller[535] from Italy, and in particular to be able to say with a clear conscience that I kept going until the end for as long as there was the slightest chance of being useful – the Museum is so full of all kinds of people that the fifty manuscripts I have had my fingers on must seem like nothing to them.

Thank you, dear Lise, for eleven years of loving companionship and for our lovely children! May the Lord bless us through them, so we see them growing up to happiness and they see in us Christian examples worthy of imitation and a pleasure to follow ... Kiss the dear children and greet the friends you meet from your

own husband
N.F.S. Grundtvig

23. To John Bowring

John Bowring (1792-1872) was an English linguist who visited Denmark in 1829 and met Grundtvig.

By the end of his first trip to England, Grundtvig believes that his own linguistic ability has improved considerably. Letter 23 is of interest in this context, with a number of the grammatical mistakes still common to Danes learning English today. Underneath the letter the translator has added a 'fair copy' with corrections.

∽

Friday morning 20th October 1829

Dear Sir!
Sending my *Kvædlinger*[536] and *Krønike-Rim* for you, I will not mention, where more of my small poems are to be met with, for in this point our *Literatur-Lexikon* is almost as good an instructor, as I might prove myself, and besides, I think, but very few of my verses will suit your purpose. Whereas I will tell you in what point of view I consider myself as a poet, for, as it very seldom shall be the case, that, speaking of his brethren, an author did quite forget himself, I also make no profession of that self-denial, and perhaps there may be no author in Denmark. of whom the opinions are more different and the ideas more confuse than just of me.

Rather than a genuine poet I would terme myself a particular compound of history and poetry, the fermentation of which not without some power has manifested itself as

---

535. John Miller (dates unknown) was a Lincoln's Inn lawyer and writer of legal works. He was eminently distinguished by his knowledge of languages and had a library "peculiarly rich in books on foreign law in the finest condition". Miller was helpful the following year with introductions for Grundtvig to various antiquarian book experts. In 1831 Grundtvig wrote to him as "if not the only at least the first of my English friends." (BTOFG II no. 349).
536. The three book references are to *Little Poems* (1815), *Rhymed Chronicle* (1829), and *Encyclopedia of Literature*.

well in the prosaic as in the metrical performances of mine, which of course with few exceptions fall short of the unity and the clearness, I have never despised, but would not buy on the expense of life and strength. How far at length I have succeeded in attaining a form wherein the workings of my mind might freely move without encroaching upon the unity, my "Krønike-Rim", I think, will better show than I, as the most partial friend of mine, should be able to tell.

The carriage is ready at the door, and recommending myself to your kind remembrance, Dear Sir, I continue

Yours
very faithfully
N.F.S. Grundtvig

Corrected version by Edward Broadbridge

Dear Sir!
In sending my *Little Poems or Small Verse* and *Rhymed Chronicle* to you, I shall omit to mention where any more of my small poems are available, for on this point our *Encyclopedia of Literature* is almost as good an instructor as I might be myself, and besides, I think only very few of my verses will suit your purpose. On the other hand, allow me to tell you from what point of view I consider myself a poet, for, as is very seldom the case when speaking of one's brothers, writers should forget themselves completely. I also do not profess such self-denial; indeed there may be no other author in Denmark about whom opinions differ so much and are so confused as about myself.

Rather than a genuine 'poet' I would call myself a particular compound of history and poetry, the fermentation of which has manifested itself powerfully both in my prose and in my poetry, which of course with few exceptions fall short of the unity and the clearness that I have never despised but would not buy at the expense of life and strength. How far I have finally succeeded in attaining a form in which the workings of my mind may freely move without encroaching upon the poem's unity, my *Rhymed Chronicle* will better show than I, being my most partial friend, can tell.

The carriage is ready at the door, and recommending myself to your kind remembrance, dear Sir, I continue to be

Yours very faithfully
N.F.S. Grundtvig

24. To Lise

On his second trip to England – from 11th May to 29th September 1830 (140 days) – Grundtvig again felt himself ignored by the English. As he wrote to Lise: "Not a soul here cares a jot for me, except when I pay my 2 guineas per week; but God be praised, it does not bother me this year any more than last year." At one point, however, his loneliness and homesickness brought him to tears.

49 Hunter St., Thursday evening 3rd June 1830

Dear good Lise!
Thank you for your fond letter of 19th May. God be praised, I could see from it that you and the children are well, as I hope and pray you still may be and remain! My daily routine is even more settled this time than last; indeed, there is no comparison! However, last Saturday my heart was as tight as at any time last year at the thought that I had still not seen anything from my loved ones, and what could the reason possibly be! I had to go out into God's fresh air and with eyes wet gaze up at the Heaven where He lives, He who does good to the ungrateful. Not only was I thereby moderately relieved, but immediately on my return home I received your letter via Salting, which naturally made me doubly happy!

Last Sunday I went with Bowring to a Socinian[537] Church that he attends. I had promised to go with him in a moment when I had forgotten that it was Whit Sunday, and I did not want to withdraw, in particular because I knew of nowhere where I could expect to hear a genuine Whitsun sermon! What a pity that I did not realise that a very famous Christian Protestant, Dr. Chalmers[538] from Edinburgh, was preaching in Irving's church,[539] which is close by! I had to tramp halfway through the city with Bowring only to hear a mediocre 'Clausen' sermon by Mr. Fox,[540] who is smaller in every sense than the little pope ...[541]

Today I have been to St. Paul's to witness an annual service with around 10,000 children[542] from all of London's charity schools, who sit on an amphitheatre platform erected for the purpose – with the girls in white bonnets and aprons. They create the most picturesque scene, and they take part in the singing, which is led by a choir that we in Copenhagen can barely conceive of! Bowring had got me a ticket (which is not easy) in the very best seats at that – under the dome in the middle of the amphitheatre! I would not have missed it for the world, even though I had to arrive so early to get my seat that I was there

---

537. Socinianism was named after two 16th century Italian theologians, Laelius and Faustus Socinus, and was developed in the Polish Reformed Church in the 16th century, and by 1676 there were at least three Socinian meeting houses in London. Socinians rejected the doctrines of the Trinity, the Atonement, Original Sin, and the Divinity of Christ.
538. Thomas Chalmers (1780-1847) was Professor of Theology at Edinburgh University, an evangelical preacher, and founder of the Free Church of Scotland.
539. Edward Irving (1792-1834) was a famous Scottish pastor who in 1833 was expelled from the Church of Scotland in separation from the national Presbyterian Church, and in 1843 was the founder of his own church in London.
540. William Johnson Fox (1786-1864) was a unitarian preacher, politician and writer, who had his own chapel in Finsbury.
541. H.N. Clausen (1793-1877), 'the little pope', was a rationalist Professor of Theology at Copenhagen University from 1822-74. Following a vicious article against Clausen for his rationalist theology, Grundtvig was found guilty of libel and placed under publishing censorship between 1826-37. In protest he resigned his pastorate in 1826.
542. Every year on the first Thursday in June, there was a special thanksgiving service at St Paul's Cathedral attended by all the poor children from the charity schools of the city, around 7,000 of them (Grundtvig's figure is undoubtedly exaggerated). The poet William Blake had attended one such service and commemorated it in his poem 'Holy Thursday' (1789) with the final injunction: "Then cherish pity, lest you drive an angel from your door." The composer Joseph Haydn had been similarly moved in 1791.

for five hours more or less! I doubt if I would be tempted to repeat the visit, for despite it having a religious touch (there was a sermon!) it is no more than a theatrical stage. ...

This year, as last year, I find the English in general like the fossils[543] they appear to be, so unless the Lord makes haste to help me, neither I nor anyone will have anything to commend ourselves for from this journey! Nevertheless, it was in His name and trusting in His aid that I undertook it, and He will not let disappoint such hope! May His Spirit lead, His wings cover, and His love fill you and

Your
N.F.S. Grundtvig

25. To Lise

On June 24th 1830, Grundtvig was invited to a dinner party by Mr and Mrs Heaton. Unaware that her husband was also present, he met 26-year-old Mrs Clara Bolton, who took his breath away with her beauty and her informed conversation on mythology. Grundtvig spoke to her just this once, but the experience inspired the lines in *The Little Ladies* (1844): "Clara's breath opened the mouth, /The rock split and the stream flowed out." In a draft for an unfinished letter dated 20th August to his dinner-party host, Grundtvig asked Mr Heaton to apologise on his behalf for not taking up the invitation to visit Clara, and added, "... since I came to the age of discretion, and that is a rather long time ago, I have not, to put it mildly, been so taken by any woman in the world."[544] Just before the draft breaks off, Grundtvig calls Clara "Queen of the Elves"![545]

Two years later Clara Bolton campaigned in vain for the great Victorian politician Benjamin Disraeli's election to Parliament. She died aged 35 in a hotel in Le Havre in 1839.

Friday 25th June 1830

... At 6.30 pm I met Michelsen[546] at the Heatons, and found a not exactly large but a pleasant and partly distinguished company who were royally treated and entertained, so it was nowhere near disbanding when I left around 1 a.m. It was so late out on the streets that I had over a mile home to walk, so I was glad when halfway there I ran into a carriage which for a shilling brought me home safe and sound.

Over the table, Mrs Heaton, one of those women who can say what she likes, asked me if my umbrella and I were completely inseparable, since she had seen me many a time on the street but never without it! I admitted, equally openly, that I had promised I

---

543. Grundtvig's word here, *Forsteninger*, means 'petrifactions/fossilizations'.
544. Bang, 1932, 70.
545. The Danish word, *Ælvedronning*, can also be translated as 'fairy queen'.
546. Captain Ove Michelsen (1800-80) was a friend of Grundtvig in London, where he was studying the use of naval artillery. He was later Admiral and Minister of Naval Affairs in Denmark.

would never allow myself to be deceived by the London sunshine and go out alone into this watery world. The people I talked to most were the man sitting next to me, Baron Roland, Secretary of the Swedish Legation, and a young lady named Mrs Bolton (I do not know whether she was a spinster or a widow).[547] After dinner she got into a conversation with me, and she is the most interesting English lady I have met so far. It is reasonable to assume that she possesses what is known here as a 'large independent fortune', which I conclude from the ease with which she treated the company and the respect with which everyone treated her. She mentioned the names of a number of literary men with whom she was well acquainted, and I imagine she will include me among them, since on our parting she asked Mrs Heaton to tell me – and she herself confirmed it – that she hoped and wished that I would pay her a visit. To this end I was given her address, and I can see that she lives in the most fashionable part of the West End. I could not possibly refuse, but I feel somewhat awkward about visiting such a brilliant young lady, so I must think over the fulfilment of the promise. What I have long thought to be the case seems to have been confirmed now: that if I come into contact with any Englishmen, it is the ladies who must look after me, a possibility which I think I never dreamed of before I arrived here. Do not be jealous of your old grey-haired, toothless husband, rather be happy that the English lack of taste may for once have beneficial consequences.

It touches me deeply to hear that when you remind the boys[548] of their father, they remember him so vividly and lovingly. If I can manage it, I shall bring our lovely Danish doll[549] the English one that she is hoping for! (I must add that yesterday evening I told Mrs Bolton I was fortunate to have both a wife and children) ... Give my best wishes to Johan, Svend, and Meta, as well as to our own Jane,[550] the sisters, brothers-in-law and their friends. And heartfelt greetings to you, with thanks for your tender mothering care for them as well as for your faithful love as fiancée and wife for your husband

N.F.S. Grundtvig

26. To Lise

London, 30th June 1830

Dear, good wife!
Thanks for your letter of the 19th which I received yesterday and to which I shall begin a reply already this evening, since time will be short tomorrow and I intend to fill all four sides, if possible.

---

547. Grundtvig assumes Clara is unmarried and of independent means, even though she has been introduced as 'Mrs Clara Bolton' and her husband is present!
548. At this point Johan is 8 and Svend 5 years old.
549. i.e. Meta, who at this point is 3 years old.
550. 'Aunty Jane' is Grundtvig's unmarried sister-in-law.

First of all, as regards the beautiful Mistress Bolton, she has doubtless left you somewhat curious! When I set out to make my visiting round last Saturday I had half thought that I might also see her, but that I would first visit the Heatons (where I had run into her) and acquire a little more information about her – and this proved a good idea. Heaton was out on business, so I visited his cheerful wife, and had barely sat down before she began to joke about my success on meeting the beautiful lady. Now I heard that not only was she married, but that her husband had been present at the dinner-party! Since he had not said a word to me, let alone asked me to visit them, I realised that there was nothing for me there. Mrs Heaton declared the opposite, and although it is indeed the custom in London for the wives to issue the invitations rather than the husbands, if I had been at a dinner-party with a stranger to whom I paid not the slightest attention, I too would have thanked him not to visit me. Whatever *Mr* Bolton thinks, I cannot visit them under the circumstances – so there will be no introductions,[551] and that is that.

Last Sunday Michelsen and I were again in Richmond, this time in a carriage with Baron Moltke,[552] who was to treat us to a picnic. Although my enjoyment was not great, I truly appreciated his intentions, and later, in a summerhouse on the banks of the Thames, our twilight dinner was excellent. Strawberries and cream may not be an English dish, but I noted how popular it was in England.

On Saturday morning the King died,[553] so the Museum is closed this week and almost everything has shut down. This evening I put crêpe round my hat, since we must all look as if we are in mourning. Actually, I have indeed mourned these past few days, but over something quite different: my idleness here! I can see an end to it, but not the point of it. But with God's help things will be better sooner than we realise.

You asked about the Archbishop,[554] but I cannot say more than that it was not until today that I visited his Palace on the south bank of the Thames.[555] I was told that he was no longer staying there but was at another address in London, upon which I sailed back and left a letter and some books at his dwelling.[556] Whether or not I shall hear from him, and about what, time will tell. On the other hand, today I have been surprised by a promising visit. While we were dining, a coach drew up at the door that created quite a stir. I paid no attention until I was told that a gentleman was looking for me and that it was a wealthy baronet, Sir Phillips,[557] who has a large collection of manuscripts, and who came to invite me out tomorrow. Last year Petrie from the Tower[558] promised to introduce me to him,

---

551. i.e. introductions to the influential London literati and others.
552. Baron Carl Moltke (1773-1858) was privy councillor in London for Frederik VI.
553. George IV (1762-1830), reigned from 1820.
554. William Howley (1811-82) was Archbishop of Canterbury from 1828-48. The archbishop has a residence both in Canterbury and in London (Lambeth Palace). Grundtvig had drafted a letter to him which he never sent.
555. Lambeth Palace is still the London residence of the Archbishop of Canterbury.
556. Conceivably, this would be a letter of introduction and collections of his own poems.
557. Sir Thomas Phillips (1792-1872) was a book collector who purchased 40,000 printed books and 60,000 manuscripts in the course of his life. Grundtvig breaks British etiquette by calling him by his title followed only by his surname; he should be given his full name, and thereafter addressed as 'Sir Thomas' (Christian name only).
558. Henry Petrie (1768-1842) was an English antiquary and official, who from 1819-42 was Keeper of the Records at the Tower of London.

but since he forgot to remind himself to do so this year, when I met him on the street one day I took the liberty of reminding him. That was over a month ago, and I thought that he had surely forgotten all about it, but he had recently spoken to Sir Phillips, and the healthy young man was now so immensely courteous as to introduce himself to me!

1st July
I have just returned home from Sir Phillips, in whose library I have spent 5 hours, until I was as hungry as a dog! Even the best hosts are not kind enough to offer anyone a glass of water or a bite unless they are expressly invited to food and drink. Otherwise the man was as courteous as could be and kept up with me all the time and showed me everything that he thought might in any way interest me ....

My English is nothing like as fluent as you imagine; I come to a halt all the time, as I am thinking in Danish and cannot remember even the most common foreign words.

The first four days this week were unusually beautiful, but yesterday afternoon the familiar rain began again. God grant that with my mission accomplished I was back with my loved ones in Christianshavn! May He whose loving-kindness is everlasting and who alone can grant this wish bless and keep you all

and your
Nik. Fred. Sev. Grundtvig

27. *From Lise*

To Grundtvig's surprise, Lise chided him for failing to seize the opportunity to meet the London literati that Mrs Heaton had presented. Both here and on other occasions Lise does not seem to be jealous of her husband's attraction to other women – or of their attraction to him.

∼

Christianshavn, 10th July 1830

Dear beloved Grundtvig!
Heartfelt thanks, dear Grundtvig, for your letter last Wednesday! It was very kind of Baron Moltke to offer to post your letters and to invite you on a pleasure trip! ...

I am really distressed that you will not be visiting Mistress Bolton; I would even scold you if it could reach your ears and bear any fruit. Can you even know how many good intentions she has had towards you? Precisely because she is married, you would have done best to visit her. Imagine if it had been Mrs Rahbek or Mrs Brun[559] – have they not often invited many a man of whom not a bad word could be said? No husband would be dishonoured, nor would it surprise anyone. Is it not possible that a brilliant literary

---

559. Kamma Rahbek (1775-1829) and Frederikke Brun (1756-1829) both held literary salons in Copenhagen.

lady and her wealthy husband would actually have *enjoyed* your visit? You can now see that instead of your wife being jealous of the beautiful lady, I am angry that you did not accept the invitation. Whoever I have spoken to about it wonders at the man who did not *go*! Perhaps you have had time to think it over and have actually made the visit – that I long to know!

It was a great honour that you enjoyed from Sir Phillips, who actually came to invite you! It seems to me that it cannot be denied that the English (and especially the ladies) are showing my dear husband great courtesy. In their eyes you may appear somewhat strange (you are laughing at this word!), and this is the hardest thing to take as a foreigner. Doubtless they can sense that you do not have complete confidence in them ...

Live well, my faithful husband. May God bless and guide you on all your ways! May His protecting hand be upon you and let all your undertakings succeed. May He gather us in His hand and in His heartfelt love!

Your faithful Lise

PS. Have your hair and side-whiskers been trimmed somewhat, so that you do not look like a wild man? As you surely remember, your wife likened you to one last year! And do not be angry at this reminder; I want my husband to look good in a foreign country.

28. To Lise

London, 8th July 1830

Dear, good wife!
I have not received a letter this week, but since I have not heard that the packet[560] has arrived, I hope that it is neither your fault nor the consequence of anything else but a headwind.

Last Friday I received a very courteous letter from the Archbishop[561] with a letter of recommendation to Exeter and permission to pay my respects to him at 11 o'clock on whichever day I choose. I did so on Monday and found His Grace very gracious! In appearance he is a mild, plain, kindly man, but, as they say, he is not very deep. He promised me a recommendation to Oxford too, and made a note of it so as not to forget, but since I have not yet received it, I am not counting on it! ...

I am getting ready to turn my back on London, but this will not happen before a week on Monday. From Molbech's letter you will see that it is doubtful whether I shall get any further than Oxford, which takes five hours to drive to from here. And then I shall only find Oxford empty, since the long vacation has begun,[562] during which all the students

---
560. A packet was a small post-boat that received mail off a ship and sailed it ashore.
561. Archbishop of Canterbury, William Howley.
562. Students would have left in mid-June and would not return until mid-October.

and a number of professors leave the city. However, it could not be otherwise – and they do not take the library with them! ...

Last Friday ... I went with Michelsen to the zoo, which was full of foreign animals and birds. I saw a multitude of living creatures that I have never set eyes on before, but the lion was asleep, the camel would not get up, there were no elephants, and the reindeer were in miniature, so all in all it did not live up to my wishes – and only to my expectation in not being grandiose ...

The King[563] is to be buried at Windsor on the 15th at midnight with immense pomp, but I do not intend to stop and stare there. And anyway it would cost more than I can spare ...

When they are being good, please bring my fatherly greetings with a motherly kiss to Johan, Svend and little Meta. Greetings also to friends! In mid-August I expect to be back in London, and only then can I dare to think about embracing my wife and children back home. May the Lord who has helped us this far be our merciful companion on our short as well as our long journeys towards the eternal dwellings!

Your
N.F.S. Grundtvig

29. To Lise

From 20th July to 9th August Grundtvig stayed in a hotel in Exeter while studying the Anglo-Saxon manuscripts in the Cathedral library. He was overwhelmed by the *Exeter Book*, a 10th century manuscript of poems, owned by Leofric, the first Bishop of Exeter. In a letter to his friend Christian Molbech, dated the same day as this one, Grundtvig wrote, "My stay in Exeter has become in every way so pleasant an episode that I am close to setting it above my actual work, for my task here was far more successful than I had any reason to expect."

∼

Exeter, 25th July 1830

Dear good wife!
If you are to have a long letter from here I had best begin in good time and spend an evening when I do not come home either tired or late to write most of it. I have never *had* such busy days and pleasant evenings in England as here! I think I mentioned in the few lines that I hope you have already received that access to the manuscript I sought was open to me. But let me explain more clearly *how* this came about. Next to the great cathedral is a so-called 'Chapter House' where the books are kept. I collect the key to this large, beautiful hall every morning and I take it back every evening – without having to account for it! This is a degree of freedom that I might almost call excessive, but since I

---

563. King George IV died at Windsor Castle on 26th June 1830.

have no intention of misusing it, in my case it is only for the best. I have also helped to ensure that the manuscript can be transported to London so as to be copied in full at the Museum. ... Bowring, who is here to visit his father, has procured me a lodging in town that lies at the end of a Peter Madsen's Passage[564] and is shamefully expensive, but I am very well served there, and almost every day I am invited out to dinner. When I am not dining anywhere else, I go to Bowring's place, close to the actual city. There I chat with him or, if he is too busy, with his aging father, a handsome, friendly old man, or with his two sisters, who are cheerful, natural girls in whose company I am quite at home and on whom I practise my English tongue as best I can! It is a kind of Athenaeum[565] to which I have gained access, so as you can imagine, I am not making haste to leave, since nowhere in England can I expect to be treated so well! ...

This trip to Exeter, which I dreaded a year ago and even this year was worried about, has been given the most desirable turn by our Lord. I ought to place in His Almighty and fatherly hand not only the whole trip but also my somewhat doubtful situation when I return home ...[566]

Kiss the little ones, Johan, Svend, and Meta, from me, give my best to Jane and all our brothers and sisters and close friends, and please accept the deepest best wishes from your husband

N.F.S. Grundtvig

30. To Bernhard Ingemann

Bernhard Severin Ingemann (1789-1862) was the youngest of 8 children born to Pastor Søren and Birgitte Ingemann. He lost his father when he was 10, his mother when he was 20 and several brothers and sisters. He studied Law at Copenhagen University and began to publish poetry, plays, and the historical novels. A grant from the King of Italy enabled him to travel to Germany, France, Switzerland, and Italy in 1818-19. He left university in 1822 to become director of Danish Literature and Language at Sorø Academy, where he spent the rest of his life. In the same year, and after a 10-year engagement, he married Lucie Mandix, but the couple had no children. Ingemann supported his wife's painting throughout their life.

He is best remembered as a hymn- and song-writer, especially for his *Morning-Songs for Children* (see Letter 33), and by his 70th birthday he was honoured as Denmark's national poet.

Grundtvig's friendship with Ingemann lasted over 50 years, beginning in 1812, much of it conducted through their lengthy correspondence. They disagreed on a number of things, but as the subsequent letters show, theirs was a genuine friendship.

---

564. Peder Madsens Gang was a famous alleyway in old Copenhagen.
565. In Ancient Athens, the temple dedicated to Athena was known as the Athenaeum, the meeting-place of poets, philosophers, and orators – and by extension an academy, learned society, even a journal and an English bookshop in Amsterdam. The private gentlemen's club of the same name was founded in London in 1824.
566. Grundtvig has been without a pastorate since he resigned from the Church of Our Saviour on 26th May 1826.

N.B. In each volume in this series the translator has included a single translation that follows Grundtvig's syntax to the letter – so with all its twists and turns the first sentence in this letter runs as follows (in the original Danish to 144 words):

∽

Christianshavn, 3rd October 1830

Dear Ingemann! ...
I could get no further with yesterday's letter before a visitor came; and since it must not be a repeat of Tuesday, I am seizing the first spare moment to thank you for your kind remembrance and for the brotherhood in Spirit which is so indescribably precious to me, because, setting aside all other considerations, it cannot be anything other than a comfort for a warrior, when he is being howled down for his cruelty, and dare not flatter himself that he has managed such a hard task as the twin-edged sword without making either an ill-judged step or a showing a lack of caution but dares to tell the world and himself: look, I am joined in loving-kindness with the most peaceful of my countrymen in witness that though I am far from perfection in the field as well as in the castle it is not because I lack a heart that can beat in harmony with anything other than drums!

I have been to England for a second time and found myself all the better there than last year – without comparison! In general I met the same coldness and indifference to everything that does not smack of profit in hard cash or tangible circumstances. However, I did meet exceptions, and I can trace some progress towards the goal of compelling England to take an interest in its own ancient history and thus in its Middle Ages. I derived no particular benefit or pleasure from Bowring, who in the one or other spiritual landscape is an antipode to me and without a living interest in anything but armchair politics. Nevertheless I have much to thank him for, since his father's house in Exeter made the three weeks that I spent on the banks of the River Exe the idyllic episode that I have always desired to experience – and be thoroughly animated by! Having sat myself tired in the Chapter House beside the majestic Cathedral, alone with ancient books and the even older manuscript from Bishop Leofric's days, I would wander out of the city, which is not big, to the friendly house in the country. Here I would smile away the hours in the company of Bowring's sisters, two natural, cheerful girls with an education that is rare in England. Both the lovely summer weather and the loveliness of the countryside, known for good reason as "the Garden of England" added to the enjoyment of life. As if by coincidence, I met in the house a young clergyman who lived in Bristol, where I was heading to meet Mr. Price,[567] who is more or less the only Anglo-Saxon scholar in the country. So together with this parson, who did me all the services he could, I travelled to Bristol and found in Price such a charming man! He had not only spent some time in

---

567. Richard Price (1790-1833) was a British barrister, as well as a philologist, antiquarian, and literary editor. He assisted Henry Petrie in his edition of the Anglo-Saxon Chronicle to 1066 in vol. I of *Monumenta Historica Britannica*, and had a wide knowledge of German and Nordic literature.

Germany and even a little in Denmark, but he had rid himself of English prejudice and made himself acquainted with both German and Nordic literature Incidentally, I *must* pay England yet another visit, not least because I still have not yet been to Cambridge: I have only been to Oxford during the dead vacation, and was fooled by my transcriber in the British Museum, so I had to depart without a copy of Layamon's *British Rhymed Chronicle*, which poetically is as beautiful as it is significant.[568] Not only does this need to be remedied, I also need to further my acquaintance with the people and the language. The prospects of me doing so are doubtful. True there is a London book-dealer who has quite unexpectedly proposed to me an edition of a whole series of Anglo-Saxon books, for which I am preparing a prospectus for printing very soon.[569] If this were successful, the publisher would naturally pay for a summer stay in England, which would be absolutely essential. But even if he could manage with just 100 subscribers, many in London do not think such a number could be found. Time will tell, but at least I have had the opportunity in the said prospectus to tell the English what I think of their unnatural indifference to what they ought to venerate, even if it were not their own teaching. If I could come back to England and talk to my knowledgeable acquaintances about it, I truly believe the matter will be pushed through. In which case everything would be printed in Copenhagen, with Beowulf in a literal English translation at the head. ...

Your friend,
N.F.S. Grundtvig

31. To Bernhard Ingemann

Already in 1827 Grundtvig was concerned about the so-called 'parish-tie' that bound parishioners to worship locally. In the cities this was difficult to enforce, but in the countryside churchgoers were not expected to worship elsewhere. In 1833 Grundtvig wrote to King Frederik VI on the issue, and he also discussed the problem in other writings from the 1830s to the 1850s.[570] Grundtvig and his allies wished to establish a freedom clause within the Church so that any individual member could 'break the parish-tie'. They succeeded through the new democratic Parliament in 1855, thus paving the way for the revivalists to remain within the over-all framework of the national Church; all members were now free to join the pastors and congregations congenial to their own religious views. In the same manner, Parliament allowed for the establishment of free schools alongside the public schools run by the government.

---

568. *The Chronicle of Britain* (written c. 1190-1215) is a Middle English poem of 16,096 lines by the Worcestershire priest, Layamon. It is based mainly on the Anglo-Norman *Roman de Brut* by Robert Wace, which in turn is a version of Geoffrey of Monmouth's Latin *Historia Regum Britanniae*. Layamon's poem is longer than both of these with an enlarged (and influential) section on the life of King Arthur and the Knights of the Round Table.
569. "Bibliotheca Anglosaxonica. Prospectus and Proposals of a Subscription for the publication of the Anglosaxon Manuscripts, illustrative of the poetry and literature of our language, most of which has never yet been printed. Edited by the Rev. N.F.S. Grundtvig of Copenhagen". London 1831.
570. Text 45 in *HCF*.

Christianshavn, 19th April 1831

Dear Ingemann!
Thanks for your friendly letter, as well as for the serious role you are taking in the Church's crisis. I am probably writing too much about it at the moment, but since there is no chance of a conversation with you, here are my thoughts.

For twenty years now I have sought to bring about a reformation in the State Church itself so that it once again could become a bearable residence for living Christians. Unfortunately, it has not become better, but worse! Never before has a pastoral teacher declared religious unity to be inhuman, Christian history to be irrelevant, and the pastoral oath to be meaningless! That is what Clausen has done! Never before has a set of Theology students – the 88 – declared themselves in agreement with those who deny the obligation of the oath! And never before has the Chancellery – as is the case with Busck's complaint – declared that the government will not uphold Church Law!

Since congregations nevertheless continue to be tied to their parish pastors, it is obvious that when a congregation gets one of these unbelieving, lawless pastors who are being hatched out shamelessly and openly, the common Christians must choose. Either they put up with the sacraments being falsified and their children being seduced from the original Baptismal Covenant to which they should have been confirmed, or they must subject themselves to a martyrdom in prison.[571] Christian pastors must not allow this to happen! It is from *them* that martyrdom begins!

It is neither the Christian love of peace nor an awareness of the danger of Church division but also our flesh and blood that counsel us as far as possible to manage with written protests against the Church's self-contradiction and its glaring constraint of conscience. And we are reluctant to pursue the matter any further than we have to, especially at my age. But if we are indeed Christ's servants, we cannot but feel that this matter must come to an end immediately: a pastor with Luther's faith cannot think like Erasmus;[572] he can leave to posterity what he himself has been called to preach.

For as long as I was in doubt about where the rock lay on which Christ built His Church,[573] I was forced to wait – and wait perhaps even to my death for the enlightenment without which no Church separation is defensible. But since I received my

---

571. Baptists, who believed only in adult baptism, could be imprisoned for their 'illegal' actions. Their leader in Copenhagen, Peter Mønster, spent two years in prison. The Church sided with the state and forcibly seized and baptised babies of Baptist believers. Grundtvig was shaken to find two Baptists incarcerated prison when he accompanied Elizabeth Fry into the Copenhagen prison (see p. 210). With the democratic constitution of 1849 came freedom of belief and worship.
572. The Renaissance is embodied in the probing thought, scholarship, and rationalism of the Christian humanist Erasmus of Rotterdam (1469-1536), the Reformation in the reforming zeal and doctrine of justification by faith of Martin Luther (1483-1546). Grundtvig was in temperament and faith a Lutheran.
573. Mt. 16:18.

vision,[574] I have fought with myself for 6 years, always postponing the crucial move because I wished, as I *should*, to avoid it. Yet at the same time I was constantly thinking: what would happen if either we undertook the least possible change to the essential elements of the Church or my previous audiences demanded that I resume my pastoral role? It would be make or break. In other words either the State Church must undergo another reformation or it must offer me an independent pastoral living. Alternatively, I could formally leave the Church – with no one, a few, or many.

Not only one but both of these conditions have now come about, and I have made my irrevocable decision. It is now only a question of the length of this brief delay.

The changes in the Altar Book may seem insignificant to many, but in what *is* unchangeable every attempt at change is an attack on the life of the Church; and it is precisely the words of the Creed and the words of institution at Baptism that have been assiduously rewritten. It was not even necessary to make the major change of turning 'the Holyspirit' into 'the Holy Spirit'[575] for me to say, "The community within which Baptism is undertaken in *that* belief is not the one into which I am baptised and will everlastingly remain so!" ...

But all things ripen for harvest, God be praised! For He is Lord of the Harvest and what is harvested without Him makes for transient satisfaction.

Your friend
N.F.S. Grundtvig

32. To Lise

If there was one place in England where Grundtvig felt at home it was Trinity College, Cambridge. Here he felt he was among both friends and equals, and it was here that his idea of a people's high school began to take serious shape. At Trinity College staff and students even dined together in the same hall. Here too he met Professor Whewell (pronounced *'you'll'*) for the first time. Whewell was Master of the college, and Grundtvig was so grateful for his help that he even wrote a poem in English to him – see no. 140 in *Living Wellsprings* (2015).

---

574. A reference to Grundtvig's 'matchless discovery' in 1825 that Christianity builds first and foremost on the living Church (including Baptism, Holy Communion, and the Apostolic Creed). To all of this the Bible is an indispensable supplement.
575. The translation attempts to render Grundtvig's Danish distinction between 'den Hellig-Aand' and 'den hellige Aand', i.e. between the Holyspirit (noun) and 'the Holy Spirit' (adjective plus noun).

Trinity College Cambridge, 19th June 1831

Dear good wife!
... For the first time since I arrived here, I have dined on my own account, and tomorrow I shall dine at the so-called King's College, where I have visited a Mr. Heath,[576] who has had a lengthy stay in Copenhagen, speaks rather good Danish, and owned a copy of most of my writings. Incidentally, I owe to the residents of Trinity College the testimony that they have treated me not as a foreigner but as an old friend who came to visit. Yesterday evening, a whole group of us went up to the Observatory,[577] where we had tea with the languorous Mrs Airy (they call her 'enchanting' over here), who also sang and played meltingly for us. On the way home we watched the fireworks in honour of the anniversary of the Battle of Waterloo.[578] I wish I could describe the dining-room here (known as 'the Hall'), high, long, and wide as it is with gates at the end for doors, and long tables alongside which the students dine – and the even longer table across for the Fellows and guests. The Fellows are all bachelors, yet the Hall also has its ladies, who do not leave us but are left *by* us, when we have dined and repaired to a table with raisins and almonds, strawberries, raspberries, baked apples, etc. Some of the ladies are cooks or chambermaids, who stay in the Hall throughout the meal (I do not know why, since there are enough waiters!), though doubtless they serve the student tables when they are occupied, and there they themselves sit, when we are finished. You can hardly imagine the hubbub! Tomorrow my patron, Professor Whewell, leaves for London, so I will probably feel somewhat abandoned ...

We have had lovely weather all the time, but the countryside around Cambridge is not pretty. The only walks are the paths by the colleges along the bank of the inconsiderable River Cam, which gives the town its name. The only hill I have seen (thrown up by the Danes, they say) by the castle ruins is locked away in a prison, so the prisoners get no further than the bottom of the hill and none of them reach the top ...

Now God speed you in Jesus' name! Best wishes to the children, Jane, and all our brothers, sisters, and friends. Tell the boys from their father to work hard (Svend is still reading Snorri) and make sure that Meta is beginning to be serious.

Your
N.F.S. Grundtvig

---

576. John Heath, Fellow of King's College, had spent a number of winters in Copenhagen, where the famous linguist Rasmus Rask had taught him Icelandic and Danish.
577. Replacing previous smaller observatories, the Cambridge Observatory was built out of town in 1823. Grundtvig met the resident Professor of Astronomy, George Biddell Airy (1801-92), who also helped to establish the Observatory library.
578. At Waterloo on 18 June 1815 an allied force of British troops under the Duke of Wellington and Prussian troops under Field Marshal Gebhard von Blücher defeated the army of Napoleon Bonaparte and forced his abdication as emperor. Both sides lost around 25,000 dead or wounded, but 6,000 French were taken prisoner and 15,000 deserted in the days that followed.

33. To Lise

London 13th July 1831

Dear good wife!
Your letter of the 1st inst., which I did not receive until the day before yesterday, told me that, God be praised, you were well and were looking forward to visiting Falster in the middle of the month, perhaps with the steamship tomorrow.[579] In God's name, both adults and children would benefit from fresh air, so I wish you good weather, good health, and all good fortune for the trip. Wherever you meet family or friends, I know you will greet them cordially from the foreigner,[580] who truly to his own surprise is so much at home in London as he would be anywhere in Denmark – outside his own house and family life. Naturally, I feel their absence cannot be replaced! But if I had you here, and a living as well, and you were as used to the country and the language as I am, I would not much mind living here for a few years, in the hope of better times for my work. To be honest, it is not because I believe that things are better here than back home, but, all things being equal, and without being insensitive to human life, one can feel more at ease in a foreign country with what one cannot change at home. ...

There is not much company or conversation in the house here, but apart from when it gets really hot, I have a nice room both for my work and for smoking my pipe or a cigar out of the open window, across to the so-called gardens in Queen Square. I am told that I chose the spot out of love for the fair sex, even though a closed square is not exactly the place to find them! ...

God grant that I may continue to hear the best from my loved ones, and to give them the news that they want, until we joyfully gather again! Best wishes to the children and whoever else is staying with you from

Your
N.F.S. Grundtvig

PS. It was wise of me not to thank Johan for the letter he promised but never sent. Do not let him play around too much in the country. Is he reading my *World History* yet?[581]

---

579. Falster is an island in the south of Denmark. The first steamship route in Denmark had begun in 1830, sailing from Copenhagen past Falster to Kiel – with max. 110 passengers, travelling at max. 8 knots (c. 9 mph).
580. Grundtvig's word, *Udlændinge*, is used in jest.
581. Grundtvig's *World History* was published in 1812. It is notable for its retention of the biblical chronology – with God's purpose as the ultimate goal of history.

34. To Lise

Queen Square, Bloomsbury, 11th August 1831

Dear good wife!
... Tomorrow is our wedding-day, the third in a row when we have been separated by broad waters! May nothing worse ever separate what God has joined together! And truly, we must *twice* declare that God has joined us together, for we can honestly say that although the threefold love-tie that our children represent is physically absent today, the hand of His almighty power and the power of His love entwines us; it gives us cause to join hands in a loving embrace and to give thanks to Him who is goodness itself and whose loving-kindness lasts for ever! Dear Lise, it is in the nature of things that married couples at our age no longer show such tenderness for one another as when they were younger. But I would be dishonest if I did not take this opportunity to say that it has truly worried me that last winter there seemed to be not just a constant cloud on your brow, but something strange placing itself between us. I do not know what it is. You will recall that I have said it before, but the only reply was a stronger impression of the hidden anguish that troubles you. Only He who has our hearts in His hand can heal your wounds, and far be it from me to say that I am innocent, as my grumpiness and my oddities must of necessity become more disagreeable as the years go by, especially in our straitened circumstances. There is doubtless blame on both sides when a Christian husband and wife, even with their beloved children around them, are no longer the shining examples of mutual tenderness that they are called to be – when they no longer smile away each other's everyday sorrows. So, dear Lise, without keeping accounts where two should make one, let each of us take the blame and ask Our Heavenly Father in Jesus' name to unite us more deeply in faith and hope and everlasting love, acknowledging that with the years the natural, earthly feelings separate more than join, since everything that is of this world decays except for that which God transfigures! Let it be so that even if the world does not see it, our dear children may see in their parents that love has a warmth that defies the winter cold, and, like the sun of Eternity with the light of life glowing in secret, breaks out into a radiance over its preserves; these do not fade with the glow of the rosy cheek or in women with fire in their eyes! Yes, my dearest, faithful partner, tender mother, tried and tested friend, all this I say from a distance in the hope to God that what seeks to separate us from each other will disappear, just as the distance that physically separates us now will, with His aid, soon disappear. Just as our present separation in all likelihood is the last one that will take place on this earth, so may all distance between us disappear and only the deepest tenderness replace it!

God bless you and the children! Greet them, kiss them, and admonish them from their father ... As you know, thirteen is not only an uneven but a notorious number, so let our thirteenth year be an exception from those that follow – as it has been from those that preceded. Let us say, God be praised, it is over and done with for Lise and her own

Frederik

35. To Bernhard Ingemann

Christianshavn, 7th January 1832

Dear Ingemann!
As a correspondent, I admit that in the past year I have been so poor at fulfilling the promises I made at its outset that it is best not to make any this year! Yet I have often longed to talk to you about all manner of things and in particular about what has occupied me for the past three months – the introduction to the *Nordic Mythology* that you have doubtless noted I was writing. You will probably smile at me for standing in the doorway so long and fearing the thought of the long talk in the draughty hallway with my feet getting cold! It was too much even for me in the end, so out of sympathy for the reader I had to begin all over again. The new version is not much shorter for you, but it is twice as long for me, despite my having to write four times more than is being printed. Nonetheless, I have enjoyed myself immensely and trust that my readers will not be so wayward as to say that I have bored them!

It was quite strange after twenty years to come back to the heights on which all youthful dreams are dreamed and all visions have their source – to see how everything in the dimmer light appears clearer and takes up a closer acquaintance with the Aesir and the Vanir.[582] We must admit that it was the product of decent, genuine natures, and that all the enthusiasm that we felt for them was more than worthy.

My introduction comprises three sections: Universal Historical Learning, Myths and Mythologies, and the Nordic Giant Spirit. You will immediately see there is enough to think, talk, and write about; in fact there is probably *too* much in the end, so one is close to losing heart over how clumsy a tool of speech a quill pen can be! It cannot utter a single sound to the reader!

Otherwise, I would like to tell you about something very important that has struck me, or become clarified for me. Even with good friends there is not much point in *writing* about what one has not first *talked* about; we and our kind can possibly understand a half-sung ballad, but an *unsung* ballad is something quite different – *none* of us understand it!

Apart from this I am busy on all sides; I go to school with Fenger, who is back from Greece and from whom I am learning a little Modern Greek instead of the old Latin, which I kill off daily, using all my powers! I did not learn this literally in England, where the classicists are the only people one raises one's hat to! Nevertheless, especially since my last visit to England and Asgaard[583] there, I have become so anti-German and pro-English – so dreadfully practical! – that although you will recognise the foundation, you will nevertheless be surprised!

---

582. In Nordic mythology there are two groups of gods: the Aesir are associated with war and conquest, the Vanir with fertility, wisdom, wealth and the future.
583. Asgaard is Odin's residence in the world of the gods.

But all this chit-chat is all the same to you! So I shall wish you and your wife a happy and blessed New Year, which is why I took up my pen in the first place! The outlook has not been good here, but I am hoping that with God's help we shall get well again. I look forward to you coming by at Easter, even though I think it a great shame that two years have passed since we last met – despite there being such a relatively short distance between Sorø and here[584] ...

Your friend
N.F.S. Grundtvig

36. To Gunni Busck

Having inherited a small fortune from his merchant father, Grundtvig's friend Gunni Busck (1798-1869) contributed to Grundtvig's upkeep on a regular basis after his censorship and resignation from his curacy at the Church of Our Saviour in 1826. Busck did his best to help Grundtvig find time to work on his *Song-Work*, published in 1837, and in a memorial poem Grundtvig praised his dear friend "who bought (sic) song-praises to God's house". The 'good thought' in the first line was yet another of these donations.

∼

15th September 1835. Christianshavn

Dear friend!
Thanks for your letter and may God bless you for the good thought! Doubtless it has come originally from Himself and is in no way 'merited', but that is precisely how He works, for He loves His own! Although He tells us quite clearly that we should not thank ourselves that we now and again prefer His 'good thoughts' to our own (and cannot do otherwise if we are wise), He nevertheless blesses us with them and we always enjoy good fortune, however undeserved it may be! So, my friend, may God bless you, for He has heard my prayer through you in this matter. May He allow you to taste His bliss in rather giving than taking!

Our God is an "orderly" God, says the Apostle,[585] and for this reason there should be order in our thoughts and deeds, so it was my wish not to receive any support for my work with the hymns before I could set aside everything else; and if others can be just a little 'orderly' towards me, I may succeed. You are doubtless well aware that nowadays people can have many good sides, yet in money matters there is seldom any outcome from this, unless one can either jest with them or quarrel with them. I am more than happy to do the former, since that is a pleasure, but I cannot do the latter, since that is

---

584. The distance from Sorø to Copenhagen is about 70 km (43 miles).
585. 1 Cor 14:33, 40. Grundtvig paraphrases Paul's "For God is not a God of disorder but of peace" and "everything should be done in a fitting and orderly way".

more tedious. Since Our Lord would not help in an 'orderly' way, I had to break off my book on medieval history, perhaps for good, and at once turn to the hymnbook instead. One might as well live *until* one begins on a work as *while* one is doing it! I have therefore been reluctantly thinking about this, since I am working on the history book for the same Master and I have asked Him to settle it for me! He always does so of course, but it is not always that we agree with Him, as in this case I must. Since I have 200 rigsdaler owing for the history book, which presumably will come in the course of the year, I have the well-founded assumption that from God's generous hand which has opened itself for the hymns I should not take more than necessary, even in advance.

In other words, God has made it plain that since you are offering me an advance and can take the necessary steps, I thank you for the 200 rigsdaler for the hymn-year,[586] of which God will grant me the fortune to save a good interest in His own coinage, which never loses its value! ...

Now, in Jesus' name, may the blessing that made Abraham rich be with you!

Your friend
N.F.S. Grundtvig.

37. To Bernhard Ingemann

In letters dated 15th November 1836 and 10th January 1837 Ingemann had taken Grundtvig to task for his lack of appreciation of the fine arts. Grundtvig was a words-only man, and had little understanding of Art, Architecture, Sculpture, Classical Music, Theatre, Opera or Ballet, which he considered mere pretence. Only in 'the living Word', breathed into Adam and all humankind, did he find the true Spirit of God. In the first ('previous') letter, Ingemann had written: "If you had stood beside me in Florence or Rome, the spirit and life, the deep religious feeling and spirituality that emanates from the works of their art schools, also in the time of the Medicis, would have astonished you, and you would hardly have condemned such monuments to the highest flights of the human spirit to the Hell of history." Ingemann's second letter thanked Grundtvig for his gift of a copy of the second booklet[587] of his *Song-Work for the Danish Church*, one of his greatest achievements. But in the light of Grundtvig's love of hymn-singing Ingemann again questions his disdain for the arts.

Grundtvig's swift response two days later again reveals his reservations towards the fine arts. He tells Ingemann that they are fundamentally in agreement – except that Ingemann is wrong!

'Word' below is interchangeable with 'language' and can be translated by either; both are God's gift to humankind, and place us above the animals.

---

586. i.e. 1836, when Grundtvig will dedicate the year to his hymn collection.
587. There were seven booklets in all, finally collected in 1837.

Christianshavn, 12th January 1837

Dear Ingemann!
I am sure that despite my not writing to wish you cordially a happy Christmas, you do not doubt any the more than I am writing now to wish you and yours a blessed New Year. The reason I did not answer your previous letter was solely my conviction that if one cannot reach clarity or concord over a question face to face, one is even more unlikely to do so in writing. There is a great danger that every attempt only complicates it and renders the disagreement or misunderstanding even more fraught. So despite you urging me this way and that to come with a definite answer, I should perhaps rather say no, or make a poor jest out of it. But since I can see that you are quite seriously vexed that we differ over the foundation of the activity of the Holy Spirit, or at least totally misunderstand each other, I think nevertheless that we are such good friends, and thus so fundamentally in agreement that it makes very little difference if the spoken word is the only living expression of the Spirit.

My relation to History in general and to the Bible in particular must guarantee that I cannot doubt, let alone *deny*, that Scripture in the service of the Spirit is a great and indispensable instrument to link the activities of the Spirit in the course of time; wherever the Spirit is found, it joyfully recognises and acknowledges its previous activity. On that we are in total agreement. However, I willingly admit that any belief that the Spirit can be found in the artistic work of the *hands* – even to a higher degree and a greater extent – is more than my eyes are created or fitted to discover. Here our way of seeing clearly already begins to differ visibly, since you place much greater emphasis than I can accept on the traces of the Spirit in buildings, paintings, and sculptures.

What seems to offend you is my claim that the spoken word is the only living, effective expression of the Spirit; so the only question that remains for us is whether or not you misunderstand my meaning; for if you understand it but cannot abide it, then there is nothing more to be done, at least in writing.

On the other hand, if it *is* a misunderstanding, it is hardly reasonable that the clarity you found wanting in my mouth should meet you in my pen! It is of course possible that, as is the custom of hermits, I had forgotten what I presumed you already knew, which gave cause for a misunderstanding that no pen could erase.

So when I speak of the activity and transmission of the Spirit, I understand 'Spirit' to mean the power-manifestation of a higher way of *seeing* life, the temporal and the tangible. I therefore distinguish sharply between traces or signs of the Spirit and its actual living expression. I argue that the only thing under the sun whereby this higher reflection on the world and life can express, transmit, and impart itself in all its vitality is in the spoken, audible word. I claim this both as an experienced truth and as a natural law, so it is impossible for me to think otherwise!

However, since all our concepts can only become slightly clearer, and never *fully* clear, on earth, so can my claim still remain somewhat obscure for others despite it now being for me as clear as sunlight. I do not therefore expect my readers or friends to do any more than allow me the same freedom that I allow them, namely the freedom to hold, express, and defend my conviction: I would like to share it with others, but impose it upon no one...

Goodnight now, and may every New Year consolidate our old friendship and renew our best hopes until they are fulfilled!

N.F.S. Grundtvig

38. To Gunni Busck

The first volume of Grundtvig's *Song-Work to the Danish Church*, published in 1837, contained 401 hymns, "collected and adapted by Nik. Fred. Sev. Grundtvig, priest". It was dedicated to "The Christian-Danish Church and especially Gunne (*sic*) Busck, friend and colleague in the name of the Lord."

22nd September 1837

My dear good friend!
Only now can I send you a complete copy of the first volume of the *Song-Work*, since Milo[588] was a long time binding it but forgot to print the first parts on writing-paper and had to do this afterwards. I do hope, dear friend, that your soul will be delighted over and over again with these same soaring tones to our Lord's praise from all times and skies, for in that union lies the "new song that God places on our lips" for us to exalt His wondrous deeds for the children of humankind!

Everything is as before here, and I am still living on Østerbro, but I long for my little nest at Christianshavn and my regular occupations, which cannot thrive here.

I hear that Muus[589] is still in town and presumably has not visited you except in a hurry. I asked him to bring your watch, which I believe is in good health, although I cannot be certain since there was no key to wind it up and test it properly.

I have heard from Norway that my little book[590] has made quite a stir and that they are actually thinking of opening a people's high school there. Whether or not the idea bears fruit is a different question and only time will tell. In that regard we too are beset by the frightful witch known as "Apathy", who sits immovably on her well-upholstered throne without our even being able to see how it is possible to defeat her. Yet the Lord's purposes and means are both better and higher than ours, and that is a considerable comfort, since He hates the witch far more than we do and will certainly blow her away in His own good time, as He told the prophet: "I shall sweep away your refuge, the lie,

---

588. Jakob Frederik Milo was the bookbinder at the publisher, Wahlske Boghandel, in Copenhagen.
589. Carl Muus (1796-1885) was a Church historian as well as being private tutor to Grundtvig's children; they had lasting fun playing on his name, which means 'mouse' in Danish.
590. i.e. *To the Norwegians concerning a Norwegian High School*, published in Oslo/Kristiania in 1837.

and water will overflow your hiding-place/Your covenant with death will be annulled; your agreement with the realm of the dead will not stand."[591]

I have been to see the King without saying anything out of the ordinary to him; I found him just as before and wait for what God will impel him to do. Since he regained his health against all expectation, Our Lord will doubtless help him to establish his praiseworthy reputation from generation to generation. None of the kings of our day either appreciate or have received such strong promises, but the prospect of them being fulfilled is so far doubtful; in the nature of things others will harvest what he has sown.

God's blessing on you and yours!
Your friend
N.F.S. Grundtvig.

39. To Bernhard Ingemann

Ingemann's *Morning-Songs for Children*[592] was published in Copenhagen in 1837. It contained 7 songs that have become classics, and an eighth, about the stork in spring, which Grundtvig admired. Three months after this letter, the censorship imposed upon him after the Clausen libel case was lifted, but at this point he still has only scorn for the police censor. The 'few pages' he refers to (in fact over 5,000 words!) are a copy of his *To the Norwegians concerning a Norwegian High School*, published in Oslo in 1837. The Danish Chancellery, the King's government, had not forbidden its publication, only the advertising of it. Grundtvig was advocating a people's high school in Norway similar to the one he was promoting in Denmark. It caused quite a stir in Norway, where the female lay preacher, Randi Solem (1775-1859), responded by assuring Grundtvig that she was hoping to purchase a farm for the purpose. Unfortunately, the plans were never realised and it was not until 1864 that the first Norwegian school opened in Sagatun, 125 km north of Oslo. The Grundtvig Society of Norway was founded in 1983.

Grundtvig was deeply upset when in 1814 Denmark had to cede Norway to Sweden after the Napoleonic wars; the twin kingdom of Denmark-Norway was broken for ever. He even contemplated taking up the offer of a teaching appointment in Oslo, and in the summer of 1851 he finally visited Norway for the first and only time.

∼

22nd September 1837

Dear Ingemann!
Thanks for your letter and the *Morning-Songs*; especially your Spring Song appeals to me! I have finally received the first volume of my own *Song-Work* and can send you a copy. Despite our individual differences of opinion, I am sure that it will be received and

---

591. Isa 28: 17. Grundtvig replaces "Hail shall sweep away" with "I shall sweep away".
592. Danish title: *Morgensange for Børn*.

regarded kindly. What pleases me most is the melting together of tones from all major churches that reached my ear and touched my heart while I was working on the book. Although I am aware that on their passage within me the various tones lost some of their individual character, I trust that traces remain to gladden the faithful soul as a prelude to the new song in which all tribes and tongues will praise Him to whom and through whom all things belong...

I am sending you a few pages that you have not seen before because the Chancellery will only allow negotiation on demeaning conditions. Yet the book has aroused some reflection on the necessity of a people's high school, whatever the result may be. I am also planning to publish two volumes of short poems in Norway,[593] partly because I have had no trouble finding a publisher and partly because I think the Norwegians can benefit from a few such books being published there, since the books can become better known and more welcome.

Incidentally, malicious rumours are saying that after a pleasant stay this summer I seem to be ready to bid a fond farewell and have therefore been "lying in the ditch". But believe me when I say that the innocent cause of such ill repute is only that I have been idle and taking the sun – as one does in Sorø! I am now seriously thinking of going into winter quarters and getting down to hard work...

Farewell and live well with your wife and your muse, whom I know are living happily together and refuting the old talk that with two sweethearts in the house who are both able, there is no chance of peace!

Your
N.F.S. Grundtvig.

40. To Jacob Lindberg

On Boxing Day 1815 the 18-year-old and already qualified theologian Jacob Lindberg (1797-1857) heard Grundtvig preach in Frederiksberg Church and was captivated. He put himself at the forefront of lay people seeking freedom within the Church, and in support of Grundtvig's views he travelled the country. From 1830 Lindberg published *Theological Monthly for Christianity and History*, and from 1833 *Nordic Church Times*, to which Grundtvig contributed a number of lengthy articles alongside Lindberg's ongoing polemics. Lindberg's translation of the Bible convinced the revivalists that the Grundtvigians took the book seriously, and between 1834-44 the two were referred to as "the Grundtvig-Lindberg partnership", though not always positively. Lindberg was 47 before he was given his first pastorate – on the island of Falster. From 1853 until his death he was a member of parliament. At his grave in 1857 Grundtvig praised him as "faithful friend, a very able worker, and a renowned warrior for our Lord's good cause".

---

593. Grundtvig's *Nordic Short Poems* was published in July 1838.

Christianshavn 28th February 1838

Dear Lindberg!
Your letter last Sunday with 150 rigsdaler from some of my audience was a very pleasant surprise, since it is valid testimony that many more than I dared to think had remembered me with gladness and gratitude for the great things that God did for us during Lent 1832. It was doubly memorable as an unerring pledge that whatever we really understand by "living a godly life", He will grant it in His own good time. We only have to believe that He will, and then ask Him to do so in the name of our Lord Jesus. Yet again He has demonstrated that His thoughts and ways are not ours, so we must ensure that ours are like His by faithfully placing everything in His divine father-hand which we know to be stretched out to feed all that lives with His blessing!

In thanking my audience for their contribution to both the freedom of the Word and my support, it is my sincere wish that no one has given beyond their means, since, as the Apostle Paul writes, the relation between the desire to give and the means to do so is what pleases the Lord. We know Him to be generous to all those who call upon His name and that He will always supply what is needed in the best possible way.

In conclusion, allow me to take this opportunity to assure my audience that I do not in the slightest share the anxiety about a new Altar Book or about any decline in the Christians' position in Denmark; on the contrary I am quite certain that the Lord is ready to comfort His people and give them every cause for gratitude!

Sincerely
N.F.S. Grundtvig

41. To Bernhard Ingemann

The 51 'history talks' on the last 50 years in Europe that Grundtvig mentions in this letter became the series later known as 'Within Living Memory' (*Mands Minde*). From here on we can talk about Grundtvig as having acquired a certain amount of popularity to go with his notoriety.

∼

Christianshavn, 27th July 1838

Dear Ingemann!
I received your latest greetings via the English priest in Elsinore[594] who visited you; I imagine you found him an uncommonly straightforward, cordial Englishman. I have

---

594. Nugent Wade (1809-93) was English chaplain at Elsinore (Helsingør) from 1833-39, where he became a friend of Grundtvig. It was Wade who helped Grundtvig on his visit to England with his son Svend in 1843.

entertained the idea of paying you a visit myself, but it will doubtless go the way of my intended visit to Norway, so for the present it will not happen. The main reason why we always never get anywhere is that we stay where we are put! There are several reasons for this, and since I am otherwise making good use of the holiday period I have a very good reason for this peace and quiet in preparing the history talks you have probably heard about. I was given a late permission to hold them and went head first into them at the last solstice. Now that it is actually happening, I consider it necessary, both out of the general ignorance of History and for the sake of the middle-class participants, to begin with the most recent history, meaning what has happened within living memory. This is an area of history that I have completely neglected and in general held in contempt, so to turn it to good use I had to go back to the roots in particular of the French Revolution and deal with this singularly most unpleasant and generally poorly treated moment in History. I am in the middle of it right now, and although I could do with a little encouragement, I nonetheless need all the time available to be ahead of events by the end of the holiday. Between the two of us, I was getting desperate, partly because there was so much to read up, and partly because my memory will not be as reliable as it was in my youth. In the case of a History lecture, which must not be read from a manuscript, but must be true story-telling, that is an embarrassment.

Even under these unfavourable circumstance I have found a number of free listeners, so I naturally hope to overcome the difficulties and begin a living historical interaction between the old and the young, which is both what is lacking, yet what is indispensable! I have reserved the right to allow great and small to go side by side – so Denmark's little, and my own far smaller story, is vouchsafed some attention that even the most right-minded German must despair over. I imagine that I can thereby sustain my own concentration and hopefully that of my audience, who to a certain extent must be interested in our fatherland and in me, if the experiment is to succeed...

Would you please accept this copy of my old verses, rather well reprinted but poorly proof-read in Norway,[595] and together with your good wife remember us old folks on Amager!

Yours
N.F.S. Grundtvig

42. To Peter Fenger

Christianshavn, 25th August 1838

Dear friend!
The other day your brother Theodor brought me your letter containing 50 rigsdaler and I thank you twice as much for your charitable participation, both in the continuation of

---

595. *Nordic Little Poems*, Kristiania 1838.

the *Song-Work* and in my position. Last winter it would have been of no use, since however much I worked on it and thought that the holes would soon be filled, something kept on turning up: the close reading of the New Testament text which I felt obliged to undertake; a repeated effort to establish a Danish People's High School, which was also a pressing matter; and a renewed concern for all our Church relations to which a new papist school in Oxford[596] elicited a response which is still not finished. Finally came the request and permission for the talks on History – my wish for 30 years now – which are a major burden, partly because my memory is declining and partly because I realised that I would have to begin with the most recent history, for which I was least prepared.

So I have spent the holidays reading, and, God willing, I shall begin with French history again on Monday and wish I could be finished, but everything is going so fast! If only God will grant courage and strength for the task, I cannot rue the difficulty, since a living talk on the latest history must needs arouse and nourish a participation in these great events without which all writing and explanation of them is a waste of time.

As soon as this lecture series, which demands every waking hour of the day, is over, I intend to get back to the *Song-Work* and hope that I can make a success of the biblical history rhymes which for so long have been humming around in my head.

My little book on the 'School for Life' has finally seen the light of day in *The Land of Our Fathers*,[597] and I shake off all the ingratitude that I receive there for my unwise talk of 'Lower Secondary Schools', since my proposal for a Danish People's High School is given unconditional praise. If we could get that established and the State Church free, then two giant strides would have been made for God's kingdom and joy, which, whether we live or die will bring us Christianity and civic success to the extent that we are predisposed for them. I really believe that will bring us further with the latter than anywhere else on earth, and with the former anywhere outside Jerusalem! Whatever stands in the way, if we have faith in God, if we call on Him, and wait upon Him, we shall, we *must*, be successful; for He who has begun His good deed, will fulfil it on the day of our Lord Jesus Christ.

Loving greetings to you and yours, wishing you God's blessing in every way

Your friend
N.F.S. Grundtvig

43. To Vilhelm Birkedal

Grundtvig was grateful not only for donations from friends but also for their gifts. Authors regularly sent first editions of their works to their friends, as is the case in this letter. Grundtvig takes the time to discuss the State Church, where the gospel may bud but not blossom. In the final

---

596. The Oxford Movement in the 1830s and 40s was a movement towards Catholicism within the Church of England. For the results of Grundtvig's study of the movement see Letter 46.
597. *The School for Life* was reviewed in *The Land of Our Fathers* (*Fædrelandet*) V, 5-6 (1838), with Grundtvig's response coming in no. 8 of the same periodical.

paragraph of his letter to Vilhelm Birkedal, Grundtvig adds that one of his main goals in England will be to make a closer analysis of the Oxford Movement founded by Dr Edward Pusey and Pastor John Newman in the 1830s to renew the Church of England in a Catholic direction. Newman later converted to Roman Catholicism and became a cardinal. In a letter dated the same day to Peter Fenger, Grundtvig describes it thus: "I regard this trip as my little part in 'the mission'; may God grant me success to the glory of the Lord and the benefit of the Church."

~

Copenhagen, 6th May 1843

Dear friend!
Many thanks for your lovely little book on the gospels of the church year! I did not know it existed until it came into my hands the other day. I immediately read it with great pleasure and even with immediate benefit, since I truly have not seen any other organism at work in our Sunday gospel texts than the historical one, which is somewhat confusing and stops at Pentecost.

I was deeply pleased to discover this new beauty in a beloved object and a precious treasure in every way, since our Sunday gospel texts make up our biblical language for the most part. From the mouth of the Lord and the Apostles this has been passed down through the Church, has established itself in our consciousness, and has partly set its stamp on our Christian proverbs and sayings so that they form the core of our biblical language over which the Spirit hovers, and therefore they cannot be replaced. In the details of your book there are several things I would do a little differently, but in its totality, which is the main thing, it is so gratifying that we have a Christian life-path from its conception in faith before Baptism to its coronation in the Communion of Saints so vitally and so intelligibly depicted. The enlightenment that it offers will, with God's help, be so productive by way of edification that it is only minor details I must direct your attention to. For example, Epiphany only ends with the gospel of the Lord's Transfiguration; the Lent gospel marks a new phase for the 'elders' in Christ, so this must be made clear to the children who might otherwise be frightened about the scruples and sufferings that will not confront them until they are mature enough to meet them; finally, Trinity, which you have only hinted at, should be assigned to 'Eternity' – from the rebirth gospel text to All Souls, which should always end our Church Year. It has to do with an awareness of eternal life, from the first shoots to its emerging as the rose of the martyrs. The rose does not blossom in the precincts of the State Church but it can and must bud even there, at least among the believing pastors who are attracted to the firm footprints of the witnesses of old.

I shall be going to England this summer, God willing, naturally with an eye on Oxford. So I am all the less willing to postpone these few friendly lines, since I know how good it is to hear from a fellow-disciple confirmation of what is afoot among us and for the moment discover that there is no particular resonance! Indeed, reading your book I truly felt that Moses had every good reason to say: "I wish that all the Lord's people were prophets and that the Lord would put his Spirit on them!"[598]

So farewell! May the Lord enlighten and strengthen you for your ministry in Him, which is never in vain when we allow ourselves not to become tired of this world but to be refreshed by the Spirit of the Lord!

Your friend
N.F.S. Grundtvig

44. To Queen Caroline Amalie

The Danish armed forces lost battles to both Lord Nelson (1801) and the Duke of Wellington (1807), yet Grundtvig condemned only the soldiers, not the English as such. The Duke of Wellington remained Commander-in-Chief of the British army until his death. In the House of Commons he was twice Prime Minister until he moved to the House of Lords. By 1843 Grundtvig is eager to tell the queen that from the public gallery in the House of Lords he has actually seen and heard the victor at Waterloo (where, as he noted elsewhere) Wellington's famous horse was actually *named* 'Copenhagen'.

The subject under discussion that day was the rights of the Church of Scotland. A month before this letter, on 18th May 1843, 121 ministers and 73 elders had left the Church of Scotland General Assembly to form the Free Church of Scotland, a process later known as 'the Disruption'.

On her own initiative Queen Caroline Amalie awarded Grundtvig a grant for his fourth trip to England in 1843, accompanied by his 18-year-old son, Svend. Father and son left Copenhagen on 8th June 1843, travelling overland to Hamburg and thence by ferry to London.

~

London, 13th June 1843.

Most Gracious Queen!
Yesterday evening I arrived in the great city by the river, where one can truly journey – like the Prophet of Nineveh.[599] I am still far too dizzy from all the creaking and crashing that I heard onboard, where the wind and the waves, especially last Sunday held an extremely noisy Sunday service ... Despite the fact that my head is still sailing, I am truly sitting in the heart of London, in a lovely quiet area and in such a cosy, elegant sitting-room that I can clearly see how my son has grown a whole inch and feels like a prince ...

Since already yesterday I found it necessary to take a day's rest, I have not seen much else than the bustle and the intense variety of life with which London always greets its visitors. However, on Tuesday I did manage to get to a session in the House of Lords which gave me a living impression of the public conversation of the learned lords.

---

598. Num 11:29.
599. i.e. Jonah in the OT, whom God twice sent to Nineveh.

I am too short-sighted to have *seen* the Duke of Wellington properly and too far away to *hear* him distinctly, since he is not an orator and moreover has lost his teeth! On the other hand I heard the Foreign Secretary, the Earl of Aberdeen, clearly, and although there was nothing brilliant about his thinking and no particular eloquence on his lips, I whole-heartedly wished that our ministers back home could use their mother-tongue so well and express themselves on important public matters with such openness, power, and clarity.

By a happy coincidence the subject was the very complex dispute between the Scottish Church and the English government,[600] which has to do with the Church of Scotland's ancient right to reject pastors who are called to a post either by the government or private persons, when they are considered unsuitable. It seems to depend on how the pastor in question is considered *suitable* for the post and is the cause of an endless dispute in which both parties may well have right on their side, but now 600 Scottish pastors, with the cleverest in the lead, have robustly decided to leave the State Church unless each congregation has the right – without offering a reason – by a majority of votes to reject the pastor who is sent to them.

Of course the Minister proposed a middle way, which he realised would displease both sides, but the main point is that all of us in the Protestant State Churches find a need for freedom that must be satisfied if the State Church is not to face a sure and impending dissolution.

In this respect no government is so fortunate as the Danish, which can both rescue its State Church and retain its influence on the civil service and have a free hand in the appointment to a pastorate, if it only makes it possible to break the parish-tie, which is quite unknown here. The individual Christian will then be able to have a clean conscience and preserve his children from temptation, even though their school teacher and parish pastor is not a believing Christian. May God open the eyes of the Danish government to this blessing before it is wasted – which at the moment can happen in the course of a day! ...

May God bless and preserve, enlighten and exalt Your Majesties and the Fatherland!

Most humbly
N.F.S. Grundtvig

45. To Johan Grundtvig

London, 16th June 1843

Dear Johan!
Although I cannot write to you as I would wish to my first-born – since you are old enough

---

600. Like many foreigners to this day Grundtvig uses 'English' to mean 'British', but it is not helpful here. No Scottish bishops are allowed to sit in the House of Lords, since the Church of Scotland is a separate entity.

to be one of your father's intimate friends – I must nevertheless write to you if for no other reason than to put on paper that this is about the relationship I wish my eldest son to have with me and into which I pray God will place him. I still hope therefore that while we are on earth, I will *see* you in that relationship, God willing. We all make mistakes, especially in the treatment of the children we endeavour to raise and develop in the best possible way, so you must in no way believe that I blame you completely for the distance that has come between us. However, I can write to you as I would wish to my first-born, but, on mature reflection, I cannot take all the blame but must give you the lion's share, since it is certain that I have given you more and greater proof of my love than you have given me of yours, so I have first claim on your trust.

Just as we are clearly in disagreement about the best way to make use of life and prepare ourselves for its pursuits, so must I fear that we share a deeper disagreement, conscious or unconscious, about the proper value and major purpose of life. But if, as I truly believe, our heart's blood is actually one, all disagreement will be allayed and for the most part gradually disappear, if you would have a mind to speak openly and kindly to your father about what troubles your heart and how you see your role in life and your future in the world. Day by day this is becoming more necessary, if we are not constantly to misunderstand each other, for it seems to me that you are moving in a spiritual torpor as you muddle towards your examinations. This is preventing you from thinking seriously about finding a useful occupation in life and a sensible preparation for it. I nevertheless hope and deeply wish that this appearance is deceptive and that you have far more serious thoughts than it would appear. When I come home, I hope, God willing, that this matter will either be clarified or will require a desperate effort, for now comes the question of whether you should study perfunctorily for a graduation examination – for which I can neither advise nor support my son – or prepare yourself for a different kind of useful occupation – for which I have advised my sons and am gladly willing to support them from my assets – and even beyond. May God preserve you! Write to me when you have thought things over! It is perhaps easier with the pen, provided that you only remember you are writing to your loving father, who grants his children all the freedom he dare!

Your father Frederik.

46. To Queen Caroline Amalie

London, 2nd July 1843

Most Gracious Queen!
I have spent the best part of a fortnight in Oxford, which was far and away the most convenient time for a foreigner to see the university in all its glory; it marked the end of all the examinations, ceremonies, and prize-givings that attract people from all parts to this capital city of the Muses...

It is the practice or rather a malpractice that on this particular day all the graduates are allowed to say what they like from the gallery, which they alone may occupy, while the hall below them is decorated like an amphitheatre with smartly-dressed ladies by the hundreds. The floor itself is filled with Masters and their good friends, among whom I was unworthily counted, beside the Vice-Chancellor and the other officials of the university in their old-fashioned finery with sceptre-carrying porters sitting in state at the feet of the ladies.

After these young John Bulls[601] had customarily clapped, booed, and bellowed their applause or displeasure at their superiors, as well as at other men known to them and at further affronts – the ladies' blue hats etc. – the solemnities began. However, as soon as the Professor of Poetry launched into his Latin speech, the bawling from the gallery became so intense that we could not hear a word of the speaker but watched him stand there grimacing, like a dumb person striving to speak, or (which is just the same) a dead language pretending to be alive. Without of course thanking the ungovernable louts I took this as a good omen, and after the dismal interruption I took part in a handsome lunch with one of the graduates who had won an academic prize but had been defrauded of his public acclamation and celebrity. I took the opportunity to impress upon the ladies present that since it is they who constitute the core of the large audience in the auditorium, they ought to have taught the university long ago to stop speaking Latin! Your Majesty will surely not doubt that I use my freedom of speech in the home of freedom (albeit in my barbaric English) to preach daily rebellion against all stick-in the-muddery,[602] in whatever shape or form. Yet although speeches in Latin are a heresy that none of the English religious sects has dared to profess, it appears to find an open ear here, despite the English placing action and real life far above all book-reading and castles-in-the-air. It must be some kind of unreasonable superstition that has made an exception of this 'classical' stick-in-the-muddery and dead alphabetic lore! Even among the wine-bottles after the meal in Oxford's rich colleges there was hearty laughter at the classical idolatry that this intrepid foreigner had exposed in all its emptiness.[603]

Anyway, my main purpose was the commotion in the church in Oxford ... From the outset, the Episcopal Church has been such a contradiction in terms – as the English character is in several respects. On the one hand, with its ancient bishops and its deep reverence for the Apostolic Creed and 'original' Christianity, it was a Church far more historical than

---

601. The character of "John Bull" was created by Dr John Arbuthnot in *The History of John Bull* (1712). He came to personify England, as a stout, middle-aged, rural, down-to-earth man.
602. Grundtvig's Danish word here is *dødbideri*, [lit. death-biting]. Acc. to the *Dictionary of the Danish Language 1700-1950* (ODS), it is a word-play of his own making on *døvbider* [lit. blunt-cutter, applied to a blunt saw].
603. In his *Life of Grundtvig* (1882) I. p. 184, Hans Brun refers to an unpublished speech that Grundtvig made on this occasion: "He began by saying that he had never so enjoyed an academic speech, in good *or* bad Latin! The graduates laughed of course, but when with his genial wit he depicted classicism as a statue of Hephaestus (Greek god of craftsmen, ed.) both blackened with soot (ink from the Latin School?) and lame in both legs as the cupbearer at the table of the gods instead of Hebe (goddess of youth, here meaning the mother-tongue, ed.), "Then did the learned fathers laugh/ like all the Olympian gods/ to see soot-blackened Hephaestus/ come halting in Hebe's steps/ to offer them nectar sweet!" From this the bard (Grundtvig, ed.) concluded that whereas in England they raise their classical wigs and their disciplined upbringing to the skies, in secret they laugh it to scorn."

any other of the Protestant State Churches, yet on the other hand, with regard to the sacraments, the signing of the cross, and the Altar and Church customs, it was almost *Calvinist* and wanted everything proven by *Scripture*.[604] This both odd yet woeful orthodoxy, which continually killed with the letter of the alphabet what the Spirit had quickened, took with the one hand what it gave with the other. It berated the Roman Catholics for what it was guilty of itself, and it praised Calvinism for what it refused to follow itself! This fundamentally suicidal orthodoxy has had its perpetual capital in Oxford, but in the 18th century it was almost displaced by a purely Calvinist doctrine emanating from Cambridge. Against this, it has primarily been a group of Oxford dons with Dr. Pusey and the eloquent Pastor Newman in their vanguard who since 1833 have incited a powerful and quite substantial insurrection. This is setting the entire Episcopal Church in a ferment and must lead to a decisive victory or defeat. In general the so-called Puseyites are accused of being true *papists*, and although in England there is little that can be called 'papist' – a smidgeon of subservience to the Mother Church that gave birth to all of us, and a smidgeon of affection for the signing of the cross and the original Church customs – after several conversations with Pusey and Newman I am in no doubt that they are on the dangerous path back to the pope. If it is not the path to Rome, then it is to the hierarchy which, without the pope, is a kingdom without a king and with only a queen (the Church and the Virgin Mary) to take the blame for whatever its bishops do.

If these main figures are papists at heart, the whole edifice is in danger either of becoming one with the Catholics or of going into liquidation. But since they are serious, reverent, and, as far as can be judged, upright and sincere men, they may be able to put themselves back on the right track when they see that Christianity in origin in both faith and creed is independent of Scripture. Far from leading to papistry, the divine activity of the sacraments excludes this. I have found such open minds to this unknown version of events among intelligent men of both opposing sides that I dare to hope that my endeavours to clarify this strangely complex church matter will, with God's help, not be in vain. It is not the case here, as it is in Denmark, that the majority do not know what we are talking about but merely appeal to the Chancellery![605] Both sides urged me to promise to return to Oxford at the end of July, when there will still be people around to talk to, and although it will delay my journey north, I am happy to have made the promise, since Oxford is the great focal point in this matter and the door there stands open. This struck me in particular when a priest from the Calvinist side, whom I had attacked the previous day as seldom before, came up to me just as I was about to leave to persuade me either to stay or to come again.

I am not quite sure what I shall be doing during these three weeks in London, since, rather than in order to occupy myself, my visit to the British Museum this time round is more to introduce it to my son, who, God be praised, seems to be enjoying himself. My hunt for newly-published Anglo-Saxon and other historically significant books is of secondary importance and is more tiring than engaging. However, I assume that Lady

---

604. Grundtvig's 'matchless discovery' of 1825 was that Christianity existed in oral form *before* Scripture was written.
605. i.e. The King's government.

Radstock,[606] who is a true sister of Mrs Browne, will keep her word and introduce me to the ladies who are worth talking to. Your Majesty knows that my preference for the fair sex is the poetic element that is closest to my heart, so when I can get on with the ladies, I can easily bear with the displeasure of the gentlemen.

The countryside around Oxford, whose closer acquaintance I incidentally made on a little walk, is so pretty – with the little River Isis (mother of the world-famous Thames), meadows, hills, and woods – that I came to think time and again of Zealand – and all I missed were the beech-trees!

The speed on the railway, which on this occasion I tried for the first time, was not particularly pleasant, yet none of these minor troubles can detract from the great pleasure Your Majesty has granted me to be able at this decisive moment to have a living access to the finest people in Europe. At every opportunity they welcome me with a goodwill that I can only be astonished by. ...

The fact that I found a 'home' so to speak, at Queen's College, Oxford was a double pleasure for me, and doubly precious is the fact that I can write to the Queen as a husband would to his wife regarding what I have experienced on this trip abroad. ...

Your most humble subject
N.F.S. Grundtvig

47. To Queen Caroline Amalie

Grundtvig and his son Svend travelled north with his English friend, Nugent Wade, who was suffering from erysipelas, a bacterial infection causing rashes; this finally required medical attention in Edinburgh. From Svend's diary we can deduce that he and his father took the following route for this trip: 31/7 stagecoach from Oxford via Stratford to Birmingham; 1/8 steam train from Birmingham via Manchester (brief visit to cathedral) to Lancaster, thence by boat along the Lancaster-Kendal canal to Kendal; 2/8 stay with Mr. Barrow,[607] local excursions; 3/8 (by means unknown) from Kendal over Bowness and along Windermere to Ambleside, thence to Keswick by Derwent Water (rowing-trip in the evening); 4/8 (by means unknown) from Keswick to Penrith (visited church and the 'giants' graves'[608]), thence by stagecoach to Carlisle; 6/8 stagecoach via 'Abbotsford' (Sir Walter Scott's home) and Melrose Abbey to Edinburgh (arrived 3 am after a 10-hour trip. Here they stayed from 6/8 to 10/8, visiting St. Giles Cathedral, Edinburgh Castle and the house of John Knox.[609] The trip home was via Newcastle and Durham (where they saw the cathedral), and

---

606. Esther Paget (1800-74) became Lady Radstock, when she married Baron Granville Radstock in 1823. Mrs Browne is her sister.
607. John Barrow (1810-81) tutor and librarian at Queen's College (1835-46).
608. Two upright columns ten to eleven feet high and fifteen feet apart. The 'Giant's Thumb' is the Norse cross (920 CE), erected as a memorial to his father by Owain [ap Dyfnwal] Caesarius, King of Cumbria from 920 to 937 AD. There is a tradition that the 'Giant's Grave' is the grave of Owain himself. The four hogback stones surrounding the grave are said to represent the wild boar he killed in nearby Inglewood Forest.
609. John Knox (c.1514-72) led the Scottish Reformation and founded the Presbyterian Church of Scotland.

then by steam train to Darlington and Leeds, thence (by means unknown) via York (where again they saw the cathedral) to London.

Edinburgh, 6th August 1843

Most gracious Queen!
Yesterday afternoon I arrived in the capital of Scotland, the furthest limit for my travel-plans, and all I know about it so far is that it is a rich city of quite striking beauty, whose location between the ocean and an elevation, twice as large as our capital city, cannot be described without writing to excess and can only be imagined. ...

If I had been an Englishman, I would have covered the whole trip of 200 miles from Oxford to Lancaster last Monday in a single day on the railway, but since I belong to the somewhat slower and even more easy-going Danes, I settled for a morning journey of 80 miles with 'living horses' to Birmingham, and spent the afternoon looking round that monstrous 'steam-engine of a city' with its 100,000 chimneys. I can think of no more suitable name for such a fearsomely drab factory city in the desert, where they only seem to think of steam as money, but since it is like this in the whole of North America, I was pleased to spend a few hours dedicated to a living idea of the pedlar's life on the other side of the ocean. At the entrance to the railway ticket office were the words in block capitals: WIPE YOUR SHOES, which reminded me of the words, "Take off your shoes, for the ground you are standing on is holy!"[610] For this was indeed the sanctuary of the people of Birmingham. From here began my only railway journey worth mentioning, as I covered the 90 or so miles to Manchester, looked around for 4-5 hours, travelled 55 miles to Lancaster, and thence a further 30 miles in a canal barge pulled by galloping horses to Kendal.[611] This 'voyage', in which one is constantly close to the hills until finally one sails *through* one of them and gains a view of the Atlantic Ocean, was more beautiful than I could ever have imagined, even though I had heard of its fame. Kendal, a little town among green hills has left behind a particularly smiling impression, despite it being a rainy day. I stayed there a few hours and made use of a few hours of sunshine until finally I paid for a delightful evening walk in a downpour!

It was one of the Oxford dons from Queen's College who gave us the invaluable advice that when we went north, we should go through Kendal. During vacations he lived there with his aging mother, who proved to be a perfect example of the old English 'matron'; thanks to him we were able to grasp this favourable opportunity. We were now so close to the famous 'lakes' between the green hills of Westmoreland and the black hills of Cumberland, and though I could not find the time to follow the English custom of staying there

---

610. Ex 3:5.
611. The Lancaster Canal was opened in 1819 and runs for 41 miles (without a lock) from Preston to Kendal. The Hincaster tunnel between the hills is 145 m long. From Slyne there is a view of the Irish Sea (not the Atlantic Ocean). Grundtvig's comparison of Birmingham with North America shows an amazing ignorance.

5-6 days for a proper round tour – so that I could say I had been in all the beautiful places as described precisely in *The Lakes' Travel Book* – I decided nevertheless to use my eyes as best I could for a whole two days, and I regret absolutely nothing! For although we left Kendal on Thursday morning with gloomy prospects and had to interrupt our going the rounds at Friday lunchtime in order to reach here yesterday, I have seen so much that is new and beautiful on this my first mountain trip[612] that I think for the moment I cannot grasp any more; in my experience one can actually see too *much* in one go ...

God save the King and bless Your Majesties with a happy life and a praiseworthy memory!

Your most humble subject
N.F.S. Grundtvig

48. To Lise

This letter was written 3 days before their silver wedding on 12th August 1843.

∼

Edinburgh, 9th August 1843

Dear Lise!
On Saturday we reached the furthest point on our journey, but already tomorrow we intend to start the homeward trip to London. Mr. Wade has erysipelas of the face and has been resting here all the while under medical care in an expensive public house, so naturally he longs for home. I had no courage whatsoever for this Scotland trip and am happy to break it off here and now; what is more, I have had a bad attack of diarrhoea, which I hope is now over but am not quite sure.

The little that Svend and I have managed to see of the city and the people has been more than adequate, since in many respects Edinburgh is the most beautiful of all European capitals. The only man we have been with, the librarian Mr Laing,[613] received us like old acquaintances, showed us round everywhere, and invited us to dinner today. I have not seen old Dr. Chalmers,[614] who is at the head of the discontents who have left the State Church, but I expect to meet him today, even though it will be brief; we shall probably find it difficult to understand each other.

---

612. Although the Danish word here, *bjerg*, covers both hills and mountains, a mountain in England is defined as anything over 600 m, so Grundtvig has certainly seen Sca Fell (964 m) Helvellyn (950 m) Skiddaw (931 m), and Cross Fell (863 m).
613. David Laing (1793-1878) was the leading Scottish expert of his time on early books and manuscripts. On his death his manuscript collection was gifted to Edinburgh University library.
614. Thomas Chalmers (1780-1847), Professor of Theology at Edinburgh University, was an evangelical preacher, and founder of the Free Church of Scotland.

I expect Svend has written to you about our mountain-trip to Westmorland and Cumberland around the beautiful inland lakes; he was completely enthralled by the things he saw and the wonderful views. I too found it all enjoyable, even though the frequent rain was unpleasant and we have all caught a cold. If with God's help we can get away to London, as I hope, then I can imagine us being home in early September. ...

Thank you, dear wife for all your love for me through 25 years and for the children you have conceived and born! By the goodness of God we still have them and have lost none. He gave us and them health into adulthood before our eyes! If the children also thank God, as we hope, for giving them loving, Christian parents, then our joy is singular and our silver wedding day a special occasion for us all, even though we are unable to be physically together. Kiss the children for me and greet our friends most affectionately wherever you are and wherever you come.

Your Frederik

49. To Queen Caroline Amalie.

In Christian VIII's Language Decree (*Sprogpatent*) of 1844 German took precedence over Danish in the Schleswig Provincial Assembly. An estimated 10,000 people met at Skamling Bank on 4th July 1844 to celebrate their Danishness and protest against the decree (see p. 30).

∽

Copenhagen 9th July 1844

Most gracious Queen!
It is my duty to acknowledge the reception of 500 rigsdaler for the Charity School; it would moreover be a pleasure for me to inform you of the ten thousand people at Skamling Bank, were I not aware that Her Majesty has unfortunately suffered damage to the ear that is turned towards Schleswig-Holstein! Your Majesty is known for her sincerity and popularity; she has a Danish motherly heart and an English, Anglo-Saxon 'shield-maid'[615] breast, All I shall therefore say is that if Your Majesty had been present and seen with your own eyes that the ten thousand stood not merely on paper but on God's green earth, waiting patiently for the voice that would speak their cause – and had she heard with her own ears the farmer's son, himself a farm hand, and the people's hero from Sommersted[616] defend the cause of the mother-tongue – she would never again borrow the ears of the Schleswig-Holsteiners to regard the most justified cause under the sun in a distorted, hostile light. Their cause has been suppressed for centuries; it is sacred and righteous,

---

615. Grundtvig regularly uses this word (*skjoldmø* in Danish) to praise true Danish women who fight the Danish cause.
616. Laurids Skau had pleaded the same cause in a speech at Sommersted Inn the year before.

yet after the latest decree, it seems hopeless. He used the same words that appear in *The Fatherland*[617] but with a deep-felt grief and an air of heroism, with a homely majesty which our daily papers least of all can adopt or convey...

The North Schleswigians, faithful guardians of the "green home of the gods", sighed at its suffering; they burned with indignation; they snorted with rage on behalf of the language of their hearts, the spirit of their forefathers, and the living spirit-laden mother-tongue. Only a handful of 'shameful boys'[618] including myself and my peers, defied all truth and justice, roused the people and disturbed the peace. Never would Your Majesty regard Denmark's resurrection from the dead and the renaissance of our mother-tongue in the spirit of our forefathers and the North with such High German eyes; nor would Your Majesty listen to these voices of the people with such Low German ears unless both those eyes and ears, in regrettable error, inconceivable blindness, and exceptional misunderstanding, had earned the applause of the last of the Danes whose eyes had sparkled under the derided Danish Dannebrog, whose tongues had brandished Mjolnir[619] against Denmark's enemies, and whose heads bore the golden crowns of the North in the golden year!

To this I can only add that just as I have never spoken to so many ears at one and the same time, nor with Dannebrog waving, the beechwoods singing, and the Baltic Sea surging before my very eyes. I have never before spoken for so long yet so fluently, so cheerfully yet so forcefully, and never in front of such an enthusiastic audience. I do not disregard the hurrahs that may come equally loud and clear but not therefore uniformly from any multitude with their mouths open. But the longer and more seriously I spoke, the more the silence and attention grew and the more it demanded immediate attention and sacrifice. This was proof as clear as sunlight to my eyes that not only is Danish the mother-tongue of North Schleswig, but that it is also loved as a mother and finds such open ears around the Skamling hills as a silver-haired queen when she last spoke to the children at the charity school...

Your most humble subject
N.F.S. Grundtvig.

50. To Peter Rørdam

Peter Rørdam (1806-83) took a degree in Theology in 1833, met Grundtvig in the Queen's Charity School, and then worked in education. With a royal grant he travelled to Germany, Holland, England and thence to Madeira. On his homecoming he became head of Queen Caroline Amalie's Charity School for Boys in 1838. He made it known that he wanted a higher position in the Copenhagen Education Authority, but in 1844 the powerful Bishop Mynster stood in the way; instead, on

---

617. The Fatherland/*Fædrelandet* was a Danish newspaper from 1834-82, first as a weekly, then as a daily for the National Liberals. It argued that Schleswig should be solely Danish and Holstein solely German (the Eider Policy). With Orla Lehmann as a leading writer it also championed a free constitution, liberalism, and scandinavianism.
618. Grundtvig uses the German word *Schand-Knaben* here.
619. Mjolnir is the god Thor's hammer.

Grundtvig's advice, he became Pastor of Mern in South Zealand. In 1850 he married Jutta Carlsen (1815-66), the sister of Marie Toft. In 1856 he moved to the parish of Lyngby, Copenhagen, where he proved to be a popular and much-loved figure, so much so that when the railway came, a special 'church train'" transported members of his congregation from Copenhagen to Lyngby in time for the Sunday service.

Rørdam's request for new works resulted in two of Grundtvig's best-known pieces: the hymn 'The forest leaves are falling fast' (1844), and the song, 'As sunshine is to the dark brown earth' (1856).

Grundtvig's breakdown in the spring and summer of 1844 was not as severe as the one in December 1810, and by August he had recovered, thanks not least to the nursing of his daughter, Meta.

∼

Copenhagen, 6th August 1844

Dear friend!
Thanks for your letter after a lengthy break; so be it. When I finally came to Mern, it seemed as though my visit would break off, rather than confirm, our friendly relations, so I too have kept silent because I was angry with you, not so much for anything you have said or done to me recently; that was all in friendship, even though it was rather disturbing for me in these heavy days. It is about the letter you sent without my knowledge to Busck, whereby you unnecessarily caused him some dark hours and me a genuine grief before I finally managed to make him see reason.

But let that all be forgotten here! I have regained all my spiritual strength, God be praised; indeed I have even had it increased. Through my walk through 'the shadow of death'[620] with the light that never abandons faithful Christians, even though they dream that it has, I have gained a new, far clearer light over life – both here and beyond. Doubtless both you and most of my friends, seeing me in my everyday life now, will merely shake your heads and not know *what* to think! However, I am used to that of old, so it is only when I myself am all at sea and do not know *what* I am to think about our Lord or humankind and myself that I am in a fix! I hope that is over for good and all, God be praised! For even though the prospects for the moment for both human life and Denmark's role in it are very gloomy, I only have to recall how mine were as black as pitch three months ago! Then the light dawns in a red sky over forest and sea and even the hills! So I have come through my latest hardship and am more the poet than I have been for the last many years and you will find much that is new singing within me. This is my swansong now, which began with my cradle-song for the little child in his earthly mother's lap. Since the small differences in it since then are major events in my spiritual life now, I shall write it down in its entirety as it now sounds in my solitude with our Lord.

---

620. Ps 23:4.

Dear child, sleep sweetly! etc.[621]

Now, my friend, I do not have much more time. Night is drawing nigh, when no one can work, and I still have much to do before I lie down to rest in His blessed name. Both within and upon me it has proved its divine power and human, yet heavenly kindness, and from now on it will show both of these far more clearly, despite it all seeming only dim in relation to the clarity it had with the Father before the foundations of the world were laid. We see only faint glimpses of the glory that shall be revealed to us when He comes to be glorious among His saints and wondrous among all His believers!

Your friend
N.F.S. Grundtvig

51. To Queen Caroline Amalie

March 1848 marks a turning-point in Danish history. King Christian VIII had died on 20th January, and was succeeded by Frederik VII. Christian had supported Grundtvig's plans for a people's high school at Sorø Academy, where Ingemann was currently principal,[622] but with the King's death, the plans fell through. The new king immediately faced demands for an *end* to absolute monarchy and a new *people's* constitution. The Dowager Queen asked Grundtvig what he thought of the February Revolution of 1848 in France – which deposed King Louis Philippe and introduced the Second Republic. Grundtvig's response is guarded; he fears the mob rule that had characterised the 1789 Revolution, but acknowledges that 'the time of the people' has come, also in Denmark. He had lived happily and beneficially under Christian and Caroline Amalie and was unsure of the effects of 'people power' in Denmark, but believed it was inevitable. In the event the King agreed to most of the people's demands, and the new Parliament and constitution came into being in 1849.

∽

Copenhagen, 8th March 1848

Most Gracious Queen!
... Your Majesty asks what I think about the day's events. Although I do not think that all of them will bring about happiness for either France or the rest of Europe, I nevertheless hope that at least both here in Denmark and in Norway we shall realise what we have so far failed to see, namely, that whatever we do, government by the common people is just around the corner. Our task is to make haste to inform and educate them to become wise and gracious masters. Your Majesty will be aware that a popular revival and popular education was precisely what I attempted to implement with a seedbed in Sorø, so I can only applaud the fact that world events are now advocating such a necessity! Now

---

621. No. 68 in *LW*.
622. For detailed information see ch. 7 in *TSFL*: 'The School for Life and the Academy at Sorø'.

and then I am tempted to think that it is too soon to begin what we can now barely do without! Yet in all things I trust in Him who is both better and much wiser than any of us, so all the good that is possible will probably also become reality, however unbelievable we may find it.

May God save Denmark and be, as He has been from time immemorial, close to all those who in truth call upon His name!

Your most humble subject
N.F.S. Grundtvig

52. To Svend Grundtvig

The First Schleswig War or Three Years' War (1848-51) centred on the duchies of Schleswig and Holstein, largely German-speaking but ruled by Denmark. Wishing the duchies to secede and form their own governments 7,000 Schleswig-Holsteiner soldiers occupied Flensborg on 31st March 1848 but were defeated by over 7,000 Danish soldiers at the Battle of Bov on 9th April. A further Danish victory at Dybbøl Hill sealed the victory and a truce was declared, ratified on the very day of this letter. Both Grundtvig's sons, Johan and Svend, fought in the war.

British mediators proposed a division of Schleswig according to language and mind-set, but the Danes refused, and the war moved into its next phase. Denmark retained the duchies until 1864, when Danish forces were swept aside by Chancellor Bismarck, and the duchies passed into German hands. Denmark lost two-fifths of its territory and over a million people, including 200,000 Danish speakers. Following Germany's defeat in the First World War, Holstein remained German, but Schleswig was granted a referendum, which resulted in a division of the duchy into a Danish area (South Jutland, aka North Schleswig) and a German area (South Schleswig). The border has been secure ever since, and indeed has flourished with Germans in Denmark and Danes in Germany on good terms and a thriving cross-border trade.

Copenhagen, 26th August 1848

Dear Svend
You cannot be really serious if you think that your father is frightened to see his sons take the path down which we alone can gain an understanding of life, or that he should wish it to be otherwise; for, in contrast to most fathers, it is precisely along this path that he has endeavoured to preserve his sons' strength and to give them all the encouragement and opportunity he could.

No, my son, when I say that at the moment my sons and I cannot talk together properly, it is not because I miss them or want them to follow in my wake; it is because, as I wrote, our life currents are not flowing parallel but only cross each other when they meet. Indeed even when all currents in our country have run parallel in recent times, we have been unable to make peace because my sons stopped the flow in themselves and have wished me to do the same, which is not possible. I therefore have good reason to say that as soon as I disapprove of anything in the present government, I must expect to be corrected by my two sons, not because they dare to *justify* the government, but because they claim that, like them, I ought to have a blind trust that the government is better informed than I am. I shall stop here, for I have no wish to be told, least of all by my sons, that I fail to appreciate or should regret the freedom of life and independent thinking they have enjoyed; for from childhood I have striven to prepare them for it and encourage them to it. Nor do I wish in any way to quarrel with my sons as to who is to blame most for this discrepancy, which could hardly have come about without blame on both sides. Whoever cannot straighten things out face to face can much less do so pen to pen, and if it *seems* to be so, it is mere appearance, whereby shadows are taken for people until they meet face to face again.

This will naturally come about, my sons, since our hearts, God be praised, have not parted, even if our ways of thinking cut across each other. At least they are willing to write to me openly on the matter and I can answer them equally openly – with the wish that we write no more about this, for it only encourages misunderstanding rather than deterring it!

Among the other books you have received is Allen's *Survey of the Language Relations in Schleswig*,[623] which you will enjoy, for it offers not only a proper justification of the historical circumstances, but also assumes the fundamental principle behind the internal coherence of our mother-tongue with the life in general of our people, which only a handful of our writers have so far addressed. ... My reading is very limited at present, since *The Dane*[624] takes up nearly all my time; I was prepared for this, since a weekly one-man journal must either be of poor quality or require one's fullest attention.

As far as I can see, not much is being published here. We have received a shortened edition of Snorri's *Edda*, which is fine, but not much, when we consider that our literature at present has as its immediate object the future existence of Denmark and all the Nordic countries.

We are being comforted or threatened by all the powers of Germany almost on a daily basis, but none of those I speak to knows anything; as for myself, you doubtless know that I fear not so much for Germany's power but more for the armistice that we have had for some time now.

Your mother and everyone here send their best wishes. Unfortunately, Meta still has a fever. Give my love to Johan, and may you both win all your battles with a healthy mind in a healthy body! You know that this pleases no one more than your

Father and Friend,
Grundtvig

---

623. In 1840 the Danish historian Carl Ferdinand Allen (1811-71) had published *Survey of the Language Relations in Schleswig*, which strongly supported the Danish cause.
624. From 1848-51 Grundtvig published a one-man weekly paper, *The Dane*, which included various writings, not least on the First Schleswig War (1848-51).

53. To his sons

Two days after Grundtvig won election to the Constituent Assembly, he wrote to his sons.

~

8th November 1848.

My dear sons!
Although I have had very little time, it has been much more my reluctance to write to you rather than a lack of time that has hindered me. In my view our country is in extreme danger, and those who *should* lift a finger to save it neither will nor dare do so. I can barely manage to talk about it, even with those who are in far greater agreement with me as to the ways and means than my sons still appear to be.

Since my battle to gain a place in the Assembly has had a successful outcome – in the easiest and most desirable way imaginable – I have taken my seat today and spoken about the sorry state of Schleswig, which is a danger to Denmark and all Danes. So even my great lack of time cannot prevent me from sending my sons a loving greeting in my own hand to tell them that I have seldom been more despondent than last Sunday evening, when I learned that with might and main the weavers' supporters were determined to elect their country boy – meaning me! Thus, I have rarely had such an enjoyable day as last Monday, when our Lord did wondrous things! I was not only elected – by nearly 600 votes to 11 – but it all ended in the friendliest, most enjoyable atmosphere among almost everyone, and most clearly with my rival!

Rørdam's election speech and all his instructions were as masterly as they were simple and inimitable. God bless you and strengthen you and all of us.

Fatherly,
Grundtvig.

54. To Johan Grundtvig

The Constituent Assembly opened on 23rd October 1848 with a speech by Frederik VII. Over 6 months later, on 25th May 1849, the new democratic constitution was finally passed by 119 votes to 6; it came into force with the royal signature on 5th June 1849.

Meanwhile Grundtvig's two sons, Johan and Svend were fighting for Denmark in the First Schleswig War (1848-51), known in Denmark as the Three Years' War. They were swiftly promoted and later decorated.

~

Copenhagen 22nd March 1849

Dear Johan!
Your letter was very dear to me – as letters always are from those whom we love when they are freely sent. For the greetings come from the heart and do good, however much or little they contain. So I am writing again today, even though time is very short and I have nothing in particular to say. I can see that you are following our negotiations in the Assembly but not with any satisfaction, and of course that is the case with me too. On the other hand, since I never expected more of our Parliament than what I have experienced, the depressing impression I have of it fortunately does not affect me. In the circumstances it is a necessary play in which I have volunteered to take part on condition that I do not have to play anyone but myself! Since it remains doubtful to what extent I shall be allowed to enjoy this right – my inalienable, my guardian's right – I appreciate that it has been granted me for the most part without a murmur. God be praised, I believe that even when we seem to be no more than actors, it nevertheless feels that for men like us – who wish for the best, know what we want, and dare what we must – this feeling is not futile since, like all who give birth, it carries its foetus for a long time *unseen*!

    As ever, I am at heart of good hope, and have far more boldness to say and do what I regard as virtuous and beneficial than ever before. The rest is in God's hands, or rather *all* things are in God's hands, and I enjoy a share in this, so I am confident of the rest. May His strength and blessing be also with you, your thoughts and deeds with the Danish army, and Denmark's future.

Mother sends her love,
from your father
Grundtvig.

55. *To his sons*

This letter sums up Grundtvig's luke-warm and self-contradictory welcome for 'democracy'. In the first five lines he claims that parliamentary business is "futile"; that "the yield seems poor"; and yet "there is no disappointment", for he considers his "time and efforts well-spent". He was doubtless not *alone* in thinking this, but he *was* alone in that he insisted on total independence outside all party lines.

Copenhagen 8th June 1849

… Now that the busy and largely futile parliamentary business is over, I feel the need to tell my sons how I am and what I think about it all.
    Looking back on the 7 months which I have spent mostly in the Constituent Assem-

bly, the yield seems poor. I have been almost alone in voting against the two proposals we have been considering without being able to vote for the third and most important one, the 'Constitution'.

However, since this was no more than I expected, there is no disappointment; moreover I consider my time and efforts well-spent, since I have kept my energy, my courage, and my freedom up to the very last day. I have given my opinion in plain language and retained enough vitality and level-headedness to do so in a way that did not immediately offend, and indeed embittered nobody except perhaps a minister or two, who nevertheless responded politely. What I managed to slip into the Constitution – which amounts to two lines about 'public access to the courts and oral proceedings therein' – will not in their present form improve our administration of justice much. However, I am pleased for them to be seen as a good portent, since they represent what I have been striving for from the beginning, and I am doubly pleased because actually I no more "slipped them in" than I forced them in! Against my expectation they actually came across as harmless, and their acceptance was partly to shut me up when I said that all my amendments to the Constitution were "lost behind the steam train".[625] It was annoying that my proposal on 'Nordic citizenship' met with such an idiotic outcome; but it almost got through before I decided to withdraw it, so I was very pleased and took it as a good omen that one day we shall have a government that appreciates the acclamation of our friends more than our enemies.

On Tuesday the Constitution was what they call "solemnly approved and confirmed" by the King, but there was nothing moving about it; no sound of joy was heard, apart from a hurrah for the King – neither when he arrived nor when he very openly and properly announced the Royal Assent. As though he was taking great pains, he made a brief pause, which, being empty of content, made a poor impression. Though this was obviously indefensible, it was nonetheless appropriate, since no one was especially happy with the idea of an Upper Chamber, which ministers have created for their own sakes or in order to humiliate the political parties.

This Upper Chamber, which without much effort the money barons will immediately take possession of, also made it impossible for me to vote for a Constitution to which, despite its lack of weight and colour, I would otherwise have resigned myself...

However, I do wish to tell my sons that my high esteem for the hidden resources of Denmark, far from causing me to withdraw in shame from the experiences of the last year, has buoyed me to step forward even more boldly than before and lament that no one knows how to make use of our riches! They lie as close to the surface as California's gold and will prove to be far more beneficial and inexhaustible. The blindness is disheartening, yet I believe in Him who Himself says that He came to judge the world to make the see-

---

625. The metaphor, meaning lost for good, is a literal translation of the Danish. The first railway line in Denmark opened in Schleswig in 1844 – from Altona/Hamburg to Kiel. Next came the Copenhagen-Roskilde line in 1847, and in 1862 the first line opened in Jutland – between Aarhus and Randers. Grundtvig was familiar with static steam engines from his trip to London in 1829. Indeed in 1843 he had ridden on a steam *train* from Birmingham to Manchester, and was not amused!

ing blind and to make the blind see. In my eyes the Danish heart was born blind, not for the sins of the past or the present but so that the acts of God's may be revealed thereby.

It gives me great pain to think of you being squeezed onto Als[626] and starved for either no good purpose or for a bloodbath more frightening than a major battle, even with a victory of doubtful significance. But soon, with God's help, the page will surely turn somehow or other, and then I hope that we shall see each other again with a joy that the whole of Denmark will share and those beyond Denmark will benefit from.

We can rarely, if ever, offer hope where hopelessness seems far more reasonable, but it always makes us happy if someone has *good hope* for what we love, so that is what I am saying!

God bless you, my children. Today I felt that I had the same to say to you both, which is the only reason why you are not receiving a letter each, since it is long enough to have been shared by two.

With all my love
Father Grundtvig.

56. To Peter Rørdam

On 6th November 1848 Grundtvig was democratically voted into the Constituent Assembly that passed the new democratic constitution on Constitution Day, 5th June 1849. Two months later, aged 65, he is preparing for the new elections to the lower house of the first Parliament. A full account of Grundtvig as a politician can be found in volume 4 of this series, *The Common Good* (2019). As the independent member for the Præstø constituency, where he had been pastor in 1821-22, Grundtvig was a commanding presence in the lower chamber, but by general agreement he talked too much – and he also lost most of his amendment votes. Nevertheless, in admonishing him for the "idiosyncratic negotiating form that the honourable member allows himself," the house speaker, Andreas Krieger added, "this will not cause me to forget the respect I owe the Bard of Denmark, Nicolai Frederik Severin Grundtvig." The later Prime Minister, Ditlev (D.G.) Monrad, called the two senior members, Grundtvig and Anton Tscherning, "the only two members to whom we would attach the designation 'genius'. It is as if I am watching a beautiful natural phenomenon, as though I am seeing erupting volcanoes!"

Copenhagen, 13th August 1849

Dear Friend!
Thanks for your letter… It is time to think about the approaching Parliament and I have already given considerable thought as to whether yet again I should risk my old skin. I have reached the conclusion that, whatever happens, I shall stand again where I was

---

626. Als is an island in south-east Jutland to which the Danish troops withdrew.

elected last time and may our Lord and the voters decide the rest. The week before last I was strengthened in this decision when Barfod[627] visited me with the question from the farmers as to whether, as they wished, I would consider standing in Præstø. They did not want anyone to stand who could increase the tension between town and country. I responded positively, on condition that they kept their word and did not work for the other side in secret. For the sake of our friendship and the cause, I hope you will keep an eye on what is going on. I remember what your opinion was in your letter to the voters, and if the July battle[628] had not happened, I would have begun to write an account of my parliamentary prospects in *The Dane*, for any *brief* account of the subject is of no benefit whatsoever. If you nonetheless think that a short, open letter to the voters is advisable, then I can have one printed at once.

My reason for standing again is not because I expect to persuade anyone of my view of the major circumstances; it is partly because I feel that I owe something to the voters who elected me last year and partly that as a Member of Parliament I am more assured of the freedom of my voice and my pen. I cannot do without these. So with God's help I shall not be entirely useless. If I cannot get the laws passed that I want on freedom of worship and freedom of speech, on education, and on farming, I can perhaps at least prevent any crackpot developments in these areas, and if I cannot prevent the government from taking a lopsided view, I can perhaps prevent Parliament as such from taking the blame.

Meta and her husband are home after a lovely trip from Mern to Als and beyond, and a number of holidaymakers are turning homeward, so I shall soon have some company again; at the moment I have no one to sit and talk to properly about everything, and that is a great loss. However, our Lord is a good man, and it is remiss of me to complain; for to be able at my age to miss people even as I keep up with the times is indeed a sign of grace. He is always there for me to turn to, so it is my own fault if I feel alone.

Your good health! Best wishes to your sister, and think kindly of

Your
N.F.S. Grundtvig

57. To Svend Grundtvig

Grundtvig believed that the solution to the Schleswig-Holstein question was to give up German-minded Holstein but retain all of Schleswig, where there was both a Danish and a German mind-set. Both his sons, Johan and Svend, volunteered for the war against Germany (1848-50) and both were sent to the front line – the border rampart known as Dannevirke. On 17th July Svend was promoted to lieutenant. Grundtvig was proud that both his boys were doing their duty for Denmark. They were involved in a skirmish at Ovre Stolk on 25th July 1850, with the loss of several Danish com-

---

627. Poul Barfod (1811-96) was a Danish historian and politician.
628. Schleswig-Holstein troops besieged Fredericia on 8th May 1849. After 6 days of fighting in July a ceasefire was agreed and the Schleswig-Holstein troops withdrew, despite having suffered fewer casualties.

manders. In a letter to his mother Johan wrote, "Schleppegrell, Læssøe, Trepka, Lieutenant-Colonel Bülow and Captain Kranold, the hope of all our army, are lost!" The Danes nevertheless pushed the Schleswig-Holsteiners back to where the Battle of Idstedt was fought on the same day. There were roughly 30,000 soldiers on either side in this, the biggest battle in the country's history. Svend wrote home, "Of the 17 officers we marched alongside yesterday morning, only 5 returned uninjured... What cost us most was the storming of Idstedt town, where the enemy was unyielding and shot from every window as we moved forward over open fields and roads... The enemy positions were very strong and our numbers not much stronger than theirs: I cannot deny that they fought against us with skill and bitterness." Svend's bravery at the Battle of Idstedt earned him the Order of Chivalry *(Ridderkorset)*. The Danish victory is commemorated by the Idstedt Lion sculpture in Flensburg. After the war Svend remained in the army and was promoted to Captain.

~

Copenhagen, 3rd August 1850

Dear Son!
This shall be as much a portent for me as it is news! Both are good, to judge from your letter written under open skies at Dannevirke, subdued yet quick-witted. That is how I both wish and hope that the Danes will pitch camp at Dannevirke, armed and ready. Since they cannot enjoy their Danish freehold in peace, they will have to assert it in war. But may they otherwise be so tired of the bloodbath that they do not seek to gain the whole world, let alone a piece of Holstein. Nor should they blow the lur[629] or sharpen the blades of their blunted swords, even if they dared to expect far better advantage from such a victory than at Ovre Stolk and Idstedt. Already with hindsight we can see that it was so dearly-bought that only the blessings of a people's spirit like the Danes' saved us; with God's help the benefits and joys of this spirit will be seen in the clear light of day to be victorious again. In my eyes this makes the battle and the sacrifice worthwhile. I have worked unfailingly, one might even say, obstinately, to get the Kingdom of Denmark to fight to the last in Schleswig to retain South Jutland. I am equally adamant in arguing that we must not relinquish an inch of what, to worthy fulfilment and clarification, Denmark has gained with its heart's blood and cannot surrender. Then we can happily sheathe our swords and leave Holstein to its own devices. The duchy will never be truly won for Denmark, even if it were far more easily conquered than at present; in my view it would cost Denmark its dying strength, which would in the event be totally wasted.

Anyway, God be praised that I have sons who have the will and the courage to put their lives and blood at stake for the country, which was so desperately needed and so clearly at stake. May my gallant sons give the honour to God, who is master of our all life and spirit and thus for all that we think, are, and do! It is a dear and unforgettable assuredness that while my eyes are still open, and even when they shall be closed, my sons

---

629. The long lur horn is a wind instrument cast in bronze dating to the Late Bronze Age (c. 1000 BCE). In the Icelandic Sagas it was used to call warriors to battle.

will work for whatever God gives them strength, courage, and fortune, in peace as in war, in good health and with untiring spirit. This has been my soul's desire all my days and so it remains. I pour God's and my own blessing upon them, and where that is received, it is never in vain.

Peace be with you! You will doubtless soon meet at some turn or other. You are as close to me now as I write as you were the first time you stood on my knees and shoulders!
From Mother, Meta and all of us the most loving wishes from your

Father and Friend,
N.F.S. Grundtvig

58. To Johan Grundtvig

Grundtvig's relationship to his eldest son, Johan, fluctuated, but in the following letter we find him sharing his experience of being a member of the new Parliament.

Copenhagen 8th October 1850

Dear son!
I have long wished to write to you, and this is truly a debt that I am making a move to repay. There have always been obstacles in the way, so it is doubtful that you would have received a letter today if I had not heard in a letter from Svend that Mother was also holding a pause. Immediately therefore I took up my pen, since today I am going to Parliament and I am not good at writing letters on such days, as I trust Mother's diligence!
On Saturday, as the oldest Member of Parliament, I opened negotiations with a few words on war and peace that I had naturally weighed, but that were also weighty. Our parliamentary officers were the same as the last time, so, as I said in my preface, there is little prospect that activity in the chambers will correspond to activity in the field! However, I refuse to give up hope, nor should anyone in Denmark do so; for however poorly Parliament has both seen and sought to carry out its task, we must never forget that we have no *better* way. If the government is intent on doing good, Parliament will not stand in its way, and if the government is to do better, then it needs Parliament. You have doubtless seen the news that yesterday Hall[630] proposed, I supported, and Parliament unanimously passed a bill to honour the army; but let me just add that I emphasised that "The Danish army has earned the gratitude of our Fatherland, old

---

630. Carl Christian Hall (1812-81) was a Danish national-liberal politician, who sat in Parliament from 1849 until his death.

Denmark!" I drew attention to the fact that it had done so from the beginning of the war, both when it won and when it lost, both when it drew on the strength of our young people, and when it had to tax their energy during a lull in the fighting. However, the people could not call the outcome 'successful' for as long as some of them were still suffering under the yoke of the enemy. Success will only come when the battle is won in South Jutland, and Dannebrog is waving over Danne-virke with promise of the fruits of peace from the flower of victory!

The fact that this was received with open appreciation and considerable applause does not mean so much, but if a good speech finds a good ear, there is always hope that it can find a good *place* to be enacted. I did not know for sure that my sons had also been transferred to Danne-virke, but I could feel it, since my heart was beating faster than usual.

Otherwise we continue here in the usual peace and quiet that you know, getting close to moving home, which is just about to happen. Yesterday in good weather, Algreen,[631] with praiseworthy precision, moved all my books out of Vimmelskaftet into Stormgaden, and already by lunchtime, when I came home from Parliament, the whole wall was lined with my 'Mammon'! Actually, the books are now more of a burden to me than a delight, but what we own we must try to find room for, and what the old people no longer enjoy they should share with the young.

Greetings to Svend, and may God strengthen and keep you in the service of our country with good hope for the future. That future lies in the hands of a better father than your own, who nevertheless deeply wishes to make your prospects light and your years fruitful in both benefit and happiness!

Mother and all our close friends send their love through

Father
Frederik.

59. To Johan and Svend Grundtvig

His wife's death came as no surprise and something of a relief to Grundtvig. He had gradually distanced himself from Lise, and she became ever more deeply depressed.[632] When she had to find the latest apartment and then move her home again in October 1850, it all became too much. The letter below was written on the same day that she died. Seen from Lise's side, she had waited patiently for him for 7 long years from engagement to wedding and had then born three children, Johan (b. 1822), Svend (1824), and Meta (1827). She had lived *with* Grundtvig through thick and thin, not least during his England trips, as the above letters show. In the letter below, Grundtvig seems more concerned with his sons, who had won a famous victory at the Battle of Idsted in July 1850; nonetheless the Schleswig-Holsteiners fought on until October and only finally capitulated in January 1851. Grundtvig hopes that his sons will now come home and console him.

---

631. Peder Algreen (1807-77) was first a teacher, then a pastor in Copenhagen, where he met Grundtvig.
632. To describe her depression Grundtvig used the Danish word *tungsindig*, lit. 'heavy-minded'.

Lise Blicher was buried in the Church of Our Saviour, where Grundtvig had been pastor from 1822-26. He himself conducted the service, and his eulogy, 'Beside My Lise's Coffin', appears as no. 48 in *Human Comes First* (2018). The grave has since been demolished, but the gravestone is immured in the church tower.

~

Copenhagen, 14th January 1851.

My dear sons!
Although I naturally have not much desire today to either speak or write, I must nevertheless send you, my children, a few friendly lines together with your mother's last greetings which Meta will bring you.

If the capitulation is genuine and most of our army discharged, then perhaps for a few months you can enjoy the repetition of life in your parents' home that I know you will never forget. Although no one knows better than you that "the woman stands for life in the home", for she was just that until you came of age, I trust that whenever it becomes possible you would wish to recall your home life at your leisure.

It has been a hard time for us all, but, God be praised that it did not last longer, as the doctors feared. As God has given me the strength, so was it good for me that I had a lot to do. With her daughter's heart Meta has given both you and me some good advice, and with filial concern, Boisen[633] has discovered that it comes of its own accord, which has indeed been a great sacrifice during this long period of time.

May God strengthen, bless, and keep you until the end, as is the natural wish of your

Father
Grundtvig

60. To Bernhard Ingemann

If we are to judge from the surviving correspondence between Grundtvig and Ingemann, Grundtvig's last letter to his friend before this one was dated 25th September 1849. Thus, including the poem referred to below, Ingemann had sent no fewer than four letters to Grundtvig without a response. When Ingemann heard of Lise's death, he wrote a poem about her (dated February 1851) and sent it to Grundtvig in an envelope with no letter enclosed. It included the words, "She who loved him most is gone, No longer does he hear the word/of love's most precious heart-voice/ from the summer of life."

~

---

633. Peter Boisen (1815-62) was the son of Grundtvig's friend, Bishop of Lolland-Falster Peter Boisen. In 1847 Peter married Grundtvig's daughter, Meta, and in 1854 he became Grundtvig's curate at Vartov Church.

Copenhagen, 18th February 1851

Dear Ingemann!
Although the parliamentary bell is ringing at this very minute, I must pick up my pen before my hand wavers again, partly because I am genuinely ashamed of my apparently obstinate silence and especially because I can see from the empty envelope that even if you are not yet angry at my unwritten letter, you are nevertheless upset.

But to the point: deepfelt thanks to you and Lucie for your kind contribution, which although I may have expected none other, it is precisely for that reason I wish to assure you of my thanks. The reason I have not responded (though Algreen has doubtless told you of my gratitude, as I bid him) is not just because I am out of the habit of writing to you and have my hands full, but also because I have of late been most unwilling to talk to anyone, even friends, about my Lise's suffering and death. For she suffered for a long, long time, and I too suffered not a little. So when "for the sake of Christ's blood God made her hour of departure good", I thanked him from my innermost being both on her and my own behalf and not for a moment would I have wished her back with "an incurable illness", as the doctors said, and, as far as I could judge, an inconsolable heart. Since in serious matters I never say anything except what I mean, I had thought that I should not write to Lise's and my old friends, who have seen what she meant to me through a whole lifetime; they could not see what lay under the cold, dead letters. Thus in their eyes I could easily assume the appearance of an unloving or unfeeling husband, which, however little I value appearances, I would not have placed upon me.

Now on the other hand, when, rather than scold me, you prefer to urge me with your kind heart to look back to the truly idyllic days – and do not even include an accompanying letter –, in God's name I must both say and write what is true, without the fear of wondering what it will look like – and that is the truth! I could no longer comfort or gladden the noble soul with the melancholic mind, nor could she comfort or gladden me. I also need far more of both than the world realises, or with God's help will ever know. That is why I mourned inwardly at her death-bed but not at her grave, where I said from deep inside my heart, "The Lord gave and the Lord has taken away!"[634]

So, as you can see, now I have written it! Your loving verses I take to have been sent with a view to publication in *The Dane*, since there is nothing else in the envelope, and unless you tell me in time, you must keep silent later when you see it in next Saturday's edition.

Dear good old friend and stable-mate! May God bless you, also for your loyal friendship to me and my house, which no vicissitude in either the outside or inside world has been able to damage! Svend is now staying with me, and I know that if he was around at this minute, he would ask me to include his greetings in this greeting from Jane and all of us to your Lucie and yourself

from your
N.F.S. Grundtvig

---

634. Job 1:21.

61. To Vilhelmine Stenersen

Following an invitation from the Norwegian Students' Association, Grundtvig made his only other trip outside Denmark on 4th June 1851, accompanied by his sons, Johan and Svend, on a steamship to Oslo. Among their hosts were his Norwegian friend, Pastor Wilhelm Wexels, and the widow of Stener Stenersen (1789-1835), Grundtvig's old university friend, who as Professor of Theology at Oslo University, had tried in vain to recruit Grundtvig as Professor of History. Grundtvig's reputation as a friend of Norway preceded him, and the 10-day visit was an enormous success. Indeed, Stenersen's daughter, Vilhelmine (1828-93), who was also involved in hosting the visit, fell in love with Johan! They were married in 1855 in Oslo with Pastor Wexels presiding, and four years later they moved to Denmark – to Grundtvig's delight. The couple had six children, the last of whom did not die until 1945. Thus, aged 67, Grundtvig's one and only trip to Norway was an unforgettable honour, for himself and his offspring.

~

17th July 1851

Daughter of my Friend, and if I am to be honest from both sides, my young friend!

One must not tell young girls that it is a good idea *not* to follow their mother's counsels, but when their mother's example is *better* than her counsel, it is best to follow the example! So I have her permission to thank you for your kind letter which your mother in a sense advised against and yet showed you the way there and urged you to take it. A second question is whether I should have anything to do with writing to young people of the fair sex! However, just as I cannot resist talking to them if they wish to talk to me, so might I just as well write to them if they allow it! I am therefore, without apology, following the good example you have furnished me with and am seizing the opportunity, as personally as it is possible with a pen, to thank you deeply for all the kindness you have shown both me and my family and for all the many signs of it that we received in the happy days we spent in the haven of your circle. They will doubtless prove to be unforgettable, since we must guard against forgetting what is delightful to remember. Overdue but gratifying is the expression I will use, for my trip to Norway has been a life-event which I shall openly cherish. So I thank not only my friends and well-wishers in the hills and mountains round and about, but first and foremost Him who is above them – who existed before they came into being and whose quickening effect I both feel and am certain can be traced back to all my undertakings. It is so with poets and bards like us that the more we strive to resemble prophets, the closer our fate is to being despised in our home and the land of our birth. Although I dare say we could not bear it to be otherwise in our day-to-day existence, so much the more is it pleasant and beneficial once in a while – or at least once in our lives – to be received and borne by the hands of our closest neighbours, as happened to me in Norway!

So thank you, dear friend, for your ardent participation in all that both honoured and delighted me – and thanks too to your dear mother and brothers. Please convey my deepest gratitude to Wexels and to whomever else you meet of our mutual friends and acquaintances!

May God bless you and keep you!

Your friend
N.F.S. Grundtvig

62. *From Queen Caroline Amalie*

The dowager queen's relationship to Grundtvig was strengthened through her presence at his Sunday services at Vartov from 1839 onwards. When Grundtvig's first wife died in 1851, she expressed her heartfelt condolences; conversely, when Grundtvig remarried soon after, she expressed her joy at his new-found love with 'Lady Toft'[635] in the letter below, which shows a friend's insight into the relationship. On the 50th anniversary of Grundtvig's ordination into the priesthood, she presented him with a memorah, a 7-branch gold candlestick, on behalf of a group of women from throughout the Nordic countries. When Grundtvig married for a third time, and his new wife started the 'friends' meetings' on Grundtvig's 80th birthday in 1863, Caroline Amalie was present, as she was at all the subsequent friends' meetings.

∼

2nd August 1851

Herr Pastor Grundtvig.
The news you send me is in no way unexpected! I assumed that I would soon hear of your contract with Lady Toft to travel the road of life together. May God bless your pact and allow you to find in your married state all the happiness and joy that you look forward to. May you in your union work even more powerfully to the revival and blossoming of Denmark and the North in their full clarity.

I imagine that the intrepid Lady Toft is a woman after your own head, just as you are a man after her own heart; two matching souls of the same nature. Your relationship will therefore be a real, and the truth is the *only*, element that should exist in all relationships in our newly revived North! It is thus that we should separate ourselves from the rest of the world with its spiritless comforts.

It pleases me greatly to hear that the Boisens are enjoying their trip, and may Meta's health be confirmed.

---

635. The Danish word here, 'Fru' is the equivalent of 'Mrs', but in translation Marie, being a manor-owner would have been addressed in English as 'Lady'.

My warmest greetings to Lady Toft. Now you will become the brother-in-law of my friend Rørdam!

God bless you!

Your heartily devoted friend
Caroline Amalie

63. To Peter Fenger

Grundtvig stood as an independent at the general election on 26th February 1853 and again at the election on 27th May, three months later, He won the first, sat for 3 months, then lost the second. The letter below was written 16 days before the first election, but he had not yet found a constituency to represent! In the event he won Sorø County's 4th constituency in Skelskør in south-west Zealand, where his friend Peter Fenger was pastor. Grundtvig helped to found the Danish Association in 1853 'for the common good' and was a regular speaker at its meetings.[636] Another alliance to promote national unity was Friends of the Farmers (*Bondevennerne*), which in the 1840s and 1850s advocated improved conditions for peasant farmers: this became a kind of political party in 1846 and was influential in the drawing-up of the new constitution.

Copenhagen, 10th February 1853

Dear good friend!
Things are so confused and skewed at the moment – though not without the hope that God will intervene for the better – so of course I must stand for election wherever and as soon as possible!

If I can be more or less sure of being elected in your constituency, then my old body will make sure it follows the movement of my thought and puts up with the winter weather on the way...

All of us here, plus the Rørdams and whoever else we can reach, are thinking seriously about starting a 'Danish Association' throughout the kingdom, with the sole aim of working as best we can for what we agree to call 'Danish'. I have complained vociferously about the lack of such an association since 1848, but as long as the others think that *without* it we have freer hands, under the name of 'the Danish cause', to pay as much or as little attention to what is Danish, we can make no progress! However, now that everyone else who wishes to save old Denmark in any way whatsoever – and with the Friends of the Farmers against them – cannot but feel the lack of a widespread and active society, both my wife and her brother[637] also believe that we can gather thousands of people in various occupations around what all Danes have in common and find not only irreplaceable but also undeniable.

---

636. For Grundtvig's speech to the Danish Society on 2nd May 1855, see no. 33c in *TCG*.
637. Master of the Royal Hunt, Hans Carlsen-Lange.

At the moment, such an association is without doubt essential to the salvation of Denmark from the imminent danger of falling into enemy hands. In calmer days and with God's help it will contribute incalculably to equalizing conditions among the Danes, to safeguarding our mother-tongue, and to promoting Danish and popular education in every direction. Therefore, my dear friend, do what you can in your circle to pave the way for this good cause, which will be taken up at the very first opportunity. My wife believes – and this is so to be desired – that many of the revivalists can be won over, if they are approached in the right way, and it is clear that they most of all will feel the misfortune if we step by step come closer to the Schleswig situation, where our mother-tongue has either been suppressed or has died and is powerless in our preaching, our songs, and our Bible.

May the Lord in whom we trust, as He who never puts our hope to shame, bless you. With loving greetings also from my wife

Your old friend
N.F.S. Grundtvig

64. To Bernhard Ingemann

On 8th September 1853, after a summer with depression, Grundtvig celebrated his 70th birthday at Gammel Køgegaard, 45 km south of Copenhagen. The manor belonged to his brother-in-law, Hans Carlsen-Lange (1810-87), Marie's elder brother. Gifts came from all over Denmark, and Grundtvig's friends donated 7000 rigsdaler towards the founding of a people's high school in his own name.

∽

Copenhagen, 13th September 1853

Dear Ingemann!
It was a great pleasure for myself and many others to see you at Gammel Køgegaard on 8th September, when my Danish friends rather surprised me with the prospect of what I had looked for in vain during this, for me, miserable summer, and had almost turned my back on. We never expected your physical presence if it were to expose your health to any danger, and I could not but feel that with regard to the body – right down to the fingertips – I have made myself guilty of many a negligence that I had best hush up any questions on the subject.

Deepfelt thanks for being present in heart and soul, for your kind greeting with Dr. [Peter] Kierkegaard, and for your more than friendly song, which contributed incalculably to making me and many others feel the day was so joyful![638]

---

638. Ingemann wrote a song of 4 stanzas for the occasion, ending with the lines: "O'er the giant poet's forehead/ still the lightning-spirit burns;/ev'ry giant resurrected/shall his name recall by turns." Grundtvig returned the compliment on Ingemann's 70th birthday in 1859.

Indeed, it was truly a refreshment for my tired soul, and if anything with God's help can get me back on my feet again, it must be the prospect and preparation for a winter seed that can give fruit in the coming year. A fog just as poisonous as the one that has brooded externally over Copenhagen this summer[639] has brooded internally over my heart and soul, so I have been a burden to myself and my nearest and dearest. Although, God be praised, it is now more bearable, I can only call it a great wonder if I were to gain a renewed lust and strength for a life of manly strides to the end. It may be no greater a wonder than what I have often witnessed so far in myself, so I am beginning to cherish the hope of the great joy that I am wont to call the golden red of the evening, which has frequently moved me to the depths as I have gazed upon it with a poet's eye.

Your song also nourished this hope, my faithful old friend, and our common hope that the God of Truth and almighty Love will not disappoint our joint hope of better days for old Denmark and all that breathes truth and love.

Loving greetings to you and yours from my wife and me,

Your friend
N.F.S. Grundtvig

65. To Gunni Busck

Grundtvig's joy at the birth of his third son is coupled with his belief that the new Frederik Lange Grundtvig (1854-1903) will follow in his father's footsteps and become a pastor, for neither Johan nor Svend had done so, much to Grundtvig's disappointment.

Frederiksholms Kanal, 16th May 1854

Dear friend!
God be praised, yesterday evening towards 9 o'clock, after a hard but brief battle, my wonderful wife gave birth to a fine, healthy boy, weighing close to 8 pounds. He has proved that he can howl as well as any, so the heavenly Father who has given him life and a voice will doubtless also give him life and a voice to praise His name vociferously when we have kept silent for too long! It has always seemed to me that were I to leave behind three sons, it would be the youngest who most clearly would adopt my spirit and continue my work in the light and service of our Lord. He is born in my old age, so his life-path will be like that of a grandson, marvellously prolonging my life in him into the next century! It would be a wonder if I were allowed to see him at the age Abraham saw Jacob, but one wonder is actually no greater than another. Our heavenly Father, who has granted and entrusted him to me, will in any case allow us to live so long together as is

---

639. i.e. the cholera outbreak, see p. 249

good for us both. So long may I feel that my day's work is not over – an essential feeling when we are to work cheerfully with all the power that the Lord gives!

Best wishes to your wife and household from us all!

Your friend
N.F.S. Grundtvig

66. To Bernhard Ingemann

Grundtvig's second wife Marie is dead. His friend Ingemann could not go to the funeral.

～

Rønnebæksholm. 21st July 1854

Thanks, dear old friend, for the testimony of your heartfelt participation in my deep grief! In the world's eyes such a testimony is superfluous, but when participation takes place it can only overflow into a testimony and can never be too much. Dear friends, you saw little of our life together here. She was so rich in all things *human*, and her love so generous in its grace that it was immediately clear that it was a joy to be loved by her, and an unutterably great joy to be loved by her as she loved her aging husband.

Yet in every sense she belonged to God. He gave and he took and, despite all the objections of the world and our self-love, the believing soul cannot but add, "God be praised!" He gave so richly as to exceed the boldest expectations, and He took so like a father as to exceed even there all expectation once He had given us, in the blessing of a little boy, a living memorial and a living hope. With His blessing, our loving Christian life together will not only be reflected in Him but will be reborn to a glorious increase.

He Himself has given us the valid reason as to why His paths are beyond tracing out and His judgements unsearchable.[640] Of necessity they are far above ours – as Heaven is above Earth – and if we forget this, the error is ours alone. Now that I look back on the wonderfully rich and generous heart that God revealed to me as a hidden source of help in my old age, then I must say: stronger legs than mine would be needed to bear such good days for long! I would have already become unrighteous towards everything in the world that was not like her, and reluctant to do anything that was not for her sake! This would have happened however much the power of her love drove me into active participation and vital activity, wherever a door stood open for what is noble in Heaven and on Earth. She was a wonderful helpmate to me in every sense, with an eye for all that is worth seeing and a heart of all that is worth loving! God be praised, I have always glorified 'woman' as mother of the living, the wellspring of human life. But that 'woman' would be all that

---

640. Rom 11:33.

she was, even for such an old man as me, was far beyond my imagination and thus far beyond my ability to treasure and draw on it properly.

So, old friend, you know that during these days of sorrow the only thing one can speak of with any spirit is what one misses and mourns. I shall therefore close here and speak of nothing else – with love to your Lucie, whom, I am pleased to say, found herself attracted to my charming Marie, and with thanks yet again for not deferring your soothing of my sadness with your loving concern and praise for the comfort and support of my old age. Given by God, and now with God, she would never have listened to any who claimed that she could be anything *without* God, who alone is good!

Your friend
N.F.S. Grundtvig.

67. To Svend Grundtvig

Two weeks after Frederik's birth Grundtvig baptised him at home, and confirmed this in Vartov Church 3 weeks later. Marie did not recover. She was first laid to rest in Carlsen's Chapel in St. Nicolai Church Køge, but in the summer of 1855 she was moved to Clara's Churchyard on Køge Ridge, where Grundtvig himself was to lie beside her in 1872.

∼

29th July 1854

Your letter, my dear son, could not do other than gladden my father's heart. Although I at no point doubted that my sons were minded to everything you gave expression to – and Meta had already told me what you were thinking – my impression corresponds to your expression, so I thank you from the heart, my children, for speaking your minds! May God, who is the best Father of all, lay in His blessing what mine cannot bear!

As for the matter itself, my heart and my thoughts are so fixed on what has happened that I cannot make any decision on what lies ahead. My state of mind seems so desperate and partly of so little consequence that there will always be time enough to think when I have to make a choice. Carlsen[641] and I agree that we should let the summer and the coming winter follow the same path as before, so I think there will be time enough this winter, if I live so long, to think about the rest. All that is clear to me is that unless it is absolutely necessary I shall not deprive my sons of the allowance which they may still need and that likewise I shall not move my son outside the family circle that I know his mother wished him to grow up in. That much stronger is the need for me, while my eyes remain open, not to be separated from the precious child; there is no other

---

641. Hans Carlsen-Lange, Marie's brother.

mother for him in our family than Meta, but she has been unable to manage what I know she would like to.

There is no question that without a moment's thought, I would wish both my sons to come out here and stay with me for a while, and you should know that I have given it some thought. But although I would rather not interrupt the healthy, vital activity of either young or old, that is not the only reason why I continue to hesitate over such an invitation. The main reason is that with a companion completely after my head and heart for the last few years as none other could be, I have been cosseted and almost disqualified from associating with my nearest and dearest, and have no wish to impose upon them a burden I myself in their place would shrink from bearing.

I must therefore first believe that I am a little more equitable and reasonable in relation to my daily society before I make loving demands on my children's company. Loneliness and silence still serve me best, or rather, they are a necessity for me in my daily existence, for I cannot as yet occupy myself either with people or books. It has been a strange yet rich life I have lived and shall rely on to my days' end, and this completely unexpected, precipitate severance from it is so much like death that whatever anyone else thinks, life in any other form is so foreign to me at present that I doubt I shall ever come to terms with it.

Otherwise, dear children, I am tolerably well, and, God be praised, I am recovering my inner balance day by day. I do not doubt that if it is God's will, I shall have a few more years left in this world, and that He will give me the strength and the desire to live and work as usual in both my inner and outer circle.

God willing, I propose to come to town on Sunday 6th August, when we can speak further on this.

Best wishes to Johan, Meta and Boisen, with love from me, your old, in heartfelt affection unchangeable

Father
N.F.S. Grundtvig

68. To Johan Grundtvig

Grundtvig's eldest son, Johan, had gained a degree in Theology in 1848, but had no wish to become a pastor. He served as a volunteer in the First Schleswig War (1848-51) and rose to the rank of Captain, but thereafter he became a civil servant and worked in the ministerial archives. The letter also reveals how little contact Grundtvig had with Johan during his marriage to Marie.

Rønnebæksholm, 2nd August 1854

God bless you, my dear son, for your loving thoughts and your fundamental honesty. May He bless your effort to break the tie on your tongue which to our detriment and the sadness or indignation of your neighbour forces us to brood in darkness over the commotion in our souls! Yes, my dear first-born! You have never lost your first-born right in my heart, and I have never surrendered the bright hope I not so much conceived *of* you as thought born *with* you. You have long been like a closed book to me, which I could not read but whose content I had to guess. Even with the best and most reasonable guesswork, the doubt adheres so strongly that despite all our efforts we cannot be free of it. So my heartfelt thanks for allowing your pen to reveal that you still regard me as your best, fatherly, friend on earth, for it was truly that which I was tempted to doubt and that is a doubt that paralyses every movement in a father's heart and hides it away. It is for me a very sad event that gives rise to this happy realisation that, God be praised, I have kept my first-born. The ways and thoughts of the Lord are as high above us as the heavens above the earth, and this sad event is also indissolubly linked to God's gift in my last-born, so I must keep silent in the presence of the Lord until I can say with a fullness of heart, The Lord gave, the Lord took, the Lord's name be praised! You can believe your father when I say that I loved the recently-departed so deeply because she felt very sincerely for my children, who were not hers, and all that I loved. It was truly a great sadness for her that before her very eyes she stood like a dividing wall between you and your father, whom she could see, with her sharp eye, you loved, but regarded as being in prison.

So, thanks be to the peace of God, it made me truly happy that you ended your letter with the best wishes for your little brother, who was born with a blessed smile and who, when God has let him grow up, will doubtless make you feel that the love-bond to which he is the living witness, also embraced all my loved ones.

Best wishes to Svend, Meta and all her household. Today she will receive my letter from yesterday, just as I received hers today. God willing, we shall happily meet in a few days time.

Your own father
N.F.S. Grundtvig

69. From Meta Bøisen (née Grundtvig)

Meta Grundtvig (1827-87) was Grundtvig's third child but first girl. As such, she was the apple of his eye, by all accounts a gentle, devoted daughter who looked after him during his depression in 1844. So much the greater was his disappointment the following year, when she announced her engagement to Peter Boisen (1815-62). Grundtvig wrote 'To my own Meta' that year, lamenting his loss, no. 133 in *Living Wellsprings* (2015). Boisen, the son of a bishop, had a degree in Theology and was a teacher at Queen Caroline Amelia's Charity School from 1841, and its principal from 1851. Grundtvig had married him and Meta at Vartov Church in 1847, and in 1854 he became Grundtvig's curate there. His interest in songs resulted in the publication of *New and Old Songs by and for the Danish People* (1849). In 1850 Grundtvig became a grandfather for the first time to Peter and Meta's firstborn, Elisabeth, who grew up quite close to Grundtvig.

In the letter below, Meta truly takes her father to task for his self-pity!

12th August 1854

Thanks, dear father, for telling me that you had safely arrived at Rønnebæksholm and that, God be praised, you found our little brother[642] well. Naturally, the rest of your letter could only distress me. You write as though you had no children whatsoever, or at least found in them no love for you worth talking about. I can understand that you feel a deep, sad loss, but I do not understand how you could speak as though our Lord had taken all earthly love from you. So often in your life you have told me that no earthly love can compare with the love between parents and children, yet now, when our Lord has not only let you keep all your children but has even granted you a little son in your old age, it makes me very sad to see you write that life has no joy in it for you. I understand it when you say you can only live in the past and the future, but your past also belongs to your children, and truly they belong together with those who love you deeply. Indeed, father, if I did not think it was proof that you place greater trust in me than in your sons, it would sadden me all the more than it already has. You have not mentioned in a single letter to me that my love for you was a joy – it seems to me as though it was more of a burden, but you had not the heart to tell me straight out. Yes, father, you do not understand the power you have over me, for a loving word from you is one of my greatest joys, just as an unloving or an unfriendly look is a great sadness to me. That is how it has been all my life and that is how it still is at the moment.

I have expressed myself openly and honestly, as I know you prefer. I am also convinced that you will see it is out of love for you that I write this letter, for it has cost me tears welling up from a deep-felt distress to realise that I could not be there for you. Live well, beloved father, may God be with you to comfort and strengthen you in your grief, and may He help your heart to feel with what great love you are regarded by

Your little Meta

Do kiss our little brother from me and give my best wishes to whoever cares for a greeting from me, especially to little Amalie.[643]

---

642. i.e. the new-born Frederik Lange Grundtvig.
643. Amalie Jørgensen was Otto and Marie Grundtvig's granddaughter. She was living with the Grundtvigs during and after the First Schleswig War (1848-51).

70. To Svend Grundtvig

On 29th May 1861 Grundtvig celebrated his 50th anniversary in the priesthood. The day began with a children's choir singing outside his home on Gammel Kongevej one of Grundtvig's best-known hymns, 'We welcome with joy this blessed day'.[644] They then hoisted the Dannebrog flag that they had sewn and shouted hurrah in his honour. At 10 am Grundtvig presided at a service of celebration in a chock-full Vartov Church. The dowager Queen Caroline Amalie presented him with a 7-armed candelabrum, a gift from his friends in Norway and Denmark, with the words, "May this gold candelabrum remind you of the light that now shines in the Danish Church." The government granted Grundtvig the rank of Bishop on the occasion, but to the King's dismay Ditlev Monrad, Minister of the Church and Culture, promoted Grundtvig to the actual *title* of Bishop, and he was then often known as 'Bishop Grundtvig', especially abroad.

Late in the afternoon a number of his friends gathered for dinner in a large well-decorated garden tent in Grundtvig's garden. A group of young people arrived and sang, and the sum of 3000 rigsdaler was handed over for the publication of Grundtvig's hymns and spiritual songs. His friend, Pastor Gunni Busck, then presented him with a gold coin minted in his honour from donations from the Vartov congregation. Grundtvig made a speech of thanks, which was followed by more singing and speeches, including greetings from the Jutland farmers and the Norwegian students. Between 10 and 11 pm torches were lit all round the garden, after which a farewell song was sung and the celebration ended.

Grundtvig's son Johan and his daughter Meta were present, but not Svend. The letter is addressed to Svend and his wife – hence the 'dear children'.

∼

3rd June 1861

Thank you, dear children, both for the absence you felt and the participation you showed as best you could on the jubilee day. It was as delightful as such a day can possibly be, and I had therefore wished so deeply that I could share it with you who are so close to my heart! Your sentiment on the day itself was a doubly joyful surprise, when I was forced to believe my own eyes and see what I had never imagined – that the telegraph really can and does convey poetry! And as the thoughtful Johan immediately remarked, it does so more faultlessly than it often does the thinnest prose! Even my bad legs wished me well on the day, or rather, I had to wish myself well with them! As Baggesen says of the happy days in Kalundborg, "even the lame walked better!". Monrad came not only with the 'bishop's letter' himself, but – although he first had to talk to the ministers of state – he arrived on time at the dining-table and called for a toast in my honour ....

---

644. No. 53 in *LW*.

In my sermon I naturally said as little as possible about myself and spoke first and foremost of the enlightenment that we have heard from the beginning of time and which we know will last to its end. I also spoke of the blessing that God confers along with this enlightenment about life and peace ...

Thanks too for your letter to my wife! She will write back, I am sure. Johan also drank to her health on the great day!

Loving greetings
from Father Grundtvig

Grundtvig's Works

Books and articles in Italics; poems, hymns, verses and lines in Normal

A Brief Chronicle of the Bible for Children and the Common Man (1828)
A Brief View of World History in Context (1812)
A child is born in Bethlehem (1820)
A Congratulation to Denmark on the Danish Dimwit and the Danish High School (1847)
All the Father does is great (1851)
An Impartial View of the Danish State Church (1834)
An Open Letter to My Children (1839)
A plain and cheerful, active life on earth (1839)
A People's Identity in Relation to Christianity (1847)
Appeal for, and Concept of, a Danish High School in Sorø (1840)
At the Funeral of My Brother Otto (1843)
Basic Christian Teachings (1855-61, 1868)
Beowulf (1820)
Bless'd were you, the eyes that saw Him (1864)
Bragi Talks on Greek and Nordic Myths (1844)
Brief Thoughts on the Edda (1806)
Childhood (1864)
Christian Marriage (1851)
Church Mirror (1860-62, pub. 1871)
Church Teachings (1842)
Consolation Letter to Denmark (1864)
Dane-woman (1848)
Danish Heroic Ballads for School Use (1847)
Danish Proverbs and Sayings (1845)
Danish Raven-Gall (1861)
Danne-Virke (1816-19)
Danskeren (1848-51)
Dare a single soul remember (1825)
Dearest ladies *(1848)*
Deeds of the Danes/Gesta Danorum (1818)
Denmark, loveliest field and meadow (1817)
Earth and heaven, be united (1868)
Enlightenment (1839)
Farewell to my friend, F.C. Sibbern (1811)
Farewell to my Pupils (1811)
Far higher are mountains elsewhere on the earth (1820)
Festival Hymns (1845 ff)
Folksongs and Other Songs for 'Danish Society' (1840-47)
Freedom for Loki as well as for Thor (1832)
Free School Song (1841)
Gather round, you maidens spry (1810)
Girl, I never dared to promise (1815)
Greek and Nordic Mythology for Young People (1846)
Gunderslev Wood (1808)
Hail, our reconciling Saviour (1837)
Handbook of World History (1833-43)
Hearts of equal disposition (1848)
High Odin, White Christ! (1808)
Hill by the beach at Egeløkke (1811)
History of the Nordic Kings (1818)
How sweet to travel the road ahead (1855)
How the Church is like God's kingdom! (1851)
Human comes first, and Christian next (1837)
Idun, A New Year Present for 1811 (1810)
In Praise of Jutland (1815)
Is Faith Truly a School Matter? (1836)
Is spelling right or wrong a light? (1839)
Jesus Christ, how we praise Your name (1837)
Jesus, where is it I find You? (1843)
Lady Marie's Monument (1855)
Land of my fathers (1848)

Lesson and Mark Book for Carl Steensen Leth (1806)
Little God's child, what troubles you? (1855)
Little Poems (1815)
Looking Back at Copenhagen (1808)
Lovely is the midnight sky (1810)
Man is not an ape (1832)
Mother's name is a heav'nly sound (1838)
My Friend-wife (1854)
My heart was also granted (1808)
My Mother (1822)
New Year's Morning (1824)
New Year's Wishes in Danish Society (1842)
N.F.S. Grundtvig's Literary Testament (1827)
Nordic Mythology 1808 (1808)
Nordic Mythology 1832 (1832)
Of the people is our watchword (1848)
O Jesus, let a stream of tears (1810-11)
Old enough have I become now (1872)
On Human Beings in the World (1817)
On Nordic Mythology (1807)
On Polemics and Tolerance or On Dispute and Resignation (1814)
On Religion and Liturgy (1807)
On Religious Freedom (1827)
On Religious Persecution (1842)
On the Advancement of Learning (1807)
On the Establishment of Sorø Academy as a People's High School (1843)
On the Union of Learning in the North (1839)
On True Christianity (1826)
Open Letter from a Friend to an English Priest (1839)
O ring in now a Christmas blessed (1817)
Our Garden at Udby (1811)
Peace (1813)
Perhaps alone from a beloved woman (1810)
Political Observations with Regard to Denmark and Holstein (1831)
Poul Dons (1843)
Rhymed Chronicle for Children (1828)

Rhymed letter to our Nordic next-of-kin (1832)
Roskilde Rhymes (1814)
Scenes from the Death of the Giants' Life in the North (1809)
Schoolmasters, The (play, 1802)
She is not dead, she sleeps awhile (1854)
Should the Lutheran Reformation Really Continue? (1830-31).
Sisterly was my first dear wife (1858)
So I look with double pleasure (1860)
Solitary state (1849)
Song for their Majesties (1840)
Song-Work for the Danish Church (1837 ff)
See the sunrise (1817)
Take the black cross from the gravestone (1832)
The Academy in Sorø – a Sweet Dream (1837)
The Church's Retort (1825)
The connecting links (1863)
The Dane (1848-51)
The Danish Four-Leaf Clover (1836)
The Divine Trinity (1858)
The Easter Lily (1817)
The Eternal Word of Life (1855-56)
The Golden Year (1839)
The King's hand, the people's voice (1839)
The Land of the Living (1824)
The Masked Ball in Denmark. A Vision (1808)
The People, the People's Church, and Popular Belief in Denmark (1851)
The Phoenix (1840)
The School for Life and the Academy at Sorø (1838)
There sat a fisherman deep in thought (1838)
The Seven Stars of Christendom (1854-55)
The Truth of Christianity (1826-27)
The University in London and the Academy at Sorø (1827)
The Year of our Fathers. A Danish Poem to His Majesty Frederik VI (1815)
To bid this world farewell aright (1845)

To my dear children (1851)
To My Dear Father, Johan Grundtvig (1810)
To my friend, Poul Dons (1808)
To My Own Meta (1845)
To My Sons (1839)
To the Fatherland concerning its State of Affairs and its Dangers (1813)
To the Norwegians concerning a Norwegian High School (1837)
Uneasy heart (1851)
We can feel we must learn daily (1855)
We greet you again, God's angels bright (1824)
We pondered both the cause of life's confusion (1811)
We welcome with joy this blessed day (1826)
What Constitutes Poetry? (1805)
What is it, my Marie? (1851)
Why has the Word of the Lord Disappeared from His Church (1810)
Within Living Memory (1838, pub.1877)
World History 1812 (1812)
World History 1817 (1817)

Indexes

The following words have too many references to be indexed:
Christian, Christianity, Church, Copenhagen, Denmark, Education, Faith, God, Grundtvig, N.F.S., History, Holy Spirit, Jesus, Nordic, School, State, University, the Word

Biblical References
Exodus 16 304
Deuteronomy 27:12-13 228
Job 1:21 252, 486
Matthew 16:18 447
Matthew 6:27 50
Matthew 14:27 122
Matthew 10:24 191
Matthew 5:15-16 405
Matthew 6:24 409
Luke 7:11-17 284
Luke 16:1-13 122
Luke 17:15-17 300
Luke 10:38-42 191
Luke 4:16-30 127
Luke 2:25-35 149
Luke 6:40 191
John 2:1-12 260
John 14:18 122
John 8:21 122
John 16:5-7 122
John 16:6-33 122
Romans 8:28 118
Romans 16:25 131
Romans 11:33 413, 492
Romans 13:11-12 146
1 Corinthians 10:6 13 83
1 Corinthians 13:12 131
1 Corinthians 14:33 453
2 Corinthians 3:17 180, 316
2 Corinthians 6:15 409
Romans 10:10 255
Ephesians 6:13 432
Revelation 1-3 278
Revelation 1:9
Revelation 1:11 305
Revelation 14:13 143

Places and peoples
America, North 19, 339, 341-343, 468
Anglo-Saxon 22, 128, 131, 160, 162-163, 165, 167, 169, 201, 250, 344, 373
Argentina 19, 344
Austria-Hungary 18
Bristol 162, 445
British Museum 159-160, 279, 429-430, 432, 445, 466
Cambridge 163-166, 188, 190-191, 201, 314, 353, 445, 447-448, 466
Canada 22, 344, 355
Cathedral, St. Paul's 162, 437
Christianshavn 62, 99, 126, 143-144, 156, 181, 376, 423-424, 430, 440-441, 444, 446, 451, 452, 454, 455, 458-460
Church, Christian's 156, 172-173, 177, 188, 293
Church, Citadel 136, 419
Church, Frederiksberg 123-124, 419, 458
Church, Garnison 419
Church, Holmens 138
Church of Our Lady 60, 144, 181
Church of Our Saviour 136, 143-145, 194, 241, 243, 293, 301, 376, 423-424, 430, 443, 452, 484
Church, Præstø 107, 138, 142-143, 194
Church, Regens 106, 405
Church, St. Knud's, Odense 136, 419
Church, Udby 42, 110, 194, 302, 410

Church, Ulse 137, 421
Church, Vartov 194, 221-222, 236-237, 251, 260, 262, 265, 277, 280, 289-290, 293, 295-296, 307, 377, 379, 423, 484, 492, 494-496
Church, Ørslev 113
Clinton, Iowa 340-341
Danish West Indies 20, 42, 94, 211, 225, 230
Denmark-Norway 16, 18, 197, 457
Dybbøl 285, 475
Egeløkke 45, 73-75, 77, 80-81, 83, 85, 87-88, 91-92, 99, 109, 111, 157-158, 213, 314, 379, 404, 408, 411-412, 429
Elers' Hall of Residence 62, 66
England 18, 20, 22, 25, 36, 41, 51-52, 86, 107, 159-169, 172, 180, 185, 188-189, 201-204, 207, 213-214, 218, 228, 243, 271, 286, 304, 309, 316-317, 344, 355, 362, 370, 372-373, 375, 377, 379, 401-402, 421, 429-430, 432, 434, 436, 439, 443-445, 447, 451, 458, 460-461, 465-466, 469, 471, 483
Europe 18, 20, 23-26, 157, 167, 209, 227, 339, 344, 346-348, 421, 458, 467, 473
Exeter 162, 442-443, 445
Falster 70, 73, 111, 113, 324, 449, 457, 484
Faroe Islands 16, 326-328
France 18, 25, 30, 159, 168, 185, 226, 330, 346, 355, 420, 429, 443, 473
Frederiksholms Kanal 16 45, 247

Funen 23, 47, 74, 287, 293, 224
Gammel Kongevej 148/Happy Home 45, 260, 263-265, 279, 295, 315, 379, 496
Gammel Køgegård 250-252, 489
Germany/German 18, 21, 23, 25, 28, 36, 51-52, 64, 66-67, 73-75, 94, 99-101, 116, 118, 129-131, 150, 159, 168-169, 172, 179, 183, 185, 224-228, 232, 237, 249, 267, 271, 283, 285, 290, 317, 323, 327-328, 332, 337, 343, 345-346, 355-356, 367, 369, 375, 401, 413, 421, 425, 429, 444-445, 471, 474-475, 480
Grand View College, Des Moines 339, 341
Great Tuborg 294-297, 379
Greece/Greek 25, 49, 54, 57, 65, 73, 103, 115-116, 131, 183, 185, 246, 250, 279, 452
Greenland 16, 28, 42, 228, 326, 328-329
Helsingør 459
Holmen's Kanal 22 122
Holstein/-ers 16, 25, 168, 189, 224-228, 283, 471, 475, 481-482
Iceland/-ic 16, 22, 63, 73, 84-85, 124, 127, 228, 250, 265, 326, 448
Idstedt 31, 228, 481
International People's College, Elsinore 342, 349
Ireland 328
Jelling 52
Jutland/-er 16, 23, 44, 47, 50-53, 54, 60-61, 63, 66, 75, 85, 111, 131, 199, 212, 228, 249, 259, 266, 283, 286, 291, 293, 232, 367, 475, 479, 481, 483, 496
Kiel 24, 102, 425, 449, 479
Køge 252, 259, 301, 492
Langeland 73, 83, 86, 92, 93, 99, 105, 111, 114, 408, 412
Lejre 31
Lolland 73, 242,

London 159-162, 165-166, 170, 189, 201, 203, 210, 213, 283, 350, 358, 429-430, 432-434, 436, 438-443, 445-446, 449, 463-465, 467-468, 470, 478
Løngangsstræde 137, 194, 237
Marie's Pleasure People's High School 75, 253, 379
North, the 52, 93, 97, 120, 124, 130, 135, 146, 148, 150, 155, 159-160, 166-167, 170-171, 188, 199, 209, 213, 219, 265, 267, 279, 292, 362, 388, 403, 413, 423, 426-427, 471, 487, 499
Norway/-egian 16-19, 24, 51-52, 84, 92, 101-103, 127-128, 135, 152, 168, 190, 197, 232, 243, 250, 255, 265-266, 285, 295-296, 317, 323, 326-326, 331, 341, 354-355, 358, 379, 413, 416-418, 425, 456-457, 459-460, 473, 486-487, 496
Nybrogade 6 241,
Nybrogade 12 246-247
Nørregade 25 233, 259
Nørre Voldgade 38 259
Oldenburg 16
Oslo 51, 101, 103, 243, 295, 366, 457, 486
Prinsessegade 52 45, 144, 156
Prussia 17, 24-25, 31, 106, 224, 283, 291
Præstø 45, 107, 122, 137-138, 141-143, 194, 231, 315, 369, 407-408, 414, 418, 423, 480
Rome/Roman 92, 133, 185, 203, 345, 454, 466
Roskilde 24, 118-121, 123, 211, 411, 479
Ryslinge People's High School 286, 289, 326, 343
Rødding People's High School 205-206, 289, 320, 323, 342-343
Rønnebæksholm 233, 236, 243, 245, 247-248, 250, 252-254, 259, 268, 314, 495, 494-495
Scandinavia/-n/-ism 17, 243, 471

Schleswig-Holstein 16, 24, 169, 224-226, 471, 474-475, 480, 483
Schleswig, North 16, 212, 224, 227-228, 283, 472, 474
Schleswig, South 224, 228, 283, 474
Schleswigians 284, 332, 472
Skamling Hill 30, 211-212, 308
Skibbinge 137
Slagelse 136, 419, 430
Sorø 96, 98, 161, 166, 175, 188-189, 197, 204, 206-207, 232, 444, 452, 457, 473, 488
Stormgade 199 237, 483
Strandgade 4B 156, 158, 201
Sweden 19, 24, 79, 102, 135, 190, 243, 255, 285, 295-296, 323, 326, 331, 354-355, 358, 457
Thyregod 21, 47-51, 54, 58, 60, 127, 217, 309-310, 371
Torkilstrup 34, 70, 73, 410
Torvegade 25 144
Trinity College 163-164, 188, 314, 448
Türkiye 131, 228, 278, 286
Udby 21, 26, 32, 36, 39-43, 45-49, 51-52, 54, 60, 63, 65, 73-74, 100, 106-108, 111-116, 126-127, 134, 142-143, 217, 309-312, 314, 367-368, 371, 378-379, 407-408, 410-411, 413-415
Uldum People's High School 30, 289
USA 19, 30, 34, 36, 185, 212, 230, 333, 339, 341-342, 344, 349, 355-356, 358, 364
Valkendorf's Hall of Residence 91, 93, 94, 99, 103, 312, 404-405, 407
Vallekilde People's High School 289, 333
Vartov 94, 136, 172, 194, 197, 222, 233, 236-237, 250, 261, 266, 289-290, 296, 317, 333-334, 352, 365, 379-380, 386, 487, 494, 496

Viborg Cathedral High School 47, 408-409
Vimmelskaftet 49 201
Vindbyholt 107
Zealand 23, 33, 35, 37, 41-42, 44-45, 51-53, 61, 63, 96, 111, 138, 166, 236, 248, 253, 291, 331, 333, 347, 430, 467, 472, 488
Ørslev 111, 113
Aalborg 136, 419
Aarhus 56-61, 63, 127, 158, 336, 363, 368, 478
Aarhus Cathedral High School 54, 57-58, 186, 311, 356, 362

Persons

Absalon, Archbishop 84
Ahlefeldt-Laurvig, Frederik 86
Andersen, Hans Christian 97, 226, 243, 308, 356
Ansgar 52, 152, 279
Baggesen, Jens 118, 134, 497
Balle, Nicolai 49, 65, 108, 118, 314, 385, 424
Barfod, Frederik 177, 185, 192, 244, 314, 376
Basedow, Johann 161
Bell, Andrew 161
Bentham, Jeremy 165
Birkedal, Vilhelm 226, 293, 310, 460-461
Bjørnson, Bjørnstjerne 265, 290
Black, Young, and Young 163, 165
Blicher, Diderik 70, 410
Blicher, Jane 70, 141, 156, 420, 423
Blicher, Lise 70, 74-75, 82, 112, 143, 410-411, 419, 421, 484
Blicher, Marie 70, 82, 112, 236
Blicher, Pouline 70
Bloch, Laura 260
Blom, Marie 156-158
Bluetooth, Harald 93, 117
Boisen, Eline 236, 250
Boisen, Nanna 250
Boisen, Peter 30, 94, 199, 213, 216, 233, 238, 247, 261, 323, 484, 494

Bolton, Clara 162, 213, 236, 303, 437-438
Bondesen, Nicolai 142
Bowring, John 161, 434
Brorson, Hans Adolph 329
Bruun, Thomas 118
Busck, Gunni 177, 181, 189, 212, 246, 250, 260, 265, 289, 312-313, 323, 376, 452, 455, 490 496
Bødtker, Christian 105
Canute 73, 157
Carlsen, Clara 259
Carlsen, Hans 251-252
Caroline Amalie 162, 193, 197, 199-200, 203-204, 206-209, 212, 221-222, 226, 239, 246, 248-249, 265, 272, 290-291, 296, 307, 318, 323, 376-377, 462-463, 465, 468, 471, 474, 487-488, 496
Chalmers, Thomas 204, 436, 470
Christian IV 121, 141, 403, 416, 419
Christian VI 29
Christian VIII 23, 197, 199-200, 204, 211, 225, 377, 473
Clausen, Henrik (H.C.) 151
Clausen, Henrik (H.N.) 152, 180, 230, 272, 437
Coleridge, Samuel Taylor 165-166
Dannebod, Thyra 131
Danneskiold-Samsøe, Christian 33, 49, 137
Datter, Malene Jens 40, 52-53, 256, 311
Dons, Poul 84, 87, 94-96, 101, 107, 112, 117, 121, 201-202, 312, 413-414
Egede, Hans 28
Faurskov, Bertel 47, 60
Feld, Christian 47
Feld, Laurids 47-48, 54, 314
Fenger, Johannes 222, 289, 328
Fenger, Peter 159, 177, 181, 194, 260, 279, 289, 293, 312, 323, 328, 376, 430, 432, 460-461, 488
Fenger, Rasmus 160, 222, 376

Fibiger, Mathilde 226, 242, 248, 303, 314
Fichte, Johann 25, 67, 80, 101, 130, 132, 368
Flor, Christian 205-206
Frederik VI 22-24, 106, 122, 135-136, 152, 159, 193, 197, 199, 221, 310, 415, 419, 423, 428, 439, 446
Fry, Elizabeth 209-211, 218, 268, 446
Glahn, Poul 33, 70, 82, 137, 410
Goldschmidt, Meir 222, 229
Gorm 52
Goethe, Johann von 25, 66, 68, 101, 164
Grundtvig, Asta (wife) 261-263, 266, 271, 282, 295-296, 301, 313, 315, 317, 323
Grundtvig, Asta (daughter) 41, 45, 296, 303
Grundtvig, Cathrine (mother) 38, 42-43, 46, 121-122, 143, 156, 405, 414, 418
Grundtvig, Frederik Lange (son) 33, 250-251, 339-341, 490, 495
Grundtvig, Jacob (brother) 35, 40, 42, 47, 407
Grundtvig, Johan (father) 37, 40-43, 46, 63, 107, 121-122, 379, 404, 407, 415
Grundtvig, Johan (son) 50, 143, 158-159, 194, 201, 213, 227-228, 231, 237-238, 243, 260, 262, 266, 298, 303, 340, 418, 438 439, 442, 444, 475 476, 481, 482-484, 486-487, 491, 493, 496
Grundtvig, Lise (wife) 27, 41, 49, 122, 127, 141, 143, 149, 156-165, 201, 213-214, 228, 235-239, 241, 249, 251, 303, 317, 401, 410-412, 422, 431-438, 441-443, 447-450 469, 485

Grundtvig, Marie (see under Toft, Marie) 233-235, 236, 240, 243-244, 251, 255, 259, 268, 472
Grundtvig, Meta (daughter) 41, 45, 94, 156, 201, 213, 216, 227, 233, 237-238, 247, 252, 261, 266, 303, 433, 438-439, 442, 444, 449, 472, 475, 488-484, 492-496
Grundtvig, Niels (brother) 35, 42, 47
Grundtvig, Otto (brother) 35, 41, 63, 70, 111-112, 127, 201-202, 410, 415, 495
Grundtvig, Svend (son) 37, 41, 45, 149, 157-159, 194-195, 201-202, 204, 227-228, 237-238, 260, 262, 266, 291, 298, 303, 327, 340, 438-439, 442, 444, 449, 459, 463, 468, 470, 475, 477, 481-484, 486, 492-493, 496-497
Grundtvig, Ulrikke (sister) 39, 46, 311
Graae, Christen 83
Gurney, Joseph 209
Hadding 146
Hansen, Hans 231
Heaton, Mr and Mrs 162, 437-439, 441
Hegel, Friedrich 101, 364, 372
Heiberg, Johan 242
Hemmings, Luise 213, 236
Herder, Johann 130
Hersleb, Svend 94, 101-103, 149, 232, 312, 416
Holberg, Ludvig 101, 189, 222, 403
Howley, William 160, 162, 431, 440, 442
Hvide, Skjalm 37, 248
Høgsbro, Sophus 264, 294
Ignatius of Antioch 150
Ingemann, Bernhard 17, 68, 95, 97, 138, 146, 163-164, 171, 179, 184, 202, 206, 214, 221, 238, 241,

246, 250, 252, 305, 312, 329, 444, 446, 451, 454, 456, 459, 485, 489
Irenaeus 9, 150
Jensen, Jens 231, 384
Kall, Abraham 47, 65
Kant, Immanuel 67, 130, 132, 318, 372
Kierkegaard, Peter 291, 323, 489
Kierkegaard, Søren 10, 17, 97, 101, 151, 222-224, 271-274, 308, 318, 345, 349, 351, 356, 361, 364
King, Martin Luther 343
Kingo, Thomas 107, 112-113, 175, 329-330
Koch, Hal 88, 109, 163, 167, 362, 369, 375
Kock, Laurids 131
Kold, Christen 233, 286-289, 293, 295, 323-326, 343, 346, 376
Kotzebue, August 106
Kragballe, Christian 272, 314
Krarup, Thure 57-59
Köster, Kristian 94
Lancaster, Joseph 161
Lehmann, Orla 226, 231, 316, 471
Leth, Carl de 73-74, 127
Leth, Carl de (junior) 74
Leth, Constance Steensen de 73-75, 127, 213, 303, 312, 379, 402, 411-412
Lindberg, Jacob 149, 458
Luther, Martin 28-29, 36, 38, 107, 111, 115-117, 134-135, 167-168, 204, 211, 219, 274-275, 293, 314, 318, 328-329, 337, 342, 345, 424, 447
Lutheran 49, 54, 87, 98, 107, 113-114, 118, 135, 142, 167-168, 179, 220, 222, 264, 273, 293, 303-304, 324-325, 329-332, 336, 341-342, 344-345, 355-356, 414, 447
Margrete I 255
Mariboe, Carl 159
Marie Sophie 138

Martensen, Hans 264-265, 271-273, 289, 306-307, 314
Maurice, Frederick (F.D.) 166
Melbye, Mads 236
Molbech, Christian 76, 92, 94-99, 101, 105, 107-108, 117, 121, 161, 312, 402, 415, 442-443
Monrad, Ditlev 231, 265, 479, 496
Mynster, Jacob 61, 65, 96, 117, 144-145, 161, 180, 184, 194, 221-222, 229, 221-222, 236, 272, 273 312, 376, 472
Møller, Jens 84, 127
Müller, Peter 106, 172, 405, 420
Münter, Frederik 108, 120, 123, 144, 160, 407
Napoleon/-ic 19, 21, 24, 60, 65, 85-86, 122, 135, 227, 448, 457
Nelson, Lord 30, 86, 462
Newman, John Henry 203-204, 461, 466
Nyerup, Professor 91
Olsen, Christen 132-133, 138, 142
Pedersen, Maren 259, 263
Peel, Sir Robert 162
Pestalozzi, Johann 161
Plum, Frederik 106
Polycarp of Smyrna 150
Pontoppidan, Erik 113, 327
Pram, Christian 137
Rahbek, Kamma 99, 117, 441
Rahbek, Knud 99, 121
Rask, Rasmus 128, 448
Reedtz, Holger 259
Rousseau, Jean-Jacques 77, 95, 372
Rudelbach, Andreas 149
Rørdam, Peter 213, 221, 231, 238, 259, 272, 289, 307, 312-313, 323, 333, 376-377, 472, 479
Rørdam, Skat 291
Rørdam, Thomas 343
Sandvig, Bertel 84
Saxo 53, 66, 84, 118, 124, 127-128, 136, 143, 158-159, 189, 279, 423-424

Schelling, Friedrich von 25, 66, 80, 101, 130, 368
Schiller, Friedrich 25, 66, 80, 129, 373
Schleiermacher, Friedrich 101, 174
Schlegel, August 166
Schlegel, Friedrich 413
Schmidt, Louise 238
Scholten, Peter von 230
Schouboe, Frederik 103
Schouboe Institute, the 91, 101, 103-104, 107, 157, 404, 423
Schouw, Joachim 24, 230
Shakespeare, William 166-167, 169, 226, 318, 322, 336, 417
Sibbern, Frederik 94, 99-101, 107-108, 208, 312, 408
Siemonsen, Lorentz 172, 175
Skougaard, Peder 66, 73, 85, 103, 311
Skrike, Louise 301, 323
Smith, Adam 165
Smith, Anthony 26
Stampe, Elise 264, 305
Steffens, Henrik 37, 66-68, 80, 85, 94-95, 147-148, 186, 312, 425
Stenersen, Stener 101, 243, 486
Stenersen, Vilhelmine 486
Stephanius, Stephanus 118, 127
Stougaard, Jens 57-59, 314
Sturluson, Snorri 53, 66, 84, 124, 127-128, 136, 143, 158, 478, 475
Sverdrup, Georg 102
Thorvaldsen, Bertel 182
Toft, Harald 235
Toft, Haralda 235, 251-253, 255
Toft, Marie 233-234, 236, 243-244, 255, 259, 268, 472
Treschow, Niels 102
Trier, Ernst 263, 298, 323, 333
Tuxen, Nicolai 230
Wade, Nugent 123, 203, 458, 467, 469
Wagner, Richard 87

Wellington, Duke of 162, 448, 462-463
Wexels, Wilhelm 152, 486-487
Weyse, Christoph 87, 430
Whewell, William 163-164, 166, 191, 314, 448-449
Willemoes, Peter 30, 86-87, 185
Willibrord 52
Wolff, Christian 129-130
Oehlenschläger, Adam 66-68, 84, 96, 100, 116, 118, 161
Ørsted, Anders 24, 99
Ørsted, Hans Christian (H.C.) 99, 118, 123
Ørsted, Sophie 101
Østrup, Wilhelm 111, 408

Grundtvig authors quoted in main text
Abrahamowitz, Finn 70, 136, 305, 310, 313
Albeck, Gustav 61, 80
Allchin, Donald 33, 163, 318, 321
Auken, Sune 128, 146, 208
Balslev-Olesen, Christian 332
Balslev-Clausen, Peter 248
Baunvig, Katrine Frøkjær 208, 330
Begtrup, Holger 167, 251, 323, 342, 351
Berntsen, Klaus 287
Bjerg, Svend 332
Borish, Steven M. 324
Borup, Johan 149, 168, 212, 306
Bradley, S.A.J (Sid) 165, 273
Brandes, Georg 308, 356
Bredsdorff, Morten 53, 166
Broadbridge, Edward 10, 12, 42, 110, 135, 145, 173, 245, 506-508
Brun, Hans 201, 214, 249, 263, 272, 316
Bruun, Niels 85
Bugge, Knud Eyvin 79, 106, 310, 327, 344, 346, 350, 356
Bønding, Sophie 208-209
Baagø, Kaj 218
Heggem, Synnøve 256-257, 292

Holm, Anders 130, 132, 134, 222, 343, 250, 358
Holt, Thyra 53
Gregersen, Niels Henrik 68, 351
Hammerich, Frederik 291, 308
Hansen, Martin A. 318,
Helweg, Hjalmar 308-309
Høirup, Henning 37, 317
Iversen, Hans Raun 10, 12, 275, 366, 370, 508
Jensen, Erik Krebs 255
Jensen, Jørgen I. 146-147
Johansen, Steen 152
Jonas, Uffe 68, 204, 232
Koch, Hal 88, 109, 163, 167
Korsgaard, Ove 26, 189, 224, 266, 315
Kullberg, Steen 167
Larsen, Birgitte Stoklund 250, 254-255, 315
Lundgreen-Nielsen, Flemming 87, 184, 193, 305, 308, 337
Manniche, Peter 342, 351
Martinsen, Lone Kølle 324
Pedersen, Kim Arne 132
Reich, Ebbe Kløvedal 306
Rønning, Frederik 68, 81, 83, 104, 112, 127, 144, 146
Schelde, Michael 334
Schrøder, Ludwig 25, 60, 96, 161, 323
Stevns, Magnus 246
Thaulow, Vanja 116, 309
Thodberg, Christian 174-175
Thyregod, Christian 55
Vind, Ole 170, 186, 219, 369
Vogel, Ulrich 309
Wigh-Poulsen, Henrik 322
Øhrgaard, Per 269

General
adscription 18, 20, 185, 187
Advent 115, 212, 144-145
Age, Golden 49, 137, 189, 198, 310, 325
agriculture 19, 27, 326, 328, 342, 345, 348, 352, 355

[505]

All-Father, the 92-93
Anti-slavery Society 211, 230, 328
Assembly/-ies, Provincial Advisory 23-24, 26, 114, 211, 224, 231
Assembly, Constituent 23, 206, 220-221, 225, 230-231, 265
Assembly/-ies, godly 28, 64, 114
Association 30, 212, 232, 324, 328-329, 341, 347-350, 486
Association, Danish 249, 328, 489
'Association Denmark' 322, 329
Atonement 436
Baptism/-t 28-29, 45, 52, 65, 115, 141, 150, 167-168, 172, 174, 179, 181, 191, 197, 204, 209-210, 212, 222, 245, 251, 264, 272, 274-275, 278, 290-291, 316, 330, 332, 414, 447-448, 462
Bard 37, 130, 133, 166, 244, 466, 479, 486
Basic Forms of Anxiety 310
Benediction, the 280, 333
Bible, the 49, 61, 64, 69, 85, 88, 99, 103, 107, 109, 111, 113, 115-117, 131-132, 134, 145, 150, 155, 157, 161, 167-168, 180-181, 184, 204, 219, 250, 274, 289, 304-305, 332, 341, 379, 447, 454, 458
Bragi 76, 207-208, 309, 370
Catholic 29, 57, 115, 162, 167, 185, 203, 264, 330, 363, 461
Chancellery 135, 172, 419-420, 446, 457, 467
Christmas 92, 107, 121, 134, 149, 158-159, 184, 207, 221-222, 250, 262, 283, 296, 298, 330, 336, 340, 408, 454
Church of England/Anglican 160, 162, 203-204, 339, 363, 431, 460-461
Church, the People's (*Folkekirken*) 28-29, 144, 174-175, 220, 293-294

aka Danish Lutheran Church 167, 222, 264, 293, 329, 331, 336, 341, 344-345
Church Collector 272
Church Society 333, 428
Church, State 28-29, 144, 152-153, 155, 172, 179-180, 203-204, 223, 273-274, 431, 446-447, 461-464, 469, 498
citizenry 20
Clergy 20-22, 27, 47, 106, 123, 163, 192, 341, 405, 411, 419-420
Catechism, Luther's Small 29, 54, 113, 150, 274
Clara Raphael. Twelve Letters 242, 248
Communion, Holy 28-29, 133, 144, 167, 197, 203-204, 220, 222, 260, 264, 275, 290-291, 330, 332, 447
Concluding Unscientific Postscript 223
confirmand 231
Confirmation 27, 29, 54, 113, 141-142, 157, 180, 183, 219, 254, 296, 298, 330, 462
constitution 20, 23, 26, 31, 102, 152, 175, 199, 206, 225-226, 230-231, 249, 266-268, 271, 273, 283, 285, 303, 317, 334, 421, 447, 471, 473, 476-479, 488
Creation 9, 68-69, 117, 129, 131, 155, 178-179, 212, 255-256, 266, 321, 326, 331-332
Creed 129, 150, 155, 168, 197, 203-204, 253, 275-276, 336, 342, 428, 447, 467
Creed, the Apostolic 150, 168, 276, 316, 333, 341, 363, 376, 447, 466
curate/-acy 41, 43, 48, 94, 106, 108-109, 111, 134, 136, 141, 144, 149, 152, 194, 261, 272, 291, 368, 376, 379, 405-408, 410, 415-416, 419, 423, 425, 452, 484, 495

Danish Literary Times 123, 128
Dane-woman 194, 236, 241, 255
Danish Hymnbook, the 329-331, 376
Danishness 23, 186, 188, 193-194, 212, 219-220, 229, 247, 427, 471
Danish Rhymed Chronicle (1495) 157
Danish Society 19, 30, 192-193, 204, 210, 232-233, 236, 305, 308, 316, 328-329, 334, 352, 488
Deeds of the Danes 84, 119, 124, 127-128, 136, 159, 189, 279, 423
democracy/-t 17, 21-22, 26, 185, 224, 230, 266-268, 283, 285, 289, 304, 316, 335, 347, 357, 478
Devil, the 108, 112, 129, 308-309, 366, 408-409
Easter 54, 58, 133-134, 174, 177, 222, 330, 430, 452
Education Act 26, 29-30, 103, 158, 197
Emile 77-78, 161
Enlightenment 65, 97, 129-130, 169, 188, 253, 268, 276, 304, 347, 349, 351, 357, 368, 429, 446, 461, 497
Epiphany 219, 461
Estates (of the realm) 20-23, 26, 316
Experience 10, 23, 25, 39, 47, 57-58, 63, 66-68, 75-78, 80, 83-85, 87, 91, 97-98, 100, 103, 105, 113, 117, 123, 131-133, 156-157, 161, 168, 178-179, 186, 190-191, 193, 209, 218, 223, 230, 245-246, 253, 256-257, 268, 276, 303-304, 308-309, 316, 330, 350, 362, 371-373, 388, 401, 413, 415, 422, 424-426, 437, 444, 469, 482
Fall, the 117, 129, 147, 183, 350
fatherland 23, 30, 37, 85, 123, 135, 147, 181, 188, 204, 206, 229, 266, 268-269, 284, 287, 332, 334, 371, 416, 420-421, 423, 426, 429-430, 459, 463, 471, 482

forefather/s 23, 33, 36-38, 41, 51, 60, 63, 74, 91, 106, 109, 112, 114, 128, 130, 135, 142, 168, 170, 174, 185-186, 293, 303, 311, 318, 424, 429, 471
Free Congregations 29, 172, 180, 272, 290, 307, 332
freedom 9, 17-23, 25-27, 83, 114, 128, 144, 155-156, 162-163, 166, 168-170, 172, 179-180, 185-187, 209, 211, 217-219, 228, 230, 232, 248, 263, 267-269, 273-274, 293, 295, 297, 302, 304, 307, 311, 313-314, 316, 318, 326, 333, 335, 344-347, 356, 363, 369, 372, 374-375, 420, 431, 443, 446-447, 455, 458, 464-465, 475, 478, 480
Freya 255
Friends' Meetings 289, 297-298, 308, 312, 317, 323, 487
Friends of the Farmers Association 232
God, image of 117, 129, 220, 250, 255, 257
Grundtvig Centre 330, 336, 509
Grundtvigian 27, 183, 199-200, 232-233, 289, 322-324, 328, 332-334, 341-342, 344, 346-347, 349, 361, 369, 380
Grundtvig's Forum 333-334, 380
Grundtvig Memorial Rooms 48, 126, 378
Grundtvig's Works, online 10
Grundtvig Times 333
heathen 17, 64, 93, 107, 130, 178, 349
Hebrew 58, 65, 115-116, 119, 183, 278, 409, 428
Historical 33, 46, 53, 63, 68, 73, 97, 118, 128-129, 132, 148, 166-167, 169, 175, 180, 203, 212, 219, 223, 346, 363, 368, 372, 426, 443, 451, 459-461, 465, 475
humankind 9, 28, 80, 84, 118, 123, 129, 150, 155, 166, 171, 178-179, 184, 186, 191-192, 248, 276, 295, 303, 310, 318, 356, 363, 368, 427, 430, 453, 455, 472

hymn 50, 53-54, 85, 107, 113, 134, 146, 149-150, 174, 181, 183, 197, 207, 212, 221-223, 233, 245-246, 248, 250, 254-257, 265, 274-275, 278-279, 287, 289, 290, 295, 301, 304, 307, 313, 318, 322, 327-328, 329-331, 333, 334, 336, 339, 344, 355-356, 358, 418, 430, 453, 455, 472, 496
Hymn-singing 113, 149, 181, 192, 221-222, 289-290, 322, 329-331, 333, 374, 453
identity 9, 26, 51, 119, 190, 219-220, 228-229, 247, 255, 267, 286, 342, 348, 356-357, 372
Independent Congregations 293-294, 332
Inner Mission 329, 341-342, 349
Institution, the Words of 197, 253, 275-276, 333, 447
justice 20, 61, 187, 268, 276, 471, 478
Language 10, 12, 23, 25-26, 51, 53, 58, 60, 66, 73-74, 76, 83, 97, 114, 128-129, 132, 160-161, 165-166, 168, 185-186, 204-206, 219, 221, 224, 232, 256, 266-267, 275, 278-279, 283, 286, 304, 307, 311, 327, 331, 339, 341, 347-348, 355, 364, 404, 413, 426, 429, 444-445, 449, 453, 461, 465, 470-171, 475, 478
Latin 25, 47, 49, 54, 57-58, 60, 65, 73, 84, 124, 127, 158, 167, 183, 188, 200, 202, 204, 229, 232, 246, 250, 266, 278, 285, 303, 314, 336, 345, 350, 428, 433, 445, 451, 465
Law, The King's 21, 150
Legacy 17, 37, 39, 41, 51, 109, 188, 261, 263, 314, 321-322, 324, 332-334, 339, 346-347, 355, 361, 368, 388, 432

Lent 39, 174, 296, 458, 462
Libel 152, 427, 437, 456
liturgy 84-85, 142, 181, 183, 264, 330-333, 355
Loki 27, 93, 170, 267
Middle Ages 20, 429, 445
manor/lords of the 18, 20, 26, 78
marriage 20, 27, 112, 165, 199, 213-214, 218, 235, 242, 246, 249, 252, 260-261, 265, 291, 313, 316, 410-411, 422, 493
matchless discovery 149, 151, 273, 316, 363, 370, 416, 447, 466
monarchy/-ist 18, 24, 26, 79, 188, 197, 199, 224, 243, 315, 473
Mosaic-Christian 129, 170, 183
mother-tongue 23, 30, 51, 85, 132, 184, 186, 188, 194, 204, 206, 228-229, 266, 327, 463, 465, 470-471, 475, 489
Mythology 17-18, 21, 25, 27, 49, 58, 66, 68, 73, 84, 87-88, 91-93, 100, 107, 111, 130-131, 146, 148, 162-163, 169-172, 179, 183, 185, 205, 207-208, 232, 255, 257, 260, 267, 271, 279, 312, 323, 325, 350, 362-365, 370, 374, 402-404, 413, 426, 437, 451
Nation-state 21, 24, 26, 170
Nature/natural 9, 21, 28, 35, 51, 53, 60, 77, 79 87, 98, 101, 146, 148, 157, 165, 171, 189-190, 194, 210-211, 230, 233, 246, 257, 268-269, 303, 309, 312-314, 356, 363, 368-370, 402-404, 409, 415, 425, 431, 443, 450-451, 479
Natural Man 130
Naturalist 160, 170, 431
Nobility 20-22, 49, 73-75, 81, 85, 189, 203, 268, 289
Norns, the 93, 402
Norwegian Students Society 243
Ny Minerva 84
Odin 92, 100, 146, 159, 185, 193, 223, 260, 279, 362, 451
Odinkar 93

Order of the Dannebrog 199
Palnatoke 93
parish/-ioners 21, 27, 29, 33, 35-36, 39-42, 47, 55, 111-115, 137, 141, 143, 155, 194, 221, 264, 269, 293, 336, 410, 415, 445-446, 464, 472
parish-tie 155, 172, 180, 269, 376, 445-446, 463
Party, National Liberal 23
peasant/-ry 19-22, 26-29, 49-51, 53, 75, 133, 177, 185, 188, 232, 253, 268, 286, 303, 307, 344, 351, 369, 488
Pentecost 58, 134, 174, 220, 222, 289, 330, 410, 461
People's High School 26, 30, 75, 85, 87, 165-166, 185-186, 189-190, 193, 197, 204-206, 232-233, 249-250, 253, 283, 286, 315, 320, 323, 328, 331, 333, 342-343, 346-348, 351-352, 379-380, 386, 448, 455-457, 460, 475, 4890
People's High School Songbook, the 87, 315, 328, 331, 386
Philosophy 25, 57, 61, 63-66, 78, 84, 88, 94, 99-102, 118, 128-129, 132, 149, 161, 164-165, 167, 169, 185-186, 188, 195, 255, 273, 345-346, 349, 353-354
pietism/-ist 28-29, 114, 148, 342, 413
Poetic Edda 84
poetry/-ic 33, 53, 61, 66, 68, 77, 83-85, 88, 91-93, 95, 99-100, 103, 108-109, 113, 121, 128, 131-132, 134, 145, 148, 157, 163-164, 166, 168-169, 174, 183, 186, 199, 206-207, 229, 266, 273, 278, 303-305, 307-308, 312-313, 321, 342, 344, 361, 364, 367, 369-370, 418, 425-427, 435-436, 443-445, 465, 467, 496

Population 18-20, 28-29, 62, 141, 177, 326, 329, 339, 344, 348
Prayer, the Lord's 212, 253, 275-276, 333
Protestant/-ism 152, 162, 257, 318, 370, 427, 436, 463, 466
pulpit 43, 110-111, 122-124, 134, 138, 145, 172-173, 192, 197, 221, 264, 274, 280, 290-291, 293, 308, 314-315
Quaker 209-211, 218
Rationalism/-t 25, 49,63-66, 80, 82, 84, 150, 152, 183, 203, 232, 376, 430-431, 437, 447
Reason 19, 42, 46, 64-65, 77, 80-81, 83, 85, 118, 128, 131, 136, 218, 249, 259, 326, 334, 336, 339, 369, 414, 420, 425, 436, 445, 453-454, 459, 462, 465, 472, 475, 479-480, 485, 491
Redeemer/Redemption 178-179, 250, 432
Reformation 25, 51-52, 57, 61, 107, 148, 167-168, 189, 203-204, 329, 331, 446-447, 467
Reformation Theology for a Post-Secular Age 331
religion 18, 20, 28, 65, 83-85, 101, 199, 279, 293, 309, 330, 352, 368, 370, 421, 424
revival/-ist 17, 28, 64, 109, 111-112, 114-117, 120, 131, 133, 233, 236, 273, 286-287, 332, 347, 370, 376, 473, 487
rhyme 38, 51, 53, 84, 157, 333, 426-427, 460
rhythm 53, 146-147
Romantic/-ism 25, 37, 66-68, 77, 80-82, 84, 87, 91, 94, 97, 100-101, 109, 129-130, 147-148, 171, 186, 321, 425
sacrament 28-29, 82, 150, 172, 177, 181, 192, 197, 253, 264, 269, 272, 274-275, 332, 446, 466
salvation 9, 28, 46, 51, 69, 93, 107, 112-113, 145-146, 179, 186,

210, 212, 223, 256, 331-332, 414, 431, 489
Saviour 88, 108, 114, 120, 134, 136, 142-145, 194, 241, 243, 253, 293, 301, 330, 376, 407-408, 418, 423-424, 430, 443, 452, 484
Scandinavian Creation Theology 68
Schleswig Aid Society, the 328
School, Charity 162, 199, 233, 261, 470-471, 494
School, Continuation 324-326
School for Life 18, 60, 78, 85, 169-170, 172, 188, 190, 307, 339, 460, 473
School for Lust 75
School for Pleasure 190
School, the People's (*Folkeskole*) 325
School, Workers' High 326
Schleswig Association 212
Scripture 152, 203, 304, 428, 454, 466
sermon 83, 106, 111, 114-116, 120, 122-123, 142, 144-145, 150, 162, 167, 172, 174, 186, 190, 192, 195, 208, 219, 221-223, 253, 272, 274-275, 292, 299, 301, 304, 333, 405, 407, 410-411, 413-414, 420, 436-437, 497
skald 130-133, 137, 273, 288, 306, 312-313
slave/-s 20, 42, 163, 211, 225, 230
slavery/-owners 20, 209, 211, 230, 268, 328
Sleipner 146, 223, 265
society 17, 19-20, 26, 30, 35, 49, 63, 97, 101, 161, 163, 166, 169, 171, 177, 185, 192-193, 204, 209, 211, 217, 230, 243, 249, 266, 268, 279, 286, 303, 328-329, 333-334, 335, 341-343, 346-347, 351-352, 355, 357, 427, 493
Society, Danish 30, 192-193, 204, 210, 232-233, 236, 305, 308, 316,

328-329, 334, 341, 347, 349, 352, 488
Sovereignty 26
Spirit, the people's 148, 169
tax 27, 29, 267, 335, 483
Testament, New 83, 115, 150, 163, 250, 274, 401, 428, 460
Testament, Old 29, 58, 111, 199, 228

Theological Monthly 150, 155, 458
Thor 27, 170, 267
Trinity/-arian 45, 85, 108, 111, 129, 143, 163-164, 183, 188, 275-276, 314, 379, 436, 461
Truth 28, 45, 49, 53, 64, 81, 85, 93, 96, 117, 123, 127, 128-129, 131, 133, 170-171, 177, 186, 223, 264, 272, 276, 305, 341, 417, 420-421, 426-427, 457, 471, 470, 486, 487, 494
Tumulus 127-128, 130
Vanir, the 171, 452
Vartov gallops 222
Word, the Living 142, 167, 193, 206, 208, 287, 370, 454
Aesir, the 155, 171, 451

N.F.S. Grundtvig. Works in English

Translated and edited by Edward Broadbridge
Published by Aarhus University Press

"The world and scholarship have been done a great service with this edition of Grundtvig's works."
Linda Woodhead, Head of the Department of Theology and Religious Studies, Kong's College London

"Scholars and general readers alike will find these translations to be not only invaluable sources for the study of the work of an influential modern genius, but also a very pleasurable reading experience, one that is inspiring and full of surprising insights."
Mark Bradshaw Busbee, Department of English Chair, Samford University, Alabama

Vol. 1. The School for Life. N.F.S. Grundtvig on Education for the People (2011)
"Edward Broadbridge and his dedicated team have delivered a long-overdue English rendition of Grundtvig's educational ideas in a sensitive and highly readable translation that retains the power of Grundtvig's voice and moreover brings the "living word" alive in the accompanying audiobook."
Chris Spicer, Chair, Folk Education Association of America

"How wonderful to welcome Edward Broadbridge's remarkable new translation entitled The School for Life. The book draws together Grundtvig's most important works on education, both prose and poetry, representing a major addition to the English language literature on educational philosophy."
Andrew Buckser, Dean of Arts and Sciences and Professor of Anthropology at State University of New York

"For those English-speaking communities interested in the origins and history of folk education and adult education in Scandinavia, The School for Life: N.F.S. Grundtvig on Education for the People provides a charming and much-needed entry point, including an excellent audio recording with the text.
What I have found through this book and its translations is a vigorous, passionate, and inquiring mind fit not only for the transformational times of the 18th and 19th centuries, but one that can inspire the transformations of the 21st century as well."
Dawn Jackman Murphy, Vice President, Folk Education Association of America

"This work has been long-awaited: a major translation of the Danish educationist, cultural philosopher, and theologian, N.F.S. Grundtvig. We can follow Grundtvig's

theological foundational principle: "Human comes first, and Christian next" through his educational writings, which emphasise the need for a cultural self-awareness along with a radical tolerance for all forms of human expression in a cultural context."
Niels Henrik Gregersen, Professor of Systematic Theology, University of Copenhagen

Vol. 2. Living Wellsprings. The Hymns, Songs, and Poems of N.F.S. Grundtvig (2015)

"I expected a lot from this book and honestly, it is much more than I expected! The Grundtvig anthology of new translations presents the tremendous depth and breadth of Grundtvig's work in a highly accessible way. Songs and poems embracing Nordic sagas, Christian spirituality, education, democracy, wisdom, nature, as well as personal tributes to his wives, children and friends and even more can be found in Living Wellsprings."
Joy Ibsen, Church and Life, May 2015

"Students of historical hymn texts will find this a rich source of material. The translations are well done, reading quite naturally for the most part."
Lydia Pedersen, The Hymn Society in The Hymn, Vol. 67/2, 2016.

"A magnificent book."
Bertel Haarder, Former Danish Minister of Education (Letter to the Editor, 2015)

"One overarching characteristic of the translations becomes very clear after a reading of all the poems and reflecting on their collective effort. Broadbridge has produced translations that recapture Grundtvig's wonder at God's creation and man's place in it. Broadbridge's achievement is that his work bears the mark of Grundtvig's call for 'a plain and cheerful, active life on earth'."
Mark Bradshaw Busbee, Department of English Chair, Samford University, Alabama

Vol. 4. The Common Good. N.F.S. Grundtvig as Politican and Contemporary Historian (2019)

"*The Common Good* should be required reading for anyone interested in the role of religion in politics ... Broadbridge's translation is so excellent and elegant that one forgets that it is not the original. Broadbridge has transformed long and long-winded sentences – Grundtvig's "torturous prose" featuring sentences that "approach 300 words" – into an English full of verve!"
Dr Ulrich Schmiedel, Senior Lecturer in Theology, Politics and Ethics

Vol. 6. Denmark's Catalyst. The Life and Letters of N.F.S. Grundtvig (2023)

N.F.S. Grundtvig is perhaps the most influential person in Danish history. He is often referred to as 'the man who most shaped Denmark' into a liberal, stable, freedom-loving society. As the culmination of the English translation series of Grundtvig's works, *Denmark's Catalyst*, is a comprehensive, thoroughly-researched, and richly-

illustrated introduction to his life, his times, and his work in building the nation – with the bonus of 70 letters to and from family, friends, opponents, churchmen, kings and an admiring queen.
Ingrid Ank, Academic Leader of the Grundtvig Academy, Copenhagen

The Life and Letters of N.F.S Grundtvig covers his multifaceted career with the lucidity and authority that come from the authors, Edward Broadbridge and Hans Raun Iversen, having spent many years researching and translating 'Denmark's catalyst'. A thorough, accessible and sensitive biography of this passionate and complex man is followed by surveys of his national and international reputation, of the institutions and organizations founded in his name throughout the world, and of Grundtvig-scholarship to the present date. It is itself a very significant contribution to that scholarship, and unrivalled as an introduction to Grundtvig for English speakers.
Neil Keeble, Professor Emeritus of English Studies, University of Stirling

Afterword

Every translation is a compromise, an approximation. Whether or not successful when it is literally 'carried over' to a new language, it nevertheless takes on a life of its own. Only time, circumstance, and scholarship are the judge of its success or failure. By its very nature a translation can never equal the original but must always fall short. Nonetheless, in successful cases the translation can become a work of art in its own right. In the English-speaking world this tenet has been universally accepted when applied to the King James version of the Bible from 1611. Scholars turned the Hebrew Old Testament and the Greek New Testament into the first 'people's Bible' in English, and with its poetic cadences it has since become the single book with the greatest influence on all English literature. Hardly a translation even, more a work of sublime genius by *several* translators – and it has countless errors!

Grundtvig himself was a brilliant translator, from Greek, Latin, Icelandic, German, and Old English. His most famous Danish translations are *Deeds of the Danes* (from Latin), the *Edda poetry* (from Icelandic), and *Beowulf* (from Old English). These were not much read at the time, but were nevertheless highly praised by the Danish Grundtvig scholar, Steen Johansen:

> The linguistic dress in which Grundtvig clothed them bore such a powerful and personal stamp of the translator's personality that in this regard they are without parallel in our translation literature. Grundtvig's Saxo was indeed, as Hersleb wrote, 'every bit as much an original work as it was a translation.' That is how the chronicles have been regarded ever since, as works by Grundtvig![652]

In 1836, in a burst of national pride and prejudice in *The Danish Four-Leaf Clover* Grundtvig himself claimed that in the case of Danish the translation task was impossible:

> I do believe that all that is beautiful and good can be translated into Danish with no loss whatsoever, while the best of Danish cannot be translated into any language, not even into English, without losing at least the half of it.

This was still the case when the present translator began working with Grundtvig in the mid-1970s. 'Too difficult. Too Danish' were the confrontational words from a number of responders to this translator, who wanted Grundtvig better-known outside the confines of the 19th century Danish language. The breakthrough came in 2008 when the Director of the Grundtvig Centre, Michael Schelde, approached the present editor and translator with a view to producing the series 'N.F.S. Grundtvig. Works in English'. This sixth

---

652. (GS 1968, 63).

volume completes the series, which amounts to a translation of over 580,000 original words by Grundtvig.

All Grundtvig's translators have been faced with the complex task of reproducing in English his contents and concepts, his metaphors and similes, his rhymes and rhythms, and the general singability of his hymns and songs. Particularly in the last two I have deliberately chosen to make the English hymns follow the metre (always), the rhyme-scheme (mostly), the imagery (frequently), and the meaning (whole-heartedly). For those who know both languages intimately the compromises are obvious from the very first page.

In the 50 years or so that I have been translating Grundtvig, I have revised some of my previous choices. Thus in 1983 I translated Grundtvig's 1807 work, *Om Videnskabelighed og dens Fremme* as *On Scholarship and its Encouragement*, whereas by 2021 this had become *On the Advancement of Learning*. Having advanced my Grundtvig scholarship by 50 years or so, my choices in the 6 volumes now remain firm and consistent. Any errors throughout this and the previous volumes must be laid at my door. Tradition plays a role here, so I fully acknowledge the use of 'Folk High School' wherever it is used, but nevertheless prefer 'People's High School' as the English translation that is closer to Grundtvig's concept and Kold's practice.

In her book *Understanding Translation* (Academica, DK 2008) Anne Schjoldager lists no fewer than six competencies required of the translator: linguistic, cultural, textual, subject-specific, research, and transfer. Thus the translator should preferably be both bi-lingual and bi-cultural; should be genre- and subject-cognisant; should have a vast library, the internet, and other expertise reserves available; and should also have a sixth sense of how to transfer meaning from the source language to the target language. I have been aware of these throughout; only time will tell if I have been successful.

Finally, I wish to record here the deepest thanks to my late wife Hanna, who first introduced me to Grundtvig, then nourished my interest, then supported me with her learning, her patience, and her love – all the way through this mutually enriching adventure.

Edward Broadbridge
Randers, June 2023